D1243641

Rosa Luxemburg Speaks

Rosa Luxemburg Speaks

Edited with an introduction by Mary-Alice Waters

A MERIT BOOK

PATHFINDER PRESS, INC.
NEW YORK 1970

Manufactured in the United States of America
Library of Congress Catalog Card Number 76-119530

First Printing 1970

A MERIT BOOK

Pathfinder Press
873 Broadway
New York, N. Y. 10003

Contents

INTRODUCTION

By Mary-Alice Waters

The Struggle Begins

Rosa Luxemburg was born in 1871 a few days before the Paris Commune was proclaimed by the French workers. She died a little more than a year after the Bolsheviks came to power in the October Revolution. Her life thus spanned a great historical epoch, the five decades which opened with the first dress rehearsal for socialist revolution and closed as a new era in the history of mankind was being born.

Throughout her life—from her political awakening as a schoolgirl in Warsaw until her murder in Berlin in 1919—Rosa Luxemburg dedicated her immense energies, capacities, and intellectual powers to the goal of world socialist revolution. She understood that the stakes were high, that the fate of humanity was at stake and, as a woman of action, she gave herself completely to the great historic battle.

As she expressed it to her comrades only two weeks before her murder: "Today we can seriously set about destroying capitalism once and for all. Nay, more; not merely are we today in a position to perform this task, not merely is its performance a duty toward the proletariat, but our solution offers the only means of saving human society from destruction."

Such was the conviction that guided her life.

To a world just emerging from the holocaust of the First World War her words had a sharp immediacy. Fifty years and several devastating wars later, the alternative she poses—socialism or extermination—still remains the choice facing humanity.

Rosa Luxemburg was born on March 5, 1871, in the small town of Zamosc in southeastern Poland. (The date of her birth has been a subject of controversy, because she often used fake documents which made her out to be older than she was. Most of her closest friends believed she was born in 1870, and this is the year often given for her birth; but it seems fairly well established now that 1871 is correct.) She was the youngest of five children—three boys and two girls—of parents who, while not well-off, were in comfortable circumstances.

Zamosc had one of the strongest and most cultured Jewish communities in Russian Poland at the time, but Rosa Luxemburg's parents, if anything, deemphasized their Jewishness. Her father, who owned a timber business, had been educated in Germany, and the two languages spoken in her home were Polish and German. Also, her mother was well read, and German classics were the common fare of the household. Rosa learned Russian as well at a very early age.

When she was two and a half her family moved to Warsaw, where she grew up. She developed a serious hip ailment at the age of five, and had to spend almost a year in bed, during which time she taught herself to read. The disease was wrongly diagnosed as tuberculosis and wrongly treated, and she never fully recovered. For the rest of her life she walked with a slight limp.

At the age of thirteen she entered the second girls' high school in Warsaw — a difficult accomplishment for a Polish Jew, since such education was reserved first and foremost for the children of the Russian administrators. She graduated in 1887 with an excellent academic record, but was denied a gold medal she had earned for academic achievement because of her "rebellious attitude" towards the authorities.

It was during her high-school years that she became active in the underground revolutionary movement. She joined one of the small cells of the relatively isolated Proletariat Party which was allied with the terrorist Narodnik, or Populist, movement in Russia. After graduation she lived at home for two years but continued her political activities. She soon became known to the police.

In 1889, with arrest imminent, she decided to leave Poland and continue her studies in Western Europe. She was smuggled across the border under a pile of straw in a peasant's cart. In this she had the aid of a Catholic priest whom she had convinced that she wanted to be baptized in order to marry her lover, but could not go through with it in Poland because of her parents' opposition.

At the end of 1889, she arrived in Zurich, which was to be her home for the next nine years. She enrolled at the University of Zurich — one of the few institutions which then admitted men and women on an equal basis — and studied mathematics and natural sciences. After a few years she shifted to the school of law, and in 1897 completed a dissertation on the industrial development of Poland, receiving her doctorate in political science. The uniqueness of her accomplishment is revealed in her own humorous accounts of subsequent apartment hunting in Berlin. Her prospective landlords considered her an oddity, since they had never before seen a woman with a doctor's degree!

But her studies in Zurich occupied only a portion of her time and energy. Switzerland was one of the main emigre centers of Western Europe, the home of the great exiled Russian Marxists Plekhanov and Axelrod and many others. While Rosa Luxemburg held herself aloof from the swirling personal intrigues of emigre politics to the best of her ability, she was in the thick of the political battles. She rapidly educated herself in Marxism, and it was not long before she locked horns with some of the "unchallenged" authorities of the Second International.

During her years in Zurich she was involved primarily in Polish politics. In 1892 she was one of the founding members of the Polish Socialist Party (PPS), the first attempt to unite all the various currents of Polish socialism into one organization. But she soon came into conflict with that organization's principal leaders over the question of Polish nationalism. In her opinion the fight for Polish independence was a dangerous trap to be avoided at all costs, since it would inevitably subordinate working-class struggles to bourgeois interests wearing the protective coloring of nationalism. In 1894 she and a small group of Polish emigres broke away from the PPS and formed the Social Democracy of the Kingdom of Poland, which five years later became the Social Democratic Party of Poland and Lithuania (SDKPiL). Rosa Luxemburg remained one of the central leaders of Polish social democracy from that time until her death, and the battle against the PPS—a party which evolved more and more toward bourgeois nationalism and further and further away from socialism—was one of the important political constants running through her life.

Among the other founders and central organizers of the Polish social democracy was Leo Jogiches, Rosa's lifelong political collaborator, who would be her husband for more than fifteen years. Shortly after Rosa escaped from Poland, he arrived in Zurich from Vilna, the Lithuanian capital, where he had already won a considerable reputation in the underground. Although they were never legally married, and often had to spend long periods apart, their marital relationship lasted until 1907, and their political relationship bound their lives together to the end. Jogiches was arrested and murdered by the German authorities two months after Rosa had suffered the same fate.

Rosa was always an orator and writer, and her public role placed her continually in the spotlight, but she was not an organizer. She had virtually no interest in the details of party functioning, finances, underground work, the complications of getting literature published, etc.—all the thousands of details and problems which must be dealt with if an effective organization is to be built. Such things she left to Jogiches, who from all accounts was competent but also rather domineering and sometimes autocratic. He kept out of the public eye, organizing the SDKPiL, and, during the war, the Spartacus League, with quiet efficiency. Jogiches was a sharp political thinker, however, and served as Rosa's "sounding board" for years. Undoubtedly many of Rosa Luxemburg's ideas were worked out in conversation and debate with him, and he was always one of her severest critics. Although he has been overshadowed by Rosa, his own role in the international socialist movement of the early twentieth century was an important one.

The early battles with the PPS over the question of nationalism reverberated throughout the Second International, beginning with a battle over delegate status at the Third Congress of the International in 1893. Rosa Luxemburg demanded the right to be seated at the congress as the representative of a definite Polish tendency with its own publication, but the powerful connections of the PPS carried the day and her demand was refused.

By the next congress in 1896, her right to delegate status was unchallenged. Her reputation had spread rapidly in the intervening years and her articles appeared more and more frequently in the major social democratic publications of Western Europe. She was soon polemicizing on the national question with Karl Kautsky, Wilhelm Liebknecht, and other acknowledged authorities in the Marxist movement.

Upon the completion of her studies in the spring of 1897, she decided to move to Germany where she could play an active role in a large and influential party, and make a living as a journalist, writing for the rapidly growing publications of the German Social Democratic Party (SPD). The first problem to be solved was citizenship status. As long as she was a foreigner the German authorities could easily prevent her from being politically active. The answer was marriage to the German son of a longtime friend. In April 1897 she married Gustav Lubeck, thereby gaining German citizenship for life, and the two parted company outside the registry office. A divorce was obtained five years later.

After an extended visit to Paris, Rosa moved to Berlin in the spring of 1898, just in time to play a significant part in the battle against Eduard Bernstein's theoretical attempts to turn social democracy into a party of capitalist reform. Two years later Jogiches was able to join her in Germany.

The story of her battles with the leaders of the German SPD is told throughout the pages of this book, both in her own words and in the accompanying summaries of the most important political events in her life. But a few additional words about the SPD are in order here.

Despite the fact that she lived almost half of her life there, Rosa Luxemburg never really liked Germany, and over the years she came more and more to identify her distaste for things German with her hatred of the conservative, stifling, reformist apparatus of the pre-World War I SPD and the social democratic trade-union leaders. When she first arrived, she described Berlin as "the most repulsive place; cold, ugly, massive — a real barracks, and the

4

charming Prussians with their arrogance as if each one of them had been made to swallow the very stick with which he had got his daily beating." [1] More than a decade later, after an argument with a German socialist intellectual and critic over whether or not Tolstoy's writings were "art" she was so angry that she wrote, "There he stands in the street like a pot-bellied public urinal [piss-rotunde]. . . . In any Serbian village you care to name there is more humanity than in the whole of German social democracy." [2]

And the leaders of the SPD did not think much more highly of Rosa Luxemburg than she of them. While they learned to respect her exceptional abilities, they generally considered her, to put it most bluntly, a cantankerous foreign youngster who, on top of everything else, was a woman. One of their first proposals to her was that she turn her attentions toward the SPD's organization for women, where they thought she properly belonged, and where they hoped she could be sidetracked and eliminated from the mainstream of the party's political life. She promptly turned down the proposal and looked for some other arena of activity.

While she understood the importance of organizing women to take part in the revolutionary struggle — one of her closest life-long friends and collaborators was Clara Zetkin, the outstanding leader of the SPD's women's organization — she steadfastly refused to be forced into any traditional woman's role within the party. Unfortunately, she rarely, if ever, wrote about the special problems of the struggle for women's liberation. She considered herself, and she was, a revolutionary leader of men *and* women, and she dismissed the insults directed against her because she was a woman as simply part of the overhead of political battle. She understood that women can achieve their full liberation only with the triumph of the socialist revolution and the elimination of their economic bondage to the family institution, and she devoted all her energies to bringing about that revolution. She felt that was the greatest contribution she could possibly make toward the elimination of the oppression of women, as well as of the working class, national minorities, peasants, and all other exploited sectors of the population.

The SPD which Rosa Luxemburg joined was a powerful and impressive organization; it was *the* great party of the Second International. While the Russians and the Poles were struggling to assemble a relative handful of members and organize them into something that functioned like a party, the SPD had an enormous power and influence, which grew steadily from the time it was founded in 1875 until it committed moral suicide with the outbreak of World War I. In 1912, for example, the SPD won four and a quarter million votes, or 34.7 percent of the total, making it the largest party in the Reichstag, with 110 deputies. By the beginning of 1914, SPD membership had passed the one million mark. The party published ninety daily papers which reached 1.4 million subscribers. It also had a large women's movement, a youth section, cooperatives, sports and cultural organizations, and several million workers in social-democratic-led trade unions. The capital assets of the SPD's various branches and activities were worth 21.5 million marks and some 3,500 people were employed in the party, trade-union, and related apparatuses.

Much like the Debsian Socialist Party of the early years of the twentieth century in the U. S., the SPD brought together under its banner every conceivable tendency within the broad socialist movement, and the antagonistic points of view clashed with each other in the party publications, at public meetings, and in congresses. While technically a member could be expelled for failure to live up to the party program, or for violating party decisions, in reality no one ever lost his or her membership for such reasons, and the most openly reformist tendencies existed comfortably within the party side by side with the revolutionaries.

Parliamentary and trade-union activities appeared to have proved their tremendous effectiveness. The results, which all could see, were reflected in membership figures and vote totals. The left wing of the party very early began to take note of all the danger signals of a rightward drift — the party's increasing adaptation to the pressure to win votes at the price of political concessions; the trade-union leadership's deathly fear of any struggle that might go beyond demanding better wages or a slight improvement in working conditions. But even the severest left-wing critics, including Rosa Luxemburg herself, did not *begin* to grasp the depth of the process taking place or to realize how meaningless the official ritual recitations of Marxist orthodoxy had become. It took the shock of World War I and the SPD's support of the war plans of German imperialism to convince the left wing that the SPD leadership was unwilling and unable to act in accordance with Marxist principles.

In retrospect, of course, it is not difficult to see how different the political swamp of the SPD was from Lenin's Bolshevik Party with its organizational and political clarity. In the light of history, it is not hard to understand why the SPD collapsed whereas the Bolsheviks were able to lead the Russian masses to victory. But in the early years of the twentieth century, the question of what kind of party was needed to assure a revolutionary victory was only being posed; the differences were not so sharp or clear. Many fundamental divergences were attributed simply to differing objective circumstances and the isolation of the Russian social democrats from the masses.

We shall return to this question, since the nature of the SPD, its apparent strengths as well as its fatal weaknesses, greatly influenced Rosa Luxemburg's political life and thought.

Another great influence on her life and thought came from her roots in the Polish movement and her comprehension of the dynamics of the struggle brewing in the czarist empire. Zinoviev, speaking at the January 18, 1919, session of the Petrograd Soviet which paid tribute to the slain leaders of the German revolution, referred to Rosa Luxemburg's discussions with the Bolshevik leaders after the 1905 Revolution, and praised her as one of the first Marxists able to evaluate the Russian Revolution correctly as a whole.

She understood the deep revolutionary significance of the events that were taking place in the czarist empire, their potential, and the example they provided for all Europe. She sought constantly to put that example before the German workers and inspire them with it. Her own strength to withstand the twenty long years of battling, often single-handed, against the reformist drift of the SPD, to maintain her profoundly revolutionary perspective in the face of the heavy pressure to retreat and find a comfortable niche in the party apparatus, must have stemmed at least in part from her deep-rooted understanding of the revolutionary prospects in the Russian Empire and their meaning for all humanity. When she sometimes became discouraged by the enormous tasks facing her in Germany, she would find hope and encouragement in the revolutionary potential of the struggles in her homeland and other parts of the czar's territory. This internationalism of her vision, crowning her other qualities, made her a truly great revolutionary.

Rosa Luxemburg's Place in History

Rosa Luxemburg was destined to be one of the most controversial figures in the history of the international socialist movement, and her rightful place of honor among the great revolutionary Marxists has often been denied her. Her detractors have come from every side, and have used virtually every means of slander and distortion to discredit her, to picture her as the opposite of the revolutionary she was.

The ruling class, of course — whether American, German, Japanese, Mexican, or any other stripe — has had no interest in telling the truth about Rosa Luxemburg. They are more than willing to see her revolutionary heritage smeared and buried. But Luxemburg's detractors have come from sources within the traditional left-wing movement as well.

The first major category of her defamers are those who have tried to turn her into an opponent of the Russian Revolution, to make her a proponent of some special school of "democratic" socialism as opposed to the "tyrannical, dictatorial" socialism of Lenin. Perhaps the most widely read modern writer in this category is Bertram D. Wolfe, the virulently anti-Leninist editor of those works by Rosa Luxemburg in which she voiced differences with the Bolsheviks. Also belonging to this category are the various branches of left-wing social democracy (the right wing of social democracy long ago gave up any pretense of being "Red Rosa's" heir).

The left-wing social democrats — unlike Rosa Luxemburg, who understood the basic social and economic transformation that took place in the Soviet Union after the October insurrection — consider the Soviet Union and other degenerated or deformed workers' states to be a form of capitalist state. They thus condemn those countries and find in them nothing that is fundamentally superior to the Western imperialist nations. In their search for some impeccable revolutionary authority to whose reputation they can hitch this un-Marxist analysis, they came up with Rosa Luxemburg, and have since tried to lay claim to her heritage on the fraudulent grounds that she also opposed the Russian Revolution. We will return to her analysis of the Russian Revolution later on, but one need only read her words of praise for the Bolsheviks to see clearly that she was anything but an opponent of the Russian Revolution.

The second major political tendency which has spared no effort in its attempt to slander and distort Rosa Luxemburg's views is Stalinism. During the early years of the Russian Revolution, when Lenin and Trotsky both played central roles in the leadership of the Bolshevik Party and the Third International, Rosa Luxemburg was held in high esteem. She was recognized as a genuine revolutionary — one who made errors to be sure, but, more importantly, a revolutionary woman of action, a fighter whose errors never carried her outside the revolutionary camp.

The fate of her posthumous image was tied to that of the Russian Revolution, however, and as the revolution itself degenerated, and Stalin rose to dominance as the leader of a powerful bureaucracy, she came under attack along with other genuine revolutionaries.

One of the themes that runs throughout Rosa Luxemburg's writings on the Russian Revolution is that without the aid of revolution in Western Europe, especially Germany, the revolutionary regime which had come to power in Russia could not hope to survive. This view was shared by Lenin, Trotsky, and many others. History proved them all correct — but in its own way, in a manner unforeseen by any of the generation of Marxists who helped to make the first socialist revolution. The Soviet regime managed to survive the civil war and invasion of hostile armies. Through incredible sacrifice and effort it managed to maintain its foundation of a nationalized economy and to industrialize the country. With a planned economy free from the built-in anarchy of capitalist production, it was unaffected by the great economic crisis of the 1930s and made tremendous material progress while the capitalist countries stagnated and decayed.

But, while the basic foundations of the Russian Revolution were never destroyed, and while they made possible the economic growth that transformed Russia from the most backward agri-

8

cultural country in Europe into the second most highly industrialized country in the world, the revolution did not survive its isolation and initial poverty unscathed. The brutal material conditions in which it was doomed to struggle, unrelieved by the help which would have come from a victorious workers' revolution elsewhere, created the basis for, and nourished the growth of, a huge bureaucratic caste which represented the interests of the middle-class layers of Soviet society. These layers were at first made up of the rich and middle peasantry. Subsequently, Stalin's bureaucratic caste became more and more based on the economically privileged officials, managers, and administrators.

In its rise to power, the wing of the party led by Stalin had to destroy the Leninist, proletarian wing, led by Trotsky. Stalin had to eliminate every last vestige of revolutionary policies and perspectives to be able to carry out his basically nationalist, rather than internationalist, program and his counterrevolutionary, rather than revolutionary, projections. His ruthlessness was total. He was willing and able to use every form of struggle from lies and frame-up to torture, concentration camps, and murder. And while destroying everything Lenin stood for, while eliminating physically the party Lenin had built and wiping out all vestiges of democratic functioning both inside the party and throughout society, Stalin claimed to be wearing Lenin's mantle!

The process taking place within the Soviet Union was reflected in every Communist Party around the world, and in each it meant the destruction of revolutionary tradition.

Along with Trotsky and others who fought uncompromisingly for revolutionary policies nationally and internationally, against the interests of the privileged layers of Soviet society, Rosa Luxemburg became an early target of Stalin and his henchmen. The fact that she was a prime target is, in its own way, a tribute to the revolutionary influence of her heritage.

In 1923, Ruth Fischer and Arkadi Maslow, leaders of the German Communist Party (KPD), launched an attack against Rosa Luxemburg's "right-wing deviations." Her influence was labeled the "syphilis bacillus" of the German Communist movement, her "errors" were "examined" and found to be almost identical to Trotsky's, and thus she was portrayed as the main source of all the defects of German Communism. It was discovered that her theoretical errors in *The Accumulation of Capital* were the source of a full-blown theory of "spontaneity" and all her organizational mistakes flowed from her economic miscalculations.

After the 1925 Congress of the Third International, Communist Parties took a swing to the right. Fischer and Maslow were soon expelled, and Rosa Luxemburg was attacked, no longer for "right-wing deviations" but as an ultraleftist.

During the ultraleft Third Period, 1928-35, when the Communist Party in Germany paved the way for Hitler's rise to power by refusing to work with the SPD to combat fascism, Rosa Luxemburg, along with the rest of the prewar left wing, was accused of differing "only formally from the social-fascist theoreticians." ("Social-fascist" was the Communist Party's designation for social democrats.)

In 1931 Stalin himself entered the debate, rewriting history the way he wanted it read, in an article entitled "Questions Concerning the History of Bolshevism." Here he decreed, contrary to historical fact as well as everything he had previously written, that Rosa Luxemburg was personally responsible for that greatest of all sins, the theory of permanent revolution, and that Trotsky had only picked it up from her. He also decreed, despite the historical record, that Rosa Luxemburg had begun the attack on Kautsky and the German SPD center in 1910 only after she had been persuaded to do so by Lenin, who saw the degeneration of the SPD much more clearly than she.

Trotsky came to Rosa Luxemburg's defense, setting the historical record straight, in the article "Hands Off Rosa Luxemburg," which is printed as an appendix to this collection. But the article by Stalin set the Communist Party line on Rosa Luxemburg for several decades. Since she was never declared an "unperson" and eliminated from the history books altogether, as were so many of her contemporaries, her image has been partially restored with the passage of time. Her anniversaries are commemorated today in Eastern Germany and Poland, but a thoroughly honest evaluation of her role and her ideas has never been and will never be made by the Stalinists. In 1922 Lenin upbraided the German party for its slowness in publishing her collected works; this task has yet to accomplished in either Poland or Germany, almost fifty years later!

The reason is not hard to divine. Rosa Luxemburg's revolutionary spirit breathes through every page she ever wrote. Her internationalism, her call to action, her high standard of truth and honesty, her devotion to the interests of the working class, her concern for freedom and the fullest possible growth of the human spirit: such things are hardly in tune with the thinking of the bureaucratic caste that dominates economic, political, social and artistic life in Eastern Europe! They prefer to ignore her revolutionary politics and leave her in the shadows of hallowed martyrdom.

Historically, Rosa Luxemburg's political record unquestionably places her in the revolutionary camp. On every important political question during her lifetime, she stood foursquare on the side of opposition to the capitalist system and all its evils. She fought tenaciously against every attempt to turn the labor movement away from the fight to abolish capitalism, against every unscientific, utopian, phony scheme to reform the system. She was fond of repeating that the greatness of Marxism was that it placed the socialist movement on a scientific basis, proving from the very laws of capitalism itself the necessity for socialism as the next form of economic organization, if man was to progress and not descend to the depths of barbarism. She remained true to that comprehension of revolutionary Marxism throughout her life.

In the debate with Bernstein and his followers over the possibility of reforming capitalism into socialism, she led the theoretical fight against his revision of Marxism.

When the Frenchman Millerand became the first socialist to enter a bourgeois cabinet, she exposed the illogic of his action and demonstrated why he would have to betray his own socialist principles.

In the fight with the German trade-union leaders she explained the material reasons for their conservatism and their rejection of a revolutionary perspective. She warned against the dangers that pure-and-simple trade unionism posed to the party.

In the debate over the value of using elections as a means of struggle against the capitalist system, she refused to concede to those forces within the SPD that wanted to subordinate everything to parliamentary politicking, and she demanded that the SPD continue to organize the masses in other forms of struggle as well.

In the debates over the character of the 1905 and the 1917 Revolutions in Russia, she stood wholeheartedly with the Bolsheviks and against the Mensheviks, asserting that the working class must lead the struggle, fighting for its own interests. She had nothing but contempt for the Menshevik temporizing and compromising with the liberal, capitalist parties.

She fully understood that in political struggle, program is decisive in the long run. She battled always for programmatic clarity and worked to develop the kind of program that would help advance the class struggle step by step towards socialist revolution.

Living during the first tremendous growth of modern militarism, she was among the first to recognize the importance of military spending as an economic safety valve for capitalism. Faced with the growing realization of the destructive capacities of the imperialist rulers, she neither dismissed the dangers as irrelevant nor surrendered to them in advance.

At the crucial hour of the First World War, one of the fundamental historical dividing lines between revolutionary and non-revolutionary, she and Karl Liebknecht led the small handful of members of the SPD who refused to support the war plans of their own imperialist government.

Years before Lenin or any of the other European revolutionary leaders, she discerned the weaknesses of Kautsky and the German SPD "center," correctly branding them as men without revolutionary principles whose open capitulation to the right wing of the party was doubtless only a matter of time.

11

While her most enduring contributions are reflected in her writings, she was far from being an armchair revolutionary. She was always in the thick of any action she could find.

Finally, she stood solidly behind the October Revolution, declaring her unconditional support for the direction taken by the Bolsheviks, and proclaiming that the future belonged to bolshevism.

Such a record was matched by only a very few prewar social democrats anywhere in Europe. And Rosa Luxemburg's errors were made within this framework of a totally revolutionary perspective and a genuine search for the swiftest and surest path to a socialist future.

The National Question

Rosa Luxemburg's major errors were centered around three questions: the right of nations to self-determination; the nature of the party and its relationship to the revolutionary masses; and certain Bolshevik policies following the October Revolution. Her theoretical errors in economics, developed in *The Accumulation of Capital*, are also important in the history of Marxism, but as her economic writings are essentially outside the scope of this book, they will be referred to only in passing.

From the beginning of her political life to the very end, Rosa Luxemburg emphatically rejected the basic Marxist position on the revolutionary significance of the struggle of oppressed national minorities and nations for self-determination. Her first writings on this question were published in 1893, and her last were set down only a few months before her death, in her pamphlet on the Russian Revolution. It can be said with certainty that this is one question on which she did not change her mind before she was murdered.

A large part of her writings on national struggles were published in Polish, and unfortunately few have been translated into other languages. Her most important article, for example, "The Question of Nationality and Autonomy," written in 1908, against which Lenin polemicized in his basic work, *The Right of Nations to Self-Determination*, has apparently never been published in any language except the original Polish. However, the *Junius Pamphlet* and the section of "The Russian Revolution" which is devoted to the national struggle contain the essence of her position. Both are included in this collection.

Briefly, without enumerating all the supporting arguments and examples, her position can be summed up as follows: The elimination of all forms of oppression, including the subjugation of one nation by another, was an incontestable goal of socialism. Without the elimination of all forms of oppression one could not even begin to talk of socialism. However, Rosa Luxemburg held that it was incorrect for revolutionary socialists to assert the unconditional right of all nations to self-determination. The demand for self-determination was unrealizable under imperialism. It would always be perverted by one or another of the major capitalist powers. Under socialism it would become largely irrelevant, as socialism would eliminate *all* national boundaries, at least in an economic sense, and the secondary problems of language and culture could be solved without great difficulty.

In a strategic sense, she thought that advocacy of the right of nations to self-determination was extremely dangerous to the international working class since it reinforced nationalist movements which must inevitably come under the domination of their own bourgeoisie. In her opinion, supporting separatist aspirations served only to divide the international working class, not to unite it in common struggle against the ruling classes of all nations. Advocacy of the right of nations to self-determination, which she described as "nothing but hollow, petty bourgeois phraseology and humbug," only corrupts class consciousness and confuses the class struggle. As she says in "The Russian Revolution," the "utopian, petty bourgeois character of this nationalist slogan" [right to national self-determination] resides in the fact "that in the midst of the crude realities of class society and when class antagonisms are sharpened to the uttermost, it is simply converted into a means of bourgeois class rule."

Lenin and the other defenders of the Marxist position answered her clearly and sharply.

It is not sufficient, they maintained, to say simply that socialists are opposed to all forms of exploitation and oppression. Every capitalist politician in the world would make the exact same assertion. As Rosa Luxemburg herself pointed out so forcefully, the entire First World War was supposedly fought under the banner of assuring self-determination for all nations. Socialists must put their words into action in order to prove to the oppressed and exploited national minorities that their slogans are not hollow and meaningless as are those of the ruling classes.

Theoretically it is incorrect to say that self-determination can *never* be achieved under capitalism. The example of Norway winning independence from Sweden in 1905, with the support of the Swedish workers, is a case in point.

A socialist government, Lenin asserted, can win the allegiance of oppressed minorities only if it is willing and able to prove its unconditional support of their right to form a separate state if they so choose. Any other policy would amount to the forcible retention of diverse nationalities within one state, to a national oppression which would in essence be no different from the national oppression practiced by imperialism. The free association of different nationalities in a single political unit can only be obtained by first guaranteeing each the right to withdraw from that union. Rosa Luxemburg, Lenin charged, tried to avoid the question of political self-determination by shifting the argument to the grounds of economic interdependence.

Paradoxically, while socialists must fight for the unconditional right of self-determination, including the right of separation, the only *party* that can lead such a fight and assure the victory of the socialist revolution is a democratic centralist party, such as the Bolsheviks built, that includes within its ranks and leadership the most conscious sectors of the working class, peasantry, and intellectuals of all the nationalities within the boundaries of the existing capitalist state. As Trotsky explained in the *History of the Russian Revolution*, "A revolutionary organization is not the prototype of the future state, but merely the instrument for its creation. . . . Thus a centralized organization can guarantee the success of revolutionary struggle—even where the task is to destroy the centralized oppression of nationalities." [3]

At the same time, Lenin pointed out, unconditional support for the right of self-determination does not mean that the socialists of the oppressed nation are obliged to fight for separation. Nor does it imply support to the national bourgeoisie of the oppressed nation, except—as Lenin explains in *The Right of Nations to Self-Determination*—insofar as the "bourgeois nationalism of *any* oppressed nation has a general democratic content that is directed *against* oppression, and it is this content that we *unconditionally* support." [4] But only the working class and its allies can lead the struggle to completion, and the oppressed masses must never rely on their own bourgeoisie which, given its ties to the ruling class of the oppressor nation and to international capital, cannot carry the struggle to its conclusion.

Lenin explained numerous times that his disagreement with Rosa Luxemburg and the Polish social democrats was not over their opposition to demanding independence for Poland, but over their attempt to deny the obligation of socialists to support the *right* of self-determination, and particularly their attempt to deny the absolute necessity for the revolutionary socialist party of an oppressor nation to guarantee that right unconditionally. Lenin points out at the end of *The Right of Nations to Self-Determination* that the Polish social democrats had been led "by their struggle against the Polish bourgeoisie, which deceives the people with its nationalist slogans, to the incorrect denial of self-determination." [5]

Finally, he argued that the right of self-determination is one of the basic democratic rights raised by the bourgeois revolution, and socialists are obligated to fight for democratic rights. "In the same way as there can be no victorious socialism that does not practice full democracy, so the proletariat cannot prepare for its victory over the bourgeoisie without an all-around, consistent, and revolutionary struggle for democracy." [6]

Rosa Luxemburg's argument that a demand for self-determination is impractical under capitalism ignores the fact that "not only the right of nations to self-determination, but *all* the fundamental demands of political democracy are only partially 'practicable' under imperialism, and then in a distorted way of exception." [7]

"There is not one of these demands which could not serve and has not served, under certain circumstances, as an instrument in the hands of the bourgeoisie for deceiving the workers." [8] But that in no way relieves socialists of the obligation to struggle for democratic rights, to expose the deceptions of the bourgeoisie, and to prove to the masses that only the socialist revolution can lead to the full realization of the basic democratic rights proclaimed by the bourgeoisie.

Rosa Luxemburg sincerely believed that the Bolshevik policy on national self-determination was disastrous and could only lead to the destruction of the revolution. But she could not have been more wrong.

The February 1917 Revolution which established a liberal republic in Russia brought about a great historical awakening of the oppressed nations within the czarist empire, but the formal equality they received from the revolution served only to emphasize to them the degree of their real oppression. And it was the refusal of the liberal bourgeois government, from February to October, to grant the right of self-determination that cemented the opposition of the oppressed nationalities to the Menshevik government in Petrograd and sealed its doom.

Only by guaranteeing self-determination, up to and including the right of separation, did the Bolshevik Party win the indestructible confidence of the small and oppressed nationalities of czarist Russia. This confidence ultimately proved decisive in the battle against the counterrevoltuion and led, not to the disintegration of the revolutionary forces, as Rosa Luxemburg feared, but to their victory within the oppressed nations as well as among the Great Russians themselves.

She totally underestimated the tremendous force of nationalism which began to awaken in Eastern Europe only in the early twentieth century. She did not comprehend that these movements were destined to explode with full force only *after* the Russian Revolution, not because the Bolsheviks encouraged them but because of the internal dynamic of the struggle generated by the awakening of the oppressed masses.

One of Rosa Luxemburg's most frequently quoted statements

from "The Russian Revolution" is her description of Ukrainian nationalism as "a mere whim, a folly of a few dozen petty bourgeois intellectuals without the slightest roots in the economic, political or psychological relationships of the country." Trotsky took her up on this in the chapter on "The Problem of Nationalities" in his *History of the Russian Revolution.*

"When Rosa Luxemburg, in her posthumous polemic against the program of the October Revolution, asserted that Ukrainian nationalism, having been formerly a mere amusement of the commonplace petty bourgeois intelligentsia, had been artificially raised up by the yeast of the Bolshevik formula of self-determination, she fell, notwithstanding her luminous mind, into a very serious historic error. The Ukrainian peasantry had not made national demands in the past for the reason that the Ukrainian peasantry had not in general risen to the height of political being. The chief service of the February Revolution — perhaps its only service, but one amply sufficient — lay exactly in this, that it gave the oppressed classes and nations of Russia at last an opportunity to speak out. This political awakening of the peasantry could not have taken place otherwise, however, than through their own native language — with all the consequences ensuing in regard to schools, courts, self-administration. To oppose this would have been to try to drive the peasants back into nonexistence."[9]

Not a few historians have tried to show that Rosa Luxemburg's position on self-determination and opposition to nationalist movements was actually put into practice in later years by Stalin, with his vicious persecution of the oppressed nations and all the attendant horrors. But, his actions were as much a perversion of Rosa Luxemburg's program as of Lenin's. As an article by the editor in the March 1935 *New International* asked: "Can one imagine Rosa in the company of those who strangled the Chinese Revolution by attributing to Chiang Kai-shek and the Chinese bourgeoisie the leading revolutionary role in 'liberating the nation from the yoke of foreign imperialism'? Can one imagine Rosa in the company of those who hailed the 1926 coup d'etat of Marshal Pilsudski as the 'great national democrat' who was establishing the 'democratic dictatorship of the proletariat and peasantry' in Poland? Can one imagine Rosa in the company of those who for years glorified and canonized every nationalist demagogue who was gracious enough to send a visiting card to the Kremlin. . . ?" [A few years later another question could have been posed: Can one imagine Rosa in the company of those who murdered virtually the entire Central Committee of the Polish Communist Party?]

And the article concludes, "How contemptible are those who dismiss a Rosa Luxemburg with smug disdain as a 'Menshevik,' when they themselves proved unable to rise to the height of her boots!" [10]

Rosa Luxemburg was wrong on the national question, but her opposition to guaranteeing the right of self-determination was not born out of hostility to revolutionary mass action that leads toward struggle to abolish capitalism. Rather she failed to comprehend the complex and contradictory aspects of the revolutionary dynamic of struggles by oppressed nationalities in the age of imperialism.

The Nature of the Revolutionary Party

Rosa Luxemburg's mistakes concerning the problem of building a revolutionary party, and the parallel problem of the relationship between that party and the working masses, were just as fundamental as her errors on the national question. Within the context of the German revolution they were probably more costly.

Her differences with the Bolsheviks concerning organizational concepts are not as easy to codify as those concerning national self-determination. She never spelled out clearly and completely, in any one place, her thinking on the type of organization needed, although most of the elements of her basic position are clearly discernible in her 1904 article, "Organizational Questions of Russian Social Democracy." Following the 1905 Revolution her ideas were further clarified.

The fact is that, despite her dispute with Lenin on the nature of the revolutionary party, she was not deeply concerned with organizational problems, and therein lies one of the clearest indications of the nature of her errors. While she understood that in political struggle, program is ultimately decisive, she did not understand, as did Lenin, that program and tactical positions are always refracted through organizational concepts.

Perhaps one of the most revealing examples of her tendency to dismiss the organizational problems of leadership is the fact that for years she refused to attend the conventions of the SDKPiL or to be elected to its Central Committee. Yet she remained one of the party's principal political leaders and its main public voice. The problem was not her location either, since the Central Committee of the SDKPiL had its headquarters in Berlin. Thus she remained a leader in effect, yet not directly accountable to any specific leading body of which she was a member.

Her attitudes on organizational matters were heavily influenced by her experiences with the SPD. She very early recognized the tremendous conservative weight of the SPD leadership, and pointed, even in her 1904 essay, to their inability to so much as consider any strategy other than continuation of the "grand old tactic" of parliamentary concerns and nothing but parliamentary concerns.

Another aspect of the SPD which greatly influenced her thinking was simply the size and scope of the organization itself, which held within its orbit any and every individual who even vaguely thought in socialist terms.

To mount an effective opposition to a leadership as strongly entrenched and secure as the SPD hierarchy was not an easy matter. It required great tactical flexibility as well as political clarity, and it was a job that Rosa Luxemburg never really tackled. Year after year she maintained a blistering political opposition, but, until the war began, she never tried to draw around her, organize, and lead a group within the SPD.

The clarity of her basic political understanding of the SPD leadership was well expressed in a letter she sent to her close friend Clara Zetkin around the beginning of 1907. This same letter illustrates equally well her inability or unwillingness to give her political comprehension an organizational form. The possibility of trying to be more than a one- or two-woman opposition doesn't seem ever to have received serious thought:

"Since my return from Russia I feel rather isolated . . . I feel the pettiness and the hesitancy of our party regime more clearly and more painfully than ever before. However, I can't get so excited about the situation as you do, because I see with depressing clarity that neither things nor people can be changed—until the whole situation has changed, and even then we shall just have to reckon with inevitable resistance if we want to lead the masses on. I have come to that conclusion after mature reflection. The plain truth is that August [Bebel], and still more so the others, have completely pledged themselves to parliament and parliamentarianism, and whenever anything happens which transcends the limits of parliamentary action they are hopeless—no, worse than hopeless, because they then do their utmost to force the movement back into parliamentary channels, and they will furiously defame as 'an enemy of the people' anyone who dares to venture beyond their own limits. I feel that those of the masses who are organized in the party are tired of parliamentarianism, and would welcome a new line in party tactics, but the party leaders and still more the upper stratum of opportunist editors, deputies, and trade-union leaders are like an incubus. We must protest vigorously against this general stagnation, but it is quite clear that in doing so we shall find ourselves against the opportunists as well as the party leaders and August. As long as it was a question of defending themselves against Bernstein and his friends, August & Co. were glad of our assistance, because they were shaking in their shoes. But when it is a question of launching an offensive against opportunism then August and the rest are with Ede [Bernstein], Vollmar, and David against us. That's how I see matters, but the chief thing is to keep your chin

up and not get too excited about it. Our job will take years." [11]
Important as the influence of the SPD was, however, it is not by itself a sufficient explanation for her organizational attitudes. Not only different objective circumstances but also different organizational concepts set her apart from Lenin.

Before discussing what her organizational theories were, however, it is worth mentioning what they were not. Rosa Luxemburg has often been credited—by those who think they agree with her as well as those who disagree—with holding a full-blown theory of "spontaneity," or even with advocacy of something akin to an anarchist position. Nothing could be a greater oversimplification and distortion of her ideas.

As mentioned earlier, the Stalinists at one time even pretended to trace her organizational errors to her theoretical mistakes in *The Accumulation of Capital*. In this, her principal economic work, Rosa Luxemburg tries to demonstrate that capitalism, considered as a closed or completed system without precapitalist or noncapitalist markets to cannibalize, could not continue to expand. Her argument is basically incorrect on the theoretical level in that she leaves out of consideration the central factors of competition among different capitals and the unevenness of the rate of development between different countries, different sectors of the economy and different enterprises—factors which constitute the driving force behind the expansion of capitalist markets. However, the Stalinists accused her of propagating a crude theory of the "automatic" and "mechanical" end of capitalism, to occur as soon as the world's noncapitalist markets were exhausted or absorbed into capitalist relations. And from this *they* made a leap into the organizational question, claiming that it followed that she could not have believed that organizing the struggle for the overthrow of capitalism was an urgent need since the automatic "breakdown" of capitalism was assured. Her own words, throughout the pages of this book, speak eloquently enough in her own defense against such crude distortions.

What was her basic conception?

She disagreed with Lenin that the party should be an organization of professional revolutionaries with deep roots in and ties to the working class, an organization holding the perspective of winning the leadership of the masses during a period of revolutionary upsurge.

On the contrary, in her view the revolutionary party should come much closer to encompassing the organized working class in its entirety.

This comes out in her 1904 essay in which she polemicizes against Lenin's definition of a revolutionary social democrat.

In *One Step Forward, Two Steps Back*, an analytical balance sheet of the Russian party's 1903 Congress at which there had been a split into "hard" and "soft," that is, Bolshevik and Men-shevik factions, over the organizational question, Lenin had taken up the "dreadful word" Jacobin (name of the left faction in the French Revolution), which had been flung at the Bolsheviks. He wrote: "A Jacobin who maintains an inseparable bond with the *organization* of the proletariat, a proletariat *conscious* of its class interests, is a *revolutionary social democrat.*" 12

In objection, Luxemburg wrote: ". . . Lenin defines his 'revolu-tionary social democrat' as a 'Jacobin joined to the organization of the proletariat, which has become conscious of its class in-terests.'

"The fact is that the social democracy is not *joined* to the orga-nizations of the proletariat. It is itself the proletariat. . . . Social democratic centralism . . . can only be the concentrated will of the individuals and groups representative of the most class-con-scious, militant, advanced sections of the working class. . . ."

In other words, she did not downplay the role of the party in providing political leadership, but tended to confine the party to the role of agitator and propagandist and to deny its central role as a day-to-day organizer of the class struggle, providing lead-ership for the masses in an organizational and technical sense as well. She did not understand the Leninist concept of a combat party — a party which recognizes that capitalism must be defeated in struggle and understands that the working masses must be led by an organization capable of standing up under the pressure of a combat; a party that is deeply rooted in the mass movement and consciously works to mobilize the combativity of the masses and help give their struggles anticapitalist direction; a party that, regardless of its size or stage of development, bases its conduct on the firm intent to become a mass working-class party capable of leading the way to victory, a party that prepares over a period of years for the role it must play in the decisive struggles; a party that understands the vital, indispensable need for *conscious* orga-nization and leadership.

Instead, Rosa Luxemburg placed great emphasis on the role of the masses themselves in action, on the steps they could take without conscious organizational leadership, on the things which she believed their combativity alone could accomplish. She as-signed to them the task of overwhelming and sweeping away the conservative, backward working-class leaders, and creating new revolutionary organizations in place of the old. She called on them to perform the task for which she herself was not willing to pave the way, except in the most general political sense.

In her mass strike pamphlet, for instance, she eloquently pic-tures the process: "From the whirlwind and the storm, out of the fire and flow of the mass strike and the street fighting, rise again, like Venus from the foam, fresh, young, powerful, buoyant trade unions." And later she warns the trade unionists that if they attempt to stand in the way of real social struggles, "the trade-union leaders, like the party leaders in the analogous case, will simply be swept aside by the rush of events, and the economic and the political struggles of the masses will be fought out without them."

As against the Bolsheviks' concept that it was necessary to organize revolution, she came closer to the Menshevik slogan of 1905 — unleash the revolution.

It was Trotsky who put her general concept in an extremely succinct form — and pointed to her central error — in a speech on "Problems of Civil War," in July 1924. Discussing the problems surrounding the timing of an insurrection, he said:

"It must be recognized that the question of the timing of the insurrection acts in many cases like a kind of litmus paper for testing the revolutionary consciousness of very many Western comrades, who have still not rid themselves of their fatalistic and passive manner of dealing with the principal problems of revolution. Rosa Luxemburg remains the most eloquent and talented example. Psychologically, this is fully understandable. She was formed, so to speak, in the struggle against the bureaucratic apparatus of the German social democracy and trade unions. Untiringly, she showed that this apparatus was stifling the initiative of the masses and she saw no alternative but that an irresistible uprising of the masses would sweep away all the barriers and defenses built by the social democratic bureaucracy. The revolutionary general strike, overflowing all the dikes of bourgeois society, became for Rosa Luxemburg synonymous with the proletarian revolution.

"However, whatever its power and mass character, the general strike does not settle the problem of power; it only poses it. To seize power, it is necessary, while relying on the general strike, to organize an insurrection. The whole of Rosa Luxemburg's evolution, of course, was going in that direction. But when she was snatched from the struggle, she had not yet spoken her last word, nor even the penultimate one." 13

Rosa Luxemburg's correct evaluation of the nature of the SPD leadership and her consequent opposition to it led her to question the centralism of a revolutionary organization as well as the centralism of a reformist one — to be skeptical of conscious organizational leadership in general.

It would be a mistake however to accuse her of rejecting any kind of centralized organization. She was concerned primarily with the *degree* of centralization, and the nature of the leadership function of the party. As Trotsky put it in the article "Luxemburg and the Fourth International," included as an appendix to this collection, "The most that can be said is that in her historical-philosophical evaluation of the labor movement, the preparatory

21

selection of the vanguard, in comparison with the mass actions that were to be expected, fell too short with Rosa; whereas Lenin —without consoling himself with the miracles of future actions— took the advanced workers and constantly and tirelessly welded them together into firm nuclei, illegally or legally, in the mass organizations or underground, by means of a sharply defined program."

The Bolsheviks answered Rosa Luxemburg, in word and deed, over the years. They pointed out that under capitalism the working class as a whole is not in a position to raise itself to the level of consciousness necessary to successfully confront the bourgeoisie in all fields, to destroy bourgeois authority. If it were, capitalism would have perished long ago.

The determination, ruthlessness, and unity of the ruling class demand that the working class create a party that is serious and professional in its concepts, that is disciplined and welded together by common political agreement on the tasks to be performed, that is trained and capable of leading the masses to victory. Such a party cannot be created spontaneously, out of the struggle itself. It is a weapon that must be fashioned before the battle begins.

Lenin labeled Rosa Luxemburg's organizational concepts her "not-to-be-taken-seriously nonsense of organization and tactics as a process." [14] By that he did not, of course, mean that an organization was created in isolation from objective circumstances, or that tactics did not evolve or change, and were not adapted to living reality. To Rosa Luxemburg's view that the historic process itself would create the organizations and tactics of struggle, Lenin counterposed a diametrically opposite relationship between historical developments and the party. As he saw it, the organization and the tactics are created not by the process but by those people who achieve an understanding of the process by means of Marxist theory and who make themselves part of the process through the elaboration of a plan based upon their understanding.

Walter Held, a leader of the German section of the Fourth International prior to the Second World War, once explained the concept by an analogy from natural science: "The power latent in a waterfall may be transformed into electricity. But not every person without more ado is capable of accomplishing this feat. Scientific education and training are indispensable. On the other hand, the scientifically trained engineers are naturally constrained to draft their plans according to the given natural conditions. What can be said, however, of a man, who, because of this, jeers at engineering science and praises instead the 'elementary force of water which produces electricity'? We should be entirely justified in laughing him out of court. Nor is it otherwise with the social process. It was for this and no other reason that Lenin used to jest about the conception of 'organization as process' which was counterposed to his conception." 15

The differing organizational theories of Lenin and Luxemburg underwent the acid test in the post-World War I revolutionary upsurge. The party Lenin had built was able to lead the masses to power. In Germany, the absence of a similar cohesive, trained, educated and disciplined party and leadership proved fatal to the German revolution and to many of the courageous revolutionaries themselves.

In retrospect the differences now seem obvious; the mistakes of Luxemburg seem underscored by history. But at the time, the issue was certainly not so clear. History itself was uttering the final word on the nature of the revolutionary party, indicating what was necessary to assure victory. And even Lenin did not think he was doing anything so unique. Prior to 1914 he viewed his efforts as being directed toward the creation of a "Bebel-Kautsky" wing in the Russian social democracy. He did not come to understand the political character of that "Bebel-Kautsky" wing of the SPD until several years after Rosa Luxemburg turned her political fire against those vacillating middle-of-the-roaders.

In the years following the Russian Revolution, however — after the lessons of the Russian and German revolutions were drawn and the questions concerning organizational concepts decided by history — many currents within the working-class movement still continue to reject the fundamental concepts of the Bolshevik Party and look to Rosa Luxemburg as the champion of a revolutionary alternative to Leninism. These basically social democratic currents — which also came to equate Leninism with Stalinism rather than recognizing them as irreconcilable opposites — have been fond of pointing out that Trotsky, too, held views similar to Luxemburg's in the years prior to 1917. Trotsky, fortunately, was alive to defend himself.

In 1904 Trotsky wrote a pamphlet, "Our Political Tasks," in which he made a statement that has been quoted by many opponents of Leninism, including Bertram D. Wolfe and Boris Souvarine. Trotsky asserted: "Lenin's methods lead to this: the party organization [the caucus] at first substitutes itself for the party as a whole; then the Central Committee substitutes itself for the organization; and finally a single 'dictator' substitutes himself for the Central Committee. . . ."16

In response to all the admiring anti-Leninists who approvingly quoted Trotsky's prognosis and saw his exile by Stalin as confirmation of the warnings he and Rosa Luxemburg had voiced in 1904, Trotsky replied: "All subsequent experience demonstrated to me that Lenin was correct in this question as against Rosa

23

Luxemburg and me. Marceau Pivert counterposes to the 'Trotskyism' of 1939, the 'Trotskyism' of 1904. But after all since that time three revolutions have taken place in Russia alone. Have we really learned nothing during these thirty-five years?"[17]

No one knows what Rosa Luxemburg might have said in the same situation, but she, too, was capable of learning from the course of history.

The Russian Revolution

The most serious of Rosa Luxemburg's criticisms of the policies of the Bolsheviks, as expressed in her draft article on the Russian Revolution, have already been dealt with — her longstanding differences on the national question, and her organizational disagreements, which are implicit in the draft. But she raises several other questions that are worth discussing. It would take a book to deal adquately with all of them, and it is in Trotsky's three-volume *History of the Russian Revolution*, in fact, that one finds the most complete answers. But the intention here is simply to indicate the direction in which the reader must search for solutions to the very complex problems of the first socialist revolution in history.

The circumstances surrounding the writing and posthumous publication of Rosa Luxemburg's article on the Russian Revolution are explained in the introductory note to that selection, but some additional comments are in order.

Incarcerated as she was in the Breslau prison, her isolation and extremely limited access to accurate information about what was going on in Russia were important factors. Even outside the jails, the truth was hard to come by. People living in the United States today, for example, can draw a parallel with the difficulties of obtaining anything resembling truthful information on happenings in Vietnam, particularly concerning the areas governed by the Provisional Revolutionary Government.

In Germany following the October Revolution in 1917, the ministry of the interior eschewed any pretense of freedom of the press and ordered "all that explains or praises the proceedings of the revolutionaries in Russia must be suppressed." [18] Anything that the German military thought would discredit the revolutionary government of Russia received wide publicity, while anything that might win sympathy was censored.

Once out of prison, with access to better information, Rosa Luxemburg retained some of her criticisms, and changed her mind about others. And on many questions it is unclear whether she altered her opinion or not, as she never mentioned them again, at least publicly. The tremendous problems facing the revolutionary leadership in Germany between November 1918 and January 1919 became her overriding concern.

What is most striking in her draft article is that she is not really suggesting alternative policies as much as she is describing what would have been the optimum course — if conditions had been different; if the proletarian revolution had occurred almost simultaneously across Europe; if the German, French, and English workers had be able to come to the aid of their Russian comrades. Under such circumstances there would have been no need for the sharp restrictions on democratic freedoms. There would have been no strong counterrevolutionary forces backed by all the major capitalist powers.

The leaders of the Russian Revolution recognized this also. Lenin and Trotsky never ceased to point out the isolation of the revolution, the tardiness — and eventually the indefinite postponement — of the German revolution. Such historical facts determined much of the course of the Russian Revolution.

During 1918 Rosa Luxemburg stressed over and over again the decisive importance of the German revolution if the Bolshevik regime was to survive:

"Everything that happens in Russia is comprehensible and represents an inevitable chain of causes and effects, the starting point and end term of which are: the failure of the German proletariat and the occupation of Russia by German imperialism. It would be demanding something superhuman from Lenin and his comrades if we should expect of them that under such circumstances they should conjure forth the finest democracy, the most exemplary dictatorship of the proletariat and a flourishing socialist economy. By their determined revolutionary stand, their exemplary strength in action, and their unbreakable loyalty to international socialism, they have contributed whatever could possibly be contributed under such devilishly hard conditions. . . . The Bolsheviks have shown that they are capable of everything that a genuine revolutionary party can contribute within the limits of the historical possibilities. They are not supposed to perform miracles. For a model and faultless proletarian revolution in an isolated land, exhausted by world war, strangled by imperialism, betrayed by the international proletariat, would be a miracle."

One could hardly ask for a clearer statement of support for the Russian Revolution or greater comprehension of its difficulties. It is within that framework that she voices her criticisms.

At another time, towards the end of November 1918, after she was released from prison, she wrote to her longtime comrade in the leadership of the SDKPiL, Adolf Warsawski, also known as A. Warski, who was at that time in Warsaw:

"If our party [SDKPiL] is full of enthusiasm for bolshevism and at the same time opposed the Bolshevik peace of Brest-Litovsk, and also opposes their propagation of national self-determination as a solution, then it is no more than enthusiasm coupled with the spirit of criticism — what more can people want from us?

"I shared all your reservations and doubts, but have dropped them in the most important questions, and in others I never went as far as you. Terrorism is evidence of grave internal weakness, but it is directed against internal enemies, who . . . get support and encouragement from foreign capitalists outside Russia. Once the European revolution comes, the Russian counterrevolutionaries lose not only this support, but — what is more important — they must lose all courage. Bolshevik terror is above all the expression of the weakness of the European proletariat. Naturally the agrarian circumstances there have created the sorest, most dangerous problem of the Russian Revolution. But here too the saying is valid — even the greatest revolution can only achieve that which has become ripe [through the development of] social circumstances. This sore too can only be healed through the European revolution. And this is coming!" [19]

Among Rosa Luxemburg's disagreements with Bolshevik policies it is those criticisms directed against the treaty of Brest-Litovsk, the dissolution of the Constituent Assembly, the distribution of land to the peasants, and the use of revolutionary violence which are most important.

She opposed the decision of the Bolsheviks to sign a separate peace treaty with the German government in early 1918 because she believed it meant surrendering large parts of revolutionary Russia to counterrevolution, to German imperialism. She feared it would only postpone the end of the war, and might possibly lead to the victory of the German armies.

Although her fears proved unfounded, she was certainly not alone in holding the position she did. It was shared by close to a majority of the Bolshevik Central Committee as well. Only after it became clear that the German army intended and had the ability to take even larger sections of Russia by continued military advances, did Lenin convince a majority of the Central Committee that the treaty of Brest-Litovsk must be signed, despite the harsh terms. The cost of continued refusal to sign a separate treaty with the Central powers, Lenin feared, would be the conclusion of a separate peace between Germany and its imperialist enemies, followed by a coalition of all the capitalist powers against revolutionary Russia.

Such fears were eventually to materialize, despite the treaty of Brest-Litovsk, but in the meantime the war-weary Russian masses were able to gain a respite, the revolutionary government was able to begin io consolidate itself, the revolutionary process in the German-occupied territories deepened and the foundations of the Red Army were laid — in short the Brest-Litovsk treaty notwithstanding the fears of all who opposed it, was the only way out for the Bolshevik government and made possible the eventual victory of the revolution. It was not choice, but iron necessity that compelled the Bolsheviks to sign the treaty.

While in prison, Rosa Luxemburg was extremely critical of the Bolshevik dissolution of the Constituent Assembly elected just after the victory of the October Revolution. But she changed her position after being released from jail. During the revolutionary upsurge of November and December 1918 in Germany, the Spartacus League rapidly came to realize that the call for a Constituent Assembly was the rallying cry of the SPD and others who opposed the revolution. To the call for a Constituent Assembly, Spartacus counterposed the demand for the transfer of power to the Workers' and Soldiers' Councils. Thus, compelled by the logic of their own struggle against the counterrevolution, Spartacus developed a position similar to that of the Bolsheviks, and Rosa Luxemburg soon realized the question was not quite so simple as it had seemed from Breslau.

In her prison essay, however, her basic error on the question of democratic practices in the revolution was to ignore the role of the Soviets, which were probably the most democratic institutions of modern times.

The Constituent Assembly was not dissolved because its majority disagreed with the Bolsheviks. If the Bolsheviks and Left Social Revolutionaries had been in the majority they would have dissolved themselves and delegated their authority to the Soviets —which held power anyway. The Constituent Assembly was disbanded because it was totally unrepresentative — as Trotsky explains in the section quoted by Rosa Luxemburg — and far from being simply another organ of workers' democracy subject to pressure from the masses, it would have rapidly become an organizing center of the counterrevolution. Once dissolved, there was no need for a new Constituent Assembly, as the Soviets had assumed the functional role of such a body.

All these things Rosa Luxemburg came to realize very rapidly through her own direct experiences in the German revolution.

Rosa Luxemburg carefully places her criticisms of the Bolsheviks' agrarian policies within the framework of the historical tasks to be accomplished and the tremendous difficulty of assuring the victory of a socialist revolution in one of the most backward capitalist countries.

In the Western European countries the destruction of feudal land relationships had been largely accomplished by the bourgeois revolutions of the nineteenth century; Russia, however, was a country where the vast majority of the peasantry owned no land. For the peasantry the February Revolution meant the opening of the struggle against the landlords, the awakening of political consciousness. At first cautious in its demands, seeking only rent reductions and similar ameliorations of intolerable conditions, the peasant movement rapidly gained in depth, scope, and political intensity. Soon estate after estate was looted, burned, and the land divided up — months before the October Revolution triumphed.

While division of the great estates was the formal program of the Social Revolutionaries, the mass radical peasant party, the SRs opposed the land seizures by the peasants because such actions jeopardized the support of the landed bourgeoisie for the coalition government to which the SRs belonged.

During the summer and fall of 1917, as the Menshevik-SR government began sending troops against the peasants to protect the landlords, the peasantry turned more and more toward the Bolsheviks who promised to support the land seizures.

In other words, the confiscation of the great estates and their division among the peasants was not a policy merely implemented by the Bolsheviks, but a *fact* already accomplished in large measure before the Bolsheviks came to power. To have opposed the division of the great estates would have meant a war against the peasantry and the defeat of the revolution — just as a similar policy by the Mensheviks had assured the downfall of the bourgeois government.

Rosa Luxemburg recognized this when she stated, "Surely the solution of the problem by the direct, immediate seizure and distribution of the land by the peasants was the shortest, simplest, most clear-cut formula to achieve two diverse things: to break down large landownership, and immediately to bind the peasants to the revolutionary government. As a political measure to fortify the proletarian socialist government, it was an excellent tactical move."

She was right, of course, in pointing to the dangers this could ultimately entail for the revolution, if the process could not be reversed, and if a significant layer of rich peasants became more and more powerful. She recognized the absolute necessity of solving the agrarian problem, which had never been accomplished by a bourgeois revolution in the czarist empire; but she did not clearly see how this task combined with the tasks of the proletarian revolution. She favored the nationalization of the large estates, but proposed they be retained intact and operated as large-scale agricultural units. While theoretically correct, such a course would have meant leaping far ahead of the historical possibilities.

The Bolsheviks were able to win the allegiance of the peasantry only by adopting the agrarian policy they did, and only with the peasants as allies was the revolution able to defeat the combined counterrevolutionary forces.

Rosa Luxemburg's final major criticism of Bolshevik policy

was directed at the use of violence against the counterrevolution. Her position was basically a moral one, a humanitarian reluctance to use force or violence, to see any life destroyed. But it would be a mistake to put her in the same category as liberal pacifists who hypocritically oppose any kind of violence.

She agreed wholeheartedly that the violence of the oppressed is in no way comparable to the violence of the oppressor. One is justified and the other is not. There was no confusion in her mind concerning the source of the greatest violence and destruction mankind had every known. She wrote in *Rote Fahne*, November 24, 1918:

"[Those] who sent 1.5 million German men and youths to the slaughter without blinking an eyelid, [those] who supported with all the means at their disposal for four years the greatest bloodletting which humanity has ever experienced — they now scream hoarsely about 'terror,' about the alleged 'monstrosities' threatened by the dictatorship of the proletariat. But these gentlemen should look at their own history."[20]

She understood full well that no revolution could consolidate itself without violently putting down the old ruling forces — that no revolution in history had ever succeeded without violence and probably never would. But she fervently wished it could be otherwise, and regretted that the revolutionary forces in the Soviet Union were so weak that they had to resort to violence against the counterrevolution.

At the same time she realized that the revolution's weakness was entirely a function of its international isolation. She realized that a successful German revolution would make violence less necessary in Russia, and that with each additional successful revolution, the forces of counterrevolution would be weaker, and less violence would have to be used against them.

Once again, her criticisms of the Bolsheviks came down to new exhortations to the German workers to come to the aid of their Russian comrades. When she wrote, "There is no doubt either . . . that Lenin and Trotsky . . . have taken many a decisive step only with the greatest inner hesitation and with most violent inner opposition," she was probably referring more than anything else to the use of violence, and reflecting very clearly her own inner revulsion against it, even though she understood it was absolutely necessary. She realized that if counterrevolutionaries were to triumph, the violence they would use would be infinitely more ruthless and barbaric than the revolutionary violence of the class that had history on its side.

Rosa Luxemburg ends her article on the Russian Revolution in the same vein as she begins it: with unequivocal support for the Bolsheviks, proclaiming that the future of the world is in the hands of bolshevism.

Only the most obtuse and hypocritical could take her words and twist them to make her appear an anticommunist. Her own phrases speak more strongly in her own defense than anything which could be added:

"Whatever a party could offer of courage, revolutionary far-sightedness and consistency in a historic hour, Lenin, Trotsky and the other comrades have given in good measure. All the revolutionary honor and capacity which Western social democracy lacked was represented by the Bolsheviks. Their October uprising was not only the actual salvation of the Russian Revolution; it was also the salvation of the honor of international socialism."

A Revolutionary

The selections that follow tell the life story of Rosa Luxemburg — in her own words. They record the main battles in which she engaged, the stands she took on each of the major political questions that divided the left in her day, and the answers she gave to those with whom she disagreed. Her record for revolutionary consistency, as noted earlier, was one that few of her contemporaries could match.

In some ways, the selections tell more about her than any biography could. They have been arranged chronologically in order to show her life and political ideas as they actually developed. The growing maturity and confidence which her writings reflect, as well as the greater clarity and smoother style, are obvious as one progresses. The earlier selections take more effort to read. They seem stiffer and more self-conscious. Throughout, her style seems somewhat long-winded, at least to the modern ear, and one often wishes she could have found some more concise way to make her point and get on with it. But, in the manner of many revolutionary intellectuals of her generation, she made her living as a journalist — sometimes simply turning out copy — and such training hardly provided great incentive to brevity.

Nevertheless, her articles are always tightly constructed with few loose ends or extraneous arguments. Her style is humorous and sharp — especially when she winds up against her arch-enemies within the SPD and gives full vent to her contempt for their cowardice, careerism, and craven scraping before the almighty power of capital.

The biographical and historical information here and in the introductory notes for each selection has been drawn in large part from the biographies of Rosa Luxemburg written by Paul Froelich and J. P. Nettl.

Froelich was also a leader of the Spartacus League in the months following the end of World War I. The League became the Communist Party of Germany and he remained in it for close to ten years. He was expelled in 1928, and subsequently went through a number of different political groups. His biography of Rosa Luxemburg was written in the late 1930s, while he was in exile in France following Hitler's rise to power. This biography contains much firsthand information, especially about the final months of Rosa Luxemburg's life, but his political judgments are distorted by his subjectivism. For example, he tends to oversimplify the reasons for the failure of the German revolution of 1919, attributing it primarily to exceptionally difficult circumstances — as if all revolutions are not made under "exceptionally difficult circumstances." He fails to deal adequately with the differences between the organization built by Rosa Luxemburg and that built by Lenin.

J. P. Nettl's two-volume biography of Rosa Luxemburg appeared in 1966, and it is an extremely valuable work from the point of view of research and academic scholarship. Nettl's biography is more reliable than Froelich's for dates, names, and other facts. It is extensively annotated and cross-referenced, and provides a wealth of information about Rosa Luxemburg's life and all her writings, including books, pamphlets, newspaper articles, and personal correspondence. His research into her Polish writings and work is particularly valuable.

Unfortunately, Nettl fails to give a comprehensive historic picture of the era in which Rosa Luxemburg lived, and he fails to grasp the main points in some of her political controversies. His ill-informed anti-Leninism is as annoying as his professorial aloofness, but his work will unquestionably remain the most comprehensive biography available for quite some time.

Little can be said about Rosa Luxemburg which, in conclusion, would not seem superfluous. Her seriousness, her unselfish devotion to the liberation of humanity, her self-discipline and courage speak for themselves throughout the pages that follow. No more honest tribute could be paid her than to say: to the depths of her being Rosa Luxemburg was a revolutionary — one of the greatest humanity has ever produced.

March, 1970

Notes

1. J. P. Nettl, *Rosa Luxemburg*, 2 vols. (London: Oxford University Press, 1966), vol. 1, p. 131.

2. Ibid., p. 387.

3. Leon Trotsky, *History of the Russian Revolution*, 3 vols. (Ann Arbor, Mich.: University of Michigan Press, 1957), vol. 3, p. 38.

4. V. I. Lenin, *The Right of Nations to Self-Determination* (Moscow: Progress Publishers, 1968), p. 54.

5. Ibid., p. 110.

6. Ibid., p. 98.

7. Ibid., p. 99.

8. Ibid., p. 103.

9. Trotsky, *History*, p. 45.

10. Max Shachtman, "Lenin and Rosa Luxemburg," *New International*, vol. 2, no. 2, March 1935, p. 64.

11. Nettl, *Rosa Luxemburg*, p. 375.

12. V. I. Lenin, *One Step Forward, Two Steps Back,* (Moscow: Foreign Language Publishing House, 1950), p. 281.

13. Leon Trotsky, "Problems of Civil War," *International Socialist Review*, vol. 31, no. 2, March-April 1970, pp. 10-11.

14. As cited by Walter Held, "The German Left and Bolshevism," *New International*, vol. 5, no. 2, February 1939, p. 47.

15. Walter Held, "Once Again—Lenin and Luxemburg," *Fourth International*, vol. 1, no. 2, June 1940, p. 49.

16. As cited by Isaac Deutscher, *The Prophet Armed, Leon Trotsky, 1879-1921* (New York: Vintage Books, 1954), p. 90.

17. Leon Trotsky, *The Writings of Leon Trotsky (1938-39)* (New York: Merit Publishers, 1969), p. 132.

18. Nettl, *Rosa Luxemburg*, vol. 2, p. 680.

19. Ibid., pp. 716-17.

20. Ibid., p. 730.

REFORM OR
REVOLUTION

Reform or Revolution was Rosa Luxemburg's first major political work, and one of her most enduring. She herself rightly considered it the work by which she would earn her political spurs in the German Social Democratic Party (SPD), and force the "old guard" to take her seriously as a political leader — despite the fact she was still in her twenties, a foreigner, and a woman.

Rosa left Switzerland, where she had recently completed her doctorate, and moved to Berlin in May 1898. Immediately she became embroiled in the growing battle over revisionism in the SPD.

During 1897-98, Eduard Bernstein published a series of articles in *Neue Zeit*, the theoretical organ of the SPD, in which he attempted to refute the basic tenets of scientific socialism, particularly the Marxist assertion that capitalism contains within itself the seeds of its own destruction, that it cannot maintain itself forever. He denied the materialist conception of history, the growing acuteness of capitalist contradictions, and the theory of class struggle. He concluded that revolution was not necessary, that socialism could be achieved by gradual reform of the capitalist system, through mechanisms like consumers' cooperatives, trade unions, and the gradual extension of political democracy. The SPD, he asserted, should be transformed from a party of social revolution into a party of social reforms. These ideas were further elaborated in his book, published in English under the title *Evolutionary Socialism*.

When Bernstein's articles began appearing, the leadership of the SPD did not take the controversy seriously. Bernstein was a close friend of the entire leadership of the party — August Bebel, Karl Kautsky, Wilhelm Liebknecht, Ignaz Auer, and others. He was one of the literary executors of Engels's estate, and a former editor of one of the SPD papers. Kautsky, the editor of *Neue Zeit*, thought highly of the articles and accepted them for publication. The attitude expressed by one of the SPD papers, *Leipziger Volkszeitung*, was quite indicative: "Interesting observations which nonetheless terminate in a mistaken conclusion; something that is always liable to happen especially to lively and critical people, but there is no more to it than that."

Although he denied it vociferously, Bernstein's writings were the first attempt to provide a systematic theoretical justification for those currents within the SPD which had in practice rejected revolutionary Marxism, the program on which the party stood. But he was certainly not an isolated individual. He had strong supporters among socialist intellectuals, trade-union leaders and the South Germans.

The position held by the South Germans within the SPD was particularly significant. The SPD itself was formed in 1875 and outlawed by the government in 1878. Despite its illegal status it continued to grow rapidly and when the antisocialist laws were repealed in 1890, the party emerged as an important, legal, political force with a significant representation in the federal Reichstag and various provincial legislatures. Under its leadership a powerful trade-union movement was built. In the International, the SPD was the unquestioned "great" party, the model looked up to by the whole International.

But the reformist current for which Bernstein became the theoretician began to develop early. During the prolonged period of European peace and relative prosperity at the end of the nineteenth century it found fertile soil in which to grow. One of its first overt manifestations was the policy of "South German exceptionalism."

The official SPD policy of "not a man nor a farthing for this system" was always translated into legislative action, on a federal level, by unconditional refusal to vote for any budgets which would tax the workers and peasants to sustain the tyranny of the German capitalist state, and maintain the courts, police and army of the rulers. But as early as 1891, SPD deputies in the provincial legislatures of Wuerttemberg, Bavaria, and Baden, pleading special conditions in southern Germany, voted for provincial budgets, arguing that since their vote was often decisive, they were thus able to use their political weight to force concessions and obtain a "better" budget to maintain capitalism. While this practice was roundly condemned within the SPD, the myth of southern exceptionalism was maintained, and motions to forbid SPD delegates to vote for *any* budgets, whether federal, provincial, or local, were defeated at national congresses in 1894 and 1895. (After the 1894 congress, even Engels protested to Wilhelm Liebknecht in a letter of November 27, 1894, sternly criticizing Georg von Vollmar, principal leader of the South Germans.)

It was such right-wing tendencies within the SPD, bent on reforming capitalism, that gave the strongest support to Bernstein's theories.

When Rosa Luxemburg arrived on the scene the battle had hardly begun. While the majority of the party executive did not agree with Bernstein, they acted as if they hoped the controversy would somehow disappear. Karl Kautsky, the SPD's leading theoretician, pleaded lack of time and begged off polemicizing against his good friend Bernstein. None of the party's journals were systematically answering Bernstein's theories, with the exception of *Saechsische Arbeiterzeitung* in which Parvus, a Russian emigre and editor of the paper, was running a slashing critique.

Rosa Luxemburg entered the battle by publishing the articles reproduced here. The first section appeared in the *Leipziger Volkszeitung* in September 1898. In April 1899 she published a second article in reply to *Evolutionary Socialism*. The two articles together were published in 1900 as *Reform or Revolution*, and a second edition appeared in 1908. The current translation, by Integer, is from the 1908 edition.

The discussion continued within the party and Second International for a number of years. The SPD executive at first encouraged a theoretical discussion, maintaining an ambivalent position, but the practical implications of Bernstein's abandonment of a revolutionary perspective could not be ignored for long. One by one most of the major German and International leaders entered the battle against revisionism. The debate spread throughout the entire International.

At the party Congresses of 1901 and 1903, and at the International Congress of 1904, resolutions condemning the theoretical basis of revisionism were adopted. However, Bernstein, Vollmar and the other proponents of revisionism remained securely within the SPD; and the extent to which the defeat of revisionism remained a hollow victory, even at that early date, was indicated by the fact that Bernstein, who had not altered his views, himself voted for the resolutions condemning revisionism.

As Ignaz Auer, SPD secretary, wrote to Bernstein in 1899, "My dear Ede, one does not formally make a decision to do the things you suggest, one doesn't *say* such things, one simply does them."

Auer's formula was unwittingly followed by the majority of the SPD, as was demonstrated fifteen years later for all the world to see when the party formally voted to support its own imperialist government in World War I, a betrayal of the most elementary principles of proletarian internationalism and revolutionary Marxism.

As Rosa Luxemburg pointed out, the Bernstein controversy posed the question of "the very existence of the social democratic movement."

That she was among the first to realize this and sound the

alarm would be sufficient to place Rosa Luxemburg in the revolutionary hall of fame, even if she had done nothing more of importance for the rest of her life.

_____

Author's Introduction

At first view the title of this work may be found surprising. Can the social democracy be against reforms? Can we counterpose the social revolution, the transformation of the existing order, our final goal, to social reforms? Certainly not. The daily struggle for reforms, for the amelioration of the condition of the workers within the framework of the existing social order, and for democratic institutions, offers to the social democracy the only means of engaging in the proletarian class war and working in the direction of the final goal — the conquest of political power and the suppression of wage labor. Between social reforms and revolution there exists for the social democracy an indissoluble tie. The struggle for reforms is its means; the social revolution, its aim.

It is in Eduard Bernstein's theory, presented in his articles on "Problems of Socialism," *Neue Zeit* of 1897-98, and in his book *Die Voraussetzungen des Sozialismus and die Aufgaben der Sozialdemokratie* [The Preconditions of Socialism and the Tasks of Social Democracy — in English published under the title *Evolutionary Socialism* — Ed.] that we find for the first time, the opposition of the two factors of the labor movement. His theory tends to counsel us to renounce the social transformation, the final goal of the social democracy and, inversely, to make of social reforms, the means of the class struggle, its aim. Bernstein himself has very clearly and characteristically formulated this viewpoint when he wrote: "The final goal, no matter what it is, is nothing; the movement is everything."

But since the final goal of socialism constitutes the only decisive factor distinguishing the social democratic movement from bourgeois democracy and from bourgeois radicalism, the only factor transforming the entire labor movement from a vain effort to repair the capitalist order into a class struggle against this order, for the suppression of this order — the question: "Reform or revolution?" as it is posed by Bernstein, equals for the social democracy the question: "To be or not to be?" In the controversy with Bernstein and his followers, everybody in the party ought to understand clearly it is not a question of this or that method of struggle, or the use of this or that set of tactics, but of the very existence of the social democratic movement.

Upon a casual consideration of Bernstein's theory, this may appear like an exaggeration. Does he not continually mention the social democracy and its aims? Does he not repeat again and again, in very explicit language, that he too strives toward the final goal of socialism, but in another way? Does he not stress particularly that he fully approves of the present practice of the social democracy?

That is all true, to be sure. It is also true that every new movement, when it first elaborates its theory and policy, begins by finding support in the preceding movement, though it may be in direct contradiction with the latter. It begins by suiting itself to the forms found at hand and by speaking the language spoken hereto. In time, the new grain breaks through the old husk. The new movement finds its own forms and its own language.

To expect an opposition against scientific socialism at its very beginning, to express itself clearly, fully, and to the last consequence on the subject of its real content; to expect it to deny openly and bluntly the theoretic basis of the social democracy —would amount to underrating the power of scientific socialism. Today he who wants to pass as a socialist, and at the same time would declare war on Marxian doctrine, the most stupendous product of the human mind in the century, must begin with involuntary esteem for Marx. He must begin by acknowledging himself to be his disciple, by seeking in Marx's own teachings the points of support for an attack on the latter, while he represents this attack as a further development of Marxian doctrine. On this account, we must, unconcerned by its outer forms, pick out the sheathed kernel of Bernstein's theory. This is a matter of urgent necessity for the broad layers of the industrial proletariat in our party.

No coarser insult, no baser aspersion, can be thrown against the workers than the remark: "Theoretic controversies are only for academicians." Some time ago Lassalle said: "Only when science and the workers, these opposite poles of society, become one, will they crush in their arms of steel all obstacles to culture." The entire strength of the modern labor movement rests on theoretic knowledge.

But doubly important is this knowledge for the workers in the present case, because it is precisely they and their influence in the movement that are in the balance here. It is their skin that is being brought to market. The opportunist theory in the party, the theory formulated by Bernstein, is nothing else than an unconscious attempt to assure predominance to the petty bourgeois elements that have entered our party, to change the policy and aims of our party in their direction. The question of reform and revolution, of the final goal and the movement, is basically, in another form, but the question of the petty bourgeois or proletarian character of the labor movement.

It is, therefore, in the interest of the proletarian mass of the

37

party to become acquainted, actively and in detail, with the present theoretic controversy with opportunism. As long as theoretic knowledge remains the privilege of a handful of "academicians" in the party, the latter will face the danger of going astray. Only when the great mass of workers take the keen and dependable weapons of scientific socialism in their own hands will all the petty bourgeois inclinations, all the opportunist currents, come to naught. The movement will then find itself on sure and firm ground. "Quantity will do it."

Berlin, April 18, 1899

Part I
The Opportunist Method

If it is true that theories are only the images of the phenomena of the exterior world in the human consciousness, it must be added, concerning Eduard Bernstein's system, that theories are sometimes inverted images. Think of a theory of instituting socialism by means of social reforms in the face of the complete stagnation of the reform movement in Germany. Think of a theory of trade-union control over production in face of the defeat of the metal workers in England. Consider the theory of winning a majority in Parliament, after the revision of the constitution of Saxony and in view of the most recent attempts against universal suffrage. However, the pivotal point of Bernstein's system is not located in his conception of the practical tasks of the social democracy. It is found in his stand on the course of the objective development of capitalist society, which, in turn is closely bound to his conception of the practical tasks of the social democracy.

According to Bernstein, a general decline of capitalism seems to be increasingly improbable because, on the one hand, capitalism shows a greater capacity of adaptation, and, on the other hand, capitalist production becomes more and more varied.

The capacity of capitalism to adapt itself, says Bernstein, is manifested first in the disappearance of general crises, resulting from the development of the credit system, employers' organizations, wider means of communication and informational services. It shows itself secondly, in the tenacity of the middle classes, which hails from the growing differentiation of the branches of production and the elevation of vast layers of the proletariat to the level of the middle class. It is furthermore proved, argues Bernstein, by the amelioration of the economic and political situation of the proletariat as a result of its trade-union activity.

From this theoretic stand is derived the following general conclusion about the practical work of the social democracy. The latter must not direct its daily activity toward the conquest of political power, but toward the betterment of the condition of the working class within the existing order. It must not expect to institute socialism as a result of a political and social crisis, but should build socialism by means of the progressive extension of social control and the gradual application of the principle of cooperation.

Bernstein himself sees nothing new in his theories. On the contrary, he believes them to be in agreement with certain declarations of Marx and Engels. Nevertheless, it seems to us that it is difficult to deny that they are in formal contradiction with the conceptions of scientific socialism.

If Bernstein's revisionism merely consisted in affirming that the march of capitalist development is slower than was thought before, he would merely be presenting an argument for adjourning the conquest of power by the proletariat, on which everybody agreed up to now. Its only consequence would be a slowing up of the pace of the struggle.

But that is not the case. What Bernstein questions is not the rapidity of the development of capitalist society, but the march of the development itself and, consequently, the very possibility of a change to socialism.

Socialist theory up to now declared that the point of departure for a transformation to socialism would be a general and catastrophic crisis. We must distinguish in this outlook two things: the fundamental idea and its exterior form.

The fundamental idea consists of the affirmation that capitalism, as a result of its own inner contradictions, moves toward a point when it will be unbalanced, when it will simply become impossible. There were good reasons for conceiving that juncture in the form of a catastrophic general commercial crisis. But that is of secondary importance when the fundamental idea is considered.

The scientific basis of socialism rests, as is well known, on three principal results of capitalist development. First, on the growing anarchy of capitalist economy, leading inevitably to its ruin. Second, on the progressive socialization of the process of production, which creates the germs of the future social order. And third, on the increased organization and consciousness of the proletarian class, which constitutes the active factor in the coming revolution.

Bernstein pulls away the first of the three fundamental supports of scientific socialism. He says that capitalist development does not lead to a general economic collapse.

He does not merely reject a certain form of the collapse. He rejects the very possibility of collapse. He says textually: "One could claim that by collapse of the present society is meant something else than a general commercial crisis, worse than all others, that is, a complete collapse of the capitalist system brought about as a result of its own contradictions." And to this he replies: "With the growing development of society a complete and almost general collapse of the present system of production becomes more and more improbable, because capitalist development increases on the one hand the capacity of adaptation and, on the other — that is, at the same time, the differentiation of industry" *(Neue Zeit,* 1897-98, vol. 18, p. 555).

But then the question arises: Why and how, in that case, shall we attain the final goal? According to scientific socialism, the historic necessity of the socialist revolution manifests itself above all in the growing anarchy of capitalism, which drives the system into an impasse. But if one admits with Bernstein that capitalist development does not move in the direction of its own ruin, then socialism ceases to be objectively necessary. There remain the other two mainstays of the scientific explanation of socialism, which are also said to be consequences of capitalism itself: the socialization of the process of production and the growing consciousness of the proletariat. It is these two matters that Bernstein has in mind when he says: "The suppression of the theory of collapse does not in any way deprive socialist doctrine of its power of persuasion. For, examined closely, what are all the factors enumerated by us that make for the suppression of the modification of the former crises? Nothing else, in fact, than the conditions, or even in part the germs of the socialization of production and exchange" (ibid., p. 554).

Very little reflection is needed to understand that here, too, we face a false conclusion. Where lies the importance of all the phenomena that are said by Bernstein to be the means of capitalist adaptation — cartels, the credit system, the development of means of communication, the amelioration of the situation of the working class, etc.? Obviously, in that they suppress or, at least, attenuate the internal contradictions of capitalist economy, and stop the development or the aggravation of these contradictions. Thus the suppression of crises can only mean the suppression of the antagonism between production and exchange on the capitalist base. The amelioration of the situation of the working class, or the penetration of certain fractions of the class into the middle layers, can only mean the attenuation of the antagonism between capital and labor. But if the mentioned factors suppress the capitalist contradictions and consequently save the system from ruin, if they enable capitalism to maintain itself — and that is why Bernstein calls them "means of adaptation" — how can cartels, the credit system, trade unions, etc., be at the same time "the conditions and even, in part, the germs" of socialism? Obviously only in the sense that they express most clearly the social character of production.

But by presenting it in its capitalist form, the same factors render superfluous, inversely, in the same measure, the transformation of this socialized production into socialist production. That is why they can be the germs or conditions of a socialist order only in a theoretic sense and not in a historic sense. They are phenomena which, in the light of our conception of socialism, we know to be related to socialism but which, in fact, not only do not lead to a socialist revolution but render it, on the contrary, superfluous.

There remains one force making for socialism — the class consciousness of the proletariat. But it, too, is in the given case not the simple intellectual reflection of the growing contradictions of capitalism and its approaching decline. It is now no more than an ideal whose force of persuasion rests only on the perfection attributed to it.

We have here, in brief, the explanation of the socialist program by means of "pure reason." We have here, to use simpler language, an idealist explanation of socialism. The objective necessity of socialism, the explanation of socialism as the result of the material development of society, falls to the ground.

Revisionist theory thus places itself in a dilemma. Either the socialist transformation is, as was admitted up to now, the consequence of the internal contradictions of capitalism, and with the growth of capitalism will develop its inner contradictions, resulting inevitably, at some point, in its collapse, (in that case the "means of adaptation" are ineffective and the theory of collapse is correct); or the "means of adaptation" will really stop the collapse of the capitalist system and thereby enable capitalism to maintain itself by suppressing its own contradictions. In that case socialism ceases to be a historic necessity. It then becomes anything you want to call it, but is no longer the result of the material development of society.

The dilemma leads to another. Either revisionism is correct in its position on the course of capitalist development, and therefore the socialist transformation of society is only a utopia, or socialism is not a utopia, and the theory of "means of adaptation" is false. There is the question in a nutshell.

The Adaptation of Capitalism

According to Bernstein, the credit system, the perfected means of communication and the new capitalist combines are the important factors that forward the adaptation of capitalist economy.

Credit has diverse applications in capitalism. Its two most important functions are to extend production and to facilitate exchange. When the inner tendency of capitalist production to extend boundlessly strikes against the restricted dimensions of private property, credit appears as a means of surmounting these limits in a particular capitalist manner. Credit, through shareholding, combines in one magnitude of capital a large number of individual capitals. It makes available to each capitalist the use of other capitalists' money — in the form of industrial credit. As commercial credit it accelerates the exchange of commodities and therefore the return of capital into production, and thus aids the entire cycle of the process of production. The manner in which these two principal functions of credit influence the formation of crises is quite obvious. If it is true that crises appear as a result of the contradiction existing between the capacity of extension, the tendency of production to increase, and the restricted consumption capacity of the market, credit is precisely, in view of what was stated above, the specific means that makes this contradiction break out as often as possible. To begin with, it increases disproportionately the capacity of the extension of production and thus constitutes an inner motive force that is constantly pushing production to exceed the limits of the market. But credit strikes from two sides. After having (as a factor of the process of production) provoked overproduction, credit (as a factor of exchange) destroys, during the crisis, the very productive forces it itself created. At the first symptom of the crisis, credit melts away. It abandons exchange where it would still be found indispensable, and appearing instead ineffective and useless, there where some exchange still continues, it reduces to a minimum the consumption capacity of the market.

Besides having these two principal results, credit also influences the formation of crises in the following ways. It constitutes the technical means of making available to an entrepreneur the capital of other owners. It stimulates at the same time the bold and unscrupulous utilization of the property of others. That is, it leads to speculation. Credit not only aggravates the crisis in its capacity as a dissembled means of exchange, it also helps to bring and extend the crisis by transforming all exchange into an extremely complex and artificial mechanism that, having a minimum of metallic money as a real base, is easily disarranged at the slightest occasion.

We see that credit, instead of being an instrument for the suppression or the attenuation of crises, is on the contrary a particularly mighty instrument for the formation of crises. It cannot be anything else. Credit eliminates the remaining rigidity of capitalist relationships. It introduces everywhere the greatest elasticity possible. It renders all capitalist forces extensible, relative, and mutually sensitive to the highest degree. Doing this, it facilitates and aggravates crises, which are nothing more or less than the periodic collisions of the contradictory forces of capitalist economy.

That leads us to another question. Why does credit generally have the appearance of a "means of adaptation" of capitalism? No matter what the relation or form in which this "adaptation" is represented by certain people, it can obviously consist only of the power to suppress one of the several antagonistic relations of capitalist economy, that is, of the power to suppress or weaken one of these contradictions, and allow liberty of movement, at one point or another, to the otherwise fettered productive forces. In fact, it is precisely credit that aggravates these contradictions to the highest degree. It aggravates the antagonism between the mode of production and the mode of exchange by stretching production to the limit and at the same time paralyzing exchange at the smallest pretext. It aggravates the antagonism between the mode of production and the mode of appropriation by separating production from ownership, that is, by transforming the capital employed in production into "social" capital and at the same time transforming a part of the profit, in the form of interest on capital, into a simple title of ownership. It aggravates the antagonism existing between the property relations (ownership) and the relations of production by putting into a small number of hands immense productive forces and expropriating a large number of small capitalists. Lastly, it aggravates the antagonism existing between the social character of production and private capitalist ownership by rendering necessary the intervention of the state in production.

In short, credit reproduces all the fundamental antagonisms of the capitalist world. It accentuates them. It precipitates their development and thus pushes the capitalist world forward to its own destruction. The prime act of capitalist adaptation, as far as credit is concerned, should really consist in breaking and suppressing credit. In fact, credit is far from being a means of capitalist adaptation. It is, on the contrary, a means of destruction of the most extreme revolutionary significance. Has not this revolutionary character of credit actually inspired plans of "socialist" reform? As such, it has had some distinguished proponents, some of whom (Isaac Pereira in France), were, as Marx put it, half prophets, half rogues.

Just as fragile is the second "means of adaptation": employers' organizations. According to Bernstein, such organizations will put an end to anarchy of production and do away with crises through their regulation of production. The multiple repercussions of the development of cartels and trusts have not been considered too carefully up to now. But they represent a problem that can only be solved with the aid of Marxist theory.

One thing is certain. We could speak of a damming up of capitalist anarchy through the agency of capitalist combines only in the measure that cartels, trusts, etc., become, even approximately, the dominant form of production. But such a possibility is excluded by the very nature of cartels. The final economic aim and result of combines is the following. Through the suppression of competition in a given branch of production, the distribution of the mass of profit realized on the market is influenced in such a manner that there is an increase of the share going to this branch of industry. Such organization of the field can increase the rate of profit in one branch of industry at the expense of another. That is precisely why it cannot be generalized, for when it is extended to all important branches of industry, this tendency suppresses its own influence.

Furthermore, within the limits of their practical application the result of combines is the very opposite of the suppression of industrial anarchy. Cartels ordinarily succeed in obtaining an increase of profit, in the home market, by producing at a lower rate of profit for the foreign market, thus utilizing the supplementary portions of capital which they cannot utilize for domestic needs. That is to say, they sell abroad cheaper than at home. The result is the sharpening of competition abroad — the very opposite of what certain people want to find. That is well demonstrated by the history of the world sugar industry.

Generally speaking, combines, treated as a manifestation of the capitalist mode of production, can only be considered a definite phase of capitalist development. Cartels are fundamentally nothing else than a means resorted to by the capitalist mode of production for the purpose of holding back the fatal fall of the rate of profit in certain branches of production. What method do cartels employ for this end? That of keeping inactive a part of the accumulated capital. That is, they use the same method which in another form is employed in crises. The remedy and the illness resemble each other like two drops of water. Indeed the first can be considered the lesser evil only up to a certain point. When the outlets of disposal begin to shrink, and the world market has been extended to its limit and has become exhausted through the competition of the capitalist countries — and sooner or later that is bound to come — then the forced partial idleness of capital will reach such dimensions that the remedy will become transformed into a malady, and capital, already pretty much "socialized" through regulation, will tend to revert again to the form of individual capital. In the face of the increased difficulties of finding markets, each individual portion of capital will prefer to take its chances alone. At that time, the large regulating organizations will burst like soap bubbles and give way to aggravated competition.

In a general way, cartels, just like credit, appear therefore as a determined phase of capitalist development, which in the last analysis aggravates the anarchy of the capitalist world and expresses and ripens its internal contradictions. Cartels aggravate the antagonism existing between the mode of production and exchange by sharpening the struggle between the producer and consumer, as is the case especially in the United States. They aggravate, furthermore, the antagonism existing between the mode of production and the mode of appropriation by opposing in the most brutal fashion, to the working class the superior force of organized capital, and thus increasing the antagonism between capital and labor.

Finally, capitalist combinations aggravate the contradiction existing between the international character of capitalist world economy and the national character of the state—insofar as they are always accompanied by a general tariff war, which sharpens the differences among the capitalist states. We must add to this the decidedly revolutionary influence exercised by cartels on the concentration of production, technical progress, etc.

In other words, when evaluated from the angle of their final effect on capitalist economy, cartels and trusts fail as "means of adaptation." They fail to attenuate the contradictions of capitalism. On the contrary, they appear to be an instrument of greater anarchy. They encourage the further development of the internal contradictions of capitalism. They accelerate the coming of a general decline of capitalism.

But if the credit system, cartels, and the rest do not suppress the anarchy of capitalism, why have we not had a major commercial crisis for two decades, since 1873? Is this not a sign that, contrary to Marx's analysis, the capitalist mode of production has adapted itself—at least, in a general way—to the needs of society? Hardly had Bernstein rejected, in 1898, Marx's theory of crises, when a profound general crisis broke out in 1900, while seven years later, a new crisis, beginning in the United States, hit the world market. Facts proved the theory of "adaptation" to be false. They showed at the same time that the people who abandoned Marx's theory of crisis only because no crisis occurred within a certain space of time merely confused the essence of this theory with one of its secondary exterior aspects—the ten-year cycle. The description of the cycle of modern capitalist industry as a ten-year period was to Marx and Engels, in 1860 and 1870, only a simple statement of facts. It was not based on a natural law but on a series of given historic circumstances that were connected with the rapidly spreading activity of young capitalism.

The crisis of 1825 was, in effect, the result of the extensive investment of capital in the construction of roads, canals, gas works, which took place during the preceding decade, particularly in England, where the crisis broke out. The following crisis of 1836-39 was similarly the result of heavy investments in the construction of means of transportation. The crisis of 1847 was provoked by the feverish building of railroads in England (from 1844 to 1847, in three years, the British Parliament gave railway concessions to the value of 15 billion dollars). In each of the three mentioned cases, a crisis came after new bases for capitalist development were established. In 1857, the same result was brought by the abrupt opening of new markets for European industry in America and Australia, after the discovery of the gold mines, and the extensive construction of railway lines especially in France, where the example of England was then closely imitated. (From 1852 to 1856, new railway lines to the value of 1250 million francs were built in France alone.) And finally we have the great crisis of 1873 — a direct consequence of the first boom of large industry in Germany and Austria, which followed the political events of 1866 and 1871.

So that up to now, the sudden extension of the domain of capitalist economy, and not its shrinking, was each time the cause of the commercial crisis. That the international crises repeated themselves precisely every ten years was a purely exterior fact, a matter of chance. The Marxist formula for crises as presented by Engels in *Anti-Duehring* and by Marx in the first and third volumes of *Capital*, applies to all crises only in the measure that it uncovers their international mechanism and their general basic causes.

Crises may repeat themselves every five or ten years, or even every eight or twenty years. But what proves best the falseness of Bernstein's theory is that it is in the countries having the greatest development of the famous "means of adaptation" — credit, perfected communications and trusts — that the last crisis (1907-08) was most violent.

The belief that capitalist production could "adapt" itself to exchange presupposes one of two things: either the world market can spread unlimitedly, or on the contrary the development of the productive forces is so fettered that it cannot pass beyond the bounds of the market. The first hypothesis constitutes a material impossibility. The second is rendered just as impossible by the constant technical progress that daily creates new productive forces in all branches.

There remains still another phenomenon which, says Bernstein, contradicts the course of capitalist development as it is indicated above. In the "steadfast phalanx" of middle-sized enterprises, Bernstein sees a sign that the development of large industry does not move in a revolutionary direction, and is not as effective from the angle of the concentration of industry as was expected by the "theory" of collapse. He is here, however,

46

the victim of his own lack of understanding. For to see the progressive disappearance of the middle-sized enterprise as a necessary result of the development of large industry is to misunderstand sadly the nature of this process.

According to Marxist theory, small capitalists play in the general course of capitalist development the role of pioneers of technical change. They possess that role in a double sense. They initiate new methods of production in well-established branches of industry; they are instrumental in the creation of new branches of production not yet exploited by the big capitalist.

It is false to imagine that the history of the middle-sized capitalist establishments proceeds rectilinearly in the direction of their progressive disappearance. The course of this development is on the contrary purely dialectical and moves constantly among contradictions. The middle capitalist layers find themselves, just like the workers, under the influence of two antagonistic tendencies, one ascendant, the other descendant. In this case, the descendant tendency is the continued rise of the scale of production, which overflows periodically the dimensions of the average-sized parcels of capital and removes them repeatedly from the terrain of world competition. The ascendant tendency is, first, the periodic depreciation of the existing capital, which lowers again, for a certain time, the scale of production, in proportion to the value of the necessary minimum amount of capital. It is represented, besides, by the penetration of capitalist production into new spheres. The struggle of the average-sized enterprise against big capital cannot be considered a regularly proceeding battle in which the troops of the weaker party continue to melt away directly and quantitatively. It should be rather regarded as a periodic mowing down of the small enterprises, which rapidly grow up again, only to be mowed down once more by large industry. The two tendencies play ball with the middle capitalist layers. The descending tendency must win in the end. The very opposite is true about the development of the working class.

The victory of the descending tendency must not necessarily show itself in an absolute numerical diminution of the middle-sized enterprises. It must show itself, first in the progressive increase of the minimum amount of capital necessary for the functioning of the enterprises in the old branches of production; second, in the constant diminution of the interval of time during which the small capitalists conserve the opportunity to exploit the new branches of production. The result as far as the small capitalist is concerned is a progressively shorter duration of his stay in the new industry and a progressively more rapid change in the methods of production as a field for investment. For the average capitalist strata, taken as a whole, there is a process

47

of more and more rapid social assimilation and dissimilation. Bernstein knows this perfectly well. He himself comments on this. But what he seems to forget is that this very thing is the law of the movement of the average capitalist enterprise. If one admits that small capitalists are pioneers of technical progress, and if it is true that the latter is the vital pulse of the capitalist economy, then it is manifest that small capitalists are an integral part of capitalist development, and they will disappear only with capitalist development. The progressive disappearance of the middle-sized enterprise — in the absolute sense considered by Bernstein — means not, as he thinks, the revolutionary course of capitalist development, but precisely the contrary, the cessation, the slowing up of this development. "The rate of profit, that is to say, the relative increase of capital," said Marx, "is important first of all for new investors of capital, grouping themselves independently. And as soon as the formation of capital falls exclusively into a handful of big capitalists, the revivifying fire of production is extinguished. It dies away."

The Realization of Socialism
through Social Reforms

Bernstein rejects the "theory of collapse" as a historic road toward socialism. Now what is the way to a socialist society that is proposed by his "theory of the adaptation of capitalism"? Bernstein answers this question only by allusion. Konrad Schmidt, however, attempts to deal with this detail in the manner of Bernstein. According to him, "the trade-union struggle for hours and wages and the political struggle for reforms will lead to a progressively more extensive control over the conditions of production," and "as the rights of the capitalist proprietor will be diminished through legislation, he will be reduced in time to the role of a simple administrator." "The capitalist will see his property lose more and more value to himself" till finally "the direction and administration of exploitation will be taken from him entirely" and "collective exploitation" instituted.

Therefore trade unions, social reforms and, adds Bernstein, the political democratization of the state are the means of the progressive realization of socialism.

But the fact is that the principal function of trade unions (and this was best explained by Bernstein himself in *Neue Zeit* in 1891) consists in providing the workers with a means of realizing the capitalist law of wages, that is to say, the sale of their labor power at current market prices. Trade unions enable the proletariat to utilize at each instant, the conjuncture of the market. But these conjunctures — (1) the labor demand determined by the state of production, (2) the labor supply created by the proletarianization of the middle strata of society and the natural reproduction of the working class, and (3) the momentary degree of productivity of labor—remain outside of the sphere of influence of the trade unions. Trade unions cannot suppress the law of wages. Under the most favorable circumstances, the best they can do is to impose on capitalist exploitation the "normal" limit of the moment. They have not, however, the power to suppress exploitation itself, not even gradually.

Schmidt, it is true, sees the present trade-union movement in a "feeble initial stage." He hopes that "in the future" the "trade-union movement will exercise a progressively increased influence over the regulation of production." But by the regulation of production we can only understand two things: intervention in the technical domain of the process of production and fixing the scale of production itself. What is the nature of the influence exercised by trade unions in these two departments? It is clear that in the technique of production, the interest of the capitalist agrees, up to a certain point, with the progress and development of capitalist economy. It is his own interest that pushes him to make technical improvements. But the isolated worker finds himself in a decidedly different position. Each technical transformation contradicts his interests. It aggravates his helpless situation by depreciating the value of his labor power and rendering his work more intense, more monotonous and more difficult. Insofar as trade unions can intervene in the technical department of production, they can only oppose technical innovation. But here they do not act in the interest of the entire working class and its emancipation, which accords rather with technical progress and, therefore, with the interest of the isolated capitalist. They act here in a reactionary direction. And in fact, we find efforts on the part of workers to intervene in the technical part of production not in the future, where Schmidt looks for it, but in the past of the trade-union movement. Such efforts characterized the old phase of English trade unionism (up to 1860), when the British organizations were still tied to medieval "corporative" vestiges and found inspiration in the outworn principle of "a fair day's wage for a fair day's labor," as expressed by Webb in his *History of Trade Unionism*.

On the other hand, the effort of the labor unions to fix the scale of production and the prices of commodities is a recent phenomenon. Only recently have we witnessed such attempts — and again in England. In their nature and tendencies, these efforts resemble those dealt with above. What does the active participation of trade unions in fixing the scale and cost of production amount to? It amounts to a cartel of the workers and entrepreneurs in a common stand against the consumer and especially against rival entrepreneurs. In no way is the effect of this any different from that of ordinary employers' associations. Basically we no longer have here a struggle between labor and capital, but the solidarity of capital and labor against the total consumers. Considered for its social worth, it is seen to be a reactionary move that cannot be a stage in the struggle for the emancipation of the proletariat, because it connotes the very opposite of the class struggle. Considered from the angle of practical application, it is found to be a utopia which, as shown by a rapid examination, cannot be extended to the large branches of industry producing for the world market.

So that the scope of trade unions is limited essentially to a struggle for an increase of wages and the reduction of labor time, that is to say, to efforts at regulating capitalist exploitation as they are made necessary by the momentary situation of the world market. But labor unions can in no way influence the process of production itself. Moreover trade-union development moves — contrary to what is asserted by Konrad Schmidt — in the direction of a complete detachment of the labor market from any immediate relation to the rest of the market.

That is shown by the fact that even attempts to relate labor contracts to the general situation of production by means of a system of sliding wage scales have been outmoded with historic development. The British labor unions are moving farther and farther away from such efforts.

Even within the effective boundaries of its activity the trade-union movement cannot spread in the unlimited way claimed for it by the theory of adaptation. On the contrary, if we examine the large factors of social development, we see that we are not moving toward an epoch marked by a victorious development of trade unions, but rather toward a time when the hardships of labor unions will increase. Once industrial development has attained its highest possible point and capitalism has entered its descending phase on the world market, the trade-union struggle will become doubly difficult. In the first place, the objective conjuncture of the market will be less favorable to the sellers of labor power, because the demand for labor power will increase at a slower rate and labor supply more rapidly than is the case at present. In the second place, the capitalists themselves, in order to make up for losses suffered on the world market will make even greater efforts than at present to reduce the part of the total product going to the workers (in the form of wages). The reduction of wages is, as pointed out by Marx, one of the principal means of retarding the fall of profit. The situation in England already offers us a picture of the beginning of the second stage of trade-union development. Trade-union action is reduced of necessity to the simple defense of already realized gains, and even that is becoming more and more difficult. Such is the general trend of things in our society. The counterpart of this tendency should be the development of the political side of the class struggle.

Konrad Schmidt commits the same error of historic perspective when he deals with social reforms. He expects that social reforms, like trade-union organizations, will "dictate to the capitalists the only conditions under which they will be able to employ labor power." Seeing reform in this light, Bernstein calls labor legislation a piece of "social control," and as such, a piece of socialism. Similarly, Konrad Schmidt always uses the term "social control" when he refers to labor protective laws. Once he has thus happily transformed the state into society, he confidently adds: "That is to say, the rising working class." As a result of this trick of substitution, the innocent labor laws enacted by the German Federal Council are transformed into transitory socialist measures supposedly enacted by the German proletariat.

The mystification is obvious. We know that the present state is not "society" representing the "rising working class." It is itself the representative of capitalist society. It is a class state. Therefore its reform measures are not an application of "social control," that is, the control of society working freely in its own labor process. They are forms of control applied by the class organization of capital to the production of capital. The so-called social reforms are enacted in the interests of capital. Yes, Bernstein and Konrad Schmidt see at present only "feeble beginnings" of this control. They hope to see a long succession of reforms in the future, all favoring the working class. But here they commit a mistake similar to their belief in the unlimited development of the trade-union movement.

A basic condition for the theory of the gradual realization of socialism through social reforms is a certain objective development of capitalist property and of the state. Konrad Schmidt says that the capitalist proprietor tends to lose his special rights with historic development, and is reduced to the role of a simple administrator. He thinks that the expropriation of the means of production cannot possibly be effected as a single historic act. He therefore resorts to the theory of expropriation by stages. With this in mind, he divides the right to property into (1) the right of "sovereignty" (ownership) — which he attributes to a thing called "society" and which he wants to extend — and (2) its opposite, the simple right of use, held by the capitalist, but which is supposedly being reduced in the hands of the·capitalists to the mere administration of their enterprises.

This interpretation is either a simple play on words, and in that case the theory of gradual expropriation has no real basis, or it is a true picture of judicial development, in which case, as we shall see, the theory of gradual expropriation is entirely false.

The division of the right of property into several component rights, an arrangement serving Konrad Schmidt as a shelter wherein he may construct his theory of "expropriation by stages," characterized feudal society, founded on natural economy. In feudalism, the total product was shared among the social classes of the time on the basis of the personal relations existing between the feudal lord and his serfs or tenants. The decomposition of property into several partial rights reflected the manner of distribution of the social wealth of that period. With the passage to the production of commodities and the dissolution of all personal bonds among the participants in the process of production, the relation between men and things (that is to say, private property) became reciprocally stronger. Since the division is no longer made on the basis of personal relations but through exchange, the different rights to a share in the social wealth are no longer measured as fragments of property rights having a common interest. They are measured according to the values brought by each on the market.

The first change introduced into juridical relations with the advance of commodity production in the medieval city communes was the development of absolute private property. The latter appeared in the very midst of the feudal juridical relations. This development has progressed at a rapid pace in capitalist production. The more the process of production is socialized, the more the process of distribution (division of wealth) rests on exchange. And the more private property becomes inviolable and closed, the more capitalist property becomes transformed from the right to the product of one's own labor to the simple right to appropriate somebody else's labor. As long as the capitalist himself manages his own factory, distribution is still, up to a certain point, tied to his personal participation in the process of production. But as the personal management on the part of the capitalist become superfluous — which is the case in the shareholding societies today — the property of capital, so far as its right to share in the distribution (division of wealth) is concerned, becomes separated from any personal relation with production. It now appears in its purest form. The capitalist right to property reaches its most complete development in capital held in the shape of shares and industrial credit.

So that Konrad Schmidt's historic schema, tracing the transformation of the capitalist "from a proprietor to a simple administrator," belies the real historic development. In historic reality, on the contrary, the capitalist tends to change from a proprietor and administrator to a simple proprietor. What happens here to Konrad Schmidt, happened to Goethe:

> What is, he sees as in a dream.
> What no longer is, becomes for him reality.

Just as Schmidt's historic schema travels, economically, backwards from a modern shareholding society to an artisan's shop, so, juridically, he wishes to lead back the capitalist world into the old feudal shell of the Middle Ages.

Also from this point of view, "social control" appears in reality under a different aspect than seen by Konrad Schmidt. What functions today as "social control"—labor legislation, the control of industrial organizations through shareholding, etc.—has absolutely nothing to do with his "supreme ownership." Far from being, as Schmidt believes, a reduction of capitalist ownership, his "social control," is, on the contrary, a protection of such ownership. Or, expressed from the economic viewpoint, it is not a threat to capitalist exploitation, but simply the regulation of this exploitation. When Bernstein asks if there is more or less of socialism in a labor protective law, we can assure him that, in the best of labor protective laws, there is no more "socialism" than in a municipal ordinance regulating the cleaning of streets or the lighting of street lamps.

Capitalism and the State

The second condition of the gradual realization of socialism is, according to Bernstein, the evolution of the state in society. It has become a commonplace to say that the present state is a class state. This, too, like everything referring to capitalist society, should not be understood in a rigorous absolute manner, but dialectically.

The state became capitalist with the political victory of the bourgeoisie. Capitalist development modifies essentially the nature of the state, widening its sphere of action, constantly imposing on it new functions (especially those affecting economic life), making more and more necessary its intervention and control in society. In this sense, capitalist development prepares little by little the future fusion of the state and society. It prepares, so to say, the return of the function of the state to society. Following this line of thought, one can speak of an evolution of the capitalist state into society, and it is undoubtedly this that Marx had in mind when he referred to labor legislation as the first conscious intervention of "society" in the vital social process, a phrase upon which Bernstein leans heavily.

But on the other hand the same capitalist development realizes another transformation in the nature of the state. The present state is, first of all, an organization of the ruling class. It assumes functions favoring social development specifically because, and in the measure that, these interests and social development coincide, in a general fashion, with the interests of the dominant class. Labor legislation is enacted as much in the immediate interest of the capitalist class as in the interest of society in general.

But this harmony endures only up to a certain point of capitalist development. When capitalist development has reached a certain level, the interests of the bourgeoisie, as a class, and the needs of economic progress begin to clash even in the capitalist sense. We believe that this phase has already begun. It shows itself in two extremely important phenomena of contemporary social life: on the one hand, the policy of tariff barriers, and on the other, militarism. These two phenomena have played an indispensable, and in that sense a progressive and revolutionary role in the history of capitalism. Without tariff protection the development of large industry would have been impossible in several countries. But now the situation is different.

At present, protection does not serve so much to develop young industry as to maintain artificially certain aged forms of production.

From the angle of capitalist development, that is, from the point of view of world economy, it matters little whether Germany exports more merchandise into England or England exports more merchandise into Germany. From the viewpoint of this development it may be said that the blackamoor has done his work and it is time for him to go his way. Given the condition of reciprocal dependence in which the various branches of industry find themselves, a protectionist tariff on any commodity necessarily results in raising the cost of production of other commodities inside the country. It therefore impedes industrial development. But that is not so from the viewpoint of the interests of the capitalist class. While industry does not need tariff barriers for its development, the entrepreneurs need tariffs to protect their markets. This signifies that at present tariffs no longer serve as a means of protecting a developing capitalist section against a more advanced section. They are now the arm used by one national group of capitalists against another group. Furthermore, tariffs are no longer necessary as an instrument of protection for industry in its movement to create and conquer the home market. They are now indispensable means for the cartelization of industry, that is, means used in the struggle of the capitalist producers against consuming society in the aggregate. What brings out in an emphatic manner the specific character of contemporary customs policies is the fact that today not industry, but agriculture plays the predominant role in the making of tariffs. The policy of customs protection has become a tool for converting and expressing the feudal interests in the capitalist form.

The same change has taken place in militarism. If we consider history as it was — not as it could have been or as it should have been — we must agree that war has been an indispensable feature of capitalist development. The United States, Germany, Italy, the Balkan States, Poland all owe the condition or the rise of their capitalist development to wars, whether resulting in victory or defeat. As long as there were countries marked by internal political division or economic isolation which had to be destroyed, militarism played a revolutionary role, considered from the viewpoint of capitalism.

But at present the situation is different. If world politics have become the stage of menacing conflicts, it is not so much a question of the opening of new countries to capitalism. It is a question of already existing *European* antagonisms, which, transported into other lands, have exploded there. The armed opponents we see today in Europe and on other continents do not range themselves as capitalist countries on one side and backward countries on the other. They are states pushed to war especially as a result of their similarly advanced capitalist development. In view of this, an explosion is certain to be fatal to this development, in the sense that it must provoke an extremely profound disturbance and transformation of economic life in all countries.

However, the matter appears entirely different when considered from the standpoint of the *capitalist class*. For the latter militarism has become indispensable. First, as a means of struggle for the defense of "national" interests in competition against other "national" groups. Second, as a method of placement for financial and industrial capital. Third, as an instrument of class domination over the laboring population inside the country. In themselves, these interests have nothing in common with the development of the capitalist mode of production. What demonstrates best the specific character of present-day militarism is the fact that it develops generally in all countries as an effect, so to speak, of its own internal, mechanical motive power, a phenomenon that was completely unknown several decades ago. We recognize this in the fatal character of the impending explosion which is inevitable in spite of the complete indecisiveness of the objectives and motives of the conflict. From a motor of capitalist development militarism has changed into a capitalist malady.

In the clash between capitalist development and the interests of the dominant class, the state takes a position alongside of the latter. Its policy, like that of the bourgeoisie, comes into conflict with social development. It thus loses more and more its character as a representative of the whole of society and is transformed at the same rate, into a pure *class* state. Or, to speak more exactly, these two qualities distinguish themselves more from each other and find themselves in a contradictory relation in the very nature of the state. This contradiction becomes progressively sharper. For, on one hand, we have the growth of the functions of a general interest on the part of the state, its intervention in social life, its "control" over society. But, on the other hand, its class character obliges the state to move the pivot of its activity and its means of coercion more and more into domains which are useful only to the class character of the bourgeoisie and have for society as a whole only a negative importance, as in the case of militarism and tariff and colonial policies. Moreover, the "social control" exercised by this state is at the same time penetrated with and dominated by its class character (see how labor legislation is applied in all countries).

The extension of democracy, which Bernstein sees as a means of realizing socialism by degrees, does not contradict but, on the contrary, corresponds perfectly to the transformation realized in the nature of the state.

Konrad Schmidt declares that the conquest of a social democratic majority in parliament leads directly to the gradual "socialization" of society. Now, the democratic forms of political life are without a question a phenomenon expressing clearly the evolution of the state in society. They constitute, to that extent, a move toward a socialist transformation. But the conflict within the capitalist state, described above, manifests itself even more emphatically in modern parliamentarism. Indeed, in accordance with its form, parliamentarism serves to express, within the organization of the state, the interests of the whole of society. But what parliamentarism expresses here is capitalist society, that is to say, a society in which capitalist interests predominate. In this society, the representative institutions, democratic in form, are in content the instruments of the interests of the ruling class. This manifests itself in a tangible fashion in the fact that as soon as democracy shows the tendency to negate its class character and become transformed into an instrument of the real interests of the population, the democratic forms are sacrificed by the bourgeoisie and by its state representatives. That is why the idea of the conquest of a parliamentary reformist majority is a calculation which, entirely in the spirit of bourgeois liberalism, preoccupies itself only with one side — the formal side — of democracy, but does not take into account the other side, its real content. All in all, parliamentarism is not a directly socialist element impregnating gradually the whole capitalist society. It is, on the contrary, a specific form of the bourgeois class state, helping to ripen and develop the existing antagonisms of capitalism.

In the light of the history of the objective development of the state, Bernstein's and Konrad Schmidt's belief that increased "social control" results in the direct introduction of socialism is transformed into a formula that finds itself from day to day in greater contradiction with reality.

The theory of the gradual introduction of socialism proposes a progressive reform of capitalist property and the capitalist state in the direction of socialism. But in consequence of the objective laws of existing society, one and the other develop in a precisely opposite direction. The process of production is increasingly so-cialized, and state intervention, the control of the state over the process of production, is extended. But at the same time, private property becomes more and more the form of open capitalist exploitation of the labor of others, and state control is penetrated with the exclusive interests of the ruling class. The state, that is to say, the *political* organization of capitalism, and the property relations, that is to say, the *juridical* organization of capitalism, become more *capitalist* and not more socialist, opposing to the theory of the progressive introduction of socialism two insurmountable difficulties.

Fourier's scheme of changing, by means of a system of phalansteries, the water of all the seas into tasty lemonade was surely a fantastic idea. But Bernstein, proposing to change the sea of capitalist bitterness into a sea of socialist sweetness, by progressively pouring into it bottles of social reformist lemonade, presents an idea that is merely more insipid but no less fantastic.

The production relations of capitalist society approach more and more the production relations of socialist society. But on the other hand, its political and juridical relations established between capitalist society and socialist society a steadily rising wall. This wall is not overthrown, but is on the contrary strengthened and consolidated by the development of social reforms and the course of democracy. Only the hammer blow of revolution, that is to say, *the conquest of political power by the proletariat, can break down this wall.*

The Consequences of Social Reformism and the General Nature of Revisionism

In the first chapter we aimed to show that Bernstein's theory lifted the program of the socialist movement off its material base and tried to place it on an idealist base. How does this theory fare when translated into practice?

Upon the first comparison, the party practice resulting from Bernstein's theory does not seem to differ from the practice followed by the social democracy up to now. Formerly, the activity of the Social Democratic Party consisted of trade-union work, of agitation for social reforms and the democratization of existing political institutions. The difference is not in the *what* but in the *how.*

At present, the trade-union struggle and parliamentary practice are considered to be the means of guiding and educating the proletariat in preparation for the task of taking over power. From the revisionist standpoint, this conquest of power is at the same time impossible and useless. And therefore, trade-union and parliamentary activity are to be carried on by the party only for their immediate results, that is, for the purpose of bettering the present situation of the workers, for the gradual reduction of capitalist exploitation, for the extension of social control.

So that if we do not consider momentarily the immediate amelioration of the workers' condition — an objective common to our party program as well as to revisionism — the difference between the two outlooks is, in brief, the following. According to the present conception of the party, trade-union and parliamentary activity are important for the socialist movement because such activity prepares the proletariat, that is to say, creates the *subjective* factor of the socialist transformation, for the task of realizing socialism. But according to Bernstein, trade unions and parliamentary activity gradually reduce capitalist exploitation itself. They remove from capitalist society its capitalist character. They realize *objectively* the desired social change.

Examining the matter closely, we see that the two conceptions are diametrically opposed. Viewing the situation from the current standpoint of our party, we say that as a result of its trade-union and parliamentary struggles, the proletariat becomes convinced of the impossibility of accomplishing a fundamental social change through such activity and arrives at the understanding that the conquest of power is unavoidable. Bernstein's theory, however, begins by declaring that this conquest is impossible. It concludes by affirming that socialism can only be introduced as a result of the trade-union struggle and parliamentary activity. For as seen by Bernstein, trade-union and parliamentary action has a socialist character because it exercises a progressively socializing influence on capitalist economy.

We tried to show that this influence is purely imaginary. The relations between capitalist property and the capitalist state develop in entirely opposite directions, so that the daily practical activity of the present social democracy loses, in the last analysis, all connection with work for socialism. From the viewpoint of a movement for socialism, the trade-union struggle and our parliamentary practice are vastly important insofar as they make socialistic the *awareness*, the consciousness, of the proletariat and help to organize it as a class. But once they are considered as instruments of the direct socialization of capitalist economy, they lose not only their usual effectiveness but cease being means of preparing the working class for the conquest of power. Eduard Bernstein and Konrad Schmidt suffer from a complete misunderstanding when they console themselves with the belief that even though the program of the party is reduced to work for social reforms and ordinary trade-union work, the final objective of the labor movement is not thereby discarded, for each forward step reaches beyond the given immediate aim and the socialist goal is implied as a tendency in the supposed advance.

That is certainly true about the present procedure of the German social democracy. It is true whenever a firm and conscious effort for the conquest of political power impregnates the trade-union struggle and the work for social reforms. But if this effort is separated from the movement itself and social reforms are made an end in themselves, then such activity not only does not lead to the final goal of socialism but moves in a precisely opposite direction.

Konrad Schmidt simply falls back on the idea that an apparently mechanical movement, once started, cannot stop by itself, because "one's appetite grows with eating," and the working class will not supposedly content itself with reforms till the final socialist transformation is realized.

Now the last-mentioned condition is quite real. Its effectiveness is guaranteed by the very insufficiency of capitalist reforms. But the conclusion drawn from it could only be true if it were possible to construct an unbroken chain of augmented reforms leading from the capitalism of today to socialism. This is, of course, sheer fantasy. In accordance with the nature of things as they are, the chain breaks quickly, and the paths that the supposed forward movement can take from that point on are many and varied.

What will be the immediate result should our party change its general procedure to suit a viewpoint that wants to emphasize the practical results of our struggle, that is, social reforms? As soon as "immediate results" become the principal aim of our activity, the clear-cut, irreconcilable point of view, which has meaning only insofar as it proposes to win power, will be found more and more inconvenient. The direct consequence of this will be the adoption by the party of a "policy of compensation," a policy of political trading, and an attitude of diffident, diplomatic conciliation. But this attitude cannot be continued for a long time. Since the social reforms can only offer an empty promise, the logical consequence of such a program must necessarily be disillusionment.

It is not true that socialism will arise automatically from the daily struggle of the working class. Socialism will be the consequence of (1) the growing contradictions of capitalist economy and (2) the comprehension by the working class of the unavoidability of the suppression of these contradictions through a social transformation. When, in the manner of revisionism, the first condition is denied and the second rejected, the labor movement finds itself reduced to a simple cooperative and reformist movement. We move here in a straight line toward the total abandonment of the class viewpoint.

This consequence also becomes evident when we investigate the general character of revisionism. It is obvious that revisionism does not wish to concede that its standpoint is that of the capitalist apologist. It does not join the bourgeois economists in denying the existence of the contradictions of capitalism. But, on the other hand, what precisely constitutes the fundamental point of revisionism and distinguishes it from the attitude taken by the social democracy up to now, is that it does not base its theory on the belief that the contradictions of capitalism will be suppressed as a result of the logical inner development of the present economic system.

We may say that the theory of revisionism occupies an intermediate place between two extremes. Revisionism does not expect to see the contradictions of capitalism mature. It does not propose to suppress these contradictions through a revolutionary transformation. It, wants to lessen, to attenuate, the capitalist contradictions. So that the antagonism existing between production and exchange is to be mollified by the cessation of crises and the formation of capitalist combines. The antagonism between capital and labor is to be adjusted by bettering the situation of the workers and by the conservation of the middle classes. And the contradiction between the class state and society is to be liquidated through increased state control and the progress of democracy.

It is true that the present procedure of the social democracy does not consist in waiting for the antagonisms of capitalism to develop and in passing on, only then, to the task of suppressing them. On the contrary, the essence of revolutionary procedure is to be guided by the direction of this development, once it is ascertained, and inferring from this direction what consequences are necessary for the political struggle. Thus the social democracy has combatted tariff wars and militarism without waiting for their reactionary character to become fully evident. Bernstein's procedure is not guided by a consideration of the development of capitalism, by the prospect of the aggravation of its contradictions. It is guided by the prospect of the attenuation of these contradictions. He shows this when he speaks of the "adaptation" of capitalist economy.

Now when can such a conception be correct? If it is true that capitalism will continue to develop in the direction it takes at present, then its contradictions must necessarily become sharper and more aggravated instead of disappearing. The possibility of the attenuation of the contradictions of capitalism presupposes that the capitalist mode of production itself will stop its progress. In short, the general condition of Bernstein's theory is the cessation of capitalist development.

This way, however, his theory condemns itself in a twofold manner.

In the first place, it manifests its *utopian* character in its stand on the establishment of socialism. For it is clear that a defective capitalist development cannot lead to a socialist transformation.

In the second place, Bernstein's theory reveals its *reactionary* character when it is referred to the rapid capitalist development that is taking place at present. Given the development of real capitalism, how can we explain, or rather state, Bernstein's position?

We have demonstrated in the first chapter the baselessness of the economic conditions on which Bernstein builds his analysis of existing social relationships. We have seen that neither the credit system nor cartels can be said to be "means of adaptation" of capitalist economy. We have seen that not even the temporary cessation of crises nor the survival of the middle class can be regarded as symptoms of capitalist adaptation. But even though we should fail to take into account the erroneous character of all these details of Bernstein's theory we cannot help but be stopped short by one feature common to all of them. Bernstein's theory does not seize these manifestations of contemporary economic life as they appear in their organic relationship with the whole of capitalist development, with the complete economic mechanism of capitalism. His theory pulls these details out of their living economic context. It treats them as the *disjecta membra* (separate parts) of a lifeless machine.

Consider, for example, his conception of the adaptive effect of credit. If we recognize credit as a higher natural stage of the process of exchange and, therefore, of the contradictions, inherent in capitalist exchange, we cannot at the same time see it as a mechanical means of adaptation existing outside of the process of exchange. It would be just as impossible to consider money, merchandise, capital as "means of adaptation" of capitalism.

However, credit, like money, commodities and capital, is an organic link of capitalist economy at a certain stage of its development. Like them, it is an indispensable gear in the mechanism of capitalist economy, and at the same time, an instrument of destruction, since it aggravates the internal contradictions of capitalism.

The same thing is true about cartels and the new, perfected means of communication.

The same mechanical view is presented by Bernstein's attempt to describe the promise of the cessation of crises as a symptom of the "adaptation" of capitalist economy. For him, crises are simply derangements of the economic mechanism. With their cessation, he thinks, the mechanism could function well. But the fact is that crises are not "derangements" in the usual sense of the word. They are "derangements" without which capitalist economy could not develop at all. For if crises constitute the only method possible in capitalism — and therefore the normal method — of solving periodically the conflict existing between the unlimited extension of production and the narrow limits of the world market, then crises are an organic manifestation inseparable from capitalist economy.

In the "unhindered" advance of capitalist production lurks a threat to capitalism that is much graver than crises. It is the threat of the constant fall of the rate of profit, resulting not from the contradiction between production and exchange, but from the growth of the productivity of labor itself. The fall in the rate of profit has the extremely dangerous tendency of rendering impossible any enterprise for small and middle-sized capitals. It thus limits the new formation and therefore the extension of placements of capital.

And it is precisely crises that constitute the other consequence of the same process. As a result of their periodic *depreciation* of capital, crises bring a fall in the prices of means of production, a paralysis of a part of the active capital, and in time the increase of profits. They thus create the possibilities of the renewed advance of production. Crises therefore appear to be the instruments of rekindling the fire of capitalist development. Their cessation—not temporary cessation, but their total disappearance in the world market—would not lead to the further development of capitalist economy. It would destroy capitalism.

True to the mechanical view of his theory of adaptation, Bernstein forgets the necessity of crises as well as the necessity of new placements of small and middle-sized capitals. And that is why the constant reappearance of small capital seems to him to be the sign of the cessation of capitalist development though, it is, in fact, a symptom of normal capitalist development.

It is important to note that there is a viewpoint from which all the above-mentioned phenomena are seen exactly as they have been presented by the theory of "adaptation." It is the viewpoint of the isolated (single) capitalist, who reflects in his mind the economic facts around him just as they appear when refracted by the laws of competition. The isolated capitalist sees each organic part of the whole of our economy as an independent entity. He sees them as they act on him, the single capitalist. He therefore considers these facts to be simple "derangements" of simple "means of adaptation." For the isolated capitalist, it is true, crises are really simple derangements; the cessation of crises accords him a longer existence. As far as he is concerned, credit is only a means of "adapting" his insufficient productive forces to the needs of the market. And it seems to him that the cartel of which he becomes a member really suppresses industrial anarchy.

Revisionism is nothing else than a theoretic generalization made from the angle of the isolated capitalist. Where does this viewpoint belong theoretically if not in vulgar bourgeois economics?

All the errors of this school rest precisely on the conception that mistakes the phenomena of competition, as seen from the angle of the isolated capitalist, for the phenomena of the whole of capitalist economy. Just as Bernstein considers credit to be a means of "adaptation," so vulgar economy considers money to be a judicious means of "adaptation" to the needs of exchange. Vulgar economy, too, tries to find the antidote against the ills of capitalism in the phenomena of capitalism. Like Bernstein, it believes that it is possible to regulate capitalist economy. And in the manner of Bernstein, it arrives in time at the desire to palliate the contradictions of capitalism, that is, at the belief in the possibility of patching up the sores of capitalism. It ends up by subscribing to a program of reaction. It ends up in utopia.

The theory of revisionism can therefore be defined in the following way. It is a theory of standing still in the socialist movement, built, with the aid of vulgar economy, on a theory of a capitalist standstill.

Part II
Economic Development and Socialism

The greatest conquest of the developing proletarian movement has been the discovery of grounds of support for the realization of socialism in the *economic condition* of capitalist society. As a result of this discovery, socialism was changed from an "ideal" dream by humanity for thousands of years to a thing of *historic necessity.*

Bernstein denies the existence of the economic conditions for socialism in the society of today. On this count his reasoning has undergone an interesting evolution. At first, in *Neue Zeit*, he simply contested the rapidity of the process of concentration taking place in industry. He based his position on a comparison of the occupational statistics of Germany in 1882 and 1895. In order to use these figures for his purpose, he was obliged to proceed in an entirely summary and mechanical fashion. In the most favorable case, he could not, even by demonstrating the persistence of middle-sized enterprises, weaken in any the Marxian analysis, because the latter does not suppose, as a condition for the realization of socialism, either a definite rate of concentration of industry — that is, a definite *delay* of the realization of socialism — or, as we have already shown, the *absolute disappearance* of small capitals, usually described as the disappearance of the small bourgeoisie.

In the course of the latest development of his ideas, Bernstein furnishes us in his book a new assortment of proofs: the statistics of *shareholding societies.* These statistics are used in order to prove that the number of shareholders increases constantly, and, as a result, the capitalist class does not become smaller but grows bigger. It is surprising that Bernstein has so little acquaintance with his material. And it is astonishing how poorly he utilizes the existing data in his own behalf.

If he wanted to disprove the Marxian law of industrial development by referring to the condition of shareholding societies, he should have resorted to entirely different figures. Anybody who is acquainted with the history of shareholding societies in Germany knows that their average foundation capital has *diminished* almost constantly. Thus while before 1871 their average foundation capital reached the figure of 10.8 million marks, it was only 4.01 million marks in 1871, 3.8 million marks in 1873, less than a million from 1882 to 1887, 0.52 million in 1891 and only 0.62 million in 1892. After this date the figures oscillated around 1 million marks, falling to 1.78 in 1895 and to 1.19 in the course of the first half of 1897 (Van de Borght: *Handwoerterbuch der Staatsswissenschaften*, 1).

These are surprising figures. Using them, Bernstein hoped to show the existence of a counter-Marxian tendency for the retransformation of large enterprises into small ones. The obvious answer to his attempt is the following. If you are to prove anything at all by means of your statistics, you must first show that they refer to the *same* branches of industry. You must show that small enterprises really replace large ones, that they do not, instead, appear only where small enterprises or even artisan industry were the rule before. This, however, you cannot show to be true. The statistical passage of immense shareholding societies to middle-sized and small enterprises can be explained only by referring to the fact that the system of shareholding societies continues to penetrate new branches of production. Before, only a small number of large enterprises were organized as shareholding societies. Gradually shareholding organization has won middle-sized and even small enterprises. Today we can observe shareholding societies with a capital below 1000 marks.

Now what is the economic significance of the extension of the system of shareholding societies? Economically the spread of shareholding societies stands for the growing socialization of production under the capitalist form — socialization not only of large but also of middle-sized and small production. The extension of shareholding does not therefore contradict Marxist theory but, on the contrary, confirms it emphatically.

What does the economic phenomenon of a shareholding society actually amount to? It represents, on one hand, the unification of a number of small fortunes into a large capital of production. It stands, on the other hand, for the separation of production from capitalist ownership. That is, it denotes that a double victory is being won over the capitalist mode of production — but still on the capitalist base.

What is the meaning, therefore, of the statistics cited by Bernstein, according to which an ever greater number of shareholders participate in capitalist enterprises? These statistics go to demonstrate precisely the following: at present a capitalist enterprise does not correspond, as before, to a single proprietor of capital but a number of capitalists. Consequently, *the economic notion of "capitalist" no longer signifies an isolated individual. The industrial capitalist of today is a collective person, composed of hundreds and even of thousands of individuals. The category "capitalist" has itself become a social category. It has become "socialized"—within the framework of capitalist society.*

In that case, how shall we explain Bernstein's belief that the phenomenon of shareholding societies stands for the dispersion and not the concentration of capital? Why does he see the extension of capitalist property where Marx saw its suppression?

This is a simple economic error. By "capitalist," Bernstein does not mean a category of production but the right to property. To him, "capitalist" is not an economic unit but a fiscal unit. And "capital" is for him not a factor of production but simply a certain quantity of money. That is why in his English sewing thread trust he does not see the fusion of 12,300 persons with money into a single capitalist unit but 12,300 different capitalists. That is why the engineer Schuze whose wife's dowry brought him a large number of shares from stockholder Mueller is also a capitalist for Bernstein. That is why for Bernstein the entire world seems to swarm with capitalists.

Here, too, the theoretic base of his economic error is his "popularization" of socialism. For this is what he does. By transporting the concept of capitalism from its productive relations to property relations, and by speaking of simple individuals instead of speaking of entrepreneurs, he moves the question of socialism from the domain of production into the domain of relations of fortune—that is, from the relation between capital and labor to the relation between poor and rich.

In this manner we are merrily led from Marx and Engels to the author of the *Evangel of the Poor Fisherman*. There is this difference, however. Weitling, with the sure instinct of the proletarian, saw in the opposition between the poor and the rich, the class antagonisms in their primitive form, and wanted to make of these antagonisms a lever of the movement for socialism. Bernstein, on the other hand, locates the realization of socialism in the possibility of making the poor rich. That is, he locates it in the attenuation of class antagonisms and, therefore, in the petty bourgeoisie.

True, Bernstein does not limit himself to the statistics of incomes. He furnishes statistics of economic enterprises, especially those of the following countries: Germany, France, England, Switzerland, Austria and the United States. But these statistics are not the

65

comparative figures of *different periods* in each country but of each period in different countries. We are not therefore offered (with the exception of Germany, where he repeats the old contrast between 1895 and 1882), a comparison of the statistics of enterprises of a given country at different epochs but the *absolute* figures for different countries: England in 1891, France in 1894, United States in 1890, etc.

He reaches the following conclusion: "Though it is true that large exploitation is already supreme in industry today, it nevertheless, represents, including the enterprises dependent on large exploitation, even in a country as developed as Prussia, *only half of the population occupied in production."* This is also true about Germany, England, Belgium, etc.

What does he actually prove here? He proves not the existence of such or such a *tendency of economic development* but merely the *absolute relation of forces* of different forms of enterprise, or, put in other words, the absolute relation of the various classes in our society.

Now if one wants to prove in this manner the impossibility of realizing socialism, his reasoning must rest on the theory according numerical material forces of the elements in struggle, that is, by the factor of *violence.* In other words, Bernstein, who always thunders against Blanquism, himself falls into the grossest Blanquist error. There is this difference, however. To the Blanquists, who represented a socialist and revolutionary tendency, the possibility of the economic realization of socialism appeared quite natural. On this possibility they built the chances of a violent revolution—even by a small minority. Bernstein, on the contrary, infers from the numerical insufficiency of a socialist majority, the impossibility of the economic realization of socialism. The social democracy, *does not, however, expect to attain its aim either as a result of the victorious violence of a minority or through the numerical superiority of a majority. It sees socialism come as a result of economic necessity—and the comprehension of that necessity—leading to the suppression of capitalism by the working masses.* And this necessity manifests itself above all in the anarchy of capitalism.

What is Bernstein's position on the decisive question of anarchy in capitalist economy? He denies only the great general crises. He does not deny partial and national crises. In other words, he refuses to see a great deal of the anarchy of capitalism; he sees only a little of it. He is—to use Marx's illustration—like the foolish virgin who had a child "who was only very small." But the misfortune is that in matters like economic anarchy little and much are equally bad. If Bernstein recognizes the existence of a little of this anarchy, we may point out to him that by the mechanism of market economy this bit of anarchy will be extended

66

to unheard-of proportions, to end in collapse. But if Bernstein hopes, while maintaining the system of commodity production, to transform gradually his bit of anarchy into order and harmony, he again falls into one of the fundamental errors of bourgeois political economy, according to which the mode of exchange is independent of the mode of production.

This is not the place for a lengthy demonstration of Bernstein's surprising confusion concerning the most elementary principles of political economy. But there is one point—to which we are led by the fundamental question of capitalist anarchy—that must be clarified immediately.

Bernstein declares that Marx's law of surplus value is a simple abstraction. In political economy a statement of this sort obviously constitutes an insult. But if surplus value is only a simple abstraction, if it is only a figment of the mind—then every normal citizen who has done military duty and pays his taxes on time has the same right as Karl Marx to fashion his individual absurdity, to make his own law of value. "Marx has as much right to neglect the qualities of commodities till they are no more than the incarnation of quantities of simple human labor as have the economists of the Boehm-Jevons school to make an abstraction of all the qualities of commodities outside of their utility."

That is, to Bernstein, Marx's social labor and Menger's abstract utility are quite similar—pure abstractions. Bernstein forgets that Marx's abstraction is not an invention. It is a discovery. It does not exist in Marx's head but in market economy. It has not an imaginary existence, but a real social existence, so real that it can be cut, hammered, weighed and put in the form of money. The abstract human labor discovered by Marx is, in its developed form, no other than *money*. That is precisely one of the greatest of Marx's discoveries, while to all bourgeois political economists, from the first of the mercantilists to the last of the classicists, the essence of money has remained a mystic enigma.

The Boehm-Jevons abstract utility is, in fact, a conceit of the mind. Or stated more correctly, it is a representation of intellectual emptiness, a private absurdity, for which neither capitalism nor any other society can be made responsible, but only vulgar bourgeois economy itself. Hugging their brainchild, Bernstein, Boehm and Jevons, and the entire subjective fraternity, can remain twenty years or more before the mystery of money, without arriving at a solution that is any different from the one reached by any cobbler, namely that money is also a "useful" thing.

Bernstein has lost all comprehension of Marx's law of value. Anybody with a small understanding of Marxian economics can see that without the law of value, Marx's doctrine is incomprehensible. Or to speak more concretely—for him who does not understand the nature of the commodity and its exchange, the entire economy of capitalism, with all its concatenations, must of necessity remain an enigma.

What precisely was the key which enabled Marx to open the door to the secrets of capitalist phenomena and solve, as if in play, problems that were not even suspected by the greatest minds of classic bourgeois political economy? It was his conception of capitalist economy as a historic phenomenon — not merely in the sense recognized in the best of cases by the classic economists, that is, when it concerns the feudal past of capitalism — but also insofar as it concerns the socialist future of the world. The secret of Marx's theory of value, of his analysis of the problem of money, of his theory of capital, of the theory of the rate of profit, and consequently of the entire existing economic system, is found in the transitory character of capitalist economy, the inevitability of its collapse, leading — and this is only another aspect of the same phenomenon — to socialism. It is only because Marx looked at capitalism from the socialist's viewpoint, that is, from the historic viewpoint, that he was enabled to decipher the hieroglyphics of capitalist economy. And it is precisely because he took the socialist viewpoint as a point of departure for his analysis of bourgeois society that he was in the position to give a scientific base to the socialist movement.

This is the measure by which we evaluate Bernstein's remarks. He complains of the "dualism" found everywhere in Marx's monumental *Capital*. "The work wishes to be a scientific study and prove, at the same time, a thesis that was completely elaborated a long time before the editing of the book; it is based on a schema that already contains the result to which he wants to lead. The return to the *Communist Manifesto* (that is, to the socialist goal! — R. L.) proves the existence of vestiges of utopianism in Marx's doctrine."

But what is Marx's "dualism" if not the dualism of the socialist future and the capitalist present? It is the dualism of capitalism and labor, the dualism of the bourgeoisie and the proletariat. It is the scientific reflection of the dualism existing in bourgeois society, the dualism of the class antagonism writhing inside the social order of capitalism.

Bernstein's recognition of this theoretic dualism in Marx as "a survival of utopianism" is really his naive avowal that he denies the historic dualism of bourgeois society, that he denies the existence of class antagonism in capitalism. It is his confession that socialism has become for him only a "survival of utopianism." What is Bernstein's "monism" — Bernstein's unity — but the eternal unity of the capitalist regime, the unity of the former socialist who has renounced his aim and has decided to find in bourgeois society, one and immutable, the goal of human development?

Bernstein does not see in the economic structure of capitalism the development that leads to socialism. But in order to conserve his socialist program, at least in form, he is obliged to take refuge in an idealist construction, placed outside of all economic development. He is obliged to transform socialism itself from a definite historic phase of social development into an abstract "principle."

That is why the "cooperative principle" — the meager decantation of socialism by which Bernstein wishes to garnish capitalist economy — appears as a concession made not to the socialist future of society, but to Bernstein's own socialist past.

Cooperatives, Unions, Democracy

Bernstein's socialism offers to the workers the prospect of sharing in the wealth of society. The poor are to become rich. How will this socialism be brought about? His articles in *Neue Zeit* "Problems of Socialism" contain only vague allusions to this question. Adequate information, however, can be found in his book.

Bernstein's socialism is to be realized with the aid of these two instruments: labor unions — or as Bernstein himself characterizes them, economic democracy — and cooperatives. The first will suppress industrial profit; the second will do away with commercial profit.

Cooperatives, especially cooperatives in the field of production, constitute a hybrid form in the midst of capitalism. They can be described as small units of socialized production within capitalist exchange.

But in capitalist economy exchange dominates production (that is, production depends to a large extent on market possibilities). As a result of competition, the complete domination of the process of production by the interests of capital — that is, pitiless exploitation — becomes a condition for the survival of each enterprise. The domination of capital over the process of production expresses itself in the following ways. Labor is intensified. The work day is lengthened or shortened, according to the situation of the market. And, depending on the requirements of the market, labor is either employed or thrown back into the street. In other words, use is made of all methods that enable an enterprise to stand up against its competitors in the market. The workers forming a cooperative in the field of production are thus faced with the contradictory necessity of governing themselves with the utmost absolutism. They are obliged to take toward themselves the role of the capitalist entrepreneur — a contradiction that accounts for the failure of production cooperatives, which either become pure capitalist enterprises or, if the workers' interests continue to predominate, end by dissolving.

69

Bernstein has himself taken note of these facts. But it is evident that he has not understood them. For, together with Mrs. Potter-Webb, he explains the failure of production cooperatives in England by their lack of "discipline." But what is so superficially and flatly called here "discipline" is nothing else than the natural absolutist regime of capitalism, which it is plain, the workers cannot successfully use against themselves.

Producers' cooperatives can survive within capitalist economy only if they manage to suppress, by means of some detour, the capitalist contradiction between the mode of production and the mode of exchange. And they can accomplish this only by removing themselves artificially from the influence of the laws of free competition. And they can succeed in doing the last only when they assure themselves beforehand of a constant circle of consumers, that is, when they assure themselves of a constant market.

It is the consumers' cooperative that can offer this service to its brother in the field of production. Here—and not in Oppenheimer's distinction between cooperatives that purchase and cooperatives that sell—is the secret sought by Bernstein: the explanation for the invariable failure of producers' cooperatives functioning inde-. pendently and their survival when they are backed by consumers' organizations.

If it is true that the possibilities of existence of producers' cooperatives within capitalism are bound up with the possibilities of existence of consumers' cooperatives, then the scope of the former is limited, in the most favorable of cases, to the small local market and to the manufacture of articles serving immediate needs, especially food products. Consumers', and therefore producers', cooperatives are excluded from the most important branches of capital production—the textile, mining, metallurgical and petroleum industries, machine construction, locomotive and shipbuilding. For this reason alone (forgetting for the moment their hybrid character), cooperatives in the field of production cannot be seriously considered as the instrument of a general social transformation. The establishment of producers' cooperatives on a wide scale would suppose, first of all, the suppression of the world market, the breaking up of the present world economy into small local spheres of production and exchange. The highly developed, widespread capitalism of our time is expected to fall back to the merchant economy of the Middle Ages.

Within the framework of present society, producers cooperatives are limited to the role of simple annexes to consumers' cooperatives. It appears, therefore, that the latter must be the beginning of the proposed social change. But this way the expected reform of society by means of cooperatives ceases to be an offensive against capitalist production. That is, it ceases to be an attack against the principal bases of capitalist economy.

It becomes, instead, a struggle against commercial capital, especially small and middle-sized commercial capital. It becomes an attack made on the twigs of the capitalist tree.

According to Bernstein, trade unions too are a means of attack against capitalism in the field of production. We have already shown that trade unions cannot give the workers a determining influence over production. Trade unions can neither determine the dimensions of production nor the technical progress of production.

This much may be said about the purely economic side of the "struggle of the rate of wages against the rate of profit," as Bernstein labels the activity of the trade union. It does not take place in the blue of the sky. It takes place within the well-defined framework of the law of wages. The law of wages is not shattered but applied by trade-union activity.

According to Bernstein, it is the trade unions that lead — in the general movement for the emancipation of the working class — the real attack against the rate of industrial profit. According to Bernstein, trade unions have the task of transforming the rate of industrial profit into "rates of wages." The fact is that trade unions are least able to execute an economic offensive against profit. Trade unions are nothing more than the organized *defense* of labor power against the attacks of profit. They express the resistance offered by the working class to the oppression of capitalist economy.

On the one hand, trade unions have the function of influencing the situation in the labor-power market. But this influence is being constantly overcome by the proletarianization of the middle layers of our society, a process which continually brings new merchandise on the labor market. The second function of the trade unions is to ameliorate the condition of the workers. That is, they attempt to increase the share of the social wealth going to the working class. This share, however, is being reduced, with the fatality of a natural process, by the growth of the productivity of labor. One does not need to be a Marxist to notice this. It suffices to read Rodbertus's *In Explanation of the Social Question.*

In other words, the objective conditions of capitalist society transform the two economic functions of the trade unions into a sort of labor of Sisyphus, which is nevertheless, indispensable. For as a result of the activity of his trade unions, the worker succeeds in obtaining for himself the rate of wages due to him in accordance with the situation of the labor-power market. As a result of trade-union activity, the capitalist law of wages is applied and the effect of the depressing tendency of economic development is paralyzed, or to be more exact, is attenuated.

However, the transformation of the trade union into an instrument for the progressive reduction of profit in favor of wages presupposes the following social conditions: first, the cessation of the proletarianization of the middle strata of our society; secondly, a stoppage of the growth of productivity of labor. We have in both cases *a return to precapitalist conditions.*

Cooperatives and trade unions are totally incapable of transforming the *capitalist mode of production.* This is really understood by Bernstein, though in a confused manner. For he refers to cooperatives and trade unions as a means of reducing the profit of the capitalists and thus enriching the workers. In this way, he renounces the struggle against the *capitalist mode of production* and attempts to direct the socialist movement to struggle against "capitalist distribution." Again and again, Bernstein refers to socialism as an effort towards a "just, juster and still more just" mode of distribution (*Vorwaerts*, March 26, 1899).

It cannot be denied that the direct cause leading the popular masses into the socialist movement is precisely the "unjust" mode of distribution characteristic of capitalism. When the social democracy struggles for the socialization of the entire economy, it aspires therewith also to a "just" distribution of the social wealth. But, guided by Marx's observation that the mode of distribution of a given epoch is a natural consequence of the mode of production of that epoch, the social democracy does not struggle against distribution in the framework of capitalist production. It struggles instead for the suppression of capitalist production itself. In a word, the social democracy wants to establish the mode of socialist distribution by suppressing the capitalist mode of production. Bernstein's method, on the contrary, proposes to combat the capitalist mode of distribution in the hope of gradually establishing, in this way, the socialist mode of production.

What, in that case, is the basis of Bernstein's program for the reform of society? Does it find support in definite tendencies of capitalist production? No. In the first place, he denies such tendencies. In the second place, the socialist transformation of production is for him the effect and not the cause of distribution. He cannot give his program a materialist base, because he has already overthrown the aims and the means of the movement for socialism, and therefore its economic conditions. As a result, he is obliged to construct himself an idealist base.

"Why represent socialism as the consequence of economic compulsion?" he complains. "Why degrade man's understanding, his feeling for justice, his will?" (*Vorwaerts*, March 26, 1899). Bernstein's superlatively just distribution is to be attained thanks to man's free will, man's will acting not because of economic necessity, since this will itself is only an instrument, but because of man's comprehension of justice, because of man's *idea of justice.*

We thus quite happily return to the principle of justice, to the old war horse on which the reformers of the earth have rocked for ages, for the lack of surer means of historic transportation. We return to that lamentable Rosinante on which the Don Quixotes of history have galloped towards the great reform of the earth, always to come home with their eyes blackened.

The relation of the poor to the rich, taken as a base for socialism, the principle of cooperation as the content of socialism, the "most just distribution" as its aim, and the idea of justice as its only historic legitimation — with how much more force, more wit and more fire did Weitling defend that sort of socialism fifty years ago. However, that genius of a tailor did not know scientific socialism. If today the conception torn into bits by Marx and Engels a half century ago is patched up and presented to the proletariat as the last word of social science, that, too, is the art of a tailor, but it has nothing of genius about it.

Trade unions and cooperatives are the economic points of support for the theory of revisionism. Its principal political condition is the growth of democracy. The present manifestations of political reaction are to Bernstein only "displacement." He considers them accidental, momentary, and suggests that they are not to be considered in the elaboration of the general directives of the labor movement.

To Bernstein, democracy is an inevitable stage in the development of society. To him, as to the bourgeois theoreticians of liberalism, democracy is the great fundamental law of historic development, the realization of which is served by all the forces of political life. However, Bernstein's thesis is completely false. Presented in this absolute form, it appears as a petty bourgeois vulgarization of results of a very short phase of bourgeois development, the last twenty-five or thirty years. We reach entirely different conclusions when we examine the historic development of democracy a little closer and consider at the same time the general political history of capitalism.

Democracy has been found in the most dissimilar social formations: in primitive communist groups, in the slave states of antiquity and in the medieval communes. And similarly absolutism and constitutional monarchy are to be found under the most varied economic orders. When capitalism began, as the first production of commodities, it resorted to a democratic constitution in the municipal-communes of the Middle Ages. Later, when it developed to manufacturing, capitalism found its corresponding political form in the absolute monarchy. Finally, as a developed industrial economy, it brought into being in France the democratic republic of 1793, the absolute monarchy of Napoleon I, the nobles' monarchy of the Restoration period (1815-1830), the bourgeois constitutional monarchy of Louis Philippe, then again the democratic republic, and again the monarchy of Napoleon III, and finally, for the third time, the republic.

In Germany, the only truly democratic institution — universal suffrage — is not a conquest won by bourgeois liberalism. Universal suffrage in Germany was an instrument for the fusion of the small states. It is only in this sense that it has any importance for the development of the German bourgeoisie, which is otherwise quite satisfied with a semifeudal constitutional monarchy. In Russia, capitalism prospered for a long time under the regime of oriental absolutism, without having the bourgeoisie manifest the least desire in the world to introduce democracy. In Austria, universal suffrage was above all a safety line thrown to a foundering and decomposing monarchy. In Belgium, the conquest of universal suffrage by the labor movement was undoubtedly due to the weakness of the local militarism, and consequently to the special geographic and political situation of the country. But we have here a "bit of democracy" that has been won not by the bourgeoisie but *against it*.

The uninterrupted victory of democracy, which to our revisionism, as well as to bourgeois liberalism, appears as a great fundamental law of human history and, especially, of modern history, is shown, upon closer examination, to be a phantom. No absolute and general relation can be constructed between capitalist development and democracy. The political form of a given country is always the result of the composite of all the existing political factors, domestic as well as foreign. It admits within its limits all variations of the scale, from absolute monarchy to the democratic republic.

We must abandon, therefore, all hope of establishing democracy as a general law of historic development, even within the framework of modern society. Turning to the present phase of bourgeois society, we observe here, too, political factors which, instead of assuring the realization of Bernstein's schema, lead rather to the abandonment by bourgeois society of the democratic conquests won up to now.

Democratic institutions — and this is of the greatest significance — have completely exhausted their function as aids in the development of bourgeois society. Insofar as they were necessary to bring about the fusion of small states and the creation of large modern states (Germany, Italy), they are no longer indispensable at present. Economic development has meanwhile effected an internal organic cicatrization.

The same thing can be said concerning the transformation of the entire political and administrative state machinery from feudal or semifeudal mechanism to capitalist mechanism. While this transformation has been historically inseparable from the development of democracy, it has been realized today to such an extent that the purely democratic "ingredients" of society, such as universal suffrage and the republican state form, may be suppressed without having the administration, the state finances, or the military organization find it necessary to return to the forms they had before the March Revolution.

If liberalism as such is now absolutely useless to bourgeois society, it has become, on the other hand, a direct impediment to capitalism from other standpoints. Two factors dominate completely the political life of contemporary states: world politics and the labor movement. Each is only a different aspect of the present phase of capitalist development.

As a result of the development of the world economy and the aggravation and generalization of competition on the world market, militarism and the policy of big navies have become, as instruments of world politics, a decisive factor in the interior as well as in the exterior life of the great states. If it is true that world politics and militarism represent a rising tendency in the present phase of capitalism, then bourgeois democracy must logically move in a descending line.

In Germany, the era of great armament, begun in 1893, and the policy of world politics, inaugurated with the seizure of Kiao-Cheou, were paid for immediately with the following sacrificial victim: the decomposition of liberalism, the deflation of the Center Party, which passed from opposition to government. The recent elections to the Reichstag of 1907, unrolling under the sign of the German colonial policy, were at the same time the historical burial of German liberalism.

If foreign politics push the bourgeoisie into the arms of reaction, this is no less true about domestic politics — thanks to the rise of the working class. Bernstein shows that he recognizes this when he makes the social democratic "legend," which "wants to swallow everything" — in other words, the socialist efforts of the working class — responsible for the desertion of the liberal bourgeoisie. He advises the proletariat to disavow its socialist aim, so that the mortally frightened liberals might come out of the mousehole of reaction. Making the suppression of the socialist labor movement an essential condition for the preservation of bourgeois democracy, he proves in a striking manner that this democracy is in complete contradiction with the inner tendency of development of the present society. He proves at the same time that the socialist movement is itself a *direct product* of this tendency.

But he proves, at the same time, still another thing. By making the renouncement of the socialist aim an essential condition of the resurrection of bourgeois democracy, he shows how inexact is the claim that bourgeois democracy is an indispensable condition of the socialist movement and the victory of socialism. Bernstein's reasoning exhausts itself in a vicious circle. His conclusion swallows his premises.

The solution is quite simple. In view of the fact that bourgeois liberalism has given up its ghost from fear of the growing labor movement and its final aim, we conclude that the socialist labor movement is today the *only* support for that which is not the goal of the socialist movement — democracy. We must conclude that democracy can have no other support. We must conclude that the socialist movement is not bound to bourgeois democracy, but that, on the contrary, the fate of democracy is bound with the socialist movement. We must conclude from this that democracy does not acquire greater chances of life in the measure that the working class renounces the struggle for its emancipation, but that, on the contrary, democracy acquires greater chances of survival as the socialist movement becomes sufficiently strong to struggle against the reactionary consequences of world politics and the bourgeois desertion of democracy. He who would strengthen democracy should want to strengthen and not weaken the socialist movement. He who renounces the struggle for socialism renounces both the labor movement and democracy.

Conquest of Political Power

The fate of democracy is bound up, we have seen, with the fate of the labor movement. But does the development of democracy render superfluous or impossible a proletarian revolution, that is, the conquest of the political power by the workers?

Bernstein settles the question by weighing minutely the good and bad sides of social reform and social revolution. He does it almost in the same manner in which cinnamon or pepper is weighed out in a consumers' cooperative store. He sees the legislative course of historic development as the action of "intelligence," while the revolutionary course of historic development is for him the action of "feeling." Reformist activity, he recognizes as a slow method of historic progress, revolution as a rapid method of progress. In legislation he sees a methodic force; in revolution, a spontaneous force.

We have known for a long time that the petty bourgeois reformer finds "good" and "bad" sides in everything. He nibbles a bit at all grasses. But the real course of events is little affected by such combination. The carefully gathered little pile of the "good sides" of all things possible collapses at the first fillip of history. Historically, legislative reform and the revolutionary method function in accordance with influences that are much more profound than the consideration of the advantages or inconveniences of one method or another.

In the history of bourgeois society, legislative reform served to strengthen progressively the rising class till the latter was sufficiently strong to seize political power, to suppress the existing juridical system, and to construct itself a new one. Bernstein, thundering against the conquest of political power as a theory of Blanquist violence, has the misfortune of labelling as a Blanquist error that which has always been the pivot and the motive force of human history. From the first appearance of class societies having the class struggle as the essential content of their history, the conquest of political power has been the aim of all rising classes. Here is the starting point and end of every historic period. This can be seen in the long struggle of the Latin peasantry against the financiers and nobility of ancient Rome, in the struggle of the medieval nobility against the bishops and in the struggle of the artisans against the nobles, in the cities of the Middle Ages. In modern times, we see it in the struggle of the bourgeoisie against feudalism.

Legislative reform and revolution are not different methods of historic development that can be picked out at pleasure from the counter of history, just as one chooses hot or cold sausages. Legislative reform and revolution are different *factors* in the development of class society. They condition and complement each other, and are at the same time reciprocally exclusive, as are the north and south poles, the bourgeoisie and the proletariat.

Every legal constitution is the *product* of a revolution. In the history of classes, revolution is the act of political creation, while legislation is the political expression of the life of a society that has already come into being. Work for reform does not contain its own force, independent from revolution. During every historic period, work for reforms is carried on only in the direction given to it by the impetus of the last revolution, and continues as long as the impulsion of the last revolution continues to make itself felt. Or, to put it more concretely, in each historic period work for reforms is carried on only in the framework of the social form created by the last revolution. Here is the kernel of the problem.

It is contrary to history to represent work for reforms as a long-drawn-out revolution and revolution as a condensed series of reforms. A social transformation and a legislative reform do not differ according to their duration but according to their content. The secret of historic change through the utilization of political power resides precisely in the transformation of simple quantitative modification into a new quality, or to speak more concretely, in the passage of a historic period from one given form of society to another.

That is why people who pronounce themselves in favor of the method of legislative reform *in place of and in contradistinction to* the conquest of political power and social revolution, do not really choose a more tranquil, calmer and slower road to the *same* goal, but a *different* goal. Instead of taking a stand for the establishment of a new society they take a stand for surface modification of the old society. If we follow the political conceptions of revisionism, we arrive at the same conclusion that is reached when we follow the economic theories of revisionism. Our program becomes not the realization of *socialism*, but the reform of *capitalism:* not the suppression of the system of wage labor, but the diminution of exploitation, that is, the suppression of the abuses of capitalism instead of the suppression of capitalism itself.

Does the reciprocal role of legislative reform and revolution apply only to the class struggles of the past? Is it possible that now, as a result of the development of the bourgeois juridical system, the function of moving society from one historic phase to another belongs to legislative reform, and that the conquest of state power by the proletariat has really become "an empty phrase," as Bernstein puts it?

The very opposite is true. What distinguishes bourgeois society from other class societies — from ancient society and from the social order of the Middle Ages? Precisely the fact that class domination does not rest on "acquired rights" but on *real economic relations* — the fact that wage labor is not a juridical relation, but purely an economic relation. In our juridical system there is not a single legal formula for the class domination of today. The few remaining traces of such formulas of class domination are (as that concerning servants) survivals of feudal society.

How can wage slavery be suppressed the "legislative way," if wage slavery is not expressed in laws? Bernstein, who would do away with capitalism by means of legislative reform, finds himself in the same situation as Uspensky's Russian policeman who tells: "Quickly I seized the rascal by the collar! But what do I see? The confounded fellow has no collar!" And that is precisely Bernstein's difficulty.

"All previous societies were based on an antagonism between an oppressing class and an oppressed class" *(Communist Manifesto)*. But in the preceding phases of modern society, this antagonism was expressed in distinctly determined juridical relations and could, especially because of that, accord, to a certain extent, a place to new relations within the framework of the old. "In the midst of serfdom, the serf raised himself to the rank of a member of the town community" *(Communist Manifesto)*. How was that made possible? It was made possible by the progressive suppression of all feudal privileges in the environs of the city: the corvee, the right to special dress, the inheritance tax, the lord's claim to the best cattle, the personal levy, marriage under duress, the right to succession, etc., which all together constituted serfdom.

In the same way, the small bourgeoisie of the Middle Ages succeeded in raising itself, while it was still under the yoke of feudal absolutism, to the rank of bourgeoisie *(Communist Manifesto)*. By what means? By means of the formal partial suppression or complete loosening of the corporative bonds, by the progressive transformation of the fiscal administration and of the army.

Consequently, when we consider the question from the abstract viewpoint, not from the historic viewpoint, we can *imagine* (in view of the former class relations) a legal passage, according to the reformist method, from feudal society to bourgeois society. But what do we see in reality? In reality, we see that legal reforms not only did not obviate the seizure of political power by the bourgeoisie, but have, on the contrary, prepared for it and led to it. A formal social-political transformation was indispensable for the abolition of slavery as well as for the complete suppression of feudalism.

But the situation is entirely different now. Now law obliges the proletariat to submit itself to the yoke of capitalism. Poverty, the lack of means of production, obliges the proletariat to submit itself to the yoke of capitalism. And no law in the world can give to the proletariat the means of production while it remains in the framework of bourgeois society, for not laws but economic development have torn the means of production from the producers' possession.

And neither is the exploitation inside the system of wage labor based on laws. The level of wages is not fixed by legislation, but by economic factors. The phenomenon of capitalist exploitation does not rest on a legal disposition, but on the purely economic fact that labor power plays in this exploitation the role of merchandise possessing, among other characteristics, the agreeable quality of producing value — *more* than the value it consumes in the form of the laborer's means of subsistence. In short, the fundamental relations of the domination of the capitalist class cannot be transformed by means of legislative reforms, on the basis of capitalist society, because these relations have not been introduced by bourgeois laws, nor have they received the form of such laws. Apparently Bernstein is not aware of this, for he speaks of "socialist reforms." On the other hand, he seems to express implicit recognition of this when he writes, on page 10 of his book, that "the economic motive acts freely today, while formerly it was masked by all kinds of relations of domination, by all sorts of ideology."

It is one of the peculiarities of the capitalist order that within it all the elements of the future society first assume, in their de-

79

velopment, a form not approaching socialism but, on the contrary, a form moving more and more away from socialism. Production takes on a progressively increasing social character. But under what form is the social character of capitalist production expressed? It is expressed in the form of the large enterprise, in the form of the shareholding concern, the cartel, within which the capitalist antagonisms, capitalist exploitation, the oppression of labor-power, are augmented to the extreme.

In the army, capitalist development leads to the extension of obligatory military service, to the reduction of the time of service and, consequently, to a material approach to a popular militia. But all of this takes place under the form of modern militarism, in which the domination of the people by the militarist state and the class character of the state manifest themselves most clearly.

In the field of political relations, the development of democracy brings — in the measure that it finds a favorable soil — the participation of all popular strata in political life and, consequently, some sort of "people's state." But this participation takes the form of bourgeois parliamentarism, in which class antagonism and class domination are not done away with, but are, on the contrary, displayed in the open. Exactly because capitalist development moves through these contradictions, it is necessary to extract the kernel of socialist society from its capitalist shell. Exactly for this reason must the proletariat seize political power and suppress completely the capitalist system.

Of course, Bernstein draws other conclusions. If the development of democracy leads to the aggravation and not to the lessening of capitalist antagonisms, "the social democracy," he answers us, "in order not to render its task more difficult, must by all means try to stop social reforms and the extension of democratic institutions." Indeed, that would be the right thing to do if the social democracy found to its taste, in the petty bourgeois manner, the futile task of picking for itself all the good sides of history and rejecting the bad sides of history. However, in that case, it should at the same time "try to stop" capitalism in general, for there is no doubt that the latter is the rascal placing all these obstacles in the way of socialism. But capitalism furnishes besides the *obstacles* also the only *possibilities* of realizing the socialist program. The same can be said about democracy.

If democracy has become superfluous or annoying to the bourgeoisie, it is on the contrary necessary and indispensable to the working class. It is necessary to the working class because it creates the political forms (autonomous administration, electoral rights, etc.) which will serve the proletariat as fulcrums in its task of transforming bourgeois society. Democracy is indispensable to the working class, because only through the exercise of its democratic rights, in the struggle for democracy, can the proletariat become aware of its class interests and its historic task.

In a word, democracy is indispensable not because it renders superfluous the conquest of political power by the proletariat, but because it renders this conquest of power both *necessary* and *possible*. When Engels, in his preface to the *Class Struggles in France*, revised the tactics of the modern labor movement and urged the legal struggle as opposed to the barricades, he did not have in mind—this comes out of every line of the preface—the question of a definite conquest of political power, but the contemporary daily struggle. He did not have in mind the attitude that the proletariat must take toward the capitalist state at the time of its seizure of power, but the attitude of the proletariat while in the bounds of the capitalist state. Engels was giving directions to the proletariat *oppressed*, and not to the proletariat victorious.

On the other hand, Marx's well-known sentence on the agrarian question in England (Bernstein leans on it heavily) in which he says: "We shall probably succeed easier by buying the estates of the landlords," does not refer to the stand of the proletariat *before, but after its victory*. For there evidently can be a question of buying the property of the old dominant class only when the workers are in power. The possibility envisaged by Marx is that of the *pacific exercise of the dictatorship of the proletariat* and not the replacement of the dictatorship with capitalist social reforms. There was no doubt for Marx and Engels about the necessity of having the proletariat conquer political power. It is left to Bernstein to consider the poultry-yard of bourgeois parliamentarism as the organ by means of which we are to realize the most formidable social transformation of history, *the passage from capitalist society to socialism*.

Bernstein introduces his theory by warning the proletariat against the danger of acquiring power too early. That is, according to Bernstein, the proletariat ought to leave the bourgeois society in its present condition and itself suffer a frightful defeat. If the proletariat came to power, it could draw from Bernstein's theory the following "practical" conclusion: to go to sleep. His theory condemns the proletariat, at the most decisive moments of the struggle, to inactivity, to a passive betrayal of its own cause.

Our program would be a miserable scrap of paper if it could not serve us in *all* eventualities, at *all* moments of the struggle, and if it did not serve us by its *application* and not by its nonapplication. If our program contains the formula of the historic development of society from capitalism to socialism, it must also formulate, in all its characteristic fundamentals, all the transitory phases of this development, and it should, consequently, be able to indicate to the proletariat what ought to be its corresponding action at every moment on the road toward socialism. There can be no time for the proletariat when it will be obliged to abandon its program or be abandoned by it.

Practically, this is manifested in the fact that there can be no time when the proletariat, placed in power by the force of events, is not in the condition, or is not morally obliged, to take certain measures for the realization of its program, that is, take transitory measures in the direction of socialism. Behind the belief that the socialist program can collapse completely at any point of the dictatorship of the proletariat lurks the other belief that *socialist program is, generally and at all times, unrealizable.*

And what if the transitory measures are premature? The question hides a great number of mistaken ideas concerning the real course of a social transformation.

In the first place, the seizure of political power by the proletariat, that is to say by a large popular class, is not produced artificially. It presupposes (with the exception of such cases as the Paris Commune, when power was not obtained by the proletariat after a conscious struggle for its goal, but fell into its hands, like a good thing abandoned by everybody else) a definite degree of maturity of economic and political relations. Here we have the essential difference between coups d'etat along Blanqui's conception, which are accomplished by an "active minority," and burst out like pistol shot, always inopportunely, and the conquest of political power by a great conscious popular mass, which can only be the product of the decomposition of bourgeois society and therefore bears in itself the economic and political legitimation of its opportune appearance.

If, therefore, considered from the angle of political effect, the conquest of political power by the working class cannot materialize itself "too early," then from the angle of conservation of power, the premature revolution, the thought of which keeps Bernstein awake, menaces us like a sword of Damocles. Against that neither prayers nor supplication, neither scares nor any amount of anguish, are of any avail. And this for two very simple reasons.

In the first place, it is impossible to imagine that a transformation as formidable as the passage from capitalist society to socialist society can be realized in one happy act. To consider that as possible is again to lend color to conceptions that are clearly Blanquist. The socialist transformation supposes a long and stubborn struggle, in the course of which, it is quite probable, the proletariat will be repulsed more than once, so that the first time, from the viewpoint of the final outcome of the struggle, it will necessarily come to power "too early."

In the second place, it will be impossible to avoid the "premature" conquest of state power by the proletariat precisely because these "premature" attacks of the proletariat constitute a factor, and indeed a very important factor, creating the political conditions of the final victory. In the course of the political crisis accompanying its seizure of power, in the course of the long and stubborn struggles, the proletariat will acquire the degree of political maturity permitting it to obtain in time a definitive victory of the revolution. Thus these "premature" attacks of the proletariat against the state power are in themselves important historic factors helping to provoke and determine the *point* of the definite victory. Considered from this viewpoint, the idea of a "premature" conquest of political power by the laboring class appears to be a political absurdity derived from a mechanical conception of the development of society, and positing for the victory of the class struggle a point fixed *outside* and *independent of* the class struggle.

Since the proletariat is not in the position to seize political power in any other way than "prematurely," since the proletariat is absolutely obliged to seize power once or several times "too early" before it can maintain itself in power for good, the objection to the "premature" conquest of power is at bottom nothing more than a *general opposition to the aspiration of the proletariat to possess itself of state power.* Just as all roads lead to Rome, so too, do we logically arrive at the conclusion that the revisionist proposal to slight the final aim of the socialist movement is really a recommendation to renounce the socialist movement itself.

Collapse

Bernstein began his revision of the social democracy by abandoning the theory of capitalist collapse. The latter, however, is the cornerstone of scientific socialism. Rejecting it, Bernstein also rejects the whole doctrine of socialism. In the course of his discussion, he abandons one after another of the positions of socialism in order to be able to maintain his first affirmation.

Without the collapse of capitalism the expropriation of the capitalist class is impossible. Bernstein therefore renounces expropriation and chooses a progressive realization of the "cooperative principle" as the aim of the labor movement.

But cooperation cannot be realized within capitalist production. Bernstein, therefore, renounces the socialization of production, and merely proposes to reform commerce and · to develop consumers' cooperatives.

But the transformation of society through consumers' cooperatives, even by means of trade unions, is incompatible with the real material development of capitalist society. Therefore, Bernstein abandons the materialist conception of history.

But his conception of the march of economic development is incompatible with the Marxist theory of surplus value. Therefore, Bernstein abandons the theory of value and surplus value and, in this way, the whole economic system of Karl Marx.

But the struggle of the proletariat cannot be carried on without a given final aim and without an economic base found in the existing society. Bernstein, therefore, abandons the class struggle and speaks of reconciliation with bourgeois liberalism.

But in a class society, the class struggle is a natural and unavoidable phenomenon. Bernstein, therefore, contests even the existence of classes in society. The working class is for him a mass of individuals, divided politically and intellectually, but also economically. And the bourgeoisie, according to him, does not group itself politically in accordance with its inner economic interest, but only because of exterior pressure from above and below.

But if there is no economic base for the class struggle and, if consequently, there are no classes in our society, not only the future, but even the past struggles of the proletariat against the bourgeoisie appear to be impossible and the social democracy and its successes seem absolutely incomprehensible, or they can be understood only as the results of political pressure by the government — that is, not as the natural consequences of historic development but as the fortuitous consequences of the policy of Hohenzollern; not as the legitimate offspring of capitalist society, but as the bastard children of reaction. Rigorously logical, in this respect, Bernstein passes from the materialist conception of history to the outlook of the *Frankfurter Zeitung* and the *Vossische Zeitung*.

After rejecting the socialist criticism of capitalist society, it is easy for Bernstein to find the present state of affairs satisfactory — at least in a general way. Bernstein does not hesitate. He discovers that at the present time reaction is not very strong in Germany, that "we cannot speak of political reaction in the countries of Western Europe," and that in all the countries of the West "the attitude of the bourgeois classes toward the socialist movement is at most an attitude of defense but not one of oppression" (*Vorwaerts*, March 26, 1899). Far from becoming worse, the situation of the workers is getting better. Indeed, the bourgeoisie is politically progressive and morally sane. We cannot speak either of reaction or oppression. It is for the best in the best of all possible worlds. . . .

Bernstein thus travels in logical sequence from A to Z. He began by abandoning the *final aim* and supposedly keeping the movement. But as there can be no socialist movement without a socialist aim, he ends by renouncing the *movement*.

And thus Bernstein's conception of socialism collapses entirely. The proud and admirable symmetric construction of socialist thought becomes for him a pile of rubbish, in which the debris of all systems, the pieces of thought of various great and small minds, find a common resting place. Marx and Proudhon, Leon von Buch and Franz Oppenheimer, Friedrich Albert Lange and Kant, Herr Prokopovich and Dr. Ritter von Neupauer, Herkner and Schulze-Gaevernitz, Lassalle and Professor Julius Wolff: all contribute something to Bernstein's system. From each he takes a little. There is nothing astonishing about that. For when he abandoned scientific socialism he lost the axis of intellectual crystallization around which isolated facts group themselves in the organic whole of a coherent conception of the world.

His doctrine, composed of bits of all possible systems, seems upon first consideration to be completely free from prejudices. For Bernstein does not like talk of "party science," or to be more exact, of class science, any more than he likes to talk of class liberalism or class morality. He thinks he succeeds in expressing human, general, abstract science, abstract liberalism, abstract morality. But since the society of reality is made up of classes, which have diametrically opposed interests, aspirations and conceptions, a general human science in social questions, an abstract liberalism, an abstract morality, are at present illusions, pure utopia. The science, the democracy, the morality, considered by Bernstein as general, human, are merely the dominant science, dominant democracy and dominant morality, that is, bourgeois science, bourgeois democracy, bourgeois morality.

When Bernstein rejects the economic doctrine of Marx in order to swear by the teachings of Brentano, Boehm-Bawerk, Jevons, Say and Julius Wolff, he exchanges the scientific base of the emancipation of the working class for the apologetics of the bourgeoisie. When he speaks of the generally human character of liberalism and transforms socialism into a variety of liberalism, he deprives the socialist movement (generally) of its class character, and consequently of its historic content, consequently of all content; and conversely, recognizes the class representing liberalism in history, the bourgeoisie, as the champion of the general interests of humanity.

And when he was against "raising of the material factors to the rank of an all-powerful force of development," when he protests against the so-called contempt for the ideal that is supposed to rule the social democracy, when he presumes to talk for idealism, for morals, pronouncing himself at the same time against the only source of the moral rebirth of the proletariat, a revolutionary class struggle — he does no more than the following: preach to the working class the quintessence of the morality of

85

the bourgeoisie, that is, reconciliation with the existing social order and the transfer of the hopes of the proletariat to the limbo of ethical simulacra.

When he directs his keenest arrows against our dialectic system, he is really attacking the specific mode of thought employed by the conscious proletariat in its struggle for liberation. It is an attempt to break the sword that has helped the proletariat to pierce the darkness of its future. It is an attempt to shatter the intellectual arm with the aid of which the proletariat, though materially under the yoke of the bourgeoisie, is yet enabled to triumph over the bourgeoisie. For it is our dialectical system that shows to the working class the transitory character of this yoke, proving to the workers the inevitability of their victory, and is already realizing a revolution in the domain of thought. Saying good-bye to our system of dialectics, and resorting instead to the intellectual seesaw of the well-known "on one hand — on the other hand," "yes — but," "although — however," "more — less," etc., he quite logically lapses into a mode of thought that belongs historically to the bourgeoisie in decline, being the faithful intellectual reflection of the social existence and political activity of the bourgeoisie at that stage. The political "on one hand — on the other hand," "yes — but" of the bourgeoisie of today resembles in a marked degree Bernstein's manner of thinking, which is the sharpest and surest proof of the bourgeois nature of his conception of the world.

But, as it is used by Bernstein, the word "bourgeois" itself is not a class expression but a general social notion. Logical to the end, he has exchanged, together with his science, politics, morals and mode of thinking, the historic language of the proletariat for that of the bourgeoisie. When he uses, without distinction, the term "citizen" in reference to the bourgeois as well as to the proletarian, intending, thereby, to refer to man in general, he identifies man in general with the bourgeois, and human society with bourgeois society.

Opportunism in Theory and Practice

Bernstein's book is of great importance to the German and the international labor movement. It is the first attempt to give a theoretic base to the opportunist currents common in the social democracy.

These currents may be said to have existed for a long time in our movement, if we take into consideration such sporadic manifestations of opportunism as the question of subsidization of steamers. But it is only since about 1890, with the suppression of the antisocialist laws, that we have had a trend of opportunism of a clearly defined character. Vollmar's "state socialism,"

86

the vote on the Bavarian budget, the "agrarian socialism" of South Germany, Heine's policy of compensation, Schippel's stand on tariffs and militarism are the high points in the development of our opportunist practice. What appears to characterize this practice above all? A certain hostility to "theory." This is quite natural, for our "theory," that is, the principles of scientific socialism, impose clearly marked limitations to practical activity—insofar as it concerns the aims of this activity, the means used in attaining these aims, and the method employed in this activity. It is quite natural for people who run after immediate "practical" results to want to free themselves from such limitations and to render their practice independent of our "theory."

However, this outlook is refuted by every attempt to apply it in reality. State socialism, agrarian socialism, the policy of compensation, the question of the army all constituted defeats to our opportunism. It is clear that, if this current is to maintain itself, it must try to destroy the principles of our theory and elaborate a theory of its own. Bernstein's book is precisely an effort in that direction. That is why at Stuttgart all the opportunist elements in our party immediately grouped themselves about Bernstein's banner. If the opportunist currents in the practical activity of our party are an entirely natural phenomenon which can be explained in light of the special conditions of our activity and its development, Bernstein's theory is no less natural an attempt to group these currents into a general theoretic expression, an attempt to elaborate its own theoretic conditions and to break with scientific socialism. That is why the published expression of Bernstein's ideas should be recognized as a theoretic test for opportunism and as its first scientific legitimation.

What was the result of this test? We have seen the result. Opportunism is not in a position to elaborate a positive theory capable of withstanding criticism. All it can do is to attack various isolated theses of Marxist theory and, just because Marxist doctrine constitutes one solidly constructed edifice, hope by this means to shake the entire system, from the top to its foundation.

This shows that opportunist practice is essentially irreconcilable with Marxism. But it also proves that opportunism is incompatible with socialism (the socialist movement) in general, that its internal tendency is to push the labor movement into bourgeois paths, that opportunism tends to paralyze completely the proletarian class struggle. The latter, considered historically, has evidently nothing to do with Marxist doctrine. For, before Marx, and independently from him, there have been labor movements and various socialist doctrines, each of which, in its way, was the theoretic expression, corresponding to the conditions of the time, of the struggle of the working class for emancipation. The theory that consists in basing socialism on the moral notion of justice, on a struggle against the mode of distribution, instead of basing it on a struggle against the mode of production, the conception of class antagonism as an antagonism between the poor and the rich, the effort to graft the "cooperative principle" on capitalist economy — all the nice notions found in Bernstein's doctrine — already existed before him. And these theories were, *in their time*, in spite of their insufficiency, effective theories of the proletarian class struggle. They were the children's seven-league boots to which the proletariat learned to walk upon the scene of history.

But after the development of the class struggle and its reflex in its social conditions had led to the abandonment of these theories and to the elaboration of the principles of scientific socialism, there could be no socialism — at least in Germany — outside of Marxist socialism, and there could be no socialist class struggle outside of the social democracy. From then on, socialism and Marxism, the proletarian struggle for emancipation, and the social democracy were identical. That is why the return to pre-Marxist socialist theories no longer signifies today a return to the seven-league boots of the childhood of the proletariat, but a return to the puny worn-out slippers of the bourgeoisie.

Bernstein's theory was the *first*, and at the same time, the *last* attempt to give a theoretic base to opportunism. It is the last, because in Bernstein's system, opportunism has gone — negatively through its renunciation of scientific socialism, positively through its marshalling of every bit of theoretic confusion possible — as far as it can. In Bernstein's book, opportunism has crowned its theoretic development (just as it completed its practical development in the position taken by Schippel on the question of militarism) and has reached its ultimate conclusion.

Marxist doctrine cannot only refute opportunism theoretically. It alone can explain opportunism as a historic phenomenon in the development of the party. The forward march of the proletariat, on a world historic scale, to its final victory is not, indeed, "so simple a thing." The peculiar character of this movement resides precisely in the fact that here, for the first time in history, the popular masses themselves, *in opposition* to the ruling classes, are to impose their will, but they must effect this outside of the present society, beyond the existing society. This *will* the masses can only form in a constant struggle against the existing order. The union of the broad popular masses with an aim reaching beyond the existing social order, the union of the daily struggle with the great world transformation, this is the task of the social democratic movement, which must logically grope on its road of development between the following two rocks: abandoning the mass character of the party or abandoning its final aim, falling into bourgeois reformism or into sectarianism, anarchism or opportunism.

In its theoretic arsenal, Marxist doctrine furnished, more than half a century ago, arms that are effective against both of these two extremes. But because our movement is a mass movement and because the dangers menacing it are not derived from the human brain but from social conditions, Marxist doctrine could not assure us, in advance and once for always, against the anarchist and opportunist tendencies. The latter can be overcome only as we pass from the domain of theory to the domain of practice, but only with the help of the arms furnished us by Marx.

"Bourgeois revolutions," wrote Marx a half century ago, "like those of the eighteenth century, rush onward rapidly from success to success, their stage effects outbid one another, men and things seem to be set in flaming brilliants, ecstasy is the prevailing spirit; but they are short-lived, they reach their climax speedily, and then society relapses into a long fit of nervous reaction before it learns how to appropriate the fruits of its period of feverish excitement. Proletarian revolutions, on the contrary, such as those of the nineteenth century, criticize themselves constantly; constantly interrupt themselves in their own course; come back to what seems to have been accomplished, in order to start anew; scorn with cruel thoroughness the half measures, weaknesses and meannesses of their first attempts; seem to throw down their adversary only to enable him to draw fresh strength from the earth and again to rise up against them in more gigantic stature; constantly recoil in fear before the undefined monster magnitude of their own objects — until finally that situation is created which renders all retreat impossible and conditions themselves cry out: 'Hic Rhodus, hic salta!' [Here is the rose. And here we must dance!]"

This has remained true even after the elaboration of the doctrine of scientific socialism. The proletarian movement has not as yet, all at once, become social democratic, even in Germany. But it is becoming more social democratic, surmounting continuously the extreme deviations of anarchism and opportunism, both of which are only determining phases of the development of the social democracy, considered as a process.

For these reasons, we must say that the surprising thing here is not the appearance of an opportunist current but rather its feebleness. As long as it showed itself in isolated cases of the practical activity of the party, one could suppose that it had a serious practical base. But now that it has shown its face in Bernstein's book, one can not help exclaim with astonishment:

"What? Is that all you have to say?" Not the shadow of an original thought! Not a single idea that was not refuted, crushed, reduced into dust, by Marxism several decades ago!

It was enough for opportunism to speak out to prove it had nothing to say. In the history of our party that is the only importance of Bernstein's book.

Thus saying good-bye to the mode of thought of the revolutionary proletariat, to dialectics and to the materialist conception of history, Bernstein can thank them for the attenuating circumstances they provide for his conversion. For only dialectics and the materialist conception of history, magnanimous as they are, could make Bernstein appear as an unconscious predestined instrument, by means of which the rising working class expresses its momentary weakness, but which, upon closer inspection, it throws aside contemptuously and with pride.

SOCIALIST CRISIS
IN FRANCE

While Eduard Bernstein developed the theoretical justification for socialists joining forces with the liberal bourgeoisie on the basis of a capitalist program, Alexandre Millerand, the French social democrat, carried Bernstein's ideas to their logical conclusion and implemented them.

In 1899, at the height of the social and political crisis created by the Dreyfus case, a new cabinet was formed by the liberal Waldeck-Rousseau. It was called the "cabinet of republican defense" to emphasize the chief justification made for its existence — that the republic was in grave danger of being overthrown by the monarchist forces.

For the first time in the history of the working-class movement, a socialist accepted a post in a bourgeois ministry. Alexandre Millerand became minister of commerce, side by side with minister of war General Gallifet, who ordered the execution of some 30,000 Communards in 1871. What was the reason given by Millerand, Jaures, Briand, Viviani and other leaders of the French socialist party? "The republic must be defended."

In a series of articles printed in *Neue Zeit* in 1900-1901 under the title "The Socialist Crisis in France," Rosa Luxemburg scathingly denounced the Millerand betrayal and demonstrated why the working class cannot defend its democratic gains by joining forces with the class enemy. Her analysis is as relevant today, as it was seventy years ago.

The Third French Republic was born out of the defeat of Napoleon III in the Franco-Prussian War of 1870-71. But unlike the first two French republics, which perished in 1799 and 1851 respectively, the Third Republic survived its infancy.

As Rosa Luxemburg explains in one of the early articles in the series, the Third Republic was able "to last long enough to enter a normal period of existence and prove to the bourgeoisie that it knows how to adapt itself to their interests, and much better than any monarchy in the world could possibly do."

As a result, by 1898 the monarchist forces had been severely diminished, winning only 12 percent of the vote as compared to 20 percent for the socialists. But the continuous scandals and corruption rampant in the ruling circles exposed the internal weakness of the government. The army more and more became an independent and powerful force.

The famous Dreyfus case began in 1894 when Captain Alfred Dreyfus, a Jewish officer of the General Staff, was convicted in a secret court-martial of selling military secrets to a foreign power, and sentenced to Devil's Island for life.

It soon became clear that he had been framed to protect another officer — a non-Jewish aristocrat — and that the highest echelons of the army had been involved. As the Dreyfus scandal unfolded, it more and more polarized French society. Against Dreyfus were ranged the army, the Catholic clergy, the monarchists and the old aristocracy. On Dreyfus's side were the liberal bourgeoisie led by Zola and Clemenceau and the section of the socialist movement led by Jaures. At the height of the agitation over the scandal, Waldeck-Rousseau stepped in to head the government, and pardoned Dreyfus.

Millerand was asked to take a portfolio in the cabinet, and the majority of the socialist forces led by Jaures and Millerand decided it was the correct move. No matter what his program may have been, once in the cabinet, Millerand limited himself to a few practical reforms of the mercantile marine, the development of trade, technical education, the postal system, and similar petty measures. Once the Socialist Party was committed — through Millerand's government post — to keeping the cabinet in power, the party compromised itself more and more, and betrayed its support of working-class struggles, with the disastrous results Rosa Luxemburg outlines so clearly.

In a few years, even Jaures became disillusioned and broke with Millerand, Briand and Viviani, who had also joined the cabinet. They were expelled from the Socialist Party, and Jaures belatedly branded them "traitors who let themselves be used to serve the interests of capitalism."

The Millerand episode, like the Bernstein controversy, went down in the history of the international Marxist movement as a major historical watershed. Later, the Communist Parties in different countries, like France, pursued the "Millerand policy" during the Popular Front period in the late 1930s and again after the Second World War, and social democratic parties are today even the governing parties of numerous capitalist countries. But such participation in bourgeois governments only provides a measure for the degree of departure from Marxist principles; the revolutionary socialist rejection of "Millerandism" and popular frontism was clearly established over seventy years ago.

The following excerpt from "The Socialist Crisis in France" is taken from the August and October 1939 issues of the *New International*. The translation is by Ernest Erber. In an initial installment, not included here, Rosa Luxemburg examines in detail the differences between the relationship of class forces during the First and Second Republics, and the Third. She shows that in 1899 the real threat to the republic came not from the monarchists but from the growing independence of the army.

At the beginning of the second installment she poses the question: how well does Waldeck-Rousseau's so-called defense of the republic stand up under scrutiny? She answers, "If the existence of the republic had depended upon the Waldeck-Rousseau cabinet, it would have perished long ago."

The cabinet has been at the helm for nineteen months. It has twice outlived the average lifespan of a French cabinet — the fatal nine months. What has it accomplished?

It is hard to imagine a more extreme contradiction between means and ends, between task and accomplishment, between the advance advertisement and the subsequent performance than is to be found in the expectations roused by the Waldeck-Rousseau cabinet and its achievements.

The whole program of reform of military justice has now been reduced to the promise of the minister of war to take into account "mitigating circumstances" in the course of court-martial proceedings. The socialist, Pastre, speaking in the Chamber on December 27 of last year, proposed the introduction of the two-year military term, a reform already introduced in semiabsolutist Germany. The Radical minister of republican defense, General Andre, answered that he could take no position on this question. The socialist, Dejeante, demanded in the same session that the clergy be removed from the military academies, that the religious personnel of the military hospital be replaced by a secular personnel, and that the distribution of religious publications by the army be ended. The minister of republican defense, whose task it was to secularize the army, answered with a blunt rejection of the proposals and a glorification of the spirituality of the army — amid the stormy applause of the Nationalists.

In February 1900, the socialists denounced a series of terrible abuses in the army, but the government rejected every proposal for a parliamentary investigation. The Radical, Vigne d'Octon, made some gruesome revelations in the Chamber (session of December 7, 1900) on the conduct of the French military regime in the colonies, particularly in Madagascar and Indochina. The government rejected the proposal for a parliamentary inquiry as being "dangerous and purposeless." Finally came the climax: the minister of war mounted the tribune of the Chamber to tell of his heroic defense of — an officer of the Dragoons who was boycotted by his colleagues for having married a divorcee.

A legal formula is devised which covers the monastic orders with the same provisions that apply in the case of open societies. Its application against the clergy will depend upon the good will and its application against the socialists upon the bad will of future ministers.

The republic has in no way weakened the authorized orders. They still have their property of almost 400 million francs, their state subsidized secular clergy headed by 87 bishops, their 87 seminaries, their 42,000 priests, and their budget for publications of about 40 million francs. The chief strength of the clergy lies in its influence upon the education of 2 million French children who are at present being poisoned in the parochial schools and made into enemies of the republic. The government bestirs itself and prohibits such instruction — by nonauthorized religious orders. But almost the entire religious instruction is precisely in the hands of the authorized orders and the Radical reform results in 15,000 out of 2 million children being rescued from the holy-water sprinklers. The capitulation of the government to the church was introduced with Waldeck-Rousseau's speech in which he paid his respects to the Pope and was sealed with the vote of confidence in the government offered by the Nationalists.

The "defense of the republic" a la Waldeck-Rousseau reached its grand climax last December with the adoption of the amnesty law.

For two years France was in a turmoil. For two years the cry went up for truth, light, and justice. For two years a judicial murder weighed upon its conscience. Society was being literally suffocated in the poisoned atmosphere of lies, perjuries, and falsifications.

At last the government of republican defense arrived on the scene. All the world held its breath. The "great sun of justice" was about to rise.

And it rose. On December 19 the government had the Chamber adopt a law which guaranteed immunity to all charged with crime, which denied legal satisfaction to those falsely accused, and quashed all trials already in process. Those who were yesterday declared the most dangerous enemies of the republic are today again taken to its bosom as prodigal sons returned home. In order to defend the republic, a general pardon is extended to all its attackers. In order to rehabilitate republican justice, all victims of the judicial frame-ups are denied the opportunity for vindication.

Petty bourgeois radicalism ran true to type. In 1893 the bourgeois radicals took the helm through the cabinet of Ribot to liquidate the crisis caused by the Panama scandal. But because the republic was declared in danger, the accused deputies were not prosecuted and the whole affair was allowed to dissolve into thin air. Waldeck-Rousseau, commissioned to handle the Dreyfus affair, dissolves it in a complete fiasco "in order to close the door to the monarchist danger."

The pattern is an old one: "The shattering overture that announces the battle loses itself in a timid growl as soon as the action is to start. The actors cease to take themselves seriously, and the performance falls flat like an inflated balloon that is pricked with a needle" (Marx, *The Eighteenth Brumaire*).

Was it to realize these grotesque, piddling, laughable measures — I speak not from the viewpoint of socialism, or even of a half-way capable radical party, but merely in comparison to the republican measures of the opportunists in the 1880s, like Gambetta, Jules Ferry, Constant, and Tirard—was it for this that a socialist, the representative of working-class power, had to be taken into the cabinet?

The opportunist Gambetta, with his moderate republicans, demanded in 1879 the removal of all monarchists from government service and, through this agitation, drove MacMahon from the presidency. In 1880 these same "respectable" republicans carried through the expulsion of the Jesuits, and a system of compulsory, free education. The opportunist Jules Ferry drove over 600 monarchist judges from the bench in his judicial reforms in 1883 and dealt a hard blow at the clergy with his law on divorce. The opportunists Constant and Tirard, in order to cut the ground from under Boulangism, reduced the term of military service from five to three years.

The radical cabinet of Waldeck-Rousseau failed to even rise to the stature of these most modest republican measures of the opportunists. In a series of equivocal maneuvers in the course of nineteen months it accomplished nothing, absolutely nothing. It did not carry out the least reorganization of military justice. It did not bring about the slightest reduction in the period of military service. It did not take one decisive step to drive the monarchists out of the army, judiciary, and administration. It did not undertake a single thorough measure against the clericals. The one thing it *did* do was to maintain its pose of fearlessness, firmness, inflexibility — the classic pose of petty bourgeois politicians when they get into hot water. Finally, after much ado, it declared that the republic is not in a position to do anything about the band of military rogues and simply must let them go. Was it for this that the collaboration of a socialist was necessary in the cabinet?

It has been said that Millerand was personally indispensable for the building of the Waldeck-Rousseau cabinet. As far as is generally known, France is not suffering from a lack of men who are covetous of a cabinet portfolio. If Waldeck-Rousseau could find two useful generals in the ranks of the rebellious army to serve as ministers of war, he could have found a half-dozen men in his own party who were eager for the post of minister of commerce. But after one has come to know the record of the cabinet, one must in any case admit that Waldeck-Rousseau could have calmly taken any agreeable Radical as a co-worker and the comedy of the "defense of the republic" would not have come out one hair worse. The Radicals have always understood how to compromise themselves without outside assistance.

We have seen that the monarchist danger, which scared everyone so much during the Dreyfus crisis, was more of a phantom than reality. The "defense" of Waldeck-Rousseau, therefore, was not necessary to save the republic from a coup d'etat. Those, however, who still today defend the entry of Millerand into the government as they did two years ago, and point to the monarchist danger as both the motive for the entry and for remaining, are playing a dangerous game. The more serious one paints the picture, the more pitiful appear the actions of the cabinet, and the more questionable the role of the socialists who participated.

If the monarchist danger was very slight, as we sought to establish, then the rescuing efforts of the government, begun with pomp and circumstance and ended in fiasco, were a farce. If, on the other hand, the danger was great and serious, then the sham actions of the cabinet were a betrayal of the republic and of the parties that placed their confidence in it.

In either case, the working class has not, in sending Millerand into the cabinet, taken over that "large share of responsibility" which Jaures and his friends speak of so proudly. It has merely fallen heir to a part of the shameful "republican" disgrace of petty bourgeois radicalism.

The contradiction between the hopes confided in the cabinet of Waldeck-Rousseau and its actual achievements has confronted the Jaures-Millerand section of French socialism with but one alternative. It could confess its disillusionment, admit the uselessness of Millerand's participation in the government, and demand his resignation. Or it could declare itself satisfied with the politics of the government, pronounce the realities to be just what it had expected, and gradually tone down its expectations and demands to correspond with the gradual evaporation of the government's will-to-action.

As long as the cabinet avoided the main question and remained in the stage of preliminary skirmishes — and this stage lasted an entire eighteen months — all political tendencies that followed its policies, including the socialists, could still drift along with it. However, the first decisive step of the government — the amnesty law — pushed matters out of their twilight zone into the clear light of day.

The outcome of the Dreyfus affair was of decisive importance for the Jaures group, whether they liked it or not. To play on this card, and this card only, had been their tactic for two full years. The Dreyfus affair was the axis of all their politics. They described it as "one of the greatest battles of the century, one of the greatest of human history!" (Jaures in *Petite Republique,* August 12, 1899). To shrink from this great task of the working class would mean "the worst abdication, the worst humiliation" (ibid., July 15, 1899). *"Toute la vérité! La pleine lumiere!"* "The whole truth, full light," that was the goal of the socialist campaign. Nothing could stop Jaures and his friends — neither difficulties nor nationalist maneuvers nor the protests of the socialist group led by Guesde and Vaillant.

"We battle onward, [Jaures called out with noble pride] and if the judges of Rennes, deceived by the detestable maneuvers of the reactionaries, should again victimize the innocent in order to save the criminal army chiefs, we will again stand up on the morrow, despite all proclamations of expulsion, despite all mealymouthed references to the falsification, distortion, and belittling of the class struggle, despite all dangers, and call out to the generals and the judges: You are hangmen and criminals!" (ibid., July 15, 1899).

During the trial at Rennes, Jaures wrote confidently: "Be it as it may, justice will triumph! The hour is drawing nigh for the freeing of the martyrs and for the punishment of the criminals!" (ibid., August 13, 1899).

As late as November of last year, shortly before the passage of the amnesty law, Jaures declared at Lille: "For my part I was prepared to go further. I wanted to continue until the poisonous beasts would be forced to spit out their poison. Yes, it was necessary to prosecute all forgers, all liars, all criminals, all traitors; it is necessary to pursue them to the extreme summits of the truth, as on the extreme point of a knife, until they were forced to admit their crimes and the ignominy of their crimes before the entire world" (*Les Deux Methodes,* Lille, 1900, p. 5).

And Jaures was right. The Dreyfus affair had awakened all the latent forces of reaction in France. The old enemy of the working class, militarism, stood completely exposed, and it was necessary to direct all spears against its body. The working class was called upon for the first time to fight out a great political battle. Jaures and his friends led the workers into the struggle and thereby opened up a new epoch in the history of French socialism.

As the amnesty law was presented to the Chamber, the right-wing socialists suddenly found themselves facing a Rubicon. It was now clear that the government that had been formed to liquidate the Dreyfus crisis, instead of "turning on the spotlight," instead of establishing the "entire truth," and instead of forcing the military despots to their knees, had extinguished truth and light and bowed its own knee to the military despots. This was a betrayal of the hopes Jaures and his friends had placed on the government. This ministerial post revealed itself to be a useless tool for socialist politics and the defense of the republic. The tool had turned against the master. If the Jaures group wanted to remain true to their position in the Dreyfus campaign and to the task of republican defense, they immediately had to turn their weapons and use every means to defeat the amnesty law. The government had laid their cards on the table. It was necessary to trump them.

But to decide on the amnesty proposal was also to decide on the existence of the cabinet. Since the Nationalists declared themselves against the amnesty, and made the question one of a vote of confidence in the government, it was easy for a majority to be formed against the proposal and lead to the downfall of the cabinet.

Jaures and his friends now had to make a choice: either fight through to the finish their two-year campaign on the Dreyfus issue, or to support the Waldeck-Rousseau cabinet, either for the "full truth" or the cabinet, either for the defense of the republic or the ministerial post of Millerand. The question balanced in the scales for only a few minutes. Waldeck-Millerand outweighed Dreyfus. The cabinet's ultimatum accomplished what the Guesde-Vaillant manifestos of excommunication had failed to accomplish: in order to save the cabinet, Jaures and his group voted for the amnesty and thereby gave up the Dreyfus campaign.

The die had been cast. With the acceptance of the amnesty law, the right-wing socialists made as the guide for their conduct, not their own political interests, but the maintenance at the helm of the Waldeck-Rousseau cabinet. The vote for the amnesty law was the Waterloo of their Dreyfus campaign. In the twinkling of an eye, Jaures had brought to naught all he accomplished in the course of two years.

After surrendering their chief political stock, the Jaures group sped merrily on their sportive way. To save the government, they gave up — reluctantly and with internal *Katzenjammer* over the costly price — the goal of two years of gigantic struggles: the "whole truth" and "complete light." But to justify their own adherence to a government of political fiascos, they had to deny the fiascos. Their next step was to justify the capitulation of the government.

The government pigeonholed the Dreyfus affair instead of fighting it through to the end. But that was necessary "in order to put an end to the now useless and boring trials and avoid sickening the people with too much publicity, which would now soon obscure the truth" (Jaures in *Petite Republique*, December 18, 1900).

It is true that two years ago the whole of "loyal and honest France" had been called upon to pledge: "I swear that Dreyfus is innocent, that the innocent shall be vindicated and the guilty shall be punished" (ibid., August 9, 1899).

But today "all these judicial trials would be an absurdity. They would only tire the country without clarifying it and hurt the cause we are trying to serve. . . . The true justification of the Dreyfus affair lies today in the work for the republic as a whole" (ibid., December 18, 1900).

Yet another step and the former heroes of the Dreyfus campaign appear to the Jaures group as troublesome ghosts of the past with whom one cannot finish quickly enough.

Zola, the "great defender of justice," "the pride of France and of humanity," the man of the thundering *J'Accuse!* [*I Accuse!*] issues a protest against the amnesty law. He insists now, as previously, on "the whole truth and the full light." He accuses once more. What confusion! Does he not see, asks Jaures, that there is already "enough light" to penetrate all intellects? Zola should forget his failure to be vindicated before a court of law and remember that he is glorified in the eyes of "that great judge, the whole of humanity," and please, be so kind as not to bother us with his eternal *J'Accuse!* Only no accusations, no empty reiterations!" (ibid., December 24, 1900). The work for the republic as a whole, that is the main thing.

The heroic Picquart, "the honor and pride of the French army," "the pure knight of truth and justice," rejects as an insult his prospective recall to the army under the amnesty law — what arrogance! Does not the government offer him, with its intended recall to the army, "the most brilliant vindication"? True enough, Picquart has a right to have the truth spread on the records of the courts. But our good friend Picquart should not forget that the truth is not only a concern of Colonel Picquart, but of the whole of humanity. And in comparison to humanity as a whole, Picquart's concern for vindication plays a little role indeed. "In fact, we must not permit ourselves, in our insistence upon justice, to be limited to individual cases" (Gerault-Richard, *Petite Republique*, December 30, 1900). The work for the republic as a whole, that is the main thing.

Dreyfus, this "example of human suffering in its deepest agony," this "incarnation of humanity itself upon the summits of misfortune and desperation," (Jaures, *Petite Republique*, August 10, 1898)—Dreyfus defended himself, bewildered, against the amnesty law, which cut off his last hope for legal rehabilitation—what rapacity! Do not his tormentors suffer enough already? Esterhazy drags himself through the streets of London, "hungry and broken in spirit." Boisdeffre was forced to flee from the general staff. Gonse is out of the top ranks and goes about dejected. DePellieux died in disgrace. Henry committed suicide by cutting his throat. Du Paty de Clam is out of the service. What more can one ask for? Are not the pangs of their conscience enough punishment for the criminals? And if Dreyfus is not content with this favorable outcome of events and insists upon punishment by human courts—just let him be patient. "There will come a time when punishment will overtake the wretches" (Jaures, *Petite Republique*, January 5, 1901). "There will come a time"—but right now the good Dreyfus must realize that there are more important problems in the world than these "useless and boring trials." "We have better things to gain from the Dreyfus affair than all this agitation and acts of revenge" (Gerault-Richard, *Petite Republique*, December 15, 1900). The work for the republic as a whole, that is the main thing.

One more step and the Jaures group regard all criticism of the government's policies, to which the Dreyfus campaign was offered as a sacrificial lamb, as frivolous playing with the "government of republican defense."

Sobering voices are gradually raised in Jaures's own camp to question the action of the cabinet in the "democratization of the army" and the "secularization of the republic"—what light-mindedness! How terrible "systematically and with nervous impatience [after eighteen months—R. L.] to discredit the first achievements of our common efforts. . . . Why discourage the proletariat?" (Jaures, *Petite Republique*, January 5, 1901). The proposal of the government on the religious orders was a capitulation to the church? Only a "dilettante and mealymouthed performer" could say that. As a matter of fact, "it is the greatest struggle between the church and bourgeois society since the laws on the secularization of the schools" (ibid., January 12, 1901).

And if, in general, the government flounders from one fiasco to another, does not the "assurance of future victories" remain? (ibid., January 5, 1901). It is not a matter of single laws—the work for the republic as a whole, that is the main thing.

Just what, after all of this procrastination, is the "work for the republic as a whole"? It is no longer the liquidation of the Dreyfus affair, nor the reorganization of the army, nor the subordination of the church. As soon as the existence of the cabinet is threatened, everything else is given up. It suffices for the government, in order to pass its favorite measures, to pose it as a vote of confidence, and Jaures and his friends are safely put into the harness.

Yesterday, the cabinet must take defensive action in order to save the republic. Today, the defense of the republic must be given up in order to save the cabinet. "The work for the republic as a whole" means, today, the mobilization of all republican forces to keep the cabinet of Waldeck-Millerand at the helm. . . .

The present attitude of the Jaures group towards the policies of the government is, in one sense, in direct contradiction to its position during the Dreyfus affair. But, in another sense, it is nothing but a direct continuation of the previous policy. The same principle — unity with the bourgeois democrats — served as the basis of socialist policy in both cases. It served during two years of unyielding struggle for a solution of the Dreyfus affair, and, today, because the bourgeois democrats have deserted the fight, it leads the socialists to also liquidate the Dreyfus affair and to give up all attempts at a fundamental reformation of the army and a change in the relations between republic and church.

Instead of making the independent political struggle of the Socialist Party the *permanent, fundamental* element and unity with bourgeois radicals the *varying* and *incidental* element, this principle caused Jaures to adopt the opposite tactic: the alliance with the bourgeois democrats became the *constant*, and the independent political struggles the *accidental* element.

Already in the Dreyfus campaign, the Jaures socialists failed to understand the line of demarcation between the bourgeois and the proletarian camps: if the question presented itself to the friends of Dreyfus as an attack upon the by-products of militarism — as the cleansing of the army and the suppression of corruption, a socialist had to view it as a struggle against the root of the evil — against the standing army itself. And if the bourgeois radicals considered justice for Dreyfus and punishment for the guilty ones as the single central point of the campaign, a socialist had to view the Dreyfus affair as the basis for an agitation in favor of the militia system.* Only thus would the Dreyfus affair

---

* The militia system, or the "people in arms," as the social democrats often phrased it, was regarded by the prewar socialist movement as the solution to the problem of militarism, i.e., the replacement of a standing army with a militia. Lenin, writing during World War I, exposed the fallacy of this demand. Contrast Luxemburg's position with that in section 43 of the war resolution adopted by the Sixth Congress of the Communist International in 1928: "In imperialist states the attitude of the proletariat toward armies is determined by the following: no matter what their form of organization may be, armies are a constituent part of the bourgeois state apparatus, which the pro-

and the admirable efforts of Jaures and his friends have been a great agitational service to socialism. Actually, however, the agitation of the socialist camp, on the whole, ran in the same shallow channels as the agitation of the bourgeois radicals with a few individual exceptions in which the deeper significance of the Dreyfus affair was touched upon. It was exactly in this sphere that the socialists, despite their greater efforts, perseverance, and brilliance, failed to be the vanguard, and acted as the co-workers and camp followers of the bourgeois radicals. With the entry of Millerand into the radical cabinet, the socialists stood entirely upon the same ground as their bourgeois allies.

The circumstance which divides socialist politics from bourgeois politics is that the socialists are opponents of the entire existing order and must function in a bourgeois parliament fundamentally as an *opposition*. The most important aim of socialist activity in a parliament, the education of the working class, is achieved by a systematic criticism of the ruling party and its politics. The socialists are too far removed from the bourgeois order to be able to achieve practical and thoroughgoing reforms of a progressive character. Therefore, principled opposition to the ruling party becomes, for every minority party and above all for the socialists, the only feasible method with which to achieve practical results.

Not having the possibility of carrying their own policies with a parliamentary majority, the socialists are forced to wring concessions from the bourgeois majority by constant struggle. They achieve this through their critical opposition in three ways. (1) Their demands are the most advanced, so that when they compete with the bourgeois parties at the polls, they bring to bear the pressure of the voting masses. (2) They constantly expose the government before the people and arouse public opinion. (3) Their agitation in and out of parliament attracts ever greater masses about them and they thus grow to become a power with which the government and the entire bourgeoisie must reckon.

The French socialists grouped about Jaures have closed all three roads to the masses by the entry of Millerand into the government.

Above all, an uncompromising criticism of the government's policies has become impossible for the Jaures socialists. If they wanted to chastise the cabinet for its weaknesses, its half measures, its treachery, the blows would beat down upon their own backs.

---

letariat in the course of its revolution, must not democratize, but break up. . . . This attitude must be maintained equally toward standing armies and democratic militia, for both these forms of military organization represent the armed forces of the bourgeoisie directed against the proletariat. . . ." [Ed.]

If the efforts of the government at republican defense are a fiasco, the question immediately arises, what is the role of a socialist in such a government? In order not to compromise the ministerial post of Millerand, Jaures and his friends must remain silent in the face of all the acts of the government that could be used to open the eyes of the working class. It is a fact that since the organization of the Waldeck-Rousseau cabinet, all criticism of the government has vanished from the organ of the right wing of the socialist movement, *Petite Republique*, and every attempt at such criticism is immediately denounced by Jaures as "nervousness," "pessimism," and "extremism." The first consequence of socialist participation in a coalition cabinet is, therefore, the renunciation of the most important task of all socialist activity and, above all, of parliamentary activity: *the political education and clarification of the masses.*

Furthermore, in those instances where they have been critical, the followers of Millerand have robbed their criticism of all practical significance. Their conduct in the matter of the amnesty proposals showed that no sacrifice is too great for them in order to keep the government in power. It revealed that they are prepared in advance to cast their votes for the government *in every instance* when the government levels a pistol, in the form of a vote of confidence, at their breast.

It is true that the socialists in a country governed by a parliament are not as free in their conduct as, for instance, in the German Reichstag where they can take a position of opposition without regard for the consequences and at all times express themselves unmistakably on it. Out of regard for the "lesser evil," the French socialists on the contrary see themselves constantly forced to defend a bourgeois government with their votes. But, on the other hand, it is specifically through the parliamentary regime that the socialists gain a sharp weapon which they can hold over the head of the government like a sword of Damocles and with which they can give their demands and their criticisms added emphasis. But in making themselves dependent upon the government through the cabinet post of Millerand, Jaures and his friends made the government independent of them. Instead of being able to use the specter of a cabinet crisis to force concessions from the government, the socialists, on the contrary, placed the government in a position where it could use the cabinet crisis as a Damocles sword over the head of the socialists to be used at any time to force them into line.

The Jaures group has become a second Prometheus bound. A striking example is the recent debate on the law regulating the right of association. Jaures's friend, Viviani, tore to pieces the government's proposals on the religious orders in a brilliant speech in the Chamber and counterposed the real solution to the problem. When, however, Jaures, on the following day, after overwhelming praise for the speech, puts into the mouth of the government the answers to Viviani's criticism, and when, without even waiting for the debate to open and before all attempts to improve the government's proposals, Jaures advises the socialists and the Radicals to guarantee the acceptance of the government's measures at any price, the entire political effect of Viviani's speech is destroyed.

The ministerial position of Millerand transforms — this is its second consequence — the socialist criticism of his friends in the Chamber into empty holiday speeches, *without any influence whatsoever upon the practical politics of the government.*

Finally, the tactic of pushing the bourgeois parties forward through the pressure of the socialists reveals itself, in this instance, as an empty dream.

In order to safeguard the future existence of the government, the supporters of Millerand think they must maintain the closest cooperation with the other groups of the Left. The Jaures group is swallowed up entirely by the general "republican" swamp of the Left, of which Jaures is the leading brain.

In the service of Millerand, his socialist friends play, at present, the role usually played by the bourgeois Radicals.

Yes, contrary to general practice, the Radicals play the role of the most thoroughgoing oppositionists within the present republican majority and the socialists play the role of the right wing, the moderate governmental elements.

D'Octon and Pellatan, both Radicals, were the ones who forcefully demanded an inquiry into the horrible colonial administration, while two socialist deputies of the right wing found it possible to vote against the inquiry. It was the Radical Vazeille who opposed the strangling of the Dreyfus affair by means of the amnesty law, while the socialists finally voted against Vazeille.

Finally, it is the socialistic Radical, Pelletan, who gives the following advice to the socialists: "The question comes down to this: does a government exist to serve the ideas of the party that supports it or to lead that party to a betrayal of its ideas? O, the men whom we maintain at the helm don't fool us! With the exception of two or three ministers, they all rule about in the same manner as a cabinet headed by Meline would. And those parties that should warn the cabinet and chastise it, crawl upon their stomachs before it. I, for my part, belong to those who view as excellent strategy the attempt of the Socialist Party to place one of its people in power, instead of isolating itself as a result of a systematic struggle against the government. Yes, I hold this strategy to be first-rate. But to what purpose? So that the progressive policies in the cabinet receive added support, and not so that the worst omissions by the cabinet find the socialists as hostages. . . . Today, Waldeck-Rousseau is no longer an ally, as we would like to believe, but the guide of the conscience of the progressive parties. And he guides them, it appears to me, a little too far. It suffices to have him pull out of his pocket the bogey-man of the cabinet crisis to make himself obeyed. Beware! The politics of the country will lose something when out of us and out of you there will be formed a new category of subopportunists" (*Depeche de Toulouse,* December 29, 1900).

Socialists who attempt to win away petty bourgeois democrats from their position of opposition to the government, and petty bourgeois democrats who accuse the socialists of crawling on their stomachs before the government and of betraying their own ideas — that is the lowest level to which socialism has yet sunk, and at the same time, the final consequence of socialist ministerialism. . . .

STAGNATION AND PROGRESS

OF MARXISM

"Stagnation and Progress of Marxism" was written in 1903, twenty years after the death of Marx. Here Rosa Luxemburg deals with a question that is often posed today, particularly in intellectual circles: Is Marxist doctrine so rigid and dogmatic that it leaves no room for intellectual creativity?

Her answer is an emphatic *No*, and she goes on to demonstrate that if in the last twenty years of the nineteenth century there were few new contributions to Marxist theory, aside from those made by Engels, it was not because Marxism was outdated or incapable of further development. On the contrary, the class struggle itself had not yet progressed to the point where new practical problems, demanding new theoretical advances, arose. "Marx, in his scientific creation, has outstripped us as a party of practical fighters. It is not true that Marx no longer suffices for our needs. On the contrary, our needs are not yet adequate for the utilization of Marx's ideas."

Her confidence that the needs of the struggle itself would produce Marxists capable of further elaborating and developing revolutionary theory was borne out in short order. In the turbulent years of the first two decades of the twentieth century, the theoretical advancements necessary to assure the victory of the Russian Revolution took place, including such contributions as Lenin's theories on the organization of the revolutionary party, his elaboration of Marxist theory on national struggles and the right of nations to self-determination, and Trotsky's development of the theory of permanent revolution.

"Stagnation and Progress of Marxism" is reprinted from *Karl Marx: Man, Thinker and Revolutionist*, a symposium edited by D. Ryazanov (International Publishers, New York, 1927). The translation is by Eden and Cedar Paul.

———

In his shallow but at times interesting causerie entitled *Die soziale Bewegung in Frankreich und Belgien* (The Socialist Movement in France and Belgium), Karl Gruen remarks, aptly enough, that Fourier's and Saint-Simon's theories had very different effects upon their respective adherents. Saint-Simon was the spiritual ancestor of a whole generation of brilliant investigators and writers in various fields of intellectual activity; but Fourier's followers were, with few exceptions, persons who blindly parroted their master's words, and were incapable of making any advance upon his teaching. Gruen's explanation of this difference is that Fourier presented the world with a finished system, elaborated in all its details; whereas Saint-Simon merely tossed his disciples a loose bundle of great thoughts. Although it seems to me that Gruen pays too little attention to the inner, the essential, difference between the theories of these two classical authorities in the domain of utopian socialism, I feel that on the whole his observation is sound. Beyond question, a system of ideas which is merely sketched in broad outline proves far more stimulating than a finished and symmetrical structure which leaves nothing to be added and offers no scope for the independent efforts of an active mind.

Does this account for the stagnation in Marxist doctrine which has been noticeable for a good many years? The actual fact is that — apart from one or two independent contributions which mark a certain theoretical advance — since the publication of the last volume of *Capital* and of the last of Engels's writings there have appeared nothing more than a few excellent popularizations and expositions of Marxist theory. The substance of that theory remains just where the two founders of scientific socialism left it.

Is this because the Marxist system has imposed too rigid a framework upon the independent activities of the mind? It is undeniable that Marx has had a somewhat restrictive influence upon the free development of theory in the case of many of his pupils. Both Marx and Engels found it necessary to disclaim responsibility for the utterances of many who chose to call themselves Marxists! The scrupulous endeavor to keep "within the bounds of Marxism" may at times have been just as disastrous to the integrity of the thought process as has been the other extreme — the complete repudiation of the Marxist outlook, and the determination to manifest "independence of thought" at all hazards.

Still, it is only where economic matters are concerned that we are entitled to speak of a more or less completely elaborated body of doctrines bequeathed us by Marx. The most valuable of all his teachings, the materialist-dialectical conception of history, presents itself to us as nothing more than a method of investigation, as a few inspired leading thoughts, which offer us glimpses into an entirely new world, which open to us endless perspectives of independent activity, which wing our spirits for bold flights into unexplored regions.

Nevertheless, even in this domain, with few exceptions the Marxist heritage lies fallow. The splendid new weapon rusts unused; and the theory of historical materialism remains as unelaborated and sketchy as it was when first formulated by its creators.

It cannot be said, then, that the rigidity and completeness of the Marxist edifice are the explanation of the failure of Marx's successors to go on with the building.

We are often told that our movement lacks the persons of talent who might be capable of further elaborating Marx's theories. Such a lack is, indeed, of long standing; but the lack itself demands an explanation, and cannot be put forward to answer the primary question. We must remember that each epoch forms its own human material; that if in any period there is a genuine need for theoretical exponents, the period will create the forces requisite for the satisfaction of that need.

But is there a genuine need, an effective demand, for a further development of Marxist theory?

In an article upon the controversy between the Marxist and the Jevonsian schools in England, Bernard Shaw, the talented exponent of Fabian semisocialism, derides Hyndman for having said that the first volume of *Capital* had given him a complete understanding of Marx, and that there were no gaps in Marxist theory — although Friedrich Engels, in the preface to the second volume of *Capital*, subsequently declared that the first volume with its theory of value, had left unsolved a fundamental economic problem, whose solution would not be furnished until the third volume was published. Shaw certainly succeeded here in making Hyndman's position seem a trifle ridiculous, though Hyndman might well derive consolation from the fact that practically the whole socialist world was in the same boat!

The third volume of *Capital*, with its solution of the problem of the rate of profit (the basic problem of Marxist economics), did not appear till 1894. But in Germany, as in all other lands, agitation had been carried on with the aid of the unfinished material contained in the first volume; the Marxist doctrine had been popularized and had found acceptance upon the basis of this first volume alone; the success of the incomplete Marxist theory had been phenomenal; and no one had been aware that there was any gap in the teaching.

Furthermore, when the third volume finally saw the light, whilst to begin with it attracted some attention in the restricted circles of the experts, and aroused here a certain amount of comment — as far as the socialist movement as a whole was concerned, the new volume made practically no impression in the wide regions where the ideas expounded in the original book had become dominant. The theoretical conclusions of volume 3 have not hitherto evoked any attempt at popularization, nor have they secured wide diffusion. On the contrary, even among the social democrats we sometimes hear, nowadays, reechoes of the "disappointment" with the third volume of *Capital* which is so frequently voiced by bourgeois economists — and thus these social democrats merely show how fully they had accepted the "incomplete" exposition of the theory of value presented in the first volume.

How can we account for so remarkable a phenomenon?

Shaw, who (to quote his own expression) is fond of "sniggering" at others, may have good reason here, for making fun of the whole socialist movement, insofar as it is grounded upon Marx! But if he were to do this, he would be "sniggering" at a very serious manifestation of our social life. The strange fate of the second and third volumes of *Capital* is conclusive evidence as to the general destiny of theoretical research in our movement.

From the scientific standpoint, the third volume of *Capital* must, no doubt, be primarily regarded as the completion of Marx's critique of capitalism. Without this third volume, we cannot understand, either the actually dominant law of the rate of profit; or the splitting up of surplus value into profit, interest, and rent; or the working of the law of value within the field of competition. But, and this is the main point, all these problems, however important from the outlook of pure theory, are comparatively unimportant from the practical outlook of the class war. As far as the class war is concerned, the fundamental theoretical problem is the origin of surplus value, that is, the scientific explanation of exploitation; together with the elucidation of the tendency towards the socialization of the process of production, that is, the scientific explanation of the objective groundwork of the socialist revolution.

Both these problems are solved in the first volume of *Capital*, which deduces the "expropriation of the expropriators" as the inevitable and ultimate result of the production of surplus value and of the progressive concentration of capital. Therewith, as far as theory is concerned, the essential need of the labor movement is satisfied. The workers, being actively engaged in the class war, have no direct interest in the question how surplus value is distributed among the respective groups of exploiters; or in the question how, in the course of this distribution, competition brings about rearrangements of production.

That is why, for socialists in general, the third volume of *Capital* remains an unread book.

But, in our movement, what applies to Marx's economic doctrines applies to theoretical research in general. It is pure illusion to suppose that the working class, in its upward striving, can of its own accord become immeasurably creative in the theoretical domain. True that, as Engels said, the working class alone has today preserved an understanding of and interest in theory. The workers' craving for knowledge is one of the most noteworthy cultural manifestations of our day. Morally, too, the working-class struggle denotes the cultural renovation of society. But active participation of the workers in the march of science is subject to the fulfillment of very definite social conditions.

In every class society, intellectual culture (science and art) is created by the ruling class; and the aim of this culture is in part to ensure the direct satisfaction of the needs of the social process, and in part to satisfy the mental needs of the members of the governing class.

In the history of earlier class struggles, aspiring classes (like the Third Estate in recent days) could anticipate political dominion by establishing an intellectual dominance, inasmuch as, while they were still subjugated classes, they could set up a new science and a new art against obsolete culture of the decadent period.

The proletariat is in a very different position. As a nonpossessing class, it cannot in the course of its struggle upwards spontaneously create a mental culture of its own while it remains in the framework of bourgeois society. Within that society, and so long as its economic foundations persist, there can be no other culture than a bourgeois culture. Although certain "socialist" professors may acclaim the wearing of neckties, the use of visiting cards, and the riding of bicycles by proletarians as notable instances of participation in cultural progress, the working class as such remains outside contemporary culture. Notwithstanding the fact that the workers create with their own hands the whole social substratum of this culture, they are only admitted to its enjoyment insofar as such admission is requisite to the satisfactory performance of their functions in the economic and social process of capitalist society.

The working class will not be in a position to create a science and an art of its own until it has been fully emancipated from its present class position.

The utmost it can do today is to safeguard bourgeois culture from the vandalism of the bourgeois reaction, and create the social conditions requisite for a free cultural development. Even along these lines, the workers, within the extant form of society, can only advance insofar as they can create for themselves the intellectual weapons needed in their struggle for liberation.

But this reservation imposes upon the working class (that is to say, upon the workers' intellectual leaders) very narrow limits in the field of intellectual activity. The domain of their creative energy is confined to one specific department of science, namely social science. For, inasmuch as "thanks to the peculiar connection of the idea of the Fourth Estate with our historical epoch," enlightenment concerning the laws of social development has become essential to the workers in the class struggle, this connection has borne good fruit in social science, and the monument of the proletarian culture of our day is—Marxist doctrine.

But Marx's creation, which as a scientific achievement is a titanic whole, transcends the plain demands of the proletarian class struggle for whose purposes it was created. Both in his detailed and comprehensive analysis of capitalist economy, and in his method of historical research with its immeasurable field of application, Marx has offered much more than was directly essential for the practical conduct of the class war.

Only in proportion as our movement progresses, and demands the solution of new practical problems do we dip once more into the treasury of Marx's thought, in order to extract therefrom and to utilize new fragments of his doctrine. But since our movement, like all the campaigns of practical life, inclines to go on working in old ruts of thought, and to cling to principles after they have ceased to be valid, the theoretical utilization of the Marxist system proceeds very slowly.

If, then, today we detect a stagnation in our movement as far as these theoretical matters are concerned, this is not because the Marxist theory upon which we are nourished is incapable of development or has become out-of-date. On the contrary, it is because we have not yet learned how to make an adequate use of the most important mental weapons which we had taken out of the Marxist arsenal on account of our urgent need for them in the earlier stages of our struggle. It is not true that, as far as the practical struggle is concerned, Marx is out-of-date, that we have superseded Marx. On the contrary, Marx, in his scientific creation, has outstripped us as a party of practical fighters. It is not true that Marx no longer suffices for our needs. On the contrary, our needs are not yet adequate for the utilization of Marx's ideas.

Thus do the social conditions of proletarian existence in contemporary society, conditions first elucidated by Marxist theory, take vengeance by the fate they impose upon Marxist theory itself. Though that theory is an incomparable instrument of intellectual culture, it remains unused because, while it is inapplicable to bourgeois class culture, it greatly transcends the needs of the working class in the matter of weapons for the daily struggle. Not until the working class has been liberated from its present conditions of existence will the Marxist method of research be socialized in conjunction with other means of production, so that it can be fully utilized for the benefit of humanity at large, and so that it can be developed to the full measure of its functional capacity.

111

ORGANIZATIONAL QUESTION
OF SOCIAL DEMOCRACY

Rosa Luxemburg was born and grew up in what was at that time Russian Poland, and the fate of the party she helped to found and lead, the Social Democratic Party of Poland and Lithuania (SDKPiL), was always intertwined with that of the Russian Social Democratic Party (RSDRP). As a result, she remained deeply interested throughout her life in what was happening in Russia itself and in the Russian social democratic movement. Even her opponents in Germany considered her the party's authority on Russia as well as Poland. As the representative of the SDKPiL to the Second International, she was frequently involved in the debates between and about the different factions of Russian Social Democracy.

She never aligned herself unreservedly with either the Bolsheviks or the Mensheviks. Most basically she stood for unity within the RSDRP. As the following article shows she disagreed with the kind of party the Bolsheviks were trying to build. But after the "dress rehearsal" Revolution of 1905-06 she was in substantial agreement with the Bolsheviks on their analysis of the revolution, and the way they had responded to the revolutionary upheaval, while she had great contempt for the theoretical and practical errors made by the Mensheviks. From that time forward she generally sided with the Bolsheviks, although she had sharp disagreements with Lenin over the Bolshevik policy of supporting the nationalist aspirations of oppressed minorities within the czarist empire. She also continued to disagree strongly with the Bolshevik policy of building a disciplined faction of professional revolutionists and their willingness, when necessary, to split the RSDRP.

The moral pressure for unity at all costs was very strong in the Second International, and it was not until the Bolsheviks had proved the correctness of their methods by leading the successful Russian Revolution that they were given credit for being anything but incorrigible, destructive factionalists.

"Organizational Questions of the Russian Social Democracy" was written in 1904 and published simultaneously in *Neue Zeit* and in *Iskra*, the central organ of the RSDRP, then controlled by the Mensheviks. It is Rosa Luxemburg's reply to Lenin's work *What Is To Be Done?* written before the Second (1903) Congress of the RSDRP, and to his pamphlet, *One Step Forward, Two Steps Back,* an analysis of the proceedings of the 1903 congress.

Two representatives of the SDKPiL attended the first part of the 1903 congress, although they left before the debate on the statutes of the RSDRP and the voting which split the party between Bolsheviks (majority) and Mensheviks (minority). The representatives of the SDKPiL had been instructed by their own party congress held several days prior to the Russian congress to try and negotiate Polish affiliation to the RSDRP.

The main problem to be negotiated was the question of how much autonomy the SDKPiL would have within the RSDRP. Although the SDKPiL leaders said they were opposed to the principle of a federated party of completely autonomous organizations, the conditions they demanded before they would join the RSDRP in effect came close to the concept of federation. They demanded that they maintain their own organization and control structure intact, and were reluctant to allow the Central Committee of the RSDRP — on which they would of course be represented — to become the ultimate governing body of the Polish party. During the negotiations at the congress itself, Rosa Luxemburg even instructed the SDKPiL representatives that she would be unwilling to allow a representative of the RSDRP to sit on the Central Committee of the SDKPiL! However, she had already determined to quash the unity move by that time and such a position may have been designed purely to hasten the end of negotiations.

The incident that provoked the decision to break off unity moves (a decision that was apparently made by Rosa Luxemburg and Leo Jogiches without consultation with the rest of the party, and which made them the center of significant criticism for a while) was the publication in the July *Iskra* of an article by Lenin on the right of nations to self-determination. The article contained nothing startlingly new. It was simply an elaboration of the basic RSDRP position which was incorporated into the statutes to be voted on by the congress (paragraph 7), and against which the Polish party had not raised strenuous objections. They had made it clear that they did not agree with the basic position, but felt it was stated in such a way that they could live with it.

However, Lenin's article, which placed stronger emphasis on the right of self-determination than had previous articles in *Iskra* written by Martov, was totally unacceptable to Rosa Luxemburg.

She immediately instructed the SDKPiL representatives to break off negotiations if they could not win agreement from the Congress to change paragraph 7 of the statutes and repudiate the interpretation given by Lenin in his article. When the SDKPiL representatives were informed that the Congress intended to confirm paragraph 7 along with Lenin's interpretation, they left a declaration of their position and departed.

It was not until the Fourth Congress of the RSDRP, following the 1905-06 Revolution, that unity moves were reopened and the SDKPiL affiliated to the RSDRP at that time.

Some of the issues raised by the organizational dispute between Luxemburg and Lenin, along with some of their other disagreements, are discussed more fully in the introduction to this collection.

The translation was made by Integer in 1934.

I

An unprecedented task in the history of the socialist movement has fallen to the lot of the Russian social democracy. It is the task of deciding on what is the best socialist tactical policy in a country where absolute monarchy is still dominant. It is a mistake to draw a rigid parallel between the present Russian situation and that which existed in Germany during the years 1878-90, when Bismarck's antisocialist laws were in force. The two have one thing in common—police rule. Otherwise, they are in no way comparable.

The obstacles offered to the socialist movement by the absence of democratic liberties are of relatively secondary importance. Even in Russia, the people's movement has succeeded in overcoming the barriers set up by the state. The people have found themselves a "constitution" (though a rather precarious one) in street disorders. Persevering in this course, the Russian people will in time attain complete victory over the autocracy.

The principal difficulty faced by socialist activity in Russia results from the fact that in that country the domination of the bourgeoisie is veiled by absolutist force. This gives socialist propaganda an abstract character, while immediate political agitation takes on a democratic revolutionary guise.

Bismarck's antisocialist laws put our movement out of constitutional bounds in a highly developed bourgeois society, where class antagonisms had already reached their full bloom in parliamentary contests. (Here, by the way, lay the absurdity of Bismarck's scheme.) The situation is quite different in Russia. The problem there is how to create a social democratic movement at a time when the state is not yet in the hands of the bourgeoisie. This circumstance has an influence on agitation, on the manner of transplanting socialist doctrine to Russian soil It also bears in a peculiar and direct way on the question of *party organization.*

Under ordinary conditions—that is, where the political domination of the bourgeoisie has preceded the socialist movement—the bourgeoisie itself instills in the working class the rudiments of political solidarity. At this stage, declares the *Communist Manifesto*, the unification of the workers is not yet the result of their own aspiration to unity but comes as a result of the activity of the bourgeoisie, "which, in order to attain its own political ends, is compelled to set the proletariat in motion. . . ."

In Russia, however, the social democracy must make up by its own efforts an entire historic period. It must lead the Russian proletarians from their present "atomized" condition, which prolongs the autocratic regime, to a class organization that would help them to become aware of their historic objectives and prepare them to struggle to achieve those objectives.

The Russian socialists are obliged to undertake the building of such an organization without the benefit of the formal guarantees commonly found under a bourgeois democratic setup. They do not dispose of the political raw material that in other countries is supplied by bourgeois society itself. Like God Almighty they must have this organization arise out of the void, so to speak.

How to effect a transition from the type of organization characteristic of the preparatory stage of the socialist movement—usually featured by disconnected local groups and clubs, with propaganda as a principal activity—to the unity of a large, national body, suitable for concerted political action over the entire vast territory ruled by the Russian state? That is the specific problem which the Russian social democracy has mulled over for some time.

Autonomy and isolation are the most pronounced characteristics of the old organizational type. It is, therefore, understandable why the slogan of the persons who want to see an inclusive national organization should be "Centralism!"

Centralism was the theme of the campaign that has been carried on by the *Iskra* group for the last three years. This campaign has produced the Congress of August 1903, which has been described as the second congress of the Russian Social Democratic Party but was, in fact, its constituent assembly.

At the party congress, it became evident that the term "centralism" does not completely cover the question of organization for the Russian social democracy. Once again we have learned that no rigid formula can furnish the solution of any problem in the socialist movement.

115

One Step Forward, Two Steps Backward, written by Lenin, an outstanding member of the *Iskra* group, is a methodical exposition of the ideas of the ultracentralist tendency in the Russian movement. The viewpoint presented with incomparable vigor and logic in this book, is that of pitiless centralism. Laid down as principles are the necessity of selecting, and constituting as a separate corps, all the active revolutionists, as distinguished from the unorganized, though revolutionary, mass surrounding this elite. Lenin's thesis is that the party Central Committee should have the privilege of naming all the local committees of the party. It should have the right to appoint the effective organs of all local bodies from Geneva to Liege, from Tomsk to Irkutsk.* It should also have the right to impose on all of them its own ready-made rules of party conduct. It should have the right to rule without appeal on such questions as the dissolution and reconstitution of local organizations. This way, the Central Committee could determine, to suit itself, the composition of the highest party organs as well as of the party congress. The Central Committee would be the only thinking element in the party. All other groupings would be its executive limbs.

Lenin reasons that the combination of the socialist mass movement with such a rigorously centralized type of organization is a specific principle of revolutionary Marxism. To support this thesis, he advances a series of arguments, with which we shall deal below.

Generally speaking it is undeniable that a strong tendency toward centralization is inherent in the social democratic movement. This tendency springs from the economic makeup of capitalism which is essentially a centralizing factor. The social democratic movement carries on its activity inside the large bourgeois city. Its mission is to represent, within the boundaries of the national state, the class interests of the proletariat, and to oppose those common interests to all local and group interests.

Therefore, the social democracy is, as a rule, hostile to any manifestations of localism or federalism. It strives to unite all workers and all worker organizations in a single party, no matter what national, religious, or occupational differences may exist among them. The social democracy abandons this principle and gives way to federalism only under exceptional conditions, as in the case of the Austro-Hungarian Empire.

---

* Many of the Russian socialists carried on their revolutionary activities from Western Europe, where they lived in self-exile due to the oppressive czarist state. Others were exiled by the government to Siberia and Central Asia, where they were allowed some political freedom. [Ed.]

116

It is clear that the Russian social democracy should not organize itself as a federative conglomerate of many national groups. It must rather become a single party for the entire empire. However, that is not really the question considered here. What we are considering is the degree of centralization necessary inside the unified, single Russian party in view of the peculiar conditions under which it has to function.

Looking at the matter from the angle of the formal tasks of the social democracy in its capacity as a party of class struggle, it appears at first that the power and energy of the party are directly dependent on the possibility of centralizing the party. However, these formal tasks apply to all active parties. In the case of the social democracy, they are less important than is the influence of historic conditions.

The social democratic movement is the first in the history of class societies which reckons, in all its phases and through its entire course, on the organization and the direct, independent action of the masses.

Because of this, the social democracy creates an organizational type that is entirely different from those common to earlier revolutionary movements, such as those of the Jacobins and the adherents of Blanqui.

Lenin seems to slight this fact when he presents in his book (ibid., p. 140) the opinion that the revolutionary social democrat is nothing else than a "Jacobin indissolubly joined to the organization of the proletariat, which has become conscious of its class interests."

For Lenin, the difference between the social democracy and Blanquism is reduced to the observation that in place of a handful of conspirators we have a class-conscious proletariat. He forgets that this difference implies a complete revision of our ideas on organization and, therefore, an entirely different conception of centralism and the relations existing between the party and the struggle itself.

Blanquism did not count on the direct action of the working class. It, therefore, did not need to organize the people for the revolution. The people were expected to play their part only at the moment of revolution. Preparation for the revolution concerned only the little group of revolutionists armed for the coup. Indeed, to assure the success of the revolutionary conspiracy, it was considered wiser to keep the mass at some distance from the conspirators. Such a relationship could be conceived by the Blanquists only because there was no close contact between the conspiratorial activity of their organization and the daily struggle of the popular masses.

The tactics and concrete tasks of the Blanquist revolutionists had little connection with the elementary class struggle. They were freely improvised. They could, therefore, be decided on in advance and took the form of a ready-made plan. In consequence of this, ordinary members of the organization became simple executive organs, carrying out the orders of a will fixed beforehand, and outside of their particular sphere of activity. They became the instruments of a Central Committee. Here we have the second peculiarity of conspiratorial centralism — the absolute and blind submission of the party sections to the will of the center, and the extension of this authority to all parts of the organization.

However, social democratic activity is carried on under radically different conditions. It arises historically out of the elementary class struggle. It spreads and develops in accordance with the following dialectical contradiction. The proletarian army is recruited and becomes aware of its objectives in the course of the struggle itself. The activity of the party organization, the growth of the proletarians' awareness of the objectives of the struggle and the struggle itself, are not different things separated chronologically and mechanically. They are only different aspects of the same process. Except for the general principles of the struggle, there do not exist for the social democracy detailed sets of tactics which a Central Committee can teach the party membership in the same way as troops are instructed in their training camps. Furthermore, the range of influence of the socialist party is constantly fluctuating with the ups and downs of the struggle in the course of which the organization is created and grows.

For this reason social democratic centralism cannot be based on the mechanical subordination and blind obedience of the party membership to the leading party center. For this reason, the social democratic movement cannot allow the erection of an airtight partition between the class-conscious nucleus of the proletariat already in the party and its immediate popular environment, the nonparty sections of the proletariat.

Now the two principles on which Lenin's centralism rests are precisely these: (1) The blind subordination, in the smallest detail, of all party organs, to the party center, which alone thinks, guides, and decides for all. (2) The rigorous separation of the organized nucleus of revolutionaries from its social revolutionary surroundings.

Such centralism is a mechanical transposition of the organizational principles of Blanquism into the mass movement of the socialist working class.

In accordance with this view, Lenin defines his "revolutionary social democrat" as a "Jacobin joined to the organization of the proletariat, which has become conscious of its class interests."

The fact is that the social democracy is not *joined* to the organization of the proletariat. It is itself the proletariat. And because of this, social democratic centralism is essentially different from Blanquist centralism. It can only be the concentrated will of the individuals and groups representative of the most class-conscious, militant, advanced sections of the working class. It is, so to speak, the "self-centralism" of the advanced sectors of the proletariat. It is the rule of the majority within its own party.

The indispensable conditions for the realization of social democratic centralism are: (1) The existence of a large contingent of workers educated in the political struggle. (2) The possibility for the workers to develop their own political activity through direct influence on public life, in a party press, and public congresses, etc.

These conditions are not yet fully formed in Russia. The first — a proletarian vanguard, conscious of its class interests and capable of self-direction in political activity — is only now emerging in Russia. All efforts of socialist agitation and organization should aim to hasten the formation of such a vanguard. The second condition can be had only under a regime of political liberty.

With these conclusions, Lenin disagrees violently. He is convinced that all the conditions necessary for the formation of a powerful and centralized party already exist in Russia. He declares that "it is no longer the proletarians but certain intellectuals in our party who need to be educated in the matters of organization and discipline" (ibid., p. 145). He glorifies the educative influence of the factory, which, he says, accustoms the proletariat to "discipline and organization" (ibid., p. 147).

Saying all this, Lenin seems to demonstrate again that his conception of socialist organization is quite mechanistic. The discipline Lenin has in mind is being implanted in the working class not only by the factory but also by the military and the existing state bureaucracy — by the entire mechanism of the centralized bourgeois state.

We misuse words and we practice self-deception when we apply the same term — discipline — to such dissimilar notions as: (1) the absence of thought and will in a body with a thousand automatically moving hands and legs, and (2) the spontaneous coordination of the conscious, political acts of a body of men. What is there in common between the regulated docility of an oppressed class and the self-discipline and organization of a class struggling for its emancipation?

The self-discipline of the social democracy is not merely the replacement of the authority of the bourgeois rulers with the authority of a socialist central committee. The working class will acquire the sense of the new discipline, the freely assumed self-

119

discipline of the social democracy, not as a result of the discipline imposed on it by the capitalist state, but by extirpating, to the last root, its old habits of obedience and servility.

Centralism in the socialist sense is not an absolute thing applicable to any phase whatsoever of the labor movement. It is a *tendency*, which becomes real in proportion to the development and political training acquired by the working masses in the course of their struggle.

No doubt, the absence of the conditions necessary for the complete realization of this kind of centralism in the Russian movement presents a formidable obstacle.

It is a mistake to believe that it is possible to substitute "provisionally" the absolute power of a Central Committee (acting somehow by "tacit delegation") for the yet unrealizable rule of the majority of conscious workers in the party, and in this way replace the open control of the working masses over the party organs with the reverse control by the Central Committee over the revolutionary proletariat.

The history of the Russian labor movement suggests the doubtful value of such centralism. An all-powerful center, invested, as Lenin would have it, with the unlimited right to control and intervene, would be an absurdity if its authority applied only to technical questions, such as the administration of funds, the distribution of tasks among propagandists and agitators, the transportation and circulation of printed matter. The political purpose of an organ having such great powers is understandable only if those powers apply to the elaboration of a uniform plan of action, if the central organ assumes the initiative of a vast revolutionary act.

But what has been the experience of the Russian socialist movement up to now? The most important and most fruitful changes in its tactical policy during the last ten years have not been the inventions of several leaders and even less so of any central organizational organs. They have always been the spontaneous product of the movement in ferment. This was true during the first stage of the proletarian movement in Russia, which began with the spontaneous general strike of St. Petersburg in 1896, an event that marks the inception of an epoch of economic struggle by the Russian working people. It was no less true during the following period, introduced by the spontaneous street demonstrations of St. Petersburg students in March 1901. The general strike of Rostov-on-Don, in 1903, marking the next great tactical turn in the Russian proletarian movement, was also a spontaneous act. "All by itself," the strike expanded into political demonstrations, street agitation, great outdoor meetings, which the most optimistic revolutionist would not have dreamed of several years before.

Our cause made great gains in these events. However, the initiative and conscious leadership of the social democratic organizations played an insignificant role in this development. It is true that these organizations were not specifically prepared for such happenings. However, the unimportant part played by the revolutionists cannot be explained by this fact. Neither can it be attributed to the absence of an all-powerful central party apparatus similar to what is asked for by Lenin. The existence of such a guiding center would have probably increased the disorder of the local committees by emphasizing the difference between the eager attack of the mass and the prudent position of the social democracy. The same phenomenon—the insignificant part played by the initiative of central party organs in the elaboration of actual tactical policy—can be observed today in Germany and other countries. In general, the tactical policy of the social democracy is not something that may be "invented." It is the product of a series of great creative acts of the often spontaneous class struggle seeking its way forward.

The unconscious comes before the conscious. The logic of the historic process comes before the subjective logic of the human beings who participate in the historic process. The tendency is for the directing organs of the socialist party to play a conservative role. Experience shows that every time the labor movement wins new terrain those organs work it to the utmost. They transform it at the same time into a kind of bastion, which holds up advance on a wider scale.

The present tactical policy of the German social democracy has won universal esteem because it is supple as well as firm. This is a sign of the fine adaptation of the party, in the smallest detail of its everyday activity, to the conditions of a parliamentary regime. The party has made a methodical study of all the resources of this terrain. It knows how to utilize them without modifying its principles.

However, the very perfection of this adaptation is already closing vaster horizons to our party. There is a tendency in the party to regard parliamentary tactics as the immutable and specific tactics of socialist activity. People refuse, for example, to consider the possibility (posed by Parvus) of changing our tactical policy in case general suffrage is abolished in Germany, an eventuality not considered entirely improbable by the leaders of the German social democracy.

Such inertia is due, in a large degree, to the fact that it is very inconvenient to define, within the vacuum of abstract hypotheses, the lines and forms of still nonexistent political situations. Evidently, the important thing for the social democracy is not the preparation of a set of directives all ready for future policy. It is important: (1) to encourage a correct historic appreciation of the forms of struggle corresponding to the given situations, and (2) to maintain an understanding of the relativity of the current phase and the inevitable increase of revolutionary tension as the final goal of the class struggle is approached.

Granting, as Lenin wants, such absolute powers of a negative character to the top organ of the party, we strengthen, to a dangerous extent, the conservatism inherent in such an organ. If the tactics of the socialist party are not to be the creation of a Central Committee but of the whole party, or, still better, of the whole labor movement, then it is clear that the party sections and federations need the liberty of action which alone will permit them to develop their revolutionary initiative and to utilize all the resources of a situation. The ultracentralism asked by Lenin is full of the sterile spirit of the overseer. It is not a positive and creative spirit. *Lenin's concern is not so much to make the activity of the party more fruitful as to control the party — to narrow the movement rather than to develop it, to bind rather than to unify it.*

In the present situation, such an experiment would be doubly dangerous to the Russian social democracy. It stands on the eve of decisive battles against czarism. It is about to enter, or has already entered, on a period of intensified creative activity, during which it will broaden (as is usual in a revolutionary period) its sphere of influence and will advance spontaneously by leaps and bounds. To attempt to bind the initiative of the party at this moment, to surround it with a network of barbed wire, is to render it incapable of accomplishing the tremendous tasks of the hour.

The general ideas we have presented on the question of socialist centralism are not by themselves sufficient for the formulation of a constitutional plan suiting the Russian party. In the final instance, a statute of this kind can only be determined by the conditions under which the activity of the organization takes place in a given epoch. The question of the moment in Russia is how to set in motion a large proletarian organization. No constitutional project can claim infallibility. It must prove itself in fire.

But from our general conception of the nature of social democratic organization, we feel justified in deducing that its spirit requires — especially at the inception of the mass party — the coordination and unification of the movement and not its rigid submission to a set of regulations. If the party possesses the gift of political mobility, complemented by unflinching loyalty to principles and concern for unity, we can rest assured that any defects in the party constitution will be corrected in practice. For us, it is not the letter, but the living spirit carried into the organization by the membership that decides the value of this or that organizational form.

II

So far we have examined the problem of centralism from the viewpoint of the general principles of the social democracy, and to some extent, in the light of conditions peculiar to Russia. However, the military ultracentralism cried up by Lenin and his friends is not the product of accidental differences of opinion. It is said to be related to a campaign against opportunism which Lenin has carried to the smallest organizational detail.

"It is important," says Lenin (ibid., p. 52), "to forge a more or less effective weapon against opportunism." He believes that opportunism springs specifically from the characteristic leaning of intellectuals to decentralization and disorganization, from their aversion for strict discipline and "bureaucracy," which is, however, necessary for the functioning of the party.

Lenin says that intellectuals remain individualists and tend to anarchism even after they have joined the socialist movement. According to him, it is only among intellectuals that we can note a repugnance for the absolute authority of a Central Committee. The authentic proletarian, Lenin suggests, finds by reason of his class instinct a kind of voluptuous pleasure in abandoning himself to the clutch of firm leadership and pitiless discipline. "To oppose bureaucracy to democracy," writes Lenin, "is to contrast the organizational principle of revolutionary social democracy to the methods of opportunist organization" (ibid., p. 151).

He declares that a similar conflict between centralizing and autonomist tendencies is taking place in all countries where reformism and revolutionary socialism meet face to face. He points in particular to the recent controversy in the German social democracy on the question of the degree of freedom of action to be allowed by the party to socialist representatives in legislative assemblies.

Let us examine the parallels drawn by Lenin.

First, it is important to point out that the glorification of the supposed genius of proletarians in the matter of socialist organization and a general distrust of intellectuals as such are not necessarily signs of "revolutionary Marxist" mentality. It is very easy to demonstrate that such arguments are themselves an expression of opportunism.

Antagonism between purely proletarian elements and the non-proletarian intellectuals in the labor movement is raised as an ideological issue by the following trends: the semianarchism of the French syndicalists, whose watchword is "Beware of the politician!"; English trade unionism, full of mistrust of the "socialist visionaries"; and, if our information is correct, the "pure economism," represented a short while ago within the Russian social democracy by *Rabochaya Mysl* (*Labor Thought*), which was printed secretly in St. Petersburg.

In most socialist parties of Western Europe there is undoubtedly a connection between opportunism and the "intellectuals," as well as between opportunism and decentralizing tendencies within the labor movement.

But nothing is more contrary to the historic-dialectic method of Marxist thought than to separate social phenomena from their historic soil and to present these phenomena as abstract formulas having an absolute, general application.

Reasoning abstractly, we may say that the "intellectual," a social element which has emerged out of the bourgeoisie and is therefore alien to the proletariat, enters the socialist movement not because of his natural class inclinations but in spite of them. For this reason, he is more liable to opportunist aberrations than the proletarian. The latter, we say, can be expected to find a definite revolutionary point of support in his class interests as long as he does not leave his original environment, the laboring mass. But the concrete form assumed by this inclination of the intellectual toward opportunism and, above all, the manner in which this tendency expresses itself in organizational questions depend every time on his given social milieu.

Bourgeois parliamentarism is the definite social base of the phenomena observed by Lenin in the German, French, and Italian socialist movements. This parliamentarism is the breeding place of all the opportunist tendencies now existing in the Western social democracy.

The kind of parliamentarism we now have in France, Italy, and Germany provides the soil for such illusions of current opportunism as overvaluation of social reforms, class and party collaboration, the hope of pacific development toward socialism, etc. It does so by placing intellectuals, acting in the capacity of parliamentarians, above the proletariat and by separating intellectuals from proletarians inside the socialist party itself. With the growth of the labor movement, parliamentarism becomes a springboard for political careerists. That is why so many ambitious failures from the bourgeoisie flock to the banners of the socialist parties. Another source of contemporary opportunism is the considerable material means and influence of the large social democratic organizations.

The party acts as a bulwark protecting the class movement against digressions in the direction of more bourgeois parliamentarism. To triumph, these tendencies must destroy the bulwark. They must dissolve the active, class-conscious sector of the proletariat in the amorphous mass of an "electorate."

That is how the "autonomist" and decentralizing tendencies arise in our social democratic parties. We notice that these tendencies suit definite political ends. They cannot be explained, as Lenin attempts, by referring to the intellectual's psychology, to his supposedly innate instability of character. They can only be explained by considering the needs of the bourgeois parliamentary politician, that is, by opportunist politics.

The situation is quite different in czarist Russia. Opportunism in the Russian labor movement is, generally speaking, not the by-product of social democratic strength or of the decomposition of the bourgeoisie. It is the product of the backward political condition of Russian society.

The milieu where intellectuals are recruited for socialism in Russia is much more declassed and by far less bourgeois than in Western Europe. Added to the immaturity of the Russian proletarian movement, this circumstance is an influence for wide theoretic wandering, which ranges from the complete negation of the political aspect of the labor movement to the unqualified belief in the effectiveness of isolated terrorist acts, or even total political indifference sought in the swamps of liberalism and Kantian idealism.

However, the intellectual within the Russian social democratic movement can only with difficulty be attracted to any act of disorganization. It is contrary to the general outlook of the Russian intellectual's milieu. There is no bourgeois parliament in Russia to favor this tendency.

The Western intellectual who professes at this moment the "cult of the ego" and colors even his socialist yearnings with an aristocratic morale, is not the representative of the bourgeois intelligentsia "in general." He represents only a certain phase of social development. He is the product of bourgeois decadence.

On the other hand, the utopian or opportunist dreams of the Russian intellectual who has joined the socialist movement tend to nourish themselves on theoretic formulas in which the "ego" is not exalted but humiliated, in which the morality of renunciation, expiation, is the dominant principle.

The *Narodniki* (Populists) of 1875 called on the Russian intelligentsia to lose themselves in the peasant mass. The ultracivilized followers of Tolstoy speak today of escape to the life of the "simple folk." Similarly, the partisans of "pure economism" in the Russian social democracy want us to bow down before the "calloused hand" of labor.

If instead of mechanically applying to Russia formulas elaborated in Western Europe, we approach the problem of organization from the angle of conditions specific to Russia, we arrive at conclusions that are diametrically opposed to Lenin's.

To attribute to opportunism an invariable preference for a def-

125

inite form of organization, that is, decentralization, is to miss the essence of opportunism.

On the question of organization, or any other question, opportunism knows only one principle: the absence of principle. Opportunism chooses its means of action with the aim of suiting the given circumstances at hand, provided these means appear to lead toward the ends in view.

If, like Lenin, we define opportunism as the tendency that paralyzes the independent revolutionary movement of the working class and transforms it into an instrument of ambitious bourgeois intellectuals, we must also recognize that in the inital stage of a labor movement this end is more easily attained as a result of rigorous centralization rather than by decentralization. It is by extreme centralization that a young, uneducated proletarian movement can be most completely handed over to the intellectual leaders staffing a Central Committee.

Also in Germany, at the start of the social democratic movement, and before the emergence of a solid nucleus of conscious proletarians and a tactical policy based on experience, partisans of the two opposite types of organization faced each other in argument. The General Association of German Workers, founded by Lassalle, stood for extreme centralization. The principle of autonomism was supported by the party which was organized at the Eisenach Congress with the collaboration of W. Liebknect and A. Bebel.

The tactical policy of the "Eisenachers" was quite confused. Yet they contributed vastly more to the awakening of class consciousness of the German masses than the Lassalleans. Very early the workers played a preponderant role in that party (as was demonstrated by the number of worker publications in the provinces), and there was a rapid extension of the range of the movement. At the same time, the Lassalleans, in spite of all their experiments with "dictators," led their faithful from one misadventure to another.

In general, it is rigorous, despotic centralism that is preferred by opportunist intellectuals at a time when the revolutionary elements among the workers still lack cohesion and the movement is groping its way, as is the case now in Russia. In a later phase, under a parliamentary regime and in connection with a strong labor party, the opportunist tendencies of the intellectuals express themselves in an inclination toward "decentralization."

If we assume the viewpoint claimed as his own by Lenin and we fear the influence of intellectuals in the proletarian movement, we can conceive of no greater danger to the Russian party than Lenin's plan of organization. *Nothing will more surely enslave a young labor movement to an intellectual elite hungry for power*

126

than this bureaucratic straitjacket, which will immobilize the movement and turn it into an automaton manipulated by a Central Committee. On the other hand, there is no more effective guarantee against opportunist intrigue and personal ambition than the independent revolutionary action of the proletariat, as a result of which the workers acquire the sense of political responsibility and self-reliance.

What is today only a phantom haunting Lenin's imagination may become reality tomorrow.

Let us not forget that the revolution soon to break out in Russia will be a bourgeois and not a proletarian revolution. This modifies radically all the conditions of socialist struggle. The Russian intellectuals, too, will rapidly become imbued with bourgeois ideology. The social democracy is at present the only guide of the Russian proletariat. But on the day after the revolution, we shall see the bourgeoisie, and above all the bourgeois intellectuals, seek to use the masses as a steppingstone to their domination.

The game of the bourgeois demagogues will be made easier if at the present stage, the spontaneous action, initiative, and political sense of the advanced sections of the working class are hindered in their development and restricted by the protectorate of an authoritarian Central Committee.

More important is the fundamental falseness of the idea underlying the plan of unqualified centralism — the idea that the road to opportunism can be barred by means of clauses in a party constitution.

Impressed by recent happenings in the socialist parties of France, Italy, and Germany, the Russian social democrats tend to regard opportunism as an alien ingredient, brought into the labor movement by representatives of bourgeois democracy. If that were so, no penalties provided by a party constitution could stop this intrusion. The afflux of nonproletarian recruits to the party of the proletariat is the effect of profound social causes, such as the economic collapse of the petty bourgeoisie, the bankruptcy of bourgeois liberalism, and the degeneration of bourgeois democracy. It is naive to hope to stop this current by means of a formula written down in a constitution.

A manual of regulations may master the life of a small sect or a private circle. A historic current, however, will pass through the mesh of the most subtly worded statutory paragraph. It is furthermore untrue that to repel the elements pushed toward the socialist movement by the decomposition of bourgeois society means to defend the interests of the working class. The social democracy has always contended that it represents not only the class interests of the proletariat but also the progressive aspirations of the whole of contemporary society. It represents the interests of all who are oppressed by bourgeois domination. This must not be understood merely in the sense that all these interests are ideally contained in the socialist program. Historic evolution translates the given proposition into reality. In its capacity as a political party, the social democracy becomes the haven of all discontented elements in our society and thus of the entire people, as contrasted to the tiny minority of the capitalist masters.

But socialists must always know how to subordinate the anguish, rancor, and hope of this motley aggregation to the supreme goal of the working class. The social democracy must enclose the tumult of the nonproletarian protestants against existing society within the bounds of the revolutionary action of the proletariat. It must assimilate the elements that come to it.

This is only possible if the social democracy already contains a strong, politically educated proletarian nucleus class conscious enough to be able, as up to now in Germany, to pull along in its tow the declassed and petty bourgeois elements that join the party. In that case, greater strictness in the application of the principle of centralization and more severe discipline, specifically formulated in party bylaws, may be an effective safeguard against the opportunist danger. That is how the revolutionary socialist movement in France defended itself against the Jauresist confusion. A modification of the constitution of the German social democracy in that direction would be a very timely measure.

But even here we should not think of the party constitution as a weapon that is, somehow, self-sufficient. It can be at most a coercive instrument enforcing the will of the proletarian majority in the party. If this majority is lacking, then the most dire sanctions on paper will be of no avail.

However, the influx of bourgeois elements into the party is far from being the only cause of the opportunist trends that are now raising their heads in the social democracy. Another cause is the very nature of socialist activity and the contradictions inherent in it.

The international movement of the proletariat toward its complete emancipation is a process peculiar in the following respect. For the first time in the history of civilization, the people are expressing their will consciously and in opposition to all ruling classes. But this will can only be satisfied beyond the limits of the existing system.

Now the mass can only acquire and strengthen this will in the course of the day-to-day struggle against the existing social order — that is, within the limits of capitalist society.

On the one hand, we have the mass; on the other, its historic goal, located outside of existing society. On one hand, we have the day-to-day struggle; on the other, the social revolution. Such are the terms of the dialectical contradiction through which the socialist movement makes its way.

It follows that this movement can best advance by tacking betwixt and between the two dangers by which it is constantly being threatened. One is the loss of its mass character; the other, the abandonment of its goal. One is the danger of sinking back to the condition of a sect; the other, the danger of becoming a movement of bourgeois social reform.

That is why it is illusory, and contrary to historic experience, to hope to fix, once for always, the direction of the revolutionary socialist struggle with the aid of formal means, which are expected to secure the labor movement against all possibilities of opportunist digression.

Marxist theory offers us a reliable instrument enabling us to recognize and combat typical manifestations of opportunism. But the socialist movement is a mass movement. Its perils are not the product of the insidious machinations of individuals and groups. They arise out of unavoidable social conditions. We cannot secure ourselves in advance against all possibilities of opportunist deviation. Such dangers can be overcome only by the movement itself—certainly with the aid of Marxist theory, but only after the dangers in question have taken tangible form in practice.

Looked at from this angle, opportunism appears to be a product and an inevitable phase of the historic development of the labor movement.

The Russian social democracy arose a short while ago. The political conditions under which the proletarian movement is developing in Russia are quite abnormal. In that country, opportunism is to a large extent a by-product of the groping and experimentation of socialist activity seeking to advance over a terrain that resembles no other in Europe.

In view of this, we find most astonishing the claim that it is possible to avoid any possibility of opportunism in the Russian movement by writing down certain words, instead of others, in the party constitution. *Such an attempt to exorcise opportunism by means of a scrap of paper may turn out to be extremely harmful—not to opportunism but to the socialist movement.*

Stop the natural pulsation of a living organism, and you weaken it, and you diminish its resistance and combative spirit—in this instance, not only against opportunism but also (and that is certainly of great importance) against the existing social order. The proposed means turn against the end they are supposed to serve.

In Lenin's overanxious desire to establish the guardianship of an omniscient and omnipotent Central Committee in order to protect so promising and vigorous a labor movement against any misstep, we recognize the symptoms of the same subjectivism that has already played more than one trick on socialist thinking in Russia.

It is amusing to note the strange somersaults that the respectable human "ego" has had to perform in recent Russian history. Knocked to the ground, almost reduced to dust, by Russian absolutism, the "ego" takes revenge by turning to revolutionary activity. In the shape of a committee of conspirators, in the name of a nonexistent Will of the People, it seats itself on a kind of throne and proclaims it is all-powerful. But the "object" proves to be the stronger. The knout is triumphant, for czarist might seems to be the "legitimate" expression of history.

In time we see appear on the scene an even more "legitimate" child of history—the Russian labor movement. For the first time, bases for the formation of a real "people's will" are laid in Russian soil.

But here is the "ego" of the Russian revolutionary again! Pirouetting on its head, it once more proclaims itself to be the all-powerful director of history—this time with the title of His Excellency the Central Committee of the Social Democratic Party of Russia.

The nimble acrobat fails to perceive that the only "subject" which merits today the role of director is the collective "ego" of the working class. The working class demands the right to make its mistakes and learn in the dialectic of history.

Let us speak plainly. Historically, the errors committed by a truly revolutionary movement are infinitely more fruitful than the infallibility of the cleverest Central Committee.

SOCIALISM AND
THE CHURCHES

Revolution broke out in Russia in January 1905. Within days it had spread to Russian Poland and the other corners of the czarist empire. Rosa Luxemburg, then in Germany, immediately turned all her attention to a twofold task: helping to lead the Social Democratic Party of Poland and Lithuania (SDKPiL) through the year's events; and reporting and interpreting the 1905 Revolution for the German working class.

She was unable to leave Germany until December 1905, when she made her way illegally to Warsaw in order to participate directly in the leadership of the Polish party. But her residence in Germany did not prevent her from continuing and expanding her role as one of the main political analysts of the SDKPiL, as well as its most prolific and skilled popularizer and educator. Throughout 1905, in addition to her voluminous articles for the German press, she wrote constantly for the publications of the SDKPiL and also produced a number of longer books and pamphlets.

The 1905 Revolution brought thousands of new recruits to the SDKPiL, workers and intellectuals who were receiving a crash course in revolutionary practice and theory. Between January 1905 and early 1906 the SDKPiL grew from several hundred members to more than 30,000, with a periphery of thousands more. Rosa Luxemburg was constantly concerned with the problem of providing a basic Marxist education for these new supporters, of answering the most fundamental questions and eliminating some of the deepest prejudices of the newly radicalizing workers.

Socialism and the Churches was one of the fruits of the year 1905 — an attempt to explain to the Polish workers who were becoming class conscious exactly why the Church is a reactionary institution, opposed to the revolution, and how it came to be one of the most wealthy and vicious exploiters of the poor. It was first published in Cracow in 1905 under the pen name Jozef

Chmura. A Russian edition was printed in Moscow in 1920, and a French edition was issued by the French Socialist Party in 1937. The translation is from the French by Juan Punto.

I

From the moment when the workers of our country and of Russia began to struggle bravely against the czarist government and the capitalist exploiters, we notice more and more often that the priests, in their sermons, come out against the workers who are struggling. It is with extraordinary vigor that the clergy fight against the socialists and try by all means to belittle them in the eyes of the workers. The believers who go to church on Sundays and festivals are compelled, more and more often, to listen to a violent political speech, a real indictment of socialism, instead of hearing a sermon and obtaining religious consolation there. Instead of comforting the people, who are full of cares and wearied by their hard lives, who go to church with faith in Christianity, the priests fulminate against the workers who are on strike, and against the opponents of the government; further, they exhort them to bear poverty and oppression with humility and patience. They turn the church and the pulpit into a place of political propaganda.

The workers can easily satisfy themselves that the struggle of the clergy against the social democrats is in no way provoked by the latter. The social democrats have placed before themselves the objective of drawing together and organizing the workers in the struggle against capital, that is to say, against the exploiters who squeeze them down to the last drop of blood, and in the struggle against the czarist government, which holds the people to ransom. But never do the social democrats drive the workers to fight against the clergy, or try to interfere with religious beliefs; not at all! The social democrats, those of the whole world and those of our own country, regard conscience and personal opinions as being sacred. Every man may hold what faith and what opinions seem likely to him to ensure happiness. No one has the right to persecute or to attack the particular religious opinion of others. That is what the socialists think. And it is for that reason, among others, that the socialists rally all the people to fight against the czarist regime, which is continually violating men's consciences, persecuting Catholics, Russian Catholics, Jews, heretics and freethinkers. It is precisely the social democrats who come out most strongly in favor of freedom of conscience. Therefore, it would seem as if the clergy ought to lend their help to the social democrats, who are trying to enlighten the toiling people. If we understand properly the teachings which the socialists bring to the working class, the hatred of the clergy towards them becomes still less understandable.

The social democrats propose to put an end to the exploitation of the toiling people by the rich. You would have thought that the servants of the Church would have been the first to make this task easier for the social democrats. Did not Jesus Christ (whose servants the priests are) teach that "it is easier for a camel to pass through the eye of a needle than for a rich man to enter the Kingdom of Heaven"? The social democrats try to bring about in all countries a social regime based on the equality, liberty, and fraternity of all the citizens. If the clergy really desire that the principle "Love thy neighbor as thyself" be applied in real life, why do they not welcome keenly the propaganda of the social democrats? The social democrats try, by a desperate struggle, by the education and organization of the people, to draw them out of the downtrodden state in which they now are and to offer a better future to their children. Everyone should admit, that at this point, the clergy should bless the social democrats, for did not he whom they serve, Jesus Christ, say, "That you do for the poor, you do for me"?

However, we see the clergy, on the one hand, excommunicating and persecuting the social democrats, and, on the other hand, commanding the workers to suffer in patience, that is, to let themselves patiently be exploited by the capitalists. The clergy storm against the social democrats, exhort the workers not to "revolt" against the overlords, but to submit obediently to the oppression of this government which kills defenseless people, which sends to the monstrous butchery of the war millions of workers, which persecutes Catholics, Russian Catholics and "Old Believers." Thus, the clergy, which makes itself the spokesman of the rich, the defender of exploitation and oppression, places itself in flagrant contradiction to the Christian doctrine. The bishops and the priests are not the propagators of Christian teaching, but the worshippers of the golden calf and of the knout which whips the poor and defenseless.

Again, everyone knows how the priests themselves make profit from the worker, extract money out of him on the occasion of marriage, baptism or burial. How often has it happened that the priest, called to the bedside of a sick man to administer the last sacraments, refused to go there before he had been paid his "fee"? The worker goes away in despair, to sell or pawn his last possession, so as to be able to give religious consolation to his kindred.

It is true that we do meet churchmen of another kind. There exist some who are full of goodness and pity and who do not seek gain; these are always ready to help the poor. But we must

133

admit these are indeed uncommon and that they can be regarded in the same way as white blackbirds. The majority of priests, with beaming faces, bow and scrape to the rich and powerful, silently pardoning them for every depravity, every iniquity. With the workers the clergy behave quite otherwise; they think only of squeezing them without pity; in harsh sermons they condemn the "covetousness" of the workers when these latter do no more than defend themselves against the wrongs of capitalism. The glaring contradiction between the actions of the clergy and the teachings of Christianity must make everyone reflect. The workers wonder how it comes about that the working class, in its struggle for emancipation, finds in the servants of the church, enemies and not allies. How does it happen that the Church plays the role of a defense of wealth and bloody oppression, instead of being the refuge of the exploited? In order to understand this strange phenomenon, it is sufficient to glance over the history of the church and to examine the evolution through which it has passed in the course of the centuries.

II

The social democrats want to bring about the state of "communism"; that is chiefly what the clergy have against them. First of all, it is striking to notice that the priests of today who fight against "communism" condemn in reality the first Christian apostles. For these latter were nothing else than ardent communists.

The Christian religion developed, as is well known, in ancient Rome, in the period of the decline of the empire, which was formerly rich and powerful, comprising the countries which today are Italy and Spain, part of France, part of Turkey, Palestine and other territories. The state of Rome at the time of the birth of Jesus Christ much resembled that of czarist Russia. On one side there lived a handful of rich people in idleness, enjoying luxury and every pleasure; on the other side was an enormous mass of people rotting in poverty; above all, a despotic government, resting on violence and corruption, exerted a vile oppression. The whole Roman Empire was plunged into complete disorder, ringed round by threatening external foes; the unbridled soldiery in power practiced its cruelties on the wretched populace; the countryside was deserted, the land lay waste; the cities, and especially Rome, the capital, were filled with the poverty-stricken who raised their eyes, full of hate, to the palaces of the rich; the people were without bread, without shelter, without clothing, without hope, and without the possibility of emerging from their poverty.

There is only one difference between Rome in her decadence

and the empire of the czars; Rome knew nothing of capitalism; heavy industry did not exist there. At that time slavery was the accepted order of things in Rome. Noble families, the rich, the financiers satisfied all their needs by putting to work the slaves with which war had supplied them. In the course of time, these rich people had laid hands on nearly all the provinces of Italy by stripping the Roman peasantry of their land. As they appropriated cereals in all the conquered provinces as tribute without cost, they profited thereby to lay out on their own estates, magnificent plantations, vineyards, pastures, orchards, and rich gardens, cultivated by armies of slaves working under the whip of the overseer. The people of the countryside, robbed of land and bread, flowed from all the provinces into the capital. But there they were in no better a position to earn a livelihood, for all the trades were carried on by slaves. Thus there was formed in Rome a numerous army of those who possessed nothing—the proletariat—having not even the possibility of selling their labor power. This proletariat, coming from the countryside, could not, therefore, be absorbed by industrial enterprises as is the case today; they became the victims of hopeless poverty and were reduced to beggary. This numerous popular mass, starving without work, crowding the suburbs and open spaces and streets of Rome, constituted a permanent danger to the government and the possessing classes. Therefore, the government found itself compelled in its own interest to relieve the poverty. From time to time it distributed to the proletariat corn and other foodstuffs stored in the warehouses of the state. Further, to make the people forget their hardships it offered them free circus shows. Unlike the proletariat of our time, which maintains the whole of society by its labors, the enormous proletariat of Rome existed on charity.

It was the wretched slaves, treated like beasts, who worked for Roman society. In this chaos of poverty and degradation, the handful of Roman magnates spent their time in orgies and debauchery. There was no way out of these monstrous social conditions. The proletariat grumbled, and threatened from time to time to rise in revolt, but a class of beggars, living on crumbs thrown from the table of the lords, could not establish a new social order. Further, the slaves who maintained by their labor the whole of society were too downtrodden, too dispersed, too crushed under the yoke, treated as beasts and lived too isolated from the other classes to be able to transform society. They often revolted against their masters, tried to liberate themselves by bloody battles, but every time the Roman army crushed these revolts, massacring the slaves in thousands and putting them to death on the cross.

In this crumbling society, where there existed no way out of their tragic situation for the people, no hope of a better life, the wretched turned to Heaven to seek salvation there. The Christian religion appeared to these unhappy beings as a life belt, a consolation and an encouragement, and became, right from the beginning, the religion of the Roman proletarians. In conformity with the material position of the men belonging to this class, the first Christians put forward the demand for property in common — communism. What could be more natural? The people lacked means of subsistence and were dying of poverty. A religion which defended the people demanded that the rich should share with the poor the riches which ought to belong to all and not to a handful of privileged people; a religion which preached the equality of all men would have great success. However, this had nothing in common with the demand which the social democrats put forward today with a view to making into common property the instruments of work the means of production, in order that all humanity may work and live in harmonious unity.

We have been able to observe that the Roman proletarians did not live by working, but from the alms which the government doled out. So the demand of the Christians for collective property did not relate to the means of production, but the means of consumption. They did not demand that the land, the workshops and the instruments of work should become collective property, but only that everything should be divided up among them, houses, clothing, food and finished products most necessary to life. The Christian communists took good care not to enquire into the origin of these riches. The work of production always fell upon the slaves. The Christian people desired only that those who possessed the wealth should embrace the Christian religion and should make their riches common property, in order that all might enjoy these good things in equality and fraternity.

It was indeed in this way that the first Christian communities were organized. A contemporary wrote, "These people do not believe in fortunes, but they preach collective property and no one among them possesses more than the others. He who wishes to enter their order is obliged to put his fortune into their common property. That is why there is among them neither poverty nor luxury — all possessing all in common like brothers. They do not live in a city apart, but in each they have houses for themselves. If any strangers belonging to their religion come there, they share their property with them, and they can benefit from it as if it were their own. Those people, even if previously unknown to each other, welcome one another, and their relations are very friendly. When travelling they carry nothing but a weapon for defense against robbers. In each city they have their steward, who distributes clothing and food to the travellers. Trade does not exist among them. However, if one of the members offers to another some object which he needs, he receives some other object in exchange. But also, each can demand what he needs even if he can give nothing in exchange."

We read in the "Acts of the Apostles" the following description of the first community at Jerusalem: "No one regarded as being his what belonged to him; everything was in common. Those who possessed lands or houses, after having sold them, brought the proceeds and laid them at the feet of the apostles. And to each was distributed according to his needs."

In 1780, the German historian Vogel wrote nearly the same thing about the first Christians: "According to the rule, every Christian had the right to the property of all the members of the community; in case of want, he could demand that the richer members should divide their fortune with him according to his needs. Every Christian could make use of the property of his brothers; the Christians who possessed anything had not the right to refuse that their brothers should use it. Thus, the Christian who had no house could demand from him who had two or three to take him in; the owner kept only his own house to himself. But because of the community of enjoyment of goods, housing accommodation had to be given to him who had none."

Money was placed in a common chest and a member of the society, specially appointed for this purpose, divided the collective fortune among all. But this was not all. Among the early Christians, communism was pressed so far that they took their means in common. Their family life was therefore done away with; all the Christian families in one city lived together, like one single large family.

To finish, let us add that certain priests attack the social democrats on the ground that we are for the community of women. Obviously, this is simply a huge lie, arising from the ignorance or the anger of the clergy. The social democrats consider that as a shameful and bestial distortion of marriage. And yet this practice was usual among the first Christians.

III

Thus the Christians of the first and second centuries were fervent supporters of communism. But this communism was based on the consumption of finished products and not on work, and proved itself incapable of reforming society, of putting an end to the inequality between men and throwing down the barrier which separated rich from poor. For, exactly as before, the riches created by labor came back to a restricted group of possessors, because the means of production (especially the land) remained individual property, because the labor—for the whole society—was furnished by the slaves. The people, deprived of means of subsistence, received only alms, according to the good pleasure of the rich.

While some, a handful (in proportion to the mass of the people), possess exclusively for their own use all the arable lands, forests and pastures, farm animals and farm buildings, all the workshops, tools, and materials of production, and while others, the immense majority, possess nothing at all that is indispensable in production, there can be no question whatever of equality between men. In such conditions society evidently finds itself divided into two classes, the rich and the poor, those of luxury and poverty. Suppose, for example, that the rich proprietors, influenced by the Christian doctrine, offered to share up between the people all the riches which they possessed in the form of money, cereals, fruit, clothing and animals. What would the result be? Poverty would disappear for several weeks and during this time the populace would be able to feed and clothe themselves. But the finished products are quickly used up. After a short lapse of time, the people, having consumed the distributed riches, would once again have empty hands. The proprietors of the land and the instruments of production could produce more, thanks to the labor power provided by the slaves, so nothing would be changed.

Well, here is why the social democrats consider these things differently from the Christian communists. They say, "We do not want the rich to share with the poor; we do not want either charity or alms; neither being able to prevent the recurrence of inequality between men. It is by no means a sharing out between the rich and the poor which we demand, but the complete suppression of rich and poor." This is possible on the condition that the source of all wealth, the land, in common with all other means of production and instruments of work, shall become the collective property of the working people which will produce for itself, according to the needs of each. The early Christians believed that they could remedy the poverty of the proletariat by means of the riches offered by the possessors. That would be to draw water in a sieve! Christian communism was incapable of changing or of improving the economic situation, and it did not last.

At the beginning, when the followers of the new Savior constituted only a small group in Roman society, the sharing of the common stock, the meals in common and the living under the same roof were practicable. But as the number of Christians spread over the territory of the empire, this communal life of its adherents became more difficult. Soon there disappeared the custom of common meals and the division of goods took on a different aspect. The Christians no longer lived like one family; each took charge of his own property, and they no longer offered the whole of their goods to the community, but only the superfluity. The gifts of the richer of them to the general body, losing their character of participation in a common life, soon became simple almsgiving, since rich Christians no longer made any use of the common property, and put at the service of the others only a part of what they had, while this part might be greater or smaller according to the goodwill of the donor. Thus in the very heart of Christian communism appeared the difference between the rich and the poor, a difference analogous to that which reigned in the Roman Empire and against which the early Christians had fought. Soon it was only the poor Christians — and the proletarian ones — who took part in the communal meals; the rich, having offered a part of their plenty, held themselves apart. The poor lived from the alms tossed to them by the rich, and society again became what it had been. The Christians had changed nothing.

The Fathers of the Church struggled for a long time, yet, with burning words, against this penetration of social inequality into the Christian community, scourging the rich and exhorting them to return to the communism of the early apostles.

St. Basil, in the fourth century after Christ, preached thus against the rich: "Wretches, how will you justify yourselves before the Heavenly Judge? You say to me, 'What is our fault, when we keep what belongs to us?' I ask you, 'How did you get that which you called your property?' How do the possessors become rich, if not by taking possession of things that belong to all? If everyone took only what he strictly needed, leaving the rest to others, there would be neither rich nor poor."

It was St. John Chrysostom, patriarch of Constantinople, (born at Antioch in 347, died in exile in Armenia in 407), who preached most ardently to the Christians the return to the first communism of the apostles. This celebrated preacher, in his Eleventh Homily on the "Acts of the Apostles," said:

"And there was a great charity among them (the apostles); none was poor among them. None considered as being his what belonged to him, all their riches were in common. . . . a great charity was in all of them. This charity consisted in that there were no poor among them, so much did those who had possessions hasten to strip themselves of them. They did not divide their fortunes into two parts, giving one and keeping the other back; they gave what they had. So there was no inequality between them; they all lived in great abundance. Everything was done with the greatest reverence. What they gave was not passed from the hand of the giver to that of the recipient; their gifts were without ostentation; they brought their goods to the feet of the apostles who became the controllers and masters of them and who used them from then on as the goods of the community and no longer as the property of individuals. By that means they cut short any attempt to get vainglory. Ah! Why have these traditions been lost? Rich and poor, we should all profit from these pious usages and we should both feel the same pleasure from conforming to them. The rich would not impoverish themselves when laying down their possessions, and the poor would be enriched. . . . But let us try to give an exact idea of what should be done. . . .

"Now, let us suppose—and neither rich nor poor need be alarmed, for I am just supposing—let us suppose that we sell all that belongs to us to put the proceeds into a common pool. What sums of gold would be piled up! I cannot say exactly how much that would make; but if all among us, without distinction between the sexes, were to bring here their treasures, if they were to sell their fields, their properties, their houses—I do not speak of slaves for there were none in the Christian community, and those who were there became free—perhaps, I say if everyone did the same, we would reach hundreds of thousands of pounds of gold, millions, enormous values.

"Well! How many people do you think there are living in this city? How many Christians? Would you agree that there are a hundred thousand? The rest being made up of Jews and Gentiles. How many should we not unite together? Now, if you count up the poor, what do you find? Fifty thousand needy people at the most. What would be needed to feed them each day? I estimate that the expense would not be excessive, if the supply and the eating of the food were organized in common.

"You will say, perhaps, 'But what will become us when these goods are used up?' So what? Would that ever happen? Would not the grace of God be a thousand times abundant? Would we not be making a heaven on earth? If formerly this community of goods existed among three to five thousand faithful and had such good results and did away with poverty amidst them, what would not result in such a great multitude as this? And among the pagans themselves who would not hasten to increase the common treasure? Wealth which is owned by a number of people is much more easily and quickly spent; the diffusion of ownership is the cause of poverty. Let us take as an example a household composed of a husband, a wife, and ten children, the wife being occupied in weaving wool, the husband in bringing in the wages of his work outside; tell me in which case this family would spend more; if they live together in common, or lived separately. Obviously, if they lived separately. Ten houses, ten tables, ten servants, and ten special allowances would be needed for the children if they were separated. What do you do, indeed, if you have many slaves? Is it not true, that, in order to keep expenses down, you feed them at a common table? The division is a cause of impoverishment; concord and the unity of wills is a cause of riches.

"In the monasteries, they still live as in the early church. And who dies of hunger there? Who has not found enough to eat there? Yet the men of our times fear living that way more than they fear falling into the sea! Why have we not tried it? We would fear it less. What a good act that would be! If a few of the faithful, hardly eight thousand dared in the face of a whole world, where they have nothing but enemies, to make a courageous attempt to live in common, without any outside help, how much more could we do it today, now that there are Christians throughout the whole world? Would there remain one single Gentile? Not one, I believe. We would attract them all and win them to us."

These ardent sermons of St. John Chrysostom were in vain. Men no longer tried to establish communism either at Constantinople or anywhere else. At the same time as Christianity expanded and became, at Rome after the fourth century, the dominant religion, the faithful went further and further away from the example of the first apostles. Even within the Christian community itself, the inequality of goods between the faithful increased.

Again, in the sixth century, Gregory the Great said: "It is by no means enough not to steal the property of others; you are in error if you keep to yourself the wealth which God has created for all. He who does not give to others what he possesses is a murderer, a killer; when he keeps for his own use what would provide for the poor, one can say that he is slaying all those who could have lived from his plenty; when we share with those who are suffering, we do not give what belongs to us, but what belongs to them. This is not an act of pity, but the payment of a debt."

These appeals remained fruitless. But the fault was by no means with the Christians of those days, who were indeed, more responsive to the words of the Fathers of the Church than are the Christians of today. This was not the first time in the history of humanity that economic conditions have shown themselves to be stronger than fine speeches.

The communism, this community of the consumption of goods, which the early Christians proclaimed, could not be brought into existence without the communal labor of the whole population, on the land, as common property, as well as in the communal workshops. At the period of the early Christians, it was impossible to inaugurate communal labor (with communal means of production) because as we have already stated, the labor rested, not upon free men, but upon the slaves, who lived on the edge of society. Christianity did not undertake to abolish the inequality between the labor of different men, nor between their property. And that is why its efforts to suppress the unequal distribution of consumption goods did not work. The voices of the Fathers of the Church proclaiming communism found no echo. Besides, these voices soon became less and less frequent and finally fell silent altogether. The Fathers of the Church ceased to preach the community, and the dividing up of goods, because the growth of the Christian community, produced fundamental changes within the Church itself.

IV

At the beginning, when the number of Christians was small, the clergy did not exist in the proper sense of the word. The faithful, who formed an independent religious community, united together in each city. They elected a member responsible for conducting the service of God and carrying out the religious rites. Every Christian could become the bishop or prelate. These functions were elective, subject to recall, honorary and carried no power other than that which the community gave of its own free will. In proportion as the number of the faithful increased and the communities became more numerous and richer, to run the business of the community and to hold office became an occupation which demanded a great deal of time and full concentration. As the office-bearers could not carry out these tasks at the same time as following their private employments, the custom grew up of electing from among the members of the community, an ecclesiastic who was exclusively entrusted with these functions. Therefore, these employees of the community had to be paid for their exclusive devotion to its affairs. Thus there formed within the Church a new order of employees of the Church, which separated itself from the main body of the faithful, the clergy. Parallel with the inequality between rich and poor, there arose another inequality, that between the clergy and the people. The ecclesiastics, at first elected among equals with a view to performing a temporary function, soon raised themselves to form a caste which ruled over the people.

The more numerous the Christian communities became in the cities of the enormous Roman Empire, the more the Christians, persecuted by the government, felt the need to unite to gain strength. The communities, scattered over all the territory of the empire, therefore organized themselves into one single Church.

This unification was already a unification of the clergy and not of the people. From the fourth century, the ecclesiastics of the communities met together in councils. The first council took place at Nicaea in 325. In this way there was formed the clergy, an order apart and separated from the people. The bishops of the stronger and richer communities took the lead at the councils. That is why the bishop of Rome soon placed himself at the head of the whole of Christianity and became the Pope. Thus an abyss separated the clergy, divided up in the hierarchy, from the people. At the same time, the economic relations between the people and the clergy underwent a great change. Before the formation of this order, all that the rich members of the Church offered to the common property belonged to the poor people. Afterwards, a great part of the funds was spent on paying the clergy and running the Church. When, in the fourth century, Christianity was protected by the government and was recognized at Rome as being the dominant religion, the persecutions of the Christians ended, and the services were no longer carried on in catacombs, or in modest halls, but in churches which began to be more and more magnificently built. These expenses thus reduced the funds intended for the poor. Already, in the fifth century, the revenues of the Church were divided into four parts; the first for the bishop, the second for the minor clergy, the third for the upkeep of the Church, and it was only the fourth part which was distributed among the needy. The poor Christian population received therefore a sum equal to what the bishop received for himself alone.

In course of time the habit was lost of giving to the poor a sum determined in advance. Moreover, as the higher clergy gained in importance, the faithful no longer had control over the property of the Church. The bishops gave to the poor according to their good pleasure. The people received alms from their own clergy. But that is not all. At the beginning of Christianity, the faithful made goodwill offerings to the common stock. As soon as the Christian religion became a state religion, the clergy demanded that gifts must be brought by the poor as well as by the rich. From the sixth century, the clergy imposed a special tax, the tithe (tenth part of the crops), which had to be paid in the Church. This tax crushed the people like a heavy burden; in the course of the Middle Ages it became a real scourge to the peasants oppressed by serfdom. The tithe was levied on every piece of land, on every property. But it was always the serf who paid it by his labor. Thus the poor people not only lost the help and support of the Church, but they saw the priests ally themselves with their other exploiters: princes, nobles, moneylenders. In the Middle Ages, while the working people sank into poverty through serfdom, the Church grew richer and richer. Besides the tithe and other taxes, the Church benefitted at this period from great donations, legacies made by rich debauchees of both sexes who wished to make up, at the last moment, for their life of sin. They gave and made over to the Church, money, houses, entire villages with their serfs, and often ground-rents or customary labor dues (corvees).

In this way the Church acquired enormous wealth. At the same time, the clergy ceased to be the "administrator" of the wealth which the Church had entrusted it. It openly declared in the twelfth century, by formulating a law which it said came from Holy Scripture, that the wealth of the Church belongs not to the faithful but is the individual property of the clergy and of its chief, the Pope, above all. Ecclesiastical positions therefore offered the best opportunities to obtain large revenues. Each ecclesiastic disposed of the property of the Church as if it were his own and largely endowed from it his relatives, sons and grandsons. By this means the goods of the Church were pillaged and disappeared into the hands of the families of the clergy. For that reason, the Popes declared themselves to be the sovereign proprietors of the fortunes of the Church and ordained the celibacy of the clergy, in order to keep it intact and to prevent their patrimony from being dispersed. Celibacy was decreed in the eleventh century, but it was not put into practice until the thirteenth century, in view of the opposition of the clergy. Further to prevent the dispersal of the Church's wealth, in 1297 Pope Boniface VIII forbade ecclesiastics to make a present of their incomes to laymen, without permission of the Pope. Thus the Church accumulated enormous wealth, especially in arable lands, and the clergy of all Christian countries became the most important landed proprietor. It often possessed a third, or more than a third, of all the lands of the country!

The peasant people paid not only the labor dues (corvee) but the tithe as well, and that not only on the lands of the princes and the nobles, but on enormous tracts where they worked directly for the bishops, archbishops, parsons and convents. Among all the mighty lords of feudal times, the Church appeared as the greatest exploiter of all. In France, for example, at the end of the eighteenth century, before the Great Revolution, the clergy possessed the fifth part of all the territory of the country, with an annual income of about 100 million francs. The tithes paid by the proprietors amounted to 23 million. This sum went to fatten 2800 prelates and bishops, 5600 superiors and priors, 60,000 parsons and curates, and 24,000 monks and 36,000 nuns who filled the cloisters. This army of priests was freed from taxation and from the requirement to perform military service. In times of "calamity"—war, bad harvest, epidemics—the Church paid to the state treasury a "voluntary" tax which never exceeded 16 million francs.

The clergy, thus privileged, formed, with the nobility, a ruling class, living on the blood and sweat of the serfs. The high posts in the Church, and those which paid best, were distributed only to the nobles and remained within the hands of the nobility. Consequently, in the period of serfdom, the clergy was the faithful ally of the nobility, giving it support and helping it to oppress the people, to whom it offered nothing but sermons, according to which they should remain humble and resign themselves to their lot. When the country and town proletariat rose up against oppression and serfdom, it found in the clergy a ferocious opponent. It is also true that even within the Church itself there existed two classes: the higher clergy who engulfed all the wealth and the great mass of the country parsons whose modest livings brought in no more than 500 to 2000 francs a year. Therefore this unprivileged class revolted against the superior clergy and in 1789, during the Great Revolution, it joined up with the people to fight against the power of the lay and ecclesiastical nobility.

V

Thus were the relations between the Church and the people modified with the passage of time. Christianity began as a message of consolation to the disinherited and the wretched. It brought a doctrine which combatted social inequality and the antagonism between rich and poor; it taught the community of riches. Soon this temple of equality and fraternity became a new source of social antagonisms. Having given up the struggle against individual property which was formerly carried on by the early apostles, the clergy itself gathered riches together; it allied itself with the possessing classes who lived by exploiting the labor of the toiling class. In feudal times the Church belonged to the nobility, the ruling class, and fiercely defended the power of the latter against revolution. At the end of the eighteenth century and the beginning of the nineteenth century, the people of Central Europe swept away serfdom and the privileges of the nobility. At that time, the Church allied itself afresh with the dominant classes—with the industrial and commercial bourgeoisie. Today, the situation has changed and the clergy no longer possess great estates, but they own capital which they try to make productive by the exploitation of the people through commerce and industry, as do the capitalists.

The Catholic Church in Austria possessed, according to its own statistics, a capital of more than 813 million crowns, of which 300 million were in arable lands and in property, 387 million of debentures, and, further, it lent at interest the sum of 70 million to factory owners and businessmen. And that is how the Church, adapting itself to modern times, changed itself into an industrial and commercial capitalist from being a feudal overlord. As formerly, it continues to collaborate with the class which enriches itself at the expense of the industrial and rural proletariat.

This change is even more striking in the organization of convents. In certain countries, such as Germany and Russia, the Catholic cloisters have been suppressed for a long time. But where they still exist, in France, Italy and Spain, all evidence points how enormous is the part played by the Church in the capitalist regime.

In the Middle Ages the convents were the refuge of the people. It was there that they sought shelter from the severity of lords and princes; it was there that they found food and protection in case of extreme poverty. The cloisters did not refuse bread and nourishment to the hungry. Let us not forget, especially, that the Middle Ages knew nothing of the commerce such as is usual in our days. Every farm, every convent produced in abundance for itself, thanks to the labor of the serfs and the craftsmen. Often the provisions in reserve found no outlet. When they had produced more corn, more vegetables, more wood than was needed for the consumption of the monks, the excess had no value. There was no buyer for it and not all products could be preserved. In these conditions, the convents freely looked after their poor, in any case offering them only a small part of what has been extracted from their serfs. (This was the usual custom in this period and nearly every farm belonging to the nobility acted similarly.) In fact the cloisters profited considerably from this benevolence; having the reputation of opening their doors to the poor, they received large gifts and legacies from the rich and powerful.

With the appearance of capitalism and production for exchange, every object acquired a price and became exchangeable. At this moment, the convents, the houses of the lords, and the ecclesiastics ceased their benefactions. The people found no refuge anywhere. Here is one reason, among others, why, at the beginning of capitalism, in the eighteenth century, when the workers were not yet organized to defend their interests, there appeared poverty so appalling that humanity seemed to have gone back to the days of the decades of the Roman Empire. But while the Catholic Church in former times undertook to bring help to the Roman proletariat, by the preaching of communism, equality and fraternity, in the capitalist period it acted in a wholly different fashion. It sought above all to profit from the poverty of the people; to put cheap labor to work. The convents became literally hells of capitalist exploitation, all the worse because they took in the labor of women and children. The law case against the Convent of the Good Shepherd in France in 1903 gave a resounding example of these abuses. Little girls twelve, ten and nine years old were compelled to work in abominable conditions, without rest, ruining their eyes and their health, and were badly nourished and subjected to prison discipline.

At present the convents are almost entirely suppressed in France and the Church loses the opportunity of direct capitalist exploitation. The tithe, the scourge of the serfs, has likewise long since been abolished. This does not stop the clergy from extorting money from the working class by other methods, and particularly through masses, marriages, burials and baptisms. And the governments which support the clergy compel the people to pay their tribute. Further, in all countries, except the U. S. A. and Switzerland, where religion is a personal matter, the Church draws from the state enormous sums which obviously come from the hard labor of the people. For instance, in France the expenditure of the clergy amounts to 40 million francs a year.

To sum up, it is the labor of millions of exploited people which assures the existence of the Church, the government, and the capitalist class. The statistics concerning the revenue of the Church in Austria give an idea of the considerable wealth of the Church, which was formerly the refuge of the poor. Five years ago (that is, in 1900) its annual revenues amounted to 60 million crowns, and its expenditure did not exceed 35 million. Thus, in the course of a single year it "put aside" 25 million — at the cost of the sweat and blood shed by the workers. Here are a few details about that sum:

The Archbishopric of Vienna, with an annual revenue of 300,000 crowns and the expenses of which were not more than half of that sum, made 150,000 crowns of "savings" a year; the fixed capital of the Archbishopric amounts to about 7 million crowns. The Archbishopric of Prague enjoys an income of over half a million and has about 300,000 in expenses; its capital reaches nearly 11 million crowns. The Archbishopric of Olomouc (Olmutz) has over half a million in revenue and about 400,000 in expenses; its fortune exceeds 14 million. The subordinate clergy which so often pleads poverty exploits the population no less. The annual incomes of the parish priests of Austria reach more than 35 million crowns, the expenses 21 million only, with the result that the "savings" of the parsons yearly reach 14 million. The parish properties make up over 450 million. Finally, the convents of five years ago possessed, with all expenses deducted, a "net revenue" of 5 million a year. These riches grew every year, while the poverty of the toilers exploited by capitalism and by the state grew from year to year. In our country and everywhere else, the state of things is exactly as in Austria.

VI

After having briefly reviewed the history of the Church, we cannot be surprised that the clergy supports the czarist government and the capitalists against the revolutionary workers who fight for a better future. The class-conscious workers, organized in the Social Democratic Party, fight to bring into reality the idea of social equality and of fraternity among men, the object which was formerly that of the Christian Church.

Nonetheless, equality cannot be realized either in a society based on slavery nor in a society based on serfdom; it becomes capable of being realized in our present period, that is, the regime of industrial capitalism. What the Christian apostles could not accomplish by their ardent discourses against the egoism of the rich, the modern proletarians, workers conscious of their class position, can start working in the near future, by the conquest of political power in all countries, by tearing the factories, the land, and all the means of production from the capitalists to make them the communal property of the workers. The communism which the social democrats have in view does not consist of the dividing-up, between beggars and rich and lazy, of the wealth produced by slaves and serfs, but in honest common united work and the honest enjoyment of the common fruits of that work. Socialism does not consist of generous gifts made by the rich to the poor, but in the total abolition of the very difference between rich and poor, by compelling all alike to work according to their capacity by the suppression of the exploitation of man by man.

For the purpose of establishing the socialist order, the workers organize themselves in the workers' Social Democratic Party which pursues this aim. And that is why the social democracy and the workers' movement meets with the ferocious hatred of the possessing classes which live at the expense of the workers.

The enormous riches piled up by the Church without any effort on its part come from the exploitation and the poverty of the laboring people. The wealth of the archbishops and bishops, the convents and the parishes, the wealth of the factory owners and the traders and the landed proprietors are bought at the price of the inhuman exertions of the workers of town and country. For what can be the only origin of the gifts and legacies which the very rich lords make to the Church? Obviously not the labor of their hands and the sweat of their brows, but the exploitation of the workers who toil for them; serfs yesterday and wageworkers today. Further, the allowance which the governments today make to the clergy come from the state treasury, made up in the greater part from the taxes wrung from the popular masses. The clergy, no less than the capitalist class, lives on the backs of the people, profits from the degradation, the ignorance and the oppression of the people. The clergy and the parasitic capitalists hate the organized working class, conscious of its rights, which fights for the conquest of its liberties. For the abolition of capitalist misrule and the establishment of equality between men would strike a mortal blow especially at the clergy which exists only thanks to exploitation and poverty. But above all, socialism aims at assuring to humanity an honest and solid happiness here below, to give to the people the greatest possible education and the first place in society. It is precisely this happiness here on earth which the servants of the Church fear like the plague.

The capitalists have shaped with hammer blows the bodies of the people, in chains of poverty and slavery. Parallel to this the clergy, helping the capitalists and serving their own needs, enchain the mind of the people, hold it down in crass ignorance, for they well understand that education would put an end to their power. Well, the clergy falsifying the early teaching of Christianity, which had as its object the earthly happiness of the lowly, tries today to persuade the toilers that the suffering and the degradation which they endure come, not from a defective social structure, but from heaven, from the will of "Providence." Thus the Church kills in the workers the strength, the hope, and the will for a better future, kills their faith in themselves and their self-respect. The priests of today, with their false and poisonous teachings, continually maintain the ignorance and degradation of the people. Here are some irrefutable proofs.

In the countries where the Catholic clergy enjoys great power over the minds of the people, in Spain and in Italy for instance, the people are held down in complete ignorance. Drunkenness and crime flourish there. For example, let us compare two provinces of Germany, Bavaria and Saxony. Bavaria is an agricultural state where the population is preponderantly under the influence of the Catholic clergy. Saxony is an industrialized state where the social democrats play a large part in the life of the workers. They win the parliamentary elections in nearly all the constituencies, a reason why the bourgeoisie shows its hatred for this "red" social democrat province. And what do we see? The official statistics show that the number of crimes committed in ultra-Catholic Bavaria is relatively much higher than that in "red Saxony." We see that in 1898, out of every 100,000 inhabitants there were:

Robbery with violence:	In Bavaria 204	In Saxony 185
Assault and battery:	" 296	" 72
Perjury:	" 4	" 1

A wholly similar situation is found when we compare the record of crime in priest-dominated Possen with that in Berlin, where the influence of social democracy is greater. In the course of the year, we see for every 100,000 inhabitants in Possen, 232 cases of assault and battery, and in Berlin 172 only.

In the Papal City, in Rome, during one single month of the year 1869 (the last year but one of the temporal power of the Popes), there were condemned: 279 for murder, 728 for assault and battery, 297 for robbery and 21 for arson. These are the results of clerical domination over the poverty-stricken people.

This does not mean to say that the clergy directly incite people to crime. Quite the contrary, in their sermons the priests often condemn theft, robbery, and drunkenness. But men do not steal, rob, or get drunk at all because they like to do so or insist upon it. It is poverty and ignorance that are the causes of it. Therefore, he who keeps alive the ignorance and poverty of the people, he who kills their will and energy to get out of this situation, he who puts all sorts of obstacles in the way of those who try to educate the proletariat, he is responsible for these crimes just as if he were an accomplice.

The situation in the mining areas of Catholic Belgium was similar until recently. The social democrats went there. Their vigorous appeal to the unhappy and degraded workers sounded through the country: "Worker, lift yourself up! Do not rob, do not get drunk, do not lower your head in despair! Read, teach yourself! Join up with your class brothers in the organization, fight against the exploiters who maltreat you! You will emerge from poverty, you will become a man!"

Thus the social democrats everywhere lift up the people and strengthen those who lose hope, rally the weak into a powerful organization. They open the eyes of the ignorant and show them the way of equality, of liberty and of love for our neighbors.

On the other hand, the servants of the Church bring to the people only words of humiliation and discouragement. And, if Christ were to appear on earth today he would surely attack the priests, the bishops and archbishops who defend the rich and live by exploiting the unfortunate, as formerly he attacked the merchants whom he drove from the temple so that their ignoble presence should not defile the House of God.

That is why there has broken out a desperate struggle between the clergy, the supporters of oppression, and the social democrats, the spokesmen of liberation. Is this fight not to be compared with that of the dark night and the rising sun? Because the priests are not capable of combatting socialism by means of intelligence or truth, they have recourse to violence and wickedness. Their Judas-talk calumniates those who rouse class consciousness. By means of lies and slander, they try to besmirch all those who give up their lives for the workers' cause. These servants and worshippers of the golden calf support and applaud the crimes of the czarist government and defend the throne of this latest despot who oppresses the people like Nero.

But it is in vain that you put yourselves about, you degenerate servants of Christianity who have become the servants of Nero. It is in vain that you help our murderers and our killers, in vain that you protect the exploiters of the proletariat under the sign of the cross. Your cruelties and your calumnies in former times could not prevent the victory of the Christian idea, the idea which you have sacrificed to the golden calf; today your efforts will raise no obstacle to the coming of socialism. Today it is you, in your lies and your teachings, who are pagans, and it is we who bring to the poor, to the exploited the tidings of fraternity and equality. It is we who are marching to the conquest of the world as he did formerly who proclaimed that it is easier for a camel to pass through the eye of a needle than for a rich man to enter the kingdom of heaven.

VII

A few final words.

The clergy has at its disposal two means to fight social democracy. Where the working-class movement is beginning to win recognition, as is the case in our country (Poland), where the possessing classes still hope to crush it, the clergy fights the socialists by threatening sermons, slandering them and condemning the "covetousness" of the workers. But in the countries where political liberties are established and the workers' party is powerful, as for example in Germany, France, and Holland, there the clergy seeks other means. It hides its real purpose and does not face the workers any more as an open enemy, but as a false friend. Thus you will see the priests organizing the workers and founding "Christian" trade unions. In this way they try to catch the fish in their net, to attract the workers into the trap of these false trade unions, where they teach humility, unlike the organizations of the social democracy which have in view struggle and defense against maltreatment.

When the czarist government finally falls under the blows of the revolutionary proletariat of Poland and Russia, and when political liberty exists in our country, then we shall see the same Archbishop Popiel and the same ecclesiastics who today thunder against the militants, suddenly beginning to organize the workers into "Christian" and "national" associations in order to mislead them. Already we are at the beginning of this underground activity of the "national democracy" which assures the future collaboration with the priests and today helps them to slander the social democrats.

The workers must, therefore, be warned of the danger so that they will not let themselves be taken in, on the morrow of the victory of the revolution, by the honeyed words of those who today from the height of the pulpit, dare to defend the czarist government, which kills the workers, and the repressive apparatus of capital, which is the principal cause of the poverty of the proletariat.

In order to defend themselves against the antagonism of the clergy at the present time, during the revolution, and against their false friendship tomorrow, after the revolution, it is necessary for the workers to organize themselves in the Social Democratic Party.

And here is the answer to all the attacks of the clergy: The social democracy in no way fights against religious beliefs. On the contrary, it demands complete freedom of conscience for every individual and the widest possible toleration for every faith and every opinion. But, from the moment when the priests use the pulpit as a means of political struggle against the working class, the workers must fight against the enemies of their rights and their liberation. For he who defends the exploiters and who helps to prolong this present regime of misery is the mortal enemy of the proletariat, whether he be in a cassock or in the uniform of the police.

THE MASS STRIKE,

THE POLITICAL PARTY

AND THE TRADE UNIONS

The Mass Strike, the Political Party and the Trade Unions was written to fulfill the second task Rosa Luxemburg outlined for herself in relation to the 1905 Revolution—to interpret the events of 1905-06 for the German workers and draw the lessons for the future of the class struggle in Germany. It was also one of Rosa Luxemburg's most effective attacks on the institutionalized conservatism of the social democratic trade-union bureaucracy in Germany.

As Rosa Luxemburg explains in the opening sections of her article, the mass strike or the general strike, as a weapon to be used by the working class in its battles, had a long history of controversy surrounding it, from the days of the First International onward. However, the Russian Revolution of 1905 threw additional light on the debate, and a Marxist analysis of those events could only lead to a greater appreciation of the role played in revolutionary struggle by mass strikes in which both economic and political factors were inextricably intermixed. While her arguments are in the main absolutely correct, she tends to go too far in the direction of equating the mass strike with the revolution itself.

Her vivid description and analysis of the unfolding of the struggle in the Russian Empire illustrates her central argument: that the mass strike is not an artificially created and sterile concept in the minds of some ossified, timid, trade-union bureaucrats, "not a crafty method discovered by subtle reasoning for the purpose of making the proletarian struggle more effective, *but the method of motion of the proletarian mass*, the phenomenal form of the proletarian struggle in the revolution."

Her arguments are chiefly directed against the leaders of the German trade unions, whom she had come to regard as her most serious opponents. Her utter contempt for the cowardice, conservatism and narrow-minded reformism of the trade-union leaders permeates every section of the pamphlet. She did not expect to change their minds, but she did hope to convince some of the other leaders of the SPD of the danger created by the growing independence of the trade-union leaders from party discipline.

Even more, she hoped to educate the German workers in the true spirit of the Russian Revolution and an understanding of the international implications of that revolution. She hoped to vaccinate them against the opportunism of their own leaders. "Those trade-union leaders and parliamentarians who regard the German proletariat as 'too weak' and German conditions 'as not ripe enough' for revolutionary mass struggles, have obviously not the least idea that the measure of the degree of ripeness of class relations in Germany and of the power of the proletariat does not lie in the statistics of German trade unionism or in election figures, but—in the events of the Russian Revolution."

An open break by the trade-union leaders with SPD policy had occurred in the fall of 1905, before Rosa Luxemburg left for Warsaw. At the party congress in Jena, after a debate on whether or not the party should include in its arsenal of potential weapons the call for a mass strike, a resolution was adopted in which such a call was approved, but only in the eventuality that the government attempted to restrict the right to vote. Even this weak resolution, proposed by the central leadership of the SPD, was enough to terrify the trade unionists. At the German Trade Union Congress in Cologne immediately following the Jena Congress, even a theoretical discussion of the general strike was labeled "playing with fire" and banned. Thus, for the first time, the trade-union congress under the leadership of SPD members, adopted a policy in open contradiction to the political position of the SPD.

Instead of being disciplined or called to order for this, however, in February 1906 the SPD and trade-union leaders agreed at a secret meeting that the Jena resolution would be quietly buried. And at the following party congress in 1906, a resolution was adopted officially stating that there was no contradiction between the Jena resolution and the Cologne trade-union position.

The mass strike pamphlet was written in August 1906 in Kuokkala, Finland, where Rosa Luxemburg had gone to recuperate from her imprisonment in Warsaw.

On March 4, 1906, Rosa had been arrested, her presence in Poland having been exposed by a conservative German newspaper. Despite her fake papers, her true identity had been revealed almost immediately by a police raid on her sister's home which turned up photographs of Rosa. She was charged with serious crimes against the state, but with the help of substantial bribes, warnings from the Polish Social Democratic Party that they would retaliate if anything happened to Rosa, and certificates confirming her failing health, she was finally released from prison in July 1906.

In August she was permitted to leave Warsaw; from there she went to Finland to join Lenin, Zinoviev, Kamenev and other Bolshevik leaders. The experiences of 1905 had brought the SDKPiL much closer to the Bolsheviks, whom they recognized as their Russian counterpart in action and theory. In April of 1906 the SDKPiL had finally joined the Russian party and aligned itself with the Bolsheviks against the Mensheviks on most questions.

Rosa Luxemburg spent the latter part of August and early September in Finland, discussing with the Bolshevik leaders and writing the mass strike pamphlet. She then returned to Germany in time to take part in the 1906 party congress where she tried unsuccessfully to reverse the SPD's capitulation to the trade unions on the mass strike question, and to reassert the authority of the party over the trade-union leaders.

The pamphlet was first published in English by the Marxist Educational Society of Detroit in 1925. The translation is by Patrick Lavin.

<hr>

I. The Russian Revolution, Anarchism and the General Strike

Almost all works and pronouncements of international socialism on the subject of the mass strike date from the time before the Russian Revolution [of 1905 — Ed.], the first historical experiment on a very large scale with this means of struggle. It is therefore evident that they are, for the most part, out-of-date. Their standpoint is essentially that of Engels who in 1873 wrote as follows in his criticism of the revolutionary blundering of the Bakuninist in Spain:

"The general strike, in the Bakuninists' program, is the lever which will be used for introducing the social revolution. One fine morning all the workers in every industry in a country, or perhaps in every country, will cease work, and thereby compel the ruling classes either to submit in about four weeks, or to launch an attack on the workers so that the latter will have the right to defend themselves, and may use the opportunity to overthrow the old society. The proposal is by no means new: French and Belgian socialists have paraded it continually since 1848, but for all that it is of English origin. During the rapid and powerful development of Chartism among the English workers that followed the crisis of 1837, the 'holy month' — a suspension of work on a national scale — was preached as early as 1839, and was received with such favor that in July 1842 the factory workers of the north of England attempted to carry it out. And at the Congress of the Alliancists at Geneva on September 1, 1873, the general strike played a great part, but it was admitted on all sides that to carry it out it was necessary to have a perfect organization of the working class and a full war chest. And that is the crux of the question. On the one hand, the governments, especially if they are encouraged by the workers' abstention from political action, will never allow the funds of the workers to become large enough, and on the other hand, political events and the encroachments of the ruling classes will bring about the liberation of the workers long before the proletariat gets the length of forming this ideal organization and this colossal reserve fund. But if they had these, they would not need to make use of the roundabout way of the general strike in order to attain their object."

Here we have the reasoning that was characteristic of the attitude of international social democracy towards the mass strike in the following decades. It is based on the anarchist theory of the general strike—that is, the theory of the general strike as a means of inaugurating the social revolution, in contradistinction to the daily political struggle of the working class—and exhausts itself in the following simple dilemma: either the proletariat as a whole are not yet in possession of the powerful organization and financial resources required, in which case they cannot carry through the general strike; or they are already sufficiently well organized, in which case they do not need the general strike. This reasoning is so simple and at first glance so irrefutable that, for a quarter of a century, it has rendered excellent service to the modern labor movement as a logical weapon against the anarchist phantom and as a means of carrying the idea of political struggle to the widest circles of the workers. The enormous strides taken by the labor movement in all capitalist countries during the last twenty-five years are the most convincing evidence of the value of the tactics of political struggle, which were insisted upon by Marx and Engels in opposition to Bakuninism; and German social democracy, in its position of vanguard of the entire international labor movement is not in the least the direct product of the consistent and energetic application of these tactics.

The Russian Revolution has now effected a radical revision of the above piece of reasoning. For the first time in the history of the class struggle it has achieved a grandiose realization of the idea of the mass strike and—as we shall discuss later—has even matured the general strike and thereby opened a new epoch in the development of the labor movement. It does not, of course, follow from this that the tactics of political struggle recommended by Marx and Engels were false or that the criticism applied by them to anarchism was incorrect. On the contrary, it is the same train of ideas, the same method, the Engels-Marxian tactics, which lay at the foundation of the previous practice of the German social democracy, which now in the Russian Revolution are producing new factors and new conditions in the class struggle. The Russian Revolution, which is the first historical experiment on the model of the mass strike, not merely does not afford a vindication of anarchism, but actually means *the historical liquidation of anarchism*. The sorry existence to which this mental tendency was condemned in recent decades by the powerful development of social democracy in Germany may, to a certain extent, be explained by the exclusive dominion and long duration of the parliamentary period. A tendency patterned entirely upon the "first blow" and "direct action," a tendency "revolutionary" in the most naked pitchfork sense, can only temporarily languish in the calm of the parliamentarian day and, on a return of the period of direct open struggle, can come to life again and unfold its inherent strength.

Russia, in particular, appeared to have become the experimental field for the heroic deeds of anarchism. A country in which the proletariat had absolutely no political rights and extremely weak organizations, a many-colored complex of various sections of the population, a chaos of conflicting interests, a low standard of education amongst the masses of the people, extreme brutality in the use of violence on the part of the prevailing regime—all this seemed as if created to raise anarchism to a sudden if perhaps short-lived power. And finally, Russia was the historical birthplace of anarchism. But the fatherland of Bakunin was to become the burial-place of its teachings. Not only did and do the anarchists in Russia not stand at the head of the mass strike movement; not only does the whole political leadership of revolutionary action and also of the mass strike lie in the hands of the social democratic organizations, which are bitterly opposed as "bourgeois parties" by the Russian anarchists, or partly in the hands of such socialist organizations as are more or less influenced by the social democracy and more or less approximate to it—such as the terrorist party, the "socialist revolutionaries"— but the anarchists simply do not exist as a serious political tendency in the Russian Revolution. Only in a small Lithuanian town with particularly difficult conditions—a confused medley of different nationalities among the workers, an extremely scattered condition of small-scale industry, a very severely oppressed proletariat—in Bialystok, there is, amongst the seven or eight different revolutionary groups a handful of half-grown "anarchists" who promote confusion and bewilderment amongst the workers to the best of their ability; and lastly in Moscow, and perhaps in two or three other towns, a handful of people of this kidney make themselves noticeable.

But apart from these few "revolutionary" groups, what is the

157

actual role of anarchism in the Russian Revolution? It has become the sign of the common thief and plunderer; a large proportion of the innumerable thefts and acts of plunder of private persons are carried out under the name of "anarchist-communism"—acts which rise up like a troubled wave against the revolution in every period of depression and in every period of temporary defensive. Anarchism has become in the Russian Revolution, not the theory of the struggling proletariat, but the ideological signboard of the counterrevolutionary lumpenproletariat, who, like a school of sharks, swarm in the wake of the battleship of the revolution. And therewith the historical career of anarchism is well-nigh ended.

On the other hand, the mass strike in Russia has been realized not as means of evading the political struggle of the working class, and especially of parliamentarism, not as a means of jumping suddenly into the social revolution by means of a theatrical coup, but as a means, firstly, of creating for the proletariat the conditions of the daily political struggle and especially of parliamentarism. The revolutionary struggle in Russia, in which mass strikes are the most important weapon, is, by the working people, and above all by the proletariat, conducted for those political rights and conditions whose necessity and importance in the struggle for the emancipation of the working class Marx and Engels first pointed out, and in opposition to anarchism fought for with all their might in the International. Thus has historical dialectics, the rock on which the whole teaching of Marxian socialism rests, brought it about that today anarchism, with which the idea of the mass strike is indissolubly associated, has itself come to be opposed to the mass strike in practice; while on the contrary, the mass strike which, as the opposite of the political activity of the proletariat, was combatted appears today as the most powerful weapon of the struggle for political rights. If, therefore, the Russian Revolution makes imperative a fundamental revision of the old standpoint of Marxism on the question of the mass strike, it is once again Marxism whose general methods and points of view have thereby, in a new form, carried off the prize. The Moor's beloved can die only by the hand of the Moor.

II. The Mass Strike, A Historical
and Not an Artificial Product

The first revision of the question of the mass strike which results from the experience of Russia relates to the general conception of the problem. Till the present time the zealous advocates of an "attempt with the mass strike" in Germany of the stamp of Bernstein, Eisner, etc., and also the strongest opponents of such an attempt as represented in the trade-union camp by, for example, Bomelburg, stand, when all is said and done, on the same conception, and that the anarchist one. The apparent polar opposites do not mutually exclude each other but, as always, condition, and at the same time, supplement each other. For the anarchist mode of thought is direct speculation on the "great *Kladderadatsch,*" on the social revolution merely as an external and inessential characteristic. According to it, what is essential is the whole abstract, unhistorical view of the mass strike and of all the conditions of the proletarian struggle generally.

For the anarchist there exist only two things as material suppositions of his "revolutionary" speculations—first imagination, and second goodwill and courage to rescue humanity from the existing capitalist vale of tears. This fanciful mode of reasoning sixty years ago gave the result that the mass strike was the shortest, surest and easiest means of springing into the better social future. The same mode of reasoning recently gave the result that the trade-union struggle was the only real "direct action of the masses" and also the only real revolutionary struggle—which, as is well known, is the latest notion of the French and Italian "syndicalists." The fatal thing for anarchism has always been that the methods of struggle improvised in the air were not only a reckoning without their host, that is, they were purely utopian, but that they, while not reckoning in the least with the despised evil reality, unexpectedly became in this evil reality, practical helps to the reaction, where previously they had only been, for the most part, revolutionary speculations.

On the same ground of abstract, unhistorical methods of observation stand those today who would, in the manner of a board of directors, put the mass strike in Germany on the calendar on an appointed day, and those who, like the participants in the trade-union congress at Cologne, would by a prohibition of "propaganda" eliminate the problem of the mass strike from the face of the earth. Both tendencies proceed on the common purely anarchistic assumption that the mass strike is a purely technical means of struggle which can be "decided" at pleasure and strictly according to conscience, or "forbidden"—a kind of pocketknife which can be kept in the pocket clasped "ready for any emergency," and according to decision, can be unclasped and used. The opponents of the mass strike do indeed claim for themselves the merit of taking into consideration the historical groundwork and the material conditions of the present situation in Germany in opposition to the "revolutionary romanticists" who hover in the air, and do not at any point reckon with the hard realities and the possibilities and impossibilities. "Facts and figures; figures and facts!" they cry, like Mr. Gadgrind in Dickens' *Hard Times.*

159

What the trade-union opponent of the mass strike understands by the "historical basis" and "material conditions" is two things — on the one hand the weakness of the proletariat, and on the other hand, the strength of Prussian-German militarism. The inadequate organization of the workers and the imposing Prussian bayonet — these are the facts and figures upon which these trade-union leaders base their practical policy in the given case. Now when it is quite true that the trade-union cash box and the Prussian bayonet are material and very historical phenomena, but the conception based upon them is not historical materialism in Marx's sense but a policemanlike materialism in the sense of Puttkammer. The representatives of the capitalist police state reckon much, and indeed, exclusively, with the occasional real power of the organized proletariat as well as with the material might of the bayonet, and from the comparative example of these two rows of figures the comforting conclusion is always drawn that the revolutionary labor movement is produced by individual demagogues and agitators; and that therefore there is in the prisons and bayonets an adequate means of subduing the unpleasant "passing phenomena."

The class-conscious German workers have at last grasped the humor of the policemanlike theory that the whole modern labor movement is an artificial, arbitrary product of a handful of conscienceless "demagogues and agitators."

It is exactly the same conception, however, that finds expression when two or three worthy comrades unite in a voluntary column of nightwatchmen in order to warn the German working class against the dangerous agitation of a few "revolutionary romanticists" and their "propaganda of the mass strike"; or, when, on the other side, a noisy indignation campaign is engineered by those who, by means of "confidential" agreements between the executive of the party and the general commission of the trade unions, believe they can prevent the outbreak of the mass strike in Germany.

If it depended on the inflammatory "propaganda" of revolutionary romanticists or on confidential or public decisions of the party direction, then we should not even yet have had in Russia a single serious mass strike. In no country in the world — as I pointed out in March 1905 in the *Sachische Arbeiterzeitung* — was the mass strike so little "propagated" or even "discussed" as in Russia. And the isolated examples of decisions and agreements of the Russian party executive which really sought to proclaim the mass strike of their own accord — as, for example, the last attempt in August of this year after the dissolution of the Duma — are almost valueless.

If, therefore, the Russian Revolution teaches us anything, it teaches above all that the mass strike is not artificially "made," not "decided" at random, not "propagated," but that it is a historical phenomenon which, at a given moment, results from social conditions with historical inevitability. It is not therefore by abstract speculations on the possibility or impossibility, the utility or the injuriousness of the mass strike, but only by an examination of those factors and social conditions out of which the mass strike grows in the present phase of the class struggle — in other words, it is not by *subjective criticism* of the mass strike from the standpoint of what is desirable, but only by *objective investigation* of the sources of the mass strike from the standpoint of what is historically inevitable, that the problem can be grasped or even discussed.

In the unreal sphere of abstract logical analysis it can be shown with exactly the same force on either side that the mass strike is absolutely impossible and sure to be defeated, and that it is possible and that its triumph cannot be questioned. And therefore the value of the evidence led on each side is exactly the same — and that is nil. Therefore the fear of the "propagation" of the mass strike, which has even led to formal anathemas against the persons alleged to be guilty of this crime, is solely the product of the droll confusion of persons. It is just as impossible to "propagate" the mass strike as an abstract means of struggle as it is to propagate the "revolution." "Revolution" like "mass strike" signifies nothing but an external form of the class struggle, which can have sense and meaning only in connection with definite political situations.

If anyone were to undertake to make the mass strike generally, as a form of proletarian action, the object of methodical agitation, and to go house-to-house canvassing with this "idea" in order to gradually win the working class to it, it would be as idle and profitless and absurd an occupation as it would be to seek to make the idea of the revolution or of the fight at the barricades the object of a special agitation. The mass strike has now become the center of the lively interest of the German and the international working class because it is a new form of struggle, and as such is the sure symptom of a thoroughgoing internal revolution in the relations of the classes and in the conditions of the class struggle. It is a testimony to the sound revolutionary instinct and to the quick intelligence of the mass of the German proletariat that, in spite of the obstinate resistance of their trade-union leaders, they are applying themselves to this new problem with such keen interest.

But it does not meet the case, in the presence of this interest and of this fine, intellectual thirst and desire for revolutionary deeds on the part of the workers, to treat them to abstract mental gymnastics on the possibility or impossibility of the mass strike; they should be enlightened on the development of the Russian

Revolution, the international significance of that revolution, the sharpening of class antagonisms in Western Europe, the wider political perspectives of the class struggle in Germany, and the role and the tasks of the masses in the coming struggles. Only in this form will the discussion on the mass strike lead to the widening of the intellectual horizon of the proletariat, to the sharpening of their way of thinking, and to the steeling of their energy.

Viewed from this standpoint however, the criminal proceedings desired by the enemies of "revolutionary romanticism" appear in all their absurdity, because, in treating of the problem, one does not adhere strictly to the text of the Jena resolution. The "practical politicians" agree to this resolution if need be, because they couple the mass strike chiefly with the fate of universal suffrage, from which it follows that they can believe two things—first, that the mass strike is of a purely defensive character, and second, that the mass strike is even subordinate to parliamentarism, that is, has been turned into a mere appendage of parliamentarism. But the real kernel of the Jena resolution in this connection is that in the present position of Germany an attempt on the part of the prevailing reaction on the parliamentary vote would in all probability be the moment for the introduction of, and the signal for, a period of stormy political struggles in which the mass strike as a means of struggle in Germany might well come into use for the first time.

But to seek to narrow and to artificially smother the social importance, and to limit the historical scope, of the mass strike as a phenomenon and as a problem of the class struggle by the wording of a congress resolution is an undertaking which for shortsightedness can only be compared with the veto on discussion of the trade-union congress at Cologne. In the resolution of the Jena Congress German social democracy has officially taken notice of the fundamental change which the Russian Revolution has effected in the international conditions of the proletarian class struggle, and has announced its capacity for revolutionary development and its power of adaptability to the new demands of the coming phase of the class struggle. Therein lies the significance of the Jena resolution. As for the practical application of the mass strike in Germany, history will decide that as it decided it in Russia—history in which German social democracy with its decisions is, it is true, an important factor, but, at the same time, only *one* factor amongst many.

III. Development of the Mass Strike
Movement in Russia

The mass strike, as it appears for the most part in the discussion in Germany, is a very clear and simply thought out, sharply sketched, isolated phenomenon. It is the political mass strike exclusively that is spoken of. What is meant by it is a single grand rising of the industrial proletariat springing from some political motive of the highest importance, and undertaken on the basis of an opportune and mutual understanding on the part of the controlling authorities of the party and of the trade unions, and carried through in the spirit of party discipline and in perfect order, and in still more perfect order brought to the directing committees as a signal given at the proper time, by which committees the regulation of support, the cost, the sacrifice—in a word, the whole material balance of the mass strike—is exactly determined in advance.

Now, when we compare this theoretical scheme with the real mass strike, as it appeared in Russia five years ago, we are compelled to say that this representation, which in the German discussion occupies the central position, hardly corresponds to a single one of the many mass strikes that have taken place, and on the other hand that the mass strike in Russia displays such a multiplicity of the most varied forms of action that it is altogether impossible to speak of "the" mass strike, of an abstract schematic mass strike. All the factors of the mass strike, as well as its character, are not only different in the different towns and districts of the country, but its general character has often changed in the course of the revolution. The mass strike has passed through a definite history in Russia, and is passing still further through it. Who, therefore, speaks of the mass strike in Russia must, above all things, keep its history before his eyes.

The present official period, so to speak, of the Russian Revolution is justly dated from the rising of the proletariat on January 22, 1905, when the demonstration of 200,000 workers ended in a frightful bloodbath before the czar's palace. The bloody massacre in St. Petersburg was, as is well known, the signal for the outbreak of the first gigantic series of mass strikes which spread over the whole of Russia within a few days and which carried the call to action of the revolution from St. Petersburg to every corner of the empire and amongst the widest sections of the proletariat. But the St. Petersburg rising of January 22 was only the critical moment of a mass strike which the proletariat of the czarist capital had previously entered upon in January 1905. This January mass strike was without doubt carried through under the immediate influence of the gigantic general strike which in December 1904 broke out in the Caucasus, in Baku, and for a long time kept the whole of Russia in suspense. The events of December in Baku were on their part only the last and powerful ramification of those tremendous mass strikes which, like a periodic earthquake, shook the whole of south Russia, and

163

whose prologue was the mass strike in Batum in the Caucasus in March 1902.

This first mass strike movement in the continuous series of present revolutionary eruptions is finally separated by five or six years from the great general strike of the textile workers in St. Petersburg in 1896 and 1897, and if this movement is apparently separated from the present revolution by a few years of apparent stagnation and strong reaction, everyone who knows the inner political development of the Russian proletariat to their present stage of class consciousness and revolutionary energy will realize that the history of the present period of the mass struggles begins with those general strikes in St. Petersburg. They are therefore important for the problems of the mass strike because they already contain, in the germ, all the principal factors of later mass strikes.

Again, the St. Petersburg general strike of 1896 appears as a purely economic partial wage struggle. Its causes were the intolerable working conditions of the spinners and weavers in St. Petersburg; a working day of thirteen, fourteen or fifteen hours, miserable piecework rates, and a whole series of contemptible chicaneries on the part of the employers. This condition of things, however, was patiently endured by the workers for a long time till an apparently trivial circumstance filled the cup to overflowing. The coronation of the present czar, Nicholas II, which had been postponed for two years through fear of the revolutionaries, was celebrated in May 1896, and on that occasion the St. Petersburg employers displayed their patriotic zeal by giving their workers three days compulsory holidays, for which, curious to relate, they did not desire to pay their employees. The workers angered at this began to move. After a conference of about three hundred of the intelligent workers in the Ekaterinhof Garden a strike was decided upon, and the following demands were formulated: first, payment of wages for the coronation holidays, second, a working day of ten hours; third, increased rates for piecework. This happened on May 24. In a week every weaving and spinning establishment was at a standstill, and 40,000 workers were in the general strike. Today this event, measured by the gigantic mass strike of the revolution, may appear a little thing. In the political polar rigidity of the Russia of that time a general strike was something unheard of; it was even a complete revolution in little. There began, of course, the most brutal persecution. About one thousand workers were arrested and the general strike was suppressed.

Here already we see all the fundamental characteristics of the later mass strikes. The next occasion of the movement was wholly accidental, even unimportant, its outbreak elementary; but in the success of the movement the fruits of the agitation, extending over several years, of the social democracy, were seen and in the course of the general strike the social democratic agitators stood at the head of the movement, directed it, and used it to stir up revolutionary agitation. Further the strike was outwardly a mere economic struggle for wages, but the attitude of the government and the agitation of the social democracy made it a political phenomenon of the first rank. And lastly, the strike was suppressed; the workers suffered a "defeat." But in January of the following year the textile workers of St. Petersburg repeated the general strike once more and achieved this time a remarkable success: the legal introduction of a working day of eleven hours throughout the whole of Russia. What was nevertheless a much more important result was this: since that first general strike of 1896 which was entered upon without a trace of organization or of strike funds, an intensive trade-union fight began in Russia proper which spread from St. Petersburg to the other parts of the country and opened up entirely new vistas to social democratic agitation and organization, and by which in the apparently deathlike peace of the following period the revolution was prepared by underground work.

The outbreak of the Caucasian strike in March 1902 was apparently as accidental and as much due to purely economic partial causes (although produced by quite other factors) as that of 1896. It was connected with the serious industrial and commercial crisis which in Russia was the precursor of the Japanese war and which, together with it, was the most powerful factor of the nascent revolutionary ferment. The crisis produced an enormous mass of unemployment which nourished the agitation amongst the proletarian masses, and therefore the government, to restore tranquility amongst the workers, undertook to transport the "superfluous hands" in batches to their respective home districts. One such measure, which was to affect about four hundred petroleum workers called forth a mass protest in Batum, which led to demonstrations, arrests, a massacre, and finally to a political trial in which the purely economic and partial affair suddenly became a political and revolutionary event. The reverberation of the wholly "fruitless" expiring and suppressed strike in Batum was a series of revolutionary mass demonstrations of workers in Nizhni Novgorod, Saratov and other towns, and therefore a mighty surge forward of the general wave of the revolutionary movement.

Already in November 1902 the first genuine revolutionary echo followed in the shape of a general strike at Rostov-on-Don. Disputes about the rates of pay in the workshops of the Vladicaucasus Railway gave the impetus to this movement. The man-

agement sought to reduce wages and therefore the Don committee of the social democracy issued a proclamation with a summons to strike for the following demands: a nine-hour day, increase of wages, abolition of fines, dismissal of obnoxious engineers, etc. Entire railway workshops participated in the strike.
Presently all other industries joined in and suddenly an unprecedented state of affairs prevailed in Rostov: every industrial work
was at a standstill, and every day monster meetings of fifteen
to twenty thousand were held in the open air, sometimes surrounded by a cordon of Cossacks, at which for the first time
social democratic popular speakers appeared publicly, inflammatory speeches on socialism and political freedom were delivered
and received with immense enthusiasm, and revolutionary appeals were distributed by tens of thousands of copies. In the
midst of rigid absolutist Russia the proletariat of Rostov won for
the first time the right of assembly and freedom of speech by
storm. It goes without saying that there was a massacre here.
The disputes over wages in the Vladicaucasus Railway workshops grew in a few days into a political general strike and a
revolutionary street battle. As an echo to this there followed immediately a general strike at the station of Tichoretzkaia on the
same railway. Here also a massacre took place and also a trial,
and thus even Tichoretzkaia has taken its place in the indissoluble chain of the factors of the revolution.

The spring of 1903 gave the answer to the defeated strikes
in Rostov and Tichoretzkaia; the whole of South Russia in May,
June and July was aflame. Baku, Tiflis, Batum, Elisavetgrad,
Odessa, Kiev, Nikolaev and Ekaterinoslav were in a general
strike in the literal meaning of those words. But here again the
movement did not arise on any preconceived plan from one another; it flowed together from individual points in each one from
different causes and in a different form. The beginning was made
by Baku where several partial wage struggles in individual factories and departments culminated in a general strike. In Tiflis
the strike was begun by 2000 commercial employees who had
a working day from six o'clock in the morning to eleven at
night. On the fourth of July they all left their shops and made
a circuit of the town to demand from the proprietors of the shops
that they close their premises. The victory was complete; the commercial employees won a working day from eight in the morning to eight in the evening, and they were immediately joined
by all the factories, workshops and offices, etc. The newspapers
did not appear, and tramway traffic could not be carried on under military protection.

In Elisavetgrad on July 4 a strike began in all the factories
with purely economic demands. These were mostly conceded, and

the strike ended on the fourteenth. Two weeks later however it broke out again. The bakers this time gave the word and they were joined by the bricklayers, the joiners, the dyers, the mill workers, and finally all factory workers.

In Odessa the movement began with a wage struggle in the course of which the "legal" workers' union, founded by government agents according to the program of the famous gendarme Zubatov, was developed. Historical dialectics had again seized the occasion to play one of its malicious little pranks. The economic struggles of the earlier period (amongst them the great St. Petersburg general strike of 1896) had misled Russian social democracy into exaggerating the importance of so-called economics, and in this way the ground had been prepared amongst the workers for the demagogic activities of Zubatov. After a time, however, the great revolutionary stream turned round the little ship with the false flag, and compelled it to ride right at the head of the revolutionary proletarian flotilla. The Zubatovian unions gave the signal for the great general strike in Odessa in the spring of 1904, as for the general strike in St. Petersburg in January 1905. The workers in Odessa, who were not to be deceived by the appearance of friendliness on the part of the government for the workers, and of its sympathy with purely economic strikes, suddenly demanded proof by example, and compelled the Zubatovian "workers union" in a factory to declare a strike for very moderate demands. They were immediately thrown on the streets, and when they demanded the protection of the authorities which was promised them by their leader, the gentleman vanished and left the workers in the wildest excitement.

The social democrats at once placed themselves at the head of affairs, and the strike movement extended to other factories. On the first of July 2500 dockers struck work for an increase of wages from eighty kopeks to two roubles, and the shortening of the working day by half an hour. On the sixteenth of July the seamen joined the movement. On the thirteenth the tramway staff began a strike. Then a meeting took place of all the strikers, seven or eight thousand men; they formed a procession which went from factory to factory, growing like an avalanche, and presently a crowd of forty to fifty thousand betook themselves to the docks in order to bring all work there to a standstill. A general strike soon reigned throughout the whole city.

In Kiev a strike began in the railway workshops on July 21. Here also the immediate cause was miserable conditions of labor, and wage demands were presented. On the following day the foundry men followed the example. On July 23 an incident occurred which gave the signal for the general strike. During the night two delegates of the railwaymen were arrested. The strik-

167

ers immediately demanded their release, and as this was not conceded, they decided not to allow trains to leave the town. At the station all the strikers with their wives and families sat down on the railway track — a sea of human beings. They were threatened with rifle salvoes. The workers bared their breasts and cried "Shoot"! A salvo was fired into the defenseless seated crowd, and thirty to forty corpses, amongst them those of women and children, remained on the ground. On this becoming known the whole town of Kiev went on strike on the same day. The corpses of the murdered workers were raised on high by the crowd and carried round in a mass demonstration. Meetings, speeches, arrests, isolated street fights — Kiev was in the midst of the revolution. The movement was soon at an end. But the printers had won a shortening of the working day by one hour and a wage increase of one rouble; in a yeast factory the eight-hour day was introduced; the railway workshops were closed by order of the ministry; other departments continued partial strikes for their demands.

In Nikolaev the general strike broke out under the immediate influence of the news from Odessa, Baku, Batum and Tiflis, in spite of the opposition of the social democratic committee who wanted to postpone the outbreak of the movement till the time came when the military should have left the town for maneuvers. The masses refused to hold back; one factory made a beginning, the strikes went from one workshop to another, the resistance of the military only poured oil on the fire. Mass processions with revolutionary songs were formed which were taken part in by all workers, employees, tramways officials, men and women. The cessation of work was complete. In Ekaterinoslav the bakers came out on strike on August 5, on the seventh the men in the railway workshops, and then all the other factories on August 8. Tramway traffic stopped, and the newspapers did not appear.

Thus the colossal general strike in south Russia came into being in the summer of 1903. By many small channels of partial economic struggles and little "accidental" occurrences it flowed rapidly to a raging sea, and changed the entire south of the czarist empire for some weeks into a bizarre revolutionary workers' republic. "Brotherly embraces, cries of delight and of enthusiasm, songs of freedom, merry laughter, humor and joy were seen and heard in the crowd of many thousands of persons which surged through the town from morning till evening. The mood was exalted; one could almost believe that a new, better life was beginning on the earth. A most solemn and at the same time an idyllic, moving spectacle." . . . .So wrote at the time the correspondent of the Liberal *Osvoboshdenye* of Peter Struve.

The year 1904 brought with it war, and for a time, an interval of quiet in the mass strike movement. At first a troubled wave of "patriotic" demonstrations arranged by the police authorities spread over the country. The "liberal" bourgeois society was for the time being struck to the ground by the czarist official chauvinism. But soon the social democrats took possession of the arena; revolutionary workers' demonstrations were opposed to the demonstrations of the patriotic lumpenproletariat which were organized under police patronage. At last the shameful defeats of the czarist army woke the liberal society from its lethargy; then began the era of democratic congresses, banquets, speeches, addresses and manifestos. Absolutism, temporarily suppressed through the disgrace of the war, gave full scope to these gentlemen, and by and by they saw everything in rosy colors. For six months bourgeois liberalism occupied the center of the stage, and the proletariat remained in the shadows. But after a long depression absolutism again roused itself, the camarilla gathered all its strength and by a single powerful movement of the Cossack's heel the whole liberal movement was driven into a corner. Banquets, speeches and congresses were prohibited out of hand as "intolerable presumption," and liberalism suddenly found itself at the end of its tether.

But exactly at the point where liberalism was exhausted, the action of the proletariat began. In December 1904 the great general strike, due to unemployment, broke out in Baku; the working class was again on the field of battle. As speech was forbidden and rendered impossible, action began. In Baku for some weeks in the midst of the general strike the social democrats ruled as absolute masters of the situation; and the peculiar events of December in the Caucasus would have caused an immense sensation if they had not been so quickly put in the shade by the rising tide of the revolution which they had themselves set in motion. The fantastic confused news of the general strike in Baku had not reached all parts of the czarist empire when in January 1905 the mass strike in St. Petersburg broke out.

Here also as is well known, the immediate cause was trivial. Two men employed at the Putilov works were discharged on account of their membership in the legal Zubatovian union. This measure called forth a solidarity strike on January 16 of the whole of the 12,000 employees in this works. The social democrats seized the occasion of the strike to begin a lively agitation for the extension of the demands and set forth demands for the eight-hour day, the right of combination, freedom of speech and of the press, etc. The unrest among the Putilov workers communicated itself quickly to the remainder of the proletariat, and in a few days 140,000 workers were on strike. Joint conferences and stormy discussions led to the working out of that proletarian charter of bourgeois freedom with the eight-hour day at its head with which, on January 22, 200,000 workers, led by Father Gapon, marched to the czar's palace. The conflict of the two Putilov workers who had been subjected to disciplinary punishment had changed within a week into the prologue of the most violent revolution of modern times.

The events that followed upon this are well known; the bloodbath in St. Petersburg called forth gigantic mass strikes and general strike in the month of January and February in all the industrial centers and towns in Russia, Poland, Lithuania, the Baltic Provinces, the Caucasus, Siberia, from north to south and east to west. On closer inspection, however, it can be seen that the mass strike was appearing in other forms than those of the previous period. Everywhere at that time the social democratic organizations went before with appeals; everywhere was revolutionary solidarity with the St. Petersburg proletariat expressly stated as the cause and aim of the general strike; everywhere, at the same time, there were demonstrations, speeches, conflicts with the military.

But even here there was no predetermined plan, no organized action, because the appeals of the parties could scarcely keep pace with the spontaneous risings of the masses; the leaders had scarcely time to formulate the watchwords of the onrushing crowd of the proletariat. Further, the earlier mass and general strikes had originated from individual coalescing wage struggles which, in the general temper of the revolutionary situation and under the influence of the social democratic agitation, rapidly became political demonstrations; the economic factor and the scattered condition of trade unionism were the starting point; all-embracing class action and political direction the result. The movement was now reversed.

The general strikes of January and February broke out as unified revolutionary actions to begin with under the direction of the social democrats; but this action soon fell into an unending series of local partial, economic strikes in separate districts, towns, departments and factories. Throughout the whole of the spring of 1905 and into the middle of the summer there fermented throughout the whole of the immense empire an uninterrupted economic strike of almost the entire proletariat against capital — a struggle which caught on the one hand, all the petty bourgeois and liberal professions, commercial employees, technicians, actors and members of artistic professions — and on the other hand, penetrated to the domestic servants, the minor police officials and even to the stratum of the lumpenproletariat, and simultaneously surged from the towns to the country districts and even knocked at the iron gates of the military barracks.

170

This is a gigantic, many-colored picture of a general arrangement of labor and capital which reflects all the complexity of social organization and of the political consciousness of every section and of every district; and the whole long scale runs from the regular trade-union struggle of a picked and tested troop of the proletariat drawn from large-scale industry, to the formless protest of a handful of rural proletarians, and to the first slight stirrings of an agitated military garrison, from the well-educated and elegant revolt in cuffs and white collars in the counting house of a bank to the shy-bold murmurings of a clumsy meeting of dissatisfied policemen in a smoke-grimed dark and dirty guardroom.

According to the theory of the lovers of "orderly and well-disciplined" struggles, according to plan and scheme, according to those especially who always ought to know better from afar "how it should have been done," the decay of the great political general strike of January 1905 into a number of economic struggles was probably "a great mistake" which crippled that action and changed it into a "straw fire." But social democracy in Russia, which had taken part in the revolution but had not "made" it, and which had even to learn its law from its course itself, was at the first glance put out of countenance for a time by the apparently fruitless ebb of the storm-flood of the general strike. History, however, which had made that "great mistake," thereby accomplished, heedless of the reasonings of its officious schoolmaster, a gigantic work for the revolution which was as inevitable as it was, in its consequences, incalculable.

The sudden general rising of the proletariat in January under the powerful impetus of the St. Petersburg events was outwardly a political act of the revolutionary declaration of war on absolutism. But this first general direct action reacted inwardly all the more powerfully as it for the first time awoke class feeling and class consciousness in millions upon millions as if by an electric shock. And this awakening of class feeling expressed itself forthwith in the circumstances that the proletarian mass, counted by millions, quite suddenly and sharply came to realize how intolerable was that social and economic existence which they had patiently endured for decades in the chains of capitalism. Thereupon there began a spontaneous general shaking of and tugging at these chains. All the innumerable sufferings of the modern proletariat reminded them of the old bleeding wounds. Here was the eight-hour day fought for, there piecework was resisted, here were brutal foremen "driven off" in a sack on a handcar, at another place infamous systems of fines were fought against, everywhere better wages were striven for and here and there the abolition of homework. Backward degraded occupations in large towns, small provincial towns, which

171

had hitherto dreamed in an idyllic sleep, the village with its legacy from feudalism — all these, suddenly awakened by the January lightning, bethought themselves of their rights and now sought feverishly to make up for their previous neglect.

The economic struggle was not here really a decay, a dissipation of action, but merely change of front, a sudden and natural alteration of the first general engagement with absolutism, in a general reckoning with capital, which in keeping with its character, assumed the form of individual, scattered wage struggles. Not political class action was broken in January by the decay of the general strike into economic strikes, but the reverse; after the possible content of political action in the given situation and at the given stage of the revolution was exhausted, it broke, or rather changed, into economic action.

In point of fact, what more could the general strike in January have achieved? Only complete thoughtlessness could expect that absolutism could be destroyed at one blow by a single "long-drawn" general strike after the anarchist plan. Absolutism in Russia must be overthrown by the proletariat. But in order to be able to overthrow it, the proletariat requires a high degree of political education, of class consciousness and organization. All these conditions cannot be fulfilled by pamphlets and leaflets, but only by the living political school, by the fight and in the fight, in the continuous course of the revolution. Further, absolutism cannot be overthrown at any desired moment in which only adequate "exertion" and "endurance" are necessary. The fall of absolutism is merely the outer expression of the inner social and class development of Russian society.

Before absolutism can, and so that it may, be overthrown, the bourgeois Russia in its interior, in its modern class divisions, must be formed. That requires the drawing together of the various social layers and interests, besides the education of the proletarian revolutionary parties, and not less of the liberal, radical petty bourgeois, conservative and reactionary parties; it requires self-consciousness, self-knowledge and the class consciousness not merely of the layers of the people, but also of the layers of the bourgeoisie. But this also can be achieved and come to fruition in no way but in the struggle, in the process of the revolution itself, through the actual school of experience, in collision with the proletariat as well as with one another, in incessant mutual friction. This class division and class maturity of bourgeois society, as well as its action in the struggle against absolutism, is on the one hand, hampered and made difficult by the peculiar leading role of the proletariat and, on the other hand, is spurred on and accelerated. The various undercurrents of the social process of the revolution cross one another, check

172

one another, and increase the internal contradictions of the revolution, but in the end accelerate and thereby render still more violent its eruptions.

This apparently simple and purely mechanical problem may therefore be stated thus; the overthrow of absolutism is a long continuous social process, and its solution demands a complete undermining of the soil of society; the uppermost part be placed lowest and the lowermost part highest, the apparent "order" must be changed to a chaos, and the apparently "anarchistic" chaos must be changed into a new order. Now in this process of the social transformation of the old Russia, not only the January lightning of the first general strike, but also the spring and summer thunderstorms that followed it, played an indispensable part. The embittered general relations of wage labor and capital contributed in equal measure to the drawing together of the various layers of the people and those of the bourgeoisie, to the class consciousness of the revolutionary proletariat and to that of the liberal and conservative bourgeoisie. And just as the urban wage struggle contributed to the formation of a strong monarchist industrial party in Moscow, so the conflagration of the violent rural rising in Livonia led to the rapid liquidation of the famous aristocratic-agrarian zemstvo liberalism.

But at the same time, the period of the ecomonic struggles of the spring and summer of 1905 made it possible for the urban proletariat, by means of active social democratic agitation and direction, to assimilate later all the lessons of the January prologue and to grasp clearly all the further tasks of the revolution. There was connected with this too, another circumstance of an enduring social character: *a general raising of the standard of life of the proletariat,* economic, social and intellectual.

The January strikes of 1905 ended victoriously almost throughout. As proof of this some data from the enormous, and still for the most part, inaccessible mass of material may be cited here relating to a few of the most important strikes carried through in Warsaw alone by the social democrats of Poland and Lithuania. In the great factories of the metal industry of Warsaw: Lilpop, Ltd.; Ran and Lowenstein; Rudzki and Co.; Borman, Schwede and Co.; Handtke, Gerlach and Pulst; Geisler Bros.; Eberherd, Wolski and Co.; Konrad and Yarnuszkiewicz Ltd.; Weber and Daehu; Ewizdzinski and Co.; Wolonski Wire Works; Gostynski and Co., Ltd; Rrun and Son; Frage Norblin; Werner; Buch; Kenneberg Bros.; Labor; Dittunar Lamp Factory; Serkowski; Weszk — twenty-two factories in all, the workers won after a strike of four to five weeks (from January 25-26) a nine-hour day, a 25 percent increase of wages and obtained various smaller concessions. In the large workshops of the timber industry of

Warsaw, namely Karmanski, Damieki, Gromel, Szerbinskik, Twemerowski, Horn, Devensee, Tworkowski, Daab and Martens—twelve workshops in all—the strikes had won by the twenty-third of February the nine-hour day; they were not satisfied with this, but insisted upon the eight-hour day, which they also won, together with an increase of wages, after a further strike of a week.

The entire bricklaying industry began a strike on February 27 and demanded, in conformity with the watchword of social democracy, the eight-hour day; they won the ten-hour day on March 11 together with an increase of wages for all categories, regular payment of wages weekly, etc. The painters, the cartwrights, the saddlers and the smiths all won the eight-hour day without decrease of wages.

The telephone workshops struck for ten days and won the eight-hour day and an increase of wages of 10 to 15 percent. The large linen-weaving establishment of Hielle and Dietrich (10,000 workers) after a strike lasting nine weeks, obtained a decrease of the working day by one hour and a wage increase of 5 to 10 percent. And similar results in endless variation were to be seen in the older branches of industry in Warsaw, Lodz, and Sosnovitz.

In Russia proper the eight-hour day was won in December 1904 by a few categories of oil workers in Baku; in May 1905 by the sugar workers of the Kiev district; in January 1905 in all the printing works in Samara (where at the same time an increase of piecework rates was obtained and fines were abolished); in February in the factory in which medical instruments for the army are manufactured, in a furniture factory and in the cartridge factory in St. Petersburg. Further the eight-hour day was introduced in the mines at Vladivostock, in March in the government mechanical workshops dealing with government stock, and in May among the employees of the Tiflis electric town railway. In the same month a working day of eight and a half hours was introduced in the large cotton-weaving factory of Morosov (and at the same time the abolition of night work and a wage increase of 8 percent were won); in June an eight-hour day in a few oil works in St. Petersburg and Moscow; in July a working day of eight and a half hours among the smiths at the St. Petersburg docks; and in November in all the private printing establishments of the town of Orel (and at the same time an increase of time rates of 20 percent and piecework rates of 100 percent, as well as the setting up of a conciliation board on which workers and employer were equally represented).

The nine-hour day in all the railway workshops (in February), in many government, military and naval workshops, in most of the factories of the town of Berdiansk, in all the printing works of the towns of Poltava and Musk; nine and a half hours in the shipyards, mechanical workshops and foundries in the town of Nikolaev, in June, after a general strike of waiters in Warsaw, in many restaurants and cafes (and at the same time a wage increase of 20 to 40 percent, with a two-week holiday in the year).

The ten-hour day in almost all the factories of the towns of Lodz, Sosnovitz, Riga, Kovno, Oval, Dorfat, Minsk, Kharkov, in the bakeries of Odessa, among the mechanics in Kishinev, at a few smelting works in St. Petersburg, in the match factories of Kovno (with an increase of wages of 10 percent), in all the government marine workshops, and amongst all the dockers.

The wage increases were in general smaller than the shortening of hours but always more significant: in Warsaw in the middle of March 1905 a general increase of wages of 15 percent was fixed by the municipal factories department; in the center of the textile industry, Ivanovo Vosnesensk, the wage increase amounted to 7 to 15 percent, in Kovno the increase affected 73 percent of the workers. A fixed minimum wage was introduced in some of the bakeries in Odessa, in the Neva shipbuilding yards in St. Petersburg, etc.

It goes without saying that these concessions were withdrawn again, now here and now there. This however was only the cause of renewed strife and led to still more bitter struggles for revenge, and thus the strike period of the spring of 1905 has of itself become the prologue to an endless series of everspreading and interlacing economic struggles which have lasted to the present day. In the period of the outward stagnation of the revolution, when the telegraph carried no sensational news from the Russian theater of war to the outside world, and when the West European laid aside his newspaper in disappointment with the remark that there "was nothing doing" in Russia, the great underground work of the revolution was in reality being carried on without cessation, day by day and hour by hour, in the very heart of the empire. The incessant intensive economic struggle effected, by rapid and abbreviated methods, the transition of capitalism from the stage of primitive accumulation, of patriarchal unmethodical methods of working, to a highly modern, civilized one.

At the present time the actual working day in Russian industry leaves behind, not only Russian factory legislation (that is the legal working day of eleven hours) but even the actual conditions of Germany. In most departments of large-scale industry in Russia the ten-hour day prevails, which in Germany is declared in social legislation to be an unattainable goal. And what is more, that longed-for "industrial constitutionalism," for which there is so much enthusiasm in Germany, and for the sake of which the advocates of opportunist tactics would keep every keen wind from the stagnant waters of their all-suffering parliamentarism, has already been born, together with political "constitutionalism," in the midst of the revolutionary storm, from the revolution itself! In actual fact it is not merely a general raising of the standard of life, or of the cultural level of the working class that has taken place. The material standard of life as a permanent stage of well-being has no place in the revolution. Full of contradictions and contrasts it brings simultaneously surprising economic victories, and the most brutal acts of revenge on the part of the capitalists; today the eight-hour day, and tomorrow wholesale lockouts and actual starvation for the million.

The most precious, because lasting, thing in this rapid ebb and flow of the wave is its mental sediment: the intellectual, cultural growth of the proletariat, which proceeds by fits and starts, and which offers an inviolable guarantee of their further irresistible progress in the economic as in the political struggle. And not only that. Even the relations of the worker to the employer are turned round; since the January general strike and the strikes of 1905 which followed upon it, the principle of the capitalist "mastery of the house" is de facto abolished. In the larger factories of all important industrial centers the establishment of workers' committees has, as if by itself, taken place, with which alone the employer negotiates and which décide all disputes.

And finally another thing, the apparently "chaotic" strikes and the "disorganized" revolutionary action after the January general strike are becoming the starting point of a feverish *work of organization.* Dame History, from afar, smilingly hoaxes the bureaucratic lay figures who keep grim watch at the gate over the fate of the German trade unions. The firm organizations which, as the indispensable hypothesis for an eventual German mass strike, should be fortified like an impregnable citadel—these organizations are in Russia, on the contrary, already born from the mass strike. And while the guardians of the German trade unions for the most part fear that the organizations will fall in pieces in a revolutionary whirlwind like rare porcelain, the Russian revolution shows us the exactly opposite picture; from the whirlwind and the storm, out of the fire and glow of the mass strike and the street fighting rise again, like Venus from the foam, fresh, young, powerful, buoyant trade unions.

Here again a little example, which, however, is typical of the whole empire. At the second conference of the Russian trade unions which took place at the end of February 1906 in St. Petersburg, the representative of the Petersburg trade unions, in his report on the development of trade-union organizations of the czarist capital said:

"January 22, 1905, which washed away the Gapon union, was

a turning point. The workers in large numbers have learned by experience to appreciate and understand the importance of organization, and that only they themselves can create these organizations. The first trade union—that of the printers—originated in direct connection with the January movement. The commission appointed to work out the tariffs framed the statutes, and on July 19 the union began its existence. Just about this time the union of office-workers and bookkeepers was called into existence.

"In addition to those organizations, which existed almost openly, there arose from January to October 1905 semilegal and illegal trade unions. To the former belonged, for example, the union of chemists' assistants and commercial employees. Amongst the illegal unions special attention must be drawn to the watchmakers' union, whose first secret session was held on April 24. All attempts to convene a general open meeting were shattered on the obstinate resistance of the police and the employers in the form of the Chamber of Commerce. This mischance has not prevented the existence of the union. It held secret meetings of members on June 9 and August 14, apart from the sessions of the executive of the union. The tailors and tailoresses union was founded in 1905 at a meeting in a wood at which seventy tailors were present. After the question of forming the union was discussed a commission was appointed which was entrusted with the task of working out the statutes. All attempts of the commission to obtain a legal existence for the union were unsuccessful. Its activities were confined to agitation and the enrolling of new members in the individual workshops. A similar fate was in store for the shoemakers' union. In July a secret night meeting was convened in a wood near the city. Over 100 shoemakers attended; a report was read on the importance of trade unionism, on its history in Western Europe and its tasks in Russia. It was then decided to form a trade union; a commission of twelve was appointed to work out the statutes and call a general meeting of shoemakers. The statutes were drawn up, but in the meantime it had not been found possible to print them nor had the general meeting been convened."

These were the first difficult beginnings. Then came the October days, the second general strike, the czar's manifesto of October 30 and the brief "constitution period." The workers threw themselves with fiery zeal into the waves of political freedom in order to use it forthwith for the purpose of the work of organization. Besides daily political meetings, debates and the formation of clubs, the development of trade unionism was immediately taken in hand. In October and November *forty* new trade unions appeared in St. Petersburg. Presently a "central bureau," that is, a trade-union council, was established, various trade-union papers

177

appeared, and since November a central organ has also been published, *The Trade Union.*

What was reported above concerning Petersburg was also true on the whole of Moscow and Odessa, Kiev and Nikolaev, Saratov and Voronezh, Samara and Nizhni Novgorod, and all the larger towns of Russia, and in still higher degree of Poland. The trade unions of different towns seek contact with one another and conferences are held. The end of the "constitution period," and the return to reaction in December 1905 put a stop for the time being to the open widespread activity of the trade unions, but did not, however, altogether extinguish them. They operate as organizations in secret and occasionally carry on quite open wage struggles. A peculiar mixture of the legal and illegal condition of trade-union life is being built up, corresponding to the highly contradictory revolutionary situation.

But in the midst of the struggle the work of organization is being more widely extended, in a thoroughgoing, not to say pedantic fashion. The trade unions of the social democracy of Poland and Lithuania, for example, which at the last congress (in July 1906) were represented by five delegates from a membership of 10,000 are furnished with the usual statutes, printed membership cards, adhesive stamps, etc. And the same bakers and shoemakers, engineers and printers of Warsaw and Lodz who in June 1905 stood on the barricades and in December only awaited the word from Petersburg to begin street fighting, find time and are eager, between one mass strike and another, between prison and lockout, and under the conditions of a siege, to go into their trade-union statutes and discuss them earnestly. These barricade fighters of yesterday and tomorrow have indeed more than once at meetings severely reprimanded their leaders and threatened them with withdrawal from the party because the unlucky trade-union membership cards could not be printed quickly enough — in secret printing works under incessant police persecution. This zeal and this earnestness continue to this day. For example, in the first two weeks of July 1906 fifteen new trade unions appeared in Ekaterinoslav, six in Kostroma, several in Kiev, Poltava, Smolensk, Cherkassy, Proskurvo, down to the most insignificant provincial towns.

In the session of the Moscow trade-union council of June 4 this year, after the acceptance of the reports of individual trade-union delegates, it was decided "that the trade unions should discipline their members and restrain from street rioting because the time is not considered opportune for the mass strike. In the face of possible provocation on the part of the government, care should be taken that the masses do not stream out in the streets." Finally, the council decided that if at any time one trade union began a strike the others should hold back from any wages movement. Most of the economic struggles are now directed by the trade unions.

Thus the great economic struggle which proceeded from the January general strike, and which has not ceased to the present day, has formed a broad background of the revolution from which, in ceaseless reciprocal action with the political agitation and the external events of the revolution, there ever arise here and there now isolated explosions, and now great general actions of the proletariat. Thus there flame up against this background the following events one after the other; at the May Day demonstration there was an unprecedented, absolute general strike in Warsaw which ended in a bloodly encounter between the defenseless crowd and the soldiers. At Lodz in June a mass outing, which was scattered by the soldiers, led to a demonstration of 100,000 workers at the funeral of some of the victims of the brutal soldiery and to a renewed encounter with the military, and finally, on June 23, 24, and 25, passed into the first barricade fight in the czarist empire. Similarly in June the first great revolt of the sailors of the Black Sea Fleet exploded in the harbor at Odessa from a trifling incident on board the armored vessel *Potemkin* which reacted immediately on Odessa and Nikolaev in the form of a violent mass strike. As a further echo followed the mass strike and the sailors' revolts in Kronstadt, Libau and Vladivostok.

In the month of October the grandiose experiment of St. Petersburg was made with the introduction of the eight-hour day. The general council of workers delegates decided to achieve the eight-hour day in a revolutionary manner. That means that on the appointed day all the workers of Petersburg should inform their employers that they were not willing to work more than eight hours a day, and should leave their places of work at the end of eight hours. The idea was the occasion of lively agitation, was accepted by the proletariat with enthusiasm and carried out, but very great sacrifices were not thereby avoided. Thus for example, the eight-hour day meant an enormous fall in wages for the textile workers who had hitherto worked eleven hours and that on a system of piecework. This, however, they willingly accepted. *Within a week the eight-hour day prevailed in every factory and workshop in Petersburg*, and the joy of the workers knew no bounds. Soon, however, the employers, stupefied at first, prepared their defenses; everywhere they threatened to close their factories. Some of the workers consented to negotiate and obtained here a working day of ten hours and there one of nine hours. The elite of the Petersburg proletariat, however, the workers in the large government engineering establishments, remained unshaken, and a lockout ensued which threw from forty-five to fifty thousand

179

men on the streets for a month. At the settlement the eight-hour day movement was carried into the general strike of December which the great lockout had hampered to a great extent.

Meanwhile, however, the second tremendous general strike throughout the whole empire follows in October as a reply to the project of the Bulygin Duma — the strike to which the railwaymen gave the summons. This second great action of the proletariat already bears a character essentially different from that of the first one in January. The element of political consciousness already plays a much bigger role. Here also, to be sure, the immediate occasion for the outbreak of the mass strike was a subordinate and apparently accidental thing: the conflict of the railwaymen with the management over the pension fund. But the general rising of the industrial proletariat which followed upon it was conducted in accordance with clear political ideas. The prologue of the January strike was a procession to the czar to ask for political freedom: the watchword of the October strike ran away with the constitutional comedy of czarism!

And thanks to the immediate success of the general strike, to the czar's manifesto of October 30, the movement does not flow back on itself, as in January but rushes over outwardly in the eager activity of newly acquired political freedom. Demonstrations, meetings, a young press, public discussions and bloody massacres as the end of the story, and thereupon new mass strikes and demonstrations — such is the stormy picture of the November and December days. In November, at the instance of the social democrats in Petersburg the first demonstrative mass strike is arranged as a protest demonstration against the bloody deeds and the proclamation of a state of siege in Poland and Livonia.

The fermentation after the brief constitutional period and the gruesome awakening finally leads in December to the outbreak of the third general mass strike throughout the empire. This time its course and its outcome are altogether different from those in the two earlier cases. Political action does not change into economic action as in January, but it no longer achieves a rapid victory as in October. The attempts of the czarist camarilla with real political freedom are no longer made, and revolutionary action therewith, for the first time, and along its whole length, knocked against the strong wall of the physical violence of absolutism. By the logical internal development of progressive experience the mass strike this time changes into an open insurrection, to armed barricades, and street fighting in Moscow. The December days in Moscow close the first eventful year of the revolution as the highest point in the ascending line of political action and of the mass strike movement.

The Moscow events show a typical picture of the logical development and at the same time of the future of the revolutionary movement on the whole: their inevitable close in a general open insurrection, which again on its part cannot come in any other way than through the school of a series of preparatory partial insurrections, which therefore meantime end in partial outward "defeats" and, considered individually, may appear to be "premature."

The year 1906 brings the elections to the Duma and the Duma incidents. The proletariat, from a strong revolutionary instinct and clear knowledge of the situation, boycotts the whole czarist constitutional farce, and liberalism again occupies the center of the stage for a few months. The situation of 1904 appears to have come again, a period of speeches instead of acts, and the proletariat for a time walk in the shadow in order to devote themselves the more diligently to the trade-union struggle and the work of organization. The mass strikes are no longer spoken of, while the clattering rockets of liberal rhetoric are fired off day after day. At last the iron curtain is torn down, the actors are dispersed, and nothing remains of the liberal rockets but smoke and vapor. An attempt of the Central Committee of the Russian social democracy to call forth a mass strike, as a demonstration for the Duma and the reopening of the period of liberal speechmaking, falls absolutely flat. The role of the political mass strike alone is exhausted, but, at the same time, the transition of the mass strike into a general popular rising is not yet accomplished. The liberal episode is past, the proletarian episode is not yet begun. The stage remains empty for the time being.

IV. The Interaction of the Political and the Economic Struggle

We have attempted in the foregoing to sketch the history of the mass strike in Russia in a few strokes. Even a fleeting glance at this history shows us a picture which in no way resembles that usually formed by the discussions in Germany on the mass strike. Instead of the rigid and hollow scheme of an arid political action carried out by the decision of the highest committees and furnished with a plan and panorama, we see a bit of pulsating like of flesh and blood, which cannot be cut out of the large frame of the revolution but is connected with all parts of the revolution by a thousand veins.

The mass strike, as the Russian Revolution shows it to us, is such a changeable phenomenon that it reflects all phases of the political and economic struggle, all stages and factors of the revolution. Its adaptability, its efficiency, the factors of its origin are constantly changing. It suddenly opens new and wide perspectives of the revolution when it appears to have already arrived in a narrow pass and where it is impossible for anyone to reckon upon it with any degree of certainty. It flows now like a broad billow over the whole kingdom, and now divides into a gigantic network of narrow streams; now it bubbles forth from under the ground like a fresh spring and now is completely lost under the earth. Political and economic strikes, mass strikes and partial strikes, demonstrative strikes and fighting strikes, general strikes of individual branches of industry and general strikes in individual towns, peaceful wage struggles and street massacres, barricade fighting—all these run through one another, run side by side, cross one another, flow in and over one another—it is a ceaselessly moving, changing sea of phenomena. And the law of motion of these phenomena is clear: it does not lie in the mass strike itself nor in its technical details, but in the political and social proportions of the forces of the revolution.

The mass strike is merely the form of the revolutionary struggle and every disarrangement of the relations of the contending powers, in party development and in class division, in the position of the counterrevolution—all this immediately influences the action of the strike in a thousand invisible and scarcely controllable ways. But strike action itself does not cease for a single moment. It merely alters its forms, its dimensions, its effect. It is the living pulsebeat of the revolution and at the same time its most powerful driving wheel. In a word, the mass strike, as shown to us in the Russian Revolution, is not a crafty method discovered by subtle reasoning for the purpose of making the proletarian struggle more effective, *but the method of motion of the proletarian mass*, the phenomenal form of the proletarian struggle in the revolution.

Some general aspects may now be examined which may assist us in forming a correct estimate of the problem of the mass strike.

1. It is absurd to think of the mass strike as one act, one isolated action. The mass strike is rather the indication, the rallying idea, of a whole period of the class struggle lasting for years, perhaps for decades. Of the innumerable and highly varied mass strikes which have taken place in Russia during the last four years, the scheme of the mass strike was a purely political movement, begun and ended after a cut and dried plan, a short single act of one variety only and that a subordinate variety—pure demonstration strike. In the whole course of the five-year period we see in Russia only a few demonstration strikes, which be it noted, were generally confined to single towns. Thus the annual May Day general strike in Warsaw and Lodz in Russia proper on the first of May has not yet been celebrated to any appreciable extent by abstention from work; the mass strike in Warsaw on September 11, 1905, as a memorial service in honor of the executed Martin Kasprzak; that of November 1905 in Petersburg

as protest demonstration against the declaration of a state of siege in Poland and Livonia; that of January 22, 1906 in Warsaw, Lodz, Czentochon and in the Dombrowa coal basin, as well as, in part those in a few Russian towns as anniversary celebrations of the Petersburg bloodbath; in addition, in July 1906 a general strike in Tiflis as demonstration of sympathy with soldiers sentenced by court-martial on account of the military revolt; and finally from the same cause, in September 1906, during the deliberations of the court-martial in Reval. All the above great and partial mass strikes and general strikes were not demonstration strikes but fighting strikes, and as such they originated for the most part spontaneously, in every case from specific local accidental causes, without plan and undesignedly, and grew with elemental power into great movements, and then they did not begin an "orderly retreat," but turned now into economic struggles, now into street fighting, and now collapsed of themselves.

In this general picture the purely political demonstration strike plays quite a subordinate role—isolated small points in the midst of a mighty expanse. Thereby, temporarily considered, the following characteristic discloses itself: the demonstration strikes which, in contradistinction to the fighting strikes, exhibit the greatest mass of party discipline, conscious direction and political thought, and therefore must appear as the highest and most mature form of the mass strike, play in reality the greatest part in the *beginnings* of the movement. Thus for example, the absolute cessation of work on May 1, 1905, in Warsaw, as the first instance of a decision of the social democrats carried throughout in such an astonishing fashion, was an experience of great importance for the proletarian movement in Poland. In the same way the sympathetic strike of the same year in Petersburg made a great impression as the first experiment of conscious systematic mass action in Russia. Similarly the "trial mass strike" of the Hamburg comrades on January 17, 1906, will play a prominent part in the history of the future German mass strike as the first vigorous attempt with the much disputed weapon, and also a very successful and convincingly striking test of the fighting temper and the lust for battle of the Hamburg working class. And just as surely will the period of the mass strike in Germany, when it has once begun in real earnest, lead of itself to a real, general cessation of work on May first. The May Day festival may naturally be raised to a position of honor as the first great demonstration under the aegis of the mass struggle.' In this sense the "lame horse," as the May Day festival was termed at the trade-union congress at Cologne, has still a great future before it and an important part to play, in the proletarian class struggle in Germany.

But with the development of the earnest revolutionary struggle

183

the importance of such demonstrations diminishes rapidly. It is precisely those factors which objectively facilitate the realization of the demonstration strike after a preconceived plan and at the party's word of command—namely, the growth of political consciousness and the training of the proletariat—make this kind of mass strike impossible; today the proletariat in Russia, the most capable vanguard of the masses, does not want to know about mass strikes; the workers are no longer in a mood for jesting and will now think only of a serious struggle with all its consequences. And when, in the first great mass strike in January 1905, the demonstrative element, not indeed in an intentional, but more in an instinctive spontaneous form, still played a great part, on the other hand, the attempt of the Central Committee of the Russian social democrats to call a mass strike in August as a demonstration for the dissolved Duma was shattered by, among other things, the positive disinclination of the educated proletariat to engage in weak half-actions and mere demonstrations.

2. When, however, we have in view the less important strike of the demonstrative kind, instead of the fighting strike as it represents in Russia today the actual vehicle of proletarian action, we see still more clearly that it is impossible to separate the economic factors from one another. Here also the reality deviates from the theoretical scheme, and the pedantic representation in which the pure political mass strike is logically derived from the trade-union general strike as the ripest and highest stage, but at the same time is kept distinct from it, is shown to be absolutely false. This is expressed not merely in the fact that the mass strikes, from that first great wage struggle of the Petersburg textile workers in 1896-97 to the last great mass strike in December 1905, passed imperceptibly from the economic field to the political, so that it is almost impossible to draw a dividing line between them.

Again, every one of the great mass strikes repeats, so to speak, on a small scale, the entire history of the Russian mass strike, and begins with a pure economic, or at all events, a partial trade-union conflict, and runs through all the stages to the political demonstration. The great thunderstorm of mass strikes in South Russia in 1902 and 1903 originated, as we have seen, in Baku from a conflict arising from the disciplinary punishment of the unemployed, in Rostov from disputes about wages in the railway workshops, in Tiflis from a struggle of the commercial employees for reduction of working hours, in Odessa from a wage dispute in one single small factory. The January mass strike of 1905 developed from an internal conflict in the Putilov works, the October strike from the struggle of the railway workers for a pension fund, and finally the December strike from the struggle of the postal and telegraph employees for the right of combination. The progress of the movement on the whole is not expressed in the circumstances that the economic initial stage is omitted, but much more in the rapidity with which all the stages to the political demonstration are run through and in the extremity of the point to which the strike moves forward.

But the movement on the whole does not proceed from the economic to the political struggle, nor even the reverse. Every great political mass action, after it has attained its political highest point, breaks up into a mass of economic strikes. And that applies not only to each of the great mass strikes, but also to the revolution as a whole. With the spreading, clarifying and involution of the political struggle, the economic struggle not only does not recede, but extends, organizes and becomes involved in equal measure. Between the two there is the most complete reciprocal action.

Every new onset and every fresh victory of the political struggle is transformed into a powerful impetus for the economic struggle, extending at the same time its external possibilities and intensifying the inner urge of the workers to better their position, and their desire to struggle. After every foaming wave of political action a fructifying deposit remains behind from which a thousand stalks of economic struggle shoot forth. And conversely. The workers' condition of ceaseless economic struggle with the capitalists keeps their fighting energy alive in every political interval; it forms, so to speak, the permanent fresh reservoir of the strength of the proletarian classes, from which the political fight ever renews its strength, and at the same time leads the indefatigable economic sappers of the proletariat at all times, now here and now there, to isolated sharp conflicts, out of which political conflicts on a large scale unexpectedly explode.

In a word: the economic struggle is the transmitter from one political center to another; the political struggle is the periodic fertilization of the soil for the economic struggle. Cause and effect here continually change places; and thus the economic and the political factor in the period of the mass strike, now widely removed, completely separated or even mutually exclusive, as the theoretical plan would have them, merely form the two interlacing sides of the proletarian class struggle in Russia. And *their unity* is precisely the mass strike. If the sophisticated theory proposes to make a clever logical dissection of the mass strike for the purpose of getting at the "purely political mass strike," it will by this dissection, as with any other, not perceive the phenomenon in its living essence, but will kill it altogether.

3. Finally, the events in Russia show us that the mass strike is inseparable from the revolution. The history of the Russian

mass strikes is the history of the Russian Revolution. When, to be sure, the representatives of our German opportunism hear of "revolution," they immediately think of bloodshed, street fighting or powder and shot, and the logical conclusion thereof is: the mass strike leads inevitably to the revolution, therefore we dare not have it. In actual fact we see in Russia that almost every mass strike in the long run leads to an encounter with the armed guardians of czarist order, and therein the so-called political strikes exactly resemble the larger economic struggle. The revolution, however, is something other and something more than bloodshed. In contradiction to the police interpretation, which views the revolution exclusively from the standpoint of street disturbances and rioting, that is, from the standpoint of "disorder," the interpretation of scientific socialism sees in the revolution above all a thoroughgoing internal reversal of social class relations. And from this standpoint an altogether different connection exists between revolution and mass strike in Russia from that contained in the commonplace conception that the mass strike generally ends in bloodshed.

We have seen above the inner mechanism of the Russian mass strike which depends upon the ceaseless reciprocal action of the political and economic struggles. But this reciprocal action is conditioned during the revolutionary period. Only in the sultry air of the period of revolution can any partial little conflict between labor and capital grow into a general explosion. In Germany the most violent, most brutal collisions between the workers and employers take place every year and every day without the struggle overleaping the bounds of the individual departments or individual towns concerned, or even those of the individual factories. Punishment of organized workers in Petersburg and unemployment as in Baku, wage struggles as in Odessa, struggles for the right of combination as in Moscow are the order of the day in Germany. No single one of these cases however changes suddenly into a common class action. And when they grow into isolated mass strikes, which have without question a political coloring, they do not bring about a general storm. The general strike of the Dutch railwaymen, which died away in spite of the warmest sympathy, in the midst of the complete impassivity of the proletariat of the country, affords a striking proof of this.

And conversely, only in the period of the revolution, when the social foundations and the walls of the class society are shaken and subjected to a constant process of disarrangement, any political class action of the proletariat can arouse from their passive condition in a few hours whole sections of the working class who have hitherto remained unaffected, and this is immediately and naturally expressed in a stormy economic struggle. The worker, suddenly aroused to activity by the electric shock of political action, immediately seizes the weapon lying nearest his hand for the fight against his condition of economic slavery: the stormy gesture of the political struggle causes him to feel with unexpected intensity the weight and the pressure of his economic chains. And while, for example, the most violent political struggle in Germany—the electoral struggle or the parliamentary struggle on the customs tariff—exercised a scarcely perceptible direct influence upon the course and the intensity of the wage struggles being conducted at the same time in Germany, every political action of the proletariat in Russia immediately expresses itself in the extension of the area and the deepening of the intensity of the economic struggle.

The revolution thus first creates the social conditions in which this sudden change of the economic struggle into the political and of the political struggle into the economic is possible, a change which finds its expression in the mass strike. And if the vulgar scheme sees the connection between mass strike and revolution only in bloody street encounters with which the mass strikes conclude, a somewhat deeper look into the Russian events shows an exactly opposite connection: in reality the mass strike does not produce the revolution, but the revolution produces the mass strike.

4. It is sufficient in order to comprehend the foregoing to obtain an explanation of the question of the conscious direction and initiative in the mass strike. If the mass strike is not an isolated act but a whole period of the class struggle, and if this period is identical with a period of revolution, it is clear that the mass strike cannot be called at will, even when the decision to do so may come from the highest committee of the strongest social democratic party. As long as the social democracy has not the power to stage and countermand revolutions according to its fancy, even the greatest enthusiasm and impatience of the social democratic troops will not suffice to call into being a real period of mass strike as a living, powerful movement of the people. On the basis of a decision of the party leadership and of party discipline, a single short demonstration may well be arranged similar to the Swedish mass strike, or to the latest Austrian strike, or even to the Hamburg mass strike of January 17. These demonstrations, however, differ from an actual period of revolutionary mass strikes in exactly the same way that the well-known demonstrations in foreign ports during a period of strained diplomatic relations differ from a naval war. A mass strike born of pure discipline and enthusiasm will, at best, merely play the role of an episode, of a symptom of the fighting mood of the working class upon which, however, the conditions of a peaceful period are reflected.

Of course, even during the revolution, mass strikes do not

187

exactly fall from heaven. They must be brought about in some way or another by the workers. The resolution and determination of the workers also play a part and indeed the initiative and the wider direction naturally fall to the share of the organized and most enlightened kernel of the proletariat. But the scope of this initiative and this direction, for the most part, is confined to application to individual acts, to individual strikes, when the revolutionary period is already begun, and indeed, in most cases, is confined within the boundaries of a single town. Thus, for example, as we have seen, the social democrats have already, on several occasions, successfully issued a direct summons for a mass strike in Baku, in Warsaw, in Lodz and in Petersburg. But this succeeds much less frequently when applied to general movements of the whole proletariat.

Further, there are quite definite limits set to initiative and conscious direction. During the revolution it is extremely difficult for any directing organ of the proletarian movement to foresee and to calculate which occasions and factors can lead to explosions and which cannot. Here also initiative and direction do not consist in issuing commands according to one's inclinations, but in the most adroit adaptability to the given situation, and the closest possible contact with the mood of the masses. The element of spontaneity, as we have seen, plays a great part in all Russian mass strikes without exception, be it as a driving force or as a restraining influence. This does not occur in Russia, however, because social democracy is still young or weak, but because in every individual act of the struggle so very many important economic, political and social, general and local, material and psychical, factors react upon one another in such a way that no single act can be arranged and resolved as if it were a mathematical problem. The revolution, even when the proletariat, with the social democrats at their head, appear in the leading role, is not a maneuver of the proletariat in the open field, but a fight in the midst of the incessant crashing, displacing and crumbling of the social foundation. In short, in the mass strikes in Russia the element of spontaneity plays such a predominant part, not because the Russian proletariat are "uneducated," but because revolutions do not allow anyone to play the schoolmaster with them.

On the other hand, we see in Russia that the same revolution which rendered the social democrats' command of the mass strike so difficult, and which struck the conductor's baton from, or pressed it into, their hand at all times in such a comical fashion — we see that it resolved of itself all those difficulties of the mass strike which, in the theoretical scheme of German discussion, are regarded as the chief concern of the "directing body": the question of "provisioning," "discovery of cost," and "sacrifice." It goes without saying that it does not resolve them in the way that they would be resolved in a quiet confidential discussion between the higher directing committees of the labor movement, the members sitting pencil in hand. The "regulation" of all these questions consists in the circumstance that the revolution brings such an enormous mass of people upon the stage that any computation or regulation of the cost of the movement such as can be effected in a civil process, appears to be an altogether hopeless undertaking.

The leading organizations in Russia certainly attempt to support the direct victims to the best of their ability. Thus, for example, the brave victims of the gigantic lockout in St. Petersburg, which followed upon the eight-hour day campaign, were supported for weeks. But all these measures are, in the enormous balance of the revolution, but as a drop in the ocean. At the moment that a real, earnest period of mass strikes begins, all these "calculations" of "cost" become merely projects for exhausting the ocean with a tumbler. And it is a veritable ocean of frightful privations and sufferings which is brought by every revolution to the proletarian masses. And the solution which a revolutionary period makes of this apparently invincible difficulty consists in the circumstances that such an immense volume of mass idealism is simultaneously released that the masses are insensible to the bitterest sufferings. With the psychology of a trade unionist who will not stay off his work on May Day unless he is assured in advance of a definite amount of support in the event of his being victimized, neither revolution nor mass strike can be made. But in the storm of the revolutionary period even the proletarian is transformed from a provident pater familias demanding support, into a "revolutionary romanticist," for whom even the highest good, life itself, to say nothing of material well-being, possesses but little in comparison with the ideals of the struggle.

If, however, the direction of the mass strike in the sense of command over its origin, and in the sense of the calculating and reckoning of the cost, is a matter of the revolutionary period itself, the directing of the mass strike becomes, in an altogether different sense, the duty of social democracy and its leading organs. Instead of puzzling their heads with the technical side, with the mechanism, of the mass strike, the social democrats are called upon to assume *political* leadership in the midst of the revolutionary period.

To give the cue for, and the direction to, the fight; to so regulate the tactics of the political struggle in its every phase and at its every moment that the entire sum of the available power

189

of the proletariat which is already released and active, will find expression in the battle array of the party; to see that the tactics of the social democrats are decided according to their resoluteness and acuteness and that they never fall below the level demanded by the actual relations of forces, but rather rise above it—that is the most important task of the directing body in a period of mass strikes. And this direction changes of itself, to a certain extent, into technical direction. A consistent, resolute, progressive tactic on the part of the social democrats produces in the masses a feeling of security, self-confidence and desire for struggle; a vacillating weak tactic, based on an underestimation of the proletariat, has a crippling and confusing effect upon the masses. In the first case mass strikes break out "of themselves" and "opportunely"; in the second case they remain ineffective amidst direct summonses of the directing body to mass strikes. And of both the Russian Revolution affords striking examples.

V. Lessons of the Working-Class Movement in Russia Applicable to Germany

Let us now see how far all these lessons which can be learned from the Russian mass strikes are applicable to Germany. The social and political conditions, the history and status of the labor movement are widely different in Germany and Russia. At first sight the inner law of the Russian mass strikes as sketched above may appear to be solely the product of specifically Russian conditions which need not be taken into account by the German proletariat. Between the political and the economic struggle in the Russian Revolution there is a very close internal connection; their unity becomes an actual fact in the period of mass strikes. But is not that simply a result of Russian absolutism? In a state in which every form and expression of the labor movement is forbidden, in which the simplest strike is a political crime, it must logically follow that every economic struggle will become a political one.

Further, when, contrariwise, the first outbreak of the political revolution has drawn after it a general reckoning of the Russian working class with the employers, that is likewise a simple result of the circumstances that the Russian worker has hitherto had a very low standard of life, and has never yet engaged in a single economic struggle for an improvement of his condition. The proletariat in Russia has first, to a certain extent, to work their way out of these miserable conditions, and what wonder that they eagerly availed themselves, with the eagerness of youth, of the first means to that end as soon as the revolution brought the first fresh breeze into the heavy air of absolutism? And finally, the stormy revolutionary course of the Russian mass strike as well as their preponderant spontaneous, elementary character is explained on the one hand by the political backwardness of Russia, by the necessity of first overthrowing the oriental despotism, and on the other hand, by the want of organization and of discipline of the Russian proletariat. In a country in which the working class has had thirty years experience of political life, a strong social democratic party of 3 million members and a quarter of a million picked troops organized in trade unions, neither the political struggle nor the mass strike can possibly assume the same stormy and elemental character as in a semibarbarous state which has just made the leap from the Middle Ages into the modern bourgeois order. This is the current conception amongst those who would read the stage of maturity of the social conditions of a country from the text of the written laws.

Let us examine the questions in their order. To begin with it is going the wrong way about the matter to date the beginning of the economic struggle in Russia only from the outbreak of the revolution. As a matter of fact, the strikes and wage disputes in Russia proper were increasingly the order of the day since the nineties of the last century, and in Russian Poland even since the eighties, and had eventually won civic rights for the workers. Of course, they were frequently followed by brutal police measures, but nevertheless they were daily phenomena. For example, in both Warsaw and Lodz as early as 1891, there was a considerable strike fund, and the enthusiasm for trade unionism in these years had even created that "economic" illusion in Poland for a short time which a few years later prevailed in Petersburg and the rest of Russia.

In the same way there is a great deal of exaggeration in the notion that the proletarian in the czarist empire had the standard of life of a pauper before the revolution. The layer of the workers in large industries in the great towns who had been the most active and jealous in the economic as in the political struggle are, as regards the material conditions of life, on a scarcely lower plane than the corresponding layer of the German proletariat, and in some occupations as high wages are to be met with in Russia as in Germany, and here and there, even higher. And as regards the length of the working day, the difference in the large-scale industries in the two countries is here and there insignificant. The notion of the presumed material and cultural condition of helotry of the Russian working class is similarly without justification in fact. This notion is contradicted, as a little reflection will show, by the facts of the revolution itself and the prominent part that was played therein by the proletariat. With paupers no revolution of this political maturity and cleverness of thought can be made, and the industrial workers of St.

Petersburg and Warsaw, Moscow and Odessa, who stand in the forefront of the struggle, are culturally and mentally much nearer to the west European type than is imagined by those who regard bourgeois parliamentarism and methodical trade-union practice as the indispensable, or even the only, school of culture for the proletariat. The modern large capitalist development of Russia and the intellectual influence, exerted for a decade and a half, of social democracy, which has encouraged and directed the economic struggle, have accomplished an important piece of cultural work without the outward guarantees of the bourgeois legal order.

The contrast, however, grows less when, on the other hand, we look a little further into the actual standard of life of the German working class. The great political mass strikes in Russia have from the first aroused the widest layers of the proletariat and thrown them into a feverish economic struggle. But are there not in Germany whole unenlightened sections amongst the workers to which the warm light of the trade unions has hitherto scarcely penetrated, whole layers which up to the present have never attempted, or vainly attempted, to raise themselves out of their social helotry by means of daily wage struggles?

Let us consider *the poverty of the miners*. Already in the quiet working day, in the cold atmosphere of the parliamentary monotony of Germany—as also in other countries, and even in the El Dorado of trade unionism, Great Britain—the wage struggle of the mine workers hardly ever expresses itself in any other way than by violent eruptions from time to time, in mass strikes of typical, elemental character. This only shows that the antagonism between labor and capital is too sharp and violent to allow of its crumbling away in the form of quiet systematic, partial trade-union struggles. The misery of the miners, with its eruptive soil which even in "normal" times is a storm center of the greatest violence, must immediately explode, in a violent economic socialist struggle, with every great political mass action of the working class, with every violent sudden jerk which disturbs the momentary equilibrium of everyday social life.

Let us take further, the case of the *poverty of the textile workers*. Here also the bitter, and for the most part fruitless, outbreaks of the wage struggle which raged through Vogtland every few years, give but a faint idea of the vehemence with which the great agglomerate mass of helots of trustified textile capital must explode during a political convulsion, during a powerful, daring mass action of the German proletariat. Again let us take the *poverty of the homeworkers, of the ready-made clothing workers, of the electricity workers*, veritable storm centers in which violent struggles will be the more certain to break out with every political atmospheric disturbance in Germany, the less frequently the pro-

192

letariat take up the struggle in tranquil times; and the more un-successfully they fight at any time, the more brutally will capital compel them to return, gnashing their teeth to the yoke of slavery. Now, however, whole great categories of the proletariat have to be taken into account which, in the "normal" course of things in Germany, cannot possibly take part in a peaceful economic struggle for the improvement of their condition and cannot pos-sibly avail themselves of the right of combination. First and foremost we give the example of the glaring poverty of the *rail-way and the postal employees*. For these government workers there exist Russian conditions in the midst of the parliamentary constitutional state of Germany, that is to say, Russian conditions as they existed only before the revolution, during the untroubled splendor of absolutism. Already in the great October strike of 1905 the Russian railwaymen in the then formally absolutist Russia, were, as regards the economic and social freedom of their movement, head and shoulders above the Germans. The Russian railway and postal employees won the de facto right of combi-nation in the storm, and if momentarily trial upon trial and vic-timization were the rule, they were powerless to affect the inner unity of the workers.

However, it would be an altogether false psychological reckon-ing if one were to assume, with the German reaction, that the slavish obedience of the German railway and postal employees will last forever, that it is a rock which nothing can wear away. When even the German trade-union leaders have become accus-tomed to the existing conditions to such an extent that they, un-troubled by an indifference almost without parallel in the whole of Europe, can survey with complete satisfaction the results of the trade-union struggle in Germany, then the deep-seated, long-suppressed resentment of the uniformed state slaves will inevitably find vent with a general rising of the industrial workers. And when the industrial vanguard of the proletariat, by means of mass strikes, grasp at new political rights or attempt to defend existing ones, the great army of railway and postal employees must of necessity bethink themselves of their own special disgrace, and at last rouse themselves for their liberation from the extra share of Russian absolutism which is specially reserved for them in Germany.

The pedantic conception which would unfold great popular movements according to plan and recipe regards the acquisition of the right of combination for the railway workers as necessary before anyone will "dare to think" of a mass strike in Germany. The actual and natural course of events can only be the opposite of this: only from a spontaneous powerful mass strike action can the right of combination for the German railway workers, as well as for the postal employees, actually be born. And the problems which in the existing conditions of Germany are insoluble will suddenly find their solution under the influence and the pressure of a universal political mass action of the proletariat.

And finally, the greatest and most important: *the poverty of the land workers.* If the British trade unions are composed exclusively of industrial workers, that is quite understandable in view of the specific character of the British national economy, and of the unimportant part that agriculture plays, on the whole, in the economic life of Britain. In Germany, a trade-union organization, be it ever so well constructed, if it comprises only industrial workers, and is inaccessible to the great army of land workers, will give only a weak, partial picture of the conditions of the proletariat. But again it would be a fatal illusion to think that conditions in the country are unalterable and immovable and that the indefatigable educational work of the social democrats, and still more, the whole internal class politics of Germany, does not continually undermine the outward passivity of the agricultural workers and that any great general class action of the German proletariat, for whatever object undertaken, may not also draw the rural proletariat into the conflict.

Similarly, the picture of the alleged economic superiority of the German over the Russian proletariat is considerably altered when we look away from the tables of the industries and departments organized in trade unions and bestow a look upon those great groups of the proletariat who are altogether outside the trade-union struggle, or whose special economic condition does not allow of their being forced into the narrow framework of the daily guerrilla warfare of the trade unions. We see there one important sphere after another, in which the sharpening of antagonisms has reached the extreme point, in which inflammable material in abundance is heaped up, in which there is a great deal of "Russian absolutism" in its most naked form, and in which economically the most elementary reckonings with capital have first to be made.

In a general political mass strike of the proletariat, then, all these outstanding accounts would inevitably be presented to the prevailing system. An artificially arranged demonstration of the urban proletariat, taking place once, a mere mass strike action arising out of discipline, and directed by the conductor's baton of a party executive, could therefore leave the broad masses of the people cold and indifferent. But a powerful and reckless fighting action of the industrial proletariat, born of a revolutionary situation, must surely react upon the deeper-lying layers, and ultimately draw all those into a stormy general economic struggle who, in normal times, stand aside from the daily trade-union fight.

But when we come back to the organized vanguard of the German industrial proletariat, on the other hand, and keep before our eyes the objects of the economic struggle which have been striven for by the Russian working class, we do not at all find that there is any tendency to look down upon the things of youth, as the oldest German trade unions had reason to do. Thus the most important general demand of the Russian strikes since January 22—the eight-hour day—is certainly not an unattainable platform for the German proletariat, but rather in most cases, a beautiful, remote ideal. This applies also to the struggle for the "mastery of the household" platform, to the struggle for the introduction of workers' committees into all the factories, for the abolition of piecework, for the abolition of homework in handicraft, for the complete observance of Sunday rest, and for the recognition of the right of combination. Yes, on closer inspection all the economic objects of struggle of the Russian proletariat are also for the German proletariat very real, and touch a very sore spot in the life of the workers.

It therefore inevitably follows that the pure political mass strike, which is operated with for preference, is, in Germany, a mere lifeless theoretical plan. If the mass strikes result, in a natural way from a strong revolutionary ferment, in a determined political struggle of the urban workers, they will equally naturally, exactly as in Russia, change into a whole period of elementary, economic struggles. The fears of the trade-union leaders, therefore, that the struggle for economic interests in a period of stormy political strife, in a period of mass strikes, can simply be pushed aside and suppressed rest upon an utterly baseless, schoolboy conception of the course of events. A revolutionary period in Germany would so alter the character of the trade-union struggle and develop its potentialities to such an extent that the present guerrilla warfare of the trade unions would be child's play in comparison. And on the other hand, from this elementary economic tempest of mass strikes, the political struggle would derive always new impetus and fresh strength. The reciprocal action of economic and political struggle, which is the mainspring of present-day strikes in Russia, and at the same time the regulating mechanism, so to speak, of the revolutionary action of the proletariat, would result also in Germany, and quite as naturally, from the conditions themselves.

VI. Cooperation of Organized and Unorganized Workers Necessary for Victory

In connection with this, the question of organization in relation to the problem of the mass strike in Germany assumes an essentially different aspect.

The attitude of many trade-union leaders to this question is generally summed up in the assertion: "We are not yet strong

195

enough to risk such a hazardous trial of strength as a mass strike." Now this position is so far untenable that it is an insoluble problem to determine the time, in a peaceful fashion by counting heads, when the proletariat are "strong enough" for any struggle. Thirty years ago the German trade unions had 50,000 members. That was obviously a number with which a mass strike on the above scale was not to be thought of. Fifteen years later the trade unions were four times as strong, and counted 237,000 members. If, however, the present trade-union leaders had been asked at the time if the organization of the proletariat was then sufficiently ripe for a mass strike, they would assuredly have replied that it was still far from it and that the number of those organized in trade unions would first have to be counted by millions.

Today the number of trade unionists already runs into the second million, but the views of the leaders are still exactly the same, and may very well be the same to the end. The tacit assumption is that the entire working class of Germany, down to the last man and the last woman, must be included in the organization before it "is strong enough" to risk a mass action, which then, according to the old formula, would probably be represented as "superfluous." This theory is nevertheless absolutely utopian, for the simple reason that it suffers from an internal contradiction, that it goes in a vicious circle. Before the workers can engage in any direct class struggle they must all be organized. The circumstances, the conditions, of capitalist development and of the bourgeois state make it impossible that, in the normal course of things, without stormy class struggles, certain sections — and these the greatest, the most important, the lowest and the most oppressed by capital, and by the state — can be organized at all. We see even in Britian, which has had a whole century of indefatigable trade-union effort without any "disturbances" — except at the beginning in the period of the Chartist movement — without any "romantic revolutionary" errors or temptations, it has not been possible to do more than organize a minority of the better-paid sections of the proletariat.

On the other hand the trade unions, like all fighting organizations of the proletariat, cannot permanently maintain themselves in any other way than by struggle, and that not struggles of the same kind as the war between the frogs and the mice in the stagnant waters of the bourgeois parliamentary period, but struggle in the troubled revolutionary periods of the mass strike. The rigid, mechanical-bureaucratic conception cannot conceive of the struggle save as the product of organization at a certain stage of its strength. On the contrary the living, dialectical explanation makes the organization arise as a product of the struggle. We have already seen a grandiose example of this phenomenon in Russia, where a proletariat almost wholly unorganized created a comprehensive network of organizational appendages in a year and a half of stormy revolutionary struggle.

Another example of this kind is furnished by the history of the German unions. In the year 1878 the number of trade-union members amounted to 50,000. According to the theory of the present-day trade-union leaders this organization, as stated above, was not nearly "strong enough" to enter upon a violent political struggle. The German trade unions however, weak as they were at the time, did take up the struggle—namely the struggle against the antisocialist law—and showed that they were "strong enough," not only to emerge victorious from the struggle, but to increase their strength fivefold: in 1891, after the repeal of the antisocialist laws, their membership was 277,659. It is true that the methods by which the trade unions conquered in the struggle against the antisocialist laws do not correspond to the ideal of a peaceful, beelike, uninterrupted process: they first went into the fight absolutely in ruins, to rise again on the next wave and to be born anew. But this is precisely the specific method of growth corresponding to the proletarian class organizations: to be tested in the struggle and to go forth from the struggle with increased strength.

On a closer examination of German conditions and of the condition of the different sections of the working class, it is clear that the coming period of stormy political mass struggles will not bring the dreaded, threatening downfall of the German trade unions, but on the contrary, will open up hitherto unsuspected prospects of the extension of their sphere of power—an extension that will proceed rapidly by leaps and bounds. But the question has still another aspect. The plan of undertaking mass strikes as a serious political class action with organized workers only is absolutely hopeless. If the mass strike, or rather, mass strikes, and the mass struggle are to be successful they must become a real *people's movement*, that is, the widest sections of the proletariat must be drawn into the fight. Already in the parliamentary form the might of the proletarian class struggle rests not on the small organized group, but on the surrounding periphery of the revolutionary-minded proletariat. If the social democrats were to enter the electoral battle with their few hundred thousand organized members alone, they would condemn themselves to futility. And although it is the tendency of social democracy wherever possible to draw the whole great army of its voters into the party organization, its mass of voters after thirty years experience of social democracy is not increased through the growth of the party organization, but on the contrary, the new sections of

197

the proletariat, won for the time being through the electoral struggle, are the fertile soil for the subsequent seed of organization. Here the organization does not supply the troops for the struggle, but the struggle, in an ever growing degree, supplies recruits for the organization.

In a much greater degree does this obviously apply to direct political mass action than to the parliamentary struggle. If the social democrats, as the organized nucleus of the working class, are the most important vanguard of the entire body of the workers and if the political clarity, the strength, and the unity of the labor movement flow from this organization, then it is not permissible to visualize the class movement of the proletariat as a movement of the organized minority. Every real, great class struggle must rest upon the support and cooperation of the widest masses, and a strategy of class struggle which does not reckon with this cooperation, which is based upon the idea of the finely stage-managed march out of the small, well-trained part of the proletariat is foredoomed to be a miserable fiasco.

Mass strikes and political mass struggles cannot, therefore, possibly be carried through in Germany by the organized workers alone, nor can they be appraised by regular "direction" from the central committee of a party. In this case, again—exactly as in Russia—they depend not so much upon "discipline" and "training" and upon the most careful possible regulation beforehand of the questions of support and cost, as upon a real revolutionary, determined class action, which will be able to win and draw into the struggle the widest circles of the unorganized workers, according to their mood and their conditions.

The overestimate and the false estimate of the role of organizations in the class struggle of the proletariat is generally reinforced by the underestimate of the unorganized proletarian mass and of their political maturity. In a revolutionary period, in the storm of great unsettling class struggles, the whole educational effect of the rapid capitalist development and of social democratic influences first shows itself upon the widest sections of the people, of which, in peaceful times the tables of the organized, and even election statistics, give only a faint idea.

We have seen that in Russia, in about two years a great general action of the proletariat can forthwith arise from the smallest partial conflict of the workers with the employers, from the most insignificant act of brutality of the government organs. Everyone, of course, sees and believes that, because in Russia "the revolution" is there. But what does that mean? It means that class feeling, the class instinct, is alive and very active in the Russian proletariat, so that immediately they regard every partial question of any small group of workers as a general question, as a class affair, and quick as lightning they react to its influence as a unity. While in Germany, France, Italy and Holland the most violent trade-union conflicts call forth hardly any general action of the working class — and when they do, only the organized part of the workers moves — in Russia the smallest dispute raises a storm. That means nothing else however, than that at present — paradoxical as it may sound — the class instinct of the youngest, least trained, badly educated and still worse organized Russian proletariat is immeasurably stronger than that of the organized, trained and enlightened working class of Germany or of any other west European country. And that is not to be reckoned a special virtue of the "young, unexhausted East" as compared with the "sluggish West," but is simply a result of direct revolutionary mass action.

In the case of the enlightened German worker the class consciousness implanted by the social democrats is *theoretical and latent*: in the period ruled by bourgeois parliamentarism it cannot, as a rule, actively participate in a direct mass action; it is the ideal sum of the four hundred parallel actions of the electoral sphere during the election struggle, of the many partial economic strikes and the like. In the revolution when the masses themselves appear upon the political battlefield this class consciousness becomes *practical and active*. A year of revolution has therefore given the Russian proletariat that "training" which thirty years of parliamentary and trade-union struggle cannot artificially give to the German proletariat. Of course, this living, active class feeling of the proletariat will considerably diminish in intensity, or rather change into a concealed and latent condition, after the close of the period of revolution and the erection of a bourgeois-parliamentary constitutional state.

And just as surely, on the other hand, will the living revolutionary class feeling, capable of action, affect the widest and deepest layers of the proletariat in Germany in a period of strong political engagement, and that the more rapidly and more deeply, more energetically the educational work of social democracy is carried on amongst them. This educational work and the provocative and revolutionizing effect of the whole present policy of Germany will express itself in the circumstances that all those groups which at present in their apparent political stupidity remain insensitive to all the organizing attempts of the social democrats and of the trade unions will suddenly follow the flag of social democracy in a serious revolutionary period. Six months of a revolutionary period will complete the work·of the training of these as yet unorganized masses which ten years of public demonstrations and distribution of leaflets would be unable to do. And when conditions in Germany have reached the critical stage for such a period, the. sections which are today unorganized and backward will, in the struggle, prove themselves the most radical, the most impetuous element, and not one that will have to be dragged along. If it should come to mass strikes in Germany, it will almost certainly not be the best organized workers — and most certainly not the printers — who will develop the greatest capacity for action, but the worst organized or totally unorganized — the miners, the textile workers, and perhaps even the land workers.

In this way we arrive at the same conclusions in Germany in relation to the peculiar tasks of *direction*, in relation to the role of social democracy in mass strikes, as in our analysis of events in Russia. If we now leave the pedantic scheme of demonstrative mass strikes artificially brought about by order of parties and trade unions, and turn to the living picture of a peoples' movement arising with elementary energy, from the culmination of class antagonisms and the political situation — a movement which passes, politically as well as economically, into mass struggles and mass strikes — it becomes obvious that the task of social democracy does not consist in the technical preparation and direction of mass strikes, but, first and foremost, in the *political leadership* of the whole movement.

The social democrats are the most enlightened, most class-conscious vanguard of the proletariat. They cannot and dare not wait, in a fatalist fashion, with folded arms for the advent of the "revolutionary situation," to wait for that which in every spontaneous peoples' movement, falls from the clouds. On the contrary, they must now, as always, hasten the development of things and endeavor to accelerate events. This they cannot do, however, by suddenly issuing the "slogan" for a mass strike at random at any odd moment, but first and foremost, by making clear to the widest layers of the proletariat the *inevitable advent* of this revolutionary period, the inner *social factors* making for it and the *political consequences* of it. If the widest proletarian layer should be won for a political mass action of the social democrats, and if, vice versa, the social democrats should seize and maintain the real leadership of a mass movement — should they become, in a *political sense,* the rulers of the whole movement, then they must, with the utmost clearness, consistency and resoluteness, inform the German proletariat of their tactics and aims in the period of coming struggle.

VII. The Role of the Mass Strike in the Revolution

We have seen that the mass strike in Russia does not represent an artificial product of premeditated tactics on the part of the social democrats, but a natural historical phenomenon on the basis of the present revolution. Now what are the factors which in Russia have brought forth this new phenomenal form of the revolution?

The Russian Revolution has for its next task the abolition of absolutism and the creation of a modern bourgeois-parliamentary constitutional state. It is exactly the same in form as that which confronted Germany at the March Revolution, and France at the Great Revolution at the end of the eighteenth century. But the condition, the historical milieu, in which these formally analogous revolutions took place, are fundamentally different from those of present-day Russia. The most decisive difference is the circumstances that between those bourgeois revolutions of the West and the present bourgeois revolution in the East, the whole cycle of capitalist development has run its course. And this development had seized not only the West European countries, but also absolutist Russia. Large-scale industry with all its consequences—modern class divisions, sharp social contrasts, modern life in large cities and the modern proletariat—has become in Russia the prevailing form, that is, in social development the decisive form of production.

The remarkable, contradictory, historical situation results from this that the bourgeois revolution, in accordance with its formal tasks will, in the first place, be carried out by a modern class-conscious proletariat, and in an international milieu whose distinguishing characteristic is the ruin of bourgeois democracy. It is not the bourgeoisie that is now the leading revolutionary element as in the earlier revolutions of the West, while the proletarian masses, disorganized amongst the petty bourgeoisie, furnish material for the army of the bourgeoisie, but on the contrary, it is the class-conscious proletariat that is the leading and driving element, while the big bourgeois sections are partly directly counterrevolutionary, partly weakly liberal, and only the rural petty bourgeoisie and the urban petty bourgeois. intelligentsia are definitely oppositional and even revolutionary minded.

The Russian proletariat, however, who are destined to play the leading part in the bourgeois revolution, enter the fight free from all illusions of bourgeois democracy, with a strongly developed consciousness of their own specific class interests, and at a time when the antagonism between capital and labor has reached its height. This contradictory situation finds expression in the fact that in this formally bourgeois revolution, the antagonism of the bourgeois society to absolutism is governed by the antagonism of the proletariat to bourgeois society, that the struggle of the proletariat is directed simultaneously and with equal energy against both absolutism and capitalist exploitation, and that the program of the revolutionary struggle concentrates with equal emphasis on political freedom, the winning of the eight-hour day, and a human standard of material existence for the proletariat. This twofold character of the Russian Revolution is expressed in that close union of the economic with the political struggle and in their mutual interaction which we have seen is a feature of the Russian events and which finds its appropriate expression in the mass strike.

In the earlier bourgeois revolutions where, on the one hand, the political training and the leadership of the revolutionary masses were undertaken by the bourgeois parties, and where, on the other hand, it was merely a question of overthrowing the old government, the brief battle at the barricades was the appropriate form of the revolutionary struggle. Today, when the working classes are being enlightened in the course of the revolutionary struggle, when they must marshall their forces and lead themselves, and when the revolution is directed as much against the old state power as against capitalist exploitation, the mass strike appears as the natural means of recruiting the widest proletarian layers for the struggle, as well as being at the same time a means of undermining and overthrowing the old state power and of stemming capitalist exploitation. The urban industrial proletariat is now the soul of the revolution in Russia. But in order to carry through a direct political struggle as a mass, the proletariat must first be assembled as a mass, and for this purpose they must come out of factory and workshop, mine and foundry, must overcome the levigation and the decay to which they are condemned under the daily yoke of capitalism.

The mass strike is the first natural, impulsive form of every great revolutionary struggle of the proletariat and the more highly developed the antagonism is between capital and labor, the more effective and decisive must mass strikes become. The chief form of previous bourgeois revolutions, the fight at the barricades, the open conflict with the armed power of the state, is in the revolution of today only the culminating point, only a moment on the process of the proletarian mass struggle. And therewith in the new form of the revolution there is reached that civilizing and mitigating of the class struggle which was prophesied by the opportunists of German social democracy — the Bernsteins, Davids, etc. It is true that these men saw the desired civilizing and mitigating of the class struggle in the light of petty bourgeois democratic illusions — they believed that the class struggle would shrink to an exclusively parliamentary contest and that street fighting would simply be done away with. History has found the solution in a deeper and finer fashion: in the advent of revolutionary mass strikes, which, of course, in no way replaces brutal street fights or renders them unnecessary, but which reduces them to a moment in the long period of political struggle, and which at the same time unites with the revolutionary period an enormous cultural work in the most exact sense of the words: the material and intellectual elevation of the whole working class through the "civilizing" of the barbaric forms of capitalist exploitation.

The mass strike is thus shown to be not a specifically Russian product, springing from absolutism but a universal form of the proletarian class struggle resulting from the present stage of capitalist development and class relations. From this standpoint the three bourgeois revolutions—the Great French Revolution, the German Revolution of March, and the present Russian Revolution—form a continuous chain of development in which the fortunes and the end of the capitalist century are to be seen. In the Great French Revolution the still wholly underdeveloped internal contradictions of bourgeois society gave scope for a long period of violent struggles, in which all the antagonisms which first germinated and ripened in the heat of the revolution raged unhindered and unrestrained in a spirit of reckless radicalism. A century later the revolution of the German bourgeoisie, which broke out midway in the development of capitalism, was already hampered on both sides by the antagonism of interests and the equilibrium of strength between capital and labor, and was smothered in a bourgeois-feudal compromise, and shortened to a brief miserable episode ending in words.

Another half century, and the present Russian Revolution stands at a point of the historical path which is already over the summit, which is on the other side of the culminating point of capitalist society, at which the bourgeois revolution cannot again be smothered by the antagonism between bourgeoisie and proletariat, but, will, on the contrary, expand into a new lengthy period of violent social struggles, at which the balancing of the account with absolutism appears a trifle in comparison with the many new accounts which the revolution itself opens up. The present revolution realizes in the particular affairs of absolutist Russia the general results of international capitalist development, and appears not so much as the last successor of the old bourgeois revolutions as the forerunner of the new series of proletarian revolutions of the West. The most backward country of all, just because it has been so unpardonably late with its bourgeois revolution, shows ways and methods of further class struggle to the proletariat of Germany and the most advanced capitalist countries.

Accordingly it appears, when looked at in this way, to be entirely wrong to regard the Russian Revolution as a fine play, as something specifically "Russian," and at best to admire the heroism of the fighting men, that is, the last accessories of the struggle. It is much more important that the German workers should learn to look upon the Russian Revolution *as their own affair,* not merely as a matter of international solidarity with the Russian proletariat, but first and foremost, as a *chapter of their own social and political history.* Those trade-union leaders and parliamentarians who regard the German proletariat as "too weak" and German conditions "as not ripe enough" for revolutionary mass struggles, have obviously not the least idea that the measure of the degree of ripeness of class relations in Germany and of the power of the proletariat does not lie in the statistics of German trade unionism or in election figures, but — in the events of the Russian Revolution. Exactly as the ripeness of French class antagonisms under the July monarchy and the June battle of Paris was reflected in the German March Revolution, in its course and its fiasco, so today the ripeness of German class antagonisms is reflected in the events and in the power of the Russian Revolution. And while the bureaucrats of the German labor movement rummage in their office drawers for information as to their strength and maturity, they do not see that that for which they seek is lying before their eyes in a great historical revolution, because, historically considered, the Russian Revolution is a reflex of the power and the maturity of the international, and therefore in the first place, of the German labor movement.

It would therefore be a too pitiable and grotesquely insignificant result of the Russian Revolution if the German proletariat should merely draw from it the lesson — as is desired by Comrades Frohme, Elm, and others — of using the extreme form of the struggle, the mass strike, and so weaken themselves as to be merely a reserve force in the event of the withdrawal of the parliamentary vote, and therefore a passive means of parliamentary defensive. When the parliamentary vote is taken from us there we will resist. That is a self-evident decision. But for this it is not necessary to adopt the heroic pose of a Danton as was done, for example, by Comrade Elm in Jena; because the defense of the modest measure of parliamentary right already possessed is less a Heaven-storming innovation, for which the frightful hecatombs of the Russian Revolution were first necessary as a means of encouragement, than the simplest and first duty of every opposition party. But the mere defensive can never exhaust the policy of the proletariat, in a period of revolution. And if it is, on the one hand, difficult to predict with any degree of certainty whether the destruction of universal suffrage would cause a situation in Germany which would call forth an immediate mass strike action, so on the other hand, it is absolutely certain that when we in Germany enter upon the period of stormy mass actions, it will be impossible for the social democrats to base their tactics upon a mere parliamentary defensive.

To fix beforehand the cause and the moment from and in which the mass strikes in Germany will break out is not in the power of social democracy, because it is not in its power to bring about historical situations by resolutions at party congresses. But what it can and must do is to make clear the political tendencies, when they once appear, and to formulate them as resolute and consistent tactics. Man cannot keep historical events in check while making recipes for them, but he can see in advance their apparent calculable consequences and arrange his mode of action accordingly.

The first threatening political danger with which the German proletariat have concerned themselves for a number of years is a coup d'etat of the reaction which will wrest from the wide masses of the people the most important political right — universal suffrage. In spite of the immense importance of this possible event, it is, as we have already said, impossible to assert with certainty that an open popular movement would immediately break out after the coup d'etat, because today innumerable circumstances and factors have to be taken into account. But when we consider the present extreme acuteness of conditions in Germany, and on the other hand, the manifold international reactions of the Russian Revolution and of the future rejuvenated Russia, it is clear that the collapse of German politics which would ensue from the repeal of universal suffrage could not alone call a halt to the struggle for this right. This coup d'etat would rather draw after it, in a longer or shorter period and with elementary power, a great general political reckoning of the insurgent and awakened mass of the people — a reckoning with bread usury, with artificially caused dearness of meat, with expenditure on a boundless militarism and "navalism," with the corruption of colonial policy, with the national disgrace of the Konigsberg trial, with the cessation of social reform, with the discharging of railway workers, the postal officials and the land workers, with the tricking and mocking of the miners, with the judgment of Lobtau and the whole system of class justice, with the brutal lockout system — in short, with the whole thirty-year-old oppression of the combined dominion of Junkerdom and large trustified capital.

But if once the ball is set rolling then social democracy, whether it wills it or not, can never again bring it to a standstill. The opponents of the mass strike are in the habit of denying that the lessons and examples of the Russian Revolution can be a criterion for Germany because, in the first place, in Russia the great step must first be taken from an Oriental despotism to a modern bourgeois legal order. The formal distance between the old and the new political order is said to be a sufficient explanation of the vehemence and the violence of the revolution in

Russia. In Germany we have long had the most necessary forms and guarantees of a constitutional state, from which it follows that such an elementary raging of social antagonisms is impossible here.

Those who speculate thus forget that in Germany when it once comes to the outbreak of open political struggles, even the historically determined goal will be quite different from that in Russia today. Precisely because the bourgeois legal order in Germany has existed for a long time, because therefore it has had time to completely exhaust itself and to draw to an end, because bourgeois democracy and liberalism have had time to die out — because of this there can no longer be any talk of a *bourgeois* revolution in Germany. And therefore in a period of open political popular struggles in Germany, the last historical necessary goal can only be the *dictatorship of the proletariat.* The distance, however, of this task from the present conditions of Germany is still greater than that of the bourgeois legal order from Oriental despotism, and therefore, the task cannot be completed at one stroke, but must similarly be accomplished during a long period of gigantic social struggles.

But is there not a gross contradiction in the picture we have drawn? On the one hand it means that in an eventual future period of political mass action the most backward layers of the German proletariat — the land workers, the railwaymen, and the postal slaves — will first of all win the right of combination, and that the worst excrescences of exploitation must first be removed, and on the other hand, the political task of this period is said to be the conquest of power by the proletariat! On one hand, economic, trade-union struggles for the most immediate interests, for the material elevation of the working class; on the other hand, the ultimate goal of social democracy! Certainly these are great contradictions, but they are not contradictions due to our reasoning, but contradictions due to capitalist development. It does not proceed in a beautiful straight line but in a lightninglike zigzag. Just as the various capitalist countries represent the most varied stages of development, so within each country the different layers of the same working class are represented. But history does not wait patiently till the backward countries, and the most advanced layers have joined together so that the whole mass can move symmetrically forward like a compact column. It brings the best prepared parts to explosion as soon as conditions there are ripe for it, and then in the storm of the revolutionary period, lost ground is recovered, unequal things are equalized, and the whole pace of social progress changed at one stroke to the double-quick.

Just as in the Russian Revolution all the grades of development and all the interests of the different layers of workers are united in the social democratic program of the revolution, and the innumerable partial struggles united in the great common class action of the proletariat, so will it also be in Germany when the conditions are ripe for it. And the task of social democracy will then be to regulate its tactics, not by the most backward phases of development but by the most advanced.

VIII. Need for United Action of Trade Unions and Social Democracy

The most important desideratum which is to be hoped for from the German working class in the period of great struggles which will come sooner or later is, after complete resoluteness and consistency of tactics, the utmost capacity for action, and therefore the utmost possible unity of the leading social democratic part of the proletarian masses. Meanwhile the first weak attempts at the preparation of great mass actions have discovered a serious drawback in this connection: the total separation and independence of the two organizations of the labor movement, the social democracy and the trade unions.

It is clear on a closer consideration of the mass strikes in Russia as well as of the conditions in Germany itself, that any great mass action, if it is not confined to a mere one-day demonstration, but is intended to be a real fighting action, cannot possibly be thought of as a so-called political mass strike. In such an action in Germany the trade unions would be implicated as much as the social democrats. Not because the trade-union leaders imagine that the social democrats, in view of their smaller organization, would have no other resources than the cooperation of one and a quarter million trade unionists and without them would be unable to do anything, but because of a much more deep-lying motive: because every direct mass action of the period of open class struggles would be at the same time both political and economic. If in Germany, from any cause and at any time, it should come to great political struggles, to mass strikes, then at that time an era of violent trade-union struggles would begin in Germany, and events would not stop to inquire whether the trade-union leaders had given their consent to the movement or not. Whether they stand aside or endeavor to resist the movement, the result of their attitude will only be that the trade-union leaders, like the party leaders in the analogous case, will simply be swept aside by the rush of events, and the economic and the political struggles of the masses will be fought out without them.

As a matter of fact the separation of the political and the economic struggle and the independence of each is nothing but an artificial product of the parliamentarian period, even if historically determined. On the one hand in the peaceful, "normal" course of bourgeois society, the economic struggle is split into a multitude of individual struggles in every undertaking and dissolved in every branch of production. On the other hand the political struggle is not directed by the masses themselves in a direct action, but in correspondence with the form of the bourgeois state, in a representative fashion, by the presence of legislative representation. As soon as a period of revolutionary struggles commences, that is, as soon as the masses appear upon the scene of conflict, the breaking up of the economic struggle into many parts, as well as the indirect parliamentary form of the political struggle ceases; in a revolutionary mass action the political and the economic struggle are one, and the artificial boundary between trade union and social democracy as two separate, wholly independent forms of the labor movement, is simply swept away. But what finds concrete expression in the revolutionary mass movement finds expression also in the parliamentary period as an actual state of affairs. There are not two different class struggles of the working class, an economic and a political one, but only *one* class struggle, which aims at one and the same time at the limitation of capitalist exploitation within bourgeois society, and at the abolition of exploitation together with bourgeois society itself.

When these two sides of the class struggle are separated from one another for technical reasons in the parliamentary period, they do not form two parallel concurrent actions, but merely two phases, two stages of the struggle for emancipation of the working class. The trade-union struggle embraces the immediate interests, and the social democratic struggle the future interests, of the labor movement. The communists, says the *Communist Manifesto*, represent, as against various group interests, national or local, of the proletariat, the common interests of the proletariat as a whole, and in the various stages of development of the class struggle, they represent the interests of the whole movement, that is, the ultimate goal — the liberation of the proletariat. The trade unions represent only the group interests and only one stage of development of the labor movement. Social democracy represents the working class and the cause of its liberation as a whole. The relation of the trade unions to social democracy is therefore a part of the whole, and when, amongst the trade-union leaders, the theory of "equal authority" of trade unions and social democracy finds so much favor, it rests upon a fundamental misconception of the essence of trade unionism itself and of its role in the general struggle for freedom of the working class.

This theory of the parallel action of social democracy and the trade unions and of their "equal authority" is nevertheless not altogether without foundation, but has its historical roots. It rests upon the illusion of the peaceful, "normal" period of bourgeois society, in which the political struggle of social democracy appears to be consumed in the parliamentary struggle. The parliamentary struggle, however, the counterpart of the trade-union struggle, is equally with it, a fight conducted exclusively on the basis of the bourgeois social order. It is by its very nature, political reform work, as that of the trade unions is economic reform work. It represents political work for the present, as trade unions represent economic work for the present. It is, like them, merely a phase, a stage of development in the complete process of the proletarian class struggle whose ultimate goal is as far beyond the parliamentarian struggle as it is beyond the trade-union struggle. The parliamentary struggle is, in relation to social democratic policy, also a part of the whole, exactly as trade-union work is. Social democracy today comprises the parliamentary and the trade-union struggle in one class struggle aiming at the abolition of the bourgeois social order.

The theory of the "equal authority" of trade unions and social democracy is likewise not a mere theoretical misunderstanding, not a mere case of confusion but an expression of the well-known tendency of that opportunist wing of social democracy which reduces the political struggle of the working class to the parliamentary contest, and desires to change social democracy from a revolutionary proletarian party into a petty bourgeois reform one.* If social democracy should accept the theory of the "equal authority" of the trade unions, it would thereby accept, indirectly and tacitly, that transformation which has long been striven for by the representatives of the opportunist tendency.

---

* As the existence of such a tendency within German social democracy is generally denied, one must be grateful for the candor with which the opportunist trend has recently formulated its real aims and wishes. At a party meeting in Mayence on September 10, 1909, the following resolution, proposed by Dr. David, was carried.

"Whereas the Social Democratic Party interprets the term 'revolution' not in the sense of violent overthrow, but in the peaceful sense of development, that is, the gradual realization of a new economic principle, the public party meeting at Mayence repudiates every kind of revolutionary romance.'

"The meeting sees in the conquest of political power nothing but the winning over of the majority of the people to the ideas and demands of the social democracy; a conquest which cannot be achieved by means of violence, but only by the revolutionizing of the mind by means of intellectual propaganda and practical reform work in all spheres of political, economic and social life.

"In the conviction that social democracy flourishes far better when it employs legal means than when it relies on illegal means and revolution, the meeting repudiates *direct mass action* as a tactical principle, and holds fast to the principle of 'parliamentary reform action,'

In Germany, however, there is such a shifting of relations within the labor movement as is impossible in any other country. The theoretical conception, according to which the trade unions are merely a part of social democracy, finds its classic expression in Germany in fact, in actual practice, and that in three directions. First, the German trade unions are a direct product of social democracy; it was social democracy which created the beginnings of the present trade-union movement in Germany and which enabled it to attain such great dimensions, and it is social democracy which supplies it to this day with its leaders and the most active promoters of its organization.

Second, the German trade unions are a product of social democracy also in the sense that social democratic teaching is the soul of trade-union practice, as the trade unions owe their superiority over all bourgeois and denominational trade unions to the idea of the class struggle; their practical success, their power, is a result of the circumstance that their practice is illuminated by the theory of scientific socialism and they are thereby raised above the level of a narrow-minded socialism. The strength of the "practical policy" of the German trade unions lies in their insight into the deeper social and economic connections of the capitalist system; but they owe this insight entirely to the theory of scientific socialism upon which their practice is based. Viewed in this way, any attempt to emancipate the trade unions from the social democratic theory in favor of some other "trade-union theory" opposed to social democracy, is, from the standpoint of the trade unions themselves and of their future, nothing but an

---

that is, it desires that the party in the future as in the past, shall earnestly endeavor to *achieve its aims by legislation and gradual organized development.*

"The indispensable condition for this reformist method of struggle is that *the possibility of participation of the dispossessed masses of the people in the legislation* of the empire and of the individual states shall not be lessened but *increased to the fullest possible extent.* For this reason, the meeting declares it to be an incontestable right of the working class to withhold its labor for a longer or shorter period to ward off attacks on its legal rights and to gain further rights, when all other means fail.

"But as the political mass strike can only be victoriously carried through when kept within *strictly legal limits* and when the strikers give no reasonable excuse to the authorities to resort to armed force, the meeting perceives the only necessary and real preparation for the exercise of this method of struggle in the further extension of the political, trade-union and cooperative organizations. Because only in this way can the conditions be created amongst the wide masses of the people which can guarantee the successful prosecution of a mass strike: conscious discipline and adequate economic support." [R. L.]

attempt to commit suicide. The separation of trade-union practice from the theory of scientific socialism would mean to the German trade unions the immediate loss of all their superiority over all kinds of bourgeois trade unions, and their fall from their present height to the level of unsteady groping and mere dull empiricism.

Thirdly and finally, the trade unions are, although their leaders have gradually lost sight of the fact, even as regards their numerical strength, a direct product of the social democratic movement and the social democratic agitation. It is true that in many districts trade-union agitation precedes social democratic agitation, and that everywhere trade-union work prepares the way for party work. From the point of view of effect, party and trade unions assist each other to the fullest extent. But when the picture of the class struggle in Germany is looked at as a whole and its more deep-seated associations, the proportions are considerably altered. Many trade-union leaders are in the habit of looking down triumphantly from the proud height of their membership of one and a quarter million on the miserable organized members of the Social Democratic Party, not yet half a million strong, and of recalling the time, ten or twelve years ago, when those in the ranks of social democracy were pessimistic as to the prospects of trade-union development.

They do see that between these two things — the large number of organized trade unionists and the small number of organized Social Democrats — *there exists in a certain degree a direct causal connection.* Thousands and thousands of workers do not join the party organizations precisely because they join the trade unions. According to the theory, all the workers must be doubly organized, must attend two kinds of meetings, pay double contributions, read two kinds of workers' papers, etc. But for this it is necessary to have a higher standard of intelligence and of that idealism which, from a pure feeling of duty to the labor movement, is prepared for the daily sacrifice of time and money, and finally, a higher standard of that passionate interest in the actual life of the party which can only be engendered by membership of the party organization. All this is true of the most enlightened and intelligent minority of social democratic workers in the large towns, where party life is full and attractive and where the workers' standard of living is high. Amongst the wider sections of the working masses in the large towns, however, as well as in the provinces, in the smaller and ·the smallest towns where local political life is not an independent thing but a mere reflex of the course of events in the capital, where consequently, party life is poor and monotonous, and where, finally, the economic standard of life of the workers is, for the most part, miserable, it is very difficult to secure the double form of organization.

For the social democratically-minded worker from the masses the question will be solved by his joining his trade union. The immediate interests of his economic struggle which are conditioned by the nature of the struggle itself cannot be advanced in any other way than by membership of a trade-union organization. The contribution which he pays, often amidst considerable sacrifice of his standard of living, bring him immediate, visible results. His social democratic inclinations, however, enable him to participate in various kinds of work without belonging to a special party organization; by voting at parliamentary elections, by attendance at social democratic public meetings, by following the reports of social democratic speeches in representative bodies, and by reading the party press. Compare in this connection the number of social democratic electors or the number of subscribers to *Vorwaerts* with the number of organized party members in Berlin!

And what is most decisive, the social democratically-minded average worker who, as a simple man, can have no understanding of the intricate and fine so-called two-soul theory, feels that he is, even in the trade union, *social democratically* organized. Although the central committees of the unions have no official party label, the workman from the masses in every city and town sees at the head of his trade union as the most active leaders, those colleagues whom he knows also as comrades and social democrats in public life, now as Reichstag, Landtag or local representatives, now as trusted men of the social democracy, members of election committees, party editors and secretaries, or merely as speakers and agitators. Further, he hears expressed in the agitational work of his trade union much the same ideas, pleasing and intelligible to him, of capitalist exploitation, class relations, etc., as those that have come to him from social democratic agitation. Indeed, the most and best loved of the speakers at trade-union meetings are those same social democrats.

Thus everything combines to give the average class-conscious worker the feeling that he, in being organized in his trade union, is also a member of his labor party and is social democratically organized, *and therein lies the peculiar recruiting strength of the German trade unions*. Not because of the appearance of neutrality, but because of the social democratic reality of their being, have the central unions been enabled to attain their present strength. This is simply through the coexistence of the various unions — Catholic, Hirsch-Dunker, etc. [Unions under "liberal" leadership. — Ed.] — founded by bourgeois parties by which it was sought to establish the necessity for that political "neutrality." When the German worker who has full freedom of choice to attach himself to a Christian, Catholic, Evangelical or Free-thinking trade union, chooses none of these but the "free trade union" instead, or leaves one of the former to join the latter, he does so only because he considers that the central unions are the avowed organizations of the modern class struggle, or, what is the same thing in Germany, that they are social democratic trade unions.

In a word the appearance of "neutrality," which exists in the minds of many trade-union leaders, does not exist for the mass of organized trade unionists. And that is the good fortune of the trade-union movement. If the appearance of "neutrality," that alienation and separation of the trade unions from social democracy, really and truly becomes a reality in the eyes of the proletarian masses, then the trade unions would immediately lose all their advantages over competing bourgeois unions, and therewith their recruiting power, their living fire. This is conclusively proved by facts which are generally known. The appearance of party-political "neutrality" of the trade unions could, as a means of attraction, render inestimable service in a country in which social democracy itself has no credit among the masses, in which the odium attaching a workers' organization injures it in the eyes of the masses rather than advantages it — where, in a word, the trade unions must first of all recruit their troops from a wholly unenlightened, bourgeois-minded mass.

The best example of such a country was, throughout the whole of the last century, and is to a certain extent today, Great Britain. In Germany, however, party relations are altogether different. In a country in which social democracy is the most powerful political party, in which its recruiting power is represented by an army of over three million proletarians, it is ridiculous to speak of the deterrent effect of social democracy and of the necessity for a fighting organization of the workers to ensure political neutrality. The mere comparison of the figures of social democratic voters with the figures of the trade-union organizations in Germany is sufficient to prove to the most simpleminded that the trade unions in Germany do not, as in England, draw their troops from the unenlightened bourgeois-minded mass, but from the mass of proletarians already aroused by the social democracy and won by it to the idea of the class struggle. Many trade-union leaders indignantly reject the idea — a requisite of the "theory of neutrality" — and regard the trade unions as a recruiting school for social democracy. This apparently insulting, but in reality, highly flattering presumption is in Germany reduced to mere fancy by the circumstance that the positions are reversed; it is the social democracy which is the recruiting school for the trade unions.

Moreover, if the organizational work of the trade unions is for the most part of a very difficult and troublesome kind, it is, with the exception of a few cases and some districts, not merely because on the whole, the soil has not been prepared by the social democratic plough, but also because the trade-union seed itself and the sower as well must also be "red," social democratic before the harvest can prosper. But when we compare in this way the figures of trade-union strength, not with those of the social democratic organizations, but—which is the only correct way—with those of the mass of social democratic voters, we come to a conclusion which differs considerably from the current view of the matter. The fact then comes to light that the "free trade unions" actually represent today but a minority of the class-conscious workers of Germany, that even with their one and a quarter million organized members they have not yet been able to draw into their ranks one-half of those already aroused by social democracy.

The most important conclusion to be drawn from the facts above cited is that the *complete unity* of the trade-union and the social democratic movements, which is absolutely necessary for the coming mass struggles in Germany, *is actually here*, and that it is incorporated in the wide mass which forms the basis at once of social democracy and trade unionism, and in whose consciousness both parts of the movement are mingled in a mental unity. The alleged antagonism between social democracy and trade unions shrinks to an antagonism between social democracy and a certain part of the trade-union officials, which is, however, at the same time an antagonism within the trade unions between this part of the trade-union leaders and the proletarian mass organized in trade unions.

The rapid growth of the trade-union movement in Germany in the course of the last fifteen years, especially in the period of great economic prosperity from 1895 to 1900 has brought with it a great independence of the trade unions, a specializing of their methods of struggle, and finally the introduction of a regular trade-union officialdom. All these phenomena are quite understandable and natural historical products of the growth of the trade unions in this fifteen-year period, and of the economic prosperity and political calm of Germany. They are, although inseparable from certain drawbacks, without doubt a historically necessary evil. But the dialectics of development also brings with it the circumstance that these necessary means of promoting trade-union growth become, on the contrary, obstacles to its further development at a certain stage of organization and at a certain degree of ripeness of conditions.

The specialization of professional activity as trade-union leaders, as well as the naturally restricted horizon which is bound up with disconnected economic struggles in a peaceful period, leads only too easily, amongst trade-union officials, to bureaucratism and a certain narrowness of outlook. Both, however, express themselves in a whole series of tendencies which may be fateful in the highest degree for the future of the trade-union movement. There is first of all the overvaluation of the organization, which from a means has gradually been changed into an end in itself, a precious thing, to which the interests of the struggles should be subordinated. From this also comes that openly admitted need for peace which shrinks from great risks and presumed dangers to the stability of the trade unions, and further, the overvaluation of the trade-union method of struggle itself, its prospects and its successes.

The trade-union leaders, constantly absorbed in the economic guerrilla war whose plausible task it is to make the workers place the highest value on the smallest economic achievement, every increase in wages and shortening of the working day, gradually lose the power of seeing the larger connections and of taking a survey of the whole position. Only in this way can one explain why many trade-union leaders refer with the greatest satisfaction to the achievements of the last fifteen years, instead of, on the contrary, emphasizing the other side of the medal; the simultaneous and immense reduction of the proletarian standard of life by land usury, by the whole tax and customs policy, by landlord rapacity which has increased house rents to such an exorbitant extent, in short, by all the objective tendencies of bourgeois policy which have largely neutralized the advantages of the fifteen years of trade-union struggle. From the *whole* social democratic truth which, while emphasizing the importance of the present work and its absolute necessity, attaches the chief importance to the criticism and the limits to this work, the *half* trade-union truth is taken which emphasizes only the positive side of the daily struggle.

And finally, from the concealment of the objective limits drawn by the bourgeois social order to the trade-union struggle, there arises a hostility to every theoretical criticism which refers to these limits in connection with the ultimate aims of the labor movement. Fulsome flattery and boundless optimism are considered to be the duty of every "friend of the trade-union movement." But as the social democratic standpoint consists precisely in fighting against uncritical trade-union optimism, as in fighting against uncritical parliamentary optimism, a front is at last made against the social democratic theory: men grope for a "new trade-union theory," that is, a theory which would open an illimitable vista of economic progress to the trade-union struggle within the capitalist system, in opposition to the social democratic doctrine. Such a theory has indeed existed for some time — the theory of Professor Sombart which was promulgated with the express intention of driving a wedge between the trade unions and the social democracy in Germany, and of enticing the trade unions over to the bourgeois position.

In close connection with these theoretical tendencies is a revolution in the relations of leaders and rank and file. In place of the direction by colleagues through local committees, with their admitted inadequacy, there appears the businesslike direction of the trade-union officials. The initiative and the power of making decisions thereby devolve upon trade-union specialists, so to speak, and the more passive virtue of discipline upon the mass of members. This dark side of officialdom also assuredly conceals considerable dangers for the party, as from the latest innovation, the institution of local party secretariats, it can quite easily result, if the social democratic mass is not careful that these secretariats may remain mere organs for carrying out decisions and not be regarded in any way the appointed bearers of the initiative and of the direction of local party life. But by the nature of the case, by the character of the political struggle, there are narrow bounds drawn to bureaucratism in social democracy as in trade-union life.

But here the technical specializing of wage struggles as, for example, the conclusion of intricate tariff agreements and the like, frequently means that the mass of organized workers are prohibited from taking a "survey of the whole industrial life," and their incapacity for taking decisions is thereby established. A consequence of this conception is the argument with which every theoretical criticism of the prospects and possibilities of trade-union practice is tabooed and which alleges that it represents a danger to the pious trade-union sentiment of the masses. From this the point of view has been developed that it is only by blind, childlike faith in the efficacy of the trade-union struggle that the working masses can be won and held for the organization. In contradistinction to social democracy which bases its influence on the unity of the masses amidst the contradictions of the existing order and in the complicated character of its development, and on the critical attitude of the masses to all factors and stages of their own class struggle, the influence and the power of the trade unions are founded upon the upside down theory of the incapacity of the masses for criticism and decision. "The faith of the people must be maintained" — that is the fundamental principle, acting upon which many trade-union officials stamp as attempts on the life of this movement all criticisms of the objective inadequacy of trade unionism.

And finally, a result of this specialization and this bureaucratism amongst trade-union officials is the great independence and the "neutrality" of the trade unions in relation to social democracy. The extreme independence of the trade-union organization has resulted as a natural condition from its growth, as a relation which has grown out of the technical division of work between the political and the trade-union forms of struggle. The "neutrality" of the German trade unions, on its part, arose as a product of the reactionary trade-union legislation of the Prusso-German police state. With time, both aspects of their nature have altered. From the condition of political "neutrality" of the trade unions imposed by the police, a theory of their voluntary neutrality has been evolved as a necessity founded upon the alleged nature of the trade-union struggle itself. And the technical independence of the trade unions which should rest upon the division of work in the unified social democratic class struggle, the separation of the trade unions from social democracy, from its views and its leadership, has been changed into the so-called equal authority of trade unions and social democracy.

This appearance of separation and equality of trade unions and social democracy is, however, incorporated chiefly in the trade-union officials, and strengthened through the managing apparatus of the trade unions. Outwardly, by the coexistence of a complete staff of trade-union officials, of a wholly independent central committee, of numerous professional press, and finally of a trade-union congress, the illusion is created of an exact parallel with the managing apparatus of the social democracy, the party executive, the party press and the party conference. This illusion of equality between social democracy and the trade union has led to, amongst other things, the monstrous spectacle that, in part, quite analogous agendas are discussed at social democratic conferences and trade-union congresses, and that on the same questions different, and even diametrically opposite, decisions are taken. From the natural division of work between the party conference, which represents the general interests and tasks of the labor movement, and the trade-union congress (which deals with the much narrower sphere of social questions and interests) the artificial division has been made of a pretended trade-union and a social democratic outlook in relation to *the same* general questions and interests of the labor movement.

Thus the peculiar position has arisen that this same trade-union movement which below, in the wide proletarian masses, is absolutely one with social democracy, parts abruptly from it above, in the superstructure of management, and sets itself up as an independent great power. The German labor movement therefore assumes the peculiar form of a double pyramid whose base and body consist of one solid mass but whose apices are wide apart.

It is clear from this presentation of the case in what way alone in a natural and successful manner that compact unity of the German labor movement can be attained which, in view of the coming political class struggles and of the peculiar interest of the further development of the trade unions, is indispensably necessary. Nothing could be more perverse or more hopeless than to desire to attain the unity desired by means of sporadic and periodical negotiations on individual questions affecting the labor movement between the Social Democratic Party leadership and the trade-union central committees. It is just the highest circles of both forms of the labor movement which as we have seen, incorporate their separation and self-sufficiency, which are themselves, therefore, the promoters of the illusion of the "equal authority" and of the parallel existence of social democracy and trade unionism.

To desire the unity of these through the union of the party executive and the general commission is to desire to build a bridge at the very spot where the distance is greatest and the crossing most difficult. Not above amongst the heads of the leading directing organizations and in their federative alliance, but below amongst the organized proletarian masses, lies the guarantee of the real unity of the labor movement. In the consciousness of the million trade unionists, the party and the trade unions are actually *one*, they represent in different forms the *social democratic* struggle for the emancipation of the proletariat. And the necessity automatically arises therefrom of removing any causes of friction which have arisen between the social democracy and a part of the trade unions, of adapting their mutual relation to the consciousness of the proletarian masses, that is, *of rejoining the trade unions to social democracy.* The synthesis of the real development which led from the original incorporation of the trade unions to their separation from social democracy will thereby be expressed, and the way will be prepared for the coming period of great proletarian mass struggles during the period of vigorous growth, of both trade unions and social democracy, and their reunion, in the interests of both, will become a necessity.

It is not, of course, a question of the merging of the trade-union organization in the party, but of the restoration of the unity of social democracy and the trade unions which corresponds to the actual relation between the labor movement as a whole and its partial trade-union expression. Such a revolution will inevitably call forth a vigorous opposition from a part of the trade-union leadership. But it is high time for the working masses of social democracy to learn how to express their capacity for decision and action, and therewith to demonstrate their ripeness for that time of great struggles and great tasks in which they, the masses, will be the actual chorus and the directing bodies will merely act the "speaking parts," that is, will only be the interpreters of the will of the masses.

The trade-union movement is not that which is reflected in the quite understandable *but irrational* illusion of a minority of the trade-union leaders, but that which lives in the consciousness of the mass of proletarians who have been won for the class struggle. In this consciousness the trade-union movement is a part of social democracy. "And what it is, that should it dare to appear."

WHAT IS ECONOMICS?

In the fall of 1906 the SPD established a special party school in Berlin. Its purpose was to take thirty students chosen each year by the party and trade unions and give them an intensive, six-month course in the history of socialism, economics, the trade-union struggle and numerous other topics. Rosa Luxemburg was not asked to teach the first year, but in the fall of 1907, when two of the teachers who were not German citizens were forbidden by the police to continue their activities at the school, Rosa Luxemburg took over the course in economics. From 1907 until the school was closed during World War I, her teaching activities occupied much of her time and provided a great deal of enjoyment.

From all reports, she was an exceptionally good teacher, and a reading of "What Is Economics?" gives a good indication why her classes were popular. Any student who has suffered through a course in economics, and tried to understand the dry, humorless, and intentionally obscure explanations of professors like those Rosa Luxemburg ridicules, will wish they could have been in her classes.

Over a period of many years she worked to compile her lectures into a comprehensive introduction to economics. She spent a great deal of her spare time on it between 1907 and 1912, frequently turning down speaking invitations in order to have more time to work. It was not until she was imprisoned during World War I, however, that she was able to polish some of the chapters for publication, including the first chapter, "What Is Economics?"

The book was to have ten chapters, but when friends attempted to assemble the incomplete manuscript after her death they found only six. The rest were probably destroyed when her apartment was sacked by counterrevolutionary troops after her murder. The incomplete manuscript was published in the 1920s by Paul Levi, but Levi was accused of having altered the original. A second version, supposedly based on the original manuscript, was published by the East German government in 1951, and the translation by T. Edwards is from the more recent version.

219

The abridged version of the first chapter included in this selection omits several sections which constitute a side polemic on the nature of the economy today as an international rather than strictly "national" entity.

I

Economics is a peculiar science. Problems and controversies arise as soon as we take the first step in this field of knowledge, as soon as the fundamental question—what is the subject matter of this science—is posed. The ordinary working man, who has only a very vague idea of what economics deals with, will attribute his haziness on this particular point to a shortcoming in his general education. Yet, in a certain sense, he shares his perplexity with many learned scholars and professors who write multivolumed works dealing with the subject of economics and who teach courses in economics to college students. It appears incredible, and yet it is true, that most professors of economics have a very nebulous idea of the actual subject matter of their erudition.

Since it is common usage among these professors adorned with academic titles and honors to operate with definitions, that is, to try to exhaust the essence of the most complex phenomena in a few neatly arranged sentences, let us experiment for a moment and attempt to learn from a representative of offical bourgeois economics what essential topics this science deals with. Let us consult first of all the head of the German professorial world, the author of an immense number of frightfully huge textbooks dealing with economics, the founder of the so-called historical school of economics, Wilhelm Roscher. In his first big work, entitled *The Principles of Political Economy, a Handbook and Textbook for Businessmen and Students*, which was first published in 1854 but which has run through twenty-three editions since then, we read as follows, in chapter 2, section 16: "By the science of national, or political economy, we understand the science which has to do with the laws of development of the economy of a nation, or with its economic national life (philosophy of the history of political economy, according to von Mangoldt). Like all the political sciences, or sciences of national life, it is connected, on the one hand, with the consideration of the individual man, and on the other, it extends its investigation to the whole of human kind" (p. 87).

Do the "businessmen and students" now understand what economics is? Why, economics is the science having to do with economic life. What are horn-rimmed glasses? Glasses with rims of horn, of course. What is a pack mule? Why, it is a mule with a pack! As a matter of fact, this is a good way to explain the meaning of more complex words to infants. It is a pity, however, that if you did not understand the meaning of the words in question in the first place that you will not be any wiser whether the words are arranged this way or that way.

Let us consult another German scholar, the present instructor in economics at the University of Berlin, a veritable shining light of official science, famous "throughout the length and the breadth of the land"—as the saying goes—Professor Schmoller. In an article on economics to be found in that large compendium of German professors, *The Hand Dictionary of Political Sciences*, published by Professors Conrad and Lexis, Schmoller answers us as follows:

"I would say that it is the science which is to describe, define, and elucidate the causes of economic phenomena, and also to comprehend them in their interrelations. This supposes, of course, that economics is defined correctly in the first place. In the center of this science we must place the typical forms, repeated among all of the modern cultured peoples, of the division and organization of labor, of commerce, of the distribution of income, of socioeconomic institutions which, supported by certain kinds of private and public law and dominated by the same or similar psychic forces, generate the same or similar arrangements of forces, which, in their complete description, would present the statistics of the present economic civilized world—a sort of average condition of the latter. Continuing from there, the science has attempted to ascertain the differences among the various national economies, one in comparison to the others, the various types of organization here and elsewhere; it has asked in what relation and in what sequence the various forms appear and has thus arrived at the conception of the causal development of these different forms, one from the other, and the historical sequence of economic conditions. And as it has, from the very beginning, arrived at the affirmation of ideals by means of moral and historical value judgments, so it has maintained, to a certain extent, this practical function to the present. Besides theory, economics has always propagated practical principles for everyday living."

Whew! Let's take a deep breath. How was that again? Socioeconomic institutions—private and public law—psychic forces—similar and same—same and similar—statistics—statics—dynamics—average conditions—causal development—moral-historical value judgments. . . . An ordinary mortal reading this passage can't help wondering why his head is spinning like a top. With blind faith in the professorial wisdom being dispensed here, and in stubborn pursuit of knowledge, one might try to decipher this jumble two times, maybe three times—with an effort, but we are afraid it would be in vain. It is but hollow phraseology and pompous prattle which we are being handed. And this in itself is an infallible sign. If you think soundly and if you have thoroughly mastered the subject under consideration, you will express yourself concisely and intelligibly. When you are not dealing with the intellectual gymnastics of philosophy or the phantasmagoric ghosts of religious mysticism, and you still express yourself in an obscure and rambling manner, you reveal that you are in the dark yourself—or that you have a motive for avoiding clarity. We shall see later that the obscurantist and perplexing terminology of the bourgeois professors is no accident, that it expresses not merely their own muddleheadedness, but also their tendentious and tenacious aversion of a real analysis of the question which we are considering.

That the precise definition of the nature of economics is a matter of dispute may be demonstrated from a purely superficial aspect—its age. The most contradictory views have been expressed about the age of this science. For example, a well-known historian and former professor of economics at the University of Paris, Adolphe Blanqui—brother of the famous socialist leader and soldier of the Commune, Auguste Blanqui—commences the first chapter of his *History of Economic Development* with the following synopsis: "Economics is older than one might think. The Greeks and Romans already had one of their own." On the other hand, other writers discussing the history of economics, e.g., Eugen Duehring, formerly lecturer at the University of Berlin, consider it important to emphasize that economics is much younger than is commonly thought—that this science had arisen as late as the latter half of the eighteenth century. In order to present socialist opinions also, let us quote Lassalle's remark, made in 1864, in the preface to his classic polemic against Schultze-Delitzsch's *Capital and Labor*: "Economics is a science the rudiments of which are in existence but which is yet to be solved definitively."

On the other hand, Karl Marx subtitled his economic main work *Capital — The Critique of Political Economy*, the first volume of which appeared, as if in fulfillment of Lassalle's pronouncement, three years later, in 1867. By means of the subtitle Marx puts his own work outside the pale of conventional economics, regarding the latter as something concluded, finished — something to be criticized conclusively.

This science, some contend, is as old as the written history of mankind. Others contend that it is barely a century and a half old. A third group insists that it is still in its infancy. Still others assert that it has already outlived its usefulness and that it is time to pass critical and final judgment on it in order to hasten its demise. Would you not admit that such a science is a unique and complicated problem?

It would be quite ill-advised to ask one of the official bourgeois representatives of this science: How do you explain the curious fact that economics—and this is the prevailing opinion these days—was started only rather recently, a mere 150 years ago? Professor Duehring, for example, will reply with a great many words, asserting that the Greeks and Romans had no scientific concepts at all about economic problems, nothing but "irresponsible, superficial, very vulgar" notions culled from everyday experience; that the Middle Ages were entirely "unscientific" to the *n*th degree. This learned explanation obviously does not help us at all; on the contrary, it is quite misleading, especially in its manner of generalizing about the Middle Ages.

An equally peculiar explanation is offered by Professor Schmoller. In his article quoted above, he contributes the following gem to the general confusion: "For centuries many separate private and social economic facts had been observed and described, a few economic truths had been recognized, and economic problems had been discussed in systems of law and of ethics. These unrelated pertinent facts were to be united into a special science when the economic problems attained a previously unheard-of importance in the management and administration of states; from the seventeenth until the nineteenth century, when numerous writers occupied themselves with them, education about them became necessary to university students, and at the same time the evolution of scientific thought in general led to the interrelating of these collected economic sayings and facts into an independent connected system by using certain fundamental notions, such as money and barter, national politics on economic matters, labor and the division of labor—this was attempted by the important writers of the eighteenth century. Since that time the theory of economics has existed as an independent science."

When we squeeze what little sense there is from this long-winded passage, we obtain the following: There were various economic observations which, at least for a while, were lying around and about, here and there, not doing much of anything. Then, all of a sudden, as soon as the "management and administration of the state"—he means the government—needed them and when, as a consequence, it became necessary to teach economics at the universities, these economic sayings were collected and taught to college students. How astounding and how typical is this explanation for a professor! First, because of the need of the right honorable government, a teaching chair is founded—which is to be filled by a right zealous professor. Then, of course, the corresponding science must be created, otherwise what would the professor teach? Reading this passage, who is not reminded of the master of court protocol who asserted that he was absolutely convinced that monarchies would have to endure forever; after all, without monarchies, what would he do for a living? The essence of the passage, then, is the following: economics came into being because the government of the modern state needed this science. A summons issued by the powers-that-be is supposed to be the birth certificate of economics—this way of thinking fits a present-day professor perfectly.

The scientific valet of the government who, at the request of that government, will beat the drums "scientifically" in favor of any navy, tariff or tax proposal, who in wartime will become the veritable hyena of the battlefield, preaching chauvinism, national hatred'and intellectual cannibalism—such a being readily imagines that the financial requirements of sovereignty, the fiscal desires of the treasury, a nod from the powers-that-be, that these were enough to create a science overnight—out of thin air! For those of us who are not in governmental employ, such notions present a few difficulties. Moreover, this explanation only poses another question: What happened in the seventeenth century that made the governments of the modern states—going along with Professor Schmoller's contention—feel the need for shaking down their beloved subjects according to scientific principles, all of a sudden; whereas for hundreds of years they had done quite well, thank you, with the old-fashioned methods? Are not things turned upside down here and is it not more likely that the new needs of the sovereign treasuries were only a modest consequence of those great historic changes which were the real cause of the birth of the new science of economics, in the middle of the eighteenth century?

In summation, we can only say that the learned professors would not tell us what subject matter economics deals with, and then, on top of that, they would not reveal why and how this science originated. . . .

V

Sometimes economics is simply defined as follows: it is the "science of the economic relations among human beings." The question of the definition of economics does not become clarified by this camouflage of the issue involved but instead becomes even more involved—the following question arises: is it necessary, and if so why, to have a special science about the economic relations of "human beings," i.e., *all* human beings, at all times and under all conditions?

Let us pick an example of human economic relations, a simple and illustrative example, if possible. Let us imagine ourselves living in that historic period when world economy did not exist as yet, when commodity exchange flourished only in the towns, while on the countryside natural economy, i.e., production for one's own use, predominated, on the great landed estates as well as on the small farms.

Let us consider, for example, conditions in the Scottish Highlands in the 1850s, as described by Dugald Stewart: "In some parts of the Highlands of Scotland. . . . many a shepherd and a cottar too, with his wife and children appeared. . . . in shoes of leather tanned by himself. . . . in clothes which had been touched by no hands but their own, since they were shorn from the sheep and sown in the flax field. In the preparation of these scarcely a single article had been purchased, except the awl, needle, thimble, and a few parts of the ironwork employed in the weaving. The dyes, too, were chiefly extracted by the women from trees, shrubs, and herbs" (Cited by Karl Marx, *Capital,* Vol. 1, p. 524, footnote 2, Everyman ed.).

Or let us take an example from Russia where only a relatively short while ago, at the end of the 1870s, the condition of the peasantry often was as follows: "The soil which he (the peasant of the district Vyasma in the province of Smolensk) cultivates supplies him with food, clothing, almost everything which he needs for subsistence: bread, potatoes, milk, meat, eggs, linen, cloth, sheepskins, and wool for warm clothing. . . . He uses money only when buying boots, a few toilet articles, like belts, caps, gloves, and also a few essential household items: earthen and wooden dishes, fire hooks, pots, and similar items" (Prof. Nikolai Siever, *David Ricardo and Karl Marx,* Moscow 1879, p. 480).

There are similar peasant households in Bosnia and Herzegovina, in Serbia, and in Dalmatia even to this day. If we were to ask such a self-sufficient farmer from the Highlands of Scotland, or from Russia, from Bosnia, or Serbia, the customary professorial questions about his "economic motives," about the "origin and distribution of his wealth" and similar problems of economics, he would lift his eyes in amazement. Why and towards what end are we working? (Or as the professors would say: "What motivates you in your economy?") The peasant most assuredly would reply as follows: Well, now, let's see. We got to live, since—as the saying goes—roast squabs aren't flying into our mouths just yet. If we didn't work, then we would die of hunger. We work so we can make out, so we can eat sufficiently, clothe ourselves neatly, so we can keep a roof over our heads. What do we produce, what "purpose" does our labor fulfill? What a silly question! We produce what we need, what every farm family needs in order to stay alive. We plant wheat and rye, oats and barley, potatoes; according to the circumstances in which we find ourselves, we keep cows and sheep, chickens and geese. In the winter there is spinning to be done—that is woman's work, while the men make whatever the household needs with axe, saw, and hammer. For all I care, you can call it "agriculture" or "handicraft," in any case, we have to do a little of everything, since we need all kinds of things around the house and for the fields.

How do we "organize" the work? Another silly question! The men, naturally, do those chores which call for the strength of men; the women take care of the house, the cows, and the chicken coop; the children help wherever they can. You don't mean that I should send the woman to cut the wood and that I should milk the cow myself? (The good man does not know — let us add on our part — that in many primitive tribes, Brazilian Indians, for instance, it is precisely the women who collect wood, dig for roots and gather fruits in the forest, while with the cattle-raising tribes of Africa and Asia it is the men who not only take care of the cattle, but also milk them. Even today, in Dalmatia, one can still see the woman carrying heavy loads on her back, while the robust man rides alongside on a donkey, puffing a pipe. This "division of labor" appears just as natural to them as it seems natural to our peasant that he should cut the wood and that his wife should milk the cows.) But let us go on: What constitutes my wealth? But every child in the village knows the answer to that! A peasant is rich when he has a full barn, a well-filled stable, a good herd of sheep, a big chicken coop; he is poor if he starts running out of flour around Easter time and when his roof starts leaking when it rains for a spell. Upon what factors does the "increase of my wealth" depend? What is there to ask? If I had a larger piece of land, I would be richer, and if in the summer, God forbid, a big hailstorm comes down, then everyone in the village will be poor, in less than twenty-four hours.

We have permitted the farmer to answer the customary questions of economics very patiently, but we may be sure that if the professor had come to the farmhouse in person, with notebook and fountain pen to do his scientific research, that he would have been shown the gate very brusquely before he ever reached the halfway mark in his questioning. And as a matter of fact, all the relations in such a peasant economy are so open and transparent that their dissection by the scalpel of economics appears indeed idle play.

Of course, one might object and assert that the example perhaps is ill-chosen, that in a tiny self-sufficient farm household the utmost simplicity is indeed a result of the scanty resources and of the small scale on which production is carried on. Well, then let us leave the small farm household which manages to keep the wolf from its doorstep in some God-forsaken, out-of-the-way locality somewhere, let us raise our field of vision until it hits the highest summit of a mighty empire, let us examine the household of Charlemagne. This emperor succeeded in making the German Empire the mightiest in Europe during the early ninth century; he organized no less than fifty-three military expeditions to extend and secure his realm, ruling not only present-day Germany, but also France, Italy, Switzerland, Northern Spain, Holland, and Belgium; this emperor was also very much concerned with economic conditions on his manors and farms.

With his own imperial hand, no less, he wrote a special decree comprising seventy paragraphs in which he laid down the principles which were to be applied to the management of his farms: the famous *Capitulare de Villis*, i.e., law about the manors; fortunately this document, a priceless treasury of historical information, has been preserved to this day, among the moulder and dust of the archives. This document deserves particular attention, for two reasons. First of all, most of the agricultural holdings of Charlemagne subsequently developed into mighty free cities: e.g., Aix-la-Chapelle, Cologne, Munich, Basel, Strasbourg, and many other German and French cities used to be the agricultural property of Charlemagne, in times long since past. Secondly, the economic regulations of Charlemagne constituted a model for all the larger ecclesiastical and secular estates of the early Middle Ages; Charlemagne's manors kept the traditions of old Rome alive and transplanted the refined culture of the Roman villas into the rough milieu of the young Teutonic nobility; his regulations about winemaking, gardening, fruit and vegetable raising, poultry breeding, and so forth, were a historic achievement of lasting significance.

Let us take a closer look at this document. The great emperor, first of all, asks that he be served honestly, that his subjects on the manors be well taken care of and protected from poverty; that they not be burdened with work over and above their normal capacities; that if they work at night, they be compensated for it. The subjects, on their part, should apply themselves diligently to grape-growing and should put the pressed grape juice into bottles, so that it not suffer deterioration. If they shirk their duties, they are to be chastised "upon the back or elsewhere." The emperor directs further that bees and geese should be kept; poultry is to be well cared for and to be increased. Careful attention is to be paid to increasing the stock of cattle and brood mares, and also to sheep raising.

We desire furthermore, writes the emperor, that our forests are managed intelligently, that they are not cut down, and that sparrow-hawks and falcons should be kept therein. Fat geese and chickens should always be kept at our disposal; eggs which are not consumed are to be sold at the markets. In each of our manors a supply of good bed feathers, mattresses, blankets, copper kitchenware, lead, iron, wood, chains, pothooks, hatchets, drills should always be on hand, so that nothing has to be borrowed from other people.

Furthermore, the emperor insists that exact accounts of the yield of his manors be kept, namely, how much of each item was produced, and he lists them: vegetables, butter, cheese, honey, oil, vinegar, beets, "and other trifles" — as the text of the famous document goes. The emperor orders further that in each of his domains various artisans, skilled in every craft, should be present in sufficient number, and again he lists the various crafts, one by one. He designates Christmas Day as the date on which he is to receive annual accounts of all his riches and the smallest peasant does not count each head of cattle or each egg on his farm with more care than the great emperor Charles. The sixty-second paragraph of the document goes as follows: "It is important that we know what and how much of each we own — of every article." And once more he lists them: oxen, mills, wood, boats, vines, vegetables, wool, linen, hemp, fruits, bees, fishes, hides, wax, and honey, new and aged wines, and other things which are delivered to him. And for the consolation of his dear vassals who are to supply him with all these things, he adds guilelessly: "We hope that all this shall not appear too difficult for you; since each of you is lord on his manor, you, in turn, may exact these things from your subjects."

Further along in the law we encounter exact instructions as to the type of container and the mode of transportation of wines — which apparently were an affair of state which was very dear to the heart of the emperor. "Wine should be carried in casks with stout iron rims and never in skins. As for flour, it is to be transported in double carts covered with leather, so that rivers may be forded without damage to the flour. I also want an exact accounting of the horns of my bucks and goats, likewise of the skins of the wolves killed in the course of the year. In the month of May do not forget to declare ruthless war on the young wolves." Finally, in the last paragraph, Charles the Great, lists all the flowers and trees and herbs which he wants to grow on his manors, such as: roses, lilies, rosemaries, cucumbers, onions, radishes, caraway seeds, etc. The famous legislative document concludes with something like the enumeration of the various brands of apples.

This, then, is the picture of the imperial household of the ninth century and even though we are dealing here with one of the mightiest and wealthiest of the sovereigns of the Middle Ages, everyone will have to admit that his household economy as well as his management principles are surprisingly reminiscent of those of the tiny farm household which we considered previously. If we were to ask our imperial host the previous questions of economics, about the nature of his wealth, the object of production, the division of labor, etc., he would extend his royal hand and point to the mountains of wheat, wool and hemp, to the casks of wine, oil, and vinegar, to the stables filled with cows, oxen, and sheep. And, in all probability, we should not be able to think up any kind of mysterious problems for the science of economics to analyze and solve there, inasmuch as all relations, cause and effect, labor and its result are crystal-clear.

Perhaps someone wishes to call our attention to the fact that we chose the wrong example again. After all, is it not evident from the document that we are not dealing with the public economic life of the German Empire, but with the private household of the emperor? But if someone were to counterpose these two concepts, he would commit a historical error as far as the Middle Ages are concerned. Certainly, the law applied to the economy of the estates and manors of Emperor Charlemagne, but he operated these households as sovereign, not as a private citizen. Or, to be more specific, the emperor was lord on his own manorial estates, but each great noble lord of the Middle Ages, especially at the time of Charlemagne, was a similar emperor on a smaller scale — because his free noble ownership of the land made him lawmaker, tax-collector, and judge over all the inhabitants of his manors. That the economic decrees of Charles were acts of government is proved by their form: they are a part of the sixty-five laws or *capitulare* of Charles, written by the emperor and promulgated at the annual imperial diet of his princes. And the regulations about radishes and about iron-rimmed casks flow from the same despotic authority and are written in the same style, as, for instance, his admonitions to the ecclesiastics in *Capitulare Episcoporum*, the "law about the bishops," where Charles grabs the servants of the Lord by the ears and lectures them sternly not to swear, not to get drunk, not to visit places of ill repute, not to keep mistresses, and not to sell the holy sacraments for too dear a price. We might search high and low in the Middle Ages, we would not be able to find anywhere an economic unit on the countryside for which Charlemagne's manors would not be models and prototypes — whether noble domains or simple peasant farms; whether we consider separate independently working peasant families or collectively laboring village communities.

What is most striking in both examples is that the needs of human existence directly guide and determine the work, and that the results correspond exactly to the intentions and the needs, and that, regardless of the scale of production, economic relations manifest an astonishing simplicity and transparency. The small farmer on his plot of land as well as the great sovereign on his manors—both of them know exactly what they want to accomplish in production. And what is more, neither has to be a genius to know it. Both want to satisfy the ordinary human requirements of food, drink, clothes, and to obtain the various comforts of life. The only difference is that the peasant sleeps on a straw mat, while the noble lord sleeps in a soft feather bed; the peasant drinks beer and mead and also plain water, while the lord drinks fine wines at his table. The difference is one of quantity and in the kinds of goods produced. The basis of the economy, however, and its main object remain the same, i.e., the direct satisfaction of human needs. The labor which achieves this purpose is in accord with its result as a foregone conclusion. And in the labor process, too, there are differences: the peasant works with his own hands in company with the members of his family; he receives as many labor products as his plot of land and his portion of the common lands are capable of producing, or, more exactly—inasmuch as we are speaking here of the medieval serf—as much as the labor services and the tithes exacted by the lord and by the church have left him. The emperor and each noble lord does not labor in person, forcing his subjects and his tenants to do his work for him, instead.

But whether the peasant families work for themselves or for the lord, under the supervision of the village elder or of the lord's steward, the result of production is merely a certain quantity of the means of subsistence (in the larger meaning of that term)—those things which are needed, and about as much as is required. We may turn and twist this economy as much as we might want to, we shall find in it no riddles—to be understood only by thoughtful analysis, by a special science. The dumbest peasant of the Middle Ages knew exactly on what his "wealth" (perhaps we should say "poverty") depended aside from the natural catastrophies which, every once in a while, hit the lord's as well as the peasant's land. The peasant knew very well that his poverty had a very simple and direct causation: first, the limitless extortions of labor services and money fees exacted by the lord; second, the thievery of the same lords perpetrated at the expense of the village common lands, communal forests, and village water rights. And what the peasant knew he screamed to the heavens when he set the red cock on the housetops of the bloodsuckers. The only matter to be determined by scientific investigation in this type of economy was the historic origin and the development of these kinds of relations—the question of how it happened that in all of Europe the formerly free peasant lands had been transformed into noble domains from which tributes and rents were exacted, how the formerly free peasantry had been transformed into an oppressed class constrained to perform labor services, to be bound to the land, even, during the later stages.

Things look entirely different as soon as we turn our attention to any phenomena of present economic life. Let us take, for example, one of the most remarkable and striking phenomena: the commercial crisis. Every one of us has lived through a few great commercial and industrial crises and we know from our own experience the process described by Friedrich Engels in a classic passage: "Commerce becomes dull, the markets are glutted, the products lie there as abundant as they are unsalable, hard cash becomes invisible, credit vanishes, the factories are closed, the working masses lack the means of subsistence, because they have produced too much of the means of subsistence, bankruptcy follows upon bankruptcy, forced sale upon forced sale. The stagnation lasts for years, productive forces and mass products are wasted and destroyed wholesale, until the accumulated masses of commodities flow off more or less depreciated in value, until production and exchange are again gradually set into motion. Little by little the pace quickens, falls into a trot, the industrial trot changes into a gallop and this again increases into the headlong gallop of a complete industrial, commercial, credit, and speculative steeplechase, in the end to land again after the most breakneck leaps — in the ditch of the crisis" (F. Engels, *Anti-Duehring*, pp. 286-7, Kerr edition).

All of us know how the specter of a commercial crisis terrifies any modern country — even the way in which the approach of such a crisis is heralded is most significant. After a few years of prosperity and of good business have elapsed, vague rumors are to be detected in the newspapers now and then; the stock exchange receives the disquieting news of a few bankruptcies; then, the hints in the press become broader; the stock exchange becomes increasingly apprehensive; the national bank increases credit rates, this signifies that credit is more difficult to get and limited in amount; in the end, the news about bankruptcies and layoffs pours down like drops of water in a cloudburst. And once the crisis is in full swing, then the argument starts about who is to blame for it. The businessmen blame the abrupt credit refusals by the banks, the speculative mania of the stock brokers; the stock brokers blame the industrialists; the industrialists blame the shortage of money, etc. And when business finally picks up again, then the stock exchange and the newspapers note the first signs of improvement with relief, until, at last, hope, peace, and security stop over for a short stay, once more.

What is noteworthy in all this is the fact that the crisis is looked upon and treated by all concerned, by all of society, as something beyond the sphere of human volition and beyond human control, as a heavy blow struck by an invisible and greater power, an ordeal sent down from the heavens, similar to a heavy thunderstorm, an earthquake, or a flood. The language customarily employed by the trade journals in reporting a crisis is studded with such expressions as: "the formerly serene sky of the business world commences to be overcast with dark clouds"; or when a sharp increase in bank credit rates is reported it is inevitably served up under the title of "storm warnings" and after the crisis we read of the passing thunderstorm and the serene business horizon. This mode of expression reveals more than the mere bad taste of the newspaper hacks of the financial page; it is absolutely typical of the attitude towards a crisis — as if the latter were the result of the workings of a natural law. Modern society notes its approach with horror; it bows its head tremblingly under the blows coming down as thick as hail; it waits for the end of the ordeal, and then lifts its head once more — at first timidly and skeptically; only much later is society almost reassured again. This is exactly the same way in which people in the Middle Ages regarded famines or plagues; the way the farmer today endures a thunderstorm: the same consternation and helplessness in the face of a severe ordeal.

But famines and pestilences are natural phenomena first and foremost, even though in the last analysis, they, too, are social phenomena — a bad harvest, the spread of disease germs and so forth. A thunderstorm is an event caused by the elements of physical nature, and no one, at least not with the present development of the natural sciences and of technology, is able to bring about or to prevent a thunderstorm. But what is a modern crisis? It consists of the fact that too many commodities have been produced. They find no purchasers, and therefore commerce and then industry stop! The manufacture of commodities, their sale, trade, industry — all these are relations of human society. It is man, himself, who produces commodities, and it is man, himself, who buys them; exchange takes place from one person to another, and we will find in the factors which make up a modern crisis not a single circumstance which would fall outside the sphere of human activity. It is, therefore, human society which periodically creates the crisis. And yet, at the same time, we know that the crisis is a real scourge of modern society, that it is awaited with horror, endured in despair, that it is not desired nor wished for by anyone. Except for a few stock exchange manipulators who attempt to enrich themselves quickly at the expense of others and who just as frequently as not are taken in themselves, the crisis, at the very least, is a risk or an inconvenience for everyone.

No one wants a crisis and yet it happens. Man creates it with his own hands, even though he does not want it for anything in the world. Here, in fact, we have before us a question of economic life which none of the participants can explain. The medieval peasant on his small plot produced, on the one hand, what his lord, and, on the other, what he himself, desired and needed: wheat and cattle, means of subsistence for himself and his family. The great lord of the Middle Ages had those things produced for himself which he wanted and needed: wheat and cattle, good wines and fine clothes, food and luxury items for himself and his household. But contemporary society produces what it neither wants nor needs: depressions. From time to time it produces means of subsistence which it cannot consume; it periodically suffers famines while immense warehouses are full of unsalable products. Needs and their gratification, the object and consequence of labor do not agree anymore; something dark and mysterious has come between them and separated them.

Let us take another example from today's life, known to everyone and only too well known by the workers of all countries: unemployment. Like the crisis, unemployment is nothing less than a cataclysm which afflicts society from time to time; to a larger or smaller extent, it is a constant everyday symptom accompanying economic life today. The best organized and best paid layers of the workers who keep track of their unemployed members note an unbroken chain of statistics of unemployed people, for every year, and every month, and for every week in the year. These numbers of unemployed workers may undergo major fluctuations, but never, not even for a second, do they drop to zero. How helplessly present-day society confronts unemployment, that dreaded chronic disease of the working class, is shown every time its spread becomes so great that the legislative bodies are forced to concern themselves with it. After much talking back and forth, these deliberations habitually end with the passing of a resolution to institute an inquiry, an investigation about the actual number of unemployed. In the main, they limit themselves to measure the current scope of the malady—just as in floods the level of the water is measured by a water gauge. At the most a weak palliative is prescribed in the form of unemployment relief (and this is done most frequently at the cost of the employed workers), in order to lessen the effects of the phenomenon without even attempting to remove the source of the ill itself!

In the beginning of the nineteenth century, that great prophet of the English bourgeoisie, the parson Malthus, proclaimed with the refreshing brutality which is so characteristic of him: "If the worker cannot get any means of existence from those relatives on whom he may justly make claims and if society does not need his labor, he who is born into a world already fully occupied has no claim to the smallest particle of food, and, as a matter of fact, does not belong upon this world. There is no place set for him at nature's great banquet table. Nature orders him to disappear, and she quickly executes her command." Present official society, with the "social-reformist" hypocrisy so peculiar to it, frowns on such harsh candidness. Actually it, too, lets the unemployed proletarian, "whose labor it does not need," "disappear" from this world, in one way or another, sooner or later — as demonstrated by the statistics about the deterioration of public health, the increase in infant mortality, the growth of crimes against property, during every crisis.

The analogy of unemployment and floods used by us points up the striking fact that we confront great natural catastrophes with *less* helplessness than our own, purely social, exclusively human affairs! The periodic floods which cause such immense damage in eastern Germany every spring, in the last analysis, result from the complete neglect of the proper countermeasures which has been in evidence up to now. Technology, even in its present stage of development, offers us adequate means with which to protect agriculture from devastation by the uncontrolled waters. Of course, in order to harness this potential force, the means offered by technology must be applied on a large scale — a great regional water control plan which would rebuild the entire danger area, move fields and pastures accordingly, erect dams and locks, and regulate rivers. This great reform is not being undertaken, partly because neither private capital nor the government care to supply the necessary funds, partly because they would encounter the obstacle of the most multifarious private property rights to the land in the extensive area under consideration. However, the means for the control of the flood danger and for the harnessing of the raging waters do exist in present society, even if it is unable to apply them.

The remedy for unemployment, on the other hand, has not as yet been found by contemporary society. And yet it is no elemental law of nature, no physical force of nature, no supernatural power, but merely a product of exclusively human economic relations. And here, once more, we are faced by an economic riddle, by an occurrence which no one purposely desires, which no one consciously intends, but which nevertheless occurs periodically with the regularity of a natural phenomenon — over the heads of men, as it were.

We need not even have recourse to such striking occurrences of present-day life, such as depressions or unemployment, i.e., calamities and events out of the ordinary — at least, current public opinion holds that these events form an exception to the normal

234

course of events. Let us take instead the most common example from everyday life, which repeats itself a thousand times in every country, fluctuations of commodity prices. Every child knows that the prices of commodities are not something fixed and unchanging, but, quite the contrary, they go up or down, almost every day, even every hour. Let us pick up any newspaper, let us turn to the commodity exchanges, and we shall read about the price movements of the previous day: wheat—weak in the morning, around noon somewhat stronger, at closing time higher, or lower. It is the same with copper, iron, sugar and grape seed oil. And similarly, with the stocks of the various industrial firms, with private or government bonds on the stock exchange.

Price fluctuations are an incessant, everyday, "normal" occurrence of economic life today. But as a result of these same price fluctuations the financial status of the owners of all these commodities changes daily and hourly. If the price of cotton increases then the wealth of all the traders and manufacturers who have cotton stocks in storage rises, for the moment; if the prices fall, their wealth declines. If copper prices go up, then the holders of copper mine stock become richer; if they go down, they become poorer. Thus, because of simple price fluctuations, as a result of a tick of the tape from the exchange, people can become millionaires or beggars within a few hours, and, of course, speculation with its frauds is based on this mechanism. The medieval proprietor would become richer or poorer by a good or a poor crop; or as a robber knight he might enrich himself if he made a good catch while kidnapping travelling merchants; or—and that was the tested and preferred method—he increased his wealth when he squeezed his bondsmen harder, by adding to the labor services and the money fees which he extorted from them.

Today, a person can become rich or poor without doing anything, without lifting a finger, without an occurrence of nature taking place, without anyone giving anyone anything, or physically robbing anything. Price fluctuations are like secret movements directed by an invisible agency behind the back of society, causing continuous shifts and fluctuations in the distribution of social wealth. This movement is observed as atmospheric pressure read on a barometer, or temperature on a thermometer. And yet commodity prices and their movements manifestly are human affairs and not black magic. No one but man himself—with his own hands—produces these commodities and determines their prices, except that, here again, something flows from his actions which he does not intend nor desire; here again, need, object, and result of the economic activity of man have come into jarring contradiction.

How does this happen, and what are the black laws which,

behind man's back, lead to such strange results of the economic activity of man today? These problems can be analyzed only by scientific investigation. It has become necessary to solve all these riddles by strenuous research, deep thought, analysis, analogy — to probe the hidden relations which give rise to the fact that the result of the economic activity of man does not correspond to his intentions, to his volition—in short, to his consciousness. In this manner the problem faced by scientific investigation becomes defined as the lack of human consciousness in the economic life of society, and here we have reached the immediate reason for the birth of economics.

Darwin, in his description of his world cruise, tells us the following about the Indians inhabiting Tierra del Fuego (on the southern tip of South America): "They often suffer from famine: I heard Mr. Low, a sealing master intimately acquainted with the natives of this country, give a curious account of the state of a party of one hundred and fifty natives on the west coast, who were very thin and in great distress. A succession of gales prevented the women from getting shellfish on the rocks, and they could not go out in their canoes to catch seal. A small party of these men one morning set out, and the other Indians explained to him, that they were going on a four days' journey for food: on their return, Low went to meet them, and he found them excessively tired, each man carrying a great square piece of putrid whale's blubber with a hole in the middle, through which they put their heads, like the Gauchos do through their ponchos or cloaks. As soon as the blubber was brought into a wigwam, an old man cut off thin slices, and muttering over them broiled them for a minute, and distributed them to the famished party, who during this time preserved a profound silence" [Darwin, *The Voyage of the Beagle*, New York, 1909, p. 229].

These are one of the most primitive peoples to be found anywhere on the face of this globe. The limits within which their volition and their conscious planning may function in their economy are still extremely narrow. Man is still tied very closely to the apron strings of mother nature, being completely dependent on her favor. And yet within these narrow limits this small society of 150 individuals observes a plan—organizing the entire social organism. The provisions for the future welfare at first take the wretched form of a supply of rotten blubber hidden someplace. But this wretched supply is divided among all of the members of the tribe, while certain ceremonies are observed; the labor of obtaining food is joined in by everyone, also under planful leadership.

Let us consider a Greek *Oikos*, a slave household economy of antiquity, an economy which actually did form a "microcosm," a small world by itself. Here, we will be able to observe great social inequalities. Primitive poverty has given way to a comfortable surplus of the fruits of human labor. Physical labor has become the damnation of one, idleness the privilege of the other; the worker has become the personal property of the nonworker. But even this master-and-slave relation yields the strictest planfulness and organization of the economy, of the labor process, of distribution. The despotic will of the master is its base, the whip of the slave driver its sanction.

In the feudal manor of the Middle Ages the despotic organization of economic life very early assumes the forms of a traditional detailed work code in which the planning and the division of labor, the duties and the rights of each are clearly and rigidly defined. On the threshold of this era in history stands the pretty document which we have considered above, the *Capitulare de Villis* by Charlemagne, which still exudes cheerfulness and good humor and revels voluptuously in the abundance of physical delights, the production of which is the sole purpose of economic life. At the end of the feudal period in history, we see that ominous code of labor services and money payments imposed by the feudal lords in their greed for money — a code which gave rise to the German Peasant Wars of the fifteenth century and which, two hundred years later, reduced the French peasant to that miserable beastlike being who would be aroused to fight for his civil rights only by the shrill tocsin of the Great French Revolution. But as long as the broom of the revolution had not swept away this feudal rubbish, then, in all of its wretchedness, the direct master-and-bondsman relation clearly and rigidly determined the conditions of feudal economy — like fate preordained.

Today, we know no masters, no slaves, no feudal lords, no bondsmen. Liberty and equality before the law have removed all despotic relations, at least in the older bourgeois states; in the colonies — as is commonly known — slavery and bondage are introduced, frequently enough for the first time, by these same states. But where the bourgeoisie is at home, free competition rules as the sole law of economic relations and any plan, any organization has disappeared from the economy. Of course, if we look into separate private enterprises, into a modern factory or a large complex of factories and workshops, like Krupp or a large-scale capitalist farm enterprise in North America, then we shall find the strictest organization, the most detailed division of labor, the most cunning planfulness based on the latest scientific information. Here, everything flows smoothly, as if arranged by magic, managed by *one* will, by *one* consciousness. But no sooner do we leave the factory or the large farm behind, when chaos surrounds us. While the innumerable units — and today a

237

private enterprise, even the most gigantic, is only a fragment of the great economic structure which embraces the entire globe—while these units are disciplined to the utmost, the entity of all the so-called national economies, i.e., world economy, is completely unorganized. In the entity which embraces oceans and continents, there is no planning, no consciousness, no regulation, only the blind clash of unknown, unrestrained forces playing a capricious game with the economic destiny of man. Of course, even today, an all-powerful ruler dominates all working men, and women: capital. But the form which this sovereignty of capital takes is not despotism but anarchy.

And it is precisely this anarchy which is responsible for the fact that the economy of human society produces results which are mysterious and unpredictable to the people involved. Its anarchy is what makes the economic life of mankind something unknown, alien, uncontrollable—the laws of which we must find in the same manner in which we analyze the phenomena of external nature—the same manner in which we have to attempt to comprehend the laws governing the life of the plant and animal kingdom, the geologic formations on the earth's surface, and the movements of the heavenly bodies. Scientific analysis must discover *ex post facto* that purposefulness and those rules governing human economic life which conscious planfulness did not impose on it beforehand.

It should be clear by now why the bourgeois economists find it impossible to point out the essence of their science, to put the finger on the gaping wound in the social organism, to denounce its innate infirmity. To recognize and to acknowledge that anarchy is the vital motive force of the rule of capital is to pronounce its death sentence in the same breath, to assert that its days are numbered. It becomes clear why the official scientific defenders of capital's rule attempt to obscure the entire matter with all kinds of semantic artifices, try to direct the investigation away from the core of the subject, take up mere external appearances and discuss "national economy" instead of the world economy. At the very first step over the threshold of economic understanding, even with the first basic premise of economics, bourgeois and proletarian economics experience a parting of the ways. With the very first question—as abstract and as impractical as it might seem at first glance in connection with the social struggles taking place today—a special bond is forged between economics as a science and the modern proletariat as a revolutionary class.

VI

If we proceed from the insight gained above, then various questions will be cleared up, which otherwise might have seemed puzzling to us.

First of all, the problem of the age of economics is solved. A science which has for its subject the discovery of the laws of the anarchy of capitalist production obviously could not arise before that mode of production itself, before the historic conditions for the class rule of the modern bourgeoisie were established, by centuries of birth pangs, of political and economic changes.

According to Professor Bucher, the rise of the present social order was a very simple matter of course, which had little to do with preceding economic phenomena: it was the product of the exalted decision and the sublime wisdom of absolutist monarchs. "The final development of 'national economy,'" Bucher tells us — and we already know that for a bourgeois professor the term "national economy" is a purposely misleading circumlocution for capitalist production—"is in its essence the fruit of the political centralization that begins at the close of the Middle Ages with the rise of the territorial state organizations, and now finds its completion in the creation of the unified national state. Economic unification of forces goes hand in hand with the bowing of private political interests to the higher aims of the nation as a whole. In Germany it is the more powerful territorial princes, as opposed to the rural nobles and the towns, who seek to realize the modern national idea. . . ." (Bucher, *The Rise of National Economy*, p. 134).

But also in the rest of Europe—in Spain, Portugal, England, France, the Netherlands—the princely power accomplished similar valorous deeds. "In all these lands, though with varying degrees of severity, appears the struggle with the independent powers of the Middle Ages—the greater nobility, the towns, the provinces, the religious and secular corporations. The immediate question, to be sure, was the annihilation of independent territorial circles which blocked the way to political unification. But deep down beneath the movement leading to the development of princely absolutism slumbers the universal idea that the greater tasks confronting modern civilization demanded an organized union of whole peoples, a grand living community of interests; and this could arise only upon the basis of common economic action" (Loc. cit.).

Here we have the prettiest flowering of that intellectual flunkeyism which we have noted previously of German professors. According to Professor Schmoller, the science of· economics came into being at the command of enlightened absolutism. According to Professor Bucher the entire capitalist mode of production itself is but an achievement of the sovereign decision and the heavenstorming plans of absolutist sovereigns. Indeed, we would do the great Spanish and French tyrants and also the German pigmydespots a great injustice by suspecting them of having been moved by some "world-historic idea" or "the greater tasks confronting human civilization" during their petty spats with insolent generals at the close of the Middle Ages, or during the costly crusades against the Dutch cities. Really, sometimes historical facts are actually stood on their heads.

The formation of bureaucratically centralized large states was an indispensable precondition for the capitalist mode of production, but their formation was a consequence of the new economic requirements, and one could turn Bucher's sentence around and say more correctly: the achievement of political centralization "in its essence" was a product of the maturing "national economy" (i.e., capitalist production).

It is characteristic of the unconscious tool of historic progress — such as absolutism — in the measure in which absolutism did take an undeniable part in this historic preparatory process, that it played its progressive role with the very same dumb thoughtlessness with which it inhibited these same tendencies at every convenient opportunity. This happened, for instance, when the medieval tyrants by-the-Grace-of-God considered the cities allied with them against the feudal nobility as mere objects of exploitation which, at the very first opportunity, they would betray to the feudal barons once more. The same sort of thing happened when, from the very beginning, they saw in the newly discovered continent, with all its populace and culture, nothing else but a suitable subject for the most brutal, insidious, and cruel spoilation — to fill their "princely treasuries" with gold nuggets in the shortest possible time for the purpose of "the greater tasks of civilization." The same took place when the tyrants by-the-Grace-of-God put up a stiff-necked resistance to their "faithful subjects" over that piece of paper called a bourgeois parliamentary constitution, which, after all, was just as necessary to the unhindered development of capital as were political unification and large centralized states.

As a matter of fact, entirely different forces were at work: large transformations in the economic life of the European peoples took place at the close of the Middle Ages, inaugurating the new mode of production.

After the discovery of America and the circumnavigation of Africa, i.e., after the discovery of the maritime route to India, had brought an undreamed-of flowering and also a relocation of the trade routes, the breakup of feudalism and of the domination of the towns by the guilds made rapid strides. The tremendous discoveries, conquests, plundering forays into the newly discovered countries, the sudden large influx of precious metals from the new continent, the extensive spice trade with India, the voluminous slave trade which supplied African Negroes to American plantations: all of these factors created new riches and new desires in Western Europe, in a very short period of time. The small workshop of the guild artisan, with its thousand-and-one restrictions, became a brake on the necessary increase of production and on its rapid progress. The big merchants overcame this obstacle by assembling the craftsmen in large manufactures beyond the jurisdiction of the cities; under the supervision of the merchants, relieved of the restrictive regulations of the guilds, the mechanics produced quicker and better.

In England, the new mode of production was introduced by a revolution in agriculture. The flowering of the wool manufactures in Flanders and the concomitant large demand for wool gave the English rural nobility the impulse for transforming large areas of previously tilled land into sheep walks; during this process the English peasantry was driven from its homes and fields on the most extensive scale imaginable. The Reformation worked in a similar manner. After the confiscation of church property in land — either given away as presents or dissipated by the court nobility and by speculators — the peasants living on this land were also driven from it, to a large extent. Thus, the manufacturers and the capitalist farmers found an abundant supply of impoverished proletarians who stood outside any feudal or guild regulations. After an extended period of martyrdom, as vagabonds or as laborers in the public workhouses, having been cruelly persecuted by law and by the police, these poor wretches found refuge in the harbor of wage slavery toiling for a new class of exploiters. Soon thereafter, the great technological revolutions took place which permitted the increased utilization of unskilled wage workers who worked alongside the highly skilled artisans, if they did not replace them entirely.

On every side, the budding and ripening of the new relations encountered feudal encumbrances and the misery of wretched conditions. The natural economy, on which feudalism was based and which flowed from its very essence, and the pauperization of the great masses of the people, caused by the unchecked pressure of serfdom, restricted the internal outlets of manufactured commodities. The guilds, in the meanwhile, hamstrung and fettered the most important condition of production: labor power. The state apparatus, split into an infinite number of political fragments, incapable of guaranteeing public safety, and the welter of tariff and commercial regulations curbed and molested the new commerce and the new mode of production at every step.

It was evident that, in one way or another, the rising bourgeoisie of Western Europe, as the representative of free world trade and of manufacturing, had to abolish these hindrances — unless it wanted to renounce its world-historic mission completely. Before smashing feudalism to smithereens in the Great French

Revolution, the bourgeoisie settled accounts with feudalism intellectually, and the new science of economics thus originates as one of the most important ideological weapons of the bourgeoisie as it struggles with the medieval state and for a modern capitalist class state. The developing economic order appeared first under the guise of new, rapidly-acquired riches which flooded society in Western Europe and which stemmed from sources much more lucrative and seemingly inexhaustible and quite different from the patriarchal methods of feudal exploitation — which, moreover, had seen its best day. At first, the most propitious source of the new 'affluence was, not the new mode of production itself, but its pacemaker: the great upswing in commerce. It is for this reason that in the most important centers of world trade in the opulent Italian commercial republics and in Spain, the first questions of economics are posed and the first attempts at their solution are made.

What is wealth? What makes a state poor, what makes it rich? This was the new problem — after the old concepts of feudal society had lost their traditional validity in the maelstrom of new relations. Wealth is gold with which one can buy anything. It is commerce which creates wealth. Those states will become wealthy which are able to import great quantities of gold and which permit none of it to leave the country. World trade, colonial conquests in the New World, manufactures which produce for export — these are the undertakings which must be fostered; the import of foreign products which lure gold out of the country must be prohibited. These were the first teachings of economics, which appear in Italy as early as the end of the sixteenth century and which gain popularity in England and in France in the seventeenth century. And crude as this doctrine still was, it represented the first open break with the ideas of the feudal natural economy and its first bold criticism — the first idealization of trade, of commodity production, and therewith of — capital; the first political program to the liking of the ascendant young bourgeoisie.

Soon, rather than the merchant, it is the commodity producing capitalist who steps to the fore — as yet quite cautiously, under the guise of the seedy servant waiting in the antechamber of the feudal prince. Wealth is not gold, at all, the French enlighteners of the eighteenth century proclaim, gold is merely a medium of exchange for commodities. What an infantile delusion to perceive in the shining metal the magic wand for peoples and for states! Is the metal able to feed me when I am hungry; can it protect me from the cold when I am freezing? Did not the Persian king Darius suffer the hellish torments of thirst while holding golden treasures in his arms, and would he not gladly have exchanged them for a drink of water? No, wealth is the bounty of nature in food and in those substances with which everyone, king and beggar, gratifies his wants. The more luxuriously the populace satisfies its needs, the richer will be the state—because the more taxes can then be pocketed by the state.

And who procures the wheat for the bread, the fibers with which we weave our clothes, the wood and the ores with which we build our houses and our tools?—Agriculture! Agriculture, not trade, constitutes the real source of riches! The mass of the agricultural population, the peasantry, the people who create the wealth of everyone else must be rescued from feudal exploitation and elevated to prosperity! (So that I might find buyers for my commodities, the manufacturing capitalist would add softly under his breath.) The great landed lords, the feudal barons, should be the only ones to pay taxes and to support the state, since all the wealth produced by agriculture flows through their hands! (So that I, who ostensibly do not create any wealth, do not have to pay taxes, the capitalist would slyly murmur to himself.) Agriculture, labor on the farm, needs only to be freed from all the restraints of feudalism in order that the fountain of riches may gush in all its natural bounteousness for state and nation. And then will come the greatest happiness of all the people, the harmony of nature will have been reestablished in the world.

The approaching thunderclouds, heralding the storming of the Bastille, were already clearly visible in these teachings of the enlighteners. Soon, the capitalist bourgeoisie felt itself powerful enough to take off its mask of submissiveness and to put itself squarely in the foreground demanding point-blank the remodeling of the entire state in its own image. Agriculture is not the sole source of wealth, at all, Adam Smith proclaims in England, at the close of the eighteenth century. Any wage labor which is engaged in commodity production creates wealth! (*Any labor*, Adam Smith said—and thereby he shows to what degree he and his disciples had turned into mere mouthpieces for the bourgeoisie; for him and his successors the laboring man was already by nature a wage worker for the capitalist!) Because wage labor, on top of the necessary wages for the maintenance of the worker, also creates the rent for the maintenance of the landlord and a profit besides, for the enrichment of the owner of capital, for the boss. And wealth becomes increased, the more workers there are in the workshops under the thumb of capital; the more detailed and painstakingly the division of labor among them has been carried out.

This, then, was the real harmony of nature, the real wealth of nations; any labor resolves itself into a wage for the workers, which keeps them barely alive and obliges them to continuing wage labor; rent, which suffices to provide the landlords with a carefree existence; and a profit, which keeps the boss in good humor so that he will persevere in his business enterprise. In this fashion, *everyone* is provided for without having to utilize the crude methods of feudalism. "The wealth of nations," then, is fostered when the wealth of the capitalist entrepreneur is promoted—the boss who keeps everything in operation, who taps the golden source of wealth: wage labor. Therefore: away with all the fetters and restrictions of the *old* good times and also with the recently instituted paternal protective measures of the state. Free cómpetition, a free hand for private capital, the entire fiscal and state apparatus in the service of the capitalist employer—and everything will turn out for the best, in the best of all possible worlds.

This, then, was the economic gospel of the bourgeoisie, divested of all its disguises—and the science of economics had been stripped down to where it showed its real physiognomy. Of course, the practical reform proposals and the suggestions which the bourgeoisie offered the feudal states failed as miserably as all historic attempts to pour new wine into old bottles have always failed. The hammer of revolution achieved in twenty-four hours, what half a century of patchwork could not achieve. It was the conquest of political power which put the ways and means of its rule into the hands of the bourgeoisie. But economics like all the philosophical, legal, and social theories of the Age of Enlightenment, and first and foremost among them, was a method of gaining consciousness, a source of bourgeois class consciousness. As such it was a precondition and a spur to revolutionary action. Even in its remotest offshoots, the bourgeois task of remodelling the world was fed by the ideas of classical political economy. In England, during the storm and stress period of the struggle for free trade, the bourgeoisie received its arguments from the arsenal of Smith-Ricardo. And the reforms of the Stein-Hardenburg-Scharnhorst period (in post-Napoleonic Germany), which were an attempt to put the feudal rubbish of Prussia into some kind of viable shape after the blows it had received from Napoleon at Jena, likewise took their ideas from the teachings of the English classical economists—the young German economist Marwitz wrote in the year 1810 that next to Napoleon, Adam Smith was the mightiest ruler in Europe.

If we understand at this point why the science of economics originated only about a century and a half ago, then, from the vantage point gained, we will also be able to construct its subsequent fate. If economics is a science dealing with the particular laws of the capitalist mode of production, then its reason for existence and its function are bound to the life span of the latter and economics will lose its base as soon as that mode of production will have ceased to exist. In other words, economics as a science will have accomplished its mission as soon as the anarchistic economy of capitalism has made way for a planful, organized economic order which will be systematically directed and managed by the entire working force of mankind. The victory of the modern working class and the realization of socialism will be the end of economics as a science. We see here the special bond between economics and the class struggle of the modern proletariat.

If it is the task and the subject matter of economics to elucidate the laws regulating the rise, growth, and extension of the capitalist mode of production, then it flows inexorably that, to be consistent, economics must also discover the laws of the decline of capitalism. Like previous modes of production, capitalism is not eternal, but a transitory historic phase, a rung in the never-ending ladder of social progress. The teachings about the rise of capitalism must logically transform themselves into the teachings about the fall of capitalism; the science of the capitalist mode of production becomes the scientific proof of socialism; the theoretical instrument of the inception of bourgeois class rule becomes a weapon in the revolutionary class struggle waged for the emancipation of the proletariat.

This second portion of the general problem of economics, of course, was solved neither by the French nor by the English, nor much less by the German wise men of the bourgeois classes. The final conclusions of the science analyzing the capitalist mode of production were drawn by a man who, from the very beginning, stood on the watchtower of the revolutionary proletariat—Karl Marx. For the first time, socialism and the modern labor movement were constructed on the indestructible rock of scientific insight.

As an ideal about a social order built on equality and fraternity for all men, as an ideal about a communist commonwealth, socialism was thousands of years old. Among the first apostles of Christianity, among the various religious sects of the Middle Ages, in the peasant wars, the socialist ideal had always flared up as the most radical expression of the revolt against contemporaneous society. But as an ideal which could be advocated at all times, in any historical milieu, socialism was only the beautiful vision of a few enthusiasts, a golden fantasy, always out of reach, like the airy image of the rainbow in the skies.

At the close of the eighteenth and in the beginning of the nineteenth centuries, the socialist idea, freed from all religious sectarian frenzy, as a reaction to the horrors and the devastations which ascendant capitalism perpetrated in society, appeared for the first time with real force behind it. But, even at that time, socialism basically was only a dream, the invention of a few bold minds. If we listen to the first vanguard fighter of the revolutionary upheavals set into motion by the proletariat, Gracchus Babeuf, who attempted a *coup de main* during the Great French Revolution for the purpose of introducing social equality forcibly, then we shall find that the sole argument on which he is able to base his communist aspirations is the crying injustice of the existing social order. In his impassioned articles, pamphlets, and also in his defense plea before the tribunal which sentenced him to death, he never tired of picking the contemporary social order to pieces. His gospel of socialism consists of an indictment of society, the denunciation of the sufferings and the torments, the wretchedness and the debasement of the working masses, on whose backs a handful of idlers grow wealthy and rule society. For Babeuf, it was enough that the existing social order well deserved to perish, i.e., it could have been overthrown a hundred years previous to his time, if only a group of determined men had been found who would seize the state power and who would introduce the regime of equality—just as the Jacobins seized political power in 1793 and introduced the republic.

In the 1820s and 1830s, socialist ideas were represented with a great deal more genius and brilliance by three great thinkers: Saint-Simon and Fourier in France, Owen in England. They based themselves on altogether different methods and yet, in essence, on the same line of reasoning as Babeuf. Of course, not one of the above-mentioned men thought even remotely of any revolutionary seizure of power for the realization of socialism. On the contrary, like the entire generation which followed the Great Revolution, they were disappointed with social overthrows and with politics, becoming express adherents of purely pacifist means and propaganda. But the postulation of the socialist idea was the same in all of them; basically, it was only a scheme, the vision of an ingenious mind who prescribes its realization to suffering humanity, for the purpose of rescuing it from the hell of the bourgeois social order.

Thus, in spite of all the power of their criticism and the magic of their futuristic ideals, these socialist ideas remained without any noticeable influence on the real movements and struggles of the times. With a handful of friends, Babeuf perished in the counterrevolutionary tidal wave, without leaving a trace, other than a short, shining inscription on the pages of revolutionary history. Saint-Simon and Fourier succeeded in establishing sects of enthusiastic and talented followers who—having sown rich and fertile seeds of social ideas, criticism and experiments—went their separate ways, looking for greener pastures. Of them all, Owen gained the greatest hold on the proletarian masses, but, after having attracted an elite group of English workers in the

246

1830s and 1840s, his influence also vanishes with hardly a trace. A new generation of socialist leaders emerged in the 1840s: Weitling in Germany, Proudhon, Louis Blanc, Blanqui in France. The working class itself had begun to take up the struggle against the clutches of capital; the class struggle had been initiated by the revolts of the silk weavers of Lyons in France, by the Chartist movement in England. However, there existed no direct link between the spontaneous movements of the exploited masses and the various socialist theories. The proletarian masses in revolt did not have a socialist goal in view, nor did the socialist theoreticians attempt to base their ideas on the political struggle of the working class. Their socialism was to be instituted by certain cunningly devised artifices, like Proudhon's People's Bank or Louis Blanc's productive associations. The only socialist who looked on the political struggle as an end towards the realization of the social revolution was Blanqui; this made him the only real representative of the proletariat and of its revolutionary class interests at the time. But, basically, even his socialism was only a scheme—attainable at will—as the fruition of the iron determination of a revolutionary minority and the outcome of a sudden coup d'etat carried through by the same minority.

The year 1848 was to be the high point and also the critical moment for the older socialism of all varieties. The Parisian proletariat, influenced by the traditions of preceding revolutionary struggles, agitated by the various socialist systems, passionately espoused some nebulous notions about a just social order. As soon as the bourgeois kingdom of Louis Philippe had been overthrown, the Parisian workers utilized the favorable relationship of forces to demand the realization of the "social republic" and a new "division of labor" from the terrified bourgeoisie. The provisional government was granted the famous three months period of grace for complying with these demands; and for three months the workers starved and waited, while the bourgeoisie and the petty bourgeoisie secretly armed themselves and prepared to crush the workers. The period of grace ended with the memorable June massacre in which the ideal of a "social republic," attainable at will at any time, was drowned in the blood of the Parisian proletariat. The revolution of 1848 did not institute the reign of social equality, but rather the political domination of the bourgeoisie and an unforeseen growth of capitalist exploitation under the Second Empire.

But, at the same time, while socialism of the old stripe seemed to be buried forever under the smashed barricades of the June insurrection, the socialist idea was placed on a completely new foundation by Marx and Engels. Neither of the latter two looked for arguments in favor of socialism in the moral depravity of the existing social order nor did they try to smuggle social equality into the country by means of inventing new and tempting schemes. They turned to the examination of the *economic* relations of society. There, in the very laws of capitalist anarchy, Marx discovered the real substantiation of socialist aspirations. While the French and English classicists of economics had discovered the laws according to which capitalist economy lives and grows, Marx continued their work a half century later, starting where they had left off. He discovered how these same laws regulating the present economy work towards its collapse, by the increasing anarchy which more and more endangers the very existence of society itself, by assembling a chain of devastating economic and political catastrophes. As Marx demonstrated, the inherent tendencies of capitalist development, at a certain point of their maturity, necessitate the transition to a planful mode of production consciously organized by the entire working force of society—in order that all of society and human civilization might not perish in the convulsions of uncontrolled anarchy. And this fateful hour is hastened by capital, at an ever-increasing rate, by mobilizing its future gravediggers, the proletarians, in ever greater numbers, by extending its domination to all countries of the globe, by establishing a chaotic world economy, and by laying the foundation for the solidarity of the proletariat of all countries into one revolutionary world power which shall sweep aside the class rule of capital. Socialism ceased being a scheme, a pretty fancy, or an experiment carried out in each country by isolated groups of workers, each on its own hook. As the common political program of action for the entire international proletariat, socialism becomes a *historic necessity*, because it is a result of the operation of the very laws of capitalist development.

It should be apparent by now, why Marx put his own economic teachings outside the pale of official economics, and named them *A Critique of Political Economy.* The laws of capitalist anarchy and of its future collapse which were developed by Marx are only the logical continuation of the science of economics as it had been created by the bourgeois scholars, but a continuation which, in its final conclusions, is in polar opposition to the point of departure of the wise men of the bourgeoisie. The Marxian doctrine is a child of bourgeois economics, but its birth cost the mother's life. In Marxist theory, economics found its perfection, but also its end as a science. What will follow — apart from the elaboration of Marxist theory in details — is only the metamorphosis of this theory into action, i.e., the struggle of the international proletariat for the institution of the socialist economic order. The consummation of economics as a science constitutes a world-historic task: its application in organizing a planful world economy. The last chapter of economics will be the social revolution of the world proletariat.

The special bond between economics and the modern working class is shown to be a reciprocal relation. If, on the one hand, the science of economics, as it was perfected by Marx, is, more than any other science, the indispensable basis of proletarian enlightenment, then, on the other hand, the class conscious proletariat is the only receptive audience these days capable of understanding the teachings of scientific economics. With the crumbling ruins of the old feudal society still before their eyes, the Quesnays and Boisguilleberts of France, the Adam Smiths and Ricardos of England surveyed the young bourgeois order with pride and enthusiasm, and with faith in the coming millenium of the bourgeoisie and its "natural" social harmony, without trepidation, they permitted their eagle eyes to scan the depths of the economic laws of capitalism.

But the growing impact of the proletarian class struggle, and especially the June insurrection of the Parisian proletariat, has long since destroyed the faith of bourgeois society in its own godlikeness. Since it has eaten of the tree of knowledge and learned about modern class contradictions, the bourgeoisie abhors the classic nakedness in which the creators of its own classical political economy once depicted it, for all the world to see. The bourgeoisie became conscious of the fact that the spokesmen of the modern proletariat had forged their deadly weapons from the arsenal of classical political economy.

Thus, it has come about that for decades not only has socialist economics preached to the deaf ears of the propertied classes, but bourgeois economics, to the extent that it once was a real science, has done the same. Unable to comprehend the teachings of their own great forebears, and even less able to accept Marxist teachings which flowed from them and which, moreover, sound the deathknell for bourgeois society, the bourgeois professors serve up a tasteless stew made from the leftovers of a hodge-podge of scientific notions and intentional circumlocutions — not intending to explore the real tendencies of capitalism, at all. On the contrary, they try only to send up a smoke screen for the purpose of defending capitalism as the best of all economic orders, and the only possible one.

Forgotten and forsaken by bourgeois society, scientific economics can find its listeners only among class-conscious proletarians, to find among them not only theoretical understanding but also concomitant action. The famous saying of Lassalle is applicable first and foremost to economics: "When science and the workers, these two opposite poles of society, shall embrace, they shall crush in their arms all social obstacles."

PEACE UTOPIAS

By 1911, when "Peace Utopias" was written, Europe was already beginning its downhill race toward World War I. The increasing tensions generated by the colonial competition of the great imperialist powers, the arms race and growing militarism, and similar signposts clearly pointed the way. The German SPD, more and more concerned with winning votes at home, seemed less and less concerned with combating the appeals to nationalist sentiment or sharply pointing to socialist revolution as the only possible alternative to the approaching imperialist war.

Rosa Luxemburg took up the challenge and denounced in scathing terms all the prevalent illusions being put forward by the official spokesmen of the SPD, including her former friend and ally Karl Kautsky, considered by all to be the most orthodox Marxist theoretician in the International. Even Lenin was not to break with Kautsky until 1914, after Kautsky supported German imperialism in World War I. But Rosa Luxemburg, being much closer to Kautsky and the deepening opportunism of the SPD, was the first leader of the International to see Kautsky and his idealistic theories for what they were and begin attacking his growing inclination to capitulate to the right wing of the SPD.

"Peace Utopias" was first published in *Leipziger Volkszeitung*, May 6 and 8, 1911. The following abridged version is reprinted from *The Labour Monthly* of July 1926.

I

What is our task in the question of peace? It does not consist merely in vigorously demonstrating at all times the love of peace of the social democrats; but first and foremost our task is to make clear to the masses of people the nature of militarism and sharply and clearly to bring out the differences in principle between the standpoint of the social democrats and that of the bourgeois peace enthusiasts.

Wherein does this difference lie? Certainly not merely in the fact that the bourgeois apostles of peace are relying on the influence of fine words, while we do not depend on words alone. Our very points of departure are diametrically opposed: the friends of peace in bourgeois circles believe that world peace and disarmament can be realized within the framework of the present social order, whereas we, who base ourselves on the materialistic conception of history and on scientific socialism, are convinced that militarism can only be abolished from the world with the destruction of the capitalist class state. From this follows the mutual opposition of our tactics in propagating the idea of peace. The bourgeois friends of peace are endeavoring—and from their point of view this is perfectly logical and explicable—to invent all sorts of "practical" projects for gradually restraining militarism, and are naturally inclined to consider every outward apparent sign of a tendency toward peace as the genuine article, to take every expression of the ruling diplomacy in this vein at its word, to exaggerate it into a basis for earnest activity. The social democrats, on the other hand, must consider it their duty in this matter, just as in all matters of social criticism, to expose the bourgeois attempts to restrain militarism as pitiful half measures, and the expressions of such sentiments on the part of the governing circles as diplomatic make-believe, and to oppose the bourgeois claims and pretences with the ruthless analysis of capitalist reality.

From this same standpoint the tasks of the social democrats with regard to the declarations of the kind made by the British government can only be to show up the idea of a partial limitation of armaments, in all its impracticability, as a half measure, and to endeavor to make it clear to the people that militarism is closely linked up with colonial politics, with tariff politics, and with international politics, and that therefore the present nations, if they really seriously and honestly wish to call a halt on competitive armaments, would have to begin by disarming in the commercial political field, give up colonial predatory campaigns and the international politics of spheres of influence in all parts of the world—in a word, in their foreign as well as in their domestic politics would have to do the exact contrary of everything which the nature of the present politics of a capitalist class state demands. And thus would be clearly explained what constitutes the kernel of the social democratic conception, that militarism in both its forms—as war and as armed peace—is a legitimate child, a logical result of capitalism, which can only be overcome with the destruction of capitalism, and that hence whoever honestly desires world peace and liberation from the tremendous burden of armaments must also desire socialism. Only in this way can real social democratic enlightenment and recruiting be carried on in connection with the armaments debate.

This work, however, will be rendered somewhat difficult and the attitude of the social democrats will become obscure and vacillating if, by some strange exchange of roles, our party tries on the contrary to convince the bourgeois state that it can quite well limit armaments and bring about peace and that it can do this from its own standpoint, from that of a capitalist class state.

It has until now been the pride and the firm scientific basis of our party that not only the general lines of our program but also the slogans of our practical everyday policy were not invented out of odds and ends as something desirable, but that in all things we relied on our knowledge of the tendencies of social development and made the objective lines of this development the basis of our attitude. For us the determining factor until now has not been the possibility from the standpoint of the relation of forces within the state, but the possibility from the standpoint of the tendencies of development of society. The limitation of armaments, the retrenchment of militarism does not coincide with the further development of international capitalism. Only those who believe in the mitigation and blunting of class antagonism, and in the checking of the economic anarchy of capitalism, can believe in the possibility of these international conflicts allowing themselves to be slackened, to be mitigated and wiped out. For the international antagonisms of the capitalist states are but the complement of class antagonisms, and the world political anarchy but the reverse side of the anarchic system of production of capitalism. Both can grow only together and be overcome only together. "A little order and peace" is, therefore, just as impossible, just as much a petty bourgeois utopia, with regard to the capitalist world market as to world politics, and with regard to the limitation of crises as to the limitation of armaments.

Let us cast a glance at the events of the last fifteen years of international development. Where do they show any tendency toward peace, toward disarmament, toward settlement of conflicts by arbitration?

During these fifteen years we had this: in 1895 the war between Japan and China, which is the prelude to the East Asiatic period of imperialism; in 1898 the war between Spain and the United States; in 1899-1902 the British Boer War in South Africa; in 1900 the campaign of the European powers in China; in 1904 the Russo-Japanese War; in 1904-07 the German Herero War in Africa; and then there was also the military intervention of Russia in 1908 in Persia; at the present moment the military intervention of France in Morocco, without mentioning the incessant colonial skirmishes in Asia and in Africa. Hence the bare facts alone show that for fifteen years hardly a year has gone by without some war activity.

But more important still is the aftereffect of these wars. The war with China was followed in Japan by a military reorganization which made it possible ten years later to undertake the war against Russia and which made Japan the predominant military power in the Pacific. The Boer War resulted in a military reorganization of England, the strengthening of her armed forces on land. The war with Spain inspired the United States to reorganize its navy and moved it to enter colonial politics with imperialist interests in Asia, and thus was created the germ of the antagonism of interests between the United States and Japan in the Pacific. The Chinese campaign was accompanied in Germany by a thorough military reorganization, the great Navy Law of 1900, which marks the beginning of the competition of Germany with England on the sea and the sharpening of the antagonisms between these two nations.

But there is another and extremely important factor besides: the social and political awakening of the hinterlands, of the colonies and the "spheres of interest," to independent life. The revolution in Turkey, in Persia, the revolutionary ferment in China, in India, in Egypt, in Arabia, in Morocco, in Mexico, all these are also starting points of world political antagonisms, tensions, military activities and armaments. It was just during the course of this fifteen years that the points of friction in international politics have increased to an unparalleled degree, a number of new states stepped into active struggle on the international stage, all the great powers underwent a thorough military reorganization. The antagonisms, in consequence of all these events, have reached an acuteness never known before, and the process is going further and further, since on the one hand the ferment in the Orient is increasing from day to day, and on the other every settlement between the military powers unavoidably becomes the starting point for fresh conflicts. The Reval Entente between Russia, Great Britain and France, which Jaures hailed as a guarantee for world peace, led to the sharpening of the crisis in the Balkans, accelerated the outbreak of the Turkish Revolution, encouraged Russia to military action in Persia and led to a rapprochement between Turkey and Germany which, in its turn, rendered the Anglo-German antagonisms more acute. The Potsdam agreement resulted in the sharpening of the crisis in China and the Russo-Japanese agreement had the same effect.

Therefore, on a mere reckoning with facts, to refuse to realize that these facts give rise to anything rather than a mitigation of the international conflicts, of any sort of disposition toward world peace, is willfully to close one's eyes.

In view of all this, how is it possible to speak of tendencies toward peace in bourgeois development which are supposed to

253

neutralize and overcome its tendencies toward war? Wherein are they expressed?

In Sir Edward Grey's declaration and that of the French Parliament? In the "armament weariness" of the bourgeoisie? But the middle and petty bourgeois sections of the bourgeoisie have always been groaning at the burden of militarism, just as they groan at the devastation of free competition, at the economic crises, at the lack of conscience shown in stock exchange speculations, at the terrorism of the cartels and trusts. The tyranny of the trust magnates in America has even called forth a rebellion of broad masses of the people and a wearisome legal procedure against the trusts on the part of the state authorities. Do the social democrats interpret this as a symptom of the beginning of the limitation of trust development, or have they not rather a sympathetic shrug of the shoulders for that petty bourgeois rebellion and a scornful smile for that state campaign? The "dialectic" of the peace tendency of capitalist development, which was supposed to have cut across its war tendency and to have overcome it, simply confirms the old truth that the roses of capitalist profit-making and class domination also have thorns for the bourgeoisie, which it prefers to wear as long as possible round its suffering head, in spite of all pain and woe, rather than get rid of it along with the head on the advice of the social democrats.

To explain this to the masses, ruthlessly to scatter all illusions with regard to attempts made at peace on the part of the bourgeoisie and to declare the proletarian revolution as the first and only step toward world peace—that is the task of the social democrats with regard to all disarmament trickeries, whether they are invented in Petersburg, London or Berlin.

II

The utopianism of the standpoint which expects an era of peace and retrenchment of militarism in the present social order is plainly revealed in the fact that it is having recourse to project making. For it is typical of utopian strivings that, in order to demonstrate their practicability, they hatch "practical" recipes with the greatest possible details. To this also belongs the project of the "United States of Europe" as a basis for the limitation of international militarism.

"We support all efforts," said Comrade Ledebour in his speech in the Reichstag on April 3, "which aim at getting rid of the threadbare pretexts for the incessant war armaments. We demand the economic and political union of the European states. I am firmly convinced that, while it is certain to come during the period of socialism, it can also come to pass before that time, that we will live to see the United States of Europe, as confronted at present by the business competition of the United

States of America. At least we demand that capitalist society, that capitalist statesmen, in the interests of capitalist development in Europe itself, in order that Europe will later not be completely submerged in world competition, prepare for this union of Europe into the United States of Europe."

And in the *Neue Zeit* of April 28, Comrade Kautsky writes: ". . . . For a lasting duration of peace, which banishes the ghost of war forever, there is only one way today: the union of the states of European civilization into a league with a common commercial policy, a league parliament, a league government and a league army—the formation of the United States of Europe. Were this to succeed, then a tremendous step would be achieved. Such a United States would possess such a superiority of forces that without any war they could compel all the other nations which do not voluntarily join them to liquidate their armies and give up their fleets. But in that case all necessity for armaments for the new United States themselves would disappear. They would be in a position not only to relinquish all further armaments, give up the standing army and all aggressive weapons on the sea, which we are demanding today, but even give up all means of defense, the militia system itself. Thus the era of permanent peace would surely begin."

Plausible as the idea of the United States of Europe as a peace arrangement may seem to some at first glance, it has on closer examination not the least thing in common with the method of thought and the standpoint of social democracy.

As adherents of the materialist conception of history, we have always adopted the standpoint that the modern states as political structures are not artificial products of a creative fantasy, like, for instance, the Duchy of Warsaw of Napoleonic memory, but historical products of economic development.

But what economic foundation lies at the bottom of the idea of a European State Federation? Europe, it is true, is a geographical and, within certain limits, a historical cultural conception. But the idea of Europe as an economic unit contradicts capitalist development in two ways. First of all there exist within Europe among the capitalist states—and will so long as these exist—the most violent struggles of competition and antagonisms, and secondly the European states can no longer get along economically without the non-European countries. As suppliers of foodstuffs, raw materials and wares, also as consumers of the same, the other parts of the world are linked in a thousand ways with Europe. At the present stage of development of the world market and of world economy, the conception of Europe as an isolated economic unit is a sterile concoction of the brain. Europe no more forms a special unit within world economy than does Asia or America.

255

And if the idea of a European union in the economic sense has long been outstripped, this is no less the case in the political sense.

The times when the center of gravity of political development and the crystallizing agent of capitalist contradictions lay on the European continent are long gone by. Today Europe is only a link in the tangled chain of international connections and contradictions. And what is of decisive significance—European antagonisms themselves no longer play their role on the European continent but in all parts of the world and on all the seas.

Only were one suddenly to lose sight of all these happenings and maneuvers, and to transfer oneself back to the blissful times of the European concert of powers, could one say, for instance, that for forty years we have had uninterrupted peace. This conception, which considers only events on the European continent, does not notice that the very reason why we have had no war in Europe for decades is the fact that international antagonisms have grown infinitely beyond the narrow confines of the European continent, and that European problems and interests are now fought out on the world seas and in the by-corners of Europe.

Hence the "United State of Europe" is an idea which directly counter both economically and politically to the course of development, and which takes absolutely no account of the events of the last quarter of a century.

That an idea so little in accord with the tendency of development can fundamentally offer no progressive solution in spite of all radical disguises is confirmed also by the fate of the slogan of the "United States of Europe." Every time that bourgeois politicians have championed the idea of Europeanism, of the union of European states, it has been with an open or concealed point directed against the "yellow peril," the "dark continent," against the "inferior races," in short, it has always been an imperialist abortion.

And now if we, as social democrats, were to try to fill this old skin with fresh and apparently revolutionary wine, then it must be said that the advantages would not be on our side but on that of the bourgeoisie. Things have their own objective logic. And the solution of the European union within the capitalist social order can objectively, in the economic sense, mean only a tariff war with America, and, in the political sense, only a colonial race war. The Chinese campaign of the united European regiments, with the World Field Marshal Waldersee at the head, and the gospel of the Hun as our standard—that is the actual and not the fantastic, the only possible expression of the "European State Federation" in the present social order.

THE JUNIUS PAMPHLET:
THE CRISIS IN THE
GERMAN SOCIAL DEMOCRACY

August 4, 1914, has long been recognized as one of the most ignominious dates in the history of the international socialist movement. For several months before that date it had been evident that war was imminent, and the Social Democratic Parties of Western Europe had been exposing the plans of their own imperialist governments.

On August 4, as the German, Austrian, French and czarist armies had already begun to march, the Reichstag was called on to approve the necessary funds to pay for the kaiser's war. With ringing phrases of condemnation, not for the German capitalist class and Prussian militarism, but for the czarist enemy, the entire SPD caucus in the Reichstag, more than a hundred deputies, voted in favor of the war credits and "defense of the fatherland."

Following in the footsteps of the SPD—that great shining jewel of the Second International, the party of unquestioned revolutionary authority to which all others looked for the example of proletarian internationalism—the majority of the social democrats of France and England also voted to support their respective governments. Only in Russia, Serbia, Poland, Italy, Bulgaria and the United States did the majorities of the Social Democratic Parties refuse to succumb to the wave of chauvinism and patriotic war hysteria.

To the revolutionary tendencies within the Second International, the vote of the social democratic Reichstag caucus was a shattering blow. When Lenin received the German newspapers carrying the news, he believed they were forgeries by the German police. Rosa Luxemburg, despite her intimate knowledge of the degree of opportunist degeneration of the SPD, was stunned. She had not dared to face the full implications of the SPD's internal rottenness, to accept the fact the largest, most influential party in the International could so utterly and completely betray the most elementary principles of revolutionary Marxism without even murmuring an embarrassed disclaimer.

Rosa set to work immediately to begin to group around her

the small nucleus of revolutionary social democrats who repudiated the official position of the SPD. The first results were meager. A month later, on September 10, a notice appeared in two Swiss papers, simply announcing that there were social democrats in Germany who opposed the official policy. It was signed by Karl Liebknecht, Franz Mehring, Clara Zetkin, and Rosa Luxemburg.

Liebknecht, an SPD deputy in the Prussian provincial parliament and in the Reichstag, had strongly opposed the vote for war credits. He led the dissent within the SPD caucus, but he had bowed to party discipline on the August 4 vote. For the last time. He immediately joined the revolutionary opposition and, because of his public office, became its most widely known spokesman. By the end of the war, the name of Liebknecht had become an international synonym for the revolutionary forces in Germany. In December 1914, when new war credits were approved by the Reichstag, Liebknecht alone cast a negative vote.

The work of organizing a tightly knit, cohesive tendency proceeded very slowly. In the spring of 1915 the first issue of *Die Internationale* appeared and was immediately banned by the German government. From then on it was circulated illegally by a network of underground distributors. Throughout the war issues of the Spartacus letters, at first mimeographed and later printed, circulated illegally. But it was not until New Year's Day, 1916, almost a year and a half after the war began, that delegates from around Germany met secretly in the law offices of Karl Liebknecht to establish the *Gruppe Internationale*, which adopted the "Theses on the Tasks of International Social Democracy" as their program and the *Junius Pamphlet* as their initial policy statement. The *Gruppe Internationale* became the Spartacus League in November 1918, and was the nucleus of the German Communist Party, founded at the end of December 1918.

Another opposition grouping also developed during the war. The middle-of-the-road bloc in the SPD Reichstag caucus — which had a few doubts about the official policy, but was not anxious to stick its neck out — became somewhat bolder as the war progressed and its unpopularity with the German working class increased. In December 1915, a year after Liebknecht registered his solitary protest, a total of twenty deputies voted against new war credits, and twenty-seven more abstained. This group, called the Ad Hoc Working Group, became the nucleus for the Independent Social Democratic Party (USPD) founded in January 1917, a formation that wavered back and forth between the SPD and the Spartacus, remaining constant only in its lack of any principles or backbone. Its leadership eventually went back into the SPD after the war, while many of the rank and file joined the German Communist Party.

258

The German government was of course anxious to silence its revolutionary critics and in the end succeeded in placing most of them in prison. When the war began Rosa Luxemburg had already been sentenced to a year in prison for an antiwar speech made earlier in 1914. In October her appeal was turned down, and although she was able to postpone serving the sentence for several months due to health, she was finally seized in February 1915. It was while serving this sentence that she wrote the *Junius Pamphlet*, as it came to be known. It was finished by April 1915 and smuggled out of prison, but due to technical difficulties with finding a printer and other problems, it was not published until April 1916.

The "Theses on the Tasks of International Social Democracy" were also written at the same time. They were intended for presentation to the 1915 Zimmerwald Conference of social democrats who opposed the war, but due to misinformation about the date of the conference, and necessary secrecy surrounding it, Rosa's friends were not able to smuggle the draft of the Theses out of her prison in time to get it to Zimmerwald.

Rosa Luxemburg was released in January 1916, remaining free for about six months. She was once again arrested in July 1916 and held without trial until she was liberated by the first wave of the German Revolution in November 1918.

Liebknecht, who was partially protected by his parliamentary immunity, remained free until May 1916. On May Day, 1916, the Spartacus forces decided to organize a demonstration in central Berlin. They had invited the Ad Hoc Working Group to go in with them, but when that group declined, Spartacus supporters went ahead on their own. Several hundred gathered in the Potsdamerplatz in time to hear Karl Liebknecht declare, "Down with the government! Down with the war!" before he was arrested. The remainder of the demonstrators were not stopped, and the May Day celebration reportedly continued for several hours.

When Liebknecht was arrested, his former SPD colleagues in the Reichstag hastened to lift his immunity. The level to which the SPD's reactionary politics sank during World War I can be gleaned from the speech made by SPD deputy Landsberg:

"Gentlemen . . . in Liebknecht we are dealing with a man who wanted, through an appeal to the masses, to force the government to make peace, a government moreover which has repeatedly expressed its sincere desire for peace before the whole world. . . . This war is a war for our very homes . . . how grotesque was this enterprise . . . how can anyone imagine that [Liebknecht] could influence the fate of the world, play at high policy by shoving handbills at people, by creating a demonstration in the Potsdamerplatz. . . . Contrast this pathological instability with our [party's official] clear-headed and sensible calm . . ." (quoted in

Rosa Luxemburg, J.P. Nettl, Oxford University Press, 1966, p. 649).

Liebknecht was sentenced in June, and his conviction set off the first major political strike during the war, to virtually everyone's surprise. In December 1916 he began serving a four-year-and-one-month sentence.

"The Crisis of the German Social Democracy" was the actual title of Rosa Luxemburg's pamphlet, and Junius was the pseudonym under which she wrote it. The name was probably taken from Lucius Junius Brutus, a legendary Roman patriot who reportedly led a republican revolution in classical Rome. The name Junius was also used by an unidentified author in England whose letters attacking the ministry of the Duke of Grafton appeared in the London *Public Advertiser* in 1769-1772.

In substance the pamphlet is less about the actual crisis of the SPD than about the roots and causes of the war. Aimed at the most class-conscious German workers, it is a careful explanation of the historical forces which made the holocaust inevitable—if the interests of the competing capitalist classes of Europe were to be served. It patiently explodes the various myths which the SPD used to justify its support for the war.

What it does not try to do, as Lenin points out in his review of the pamphlet, which is printed as an appendix to this collection, is to offer a clear explanation for the collapse of the SPD, or to deal with the role played by the bloc around Kautsky, which had over the years increasingly capitulated to the right wing of the party. The foundations for August 4, 1914, had been laid, politically and organizationally, during a period of a quarter of a century. And the pamphlet also fails to offer a clear perspective on what to do now, where to begin. But, as Lenin, who was not prone to extravagant praise, describes it, "on the whole, the *Junius Pamphlet* is a splendid Marxist work."

In his review he deals at length with two errors which he considered important to correct—the error of asserting that there could be no more national wars, and the error of making any concession whatsoever to the demand for "defense of the fatherland."

Lenin fully recognized the importance of such a work appearing in Germany and the role it would play in the struggle against the SPD. He extended warm greetings to its author, whose identity he probably did not know, and put forward his criticisms in the spirit of fraternal collaboration with those isolated individuals who were obviously making the attempt to think revolutionary slogans through to their conclusion.

The English translation was first published by the Socialist Publication Society in New York, 1918, under the names of Karl Liebknecht, Rosa Luxemburg, and Franz Mehring. We have omitted chapter 4, which provides a fairly long and detailed historical review of German imperialism's increasing domination of the Balkan states and Asia Minor, especially Turkey, during the twenty-year period prior to the war.

The Theses follow the translation published in the *Fourth International* (Amsterdam, Winter 1959-60).

I

The scene has thoroughly changed. The six weeks' march to Paris has become world drama. Mass murder has become a monotonous task, and yet the final solution is not one step nearer. Capitalist rule is caught in its own trap, and cannot ban the spirit that it has invoked.

Gone is the first mad delirium. Gone are the patriotic street demonstrations, the chase after suspicious-looking automobiles, the false telegrams, the cholera-poisoned wells. Gone the mad stories of Russian students who hurl bombs from every bridge of Berlin, or Frenchmen flying over Nuremberg; gone the excesses of a spy-hunting populace, the singing throngs, the coffee shops with their patriotic songs; gone the violent mobs, ready to denounce, ready to persecute women, ready to whip themselves into a delirious frenzy over every wild rumor; gone the atmosphere of ritual murder, the Kishinev air that left the policeman at the corner as the only remaining representative of human dignity.*

The show is over. The curtain has fallen on trains filled with reservists, as they pull out amid the joyous cries of enthusiastic maidens. We no longer see their laughing faces, smiling cheerily from the train windows upon a war-mad population. Quietly they trot through the streets, with their sacks upon their shoulders. And the public, with a fretful face, goes about its daily task.

Into the disillusioned atmosphere of pale daylight there rings a different chorus; the hoarse croak of the hawks and hyenas of the battlefield. Ten thousand tents, guaranteed according to specifications, 100,000 kilos of bacon, cocoa powder, coffee substitute, cash on immediate delivery. Shrapnel, drills, ammunition bags, marriage bureaus for war widows, leather belts, war orders — only serious propositions considered. And the cannon fodder that was loaded upon the trains in August and September is

---

* References are to official and semiofficial rumors circulating in the first few days of August 1914 to justify Germany's declaration of war: that Russian troops had crossed into Germany, that French armies had bombed Nuremburg, that a French doctor had poisoned the wells at Montsigny, that two Frenchmen had been shot while trying to blow up a railroad tunnel. The "Kishinev air" symbolizes a pogrom atmosphere. [Ed.]

rotting on the battlefields of Belgium and the Vosges, while profits are springing, like weeds, from the fields of the dead.

Business is flourishing upon the ruins. Cities are turned into shambles, whole countries into deserts, villages into cemeteries, whole nations into beggars, churches into stables; popular rights, treaties, alliances, the holiest words and the highest authorities have been torn into scraps; every sovereign by the grace of God is called a fool, an unfaithful wretch, by his cousin on the other side; every diplomat calls his colleague in the enemy's country a desperate criminal; each government looks upon the other as the evil genius of its people, worthy only of the contempt of the world. Hunger revolts in Venetia, in Lisbon, in Moscow, in Singapore, pestilence in Russia, misery and desperation everywhere.

Shamed, dishonored, wading in blood and dripping with filth, thus capitalist society stands. Not as we usually see it, playing the roles of peace and righteousness, of order, of philosophy, of ethics — as a roaring beast, as an orgy of anarchy, as a pestilential breath, devastating culture and humanity — so it appears in all its hideous nakedness.

And in the midst of this orgy a world tragedy has occurred: the capitulation of the social democracy. To close one's eyes to this fact, to try to hide it, would be the most foolish, the most dangerous thing that the international proletariat could do. "The democrat (i.e., the revolutionary middle class)," says Karl Marx, "emerges from the most shameful downfall as spotlessly as he went innocently into it. With the strengthened confidence that he must win, he is more than ever certain that he and his party need no new principles, that events and conditions must finally come to meet them." Gigantic as his problems are his mistakes. No firmly fixed plan, no orthodox ritual that holds good for all times, shows him the path that he must travel. Historical experience is his only teacher, his *Via Dolorosa* to freedom is covered not only with unspeakable suffering, but with countless mistakes. The goal of his journey, his final liberation, depends entirely upon the proletariat, on whether *it* understands to learn from *its* own mistakes. Self-criticism, cruel, unsparing criticism that goes to the very root of the evil is life and breath for the proletarian movement. The catastrophe into which the world has thrust the socialist proletariat is an unexampled misfortune for humanity. But socialism is lost only if the international proletariat is unable to measure the depths of the catastrophe and refuses to understand the lesson that it teaches.

The last forty-five years in the development of the labor movement are at stake. The present situation is a closing of its accounts, a summing-up of the items of half a century of work. In the grave of the Paris Commune lies buried the first phase of the European labor movement and the First International. Instead of spontaneous revolution, revolts, and barricades, after each of which the proletariat relapsed once more into its dull passiveness, there came the systematic daily struggle, the utilization of bourgeois parliamentarism, mass organization, the welding of the economic with the political struggle, of socialist ideals with the stubborn defense of most immediate interests. For the first time the cause of the proletariat and its emancipation were led by the guiding star of scientific knowledge. In place of sects and schools, utopian undertakings and experiments in every country, each altogether and absolutely separate from each other, we found a uniform, international, theoretical basis that united the nations. The theoretical works of Marx gave to the working class of the whole world a compass by which to fix its tactics from hour to hour, in its journey toward the one unchanging goal.

The bearer, the defender, the protector of this new method was the German social democracy. The war of 1870 and the downfall of the Paris Commune had shifted the center of gravity of the European labor movement to Germany. Just as France was the classic country of the first phase of the proletarian class struggle, as Paris was the torn and bleeding heart of the European working class of that time, so the German working class became the vanguard of the second phase. By innumerable sacrifices in the form of agitational work, it has built up the strongest, the model organization of the proletariat, has created the greatest press, has developed the most effective educational and propaganda methods. It has collected under its banners the most gigantic labor masses, and has elected the largest representative groups to its national parliament.

The German social democracy has been generally acknowledged to be the purest incarnation of Marxian socialism. It has held and wielded a peculiar prestige as teacher and leader in the Second International. Friedrich Engels wrote in his famous foreword to Marx's *Class Struggles in France*: "Whatever may occur in other countries, the German social democracy occupies a particular place and, for the present at least, has therefore a particular duty to perform. The two million voters that it sends to the ballot boxes, and the young girls and women who stand behind them as nonvoters, are numerically the greatest, the most compact mass, the most decisive force of the proletarian international army." The German social democracy was, as the *Wiener Arbeiterzeitung* wrote on August 5, 1914, the jewel of the organization of the class-conscious proletariat. In its footsteps the French, the Italian, and the Belgian social democracies, the labor movements of Holland, Scandinavia, Switzerland, and the United States followed more or less eagerly. The Slav nations, the Russians, and the social democrats of the Balkans looked up to the German movement in boundless, almost unquestioning admiration.

In the Second International the German social democracy was the determining factor. In every congress, in the meetings of the International Socialist Bureau, everything waited upon the opinion of the German group.

Particularly in the fight against militarism and war the position taken by the German social democracy has always been decisive. "We Germans cannot accept that," was usually sufficient to determine the orientation of the International. Blindly confident, it submitted to the leadership of the much admired, mighty German social democracy. It was the pride of every socialist, the horror of the ruling classes of all countries.

And what happened in Germany when the great historical crisis came? The deepest fall, the mightiest cataclysm. Nowhere was the organization of the proletariat made so completely subservient to imperialism. Nowhere was the state of siege so uncomplainingly borne. Nowhere was the press so thoroughly gagged, public opinion so completely choked off; nowhere was the political and industrial class struggle of the working class so entirely abandoned as in Germany.

But the German social democracy was not only the strongest body, it was the thinking brain of the International as well. Therefore the process of self-analysis and appraisement must begin in its own movement, with its own case. It is in honor bound to lead the way to the rescue of international socialism, to proceed with the unsparing criticism of its own shortcomings.

No other party, no other class in capitalist society can dare to expose its own errors, its own weaknesses, before the whole world in the clear mirror of reason, for the mirror would reflect the historical fate that is hidden behind it. The working class can always look truth in the face even when this means bitterest self-accusation; for its weakness was but an error and the inexorable laws of history give it strength and assure its final victory.

This unsparing self-criticism is not only a fundamental necessity, but the highest duty of the working class as well. We have on board the highest treasure of humanity, and the proletariat is their ordained protector. While capitalist society, shamed and dishonored, rushes through the bloody orgy to its doom, the international proletariat will gather the golden treasures that were allowed to sink to the bottom in the wild whirlpool of the world war in the moment of confusion and weakness.

One thing is certain. It is a foolish delusion to believe that we need only live through the war, as a rabbit hides under the bush to await the end of a thunderstorm, to trot merrily off in his old accustomed gait when all is over. The world war has changed the condition of our struggle, and has changed *us* most of all.

Not that the laws of capitalist development or the life-and-death conflict between capital and labor have been changed or minimized. Even now, in the midst of the war, the masks are falling, and the old well-known faces grinning at us. But evolution has received a mighty forward impetus through the outbreak of the imperialist volcano. The enormity of the tasks that tower before the socialist proletariat in the immediate future make the past struggles of the labor movement seem but a delightful idyll in comparison.

Historically the war is ordained to give to the cause of labor a mighty impetus. Marx, whose prophetic eyes foresaw so many historic events as they lay in the womb of the future, writes in *Class Struggles in France* the following significant passage: "In France the middle class does what should normally be done by the industrial bourgeoisie (i.e., to fight for the democratic republic); but who shall solve the problems of labor? They will not be solved in France. They will be proclaimed in France. They will nowhere be solved within national boundaries. Class war in France will revert into a world war. The solution will begin only when the world war has driven the proletariat into the leadership of that nation which controls the world market, to the leadership of England. The revolution that will here find, not its end, but its organizational beginning, is no short-lived one. The present generation is like the Jews who were led by Moses through the wilderness. Not only must it conquer a new world, it must go down to make way for those who will be better able to cope with its problems."

This was written in 1850, at a time when England was the only capitalistically developed nation, when the English proletariat was the best organized and seemed destined through the industrial growth of its nation to take the leadership in the international labor movement. Read Germany instead of England, and the words of Karl Marx become an inspired prophecy of the present world war. It is ordained to drive the German proletariat "to the leadership of the people, and thus to create the organizational beginning of the great international conflict between labor and capital for the political supremacy of the world."

Have we ever had a different conception of the role to be played by the working class in the great world war? Have we forgotten how we were wont to describe the coming event, only a few short years ago? "Then will come the catastrophe. All Europe will be called to arms, and sixteen to eighteen million men, the flower of the nations, armed with the best instruments of murder will make war upon each other. But I believe that behind this march there looms the final crash. Not we, but they themselves will bring it. They are driving things to the extreme, they are leading us straight into a catastrophe. They will harvest what they have sown. The *Goetterdaemmerung* of the bourgeois world is at hand. Be sure of that. It is coming." Thus spoke Bebel, the speaker of our group in the Reichstag in the Morocco debate.

An official leaflet published by the party, *Imperialism and Socialism*, that was distributed in hundreds of thousands of copies only a few years ago, closes with the words: "Thus the struggle against militarism daily becomes more and more clearly a decisive struggle between capital and labor. War, high prices and capitalism — peace, happiness for all, socialism! Yours is the choice. History is hastening onward toward a decision. The proletariat must work unceasingly at its world mission, must strengthen the power of its organization and the clearness of its understanding. Then, come what will, whether it will succeed, by its power, in saving humanity from the horrible cruelties of the world war, or whether capitalism shall sink back into history, as it was born, in blood and violence, the historic moment will find the working class prepared, and preparedness is everything."

The official handbook for socialist voters, in 1911, the date of the last Reichstag elections, contains, on page 42, the following comments on the expected world war: "Do our rulers and our ruling classes dare to demand this awful thing of the people? Will not a cry of horror, of fury and of indignation fill the country and lead the people to put an end to this murder? Will they not ask: 'For whom and for what? Are we insane that we should be treated thus or should tolerate such treatment?' He who dispassionately considers the possibility of a great European world war can come to no other conclusion.

"The next European war will be a game of *va banque*, whose equal the world has never seen before. It will be, in all probability, the last war."

With such words the Reichstag representatives won their 110 seats in the Reichstag.

When in the summer of 1911, the *Panther* made its spring to Agadir, and the noisy clamor of German imperialists brought Europe to the precipice of war,* an international meeting in London, on the fourth of August, adopted the following resolution:

"The German, Spanish, English, Dutch and French delegates of labor organizations hereby declare their readiness to oppose every declaration of war with every means in their power. Every

---

* In July 1911 the German gunboat *Panther* sailed to Agadir, Morocco "to protect German interests," i.e., to secure sources of iron ore for Mannesmann Steel. War almost broke out between France and Germany, but on the threat of British intervention, Germany withdrew. At the Treaty of Berlin, November 1911, Germany was given a slice of the Cameroons and gave up her claims to Morocco. [Ed.]

nationality here represented pledges itself, in accordance with the decisions of its national and international congresses to oppose all criminal machinations on the part of the ruling classes."

But when in November 1912, the International Peace Congress met at Basel,* when the long train of labor representatives entered the Minster, a presentiment of the coming hour of fate made them shudder and the heroic resolve took shape in every breast.

The cool, skeptical Victor Adler cried out: "Comrades, it is most important that we here, at the common source of our strength, that we, each and every one of us, take from hence the strength to do in his country what he can, through the forms and means that are at his disposal, to oppose this crime of war, and if it should be accomplished, if we should really be able to prevent war, let this be the cornerstone of our coming victory. That is the spirit that animates the whole International.

"And when murder and arson and pestilence sweep over civilized Europe—we can think of it only with horror and indignation, and protests ring from our hearts. And we ask, are the proletarians of today really nothing but sheep to be led mutely to the slaughter?"

Troelstra spoke in the name of the small nations, in the name of the Belgians as well: "With their blood and with all that they possess the proletariat of the small nations swear their allegiance to the International in everything that it may decide to prevent war. Again we repeat that we expect, when the ruling classes of the large nations call the sons of the proletariat to arms to satiate the lust for power and the greed of their rulers, in the blood and on the lands of the small peoples, we expect that then the sons of the proletariat, under the powerful influence of their proletarian parents and of the proletarian press, will think thrice before they harm us, their friends, in the service of the enemies of culture."

And Jaures closed his speech, after the antiwar manifesto of the International Bureau had been read: "The International represents the moral forces of the world! And when the tragic hour strikes, when we must sacrifice ourselves, this knowledge will

---

* The Peace Congress at Basel, Switzerland was held at the Basel Minster on November 24 and 25, 1912. The immediate occasion was the fear of general European war, as Montenegro had declared war on Turkey in October, embroiling the Balkans. It was the last prewar general meeting of the Second International, and its significance is that for the first time a socialist peace conference had recognized that the period of national wars in Europe was over and that all future wars would be imperialist wars. [Ed.]

support and strengthen us. Not lightly, but from the bottom of our hearts we declare that we are ready for all sacrifices!"

It was like a Ruetli pledge. The whole world looked toward the Minster of Basel, where the bells, slowly and solemnly, rang to the approaching great fight between the armies of labor and capital.

On the third of September, 1912, the social democratic deputy, David, spoke in the German Reichstag: "That was the most beautiful hour of my life. That I here avow. When the chimes of the Minster rang in the long train of international social democrats, when the red flags were planted in the nave of the church about the altar, when the emissaries of the people were greeted by the peals of the organ that resounded the message of peace, that was an impression that I can never forget. . . .

"You must realize what it was that happened here. The masses have ceased to be will-less, thoughtless herds. That is new in the history of the world. Hitherto the masses have always blindly followed the lead of those who were interested in war, who drove the peoples at each other's throats to mass murder. That will stop. The masses have ceased to be the instruments, the yeomen of war profiteers."

A week before the war broke out, on the twenty-sixth of July, 1914, the German party papers wrote: "We are no marionettes; we are fighting with all our might, against a system that makes men the powerless tools of blind circumstances, against this capitalism that is preparing to change Europe, thirsty for peace, into a smoking battlefield. If destruction takes its course, if the determined will for peace of the German, of the international proletariat, that will find expression in the next few days in mighty demonstrations, should not be able to prevent the world war, then it must be at least, the last war, it must be the *Goetterdaemmerung* of capitalism."

On the thirtieth of July, 1914, the central organ of the German social democracy cried out: "The socialist proletariat rejects all responsibility for the events that are being precipitated by a ruling class that is blinded, and on the verge of madness. We know that for us new life will spring from the ruins. But the responsibility falls upon the rulers of today.

"For them it is a question of existence!

"World history is the last judgment!"

And then came the awful, the incredible fourth of August, 1914.

Did it *have* to come? An event of such importance cannot be a mere accident. It must have its deep, significant, objective causes. But perhaps these causes may be found in the errors of the leader of the proletariat, the social democracy itself, in the fact that our readiness to fight has flagged, that our courage and our convictions have forsaken us. Scientific socialism has taught us to recognize the objective laws of historical development. Man does not make history of his own volition, but he makes history nevertheless. The proletariat is dependent in its actions upon the degree of righteousness to which social evolution has advanced. But again, social evolution is not a thing apart from the proletariat; it is in the same measure its driving force and its cause as well as its product and its effect. And though we can no more skip a period in our historical development than a man can jump over his shadow, it lies within our power to accelerate or to retard it.

Socialism is the first popular movement in the world that has set itself a goal and has established in the social life of man a conscious thought, a definite plan, the free will of mankind. For this reason Friedrich Engels calls the final victory of the socialist proletariat a stride by humankind from the animal kingdom into the kingdom of liberty. This step, too, is bound by unalterable historical laws to the thousands of rungs of the ladder of the past with its tortuous sluggish growth. But it will never be accomplished, if the burning spark of the conscious will of the masses does not spring from the material conditions that have been built up by past development. Socialism will not fall as manna from heaven. It can only be won by a long chain of powerful struggles, in which the proletariat, under the leadership of the social democracy, will learn to take hold of the rudder of society to become instead of the powerless victim of history, its conscious guide.

Friedrich Engels once said: "Capitalist society faces a dilemma, either an advance to socialism or a reversion to barbarism." What does a "reversion to barbarism" mean at the present stage of European civilization? We have read and repeated these words thoughtlessly without a conception of their terrible import. At this moment one glance about us will show us what a reversion to barbarism in capitalist society means. *This world war* means a reversion to barbarism. The triumph of imperialism leads to the destruction of culture, sporadically during a modern war, and forever, if the period of world wars that has just begun is allowed to take its damnable course to the last ultimate consequence. Thus we stand today, as Friedrich Engels prophesied more than a generation ago, before the awful proposition: either the triumph of imperialism and the destruction of all culture, and, as in ancient Rome, depopulation, desolation, degeneration, a vast cemetery; or, the victory of socialism, that is, the conscious struggle of the international proletariat against imperialism, against its methods, against war. This is the dilemma of world history, its inevitable choice, whose scales are trembling in the balance awaiting the decision of the proletariat. Upon it depends the future of culture and humanity. In this war imperialism has been victorious. Its brutal sword of murder has dashed the scales, with overbearing brutality, down into the abyss of shame and misery. If the proletariat learns *from* this war and in this war to exert itself, to cast off its serfdom to the ruling classes, to become the lord of its own destiny, the shame and misery will not have been in vain.

The modern working class must pay dearly for each realization of its historic mission. The road to the Golgotha of its class liberation is strewn with awful sacrifices. The June combatants, the victims of the Commune, the martyrs of the Russian Revolution—an endless line of bloody shadows. They have fallen on the field of honor, as Marx wrote of the heroes of the Commune, to be enshrined forever in the great heart of the working class. Now millions of proletarians are falling on the field of dishonor, of fratricide, of self-destruction, the slave-song on their lips. And that too has not been spared us. We are like the Jews whom Moses led through the desert. But we are not lost, and we will be victorious if we have not forgotten how to learn. And if the modern leaders of the proletariat do not know how to learn, they will go down "to make room for those who will be more able to cope with the problems of a new world."

II

"We are now facing the irrevocable fact of war. We are threatened by the horrors of invasion. The decision, today, is not for or against war; for us there can be but one question: by what means is this war to be conducted? Much, aye everything, is at stake for our people and its future, if Russian despotism, stained with the blood of its own people, should be the victor. This danger must be averted, the civilization and the independence of our people must be safeguarded. Therefore we will carry out what we have always promised: in the hour of danger we will not desert our fatherland. In this we feel that we stand in harmony with the International, which has always recognized the right of every people to its national independence, as we stand in agreement with the International in emphatically denouncing every war of conquest. Actuated by these motives, we vote in favor of the war credits demanded by the Government."

With these words the Reichstag group issued the countersign that determined and controlled the position of the German working class during the war. Fatherland in danger, national defense, people's war for existence, *Kultur* [national German culture—Ed.], liberty—these were the slogans proclaimed by the parliamentary representatives of the social democracy. What followed was but the logical sequence. The position of the party and the labor union press, the patriotic frenzy of the masses, the civil peace, the disintegration of the International, all these things were the inevitable consequence of that momentous orientation in the Reichstag.

If it is true that this war is really a fight for national existence, for freedom, if it is true that these priceless possessions can be defended only by the iron tools of murder, if this war is the holy cause of the people, then everything else follows as a matter of course, we must take everything that the war may bring as a part of the bargain. He who desires the purpose must be satisfied with the means. War is methodical, organized, gigantic murder. But in normal human beings this systematic murder is possible only when a state of intoxication has been previously created. This has always been the tried and proven method of those who make war. Bestiality of action must find a commensurate bestiality of thought and senses; the latter must prepare and accompany the former. Thus the *Wahre Jacob* of August 28, 1914, with its brutal picture of the German thresher, the party papers of Chemnitz, Hamburg, Kiel, Frankfurt, Koburg and others, with their patriotic drive in poetry and prose, were the necessary narcotic for a proletariat that could rescue its existence and its liberty only by plunging the deadly steel into its French and English brothers. These chauvinistic papers are after all a great deal more logical and consistent than those others who attempted to unite hill and valley, war with humanity, murder with brotherly love, the voting for war credits with socialist internationalism.

If the stand taken by the German Reichstag group on the fourth of August was correct, then the death sentence of the proletarian International has been spoken, not only for this war, but forever. For the first time since the modern labor movement exists there yawns an abyss between the commandments of international solidarity of the proletariat of the world and the interests of freedom and nationalist existence of the people; for the first time we discover that the independence and liberty of the nations command that working men kill and destroy each other. Up to this time we have cherished the belief that the interests of the peoples of all nations, that the class interests of the proletariat are a harmonious unit, that they are identical, that they cannot possibly come into conflict with one another. That was the basis of our theory and practice, the soul of our agitation. Were we mistaken in the cardinal point of our whole world philosophy? We are holding an inquest over international socialism.

This world war is not the first crisis through which our international principles have passed. Our party was first tried forty-five years ago. At that time, on the twenty-first of July, 1870, Wilhelm Liebknecht and August Bebel made the following historical declaration before the Reichstag: "The present war is

271

a dynastic war in the interest of the Bonaparte dynasty as the war of 1866 was conducted in the interest of the Hohenzollern dynasty.

"We cannot vote for the funds which are demanded from the Reichstag to conduct this war because this would be, in effect, a vote of confidence in the Prussian government. And we know that the Prussian government by its action in 1866 prepared this war. At the same time we cannot vote against the budget, lest this be construed to mean that we support the conscienceless and criminal policies of Bonaparte.

"As opponents, on principle, of every dynastic war, as socialist republicans and members of the International Workingmen's Association which, without regard to nationality, has fought all oppressors, has tried to unite all the oppressed into a great band of brothers, we cannot directly or indirectly lend support to the present war. We therefore refuse to vote, while expressing the earnest hope that the peoples of Europe, taught by the present unholy events, will strive to win the right to control their own destinies, to do away with the present rule of might and class as the cause of all social and national evil."

With this declaration the representatives of the German proletariat put their cause clearly and unreservedly under the banner of the International and definitely repudiated the war against France as a national war of independence. It is well known that Bebel, many years later, in his memoirs, stated that he would have voted against the war loan had he known, when the vote was taken, the things that were revealed in the years that followed.

Thus, in a war that was considered by the whole bourgeois public, and by a powerful majority of the people under the influence of Bismarckian strategy, as a war in the national life interest of Germany, the leaders of the German social democracy held firmly to the conviction that the life interest of a nation and the class interest of the proletariat are one, that both are opposed to war. It was left to the present world war and to the social democratic Reichstag group to uncover, for the first time, the terrible dilemma: either you are for national liberty—or for international socialism.

Now the fundamental fact in the declaration of our Reichstag group was, in all probability, a sudden inspiration. It was simply an echo of the crown speech and of the chancellor's speech of August 4. "We are not driven by the desire for conquest," we hear in the crown speech, "we are inspired by the unalterable determination to preserve the land upon which God has placed us for ourselves, and for all coming generations. From the documents that have been presented to you, you will have seen how my government, and above all my chancellor strove, to the last, to avert the utmost. We grasp the sword in self-defense, with a clear conscience and a clean hand." And Bethmann-Hollweg declared: "Gentlemen, we are acting in self-defense, and necessity knows no law. He who is threatened as we are threatened, he who is fighting for the highest aims can be guided by but one consideration, how best to beat his way out of the struggle. We are fighting for the fruits of our peaceful labor, for the heritage of our great past, for the future of our nation."

Wherein does this differ from the social democratic declaration? (1) We have done everything to preserve peace, the war was forced upon us by others. (2) Now that the war is here we must act in self-defense. (3) In this war the German people are in danger of losing everything. This declaration of our Reichstag group is an obvious rehashing of the government declaration. As the latter based their claims upon diplomatic negotiations and imperial telegrams, so the socialist group points to peace demonstrations of the social democracy before the war. Where the crown speech denies all aims of conquest, the Reichstag group repudiates a war of conquest by standing upon its socialism. And when the emperor and chancellor cry out, "We are fighting for the highest principles. We know no parties, we know only Germans," the social democratic declaration echoes: "Our people risk everything. In this hour of danger we will not desert our fatherland."

Only in one point does the social democratic declaration differ from its government model: it placed the danger of Russian despotism in the foreground of its orientation, as a danger to German freedom. The crown speech says, regarding Russia: "With a heavy heart I have been forced to mobilize against a neighbor with whom I have fought upon so many battlefields. With honest sorrow I have seen a friendship faithfully kept by Germany fall to pieces." The social democratic group changed this sorrowful rupture of a true friendship with the Russian czar into a fanfare for liberty against despotism, used the revolutionary heritage of socialism to give to the war a democratic mantle, a popular halo. Here alone the social democratic declaration gives evidence of independent thought on the part of our social democrats.

As we have said, all these things came to the social democracy as a sudden inspiration on the fourth of August. All that they had said up to this day, every declaration that they had made, down to the very eve of the war, was in diametrical opposition to the declaration of the Reichstag group. The *Vorwaerts* wrote on July 25, when the Austrian ultimatum to Serbia was published: "They want the war, the unscrupulous elements that influence and determine the Wiener Hofburg. They want the war — it has been ringing out of the wild cries of the black-yellow press for weeks. They want the war—the Austrian ultimatum to Serbia makes it plain and clear to the world.

"Because the blood of Franz Ferdinand and his wife flowed under the shots of an insane fanatic, shall the blood of thousands of workers and farmers be shed? Shall one insane crime be purged by another even more insane? . . . The Austrian ultimatum may be the torch that will set Europe in flames at all four corners.

"For this ultimatum, in its form and in its demands, is so shameless, that a Serbian government that should humbly retreat before this note, would have to reckon with the possibility of being driven out by the masses of the people between dinner and dessert. . . .

"It was a crime of the chauvinistic press of Germany to egg on our dear ally to the utmost in its desire for war. And beyond a doubt, Herr von Bethmann-Hollweg promised Herr Berchtold our support. But Berlin is playing a game as dangerous as that being played by Vienna."

The *Leipziger Volkszeitung* wrote on July 24: "The Austrian military party has staked everything on one card, for in no country in the world has national and military chauvinism anything to lose. In Austria chauvinistic circles are particularly bankrupt; their nationalistic howls are a frantic attempt to cover up Austria's economic ruin, the robbery and murder of war to fill its coffers. . . ."

The *Dresden Volkszeitung* said, on the same day: "Thus far the war maniacs of the Wiener Ballplatz have failed to furnish proof that would justify Austria in the demands it has made upon Serbia. So long as the Austrian government is not in a position to do this, it places itself, by its provocative and insulting attacks upon Serbia, in a false position before all Europe. And even if Serbia's guilt was proven, even if the assassination in Sarajevo had actually been prepared under the eyes of the Serbian government, the demands made in the note are far in excess of normal bounds. Only the most unscrupulous war lust can explain such demands upon another state. . . ."

The *Muenchener Post*, on July 25, wrote: "This Austrian note is a document unequalled in the history of the last two centuries. Upon the findings of an investigation whose contents have, till now, been kept from the European public, without court proceedings against the murderer of the heir presumptive and his spouse, it makes demands on Serbia, the acceptance of which would mean national suicide to Serbia. . . ."

The *Schleswig-Holstein Volkszeitung* declared, on the twenty-fourth of July: "Austria is provoking Serbia. Austria-Hungary wants war, and is committing a crime that may drown all Europe in blood. . . . Austria is playing *va banque*. It dares a provocation of the Serbian state that the latter, if it is not entirely defenseless, will certainly refuse to tolerate. . . .

"Every civilized person must protest emphatically against the criminal behavior of the Austrian rulers. It is the duty of the workers above all, and of all other human beings who honor peace and civilization, to try their utmost to prevent the consequences of the bloody insanity that has broken out in Vienna."

The *Magdeburger Volksstimme* of July 25 said: "Any Serbian government that even pretended to consider these demands seriously would be swept out in the same hour by the parliament and by the people.

"The action of Austria is the more despicable because Berchtold is standing before the Serbian government and before Europe with empty hands.

"To precipitate a war such as this at the present time means to invite a world war. To act thus shows a desire to disturb the peace of an entire hemisphere. One cannot thus make moral conquests, or convince nonparticipants of one's own righteousness. It can be safely assumed that the press of Europe, and with it the European governments, will call the vainglorious and senseless Viennese statesmen energetically and unmistakably to order."

On July 24 the *Frankfurter Volksstimme* wrote: "Upheld by the agitation of the clerical press, which mourns in Franz Ferdinand its best friend and demands that his death be avenged upon the Serbian people, upheld by German war patriots whose language becomes daily more contemptible and more threatening, the Austrian government has allowed itself to be driven to send an ultimatum to Serbia couched in language that, for presumptiousness, leaves little to be desired; containing demands whose fulfillment by the Serbian government is manifestly impossible."

On the same day the *Elberfelder Freie Presse* wrote: "A telegram of the semiofficial Wolff Bureau reports the terms of the demands made on Serbia by Austria. From these it may be gathered that the rulers in Vienna are pushing toward war with all their might. For the conditions imposed by the note that was presented in Belgrade last night are nothing short of a protectorate of Austria over Serbia. It is eminently necessary that the diplomats of Berlin make the war agitators of Vienna understand that Germany will not move a finger to support such outrageous demands, that a withdrawal of the threats would be advisable."

The *Bergische Arbeiterstimme* of Solingen writes: "Austria demands a conflict with Serbia, and uses the assassination at Sarajevo as a pretext for putting Serbia morally in the wrong. But the whole matter has been approached too clumsily to influence European public opinion.

"But if the war agitators of the Wiener Ballplatz believe that their allies of the Triple Alliance, Germany and Italy, will come to their assistance in a conflict in which Russia, too, will be involved, they are suffering from a dangerous illusion. Italy would welcome the weakening of Austria-Hungary, its rival on the Adriatic and in the Balkans, and would certainly decline to burn its fingers to help Austria. In Germany, on the other hand, the powers that be — even should they be so foolish as to wish it — would not dare to risk the life of a single soldier to satisfy the criminal lust for power of the Habsburgers without arousing the fury of the entire people."

Thus the entire working-class press, without exception, judged the war's causes a week before its outbreak. Obviously the question was one of neither the existence nor the freedom of Germany, but a shameful adventure of the Austrian war party; not a question of self-defense, national protection and a holy war forced upon us in the name of freedom, but a bold provocation, an abominable threat against foreign, Serbian independence and liberty.

What was it that happened on August 4 to turn this clearly defined and so unanimously accepted attitude of the social democracy upside down? Only one new factor had appeared — the *White Book* that was presented to the Reichstag by the German government on that day. And this contained, on page 4, the following:

"Under these circumstances Austria must say to itself that it is incompatible with the dignity and the safety of the monarchy to remain inactive any longer in the face of the occurrences across the border. The Austrian imperial government has notified us of this, their attitude, and has begged us to state our views. Out of a full heart we could but assure our ally of our agreement with this interpretation of conditions and assure him that any action that would seem necessary to put an end to Serbian attempts against the existence of the Austrian monarchy would meet with our approval. We fully realized that eventual war measures undertaken by Austria must bring Russia into the situation and that we, in order to carry out our duty as ally, might be driven into war. But we could not, realizing as we did that the most vital interests of Austria-Hungary were threatened, advise our ally to adopt a policy of acquiescence, that could not possibly be brought into accord with its dignity, nor could we refuse to lend our aid in this attitude.

"And we were particularly prevented from taking this stand by the fact that the persistent subversive Serbian agitation seriously jeopardized us. If the Serbians had been permitted, with the aid of Russia and France, to continue to threaten the existence of the neighboring monarchy, there would have ensued a gradual collapse of Austria and a subjection of all the Slavic races under the Russian scepter, which would have rendered untenable the situation of the Germanic race in Central Europe. A morally weakened Austria, succumbing before the advance of Russian Pan-Slavism, would no longer be an ally on which we could count and depend, as we are obliged to do in view of the increasingly menacing attitude of our neighbors to the East and to the West. We therefore gave Austria a free hand in her proceedings against Serbia. We have had no share in the preparations."

These were the words that lay before the social democratic Reichstag group on August 4, the only important and determining phrases in the entire *White Book*, a concise declaration of the German government beside which all other yellow, grey, blue, orange books on the diplomatic passages that preceded the war and its most immediate causes become absolutely irrelevant and insignificant. Here the Reichstag group had the key to a correct judgment of the situation in hand. The entire social democratic press, a week before, had cried out that the Austrian ultimatum was a criminal provocation of the world war and demanded preventive and pacific action on the part of the German government. The entire socialist press assumed that the Austrian ultimatum had descended upon the German government like a bolt from the blue as it had upon the German public.

But now the White Book declared, briefly and clearly: (1) That the Austrian government had requested German sanction before taking a final step against Serbia. (2) That the German government clearly understood that the action undertaken by Austria would lead to war with Serbia, and ultimately, to European war. (3) That the German government did not advise Austria to give in, but on the contrary declared that an acquiescent, weakened Austria could not be regarded as a worthy ally of Germany. (4) That the German government assured Austria, before it advanced against Serbia, of its assistance under all circumstances, in case of war, and finally, (5) That the German government, withal, had not reserved for itself control over the decisive ultimatum from Austria to Serbia, upon which the whole world war depended, but had left to Austria "an absolutely free hand."

All of this our Reichstag group learned on August 4. And still another fact it learned from the government — that German forces already had invaded Belgium. And from all this the social democratic group concluded that this is a war of defense against foreign invasion, for the existence of the fatherland, for "Kultur," a war for liberty against Russian despotism.

Was the obvious background of the war, and the scenery that so scantily concealed it, was the whole diplomatic performance that was acted out at the outbreak of the war, with its clamor about a world of enemies, all threatening the life of Germany, all moved the one desire to weaken, to humiliate, to subjugate the German people and nation — were all these things such a complete surprise? Did these factors actually call for more judgment, more critical sagacity than they possessed? Nowhere was this less true than of our party. It had already gone through two great German wars, and in both of them had received memorable lessons.

Even a poorly informed student of history knows that the war of 1866 against Austria was systematically prepared by Bismarck long before it broke out, and that his policies, from the very beginning, led inevitably to a rupture and to war with Austria. The crown prince himself, later Emperor Frederick, in his memoirs under the date of November 14 of that year, speaks of this purpose of the chancellor: "He (Bismarck), when he went into office, was firmly resolved to bring Prussia to a war with Austria, but was very careful not to betray this purpose, either at that time or on any other premature occasion to His Majesty, until the time seemed favorable."

"Compare with this confession," says Auer in his brochure *Die Sedanfeier und die Sozialdemokratie* [The Sedan Commemoration and the Social Democracy] "the proclamation that King William sent out '*to my people.*'"

"The fatherland is in danger! Austria and a large part of Germany have risen in arms against us.

"It is only a few years ago since I, of my own free will, without thinking of former misunderstandings, held out a fraternal hand to Austria in order to save a German nation from foreign domination. But my hopes have been blasted. Austria cannot forget that its lords once ruled Germany; it refuses to see in the younger, more virile Prussia an ally, but persists in regarding it as a dangerous rival. Prussia — so it believes — must be opposed in all its aims, because whatever favors Prussia harms Austria. The old unholy jealousy has again broken out; Prussia is to be weakened, destroyed, dishonored. All treaties with Prussia are void, German lords are not only called upon, but persuaded, to sever their alliance with Prussia. Wherever we look in Germany, we are surrounded by enemies whose war cry is — Down with Prussia!"

Praying for the blessings of heaven, King William ordered a general day of prayer and penance for the eighteenth of July, saying: "It has not pleased God to crown with success my attempts to preserve the blessings of peace for my people."

Should not the official accompaniment to the outbreak of the war on August 4 have awakened in the minds of our group vivid memories of long remembered words and melodies? Had they completely forgotten their party history?

But not enough! In the year 1870 there came the war with France, and history has united its outbreak with an unforgettable occurrence: the Ems dispatch, a document that has become a classic byword for capitalist government art in war making, and which marks a memorable episode in our party history. Was it not old Liebknecht, was it not the German social democracy who felt in duty bound, at that time, to disclose these facts and to show to the masses "how wars are made"?

Making war simply and solely for the protection of the fatherland was, by the way, not Bismarck's invention. He only carried out, with characteristic unscrupulousness, an old, well-known and truly international recipe of capitalist statesmanship. When and where has there been a war since so-called public opinion has played a role in governmental calculations, in which each and every belligerent party did not, with a heavy heart, draw the sword from its sheath for the single and sole purpose of defending its fatherland and its own righteous cause from the shameful attacks of the enemy? This legend is as inextricably a part of the game of war as powder and lead. The game is old. Only that the Social Democratic Party could play it is new.

III

Our party should have been prepared to recognize the real aims of this war, to meet it without surprise, to judge it by its deeper relationship according to their wide political experience. The events and forces that led to August 4, 1914, were no secrets. The world had been preparing for decades, in broad daylight, in the widest publicity, step by step, and hour by hour, for the world war. And if today a number of socialists threaten with horrible destruction the "secret diplomacy" that has brewed this devilry behind the scenes, they are ascribing to these poor wretches a magic power that they little deserve, just as the Botokude whips his fetish for the outbreak of a storm. The so-called captains of nations are, in this war, as at all times, merely chessmen, moved by all-powerful historic events and forces, on the surface of capitalist society. If ever there were persons capable of understanding these events and occurrences, it was the members of the German social democracy.

Two lines of development in recent history lead straight to the present war. One has its origin in the period when the so-called national states, i.e., the modern states, were first constituted, from the time of the Bismarckian war against France. The war of 1870, which, by the annexation of Alsace-Lorraine, threw the French republic into the arms of Russia, split Europe into two opposing camps and opened up a period of insane competitive armament, first piled up the firebrands for the present world conflagration.

Bismarck's troops were still stationed in France when Marx wrote to the *Braunschweiger Ausschuss*: "He who is not deafened by the momentary clamor, and is not interested in deafening the German people, must see that the war of 1870 carries with it, of necessity, a war between Germany and Russia, just as the war of 1866 bore the war of 1870. I say of necessity, unless the unlikely should happen, unless a revolution breaks out in Russia before that time. If this does not occur, a war between Germany and Russia may even now be regarded as *un fait accompli*. It depends entirely upon the attitude of the German victor to determine whether this war has been useful or dangerous. If they take Alsace-Lorraine, then France with Russia will arm against Germany. It is superfluous to point out the disastrous consequences."

At that time this prophecy was laughed down. The bonds which united Russia and Prussia seemed so strong that it was considered madness to believe in a union of autocratic Russia with republican France. Those who supported this conception were laughed at as madmen. And yet everything that Marx has prophesied has happened, to the last letter. "For that is," says Auer in his *Sedanfeier*, "social democratic politics, seeing things clearly as they are, and differing therein from the day-by-day politics of the others, bowing blindly down before every momentary success."

This must not be misunderstood to mean that the desire for revenge for the robbery accomplished by Bismarck has driven the French into a war with Germany, that the kernel of the present war is to be found in the much discussed "revenge for Alsace-Lorraine." This is the convenient nationalist legend of the German war agitator, who creates fables of a darkly-brooding France that "cannot forget" its defeat, just as the Bismarckian press-servants ranted of the dethroned Princess Austria who could not forget her erstwhile superiority over the charming Cinderella Prussia. As a matter of fact revenge for Alsace-Lorraine has become the theatrical property of a couple of patriotic clowns, the "Lion de Belfort" nothing more than an ancient survival.

The annexation of Alsace-Lorraine long ago ceased to play a role in French politics, being superseded by new, more pressing cares; and neither the government nor any serious party in France thought of a war with Germany because of these territories. If, nevertheless, the Bismarck heritage has become the firebrand that started this world conflagration, it is rather in the sense of having driven Germany on the one hand, and France, and with it all of Europe, on the other, along the downward path of military competition, of having brought about the Franco-Russian alliance, of having united Austria with Germany as an inevitable consequence. This gave to Russian czarism a tremendous prestige as a factor in European politics. Germany and France have systematically fawned before Russia for her favor. At that time the links were forged that united Germany with Austria-Hungary, whose strength, as the words quoted from the *White Book* show, lie in their "brotherhood in arms," in the present war.

Thus the war of 1870 brought in its wake the outward political grouping of Europe about the axes of the Franco-German antagonism, and established the rule of militarism in the lives of the European peoples. Historical development has given to this rule and to this grouping an entirely new content. The second line that leads to the present world war, and which again brilliantly justifies Marx's prophecy, has its origin in international occurrences that Marx did not live to see, in the imperialist development of the last twenty-five years.

The growth of capitalism, spreading out rapidly over a reconstituted Europe after the war period of the sixties and seventies, particularly after the long period of depression that followed the inflation and the panic of the year 1873, reaching an unnatural zenith in the prosperity of the nineties opened up a new period of storm and danger among the nations of Europe. They were competing in their expansion toward the noncapitalist countries and zones of the world. As early as the eighties a strong tendency toward colonial expansion became apparent. England secured control of Egypt and created for itself, in South Africa, a powerful colonial empire. France took possession of Tunis in North Africa and Tonkin in East Asia; Italy gained a foothold in Abyssinia; Russia accomplished its conquests in Central Asia and pushed forward into Manchuria; Germany won its first colonies in Africa and in the South Sea, and the United States joined the circle when it procured the Philippines with "interests" in Eastern Asia. This period of feverish conquests has brought on, beginning with the Chinese-Japanese War in 1895, a practically uninterrupted chain of bloody wars, reaching its height in the Great Chinese Invasion, and closing with the Russo-Japanese War of 1904.

All these occurrences, coming blow upon blow, created new, extra-European antagonisms on all sides: between Italy and France in Northern Africa, between France and England in Egypt, between England and Russia in Central Asia, between Russia and Japan in Eastern Asia, between Japan and England in China, between the United States and Japan in the Pacific Ocean — a very restless ocean, full of sharp conflicts and temporary alliances, of tension and relaxation, threatening every few years to break out into a war between European powers. It was clear to everybody, therefore, (1) that the secret underhand war of each capitalist nation against every other, on the backs of Asiatic and African peoples must sooner or later lead to a general reckoning, that the wind that was sown in Africa and Asia would return to Europe as a terrific storm, the more certainly since increased armament of the European states was the constant associate of these Asiatic and African occurrences; (2) that the European world war would have to come to an outbreak as soon as the partial and changing conflicts between the imperialist states found a centralized axis, a conflict of sufficient magnitude to group them, for the time being, into large, opposing factions. This situation was created by the appearance of German imperialism.

In Germany one may study the development of imperialism, crowded as it was into the shortest possible space of time, in concrete form. The unprecedented rapidity of German industrial and commercial development since the foundation of the empire brought out during the eighties two characteristically peculiar forms of capitalist accumulation: the most pronounced growth of monopoly in Europe and the best developed and most concentrated banking system in the whole world. The monopolies have organized the steel and iron industry, i.e., the branch of capitalist endeavor most interested in government orders, in militaristic equipment and in imperialistic undertakings (railroad building, the exploitation of mines, etc.) into the most influential factor in the nation. The latter has cemented the money interests into a firmly organized whole, with the greatest, most virile energy, creating a power that autocratically rules the industry, commerce and credit of the nation, dominant in private as well as public affairs, boundless in its powers of expansion, ever hungry for profit and activity, impersonal, and therefore, liberal-minded, reckless and unscrupulous, international by its very nature, ordained by its capacities to use the world as its stage.

Germany is under a personal regime, with strong initiative and spasmodic activity, with the weakest kind of parliamentarism, incapable of opposition, uniting all capitalist strata in the sharpest opposition to the working class. It is obvious that this live, unhampered imperialism, coming upon the world stage at a time when the world was practically divided up, with gigantic appetites, soon became an irresponsible factor of general unrest.

This was already foreshadowed by the radical upheaval that took place in the military policies of the empire at the end of the nineties. At that time two naval budgets were introduced which doubled the naval power of Germany and provided for a naval program covering almost two decades. This meant a sweeping change in the financial and trade policy of the nation. In the first place, it involved a striking change in the foreign policy of the empire. The policy of Bismarck was founded upon the principle that the empire is and must remain a land power, that the German fleet, at best, is but a very dispensable requisite for coastal defense. Even the secretary of state, Hollmann, declared in March 1897, in the Budget Commission of the Reichstag: "We need no navy for coastal defense. Our coasts protect themselves."

With the two naval bills an entirely new program was promulgated: on land and sea, Germany first! This marks the change from Bismarckian continental policies to *Welt Politik* [world politics], from the defensive to the offensive as the end and aim of Germany's military program. The language of these facts was so unmistakable that the Reichstag itself furnished the necessary commentary. Lieber, the leader of the Center at that time, spoke on the eleventh of March, 1896, after a famous speech of the emperor on the occasion of the twenty-fifth anniversary of the founding of the German empire, which had developed the new program as a forerunner to the naval bills, in which he mentioned "shoreless naval plans" against which Germany must be prepared to enter into active opposition. Another Center leader, Schadler, cried out in the Reichstag on March 23, 1898, when the first naval bill was under discussion, "The nation believes that we cannot be first on land and first on sea. You answer, gentlemen, that is not what we want! Nevertheless, gentlemen, you are at the beginning of such a conception, at a very strong beginning!"

When the second bill came, the same Schadler declared in the Reichstag on the fifth of February, 1900, referring to previous promises that there would be no further naval bills, "and today comes this bill, which means nothing more and nothing less than the inauguration of a world fleet, as a basis of support for world policies, by doubling our navy and binding the next two decades by our demands." As a matter of fact the government openly defended the political program of its new course of action. On December 11, 1899, von Buelow, at that time state secretary of the foreign office, in a defense of the second naval bill stated, "when the English speak of 'a greater Britain,' when the French talk of 'The New France,' when the Russians open up Asia for themselves, we too have a right to aspire to a greater Germany. If we do not create a navy sufficient to protect our trade, our natives in foreign lands, our missions and the safety of our shores, we are threatening the most vital interests of our nation. In the coming century the German people will be either the hammer or the anvil." Strip this of its coastal defense ornamentation, and there remains the colossal program: greater Germany, as the hammer upon other nations.

It is not difficult to determine the direction toward which these provocations, in the main, were directed. Germany was to become the rival of the world's great naval force — England. And England did not fail to understand. The naval reform bills, and the speeches that ushered them in, created a lively unrest in England, an unrest that has never again subsided. In March 1910, Lord Robert Cecil said in the House of Commons during a naval debate: "I challenge any man to give me a plausible reason for the tremendous navy that Germany is building up, other than to take up the fight against England." The fight for supremacy on the ocean that lasted for one and a half decades on both sides and culminated in the feverish building of dreadnoughts and superdreadnoughts, was, in effect, the war between Germany and England. The naval bill of December 11, 1899, was a declaration of war by Germany, which England answered on August 4, 1914.

It should be noted that this fight for naval supremacy had nothing in common with the economic rivalry for the world market. The English "monopoly of the world market" which ostensibly hampered German industrial development, so much discussed at the present time, really belongs to the sphere of those war legends of which the ever green French "revenge" is the most useful. This "monopoly" had become an old time fairy tale, to the lasting regret of the English capitalists. The industrial development of France, Belgium, Italy, Russia, India and Japan, and above all, of Germany and America, had put an end to this monopoly of the first half of the nineteenth century. Side by side with England, one nation after another stepped into the world market, capitalism developed automatically, and with gigantic strides, into world economy.

English supremacy on the sea, which has robbed so many social democrats of their peaceful sleep, and which, it seems to these gentlemen, must be destroyed to preserve international socialism, had, up to this time, disturbed German capitalism so little that the latter was able to grow up into a lusty youth, with bursting cheeks, under its "yoke." Yes, England itself, and its colonies, were the cornerstones for German industrial growth. And similarly, Germany became, for the English nation, its most important and most necessary customer. Far from standing in each other's way, British and German capitalist development were mutually highly interdependent, and united by a far-reaching system of division of labor, strongly augmented by England's free trade policy. German trade and its interests in the world market, therefore, had nothing whatever to do with a change of front in German politics and with the building of its fleet.

Nor did German colonial possessions at that time come into conflict with the English control of the seas. German colonies were not in need of protection by a first-class sea power. No one, certainly not England, envied Germany her possessions. That they were taken during the war by England and Japan, that the booty had changed owners, is but a generally accepted war measure, just as German imperialist appetites clamor for Belgium, a desire that no man outside of an insane asylum would have dared to express in time of peace. Southeast and Southwest Africa, Wilhelmsland or Tsingtau would never have caused any war, by land or by sea, between Germany and England. In fact, just before the war broke out, a treaty regulating a peaceable division of the Portuguese colonies in Africa between these two nations had been practically completed.

When Germany unfolded its banner of naval power and world policies it announced the desire for new and far-reaching conquest in the world by German imperialism. By means of a first-class aggressive navy, and by military forces that increased in a parallel ratio, the apparatus for a future policy was established, opening wide the doors for unprecedented possibilities. Naval building and military armaments became the glorious business of German industry, opening up a boundless prospect for further operations by trust and bank capital in the whole wide world. Thus, the acquiescence of all capitalist parties and their rallying under the flag of imperialism was assured. The Center followed the example of the National Liberals, the staunchest defenders of the steel and iron industry, and, by adopting the naval bill it had loudly denounced in 1900, became the party of the government. The Progressives trotted after the Center when the successor to the naval bill—the high-tariff party—came up; while the Junkers, the staunchest opponents of the "horrid navy" and of the canal brought up the rear as the most enthusiastic porkers and parasites of the very policy of sea-militarism and colonial robbery they had so vehemently opposed. The Reichstag election of 1907, the so-called Hottentot Elections, found the whole of Germany in a paroxysm of imperialistic enthusiasm, firmly united under one flag, that of the Germany of von Buelow, the Germany that felt itself ordained to play the role of the hammer in the world. These elections, with their spiritual pogrom atmosphere, were a prelude to the Germany of August 4, a challenge not only to the German working class, but to other capitalist nations as well, a challenge directed to no one in particular, a mailed fist shaken in the face of the entire world. . . .

V

But czarism! In the first moments of the war this was undoubtedly the factor that decided the position of our party. In its declaration, the social democratic group had given the slogan: against czarism! And out of this the socialist press has made a fight for European culture.

The *Frankfurter Volksstimme* wrote on July 31: "The German social democracy has always hated czardom as the bloody guardian of European reaction: from the time that Marx and Engels followed, with far-seeing eyes, every movement of this barbarian government, down to the present day, where its prisons are filled with political prisoners, and yet it trembles before every labor movement. The time has come when we must square accounts with these terrible scoundrels, under the German flag of war."

The *Pfaelzische Post* of Ludwighafen wrote on the same day: "This is a principle that was first established by our August Bebel. This is the struggle of civilization against barbarism, and in this struggle the proletariat will do its share."

The *Muenchener Post* of August 1: "When it comes to defending our country against the bloody czardom we will not be made citizens of the second class."

The *Halle Volksblatt* wrote on August 5: "If this is so, if we have been attacked by Russia, and everything seems to corroborate this statement—then the social democracy, as a matter of course, must vote in favor of all means of defense. With all our strength we must fight to drive czarism from our country!"

And on August 18: "Now that the die is cast in favor of the sword, it is not only the duty of national defense and national existence that puts the weapon into our hands as into the hands of every German, but also the realization that in the enemy whom we are fighting in the east we are striking a blow at the foe of all culture and all progress. . . . The overthrow of Russia is synonymous with the victory of freedom in Europe."

On August 5, the *Braunschweiger Volksfreund* wrote: "The irresistible force of military preparation drives everything before it. But the class-conscious labor movement obeys, not an outside force, but its own conviction, when it defends the ground upon which it stands from attack in the east."

The *Essener Arbeiterzeitung* cried out on August 3: "If this country is threatened by Russia's determination, then the social democrats, since the fight is against Russian blood-czarism, against the perpetrator of a million crimes against freedom and culture, will allow none to excel them in the fulfillment of their duty, in their willingness to sacrifice. Down with czarism! Down with the home of barbarism! Let that be our slogan!"

Similarly the *Bielefelder Volkswacht* writes on August 4: "Everywhere the same cry: against Russian despotism and faithlessness."

The Elberfeld party organ on August 5: "All Western Europe is vitally interested in the extermination of rotten murderous czarism. But this human interest is crushed by the greed of England and France to check the profits that have been made possible by German capital."

The *Rheinische Zeitung* in Cologne: "Do your duty, friends, wherever fate may place you. You are fighting for the civilization of Europe, for the independence of your fatherland, for your own welfare."

The *Schleswig-Holstein Volkszeitung* of August 7 writes: "Of course we are living in an age of capitalism. Of course we will continue to have class struggles after the great war is over. But these class struggles will be fought out in a freer state, they will be far more confined to the economic field than before. In the future the treatment of socialists as outcasts, as citizens of the second class, as politically rightless will be impossible, once the czardom of Russia has vanished."

On August 11, the *Hamburger Echo* cried: "We are fighting to defend ourselves not so much against England and France as against czarism. But this war we carry on with the greatest enthusiasm, for it is the war for civilization."

And the Luebeck party organ declared, as late as September 4: "If European liberty is saved, then Europe will have German arms to thank for it. Our fight is a fight against the worst enemy of all liberty and all democracy."

Thus the chorus of the German party press sounded and resounded.

In the beginning of the war the German government accepted the profferred assistance. Nonchalantly it fastened the laurels of the liberator of European culture to its helmet. Yes, it endeavored to carry through the role of the "liberator of nations," though often with visible discomfort and rather awkward grace. It flattered the Poles and the Jews in Russia, and egged one nation on against the other, using the policies that had proven so successful in their colonial warfare, where again and again they played up one chief against the other. And the social democrats followed each leap and bound of German imperialism with remarkable agility. While the Reichstag group covered up every shameful outrage with a discrete silence, the social democratic press filled the air with jubilant melodies, rejoicing in the liberty that "German riflebutts" had brought to the poor victims of czarism.

Even the theoretical organ of the party, *Neue Zeit*, wrote on the twenty-eighth of August: "The border population of the 'little father's' [i.e., the czar — Ed.] realm greeted the coming of the German troops with cries of joy. For these Poles and Jews have but one conception of their fatherland, that of corruption and rule by the knout. Poor devils, really fatherlandless creatures, these downtrodden subjects of bloody Nicholas. Even should they desire to do so, they could find nothing to defend but their chains. And so they live and toil, hoping and longing that German rifles, carried by German men, will crush the whole czarist system. . . . A clear and definite purpose still lives in the German working class, though the thunder of a world war is crashing over its head. It will defend itself from the allies of Russian barbarism in the west to bring about an honorable peace. It will give to the task of destroying czarism the last breath of man and beast."

After the social democratic group had stamped the war as a war of defense for the German nation and European culture, the social democratic press proceeded to hail it as the "savior of the oppressed nations." Hindenburg became the executor of Marx and Engels.

287

The memory of our party has played it a shabby trick. It forgot all its principles, its pledges, the decision of international congresses just at the moment when they should have found their application. And to its great misfortune, it remembered the heritage of Karl Marx and dug it out of the dust of passing years at the very moment when it could serve only to decorate Prussian militarism, for whose destruction Karl Marx was willing to sacrifice "the last breath of man and beast." Long forgotten chords that were sounded by Marx in the *Neue Rheinische Zeitung* against the vassal state of Nicholas I, during the German March Revolution of 1848, suddenly reawakened in the ears of the German social democracy in the year of Our Lord 1914, and called them to arms arm in arm with Prussian junkerdom, against the Russia of the Great Revolution of 1905.

This is where a revision should have been made; the slogans of the March Revolution should have been brought into accord with the historical experiences of the last seventy years.

In 1848 Russian czarism was, in truth, "the guardian of European reaction." The product of Russian social conditions, firmly rooted in its medieval, agricultural state, absolutism was the protector and at the same time the mighty director of monarchical reaction. This was weakened, particularly in Germany where a system of small states still obtained. As late as 1851 it was possible for Nicholas I to assure Berlin through the Prussian consul von Rochow "that he would, indeed, have been pleased to see the revolution destroyed by the roots when General von Wrangel advanced upon Berlin in November, 1848." At another time, in a warning to Manteuffel, the czar stated, "that he relied upon the imperial ministry, under the leadership of His Highness, to defend the rights of the crown against the chambers, and give to the principles of conservatism their due." It was possible for the same Nicholas I to bestow the Order of Alexander Nevski on a Prussian ministerial president in recognition of his "constant efforts to preserve legal order in Prussia."

The Crimean War worked a noticeable change in this respect. It ended with the military and therefore with the political bankruptcy of the old system. Russian absolutism was forced to grant reforms, to modernize its rule, to adjust itself to capitalist conditions. In so doing, it gave its little finger to the devil who already holds it firmly by the arm, and will eventually get it altogether. The Crimean War was, by the way, an instructive example of the kind of liberation that can be brought to a downtrodden people "at the point of a gun." The military overthrow at Sedan brought France its republic. But this republic was not the gift of the Bismarck soldiery. Prussia, at that time as today, can give to other peoples nothing but its own junker rule. Republican France was the ripe fruit of inner social struggles and of the three revolutions that had preceded it. The crash at Sevastopol was in effect similar to that of Jena. But because there was no revolutionary movement in Russia, it led to the outward renovation and reaffirmation of the old regime. But the reforms that opened the road for capitalist development in Russia during the sixties were possible only with the money of a capitalist system. This money was furnished by Western European capital. It came from Germany and France, and has created a new relationship that has lasted down to the present day. Russian absolutism is now subsidized by the western European bourgeoisie. No longer does the Russian ruble "roll in diplomatic chambers" as Prince William of Prussia bitterly complained in 1854, "into the very chambers of the king." On the contrary, German and French money is rolling to Petersburg to feed a regime that would long ago have breathed its last without this life-giving juice. Russian czarism is today no longer the product of Russian conditions; its root lies in the capitalist conditions of Western Europe. And the relationship is shifting from decade to decade. In the same measure as the old root of Russian absolutism in Russia itself is being destroyed, the new, West European root is growing stronger and stronger. Besides lending their financial support, Germany and France, since 1870, have been vying with each other to lend Russia their political support as well. As revolutionary forces arise from the womb of the Russian people itself to fight against Russian absolutism, they meet with an ever growing resistance in Western Europe, which stands ready to lend to threatened czarism its moral and political support. So when, in the beginning of the eighties the older Russian socialist movement severely shook the czarist government and partly destroyed its authority within and without, Bismarck made his treaty with Russia and strengthened its position in international politics.

Capitalist development, tenderly nurtured by czarism with its own hands, finally bore fruit: in the nineties the revolutionary movement of the Russian proletariat began. The erstwhile "guardian of reaction" was forced to grant a meaningless constitution, to seek a new protector from the rising flood in its own country. And it found this protector—in Germany. The Germany of Buelow must pay the debt of gratitude that the Prussia of Wrangel and Manteuffel had incurred. Relations were completely reversed. Russian support against the revolution in Germany is superseded by German aid against the revolution in Russia. Spies, outrages, betrayals—a demagogic agitation, like that which blessed the times of the Holy Alliance, was unleashed in Germany against the fighters for the cause of Russian freedom, and followed to the very doorsteps of the Russian Revolution. In the Konigsberg trial of 1904 this wave of persecution was at its height. This trial threw a scathing light upon a whole historical development since 1848 and showed the complete change of relations between Russian absolutism and European reaction. *"Tua res agitur'"* ["Your problem is being attended to!"] cried a Prussian minister of justice to the ruling classes of Germany, pointing to the tottering foundation of the czarist regime. "The establishment of a democratic republic in Russia would strongly influence Germany," declared First District Attorney Schulze in Konigsberg. "When my neighbor's home burns my own is also in danger." And his assistant Casper also emphasized: "It is naturally not indifferent to Germany's public interests whether this bulwark of absolutism stands or falls. Certainly the flames of a revolutionary movement may easily spring over into Germany. . . ."

The revolution was overthrown, but the very causes that led to its temporary downfall are valuable in a discussion of the position taken by the German social democracy in this war. That the Russian uprising in 1905-06 was unsuccessful in spite of its unequalled expenditure of revolutionary force, its clearness of purpose and tenacity can be ascribed to two distinct causes. The one lies in the inner character of the revolution itself, in its enormous historical program, in the mass of economic and political problems that it was forced to face. Some of them, for instance, the agrarian problem, cannot possibly be solved within capitalist society. There was the difficulty furthermore of creating a class state for the supremacy of the modern bourgeoisie against the counterrevolutionary opposition of the bourgeoisie as a whole. To the onlooker it would seem that the Russian Revolution was doomed to failure because it was a proletarian revolution with bourgeois duties and problems, or if you wish, a bourgeois revolution waged by socialist proletarian methods, a crash of two generations amid lightning and thunder, the fruit of the delayed industrial development of class conditions in Russia and their overripeness in Western Europe. From this point of view its downfall in 1906 signifies not its bankruptcy, but the natural closing of the first chapter, upon which the second must follow with the inevitability of a natural law.

The second cause was of external nature; it lay in Western Europe. European reaction once more hastened to help its endangered protege; not with lead and bullets, although "German guns" were in German fists even in 1905 and only waited for a signal from Petersburg to attack the neighboring Poles. Europe rendered an assistance that was equally valuable: financial subsidy and political alliances were arranged to help czarism in Russia. French money paid for the armed forces that broke down the Russian Revolution; from Germany came the moral and political support that helped the Russian government to clamber out from the depths of shame into which Japanese torpedoes and Russian proletarian fists had thrust it. In 1910, in Potsdam, official Germany received Russian czarism with open arms. The reception of the blood-stained monarch at the gates of the German capital was not only the German blessing for the throttling of Persia, but above all for the hangman's work of the Russian counterrevolution. It was the official banquet of German and European "Kultur" over what they believed to be the grave of the Russian Revolution.

And strange! At that time, when this challenging feast upon the grave of the Russian Revolution was held in its own home, the German social democracy remained silent, and had completely forgotten "the heritage of our masters" from 1848. At that time, when the hangman was received in Potsdam, not a sound, not a protest, not an article vetoed this expression of solidarity with the Russian counterrevolution. Only since this war has begun, since the police permits it, the smallest party organ intoxicates itself with bloodthirsty attacks upon the hangman of Russian liberty. Yet nothing could have disclosed more clearly than did this triumphal tour of the czar in 1910 that the oppressed Russian proletariat was the victim, not only of domestic reaction, but of Western European reaction as well. Their fight, like that of the March revolutionists of 1848, was against reaction, not only in their own country, but against its guardians in all other European countries.

After the inhuman crusades of the counterrevolution had somewhat subsided, the revolutionary ferment in the Russian proletariat once more became active. The flood began to rise and to boil. Economic strikes in Russia, according to the official reports, involved 46,623 workers and 256,385 days in 1910; 96,730 workers and 768,556 days in 1911; and 89,771 workers and 1,214,881 days in the first five months of 1912. Political mass strikes, protests and demonstrations comprised 1,005,000 workers in 1912, 1,272,000 in 1913. In 1914 the flood rose higher and higher. On January 22, the anniversary of the beginning of the revolution, there was a demonstration mass strike of 200,000 workers. As in the days before the revolution of 1905, the flame broke out in June, in the Caucasus. In Baku, 40,000 workers were on a general strike. The flames leaped over to Petersburg. On the seventeenth of June 80,000 workers in Petersburg laid down their tools, on the twentieth of July, 200,000 were out; July 23 the general strike movement was spreading out all over Russia, barricades were being built, the revolution was on its way. A few more months and it would have come, its flags fluttering in the wind. A few more years, and perhaps the whole world political constellation would have been changed, imperialism perhaps would have received a firm check on its mad impulse.

But German reaction checked the revolutionary movement. From Berlin and Vienna came declarations of war, and the Russian Revolution was buried beneath its wreckage. "German guns" are shattering, not czarism, but its most dangerous enemy. The hopefully fluttering flag of the revolution sank down amid a wild whirlpool of war. But it sank honorably, and it will rise again out of the horrible massacre, in spite of "German guns," in spite of victory or defeat for Russia on the battlefields.

The national revolts in Russia which the Germans tried to foster, too, were unsuccessful. The Russian provinces were evidently less inclined to fall for the bait of Hindenburg's cohorts than the German social democracy. The Jews, practical people that they are, were able to count on their fingers that "German fists" which have been unable to overthrow their own Prussian reaction, can hardly be expected to smash Russian absolutism. The Poles, exposed to the triple-headed war, were not in a position to answer their "liberators" in audible language. But they will have remembered that Polish children were taught to say the Lord's prayer in the German language with bloody welts on their backs, will not have forgotten the liberality of Prussian anti-Polish laws. All of them, Poles, Jews and Russians, had no difficulty in understanding that the "German gun," when it descends upon their heads, brings not liberty, but death.

To couple the legend of Russian liberation with its Marxian heritage is worse than a poor joke on the part of the German social democracy. It is a crime. To Marx, the Russian revolution was a turning point in the history of the world. Every political and historical perspective was made dependent upon the one consideration, "provided the Russian revolution has not already broken out." Marx believed in the Russian revolution and expected it even at a time when Russia was only a state of vassals. When the war broke out the Russian Revolution had occurred. Its first attempt had not been victorious; but it could not be ignored; it is on the order of the day. And yet our German social democrats came with "German guns," declaring the Russian Revolution null and void, struck it from the pages of history. In 1848 Marx spoke from the German barricades; in Russia there was a hopeless reaction. In 1914 Russia was in the throes of a revolution; while its German "liberators" were cowed by the fists of Prussian junkerdom.

But the liberating mission of the German armies was only an episode. German imperialism soon raised its uncomfortable mask and turned openly against France and England. Here, too, it was supported valiantly by a large number of the party papers. They ceased railing against the bloody czar, and held up "perfidious Albion" and its merchant soul to the public disdain. They set out to free Europe, no longer from Russian absolutism, but from English naval supremacy. The hopeless confusion in which the party had become entangled found a drastic illustration in the desperate attempt made by the more thoughtful portion of our party press to meet this new change of front. In vain they tried to force the war back into its original channels, to nail it down to the "heritage of our masters"—that is, to the myth that they, the social democracy, had themselves created. "With heavy heart I have been forced to mobilize the army against a neighbor at whose side I have fought on so many battlefields. With honest sorrow I saw a friendship, truly served by Germany, break." That was simple, open, honest. But when the rhetoric of the first weeks of war backed down before the lapidary language of imperialism, the German social democracy lost its only plausible excuse.

VI

Of equal importance in the attitude of the social democracy was the official adoption of a program of civil peace, i.e., the cessation of the class struggle for the duration of the war. The declaration that was read by the social democratic group in the Reichstag on the fourth of August had been agreed upon in advance with representatives of the government and the capitalist parties. It was little more than a patriotic grandstand play, prepared behind the scenes and delivered for the benefit of the people at home and in other nations.

To the leading elements in the labor movement, the vote in favor of the war credits by the Reichstag group was a cue for the immediate settlement of all labor controversies. Nay more, they announced this to the manufacturers as a patriotic duty incurred by labor when it agreed to observe a civil peace. These same labor leaders undertook to supply city labor to farmers in order to assure a prompt harvest. The leaders of the social democratic women's movement united with capitalist women for "national service" and placed the most important elements that remained after the mobilization at the disposal of national Samaritan work. Socialist women worked in soup kitchens and on advisory commissions instead of carrying on agitation work for the party.

Under the antisocialist laws the party had utilized parliamentary elections to spread its agitation and to keep a firm hold upon the population in spite of the state of siege that had been declared against the party and the persecution of the socialist press. In this crisis the social democratic movement has voluntarily relinquished all propaganda and education in the interest of the proletarian class struggle, during Reichstag and Landtag elections. Parliamentary elections have everywhere been reduced to the simple bourgeois formula; the catching of votes for the candidates of the party on the basis of an amicable and peaceful settlement with its capitalist opponents. When the social democratic representatives in the Landtag and in the municipal commissions — with the laudable exceptions of the Prussian and Alsatian Landtag — with high sounding references to the existing state of civil peace, voted their approval of the war credits that had been demanded, it only emphasized how completely the party had broken with things as they were before the war.

The social democratic press, with a few exceptions, proclaimed the principle of national unity as the highest duty of the German people. It warned the people not to withdraw their funds from the savings banks lest by so doing they unbalance the economic life of the nation, and hinder the savings banks in liberally buying war-loan bonds. It pleaded with proletarian women that they should spare their husbands at the front the tales of suffering that they and their children were being forced to undergo, to bear in silence the neglect of the government, to cheer the fighting warriors with happy stories of family life and favorable reports of prompt assistance through government agencies. They rejoiced that the educational work that had been conducted for so many years in and through the labor movement had become a conspicuous asset in conducting the war. Something of this spirit the following example will show:

"A friend in need is a friend indeed. This old adage has once more proven its soundness. The social democratic proletariat that has been prosecuted and clubbed for its opinions went, like one man, to protect our homes. German labor unions that had so often suffered both in Germany and in Prussia report unanimously that the best of their members have joined the colors. Even capitalist papers like the *General-Anzeiger* note the fact and express the conviction that "these people" will do their duty as well as any man, that blows will rain most heavily where they stand.

"As for us, we are convinced that our labor unionists can do more than deal out blows. Modern mass armies have by no means simplified the work of their generals. It is practically impossible to move forward large troop divisions in close marching order under the deadly fire of modern artillery. Ranks must be carefully widened, must be more accurately controlled. Modern warfare requires discipline and clearness of vision not only in the divisions but in every individual soldier. The war will show how vastly human material has been improved by the educational work of the labor unions, how well their activity will serve the nation in these times of awful stress. The Russian and the French soldier may be capable of marvellous deeds of bravery. But in cool, collected consideration none will surpass the German labor unionists. Then too, many of our organized workers know the ways and byways of the borderland as well as they know their own pockets, and not a few of them are accomplished linguists. The Prussian advance in 1866 has been termed a schoolmasters' victory. This will be a victory of labor union leaders" (*Frankfurter Volksstimme,* August 18, 1914).

In the same strain *Neue Zeit,* the theoretical organ of the party, declared (no. 23, September 25, 1914): "Until the question of victory or defeat has been decided, all doubts must disappear, even as to the causes of the war. Today there can be no difference of party, class and nationality within the army or the population."

And in number 8, November 27, 1914, the same *Neue Zeit* declared in a chapter on "The Limitations of the International": "The world war divides the socialists of the world into different camps and especially into different national camps. The International cannot prevent this. In other words, the International ceases to be an effective instrument in times of war. It is, on the whole, a peace instrument. Its great historic problem is the struggle for peace and the class struggle in times of peace."

Briefly, therefore, beginning with the fourth of August until the day when peace shall be declared, the social democracy has declared the class struggle extinct. The first thunder of Krupp cannons in Belgium welded Germany into a wonderland of class solidarity and social harmony.

How is this miracle to be understood? The class struggle is known to be not a social democratic invention that can be arbitrarily set aside for a period of time whenever it may seem convenient to do so. The proletarian class struggle is older than the social democracy, is an elementary product of class society. It flamed up all over Europe when capitalism first came into power. The modern proletariat was not led by the social democracy into the class struggle. On the contrary the international social democratic movement was called into being by the class struggle to bring a conscious aim and unity into the various local and scattered fragments of the class struggle.

What then has changed in this respect when the war broke out? Have private property, capitalist exploitation and class rule ceased to exist? Or have the propertied classes in a spell of patriotic fervor declared: in view of the needs of the war we hereby turn over the means of production, the earth, the factories and the mills therein, into the possession of the people? Have they relinquished the right to make profits out of these possessions? Have they set aside all political privileges, will they sacrifice them upon the altar of the fatherland, now that it is in danger? It is, to say the least, a rather naive hypothesis, and sounds almost like a story from a kindergarten primer. And yet the declaration of our official leaders that the class struggle has been suspended permits no other interpretation. Of course nothing of the sort has occurred. Property rights, exploitation and class rule, even political oppression in all its Prussian thoroughness, have remained intact. The cannons in Belgium and in Eastern Prussia have not had the slightest influence upon the fundamental social and political structure of Germany.

The cessation of the class struggle was, therefore, a deplorably one-sided affair. While capitalist oppression and exploitation, the worst enemies of the working class, remain; socialist and labor union leaders have generously delivered the working class, without a struggle, into the hands of the enemy for the duration of the war. While the ruling classes are fully armed with the property and supremacy rights, the working class, at the advice of the social democracy, has laid down its arms.

Once before, in 1848 in France, the proletariat experienced this miracle of class harmony, this fraternity of all classes of a modern capitalist state of society. In his *Class Struggles in France,* Karl Marx writes: "In the eyes of the proletariat, who confused the moneyed aristocracy with the bourgeoisie, in the imagination of republican idealists, who denied the very existence of classes, or attributed them to a monarchical form of government, in the deceitful phrases of those bourgeois who had hitherto been excluded from power, the rule of the bourgeoisie was ended when the republic was proclaimed. At that time all royalists became republican, all millionaires in Paris became laborers. In the word *Fraternite,* the brotherhood of man, this imaginary destruction of classes found official expression. This comfortable abstraction from class differences, this sentimental balancing of class interests, this utopian disregard of the class struggle, this *Fraternite* was the real slogan of the February Revolution. . . . The Parisian proletariat rejoiced in an orgy of brotherhood. . . . The Parisian proletariat, looking upon the republic as its own creation, naturally acclaimed every act of the provisional bourgeois government. Willingly it permitted Caussidiere to use its members as policemen to protect the property of Paris. With unquestioning faith it allowed Louis Blanc to regulate wage differences between workers and masters. In their eyes it was a matter of honor to preserve the fair name of the republic before the peoples of Europe."

Thus in February 1848, a naive Parisian proletariat set aside the class struggle. But let us not forget that even they committed this mistake only after the July monarchy had been crushed by their revolutionary action, after a republic had been established. The fourth of August, 1914, is an inverted February Revolution. It is the setting aside of class differences, not under a republic, but under a military monarchy, not after a victory of the people over reaction, but after a victory of reaction over the people, not with the proclamation of *Liberte, Egalite, Fraternite,* but with the proclamation of a state of siege, after the press had been choked and the constitution annihilated.

Impressively the government of Germany proclaimed a civil peace. Solemnly the parties promised to abide by it. But as experienced politicians these gentlemen know full well that it is fatal to trust too much to promises. They secured civil peace for themselves by the very real measure of a military dictatorship. This too the social democratic group accepted without protest or opposition. In the declarations of August 4 and December 2 there is not a syllable of indignation over the affront contained in the proclamation of military rule. When it voted for civil peace and war credits, the social democracy silently gave its consent to military rule as well, and laid itself, bound and gagged, at the feet of the ruling classes. The declaration of military rule was purely an antisocialist measure. From no other side were resistance, protest, action, and difficulties to be expected. As a reward for its capitulation the social democracy merely received what it would have received under any circumstances, even after an unsuccessful resistance, namely, military rule. The impressive declaration of the Reichstag group emphasizes the old socialist principle of the right of nations to self-determination, as an explanation of their vote in favor of war credits. Self-determination for the German proletariat was the straightjacket of a siege. Never in the history of the world has a party made itself more ridiculous.

But, more! In refuting the existence of the class struggle, the social democracy has denied the very basis of its own existence. What is the very breath of its body, if not the class struggle? What role could it expect to play in the war, once having sacrificed the class struggle, the fundamental principle of its existence? The social democracy has destroyed its mission, for the period of the war, as an active political party, as a representative of working-class politics. It has thrown aside the most important weapon it possessed, the power of criticism of the war from the peculiar point of view of the working class. Its only mission now is to play the role of the gendarme over the working class under a state of military rule.

German freedom, that same German freedom for which, according to the declaration of the Reichstag group, Krupp cannons are now fighting, has been endangered by this attitude of the social democracy far beyond the period of the present war. The leaders of the social democracy are convinced that democratic liberties for the working class will come as a reward for its allegiance to the fatherland. But never in the history of the world has an oppressed class received political rights as a reward for service rendered to the ruling classes. History is full of examples of shameful deceit on the part of the ruling classes, even when solemn promises were made before the war broke out. The social democracy has not assured the extension of liberty in Germany. It has sacrificed those liberties that the working class possessed before the war broke out.

The indifference with which the German people have allowed themselves to be deprived of the freedom of the press, of the right of assembly and of public life, the fact that they not only calmly bore, but even applauded, the state of siege is unexampled in the history of modern society. In England the freedom of the press has nowhere been violated, in France there is incomparably more freedom of public opinion than in Germany. In no country has public opinion so completely vanished, nowhere has it been so completely superseded by official opinion, by the order of the government, as in Germany. Even in Russia there is only the destructive work of a public censor who effectively wipes out opposition of opinion. But not even there have they descended to the custom of providing articles ready for the press to the opposition papers.

In no other country has the government forced the opposition press to express in its columns the politics that have been dictated and ordered by the government in "Confidential Conferences." Such measures were unknown even in Germany during the war of 1870. At that time the press enjoyed unlimited freedom, and accompanied the events of the war, to Bismarck's active resentment, with criticism that was often exceedingly sharp. The newspapers were full of active discussion on war aims, on questions of annexation, and constitutionality. When Johann Jacobi was arrested, a storm of indignation swept over Germany, so that even Bismarck felt obliged to disavow all responsibility for this "mistake" of the powers of reaction. Such was the situation in Germany at a time when Bebel and Liebknecht, in the name of the German working class, had declined all community of interests with the ruling jingoes. It took a social democracy with four and a half million votes to conceive of the touching *Burgfrieden*, to assent to war credits, to bring upon us the worst military dictatorship that was ever suffered to exist. That such a thing is possible in Germany today, that not only the bourgeois press, but the highly developed and influential socialist press as well, permits these things without even the pretense of opposition bears a fatal significance for the future of German liberty. It proves that society in Germany today has within itself no foundation for political freedom, since it allows itself to be thus lightly deprived of its most sacred rights.

Let us not forget that the political rights that existed in Germany before the war were not won, as were those of France and England, in great and repeated revolutionary struggles, are not firmly anchored in the lives of the people by the power of revolutionary tradition. They are the gift of a Bismarckian policy granted after a period of victorious counterrevolution that lasted over twenty years. German liberties did not ripen on the field of revolution, they are the product of diplomatic gambling by Prussian military monarchy, they are the cement with which this military monarchy has united the present German empire. Danger threatens the free development of German freedom not, as the German Reichstag group believes, from Russia, but in Germany itself. It lies in the peculiar counterrevolutionary origin of the German constitution, and looms dark in the reactionary powers that have controlled the German state since the empire was founded, conducting a silent but relentless war against these pitiful "German liberties."

The Junkers of East of the Elbe, the business jingoes, the archreactionaries of the Center, the degraded "German liberals," the personal rulership, the sway of the sword, the Zabern policy that triumphed all over Germany before the war broke out, these are the real enemies of culture and liberty; and the war, the state of seige and the attitude of the social democracy are strengthening the powers of darkness all over the land. The liberal, to be sure, can explain away this graveyard quietly in Germany with a characteristically liberal explanation; to him it is only a temporary sacrifice, for the duration of the war. But to a people that are politically ripe, a sacrifice of their rights and their public life, even temporarily, is as impossible as for a human being to give up, for a time, his right to breathe. A people that give silent consent to military government in times of war thereby admit that political independence at any time is superfluous. The passive submission of the social democracy to the present state of siege and its vote for war credits without attaching the slightest condition thereto, its acceptance of a civil peace, has demoralized the masses, the only existing pillar of German constitutional government, has strengthened the reaction of its rulers, the enemies of constitutional government.

By sacrificing the class struggle, our party has moreover, once and for all, given up the possibility of making its influence effectively felt in determining the extent of the war and the terms of peace. To its own official declaration, its acts have been a stinging blow. While protesting against all annexations, which are, after all, the logical consequences of an imperialist war that is successful from the military point of view, it has handed over every weapon that the working class possessed that might have empowered the masses to mobilize public opinion in their own direction, to exert an effective pressure upon the terms of war and of peace. By assuring militarism of peace and quiet at home, the social democracy has given its military rulers permission to follow their own course without even considering the interests of the masses, has unleashed in the hearts of the ruling classes the most unbridled imperialistic tendencies. In other words, when the social democracy adopted its platform of civil peace, and the political disarmament of the working class, it condemned its own demand of no annexations to impotency.

Thus the social democracy has added another crime to the heavy burden it already has to bear, namely the lengthening of the war. The commonly accepted dogma that we can oppose the war only so long as it is threatened has become a dangerous trap. As an inevitable consequence, once the war has come, social democratic political action is at an end. There can be, then, but one question, victory or defeat, i.e., the class struggle must stop for the period of the war. But actually the greatest problem for the political movement of the social democracy begins only after the war has broken out. At the International congresses held in Stuttgart in 1907 and in Basel in 1912, the German party and labor union leaders unanimously voted in favor of a resolution which says: "Should war nevertheless break out, it shall be the duty of the social democracy to work for a speedy peace, and to strive with every means in its power to utilize the industrial and political crisis to accomplish the awakening of the people, thus hastening the overthrow of the capitalist class rule."

What has the social democracy done in this war? Exactly the contrary. By voting in favor of war credits and entering upon a civil peace, it has striven, by all the means in its power, to prevent the industrial and political crisis, to prevent an awakening of the masses by the war. It strives "with all the means in its power" to save the capitalist state from its own anarchy to reduce the number of its victims. It is claimed — we have often heard this argument used by Reichstag deputies — that not one man less would have fallen upon the battlefields if the social democratic group had voted against the war credits. Our party press has steadfastly maintained that we must support and join in the defense of our country in order to reduce the number of bloody victims that this war shall cost.

But the policy that we have followed out has had exactly the opposite effect. In the first place, thanks to the civil peace, and the patriotic attitude of the social democracy, the imperialist war unleashed its furies without fear. Hitherto, fear of restiveness at home, fear of the fury of the hungry populace have been a load upon the minds of the ruling classes that effectively checked them in their bellicose desires. In the well-known words of Buelow: "They are trying to put off the war chiefly because they fear the social democracy." Rohrbach says in his *Krieg und die Deutsche Politik* [The War and German Policy], page 7, "unless elemental catastrophies intervene, the only power that can force Germany to make peace is the hunger of the breadless." Obviously, he meant a hunger that attracts attention, that forces itself unpleasantly upon the ruling classes in order to force them to pay heed to its demands. Let us see, finally, what a prominent military theoretician, General Bernhardi, says, in his great work *Vom Heutigen Kriege* [On the Present War]: "Thus modern mass armies make war difficult for a variety of reasons. Moreover they constitute, in and of themselves, a danger that must never be underestimated.

"The mechanism of such an army is so huge and so complicated, that it can remain efficient and flexible only so long as its cogs and wheels work, in the main, dependably, and obvious moral confusion is carefully prevented. These are things that cannot be completely avoided, as little as we can conduct a war exclusively with victorious battles. They can be overcome if they appear only within certain restricted limits. But when great, compact masses once shake off their leaders, when a spirit of panic becomes widespread, when a lack of sustenance becomes extensively felt, when the spirit of revolt spreads out among the masses of the army, then the army becomes not only ineffectual against the enemy, it becomes a menace to itself and to its leaders. When the army bursts the bands of discipline, when it voluntarily interrupts the course of military operation, it creates problems that its leaders are unable to solve.

"War, with its modern mass armies, is, under all circumstances, a dangerous game, a game that demands the greatest possible sacrifice, personal and financial sacrifice the state can offer. Under such circumstances it is clear that provision must be made everywhere that the war, once it has broken out, be brought to an end as quickly as possible, to release the extreme tension that must accompany this supreme effort on the part of whole nations."

Thus capitalist politicians and military authorities alike believe war, with its modern mass armies, to be a dangerous game. And therein lay for the social democracy the most effectual opportunity to prevent the rulers of the present day from precipitating war and to force them to end it as rapidly as possible. But the position of the social democracy in this war cleared away all doubts, has torn down the dams that held back the storm-flood of militarism. In fact it has created a power for which neither Bernhardi nor any other capitalist statesman dared hope in his wildest dreams. From the camp of the social democrats came the cry: "Durchhalten" [see it through], i.e., the continuation of this human slaughter. And so the thousands of victims that have fallen for months on battlefields lie upon our conscience.

VII

"But since we have been unable to prevent the war, since it has come in spite of us, and our country is facing invasion, shall we leave our country defenseless! Shall we deliver it into the hands of the enemy? Does not socialism demand the right of nations to determine their own destinies? Does it not mean that every people is justified, nay more, is in duty bound, to protect its liberties, its independence? 'When the house is on fire, shall we not first try to put out the blaze before stopping to ascertain the incendiary?'"

These arguments have been repeated, again and again in defense of the attitude of the social democracy in Germany and in France.

Even in the neutral countries this argument has been used. Translated into Dutch we read for instance: "When the ship leaks must we not seek, first of all, to stop the hole?"

To be sure. Fie upon a people that capitulates before invasion and fie upon a party that capitulates before the enemy within.

But there is one thing that the firemen in the burning house have forgotten: that in the mouth of a socialist, the phrase "defending one's fatherland" cannot mean playing the role of cannon fodder under the command of an imperialistic bourgeoisie.

Is an invasion really the horror of all horrors, before which all class conflict within the country must subside as though spellbound by some supernatural witchcraft? According to the police theory of bourgeois patriotism and military rule, every evidence of the class struggle is a crime against the interests of the country because they maintain that it constitutes a weakening of the stamina of the nation. The social democracy has allowed itself to be perverted into this same distorted point of view. Has not the history of modern capitalist society shown that in the eyes of capitalist society, foreign invasion is by no means the unmitigated terror as it is generally painted; that on the contrary, it is a measure to which the bourgeoisie has frequently and gladly resorted as an effective weapon against the enemy within? Did not the Bourbons and the aristocrats of France invite foreign invasion against the Jacobins? Did not the Austrian counterrevolution in 1849 call out the French invaders against Rome, the Russian against Budapest? Did not the "Party of Law and Order" in France in 1850 openly threaten an invasion of the Cossacks in order to bring the National Assembly to terms? And was not the Bonaparte army released, and the support of the Prussian army against the Paris Commune assured, by the famous contract between Jules Favre, Thiers and Co., and Bismarck?

This historical evidence led Karl Marx, forty-five years ago, to expose the "national wars" of modern capitalist society as miserable frauds. In his famous address to the General Council of the International on the downfall of the Paris Commune, he said: "That, after the greatest war of modern times the belligerent armies, the victor and the vanquished, should unite for the mutual butchery of the proletariat—this incredible event proves, not as Bismarck would have us believe, the final overthrow of the new social power, but the complete disintegration of the old bourgeois society. The highest heroic accomplishment of which the old order is capable is the national war. And this has now proved to be a fraud perpetrated by government for no other purpose than to put off the class struggle, a fraud that is bared as soon as the class struggle flares up in a civil war. Class rule can no longer hide behind a national uniform. The national governments are united against the proletariat."

In capitalist history, invasion and class struggle are not opposites, as the official legend would have us believe, but one is the means and the expression of the other. Just as invasion is the true and tried weapon in the hands of capital against the class struggle, so on the other hand the fearless pursuit of the class struggle has always proven the most effective preventive of foreign invasions. On the brink of modern times are the examples of the Italian cities, Florence and Milan, with their century of bitter struggle against the Hohenstaufen. The stormy history of these cities, torn by inner conflicts, proves that the force and the fury of inner class struggles not only does not weaken the defensive powers of the community, but that, on the contrary, from their fires shoot the only flames that are strong enough to withstand every attack from a foreign foe.

But the classic example of our own times is the Great French Revolution. In 1793 Paris, the heart of France, was surrounded by enemies. And yet Paris and France at that time did not succumb to the invasion of a stormy flood of European coalition; on the contrary, it welded its force in the face of the growing danger to a more gigantic opposition. If France, at that critical time, was able to meet each new coalition of the enemy with a new miraculous and undiminished fighting spirit, it was only because of the impetuous loosening of the inmost forces of society in the great struggle of the classes of France. Today, in the perspective of a century, it is clearly discernible that only this intensification of the class struggle, that only the dictatorship of the French people and their fearless radicalism, could produce means and forces out of the soil of France, sufficient to defend and to sustain a newborn society against a world of enemies, against the intrigues of a dynasty, against the traitorous machinations of the aristocrats, against the attempts of the clergy, against the treachery of their generals, against the opposition of sixty departments and provincial capitals, and against the united armies

303

and navies of monarchical Europe. The centuries have proven that not the state of siege, but relentless class struggle, is the power that awakens the spirit of self-sacrifice, the moral strength of the masses; that the class struggle is the best protection and the best defense against a foreign enemy.

This same tragic *quid pro quo* victimized the social democracy when it based its attitude in this war upon the doctrine of the right of national self-determination.

It is true that socialism gives to every people the right of independence and the freedom of independent control of its own destinies. But it is a veritable perversion of socialism to regard present-day capitalist society as the expression of this self-determination of nations. Where is there a nation in which the people have had the right to determine the form and conditions of their national, political and social existence? In Germany the determination of the people found concrete expression in the demands formulated by the German revolutionary democrats of 1848; the first fighters of the German proletariat, Marx, Engels, Lassalle, Bebel and Liebknect, proclaimed and fought for a united German Republic. For this ideal the revolutionary forces in Berlin and in Vienna, in those tragic days of March, shed their heart's blood upon the barricades. To carry out this program, Marx and Engels demanded that Prussia take up arms against czarism. The foremost demand made in the national program was for the liquidation of "the heap of organized decay, the Habsburg monarchy," as well as of two dozen other dwarf monarchies within Germany itself. The overthrow of the German revolution, the treachery of the German bourgeoisie to its own democratic ideals, led to the Bismarck regime and to its creature, present-day Greater Prussia, twenty-five fatherlands under one helm, the German Empire.

Modern Germany is built upon the grave of the March Revolution [of 1848 — Ed.] upon the wreckage of the right of self-determination of the German people. The present war, supporting Turkey and the Habsburg monarchy, and strengthening German military autocracy is a second burial of the March revolutionists, and of the national program of the German people. It is a fiendish jest of history that the social democrats, the heirs of the German patriots of 1848, should go forth in this war with the banner of "self-determination of nations" held aloft in their hands. But, perhaps the Third French Republic, with its colonial possessions in four continents and its colonial horrors in two, is the expression of the self-determination of the French nation? Or the British nation, with its India, with its South African rule of a million whites over a population of five million colored people? Or perhaps Turkey, or the empire of the czar?

Capitalist politicians, in whose eyes the rulers of the people and the ruling classes are the nation, can honestly speak of the "right of national self-determination" in connection with such colonial empire. To the socialist, no nation is free whose national existence is based upon the enslavement of another people, for to him colonial peoples, too, are human beings, and, as such, parts of the national state. International socialism recognizes the right of free independent nations, with equal rights. But socialism alone can create such nations, can bring self-determination of their peoples. This slogan of socialism is like all its others, not an apology for existing conditions, but a guidepost, a spur for the revolutionary, regenerative, active policy of the proletariat. So long as capitalist states exist, i.e., so long as imperialistic world policies determine and regulate the inner and the outer life of a nation, there can be no "national self-determination" either in war or in peace.

In the present imperialistic milieu there can be no wars of national self-defense. Every socialist policy that depends upon this determining historic milieu, that is willing to fix its policies in the world whirlpool from the point of view of a single nation, is built upon a foundation of sand.

We have already attempted to show the background for the present conflict between Germany and her opponents. It was necessary to show up more clearly the actual forces and relations that constitute the motive power behind the present war, because this legend of the defense of the existence, the freedom and civilization of Germany plays an important part in the attitude of our group in the Reichstag and our socialist press. Against this legend historical truth must be emphasized to show that this is a war that has been prepared by German militarism and its world political ideas for years, that it was brought about in the summer of 1914, by Austrian and German diplomacy, with a full realization of its import.

In a discussion of the general causes of the war, and of its significance, the question of the "guilty party" is completely beside the issue. Germany certainly has not the right to speak of a war of defense, but France and England have little more justification. They too are protecting, not their national, but their world political existence, their old imperialistic possessions, from the attacks of the German upstart. Doubtless the raids of German and Austrian imperialism in the Orient started the conflagration, but French imperialism, by devouring Morocco, and English imperialism, in its attempts to rape Mesopotamia, and all the other measures that were calculated to secure its rule of force in India, Russia's Baltic policies, aiming toward Constantinople, all of these factors have carried together and piled up, brand for brand, the firewood that feeds the conflagration. If capitalist armaments have played an important role as the mainspring that times the outbreak of the catastrophe, it was a competition of armaments in all nations. And if Germany laid the cornerstone for European competitive armaments by Bismarck's policy of 1870, this policy was furthered by that of the second empire and by the military-colonial policies of the third empire, by its expansions in East Asia and in Africa.

The French socialists have some slight foundation for their illusion of "national defense," because neither the French government nor the French people entertained the slightest warlike desires in July 1914. "Today everyone in France is honestly, uprightly and without reservation for peace," insisted Jaures in the last speech of his life, on the eve of the war, when he addressed a meeting in the People's House in Brussels. This was absolutely true, and gives the psychological explanation for the indignation of the French socialists when this criminal war was forced upon their country. But this fact was not sufficient to determine the socialist attitude on the world war as a historic occurrence.

The events that bore the present war did not begin in July 1914 but reach back for decades. Thread by thread they have been woven together on the loom of an inexorable natural development until the firm net of imperialist world politics has encircled five continents. It is a huge historical complex of events, whose roots reach deep down into the Plutonic deeps of economic creation, whose outermost branches spread out and point away into a dimly dawning new world, events before whose all-embracing immensity, the conception of guilt and retribution, of defense and offense, sink into pale nothingness.

Imperialism is not the creation of any one or of any group of states. It is the product of a particular stage of ripeness in the world development of capital, an innately international condition, an indivisible whole, that is recognizable only in all its relations, and from which no nation can hold aloof at will. From this point of view only is it possible to understand correctly the question of "national defense" in the present war.

The national state, national unity and independence were the ideological shield under which the capitalist nations of central Europe constituted themselves in the past century. Capitalism is incompatible with economic and political divisions, with the accompanying splitting up into small states. It needs for its development large, united territories, and a state of mental and intellectual development in the nation that will lift the demands and needs of society to a plane corresponding to the prevailing stage of capitalist production, and to the mechanism of modern capitalist class rule. Before capitalism could develop, it sought to create for itself a territory sharply defined by national limitations. This program was carried out only in France at the time of the great revolution, for in the national and political heritage left to

Europe by the feudal middle ages, this could be accomplished only by revolutionary measures. In the rest of Europe this nationalization, like the revolutionary movement as a whole, remained the patchwork of half-kept promises. The German Empire, modern Italy, Austria-Hungary, and Turkey, the Russian Empire and the British world empire are all living proofs of this fact. The national program could play a historic role only so long as it represented the ideological expression of a growing bourgeoisie, lusting for power, until it had fastened its class rule, in some way or other, upon the great nations of central Europe and had created within them the necessary tools and conditions of its growth. Since then, imperialism has buried the old bourgeois democratic program completely by substituting expansionist activity irrespective of national relationships for the original program of the bourgeoisie in all nations. The national phase, to be sure, has been preserved, but its real content, its function, has been perverted into its very opposite. Today the nation is but a cloak that covers imperialistic desires, a battle cry for imperialistic rivalries, the last ideological measure with which the masses can be persuaded to play the role of cannon fodder in imperialistic wars.

This general tendency of present-day capitalist policies determines the policies of the individual states as their supreme blindly operating law, just as the laws of economic competition determine the conditions under which the individual manufacturer shall produce.

Let us assume for a moment, for the sake of argument, for the purpose of investigating this phantom of "national wars" that controls social democratic politics at the present time, that in one of the belligerent states, the war at its outbreak was purely one of national defense. Military success would immediately demand the occupation of foreign territory. But the existence of influential capitalist groups interested in imperialistic annexations will awaken expansionist appetites as the war goes on. The imperialistic tendency that, at the beginning of hostilities, may have been existent only in embryo, will shoot up and expand in the hothouse atmosphere of war until they will in a short time determine its character, its aims and its results.

Furthermore, the system of alliance between military states that has ruled the political relations of these nations for decades in the past makes it inevitable that each of the belligerent parties, in the course of war, should try to bring its allies to its assistance, again purely from motives of self-defense. Thus one country after another is drawn into the war, inevitably new imperialistic circles are touched and others are created. Thus England drew in Japan, and, spreading the war into Asia, has brought China into the circle of political problems and has influenced the existing rivalry between Japan and the United States, between England and Japan, thus heaping up new material for future conflicts. Thus Germany has dragged Turkey into the war, bringing the question of Constantinople, of the Balkans and of Western Asia directly into the foreground of affairs.

Even he who did not realize at the outset that the world war, in its causes, was purely imperialistic, cannot fail to see after a dispassionate view of its effects that war, under the present conditions, automatically and inevitably develops into a process of world division. This was apparent from the very first. The wavering balance of power between the two belligerent parties forces each, if only for military reasons, in order to strengthen its own position, or in order to frustrate possible attacks, to hold the neutral nations in check by intensive deals in peoples and nations, such as the German-Austrian offers to Italy, Rumania, Bulgaria and Greece on the one hand, and the English-Russian bids on the other. The "national war of defense" has the surprising effect of creating, even in the neutral nations, a general transformation of ownership and relative power, always in direct line with expansionist tendencies. Finally the fact that all modern capitalist states have colonial possessions that will, even though the war may have begun as a war of national defense, be drawn into the conflict from purely military considerations, the fact that each country will strive to occupy the colonial possessions of its opponent, or at least to create disturbances therein, automatically turns every war into an imperialistic world conflagration.

Thus the conception of even that modest, devout fatherland-loving war of defense that has become the ideal of our parliamentarians and editors is pure fiction, and shows, on their part, a complete lack of understanding of the whole war and its world relations. The character of the war is determined, not by solemn declaration, not even by the honest intentions of leading politicians, but by the momentary configuration of society and its military organizations. At the first glance the term "national war of defense" might seem applicable in the case of a country like Switzerland. But Switzerland is no national state, and, therefore, no object of comparison with other modern states. Its very "neutral" existence, its luxury of a militia are after all only the negative fruits of a latent state of war in the surrounding great military states. It will hold this neutrality only so long as it is willing to oppose this condition. How quickly such a neutral state is crushed by the military heel of imperialism in a world war the fate of Belgium shows.

This brings us to the peculiar position of the "small nation." A classic example of such "national wars" is Serbia. If ever a state, according to formal considerations, had the right of national defense on its side, that state is Serbia. Deprived through

Austrian annexations of its national unity, threatened by Austria in its very existence as a nation, forced by Austria into war, it is fighting, according to all human conceptions, for existence, for freedom, and for the civilization of its people. But if the social democratic group is right in its position, then the Serbian social democrats who protested against the war in the parliament at Belgrade and refused to vote war credits are actually traitors to the most vital interests of their own nation. In reality the Serbian socialists Laptchevic and Kaclerovic have not only enrolled their names in letters of gold in the annals of the international socialist movement, but have shown a clear historical conception of the real causes of the war. In voting against war credits they therefore have done their country the best possible service. Serbia is formally engaged in a national war of defense. But its monarchy and its ruling classes are filled with expansionist desires as are the ruling classes in all modern states. They are indifferent to ethnic lines, and thus their warfare assumes an aggressive character. Thus Serbia is today reaching out toward the Adriatic coast where it is fighting out a real imperialistic conflict with Italy on the backs of the Albanians, a conflict whose final outcome will be decided not by either of the powers directly interested, but by the great powers that will speak the last word on terms of peace. But above all this we must not forget: behind Serbian nationalism stands Russian imperialism. Serbia itself is only a pawn in the great game of world politics. A judgment of the war in Serbia from a point of view that fails to take these great relations and the general world political background into account is necessarily without foundation.

The same is true of the recent Balkan War. Regarded as an isolated occurrence, the young Balkan states were historically justified in defending the old democratic program of the national state. In their historical connection, however, which makes the Balkan the burning point and the center of imperialistic world policies, these Balkan wars, also, were objectively only a fragment of the general conflict, a link in the chain of events that led, with fatal necessity, to the present world war. After the Balkan war the international social democracy tendered to the Balkan socialists, for their determined refusal to offer moral or political support to the war, a most enthusiastic ovation at the peace congress at Basel. In this act alone the International condemned in advance the position taken by the German and French socialists in the present war.

All small states, as for instance Holland, are today in a position like that of the Balkan states. "When the ship leaks, the hole must be stopped"; and what, forsooth, could little Holland fight for but for its national existence and for the independence of its people? If we consider here merely the determination of the Dutch

309

people, even of its ruling classes, the question is doubtlessly one purely of national defense. But again proletarian politics cannot judge according to the subjective purposes of a single country. Here again it must take its position as a part of the International, according to the whole complexity of the world's political situation. Holland, too, whether it wishes to be or not, is only a small wheel in the great machine of modern world politics and diplomacy. This would become clear at once, if Holland were actually torn into the maelstrom of the world war. Its opponents would direct their attacks against its colonies. Automatically Dutch warfare would turn to the defense of its present possessions. The defense of the national independence of the Dutch people on the North Sea would expand concretely to the defense of its rule and right of exploitation over the Malays in the East Indian Archipalego. But not enough: Dutch militarism, if forced to rely upon itself, would be crushed like a nutshell in the whirlpool of the world war. Whether it wished to or not it would become a member of one of the great national alliances. On one side or the other it must be the bearer and the tool of purely imperialistic tendencies.

Thus it is always the historic milieu of modern imperialism that determines the character of the war in the individual countries, and this milieu makes a war of national self-defense impossible.

Kautsky also expressed this, only a few years ago, in his pamphlet *Patriotism and Social Democracy*, Leipzig, 1907, pages 12-14: "Though the patriotism of the bourgeoisie and of the proletariat are two entirely different, actually opposite, phenomena, there are situations in which both kinds of patriotism may join forces for united action, even in times of war. The bourgeoisie and the proletariat of a nation are equally interested in their national independence and self-determination, in the removal of all kinds of oppression and exploitation at the hands of a foreign nation. In the national conflicts that have sprung from such attempts, the patriotism of the proletariat has always united with that of the bourgeoisie. But the proletariat has become a power that may become dangerous to the ruling classes at every great national upheaval; revolution looms dark at the end of every war, as the Paris Commune of 1871 and Russian terrorism after the Russo-Japanese war have proven.

In view of this the bourgeoisie of those nations which are not sufficiently united have actually sacrificed their national aims where these can be maintained only at the expense of the government for they hate and fear the revolution even more than they love national independence and greatness. For this reason, the bourgeoisie sacrifices the independence of Poland and permits ancient constellations like Austria and Turkey to remain in existence, though they have been doomed to destruction for more than a generation. National struggles as the bringers of revolution have ceased in civilized Europe. National problems that today can be solved only by war or revolution will be solved in the future only by the victory of the proletariat. But then, thanks to international solidarity, they will at once assume a form entirely different from that which prevails today in a social state of exploitation and oppression. In capitalist states this problem needs no longer to trouble the proletariat in its practical struggles. It must divert its whole strength to other problems."

"Meanwhile the likelihood that proletarian and bourgeois patriotism will unite to protect the liberty of the people is becoming more and more rare." Kautsky then goes on to say that the French bourgeoisie has united with czarism, that Russia has ceased to be a danger for western Europe because it has been weakened by the revolution. "Under these circumstances a war in defense of national liberty in which bourgeois and proletarian may unite is nowhere to be expected" (ibid., p.16).

"We have already seen that conflicts which, in the nineteenth century, might still have led some liberty-loving peoples to oppose their neighbors, by warfare, have ceased to exist. We have seen that modern militarism nowhere aims to defend important popular rights, but everywhere strives to support profits. It activities are dedicated not to assure the independence and invulnerability of its own nationality, that is nowhere threatened, but to the assurance and the extension of overseas conquests that again only serve the aggrandizement of capitalist profits. At the present time the conflicts between states can bring no war that proletarian interests would not, as a matter of duty, energetically oppose" (ibid., p.23).

In view of all these considerations, what shall be the practical attitude of the social democracy in the present war? Shall it declare: since this is an imperialist war, since we do not enjoy in our country, any socialist self-determination, its existence or nonexistence is of no consequence to us, and we will surrender it to the enemy? Passive fatalism can never be the role of a revolutionary party like the social democracy. It must neither place itself at the disposal of the existing class state, under the command of the ruling classes, nor can it stand silently by to wait until the storm is past. It must adopt a policy of active class politics, a policy that will whip the ruling classes forward in every great social crisis and that will drive the crisis itself far beyond its original extent. That is the role that the social democracy must play as the leader of the fighting proletariat. Instead of covering this imperialist war with a lying mantle of national self-defense, the social democracy should have demanded

311

the right of national self-determination seriously, should have used it as a lever against the imperialist war.

The most elementary demand of national defense is that the nation takes its defense into its own hands. The first step in this direction is the militia; not only the immediate armament of the entire adult male populace, but above all, popular decision in all questions of peace and war. It must demand, furthermore, the immediate removal of every form of political oppression, since the greatest political freedom is the best basis for national defense. To proclaim these fundamental measures of national defense, to demand their realization, that was the first duty of the social democracy.

For forty years we have tried to prove to the ruling classes as well as to the masses of the people that only the militia is really able to defend the fatherland and to make it invincible. And yet, when the first test came, we turned over the defense of our country, as a matter of course, into the hands of the standing army to be the cannon fodder under the club of the ruling classes. Our parliamentarians apparently did not even notice that the fervent wishes with which they sped these defenders of the fatherland to the front were, to all intents and purposes, an open admission that the imperial Prussian standing army is the real defender of the fatherland. They evidently did not realize that by this admission they sacrificed the fulcrum of our political program, that they gave up the militia and dissolved the practical significance of forty years of agitation against the standing army into thin air. By the act of the social democratic group our military program became a utopian doctrine, a doctrinaire obsession, that none could possibly take seriously.

The masters of the international proletariat saw the idea of the defense of the fatherland in a different light. When the proletariat of Paris, surrounded by Prussians in 1871, took the reins of the government into its own hands, Marx wrote enthusiastically:

"Paris, the center and seat of the old government powers, and simultaneously the social center of gravity of the French working class, Paris has risen in arms against the attempt of Monsieur Thiers and his Junkers to reinstate and perpetuate the government of the old powers of imperial rule. Paris was in a position to resist only, because through a state of seige, it was rid of its army, because in its place there had been put a national guard composed chiefly of working men. It was necessary that this innovation be made a permanent institution. The first act of the Commune was, therefore, the suppression of the standing army and the substitution of an armed people. . . . If now, the Commune was the true representative of all healthy elements of French society and, therefore, a true national government,

it was likewise, as a proletarian government, as the daring fighter for the liberation of labor, international in the truest sense
of that word. Under the eyes of the Prussian army, which has
annexed two French provinces to Germany, the Commune has
annexed the workers of a whole world to France" *(Address of
the General Council of the International).*

But what did our masters say concerning the role to be played
by the social democracy in the present war? In 1892 Friedrich
Engels expressed the following opinion concerning the fundamental lines along which the attitude of proletarian parties in a great
war should follow: "A war in the course of which Russians and
Frenchmen should invade Germany would mean for the latter
a life and death struggle. Under such circumstances it could
assure its national existence only by using the most revolutionary methods. The present government, should it not be forced
to do so, will certainly not bring on the revolution, but we have
a strong party that may force its hand, or that, should it be
necessary, can replace it, the Social Democratic Party.

"We have not forgotten the glorious example of France in 1793.
The one hundredth anniversary of 1793 is approaching. Should
Russia's desire for conquest, or the chauvinistic impatience of
the French bourgeoisie check the victorious but peaceable march
of the German socialists, the latter are prepared — be assured
of that — to prove to the world that the German proletarians of
today are not unworthy of the French Sansculottes, that 1893
will be worthy of 1793. And should the soldiers of Monsieur
Constans set foot upon German territory we will meet them with
the words of the "Marsellaise":

> Shall hateful tyrants, mischief breeding,
> With hireling host, a ruffian band,
> Affright and desolate the land?

"In short, peace assures the victory of the Social Democratic
Party in about ten years. The war will bring either victory in
two or three years or its absolute ruin for at least fifteen or twenty years."

When Engels wrote these words, he had in mind a situation
entirely different from the one existing today. In his mind's eye,
ancient czarism still loomed threateningly in the background.
We have already seen the great Russian Revolution. He thought,
furthermore, of a real national war of defense, of a Germany
attacked on two sides, on the east and on the west by two enemy forces. Finally, he overestimated the ripeness of conditions
in Germany and the likelihood of a social revolution, as all true
fighters are wont to overrate the real tempo of development. But
for all that, his sentences prove with remarkable clearness, that

Engels meant by national defense, in the sense of the social democracy, not the support of a Prussian Junker military government and its Generalstab, but a revolutionary action after the example of the French Jacobins.

Yes, socialists should defend their country in great historical crises, and here lies the great fault of the German social democratic Reichstag group. When it announced on the fourth of August, "in this hour of danger, we will not desert our fatherland," it denied its own words in the same breath. For truly it has deserted its fatherland in its hour of greatest danger. The highest duty of the social democracy toward its fatherland demanded that it expose the real background of this imperialist war, that it rend the net of imperialist and diplomatic lies that covers the eyes of the people. It was their duty to speak loudly and clearly, to proclaim to the people of Germany that in this war victory and defeat would be equally fatal, to oppose the gagging of the fatherland by a state of siege, to demand that the people alone decide on war and peace, to demand a permanent session of parliament for the period of the war, to assume a watchful control over the government by parliament, and over parliament by the people, to demand the immediate removal of all political inequalities, since only a free people can adequately govern its country, and finally, to oppose to the imperialist war, based as it was upon the most reactionary forces in Europe, the program of Marx, of Engels, and Lassalle.

That was the flag that should have waved over the country. That would have been truly national, truly free, in harmony with the best traditions of Germany and the international class policy of the proletariat.

The great historical hour of the world war obviously demanded unanimous political accomplishment, a broad-minded, comprehensive attitude that only the social democracy is destined to give. Instead, there followed, on the part of the parliamentary representatives of the working class, a miserable collapse. The social democracy did not adopt the wrong policy — it had no policy whatsoever. It has wiped itself out completely as a class party with a world conception of its own, has delivered the country, without a word of protest, to the fate of imperialist war without, to the dictatorship of the sword within. Nay more, it has taken the responsibility for the war upon its own shoulders. The declaration of the "Reichstag group" says: "We have voted only the means for our country's defense. We decline all responsibility for the war." But as a matter of fact, the truth lies in exactly the opposite direction. The means for "national defense," i.e., for imperialistic mass butchery by the armed forces of the military monarchy, were not voted by the social democracy. For the availability of the war credits did not in the least depend upon the social democracy. They, as a minority, stood against a compact three-quarters majority of the capitalist Reichstag. The social democratic group accomplished only one thing by voting in favor of the war credits. It placed upon the war the stamp of democratic fatherland defense, and supported and sustained the fictions that were propagated by the government concerning the actual conditions and problems of the war.

Thus the serious dilemma between the national interests and international solidarity of the proletariat, the tragic conflict that made our parliamentarians fall "with heavy heart" to the side of imperialistic warfare, was a mere figment of the imagination, a bourgeois nationalist fiction. Between the national interests and the class interests of the proletariat, in war and in peace, there is actually complete harmony. Both demand the most energetic prosecution of the class struggle, and the most determined insistence on the social democratic program.

But what action should the party have taken to give to our opposition to the war and to our war demands weight and emphasis? Should it have proclaimed a general strike? Should it have called upon the soldiers to refuse military service? Thus the question is generally asked. To answer with a simple yes or no were just as ridiculous as to decide: "When war breaks out we will start a revolution." Revolutions are not "made" and great movements of the people are not produced according to technical recipes that repose in the pockets of the party leaders. Small circles of conspirators may organize a riot for a certain day and a certain hour, can give their small group of supporters the signal to begin. Mass movements in great historical crises cannot be initiated by such primitive measures.

The best prepared mass strike may break down miserably at the very moment when the party leaders give the signal, may collapse completely before the first attack. The success of the great popular movements depends, aye, the very time and circumstance of their inception is decided, by a number of economic, political and psychological factors. The existing degree of tension between the classes, the degree of intelligence of the masses and the degree or ripeness of their spirit of resistance — all these factors, which are incalculable, are premises that cannot be artificially created by any party. That is the difference between the great historical upheavals, and the small show-demonstrations that a well-disciplined party can carry out in times of peace, orderly, well-trained performances, responding obediently to the baton in the hands of the party leaders. The great historical hour itself creates the forms that will carry the revolutionary movements to a successful outcome, creates and improvises new weapons, enriches the arsenal of the people with weapons unknown and unheard of by the parties and their leaders.

What the social democracy as the advance guard of the class-conscious proletariat should have been able to give was not ridiculous precepts and technical recipes, but a political slogan, clearness concerning the political problems and interests of the proletariat in times of war.

For what has been said of mass strikes in the Russian Revolution is equally applicable to every mass movement: "While the revolutionary period itself commands the creation and the computation and payment of the cost of a mass strike, the leaders of the social democracy have an entirely different mission to fill. Instead of concerning itself with the technical mechanism of the mass movement, it is the duty of the social democracy to undertake the political leadership even in the midst of a historical crisis. To give the slogan, to determine the direction of the struggle, to so direct the tactics of the political conflict that in its every phase and movement the whole sum of available and already mobilized active force of the proletariat is realized and finds expression in the attitude of the party, that the tactics of the social democracy in determination and vigor shall never be weaker than is justified by the actual power at its back, but shall rather hasten in advance of its actual power, that is the important problem of the party leadership in a great historical crisis. Then this leadership will become, in a sense, the technical leadership. A determined, consistent, progressive course of action on the part of the social democracy will create in the masses assurance, self-confidence and a fearless fighting spirit. A weakly vacillating course, based upon a low estimate of the powers of the proletariat, lames and confuses the masses. In the first case mass action will break out 'of its own accord' and 'at the right time'; in the second, even a direct call to action on the part of the leaders often remains ineffectual" (*The Mass Strike, The Political Party and the Trade Unions*).

Far more important than the outward, technical form of the action is its political content. Thus the parliamentary stage, for instance, the only far reaching and internationally conspicuous platform, could have become a mighty motive power for the awakening of the people, had it been used by the social democratic representatives to proclaim loudly and distinctly the interests, the problems and the demands of the working class.

"Would the masses have supported the social democracy in its attitude against the war?" That is a question that no one can answer. But neither is it an important one. Did our parliamentarians demand an absolute assurance of victory from the generals of the Prussian army before voting in favor of war credits? What is true of military armies is equally true of revolutionary armies. They go into the fight, wherever necessity demands it, without previous assurance of success. At the worst, the party would have been doomed, in the first few months of the war, to political ineffectuality.

Perhaps the bitterest persecutions would have been inflicted upon our party for its manly stand, as they were, in 1870, the reward of Liebknecht and Bebel. "But what does that matter," said Ignaz Auer, simply, in his speech on the Sedanfeier in 1895. "A party that is to conquer the world must bear its principles aloft without counting the dangers that this may bring. To act differently is to be lost!"

"It is never easy to swim against the current," said the older Liebknecht. "And when the stream rushes on with the rapidity and the power of a Niagara it does not become easier. Our older comrades still remember the hatred of that year of greatest national shame, under the socialist exception laws of 1878. At that time millions looked upon every social democrat as having played the part of a murderer and vile criminal in 1870; the socialist had been in the eyes of the masses a traitor and an enemy. Such outbreaks of the 'popular soul' are astounding, stunning, crushing in their elemental fury. One feels powerless, as before a higher power. It is a real *force majeure*. There is no tangible opponent. It is like an epidemic, in the people, in the air, everywhere.

"The outbreak of 1878 cannot, however, be compared with the outbreak in 1870. This hurricane of human passions, breaking, bending, destroying all that stands in its way — and with it the terrible machinery of militarism, in fullest, most horrible activity; and we stand between the crushing iron wheels, whose touch means instant death, between iron arms, that threaten every moment to catch us. By the side of this elemental force of liberated spirits stood the most complete mechanism of the art of murder the world had hitherto seen; and all in the wildest activity, every boiler heated to the bursting point. At such a time, what is the will and the strength of the individual? Especially, when one feels that one represents a tiny minority, that one possesses no firm support in the people itself.

"At that time our party was still in a period of development. We were placed before the most serious test, at a time when we did not yet possess the organization necessary to meet it. When the antisocialist movement came in the year of shame of our enemies, in the year of honor for the social democracy, then we had already a strong, widespread organization. Each and every one of us was strengthened by the feeling that he possessed a mighty support in the organized movement that stood behind him, and no sane person could conceive of the downfall of the party.

"So it was no small thing at that time to swim against the current. But what is to be done, must be done. And so we gritted our teeth in the face of the inevitable. There was no time for fear. . . . Certainly Bebel and I. . . . never for a moment thought of the warning. We did not retreat. We had to hold our posts, come what might!"

They stuck to their posts, and for forty years the social democracy lived upon the moral strength with which it had opposed a world of enemies.

The same thing would have happened now. At first we would perhaps have accomplished nothing but to save the honor of the proletariat, and thousands upon thousands of proletarians who are dying in the trenches in mental darkness would not have died in spiritual confusion, but with the one certainty that that which has been everything in their lives, the international, liberating social democracy is more than the figment of a dream.

The voice of our party would have acted as a wet blanket upon the chauvinistic intoxication of the masses. It would have preserved the intelligent proletariat from delirium, would have it more difficult for imperialism to poison and to stupefy the minds of the people. The crusade against the social democracy would have awakened the masses in an incredibly short time.

And as the war went on, as the horror of endless massacre and bloodshed in all countries grew and grew, as its imperialistic hoof became more and more evident, as the exploitation by bloodthirsty speculators became more and more shameless, every live, honest, progressive and humane element in the masses would have rallied to the standard of the social democracy. The German social democracy would have stood in the midst of this mad whirlpool of collapse and decay, like a rock in a stormy sea, would have been the lighthouse of the whole International, guiding and leading the labor movements of every country of the earth. The unparalleled moral prestige that lay in the hands of the German socialists would have reacted upon the socialists of all nations in a very short time. Peace sentiments would have spread like wildfire and the popular demand for peace in all countries would have hastened the end of the slaughter, would have decreased the number of its victims.

The German proletariat would have remained the lighthouse keeper of socialism and of human emancipation.

Truly this was a task not unworthy of the disciples of Marx, Engels and Lassalle.

VIII

In spite of military dictatorship and press censorship, in spite of the downfall of the social democracy, in spite of fratricidal war, the class struggle arises from civil peace with elemental force: from the blood and smoke of the battlefields the solidarity of international labor arises. Not in weak attempts to artificially galvanize the old International, not in pledges rendered now here, now there, to stand together after the war is over. No, here, in the war, out of the war, arises, with a new might and intensity, the recognition that the proletarians of all lands have one and the same interest. The world war, itself, utterly disproves the falsehoods it has created.

Victory or defeat? It is the slogan of all-powerful militarism in every belligerent nation, and, like an echo, the social democratic leaders have adopted it. Victory or defeat has become the highest motive of the workers of Germany, of France, of England and of others, just as for the ruling classes of these nations. When the cannons thunder, all proletarian interests subside before the desire for victory of their own, i.e., for the defeat of the other countries. And yet, what can victory bring to the proletariat?

According to the official version of the leaders of the social democracy, that was so readily adopted without criticism, victory of the German forces would mean, for Germany, unhampered, boundless industrial growth; defeat, however, industrial ruin. On the whole, this conception coincides with that generally accepted during the war of 1870. But the period of capitalist growth that followed the war of 1870 was not caused by the war, but resulted rather from the political union of the various German states, even though this union took the form of the crippled figure that Bismarck established as the German Empire. Here the industrial impetus came from this union, in spite of the war and the manifold reactionary hindrances that followed in its wake. What the victorious war itself accomplished was to firmly establish the military monarchy and Prussian junkerdom in Germany; the defeat of France led to the liquidation of its empire and the establishment of a republic.

But today the situation is different in all of the nations in question. Today war does not function as a dynamic force to provide for rising young capitalism the indispensable political conditions for its "national" development. Modern war appears in this role only in Serbia, and there only as an isolated fragment. Reduced to its objective historic significance, the present world war as a whole is a competitive struggle of a fully developed capitalism for world supremacy, for the exploitation of the last remnant of noncapitalistic world zones. This fact gives to the war and its political aftereffects an entirely new character. The high stage of world industrial development in capitalist production finds expression in the extraordinary technical development and destructiveness of the instruments of war, as in their practically uniform degree of perfection in all belligerent countries. The international organization of war industries is reflected in the military instability that persistently brings back the scales, through all partial decisions and variations, to their true balance, and pushes a general decision further and further into the future. The indecision of military results, moreover, has the effect that a constant stream of new reserves, from the belligerent nations as well as from nations hitherto neutral, are sent to the front. Everywhere war finds material enough for imperialist desires and conflicts, itself creates new material to feed the conflagration that spreads out like a prairie fire. But the greater the masses, and the greater the number of nations that are dragged into this world war, the longer will it rage.

All of these things together prove, even before any military decision of victory or defeat can be established, that the result of the war will be: the economic ruin of all participating nations, and, in a steadily growing measure, of the formally neutral nations, a phenomenon entirely distinct from the earlier wars of modern times. Every month of war affirms and augments this effect, and thus takes away, in advance, the expected fruits of military victory for a decade to come. This, in the last analysis, neither victory nor defeat can alter; on the contrary, it makes a purely military decision altogether doubtful, and increases the likelihood that the war will finally end through a general and extreme exhaustion. But even a victorious Germany, under such circumstances, even if its imperialist war agitators should succeed in carrying on the mass murder to the absolute destruction of their opponents, even if their most daring dreams should be fulfilled — would win but a Pyrrhic victory. A number of annexed territories, impoverished and depopulated, and a grinning ruin under its own roof, would be its trophies. Nothing can hide this, once the painted stage properties of financial war bond transactions, and the Potemkin villages of an "unalterable prosperity" kept up by war orders, are pushed aside.

The most superficial observer cannot but see that even the most victorious nation cannot count on war indemnities that will stand in any relation to the wounds that the war has inflicted. Perhaps they may see in the still greater economic ruin of the defeated opponents, England and France, the very countries with which Germany was most closely united by industrial relations, upon whose recuperation its own prosperity so much depends, a substitute and an augmentation for their victory. Such are the circumstances under which the German people, even after a victorious war, would be required to pay, in cold cash, the war bonds that were "voted" on credit by the patriotic parliament; i.e., to take upon their shoulders an immeasurable burden of taxation, and a strengthened military dictatorship as the only permanent tangible fruit of victory.

Should we now seek to imagine the worst possible effects of a defeat, we shall find that they resemble, line for line, with the exception of imperialistic annexations, the same picture that presented itself as the irrefutable consequence of victory: the effects of war today are so far-reaching, so deeply rooted, that its military outcome can alter but little in its final consequences.

But let us assume, for the moment, that the victorious nation should find itself in the position to avoid the great catastrophe for its own people, should be able to throw the whole burden of the war upon the shoulders of its defeated opponent, should be able to choke off the industrial development of the latter by all sorts of hindrances. Can the German labor movement hope for successful development, so long as the activity of the French, English, Belgian and Italian laborers is hampered by industrial retrogression? Before 1870 the labor movements of the various nations grew independently of each other. The action of the labor movement of a single city often controlled the destinies of the whole labor movement. On the streets of Paris the battles of the working class were fought out and decided.

The modern labor movement, its laborious daily struggle in the industries of the world, its mass organization, are based upon the cooperation of the workers in all capitalistically producing countries. If the truism that the cause of labor can thrive only upon a virile, pulsating industrial life applies, then it is true not only for Germany, but for France, England, Belgium, Russia, and Italy as well. And if the labor movement in all of the capitalist states of Europe becomes stagnant, if industrial conditions there result in low wages, weakened labor unions, and a diminished power of resistance on the part of labor, labor unionism in Germany cannot possibly flourish. From this point of view the loss sustained by the working class in its industrial struggle is in the last analysis identical, whether German capital be strengthened at the expense of the French or English capital at the expense of the German.

But let us investigate the political effects of the war. Here differentiation should be less difficult than upon the economic side, for the sympathies and the partisanship of the proletariat have always tended toward the side that defended progress against reaction. Which side, in the present war, represents progress, which side reaction? It is clear that this question cannot be decided according to the outward insignias that mark the political character of the belligerent nations as "democracy" and absolutism. They must be judged solely according to the tendencies of their respective world policies.

Before we can determine what a German victory can win for the German proletariat we must consider its effect upon the general status of political conditions all over Europe. A decisive victory for Germany would mean, in the first place, the annexation of Belgium, as well as of a possible number of territories in the east and west and a part of the French colonies; the sustaining of the Habsburg Monarchy and its aggrandizement by a number of new territories; finally the establishment of a fictitious "integrity" of Turkey, under a German protectorate—i.e., the conversion of Asia Minor and Mesopotamia, in one form or another, into German provinces. In the end this would result in the actual military and economic hegemony of Germany in Europe. Not because they are in accord with the desires of imperialist agitators are these consequences of an absolute German military victory to be expected, but because they are the inevitable outgrowth of the world political position that Germany has adopted, of conflicting interests with England, France and Russia, in which Germany has been involved, and which have grown, during the course of the war, far beyond the original dimensions. It is sufficient to recall these facts to realize that they could under no circumstances establish a permanent world political equilibrium. Though this war may mean ruin for all of its participants, and worse for its defeated, the preparations for a new world war, under England's leadership, would begin on the day after peace is declared, to shake off the yoke of Prussian-German militarism that would rest upon Europe and Asia. A German victory would be the prelude to an early second world war, and therefore, for this reason, but the signal for new feverish armaments, for the unleashing of the blackest reaction in every country, but particularly in Germany.

On the other hand a victory of England or France would mean, in all likelihood, for Germany, the loss of a part of her colonies, as well as of Alsace-Lorraine, and certainly the bankruptcy of the world political position of German militarism. But this would mean the disintegration of Austria-Hungary and the total liquidation of Turkey. Reactionary as both of these states are, and much as their disintegration would be in line with the demands of progressive development, in the present world political milieu, the disintegration of the Habsburg Monarchy and the liquidation of Turkey would mean the bartering of their peoples to the highest bidder — Russia, England, France, or Italy. This enormous redivision of the world and shifting of the balance of power in the Balkan states and along the Mediterranean would be followed inevitably by another in Asia: the liquidation of Persia and a redivision of China. This would bring the Anglo-Russian as well as the Anglo-Japanese conflict into the foreground of international politics, and may mean, in direct connection with the liquidation of the present war, a new world war, perhaps for Constantinople; would certainly bring it about, inescapably, in the immediate future. So a victory on this side, too, would lead to new, feverish armaments in all nations — defeated Germany, of course, at the head — and would introduce an era of undivided rule for militarism and reaction all over Europe, with a new war as its final goal.

So the proletariat, should it attempt to cast its influence into the balance on one side or the other, for progress or democracy, viewing the world policies in their widest application, would place itself between Scylla and Charybdis. Under the circumstances the question of victory or defeat becomes, for the European working class, in its political exactly as in its economic aspects, a choice between two beatings. It is, therefore, nothing short of a dangerous madness for the French socialists to believe that they can deal a death blow to militarism and imperialism, and clear the road for peaceful democracy by overthrowing Germany. Imperialism, and its servant militarism, will reappear after every victory and after every defeat in this war. There can be but one exception: if the international proletariat, through its intervention, should overthrow all previous calculations.

The important lesson to be derived by the proletariat from this war is the one unchanging fact, that it can and must not become the uncritical echo of the "victory and defeat" slogan, neither in Germany nor in France, neither in England nor in Austria. For it is a slogan that has reality only from the point of view of imperialism, and is identical, in the eyes of every large power, with the question: gain or loss of world political power, of annexations, of colonies, of military supremacy.

For the European proletariat as a class, victory or defeat of either of the two war groups would be equally disastrous. For war as such, whatever its military outcome may be, is the greatest conceivable defeat of the cause of the European proletariat. The overthrow of war, and the speedy forcing of peace, by the international revolutionary action of the proletariat, alone can bring to it the only possible victory. And this victory, alone, can truly rescue Belgium, can bring democracy to Europe.

For the class-conscious proletariat to identify its cause with either military camp is an untenable position. Does that mean that the proletarian policies of the present day demand a return to the "status quo," that we have no plan of action beyond the fond hope that everything may remain as it was before the war? The existing conditions have never been our ideal, they have never been the expression of the self-determination of the people. And more, the former conditions cannot be reinstated, even if the old national boundaries should remain unchanged. For even before its formal ending this war has brought about enormous changes, in mutual recognition of one another's strength, in alliances and in conflict. It has sharply revised the relations of countries to one another, of classes within society, has destroyed so many old illusions and portents, has created so many new forces and new problems, that a return to the old Europe that existed before August 4, 1914, is as impossible as the return to prerevolutionary conditions, even after an unsuccessful revolution. The proletariat knows no going back, can only strive forward and onward, for a goal that lies beyond even the most newly created conditions. In this sense, alone, is it possible for the proletariat to oppose, with its policy, both camps in the imperialist world war.

But this policy cannot concern itself with recipes for capitalist diplomacy worked out individually by the social democratic parties, or even together in international conferences, to determine how capitalism shall declare peace in order to assure future peaceful and democratic development. All demands for complete or gradual disarmament, for the abolition of secret diplomacy, for the dissolution of the great powers into smaller national entities, and all other similar propositions, are absolutely utopian so long as capitalist class-rule remains in power. For capitalism, in its present imperialist course, to dispense with present-day militarism, with secret diplomacy, with the centralization of many national states is so impossible that these postulates might, much more consistently, be united into the simple demand, "abolition of capitalist class society." The proletarian movement cannot reconquer the place it deserves by means of utopian advice and projects for weakening, taming or quelling imperialism within capitalism by means of partial reforms.

The real problem that the world war has placed before the socialist parties, upon whose solution the future of the working-class movement depends, *is the readiness of the proletarian masses to act in the fight against imperialism.* The international proletariat suffers, not from a dearth of postulates, programs, and slogans, but from a lack of deeds, of effective resistance, of the power to attack imperialism at the decisive moment, just in times of war. It has been unable to put its old slogan, war against war, into actual practice. Here is the Gordian knot of the proletarian movement and of its future.

Imperialism, with all its brutal policy of force, with the incessant chain of social catastrophe that it itself provokes, is, to be sure, a historic necessity for the ruling classes of the present world. Yet nothing could be more detrimental than that the proletariat should derive, from the present war, the slightest hope or illusion of the possibility of an idyllic and peaceful development of capitalism. There is but one conclusion that the proletariat can draw from the historic necessity of imperialism. To capitulate before imperialism will mean to live forever in its shadow, off the crumbs that fall from the tables of its victories.

Historic development moves in contradictions, and for every necessity puts its opposite into the world as well. The capitalist

324

state of society is doubtless a historic necessity, but so also is the revolt of the working class against it. Capital is a historic necessity, but in the same measure is its gravedigger, the socialist proletariat. The world rule of imperialism is a historic necessity, but likewise its overthrow by the proletarian international. Side by side the two historic necessities exist in constant conflict with each other. And ours is the necessity of socialism. Our necessity receives its justification with the moment when the capitalist class ceases to be the bearer of historic progress, when it becomes a hindrance, a danger, to the future development of society. That capitalism has reached this stage the present world war has revealed.

Capitalist desire for imperialist expansion, as the expression of its highest maturity in the last period of its life, has the economic tendency to change the whole world into capitalistically producing nations, to sweep away all superannuated, precapitalistic methods of production and society, to subjugate all the riches of the earth and all means of production to capital, to turn the laboring masses of the peoples of all zones into wage slaves. In Africa and in Asia, from the most northern regions to the southernmost point of South America and in the South Seas, the remnants of old communistic social groups, of feudal society, of patriarchal systems, and of ancient handicraft production are destroyed and stamped out by capitalism. Whole peoples are destroyed, ancient civilizations are levelled to the ground, and in their place profiteering in its most modern forms is being established.

This brutal triumphant procession of capitalism through the world, accompanied by all the means of force, of robbery, and of infamy, has one bright phase: it has created the premises for its own final overthrow, it has established the capitalist world rule upon which, alone, the socialist world revolution can follow. This is the only cultural and progressive aspect of the great so-called works of culture that were brought to the primitive countries. To capitalist economists and politicians, railroads, matches, sewerage systems and warehouses are progress and culture. Of themselves such works, grafted upon primitive conditions, are neither culture nor progress, for they are too dearly paid for with the sudden economic and cultural ruin of the peoples who must drink down the bitter cup of misery and horror of two social orders, of traditional agricultural landlordism, of supermodern, superrefined capitalist exploitation, at one and the same time. Only as the material conditions for the destruction of capitalism and the abolition of class society can the effects of the capitalist triumphal march through the world bear the stamp of progress in a historical sense. In this sense imperialism, too, is working in our interest.

The present world war is a turning point in the course of imperialism. For the first time the destructive beasts that have been loosed by capitalist Europe over all other parts of the world have sprung with one awful leap, into the midst of the European nations. A cry of horror went up through the world when Belgium, that priceless little jewel of European culture, when the venerable monuments of art in northern France, fell into fragments before the onslaughts of a blind and destructive force. The "civilized world" that has stood calmly by when this same imperialism doomed tens of thousands of heroes to destruction, when the desert of Kalahari shuddered with the insane cry of the thirsty and the rattling breath of the dying, when in Putumayo, within ten years, forty thousand human beings were tortured to death by a band of European industrial robber barons, and the remnants of a whole people were beaten into cripples, when in China an ancient civilization was delivered into the hands of destruction and anarchy, with fire and slaughter, by the European soldiery, when Persia gasped in the noose of the foreign rule of force that closed inexorably about her throat, when in Tripoli the Arabs were mowed down, with fire and swords, under the yoke of capital while their homes were razed to the ground—this civilized world has just begun to know that the fangs of the imperialist beast are deadly, that its breath is frightfulness, that its tearing claws have sunk deeper into the breasts of its own mother, European culture. And this belated recognition is coming into the world of Europe in the distorted form of bourgeois hypocrisy, that leads each nation to recognize infamy only when it appears in the uniform of the other. They speak of German barbarism, as if every people that goes out for organized murder did not change into a horde of barbarians! They speak of Cossack horrors, as if war itself were not the greatest of all horrors, as if the praise of human slaughter in a socialist periodical were not mental Cossackdom in its very essence.

But the horrors of imperialist bestiality in Europe have had another effect, that has brought to the "civilized world" no horror-stricken eyes, no agonized heart. It is the mass destruction of the European proletariat. Never has a war killed off whole nations; never, within the past century, has it swept over all of the great and established lands of civilized Europe. Millions of human lives were destroyed in the Vosges, in the Ardennes, in Belgium, in Poland, in the Carpathians and on the Save; millions have been hopelessly crippled. But nine-tenths of these millions come from the ranks of the working class of the cities and the farms. It is our strength, our hope that was mowed down there, day after day, before the scythe of death. They were the best, the most intelligent, the most thoroughly schooled forces of international socialism, the bearers of the holiest traditions, of the highest heroism, the modern labor movement, the vanguard of the whole world proletariat, the workers of England, France, Belgium, Germany and Russia who are being gagged and butchered in masses.

Only from Europe, only from the oldest capitalist nations, when the hour is ripe, can the signal come for the social revolution that will free the nations. Only the English, the French, the Belgian, the German, the Russian, the Italian workers together can lead the army of the exploited and oppressed. And when the time comes they alone can call capitalism to account for centuries of crime committed against primitive peoples; they alone can avenge its work of destruction over a whole world. But for the advance and victory of socialism we need a strong, educated, ready proletariat, masses whose strength lies in knowledge as well as in numbers. And these very masses are being decimated all over the world. The flower of our youthful strength, hundreds of thousands whose socialist education in England, in France, in Belgium, in Germany and in Russia was the product of decades of education and propaganda, other hundreds of thousands who were ready to receive the lessons of socialism have fallen, and are rotting upon the battlefields. The fruit of the sacrifices and toil of generations is destroyed in a few short weeks, the choicest troops of the international proletariat are torn out by the life roots.

The bloodletting of the June battle laid low the French labor movement for a decade and a half. The bloodletting of the Commune massacre again threw it back for more than a decade. What is happening now is a massacre such as the world has never seen before, that is reducing the laboring population in all of the leading nations to the aged, the women and the maimed; a bloodletting that threatens to bleed white the European labor movement.

Another such war, and the hope of socialism will be buried under the ruins of imperialistic barbarism. That is more than the ruthless destruction of Liege and of the Rheims Cathedral. That is a blow, not against capitalist civilization of the past, but against socialist civilization of the future, a deadly blow against the force that carries the future of mankind in its womb that alone can rescue the precious treasures of the past over into a better state of society. Here capitalism reveals its death's head, here it betrays that it has sacrificed its historic right of existence, that its rule is no longer compatible with the progress of humanity.

But here is proof also that the war is not only a grandiose murder, but the suicide of the European working class. The soldiers of socialism, the workers of England, of France, of Germany, of Italy, of Belgium are murdering each other at the bidding of capitalism, are thrusting cold, murderous irons into each other's breasts, are tottering over their graves, grappling in each other's death-bringing arms.

"Deutschland, Deutschland uber alles," [Germany, Germany above everything] "long live democracy," "long live the czar and slavery," "ten thousand tent cloths, guaranteed according to specifications," "hundred thousand pounds of bacon," "coffee substitute, immediate delivery". . . . dividends are rising — proletarians falling; and with each one there sinks a fighter of the future, a soldier of the revolution, a savior of humanity from the yoke of capitalism, into the grave.

This madness will not stop, and this bloody nightmare of hell will not cease until the workers of Germany, of France, of Russia and of England will wake up out of their drunken sleep; will clasp each others' hands in brotherhood and will drown the bestial chorus of war agitators and the hoarse cry of capitalist hyenas with the mighty cry of labor, "Proletarians of all countries, unite!"

Theses on the Tasks of International
Social Democracy

A large number of comrades from different parts of Germany have adopted the following theses, which constitute an application of the Erfurt program to the contemporary problems of international socialism.

1. The world war has annihilated the work of forty years of European socialism: by destroying the revolutionary proletariat as a political force; by destroying the moral prestige of socialism; by scattering the workers' International; by setting its sections one against the other in fratricidal massacre; and by tying the aspirations and hopes of the masses of the people of the main countries in which capitalism has developed to the destinies of imperialism.

2. By their vote for war credits and by their proclamation of national unity, the official leaderships of the socialist parties in Germany, France and England (with the exception of the Independent Labor Party) have reinforced imperialism, induced the masses of the people to suffer patiently the misery and horrors of the war, contributed to the unleashing, without restraint, of imperialist frenzy, to the prolongation of the massacre and the increase in the number of its victims, and assumed their share in the responsibility for the war itself and for its consequences.

3. This tactic of the official leaderships of the parties in the belligerent countries, and in the first place in Germany, until recently at the head of the International, constitutes a betrayal of the elementary principles of international socialism, of the vital interests of the working class, and of all the democratic interests of the peoples. By this alone socialist policy is con-

demned to impotence even in those countries where the leaders have remained faithful to their principles: Russia, Serbia, Italy and — with hardly an exception — Bulgaria.

4. By this alone official social democracy in the principal countries has repudiated the class struggle in wartime and adjourned it until after the war; it has guaranteed to the ruling classes of all countries a delay in which to strengthen, at the proletariat's expense, and in a monstrous fashion, their economic, political and moral positions.

5. The world war serves neither the national defense nor the economic or political interests of the masses of the people whatever they may be. It is but the product of the imperialist rivalries between the capitalist classes of the different countries for world hegemony and for the monopoly in the exploitation and oppression of areas still not under the heel of capital. In the era of the unleashing of this imperialism, national wars are no longer possible. National interests serve only as the pretext for putting the laboring masses of the people under the domination of their mortal enemy, imperialism.

6. The policy of the imperialist states and the imperialist war cannot give to a single oppressed nation its liberty and its independence. The small nations, the ruling classes of which are the accomplices of their partners in the big states, constitute only the pawns on the imperialist chessboard of the great powers, and are used by them, just like their own working masses, in wartime, as instruments, to be sacrificed to capitalist interests after the war.

7. The present world war signifies, under these conditions, either in the case of "defeat" or of "victory," a defeat for socialism and democracy. It increases, whatever the outcome — excepting the revolutionary intervention of the international proletariat — and strengthens militarism, national antagonisms, and economic rivalries in the world market. It accentuates capitalist exploitation and reaction in the domain of internal policy, renders the influence of public opinion precarious and derisory, and reduces parliaments to tools more and more obedient to imperialism. The present world war carries within itself the seeds of new conflicts.

8. World peace cannot be assured by projects utopian or, at bottom, reactionary, such as tribunals of arbitration by capitalist diplomats, diplomatic, "disarmament" conventions, "the freedom of the seas," abolition of the right of maritime arrest, "the United States of Europe," a "customs union for central Europe," buffer states, and other illusions. Imperialism, militarism and war can never be abolished nor attenuated so long as the capitalist class exercises, uncontested, its class hegemony. The sole means of successful resistance, and the only guarantee of the peace of the world, is the capacity for action and the revolutionary will

of the international proletariat to hurl its full weight into the balance.

9. Imperialism, as the last phase in the life, and the highest point in the expansion of the world hegemony of capital, is the mortal enemy of the proletariat of all countries. But under its rule, just as in the preceding stages of capitalism, the forces of its mortal enemy have increased in pace with its development. It accelerates the concentration of capital, the pauperization of the middle classes, the numerical reinforcement of the proletariat, arouses more and more resistance from the masses; and leads thereby to an intensified sharpening of class antagonisms. In peace time as in war, the struggle of the proletariat as a class has to be concentrated first of all against imperialism. For the international proletariat, the struggle against imperialism is at the same time the struggle for power, the decisive settling of accounts between socialism and capitalism. The final goal of socialism will be realized by the international proletariat only if it opposes imperialism all along the line, and if it makes the issue "war against war" the guiding line of its practical policy; and on condition that it deploys all its forces and shows itself ready, by its courage to the point of extreme sacrifice, to do this.

10. In this framework, socialism's principal mission today is to regroup the proletariat of all countries into a living revolutionary force; to make it, through a powerful international organization which has only one conception of its tasks and interests, and only one universal tactic appropriate to political action in peace and war alike, the decisive factor in political life: so that it may fulfill its historic mission.

11. The war has smashed the Second International. Its inadequacy has been demonstrated by its incapacity to place an effective obstacle in the way of the segmentation of its forces behind national boundaries in time of war, and to carry through a common tactic and action by the proletariat in all countries.

12. In view of the betrayal, by the official representatives of the socialist parties in the principal countries, of the aims and interests of the working class; in view of their passage from the camp of the working-class International to the political camp of the imperialist bourgeoisie; it is vitally necessary for socialism to build a new workers' International, which will take into its own hands the leadership and coordination of the revolutionary class struggle against world imperialism.

To accomplish its historic mission, socialism must be guided by the following principles:

1. The class struggle against the ruling classes within the boundaries of the bourgeois states, and international solidarity of the workers of all countries, are the two rules of life, inherent in the

working class in struggle and of world-historic importance to it for its emancipation. There is no socialism without international proletarian solidarity, and there is no socialism without class struggle. The renunciation by the socialist proletariat, in time of peace as in time of war, of the class struggle and of international solidarity, is equivalent to suicide.

2. The activity of the proletariat of all countries as a class, in peace time as in wartime, must be geared to the fight against imperialism and war as its supreme goal. Parliamentary and trade-union action, like every activity of the workers' movement, must be subordinated to this aim, so that the proletariat in each country is opposed in the sharpest fashion to its national bourgeoisie, so that the political and spiritual opposition between the two becomes at each moment the main issue, and international solidarity between the workers of all countries is underlined and practiced.

3. The center of gravity of the organization of the proletariat as a class is the International. The International decides in time of peace the tactics to be adopted by the national sections on the questions of militarism, colonial policy, commercial policy, the celebration of May Day, and finally, the collective tactic to be followed in the event of war.

4. The obligation to carry out the decisions of the International takes precedence over all else. National sections which do not conform with this place themselves outside the International.

5. The setting in motion of the massed ranks of the proletariat of all countries is alone decisive in the course of struggles against imperialism and against war.

Thus the principal tactic of the national sections aims to render the masses capable of political action and resolute initiative; to ensure the international cohesion of the masses in action; to build the political and trade-union organizations in such a way that, through their mediation, prompt and effective collaboration of all the sections is at all times guaranteed, and so that the will of the International materializes in action by the majority of the working-class masses all over the world.

6. The immediate mission of socialism is the spiritual liberation of the proletariat from the tutelage of the bourgeoisie, which expresses itself through the influence of nationalist ideology. The national sections must agitate in the parliaments and the press, denouncing the empty wordiness of nationalism as an instrument of bourgeois domination. The sole defense of all real national independence is at present the revolutionary class struggle against imperialism. The workers' fatherland, to the defense of which all else must be subordinated, is the socialist International.

LETTERS FROM PRISON

During her second and longest wartime imprisonment, from July 1916 to November 1918, Rosa Luxemburg's correspondence and writing became her sole emotional and intellectual outlet. Prevented from participating in political activity — although she was able to write fairly regularly for the Spartacus letters — she consciously turned her immense energies and dominating personality toward her many other interests, and tried to keep up the spirits of her friends while she waited for her eventual release.

One of her closest confidantes and friends was Karl Liebknecht's wife Sonya (or Sonichka or Sonyusha as she often called her). During the long war years while Karl was also imprisoned — under much harsher conditions than Rosa — she obviously felt it her responsibility to try and keep Sonya from despairing, and wrote her often and at length.

Rosa Luxemburg's letters from prison reveal a side of her personality that finds little overt expression in most of her writings. It is not a contradictory side of her, as some have tried to prove, not an inexplicable antithesis to the "public" Rosa, the great woman revolutionary who seemed to her opponents to be so sharp and full of caustic venom. On the contrary, it is an integral part of her personality that influenced her every action.

As Che Guevara expressed it many years later, "At the risk of seeming ridiculous, let me say that the true revolutionary is guided by a great feeling of love. It is impossible to think of a genuine revolutionary lacking this quality."

Rosa's letters reveal how deep her love of life in all its forms was, and how keenly she felt both its beauty and its cruelty. She often said she would have liked to have been a biologist, had she not been born in a period of revolutionary upheaval, and her prison letters show her absorbing interest in all the forms of life around her.

The South End she refers to is the section of Berlin where she had an apartment for many years. Hans Diefenback was a close personal friend, a surgeon, who was killed at the front in 1917. The letters were translated by Eden and Cedar Paul in 1921. Selections here are taken from the 1946 edition published by the Socialist Book Center in London.

————

Wronke, February 18, 1917

. . . . It is long since I have been shaken by anything as by Martha's brief report on your visit to Karl, how you had to see him through a grating, and the impression it made on you. Why didn't you tell me about it? I have a right to share in anything which hurts you, and I wouldn't allow anyone to curtail my proprietary rights!

Besides, Martha's account reminded me so vividly of the first time my brother and my sister came to see me ten years ago in the Warsaw Citadel. There they put you in a regular cage consisting of two layers of wire mesh; or rather, a small cage stands freely inside a larger one, and the prisoner only sees the visitor through this double trellis-work. It was just at the end of a six-day hunger strike, and I was so weak that the commanding officer of the fortress had almost to carry me into the visitors' room. I had to hold on with both hands to the wires of the cage, and this must certainly have strengthened the resemblance to a wild beast in the zoo. The cage was standing in a rather dark corner of the room, and my brother pressed his face against the wires. "Where are you?" he kept on asking, continually wiping away the tears that clouded his glasses. How glad I should be if I could only take Karl's place in the cage of Luckau prison, so as to save him from such an ordeal!

Convey my most grateful thanks to Pfemfert for Galsworthy's book. I finished it yesterday and liked it so much. Not as much as *The Man of Property*. It pleased me less, precisely because in it social criticism is more preponderant. When I am reading a novel I am less concerned with any moral it may convey than with its purely artistic merits. What troubles me in the case of *Fraternity* is that Galsworthy's intelligence overburdens the book. This criticism will surprise you. I regard Galsworthy as of the same type as Bernard Shaw and Oscar Wilde, a type which now has many representatives among the British intelligentsia. They are able, ultracivilized, a trifle bored with the world, and they are inclined to regard anything with a humorous skepticism. The subtly ironical remarks that Galsworthy makes concerning his own *dramatis personae*, remaining himself apparently quite serious the while, often makes me burst out laughing. But persons who are truly well bred rarely or never make fun of their own associates, even though they do not fail to note anything ludicrous; in like manner, a supreme artist never makes a butt of his own creations.

Don't misunderstand me, Sonichka; don't think that I am objecting to satire in the grand style! For example, Gerhart Hauptmann's *Emanuel Quint* is the most ferocious satire of modern society that has been written for a hundred years. But the author himself is not on the grin as he writes. At the close he stands with lips a-tremble, and the tears glisten in his widely open eyes. Galsworthy, on the other hand, with his smartly-phrased interpolations, makes me feel as I have felt at an evening party when my neighbor, as each new guest has entered, has whispered some appropriate piece of spite into my ear . . . .

This is Sunday, the deadliest of days for prisoners and solitaries. I am sad at heart, but I earnestly hope that both you and Karl are free from care. Write soon to let me know when and where you are at length going for a change.

All my love to you and the children.

[P. S.] Do you think Pfemfert could send me something else worth reading? Perhaps one of Thomas Mann's books? I have not read any of them yet.

One more request. I am beginning to find the sun rather trying when I go out; could you send me a yard of black spotted veiling?

Thanks in advance.

Wronke, May 2, 1917

. . . . Do you remember how, in April last year, I called you up on the telephone at ten in the morning to come at once to the botanical gardens and listen to the nightingale which was giving a regular concert there? We hid ourselves in a thick shrubbery, and sat on the stones beside a trickling streamlet. When the nightingale had ceased singing, there suddenly came a plaintive, monotonous cry that sounded something like "Gligligligligliglick!" I said I thought it must be some kind of marsh bird, and Karl agreed; but we never learned exactly what bird it was. Just fancy, I heard the same call suddenly here from somewhere close at hand a few days ago in the early morning, and I burned with impatience to find out what the bird was. I could not rest until I had done so. It is not a marsh bird after all.

It is a wryneck, a grey bird, larger than a sparrow. It gets its name because of the way in which, when danger threatens, it tries to intimidate its enemies by quaint gestures and writhings of the neck. It lives only on ants, collecting them with its sticky tongue, just like an anteater. The Spaniards call it hormiguero — the antbird. Moerike has written some amusing verses on the wryneck, and Hugo Wolf has set them to music. Now that I've found out what bird it is that gave the plaintive cry, I am as pleased as it some one had given me a present. You might write to Karl about it, he will like to know.

You ask what I am reading. Natural science for the most part; I am studying the distribution of plants and animals.

Yesterday I was reading about the reasons for the disappearance of song birds in Germany. The spread of scientific forestry, horticulture, and agriculture, have cut them off from their nesting places and their food supply. More and more, with modern methods, we are doing away with hollow trees, wastelands, brushwood, fallen leaves. I felt sore at heart. I was not thinking so much about the loss of pleasure for human beings, but I was so much distressed at the idea of the stealthy and inexorable destruction of these defenseless little creatures that the tears came into my eyes. I was reminded of a book I read in Zurich, in which Professor Sieber describes the dying out of the Redskins in North America. Just like the birds, they have been gradually driven from their hunting grounds by civilized men.

I suppose I must be out of sorts to feel everything so deeply. Sometimes, however, it seems to me that I am not really a human being at all, but like a bird or a beast in human form. I feel so much more at home even in a scrap of garden like the one here, and still more in the meadows when the grass is humming with bees than—at one of our party congresses. I can say that to you, for you will not promptly suspect me of treason to socialism! You know that I really hope to die at my post, in a street fight or in prison.

But my innermost personality belongs more to my tomtits than to the comrades. This is not because, like so many spiritually bankrupt politicians, I seek refuge and find repose in nature. Far from it, in nature at every turn I see so much cruelty that I suffer greatly.

Take the following episode, which I shall never forget. Last spring I was returning from a country walk when, in the quiet, empty road, I noticed a small dark patch on the ground. Leaning forward I witnessed a voiceless tragedy. A large beetle was lying on its back and waving its legs helplessly, while a crowd of little ants were swarming round it and eating it alive! I was horror stricken, so I took my pocket handkerchief and began to flick the little brutes away. They were so bold and stubborn that it took me some time, and when at length I had freed the poor wretch of a beetle and had carried it to a safe distance on the grass, two of its legs had already been gnawed off. . . .

I fled from the scene feeling that in the end I had conferred a very doubtful boon.

The evening twilight lasts so long now. I love this hour of the gloaming. In the South End I had plenty of blackbirds, but here there are none to be seen or heard. I was feeding a pair all through the winter, but they have vanished.

In the South End I used to stroll through the streets at this hour. It always fascinates me when, during the last violet gleam of daylight, the ruddy gas lamps suddenly flash out, still looking so strange in the half light as if they were almost ashamed of themselves. Then one sees indistinctly a figure moving swiftly through the street, perhaps a servant maid hastening to fetch something from the baker or the grocer before the shops close. The bootmaker's children, who are friends of mine, used to go on playing in the streets after dark, until a loud call summoned them in. And there was always a belated blackbird which could not settle down, but like a naughty child would go on wailing, or would wake with a start and fly noisily from tree to tree.

For my part, I would continue standing in the middle of the street numbering the stars as they came out, unwilling to leave the mild air, and the twilight in which day and night were so gently caressing one another.

Sonyusha, I will write again soon. Make your mind easy, everything will turn out all right, for Karl too. Good-bye till the next letter.

Wronke, June 1, 1917

. . . . I know the different kinds of orchids well. I studied them once for several days in the wonderful hothouses at Frankfort-on-the-Main, where a whole section is filled with them. It was after the trial in which I was sentenced to one year's imprisonment.

Their slender grace and their fantastic, almost unnatural forms, make them seem to me overrefined and decadent. They produce on me the impression of a dainty marquise of the powder-and-patch period.

The admiration I feel for them has to encounter an internal resistance, and is attended with a certain uneasiness, for by disposition I am antagonistic to everything decadent and perverse. A common dandelion gives me far more pleasure. It has so much sunshine in its color; like me, it expands gratefully in the sun, and furls its petals shyly at the least shade.

What lovely evenings and what glorious nights we are having now! Yesterday everything seemed under the influence of an indescribable charm. Long after the sun had set, huge rays of a vague but brilliant tint — a sort of opal — were still spreading across the sky; it looked like a huge palette upon which a painter had squeezed the color out of his brushes after a long day's work.

The atmosphere was sultry; there was a slight feeling of tension, producing a sense of oppression; the shrubs were motionless, the nightingale was silent, but the indefatigable black-cap was still hopping from twig to twig uttering its clear call. There was a general feeling of expectation. I stood at the window and waited too, though I haven't the slightest idea what I was waiting for. After "closing time" at six I have nothing more to expect betwixt heaven and earth.

Breslau, Mid-November, 1917

I hope soon to have a chance of sending you this letter at long last, so I hasten to take up my pen. For how long a time I have been forced to forbear my habit of talking to you — on paper at least. I am allowed to write a few letters, and I had to save up my chances for Hans D. who was expecting to hear from me. But now all is over. My last two letters to him were addressed to a dead man, and one has already been returned to me. His loss still seems incredible. But enough of this. I prefer to consider such matters in solitude. It only annoys me beyond expression when people try, as N. tried, "to break the news" to me, and to make a parade of their own grief by way of "consolation." Why should my closest friends understand me so little and hold me so cheaply as to be unable to realize that the best way in such cases is to say quickly, briefly, and simply: "He is dead"? . . .

How I deplore the loss of all these months and years in which we might have had so many joyful hours together, notwithstanding all the horrors that are going on throughout the world. Do you know, Sonichka, the longer it lasts, and the more the infamy and monstrosity of the daily happenings surpasses all bounds, the more tranquil and more confident becomes my personal outlook. I say to myself that it is absurd to apply moral standards to the great elemental forces that manifest themselves in a hurricane, a flood, or an eclipse of the sun. We have to accept them simply as data for investigation, as subjects of study.

Manifestly, objectively considered, these are the only possible lines along which history can move, and we must follow the movement without losing sight of the main trend. I have the feeling that all this moral filth through which we are wading, this huge madhouse in which we live, may all of a sudden, between one day and the next, be transformed into its very opposite, as if by the stroke of a magician's wand; may become something stupendously great and heroic; must inevitably be transformed, if only the war lasts a few years longer. . . . Read Anatole France's *The Gods are Athirst*. My main reason for admiring this work so much is because the author, with the insight of genius into all that is universally human, seems to say to us: "Behold out of these petty personalities, out of these trivial commonplaces, arise, when the hour is ripe, the most titanic events and the most monumental gestures of history." We have to take everything as it comes both in social life and in private life; to accept what happens, tranquilly, comprehensively, and with a smile. I feel absolutely convinced that things will take the right turn when the war ends, or not long afterwards; but obviously we have first to pass through a period of terrible human suffering.

What I have just written reminds me of an incident I wish to tell you of, for it seems to me so poetical and so touching. I was recently reading a scientific work upon the migrations of birds, a phenomenon which has hitherto seemed rather enigmatic. From this I learned that certain species, which at ordinary times live at enmity one with another (because some are birds of prey, while others are victims), will keep the peace during their great southward flight across the sea. Among the birds that come to winter in Egypt — come in such numbers that the sky is darkened by their flight — are, besides hawks, eagles, falcons and owls, thousands of little song birds such as larks, gold-crested wrens, and nightingales, mingling fearlessly with the great birds of prey. A "truce of God" seems to have been declared for the journey. All are striving towards the common goal, to drop, half dead from fatigue, in the land of the Nile, and subsequently to assort themselves by species and localities. Nay more, during the long flight the large birds have been seen to carry smaller birds on their backs, for instance, cranes have passed in great numbers with a twittering freight of small birds of passage. Is not that charming? . . .

In a tasteless jumble of poems I was looking at recently, I came across one by Hugo von Hofmannsthal. As a rule I do not care for his writings, I consider them artificial, stilted, and obscure; I simply can't understand him. But this poem is an exception; it pleased me greatly and made a strong impression on me. I am sending you a copy of it, for I think you will like it too.

I am now deep in the study of geology. Perhaps you will think that must be a dry subject, but if so, you are mistaken. I am reading it with intense interest and passionate enjoyment; it opens up such wide intellectual vistas and supplies a more perfectly unified and more comprehensive conception of nature than any other science. There are so many things I should like to tell you about it, but for that we should have to have a real talk — taking a morning stroll together through the country at the South End, or seeing one another home several times in succession on a calm moonlit night. What are you reading now? How are you getting on with the *Lessing Legende*? I want to know everything about you. Write at once, if you can, by the same route, or, failing that, by the official route, without mentioning this letter. I am already counting the weeks till I can hope to see you here again. I suppose it will be soon after the New Year?

What news have you from Karl? When do you expect to see him? Give him a thousand greetings from me. All my love to you, my dear, dear Sonichka. Write soon and copiously.

Breslau, October 18, 1918

I wrote to you the day before yesterday. So far I have had no answer to the telegram I sent to the imperial chancellor; I may have to wait several days for an answer. But this much is certain, in my present mood I can no longer endure to receive my friends' visits under the supervision of the warders. I have borne it patiently all these years, and in other circumstances I should have continued to bear it. But the complete change in the general situation has had its reaction upon my own psychology. To carry on a conversation under supervision, to find it impossible to talk about the things that really interest me would now be intolerable. I would rather forego having visitors until we are all at liberty once more.

Things can't go on like this much longer. Now that Dittman and Kurt Eisner have been set free, I am sure that the door will soon be open for myself, and for Karl too. We had better wait until we can meet in Berlin.

Till then, much love.

THE SPIRIT OF
RUSSIAN LITERATURE:
LIFE OF KOROLENKO

While Rosa Luxemburg was in prison, her publisher asked her
to write something about Tolstoy, and she replied to him, "Your
idea . . . doesn't appeal to me at all. For whom? Why? Everyone
can read Tolstoy's books, and if they don't get a strong breath
of life from them, then they won't get it from any commentary."

But she did agree, after some persuading, to translate a work
by a lesser known Russian literary figure, and to write a preface
to the translation. She set to work on Vladimir Korolenko's auto-
biographical *A History of My Contemporary*, and the preface
she wrote deserves to be recognized as a classic of Marxist cultural criticism.

In it she provides a sweeping historical panorama of nineteenth-
century Russian society, culture, and politics; contrasts Russian
and European literature; and examines what is essential, not
exceptional, in that great body of Russian literary work.

Her essay is especially valuable as an implicit condemnation
of the perversion of Marxist cultural criticism that dominates
official Soviet attitudes towards art today. (The condemnation is
implicit only because it was written in 1918, when the suppression
of artistic expression by a government that considered itself socialist would have been inconceivable to Rosa Luxemburg, Lenin,
Trotsky, or any Marxist.) She skillfully and flexibly employs her
understanding of Marxist method to produce a critical review
that does justice to both the sociological and artistic qualities of
the literary works discussed.

Rosa Luxemburg's main thesis is stated clearly. "The chief
characteristic of this sudden emergence of Russian literature is
that it was born out of opposition to the Russian regime, out
of the spirit of struggle . . . Russian literature became, under
czarism, a power in public life as in no other country and in
no other time." What dominated that body of literature more
than anything else was its rejection of the status quo and search
for alternatives, and it became one of the most powerful forces

for undermining the ideological and moral foundation of czarist absolutism.

Although a regime of a different class character is involved in the Soviet Union today—one built on the foundations established by the destruction of capitalism—much of Rosa Luxemburg's analysis of nineteenth-century Russian literature could, with little alteration, be applied to the best of Soviet literature today—the works of Sinyavsky, Daniel, Solzhenitsyn, and others, most of which are banned from publication in the Soviet Union itself.

Rosa Luxemburg's views have nothing in common with the dogmatic, bureaucratic strictures placed on art in most of the workers' states today, where freedom of expression is allowed only if it serves to bolster the grip of the bureaucratic ruling caste on all aspects of social, political, economic, and artistic life. Her views are far from the caricature of art which has come to be known as "socialist realism," far from the essentially utilitarian and undialectical notion of "proletarian culture" against which Lenin and Trotsky fought in the early years of the revolution.

While she identifies "opposition to the regime" as the main characteristic of Russian literature of the nineteenth century, she does not mean something narrowly political. "Nothing, of course, could be more erroneous than to picture Russian literature as a tendentious art in a crude sense, nor to think of all Russian poets as revolutionists, or at least as progressives. Patterns such as 'revolutionary' or 'progressive' in themselves mean very little in art." In discussing Dostoyevsky she clarifies her point: ". . . With the true artist, the social formula that he recommends is a matter of secondary importance: the source of his art, its animating spirit, is decisive." There is certainly nothing tendentious, crude or narrow-minded in Rosa Luxemburg's critical vision.

The following has been reprinted from the winter 1943 issue of the now defunct *New Essays: A Quarterly Devoted to the Study of Modern Society.* The translation is by Frieda Mattick.

I

"My soul, of a threefold nationality, has at last found a home—and this above all in the literature of Russia," Korolenko says in his memoirs. This literature, which to Korolenko was fatherland, home, and nationality, and which he himself adorns, was historically unique.

For centuries, throughout the Middle Ages and down to the last third of the eighteenth century, Russia was enveloped in a cryptlike silence, in darkness and barbarism. She had no cultivated literary language, no scientific literature, no publishing houses, no libraries, no journals, no centers of cultural life. The gulf stream of the Renaissance, which had washed the shores of all other European countries and was responsible for a flowering garden of world literature, the rousing storms of the Reformation, the fiery breath of eighteenth-century philosophy — all this had left Russia untouched. The land of the czars possessed as yet no means for apprehending the light rays of Western culture, no mental soil in which its seeds could take root. The sparse literary monuments of those times, in their outlandish ugliness, appear today like native products of the Solomon Islands or the New Hebrides. Between them and the art of the Western world, there apparently exists no essential relation, no inner connection.

But then something like a miracle took place. After several faltering attempts toward the end of the eighteenth century to create a national consciousness, the Napoleonic wars flashed up like lightning. Russia's profound humiliation, arousing for the first time in czardom a national consciousness, just as the triumph of the Coalition did later, resulted in drawing the Russian intellectuals toward the West, toward Paris, into the heart of European culture, and bringing them into contact with a new world. Overnight a Russian literature blossomed forth, springing up complete in glistening armor like Minerva from the head of Jupiter; and this literature, combining Italian melody, English virility, and German nobility and profundity, soon overflowed with a treasure of talents, radiant beauty, thought and emotion.

The long dark night, the deathlike silence, had been an illusion. The light rays from the West had remained obscure only as a latent power; the seeds of culture had been waiting to sprout at the appropriate moment. Suddenly, Russian literature stood there, an unmistakable member of the literature of Europe, in whose veins circulated the blood of Dante, Rabelais, Shakespeare, Byron, Lessing, and Goethe. With the leap of a lion it atoned for the neglect of centuries; it stepped into the family circle of world literature as an equal.

The chief characteristic of this sudden emergence of Russian literature is that it was born out of opposition to the Russian regime, out of the spirit of struggle. This feature was obvious throughout the entire nineteenth century. It explains the richness and depth of its spiritual quality, the fullness and originality of its artistic form, above all, its creative and driving social force. Russian literature became, under czarism, a power in public life as in no other country and in no other time. It remained at its post for a century until it was relieved by the material power of the masses, when the word became flesh.

It was this literature which won for that half-Asiatic, despotic state a place in world culture. It broke through the Chinese Wall erected by absolutism and built a bridge to the West. Not only does it appear as a literature that borrows, but also as one that creates; not only is it a pupil, but also a teacher. One has only to mention three names to illustrate this: Tolstoy, Gogol, and Dostoyevsky.

In his memoirs, Korolenko characterizes his father, a government official at the time of serfdom in Russia, as a typical representative of the honest people in that generation. Korolenko's father felt responsible only for his own activities. The gnawing feeling of responsibility for social injustice was strange to him. "God, Czar, and the Law" were beyond all criticism. As a district judge he felt called upon only to apply the law with the utmost scrupulousness. "That the law itself may be inefficient is the responsibility of the czar before God. He, the judge, is as little responsible for the law as for the lightning of the high heavens, which sometimes strikes an innocent child. . . ." To the generation of the eighteen-forties and fifties, social conditions as a whole were fundamental and unshakable. Under the scourge of officialdom, those who served loyally, without opposition, knew they could only bend as under the onslaught of a tornado, hoping and waiting that the evil might pass. "Yes," said Korolenko, "that was a view of the world out of a single mold, a kind of imperturbable equilibrium of conscience. Their inner foundations were not undermined by self-analysis; the honest people of that time did not know that deep inner conflict which comes with the feeling of being personally responsible for the whole social order." It is this kind of view that is supposed to be the true basis of czar and God, and as long as this view remains undisturbed, the power of absolutism is great indeed.

It would be wrong, however, to regard as specifically Russian or as pertaining only to the period of serfdom the state of mind that Korolenko describes. That attitude toward society which enables one to be free of gnawing self-analysis and inner discord and considers "God-willed conditions" as something elemental, accepting the acts of history as a sort of divine fate, is compatible with the most varied political and social systems. In fact it is found even under modern conditions and was especially characteristic of German society throughout the world war.

In Russia, this "imperturbable equilibrium of conscience" had already begun to crumble in the eighteen-sixties among wide circles of the intelligentsia. Korolenko describes in an intuitive manner this spiritual change in Russian society, and shows just how this generation overcame the slave psychology and was seized by the trend of a new time, the predominant characteristic of which was the "gnawing and painful, but creative spirit of social responsibility."

343

To have aroused this high sense of citizenship, and to have undermined the deepest psychological roots of absolutism in Russian society, is the great merit of Russian literature. From its first days, at the beginning of the nineteenth century, it never denied its social responsibility—never forgot to be socially critical. Ever since its unfolding with Pushkin and Lermontov, its life principle was a struggle against darkness, ignorance, and oppression. With desperate strength it shook the social and political chains, bruised itself sore against them, and paid for the struggle in blood.

In no other country did there exist such a conspicuously early mortality among prominent representatives of literature as in Russia. They died by the dozens in the bloom of their manhood, at the youthful age of twenty-five or twenty-seven, or at the oldest around forty, either on the gallows or as suicides—directly or disguised as duels—some through insanity, others by premature exhaustion. So died the noble poet of liberty, Ryleyev, who in the year 1826 was executed as the leader of the Decembrist uprising. Thus, too, Pushkin and Lermontov, those brilliant creators of Russian poetry—both victims of duels—and their whole prolific circle. So died Belinsky, the founder of literary criticism and proponent of Hegelian philosophy in Russia, as well as Dobrolyubov; and so the excellent and tender poet Kozlov, whose songs grew into Russian folk poetry like wild garden flowers; and the creator of Russian comedy, Griboyedov, as well as his greater successor, Gogol; and in recent times, those sparkling short-story writers, Garshin and Chekhov. Others pined away for decades in penitentiaries, jails, or in exile, like the founder of Russian journalism, Novikov; like the leader of the Decembrists, Bestuzhev; like Prince Odoyevsky, Alexander von Herzen, Dostoyevsky, Chernyshevsky, Shevchenko, and Korolenko.

Turgenev relates, incidentally, that the first time he fully enjoyed the song of the lark he was somewhere near Berlin. This casual remark seems very characteristic. Larks warble in Russia no less beautifully than in Germany. The huge Russian empire contains such great and manifold beauties of nature that an impressionable poetic soul finds deep enjoyment at every step. What hindered Turgenev from enjoying the beauty of nature in his own country was just that painful disharmony of social relations, that ever-present awareness of responsibility for those outrageous social and political conditions, of which he could not rid himself, and which, piercing deeply, did not permit for a moment any indulgence in complete self-oblivion. Only away from Russia, when the thousands of depressing pictures of his homeland were left behind, only in a foreign environment, the orderly exterior and material culture of which had always naively impressed his countrymen, could a Russian poet give himself up to the enjoyment of nature, untroubled and wholeheartedly.

Nothing, of course, could be more erroneous than to picture Russian literature as a tendentious art in a crude sense, nor to think of all Russian poets as revolutionists, or at least as progressives. Patterns such as "revolutionary" or "progressive" in themselves mean very little in art.

Dostoyevsky, especially in his later writings, is an outspoken reactionary, a religious mystic and hater of socialists. His depictions of Russian revolutionaries are malicious caricatures. Tolstoy's mystic doctrines reflect reactionary tendencies, if not more. But the writings of both have, nevertheless, an inspiring, arousing, and liberating effect upon us. And this is because their starting points are not reactionary, their thoughts and emotions are not governed by the desire to hold on to the status quo, nor are they motivated by social hatred, narrow-mindedness, or caste egotism. On the contrary, theirs is the warmest love for mankind and the deepest response to social injustice. And thus the reactionary Dostoyevsky becomes the artistic agent of the "insulted and injured," as one of his works is called. Only the conclusions drawn by him and Tolstoy, each in his own way, only the way out of the social labyrinth which they believe they have found, leads them into the bypaths of mysticism and asceticism. But with the true artist, the social formula that he recommends is a matter of secondary importance; the source of his art, its animating spirit, is decisive.

Within Russian literature one also finds a tendency which, though on a considerably smaller scale and unlike the deep and world-embracing ideas of a Tolstoy or Dostoyevsky, propagates more modest ideals, that is, material culture, modern progress, and bourgeois proficiency. Of the older generation the most talented representative of this school is Goncharov, and of the younger one, Chekhov. The latter, in opposition to Tolstoy's ascetic and moralizing tendency, made the characteristic remark that "steam and electricity hold more love for humanity than sexual chastity and vegetarianism." In its youthful, rousing drive for culture, personal dignity, and initiative, this somewhat sober, "culture-carrying" Russian movement differs from the smug philistinism and banality of the French and German delineators of the *juste milieu*. Goncharov particularly, in his book *Oblomov*, reached such heights in picturing human indolence that the figure he drew earned a place of universal validity in the gallery of great human types.

Finally, there are also representatives of decadence in Russia's literature. One of the most brilliant talents of the Gorky generation is to be found among them, Leonid Andreyev, whose art

345

emanates a sepulchral air of decay in which all will to live has wilted away. And yet the root and substance of this Russian decadence is diametrically opposed to that of a Baudelaire or a D'Annunzio, where the basis is merely oversaturation with modern culture, where egotism, highly cunning in expression, quite robust in its essence, no longer finds satisfaction in a normal existence and reaches out for poisonous stimuli. With Andreyev hopelessness pours forth from a temperament which, under the onslaught of oppressive social conditions, is overpowered by pain. Like the best of the Russian writers, he has looked deeply into the sufferings of mankind. He lived through the Russo-Japanese war, through the first revolutionary period and the horrors of the counterrevolution from 1907 to 1911. He describes them in such stirring pictures as *The Red Laugh, The Seven Who Were Hanged*, and many others. And like his Lazarus, having returned from the shores of shadowland, he cannot overcome the dank odor of the grave; he walks among the living like "something half-devoured by death." The origin of this kind of decadence is typically Russian: it is that full measure of social sympathy under which the energy and resistance of the individual break down.

It is just this social sympathy which is responsible for the singularity and artistic splendor of Russian literature. Only one who is himself affected and stirred can affect and stir others. Talent and genius, of course, are in each case a "gift of God." Great talent alone, however, is not sufficient to make a lasting impression. Who would deny a Monti talent or even genius, though he hailed, in Dantean *terza rima*, first the assassination by a Roman mob of the ambassador of the French Revolution and then the victories of this same revolution; at one time the Austrians, and later the Directory; now the extravagant Suvarov, then again Napoleon and the Emperor Franz; each time pouring out to the victor the sweetest tones of a nightingale? Who would doubt the great talent of a Sainte-Beuve, the creator of the literary essay who, in the course of time, put his brilliant pen to the service of almost every political group of France, demolishing today what he worshiped yesterday and vice versa?

For a lasting effect, for the real education of society, more than talent is needed. What is required is poetic personality, character, individuality, attributes which are anchored deeply in a great and well-rounded view of the world. It is just this view of the world, just this sensitive social consciousness which sharpened so greatly the insight of Russian literature into the social conditions of people and into the psychology of the various characters and types. It is this almost aching sympathy that inspires its descriptions with colors of glowing splendor; it is the restless search, the brooding over the problems of society which enables it to observe artistically the enormity and inner complexity of the social structure and to lay it down in great works of art.

Murder and crimes are committed everywhere and every day. "Barber X murdered and robbed wealthy Mrs. Y. Criminal Court Z condemned him to die." Everyone has read such announcements of three lines in the morning paper, has gone over them with an indifferent glance in order to look for the latest news from the racetracks or the new theater schedule. Who else is interested in murders besides the police, the public prosecutor, and the statisticians? Mostly writers of detective stories and movies.

The fact that one human being can murder another, that this can happen near us every day, in the midst of our "civilization," next door to our home sweet home, moves Dostoyevsky to the very bottom of his soul. As with Hamlet, who through his mother's crime finds all the bonds of humanity untied and the world out of joint, so it is for Dostoyevsky when he faces the fact that one human being can murder another. He finds no rest, he feels the responsibility for this dreadfulness weighing upon him, as it does on every one of us. He must elucidate the soul of the murderer, must trace his misery, his afflictions, down to the most hidden folds of his heart. He suffers all his tortures and is blinded by the terrible understanding that the murderer himself is the most unhappy victim of society. With a mighty voice, Dostoyevsky sounds an alarm. He awakens us from the stupid indifference of civilized egotism that delivers the murderer to the police inspector, to the public prosecutor and his henchmen, or to the penitentiary with the hope that thereby we shall all be rid of him. Dostoyevsky forces us to go through all the tortures the murderer goes through and in the end leaves us all crushed. Whoever has experienced his Raskolnikov, or the cross-examination of Dmitri Karamazov the night after the murder of his father, or the *Memoirs from a Deathhouse,* will never again find his way back to the supporting shell of philistine and self-satisfying egotism. Dostoyevsky's novels are furious attacks on bourgeois society, in whose face he shouts: The real murderer, the murderer of the human soul, is you!

No one has taken such merciless revenge on society for the crimes committed on the individual, nobody has put society on the rack so cunningly as Dostoyevsky. This is his specific talent. But the other leading spirits of Russian literature also perceive the act of murder as an accusation against existing conditions, as a crime committed upon the murderer as a human being, for which we are all responsible—each one of us. That is why the greatest talents again and again return to the subject of crime as if fascinated by it, putting it before our eyes in the highest works of art in order to arouse us from our thoughtless indifference. Tolstoy did it in *The Power of Darkness* and in *Resurrection*, Gorky in *The Lower Depths* and in *Three of Them*, Korolenko in his story *The Rustling of the Woods* and in his wonderful Siberian *Murderer*.

Prostitution is as little specifically Russian as tuberculosis; it is rather the most international institution of social life. But although it plays an almost controlling part in our modern life, officially, in the sense of the conventional lie, it is not approved of as a normal constituent of present-day society. Rather it is treated as the scum of humanity, as something allegedly beyond the pale. Russian literature deals with the prostitute not in the pungent style of the boudoir novel, nor the whining sentimentality of tendentious literature, nor as the mysterious, rapacious vampire as in Wedekind's *Erdgeist*. No literature in the world contains descriptions of fiercer realism than the magnificent scene of the orgy in the *Brothers Karamazov* or in Tolstoy's *Resurrection*. In spite of this, the Russian artist, however, does not look at the prostitute as a "lost soul," but as a human being whose suffering and inner struggles need all his sympathy. He dignifies the prostitute and rehabilitates her for the crime that society has committed on her by letting her compete with the purest and loveliest types of womanhood for the heart of the man. He crowns her head with roses and elevates her, as does Mahado his Bajadere from the purgatory of corruption and her own agony to the heights of moral purity and womanly heroism.

Not only the exceptional person and situation that stands out crassly from the gray background of everyday life, but life itself, the average man and his misery, awakens a deep concern in the Russian writer whose senses are strongly aware of social injustice. "Human happiness," says Korolenko in one of his stories, "honest human happiness is salubrious and elevating to the soul. And I always believe, you know, that man is rather obliged to be happy." In another story, called *Paradox*, a cripple, born without arms, says, "Man is created for happiness, as a bird for flight." From the mouth of the miserable cripple such a maxim is an obvious "paradox." But for thousands and millions of people it is not accidental physical defects which make their "vocation of happiness" seem so paradoxical but the social conditions under which they must exist.

That remark of Korolenko actually contains an important element of social hygiene: happiness makes people spiritually healthy and pure, as sunlight over the open sea effectively disinfects the water. Furthermore, under abnormal social conditions —and all conditions based on social inequality are fundamentally abnormal—most heterogeneous deformations of the soul are apt to be a mass phenomenon. Permanent oppression, insecurity, injustice, poverty, and dependence, as well as that division of labor which leads to one-sided specialization, mold people in a certain manner. And this goes for both the oppressor and the oppressed, the tyrant and the slave, the boaster and the parasite, the ruthless opportunist and the indolent idler, the pedant and the jester — all alike are products and victims of their circumstances.

It is just the peculiar psychological abnormality, the warped development of the human soul under the influence of everyday social conditions, which aroused writers like Gogol, Dostoyevsky, Goncharov, Saltykov, Uspensky, Chekhov, and others to descriptions of Balzacian fervor. The tragedy of the triviality of the average man, as described by Tolstoy in his *Death of Ivan Ilyich*, is unsurpassed in world literature.

There are, for example, those rogues who, without a vocation and unfit to make a normal living, are torn between a parasitic existence and occasional conflicts with the law, forming the scum of bourgeois society for whom the Western world puts up signs, "No beggars, peddlers, or musicians allowed." For this category — the type of Korolenko's ex-official Popkov — Russian literature always had a lively and artistic interest and good-natured smile of understanding. With the warm heart of a Dickens, but without his bourgeois sentimentality, Turgenev, Uspensky, Korolenko, and Gorky look upon these "stranded" folk, the criminal as well as the prostitute, with a broad-minded realism, as equals in human society, and achieve, just because of this genial approach, works of a high artistic effect.

Russian literature treats the world of the child with exceptional tenderness and affection, as is shown in Tolstoy's *War and Peace* and *Anna Karenina*, in Dostoyevsky's *Karamazov*, Goncharov's *Oblomov*, Korolenko's *In Bad Company* and *At Night*, and in Gorky's *Three of Them*. Zola, in his novel *Page d'amour*, from the Rougon-Macquart cycle, describes the sufferings of a neglected child. But here the sickly and hypersensitive child, morosely affected by the love affair of an egotistic mother, is only a "means of evidence" in an experimental novel, a subject to illustrate the theory of inheritance.

To the Russian, however, the child and its soul is an independent entity, the object of artistic interest to the same extent as the adult, only more natural, less spoiled and certainly more helplessly exposed to the evils of society. "Whoso shall offend one of these little ones . . . it were better for him that a millstone were hanged about his neck," and so on. Present society offends millions of those little ones by robbing them of what is most precious and irretrievable, a happy, sorrowless, harmonious childhood.

As a victim of social conditions, a child's world with its misery and happiness is especially near to the Russian artist's heart. He does not stoop to the child in the false and playful manner which most adults believe necessary, but treats it with honest and sincere comradeship, yes, even with an inner shyness and respect for the untouched little being.

The manner in which literary satire is expressed is an important indicator of the cultural level of a nation. Here England and Germany represent the two opposing poles in European literature. In tracing the history of satire from Von Hutten to Heinrich Heine, one may also include Grimmelshausen. But in the course of the last three centuries, the connecting links in this chain display a frightful picture of decline. Beginning with the ingenious and rather fantastic Fischart, whose exuberant nature distinctly reveals the influence of the Renaissance, to Mosherosh, and from the latter, who at least dares to pull the bigwig's whiskers, to that small philistine Rabener — what a decline! Rabener, who gets excited about the people who dare to ridicule princelings, the clergy, and the "upper classes" because a well-behaved satirist should first of all learn to be "a loyal subject," exposes the mortal spot of German satire. In England, however, satire has taken an unparalleled upswing since the beginning of the eighteenth century, that is, after the great revolution. Not only has British literature produced a string of such masters as Mandeville, Swift, Sterne, Sir Philip Francis, Byron, and Dickens, among whom Shakespeare, naturally, deserves first place for his Falstaff, but satire has turned from the privilege of the intellectuals into a universally owned property. It has become, so to speak, nationalized. It sparkles in political pamphlets, leaflets, parliamentary speeches, and newspaper articles, as well as in poetry. Satire has become the very life and breath for the Englishman, so much so that even the stories of a Croker, written for the adolescent girl of the upper middle classes, contain the same acid descriptions of English aristocracy as those of Wilde, Shaw, or Galsworthy.

This tendency towards satire has been derived from, and can be explained by, England's political freedom of long standing. As Russian literature is similar to the English in this respect, it shows that not the constitution of a country, nor its institutions, but the spirit of its literature and the attitude of the leading social circles of society are the determining factors. Since the beginning of modern literature in Russia, satire has been mastered in all its phases and has achieved excellent results in every one of them. Pushkin's poem *Eugene Onegin*, Lermontov's short stories and epigrams, Krylov's fables, Nekrasov's poems, and Gogol's comedies are just so many masterpieces, each in its own way. Nekrasov's satiric epic *Who Can Be Happy and Free in*

Russia? reveals the delightful vigor and richness of his creations. In Saltykov-Shchedrin Russian satire has finally produced its own genius who, for a grimmer scourging of despotism and bureaucracy, invented a very peculiar literary style and a unique and untranslatable language of his own and, by so doing, profoundly influenced intellectual development. Thus, with a highly moral pathos, Russian literature combined within itself an artistic comprehension that covers the entire scale of human emotions. It created in the midst of that huge prison, the material poverty of czarism, its own realm of spiritual freedom and an exuberant culture wherein one may breathe and partake of the intellectual and cultural life. It was thus able to become a social power and, by educating generation after generation, to become a real fatherland for the best of men, such as Korolenko.

II

Korolenko's nature is truly poetic. Around his cradle gathered the dense fog of superstition. Not the corrupt superstition of modern cosmopolitan decadence as practiced in spiritualism, fortune-telling, and Christian Science, but the naive superstition found in folklore—as pure and spice-scented as the free winds of the Ukrainian plains, and the millions of wild iris, yarrows, and sage that grow luxuriantly among the tall grass. The spooky atmosphere in the servants' quarters and the nursery of Korolenko's father's house reveals distinctly that his cradle stood not far from Gogol's fairyland, with its elves and witches and its heathen Christmas spook.

Descended at once from Poland, Russia, and the Ukraine, Korolenko had to bear, even as a child, the brunt of the three "nationalisms," each one expecting him "to hate or persecute someone or other." He failed these expectations, however, thanks to his healthy common sense. The Polish traditions, with their dying breath of a historically vanquished past, touched him but vaguely. His straightforwardness was repelled by that mixture of clownish tomfoolery and reactionary romanticism of Ukrainian nationalism. The brutal methods used in Russifying the Ukraine served as an effective warning against Russian chauvinism, because the tender boy instinctively felt himself drawn toward the weak and oppressed, not toward the strong and triumphant. And thus, from the conflict of three nationalities that fought in his native land of Volhynia, he made his escape into humanitarianism.

Fatherless at the age of seventeen, depending on nobody but himself, he went to Petersburg where he threw himself into the whirlpool of university life and political activity. After studying for three years at a school of technology, he moved on to the Academy of Agriculture in Moscow. Two years later his plans were crossed by the "supreme power," as happened to many others of his generation. Arrested as a spokesman of a student demonstration, Korolenko was expelled from the Academy and exiled to the district of Vologda in the far north of European Russia. When released, he was obliged to reside in Kronstadt, under police parole. Years later he returned to Petersburg and, planning a new life again, learned the cobbler's trade in order to be closer to the working people and to develop his personality in other directions. In 1879 he was arrested again and was sent even further northeastward, to a hamlet in the district of Vyatka, at the end of the world.

Korolenko took it gracefully. He tried to make the best of it by practicing his newly acquired cobbler's trade, which helped him to make a living. But not for long. Suddenly, and apparently without reason, he was sent to western Siberia, from there back to Perm, and finally to the remotest spot of far eastern Siberia.

But even this did not mark the end of his wanderings. After the assassination of Alexander II in 1881, the new czar, Alexander III, ascended the throne. Korolenko, who in the meantime had advanced to the position of railway official, took the obligatory oath to the new government, together with the other employees. But this was declared insufficient. He was requested to pledge the oath again as a private individual and political exile. Like all the other exiles, Korolenko refused to do so and as a result was sent to the ice-wastes of Yakutsk.

There can be no doubt that the whole procedure was only an "empty gesture," though Korolenko did not try to be demonstrative. Social conditions are not altered directly or materially regardless of whether or not an isolated exile, somewhere in the Siberian taiga near the polar region, swears allegiance to the czar's government. However, it was the custom in czarist Russia to insist on such empty gestures. And not only in Russia alone. The stubborn *Eppur si muove!* of a Galileo reminds us of a similar empty gesture, having no other effect than the vengeance of the Holy Inquisition wreaked on a tortured and incarcerated man. And yet for thousands of people who have only the vaguest idea of Copernicus's theory, the name Galileo is forever identical with this beautiful gesture, and it is absolutely immaterial that it did not happen at all. The very existence of such legends with which men adorn their heroes is proof enough that such "empty gestures" are indispensable in our spiritual realm.

For his refusal to take the oath, Korolenko suffered exile for four years among half-savage nomads at a miserable settlement on the banks of the Aldan, a branch of the river Lena, in the heart of the Siberian wasteland, and under the hardships of sub-zero weather. But privations, loneliness, all the sinister scenery of the taiga, and isolation from the world of civilization did not change the mental elasticity of Korolenko nor his sunny disposition. He eagerly took part in the interests of the Yakuts and shared their destitute life. He worked in the field, cut hay, and milked cows. In winter he made shoes for the natives — and even icons. The exile's life in Yakutsk, which George Kennan called a period of "being buried alive," was described by Korolenko without lament or bitterness, but with humor and in pictures of the most tender and poetic beauty. This was the time when his literary talent ripened, and he gathered a rich booty in studying men and nature.

In 1885, after his return from exile, which lasted (with short interruptions) almost ten years, he published a short story, *Makar's Dream*, which at once established him among the masters of Russian literature. This first, yet fully matured product of a young talent burst upon the leaden atmosphere of the eighties like the first song of a lark on a gray day in February. In quick succession other sketches and stories followed — *Notes of a Siberian Traveler, The Rustling of the Woods, In Pursuit of the Icon, At Night, Yom Kippur, The River Roars,* and many others. All of them show the identical characteristics of Korolenko's creations: enchanting descriptions of nature, lovable simplicity, and a warmhearted interest in the "humiliated and disinherited."

Although of a highly critical nature, Korolenko's writings are by no means polemical, educational, or dogmatic, as is the case with Tolstoy. They reveal simply his love for life and his kind disposition. Aside from being tolerant and good-natured in his conceptions, and apart from his dislike of chauvinism, Korolenko is through and through a Russian poet, and perhaps the most "nationalistic" among the great Russian prose writers. Not only does he love his country, he is in love with it like a young man; he is in love with its nature, with all the intimate charms of this gigantic country, with every sleepy stream and every quiet wood-fringed valley; he is in love with its simple people and their naive piety, their rugged humor and brooding melancholy. He does not feel at home in the city nor in a comfortable train compartment. He hates the haste and rumble of modern civilization; his place is on the open road. To walk briskly with knapsack and hand-cut hiking staff, to give himself entirely to the accidental — following a group of pious pilgrims to a thaumaturgical image of a saint, chatting with fishermen at night by a fire, or mixing with a colorful crowd of peasants, lumbermen, soldiers, and beggars on a little battered steamboat and listening to their conversation — such is the life that suits him best. But unlike Turgenev, the elegant and perfectly groomed aristocrat, he is no silent observer. He finds no difficulty in mingling with people, knowing just what to say to make friends and how to strike the right note.

In this manner he wandered all over Russia. With every step he experienced the wonders of nature, the naive poetry of simplicity, which had also brought smiles to Gogol's face. Enraptured, he observed the elementary, fatalistic indolence characteristic of the Russian people, which in times of peace seems unceasing and profound, but in stormy times turns into heroism, grandeur, and steel-like power. It was here that Korolenko filled his diary with vivid and colorful impressions which, growing into sketches and novels, were still covered with dewdrops and heavy with the scent of the soil.

One peculiar product of Korolenko's writings is his *Blind Musician*. Apparently a purely psychological experiment, it deals with no artistic problem. Being born a cripple may be the cause of many conflicts, but is, in itself, beyond all human interference and beyond guilt or vengeance. In literature as well as in art, physical defects are only casually mentioned, either in a sarcastic manner to make an ugly character more loathsome, as Homer's Thersites and the stammering judges in the comedies of Moliere and Beaumarchais, or with good-natured ridicule as in genre paintings of the Dutch Renaissance, for instance, the sketch of a cripple by Cornelius Dussart.

Not so with Korolenko. The anguish of a man born blind and tormented with an irresistible longing for light is the center of interest. Korolenko finds a solution, which unexpectedly shows the keynote of his art and which is, incidentally, characteristic of all Russian literature. The blind musician experiences a spiritual rebirth._ While detaching himself from the egotism of his own hopeless suffering by making himself the spokesman for the blind and for their physical and mental agonies, he attains his own enlightenment. The climax is the first public concert of the blind man, who surprises his listeners by choosing the well-known songs of the blind minstrels for his improvisations, thus arousing a stirring compassion. Sociality and solidarity with the misery of men mean salvation and enlightenment for the individual as well as for the masses.

III

The sharply defined line of demarcation between belletristic and journalistic writers, observed nowadays in Western Europe, is not so strictly adhered to in Russia because of the polemical nature of its literature. Both forms of expression are often combined in making pathways for new ideas, as they were in Germany at the time when Lessing guided the people through the medium of theater reviews, drama, philosophical-theological treatises, or essays on aesthetics. But whereas it was Lessing's tragic fate to remain alone and misunderstood all his life, in Russia a great number of outstanding talents in various fields of literature worked successfully as advocates of a liberal view of the world.

Alexander von Herzen, famous as a novelist, was also a gifted journalist. He was able, during the eighteen-fifties and sixties, to arouse the entire intelligentsia of Russia with his *Bell*, a magazine he published abroad. Possessed with the same fighting spirit and alertness, the old Hegelian Chernyshevsky was equally at home in journalistic polemics, treatises on philosophy and national economy, and political novels. Both Belinsky and Dobrolyubov used literary criticism as an excellent weapon to fight backwardness and to propagate systematically a progressive ideology. They were succeeded by the brilliant Mikhaylovsky, who for several decades governed public opinion and was also influential in Korolenko's development. Besides his novels, short stories, and dramas, Tolstoy, too, availed himself of polemical pamphlets and moralizing fairy tales. Korolenko, on his part, constantly exchanged the palette and brush of the artist for the sword of the journalist in order to work directly on social problems of the day.

Some of the features of old czarist Russia were chronic famine, drunkenness, illiteracy, and a deficit in the budget. As a result of the ill-conceived peasant reform introduced after the abolition of serfdom, stifling taxes combined with the utmost backwardness in agricultural practices afflicted the peasants with crop failure regularly during the entire eighth decade. The year 1891 saw the climax: in twenty provinces an exceptionally severe drought was followed by a crop failure resulting in a famine of truly biblical dimensions.

An offical inquiry to determine the extent of the losses yielded more than seven hundred answers from all parts of the country, among which was the following description from the pen of a simple parson:

"For the last three years, bad harvests have been sneaking up on us and one misfortune after another plagues the peasants. There is the insect pest. Grasshoppers eat up the grain, worms nibble on it, and bugs do away with the rest. The harvest has been destroyed in the fields and the seeds have been parched in the ground; the barns are empty and there is no bread. The animals groan and collapse, cattle move meekly, and the sheep perish from thirst and want of fodder. . . . Millions of trees and thousands of farmhouses have become a prey to flames. A wall of fire and smoke surrounded us. . . . It is written by the prophet Zephania: 'I will destroy everything from the face of the earth, saith the Lord, man, cattle, and wild beasts, the birds and the fish.

"How many of the feathered ones have perished in the forest fires, how many fish in the shallow waters! . . . The elk has fled from our woods, the raccoon and the squirrel have died. Heaven has become barren and hard as ore; no dew falls, only drought and fire. The fruit trees have withered away and so also the grass and the flowers. No raspberries ripen any more, there are no blackberries, blueberries, or whortleberries far and wide; bogs and swamps have burned out. . . . Where are you, green of the forests, oh delicious air, balsam scent of the firs that gave relief to the ailing? All is gone!"

The writer, as an experienced Russian subject, devoutly asked at the end of his letter that he not be held "responsible for the above description." His apprehension was not unfounded, because a powerful nobility declared the famine, unbelievable as it may seem, to be a malevolent invention of "provocateurs," and that any sort of help would be superfluous.

In consequence a war flared up between the reactionary groups and the progressive intelligentsia. Russian society was gripped with excitement; writers sounded the alarm. Relief committees were established on a grand scale; doctors, writers, students, teachers, and women of intellectual pursuits rushed by the hundreds into the country to nurse the sick, to set up feeding stations, to distribute seeds, and to organize the purchase of grain at low prices.

All this, however, was not easy. All the disorder, all the time-honored mismanagement of a country ruled by bureaucrats and the army came to the fore. There was rivalry and antagonism between state and county administrations, between government and rural offices, between the village scribes and the peasants. Added to this, the chaos of ideas, demands, and expectations of the peasants themselves, their distrust of city people, the differences existing between the rich kulaks and the impoverished peasants — everything conspired to erect thousands of barriers and obstacles in the way of those who had come to help. No wonder they were driven to despair. All the numerous local abuses and suppressions with which the daily life of the peasants had been normally confronted, all the absurdities and contradictions of the bureaucracy came to light. The fight against hunger, in itself merely a simple charitable act, changed at once into a struggle against the social and political conditions of the absolutist regime.

Korolenko, like Tolstoy, headed the progressive groups and devoted to this cause not only his writings but his whole personality. In the spring of 1892, he went to a district of the province Nizhni Novgorod, the wasp's nest of the reactionary nobility, in order to organize soup kitchens in the stricken villages. Although completely unacquainted with local circumstances, he soon learned every detail and began a tenacious struggle against the thousands of obstacles that barred his way. He spent four months in this area, wandering from one village to another, from one government office to another. After the day's work, he wrote in his notebooks in old farmhouses far into the night by the dim light of a smoky lamp, and at the same time conducted, in the newspapers of the capital, a vigorous campaign against backwardness. His diary, which became an immortal monument of the czarist regime, presents a gruesome picture of the entire Golgotha of the Russian village with its begging children, silent mothers steeped in misery, wailing old men, sickness and hopelessness.

Famine was followed immediately by the second of the apocalyptic horsemen, the plague. It came from Persia in 1893, covered the lowlands of the Volga and crept up the river, spreading its deadly vapors over starved and paralyzed villages. The new enemy created a peculiar reaction among the representatives of the government which, bordering on the ridiculous, is nevertheless the bitter truth. The governor of Baku fled into the mountains when the plague broke out, the governor of Saratov kept in hiding on a riverboat during the ensuing uprisings. The governor of Astrakhan, however, took the prize: fearing that ships on their way from Persia and the Caucasus might bring the plague with them, he ordered patrol boats to the Caspian Sea to bar the entrance of the Volga to all water traffic. But he forgot to supply bread and drinking water for those thus quarantined. More than four hundred steamboats and barges were intercepted, and ten thousand people, healthy and sick, were destined to die of hunger, thirst, and the plague. Finally, a boat came down the Volga toward Astrakhan, a messenger of governmental thoughtfulness. The eyes of the dying looked with new hope to the rescue ship. Its cargo was coffins.

The people's wrath burst forth like a thunderstorm. News about the blockade and the sufferings of the quarantined prisoners swept like fire up the Volga river, followed by the cry of despair that the government was intentionally helping to spread the plague in order to diminish its population. The first victims of the "plauge uprising" were the Samaritans, those self-sacrificing men and women who had heroically rushed to the stricken areas to nurse the sick and administer precautions to safeguard the healthy. Hospital barracks went up in flames; doctors and nurses were slain. Afterwards, there was the usual procedure—penalty expeditions, bloodshed, martial law, and executions. In Saratov alone twenty death sentences were pronounced. The beautiful country of the Volga once more was changed into a Dantean Inferno.

To bring sense and enlightenment into this bloody chaos required a personality of the highest integrity and a profound understanding of the peasants and their distress. Next to Tolstoy, nobody in Russia was better suited to accomplish the task than Korolenko. One of the first on the spot, he exposed those who were in truth responsible for the uprisings — the government officials. Recording his observations, he once again presented to the public a stirring document, equally great in its historic as well as artistic value — *The Cholera Quarantine.*

In old Russia, the death penalty for ordinary crimes had long been abolished. Normally, an execution was an honor reserved for political offenses. In the late seventies, however, death penalties were in favor again, especially at the beginning of the terrorist movement. After the assassination of Czar Alexander II, the government did not hesitate to sentence even women to the gallows, as in the case of the famous Sophie Perovskaya, and later Hessa Helfman. These executions were exceptional, but they left a deep impression upon the people. Again, horror swept over the country when four soldiers of the "Penalty Battalion" were executed for murdering their sergeant who had tortured them. Even in the subjugated and depressed atmosphere of these years, public opinion could be shocked by such measures.

This situation changed with the Revolution of 1905. In 1907, after the absolutist powers had regained the upper hand, a bloody revenge set in. Military tribunals convened day and night; the gallows found no rest. The "assassins," men who had taken part in armed revolts, but especially so-called expropriators — half-grown boys — were executed by the hundreds. It was done in a most haphazard way and with very little observance of the formalities. The hangmen were inexperienced, the ropes defective, the gallows improvised in a most fantastic manner. The counter-revolution indulged in orgies.

It was at this time that Korolenko raised his voice in a strong protest against the triumphant reaction. A series of articles, published in 1909 in pamphlet form with the title *An Ordinary Occurrence,* is characteristic of him. Like his articles on the famine and the plague, it contains no set phrases, no hollow pathos. Simplicity and a matter-of-factness prevail throughout. Actual reports, letters of the executed, and impressions of prisoners make up this booklet. And yet it is outstanding in its compassion for human suffering and its understanding of the tortured heart. Exposing the crimes of society, which are contained in every death sentence, this little work, full of warmth and highest ethics, became a most stirring accusation.

Tolstoy, then eighty-two years old, wrote to Korolenko, when still strongly impressed by the pamphlet: "Your work on the death penalty has just been read to me and, though I tried, I could not hold back my tears. I find no words to express my gratitude and love for a work which is equally excellent in expression, thought, and feeling. It must be printed and distributed in millions of copies. No Duma speeches, no dissertations, dramas, or novels could produce such good results as this work.

"It is so very effective because it arouses such intense compassion for the victims of human insanity that one is ready to forgive those victims no matter what they might have done. However, even if one would try, it is not possible to forgive those responsible for such horrors. With amazement we learn of their conceit and self-delusion, of the senselessness of their actions, because you are making it quite clear that all these pitiful cruelties effected only the opposite of what had been intended. Aside from all this, there is one more thought your work had made me strongly aware of— a feeling of pity not only for the murdered but also for those poor, misguided and deceived people, the prison wardens, hangmen, and soldiers, who committed the atrocities without knowing what they were doing.

"There is only one satisfaction to note: that a book like yours will unite a great number of still unaffected and eager people into a group that strives for the highest ideals of virtue and truth, an inspired group which, in spite of its enemies, will shed an ever growing light."

About fifteen years ago, in 1903, a German daily paper sent out a questionnaire regarding the death penalty to many eminent representatives of the arts and sciences. They were the most brilliant names in literature and jurisprudence, the flower of intelligence in the land of thinkers and poets, and all of them spoke fervently in favor of the death penalty. To any thinking observer this was one of the many symptoms of the things to come in Germany during the world war.

It is one of the features of modern civilization that the mass of people, whenever the shoe pinches for one reason or another, make a scapegoat of members of another race, religion, or color in order to release its pent-up ill temper. It is then able to return refreshed to the regular daily life. It is understood that those best suited to serve as scapegoats are national minorities that have previously been socially neglected and mistreated. And just because of their weakness and the precedent of mistreatment, further cruelties are easily administered without fear of reproach. In the United States it is the Negro who is discriminated against and persecuted. In Western Europe this role has often been forced on the Italian.

It was around the turn of the century, in the proletarian section of Zurich, in Aussersihl, that a pogrom flared up against the

Italians in the wake of the murder of a child. In France, the name of the town Aiguesmortes recalls a memorable riot of workers who, embittered by the frugal habits of the Italian migratory workers which led to general wage-cutting, tried to teach them the need for a better standard of living in the style of their ancestor, the *Homo hauseri* of Dordogne. With the outbreak of the world war, traditions of the Neanderthal man unexpectedly became very popular. In the land of thinkers and poets, the "great time" was accompanied by a sudden return to the instincts of the contemporaries of the mammoth, the cave bear, and the wooly rhinoceros.

To be sure, the Russia of the czars was not as yet so highly civilized a state, and the mistreatment of foreigners and other public activities were not expressions of the psyche of the people. It was, rather, the monopoly of the government, fostered and organized at the proper moment by state institutions and encouraged with the help of government vodka.

There was, for example, the famous trial of the "Multan Votiaks" that took place in the nineties. Seven Votiak peasants from the village of Great Multan in the province of Vyatka, half heathens and savages, had been accused of a ritual murder and thrown into jail. This so-called ritual murder trial was, of course, only a small and casual incident of the government policy, which tried to change the depressed mood of the hungry and enslaved masses by offering them a little diversion. But here again, the Russian intelligentsia, with Korolenko in the lead once more, took up the cause of the half-savage Votiaks. Korolenko eagerly threw himself into the fight, unraveling the maze of misunderstandings and deceit. He worked patiently and with an infallible instinct for finding the truth, which reminds one of Jaures in the Dreyfus case. He mobilized the press and public opinion, obtained a resumption of the trial, and by personally taking over the defense, finally won an acquittal.

In Eastern Europe the subject most preferred for diverting the people's bad disposition has always been the Jews, and it is questionable whether they have yet played their role to the end. The circumstances under which the last public scandal — the famous Beyliss trial — took place was definitely still in style. This Jewish ritual murder case in 1913 was, so to speak, the last performance of a despotic government on its way out. One could call it the "necklace affair" of the Russian *ancien regime*. As a belated follow-up to the dark days of the 1907-1911 counterrevolution, and at the same time as a symbolic forerunner of the world war, this ritual murder case of Kishinev immediately became the center of public interest. The progressive intelligentsia in Russia identified itself with the cause of the Jewish butcher from Kishinev. The trial turned into a battlefield between the progressive and the reactionary camps of Russia. The shrewdest lawyers and best journalists gave their services to this cause. Needless to say, Korolenko, too, was one of the leaders of the fight. Thus shortly before the bloody curtain of world war was to be raised, Russian reaction suffered one more crushing moral defeat. Under the onslaught of the oppositional intelligentsia, the the murder indictment collapsed. There was revealed also at the same time the whole hypocrisy of the czarist regime, which, already dead and rotten internally, was only waiting for the *coup de grace* to be administered by the movement for freedom.

During the eighties, after the assassination of Alexander II, a period of paralyzing hopelessness enveloped Russia. The liberal reforms of the sixties with regard to the judiciary and to rural self-administration were everywhere repealed. A deathlike silence prevailed during the reign of Alexander III. Discouraged by both the failure to realize peaceful reforms and the apparent ineffectiveness of the revolutionary movement, the Russian people were completely overcome with depression and resignation.

In this atmosphere of apathy and despondency, the Russian intelligentsia began to develop such metaphysical-mystical tendencies as were represented by Soloviev's philosophy. Nietzsche's influence was clearly noticeable. In literature the pessimistic undertones of Garshin's novels and Nadson's poetry predominated. Fully in accord with the prevailing spirit was Dostoyevsky's mysticism, as expressed in *The Brothers Karamazov*, and also in Tolstoy's ascetic doctrines. The idea of "nonresistance to evil," the repudiation of violence in the struggle against powerful reaction, which was now to be opposed by the "purified soul" of the individual, such theories of social passivity became a serious danger for the Russian intelligentsia of the eighties — the more so since it was presented by such captivating means as Tolstoy's literary genius and moral authority.

Mikhaylovsky, the spiritual leader of the People's Will organization, directed an extremely angry polemic against Tolstoy. Korolenko, too, came to the fore. He, the tender poet who never could forget an incident of his childhood, be it a rustling forest, a walk in the evening through the quiet fields, or the memory of a landscape in its manifold lights and moods, Korolenko, who fundamentally despised all politics, now raised his voice with determination, preaching aggressive, saber-sharp hatred and belligerent opposition. He replied to Tolstoy's legends, parables, and stories in the style of the gospel with the *Legend of Florus*.

The Romans governed Judea with fire and sword, exploiting land and people. The people moaned and bent under the hated yoke. Stirred by the sight of his suffering people, Menachem the

Wise, son of Yehuda, appealed to the heroic traditions of their forebears and preached rebellion against the Romans, a "holy war." But then up spoke the sect of the gentle Sossaians (who, like Tolstoy, repudiated all violence and saw a solution only in the purification of the soul, in isolation and self-denial). "You are sowing great misery when you call men to battle," they said to Menachem. "If a city is besieged and shows resistance, the enemy will spare the lives of the humble, but will put to death all those who are defiant. We teach the people to be submissive, so that they may be saved from destruction. . . . One cannot dry water with water nor quench fire with fire. Therefore, violence will not be overcome with violence, it is evil itself."

To which Menachem answered unswervingly: "Violence is neither good nor evil, it is violence. Good or evil is only its application. The violence of the arm is evil when it is lifted to rob or suppress the weak; but if it is lifted for work or in defense of thy neighbor, then violence is welfare. It is true, one does not quench fire with fire nor dry water with water, but stone is shattered with stone and steel must be parried with steel, and violence with violence. Knoweth this: The power of the Romans is the fire but your humbleness is . . . wood. And the fire will not stop until it has eaten all the wood."

The *Legend* closes with Menachem's prayer: "O Adonai, Adonai! Let us never as long as we live fail the holy command: to fight against injustice. . . . Let us never speak these words: Save yourself and leave the weak to their destiny. . . . I too believe, O Adonai, that your kingdom will be on earth. Violence and suppression will disappear and the people will gather to celebrate the feast of brotherhood. And never again shall man's blood be shed by man's hand."

Like a refreshing breeze, this defiant creed stormed through the deep fog of indolence and mysticism. Korolenko was ready for the new historic "violence" in Russia which soon was to lift its beneficient arm, the arm to work and fight for liberty.

IV

Maxim Gorky's *My Childhood* is in many respects an interesting counterpart to Korolenko's *History of a Contemporary*. Artistically, they are poles apart. Korolenko, like his adored Turgenev, has an utterly lyrical nature, is a tender soul, a man of many moods. Gorky, in the Dostoyevsky tradition, has a profoundly dramatic view of life; he is a man of concentrated energy and action. Although Korolenko is strongly aware of all the dreadfulness of social life, he has Turgenev's capacity to present even the cruelest incidents in the mood of an ameliorating perspective, enveloped in the vapors of poetic vision and all charm of natural scenery. For Gorky as well as for Dostoyevsky, even sober everyday events are full of gruesome ghosts and torturing visions, presented in thoughts of merciless pungency, relentless, without perspective, and almost devoid of all natural scenery.

If, according to Ulrici, drama is the poetry of action, the dramatic element is positively evident in Dostoyevsky's novels. They are bursting with action, experience, and tension to such an extent that their complex and irritating compilations seem at times to crush the epic element of the novel, to break through its boundaries at any moment. After reading with breathless anxiety one or two of his voluminous books, it seems incredible that one has lived through the events of only two or three days. It is equally characteristic of Dostoyevsky's dramatic aptitude to present both the main problem of the plot and the great conflicts which lead to the climax at the beginning of the novel. The preliminaries of the story, its slow development, the reader does not experience directly. It is left to him to deduce them from the action in retrospect. Gorky, too, even in portraying complete inertia, the bankruptcy of human energy, as he did in *The Lower Depths*, chooses the drama as his medium and actually succeeds in putting life into the pale countenance of his types.

Korolenko and Gorky not only represent two literary personalities but also two generations of Russian literature and freedom-loving ideology. Korolenko's interest still centers around the peasant; Gorky, enthusiastic pupil of German scientific socialism, is interested in city proletarians and in their shadows, the lumpenproletariat. Whereas nature is the normal setting for Korolenko's stories, for Gorky it is the workshop, the garret, and the flophouse.

The key to both artists' personalities is the fundamental difference in their backgrounds. Korolenko grew up in comfortable, middle-class surroundings. His childhood provided him with the normal feeling that the world and all that is in it is solid and steady, which is so characteristic of all happy children. Gorky, partly rooted in the petty bourgeoisie and partly in the lumpenproletariat, grew up in a truly Dostoyevskian atmosphere of horror, crime, and sudden outbreaks of human passion. As a child, he already behaved like a little hunted wolf baring his sharp teeth to fate. His youth, full of deprivations, insults, and oppression, of uncertainty and abuse, was spent close to the scum of society and embraced all the typical features of the life of the modern proletariat. Only those who have read Gorky's autobiography are able to conceive fully his amazing rise from the depths of society to the sunny heights of modern education, ingenious artistry, and an outlook on life based on science. The vicissitudes of his life are symbolic of the Russian proletariat

363

as a class, which in the remarkably short time of two decades has also worked its way up from the uncultured, uncouth, and difficult life under the czar through the harsh school of struggles to historical actions. This is surely quite inconceivable to all the culture-philistines who think that proper street illumination, trains that run on time, clean collars, and the industrious clatter of the parliamentary mills stand for political freedom.

The great charm of Korolenko's poetic writing also constitutes its limitations. He lives wholly in the present, in the happenings, of the moment, in sensual impressions. His stories are like a bouquet of freshly gathered field flowers. But time is hard on their gay colors, their delicate fragrance. The Russia Korolenko describes no longer exists; it is the Russia of yesterday. The tender and poetic mood which envelops his land and his people is gone. A decade and a half ago it made room for the tragic and thunder-laden atmosphere of the Gorkys and their like, the screeching storm birds of the revolution. It was replaced in Korolenko himself by a new belligerency. In him, as in Tolstoy, the social fighter triumphed in the end; the great fellow citizen succeeded the poet and dreamer. When in the eighties Tolstoy began to preach his moral gospel in a new literary form as folklore, Turgenev wrote letters imploring the wise man of Yasnaya Polyana in the name of the fatherland to turn back to the realm of pure art. The friends of Korolenko, too, grieved when he abandoned his fragrant poetry and threw himself eagerly into journalism. But the spirit of Russian literature, the feeling of social responsibility, proved to be stronger in this richly endowed poet than his love for nature, his longing for an unhampered life of wandering, and his poetic desires.

Carried along by the rising revolutionary flood at the turn of the century, the poet in him was slowly silenced while he unsheathed his sword as a fighter for liberty, as the spiritual center of the opposition movement of the Russian intellectuals. The *History of a Contemporary*, published in his review, *The Russian Treasury*, is the last product of his genius, only half poetry but wholly the truth, like everything else in Korolenko's life.

THE RUSSIAN REVOLUTION

In February 1917 the Russian Revolution began with the over-throw of czarism and the establishment of a bourgeois democracy. But the social contradictions in Russia were so acute that no capitalist government could hope to solve them. Under Lenin and Trotsky's leadership the Bolshevik Party relentlessly explained the contradictions and errors of the liberal bourgeois government to the masses and pointed to the only solution: the socialist revolution.

In October the Bolsheviks took state power and proceeded to meet the demands of the peasants, soldiers and workers for land, peace, and bread. They were rapidly plunged into a bitter and devastating struggle for the survival of the revolution. They had to fight off the counterrevolutionary White Army backed by the invading troops of fourteen nations.

Rosa Luxemburg, still securely locked in her prison cell in Germany, watched the unfolding revolution with tremendous enthusiasm — and with fear that it could not survive the onslaught of its enemies if it had to hold out too long unaided by revolution in Western Europe, especially Germany. Everything she wrote about Russia from February 1917 to November 1918 was aimed at drawing the lessons of the Russian Revolution and mobilizing the German workers, urging them on to action in their own behalf and in behalf of the struggling vanguard of the world revolution, the Russian proletariat.

She minced no words in her condemnation of the "Russian Kautskys" — the Mensheviks — who declared Russia was not capable of progressing to the socialist revolution and sabotaged all efforts to move forward. And her praise of the Bolsheviks, her recognition of the world historic task they had accomplished, was unreserved. When she concludes her pamphlet by saying "the future everywhere belongs to 'bolshevism,'" she means exactly that.

Rosa Luxemburg recognized clearly the essential greatness of

365

the Russian Revolution, and recognized also that the course of the revolution could have been far different had the German workers come to the aid of their Russian comrades. At the same time, she was highly critical of some of the policies of the Bolshevik government—as she outlines in her unfinished rough draft on "The Russian Revolution."

The issues she raises and the circumstances surrounding the pamphlet are discussed at length in the introduction to this collection, but a few facts should be noted here.

As we know, the pamphlet was written in prison where access to information about current events was severely restricted. Even outside the prison walls the German government had no interest in providing the increasingly rebellious German workers with a day-by-day news account of how to make a revolution. The leaders of the Spartacus League who were not in jail adopted a policy of extreme caution toward any criticisms of the Bolsheviks, because of the difficulty of obtaining unbiased, accurate information, and because their primary responsibility was to defend the Russian Revolution and explain its significance to the German workers. That was essential, and they wanted no ambiguity as to who in Germany supported the Russian Revolution.

Articles criticizing some of the Bolshevik policies did appear in the Spartacus letters, but one of the articles written in prison by Rosa Luxemburg was turned down by the editors, and Paul Levi made a special trip to Breslau to dissuade her from publishing it. She agreed, because Levi convinced her that she was providing weapons for the enemies of the Russian Revolution by adding her moral authority to attacks on the Bolshevik policies, especially the conclusion of the treaty of Brest-Litovsk.

After Levi left she drafted her pamphlet on the Russian Revolution and sent it to him with a note saying "I am writing this only for you and if I can convince *you*, then the effort isn't wasted." She never published, or tried to publish it in her lifetime, and it was only after Levi was expelled from the German Communist Party that he published it on his own in 1922. On some of the questions, though not all, Rosa Luxemburg definitely changed her mind during the last few months of her life.

The chapter on the "Nationalities Question" provides one of her clearest and sharpest attacks on the Bolshevik support for the right of nations to self-determination.

The translation is by Bertram D. Wolfe and was first printed by the Workers Age Publishers in 1940. In 1961 it was issued by Ann Arbor Paperbacks (University of Michigan Press). In a number of places the draft consists only of rough notes which were never fully elaborated, but in most cases the author's meaning is clear.

I. Fundamental Significance of the Russian Revolution

The Russian Revolution is the mightiest event of the World War. Its outbreak, its unexampled radicalism, its enduring consequences, constitute the clearest condemnation of the lying phrases which official social democracy so zealously supplied at the beginning of the war as an ideological cover for German imperialism's campaign of conquest. I refer to the phrases concerning the mission of German bayonets, which were to overthrow Russian czarism and free its oppressed peoples.

The mighty sweep of the revolution in Russia, the profound results which have transformed all class relationships, raised all social and economic problems, and, with the fatality of their own inner logic developed consistently from the first phase of the bourgeois republic to ever more advanced stages, finally reducing the fall of czarism to the status of a mere minor episode — all these things show as plain as day that the freeing of Russia was not an achievement of the war and the military defeat of czarism, not some service of "German bayonets in German fists," as *Neue Zeit* under Kautsky's editorship once promised in an editorial. They show, on the contrary, that the freeing of Russia had its roots deep in the soil of its own land and was fully matured internally. The military adventure of German imperialism under the ideological blessing of German social democracy did not bring about the revolution in Russia but only served to interrupt it at first, to postpone it for a while after its first stormy rising tide in the years 1911-13, and then, after its outbreak, created for it the most difficult and abnormal conditions.

Moreover, for every thinking observer, these developments are a decisive refutation of the doctrinaire theory which Kautsky shared with the government social democrats, according to which Russia, as an economically backward and predominantly agrarian land, was supposed not to be ripe for social revolution and proletarian dictatorship. This theory, which regards only a *bourgeois* revolution as feasible in Russia, is also the theory of the opportunist wing of the Russian labor movement, of the so-called Mensheviks, under the experienced leadership of Axelrod and Dan. And from this conception follow the tactics of the coalition of the socialists in Russia with bourgeois liberalism. On this basic conception of the Russian Revolution, from which follow automatically their detailed positions on questions of tactics, both the Russian and the German opportunists find themselves in agreement with the German government socialists. According to the opinion of all three, the Russian Revolution should have called a halt at the stage which German imperialism in its conduct of the war

367

had set as its noble task, according to the mythology of the German social democracy, i.e., it should have stopped with the overthrow of czarism. According to this view, if the revolution has gone beyond that point and has set as its task the dictatorship of the proletariat, this is simply a mistake of the radical wing of the Russian labor movement, the Bolsheviks. And all difficulties which the revolution has met with in its further course, and all disorders it has suffered, are pictured as purely a result of this fateful error.

Theoretically, this doctrine (recommended as the fruit of "Marxist thinking" by the *Vorwaerts* of Stampfer and by Kautsky alike) follows from the original "Marxist" discovery that the socialist revolution is a national and, so to speak, a domestic affair in each modern country taken by itself. Of course, in the blue mists of abstract formulas, a Kautsky knows very well how to trace the worldwide economic connections of capital which make of all modern countries a single integrated organism. The problems of the Russian Revolution, moreover—since it is a product of international developments plus the agrarian question—cannot possibly be solved within the limits of bourgeois society.

Practically, this same doctrine represents an attempt to get rid of any responsibility for the course of the Russian Revolution, so far as that responsibility concerns the international, and especially the German, proletariat, and to deny the international connections of this revolution. It is not Russia's unripeness which has been proved by the events of the war and the Russian Revolution, but the unripeness of the German proletariat for the fulfillment of its historic tasks. And to make this fully clear is the first task of a critical examination of the Russian Revolution.

The fate of the revolution in Russia depended fully upon international events. That the Bolsheviks have based their policy entirely upon the world proletarian revolution is the clearest proof of their political farsightedness and firmness of principle and of the bold scope of their policies. In it is visible the mighty advance which capitalist development has made in the last decade. The Revolution of 1905-07 roused only a faint echo in Europe. Therefore, it had to remain a mere opening chapter. Continuation and conclusion were tied up with the further development of Europe.

Clearly, not uncritical apologetics but penetrating and thoughtful criticism is alone capable of bringing out the treasures of experiences and teachings. Dealing as we are with the very first experiment in proletarian dictatorship in world history (and one taking place at that under the hardest conceivable conditions, in the midst of the worldwide conflagration and chaos of the imperialist mass slaughter, caught in the coils of the most reactionary military power in Europe, and accompanied by the completest failure on the part of the international working class), it would be a crazy idea to think that every last thing done or left undone in an experiment with the dictatorship of the proletariat under such abnormal conditions represented the very pinnacle of perfection. On the contrary, elementary conceptions of socialist politics and an insight into their historically necessary prerequisites force us to understand that under such fatal conditions even the most gigantic idealism and the most storm-tested revolutionary enemy are incapable of realizing democracy and socialism but only distorted attempts at either.

To make this stand out clearly in all its fundamental aspects and consequences is the elementary duty of the socialists of all countries; for only on the background of this bitter knowledge can we measure the enormous magnitude of the responsibility of the international proletariat itself for the fate of the Russian Revolution. Furthermore, it is only on this basis that the decisive importance of the resolute international action of the proletarian revolution can become effective, without which action as its necessary support, even the greatest energy and the greatest sacrifices of the proletariat in a single country must inevitably become tangled in a maze of contradiction and blunders.

There is no doubt either that the wise heads at the helm of the Russian Revolution, that Lenin and Trotsky on their thorny path beset by traps of all kinds, have taken many a decisive step only with the greatest inner hesitation and with most violent inner opposition. And surely nothing can be farther from their thoughts than to believe that all the things they have done or left undone under the conditions of bitter compulsion and necessity in the midst of the roaring whirlpool of events, should be regarded by the International as a shining example of socialist policy toward which only uncritical admiration and zealous imitation are in order.

It would be no less wrong to fear that a critical examination of the road so far taken by the Russian Revolution would serve to weaken the respect for and the attractive power of the example of the Russian Revolution, which alone can overcome the fatal inertia of the German masses. Nothing is farther from the truth. An awakening of the revolutionary energy of the working class in Germany can never again be called forth in the spirit of the guardianship methods of the German social democracy of late-lamented memory. It can never again be conjured forth by any spotless authority, be it that of our own "higher committees" or that of "the Russian example." Not by the creation of a revolutionary hurrah-spirit, but quite the contrary: only by an insight into all the fearful seriousness, all the complexity of the tasks involved, only as a result of political maturity and independence of spirit, only as a result of a capacity for critical judgment on the part of the masses, which capacity was systematically killed by the social democracy for decades under various pretexts, only thus can the genuine capacity for historical action be born in the German proletariat. To concern oneself with a critical analysis of the Russian Revolution in all its historical connections is the best training for the German and the international working class for the tasks which confront them as an outgrowth of the present situation.

The first period of the Russian Revolution, from its beginning in March to the October Revolution, corresponds exactly in its general outlines to the course of development of both the Great English Revolution and the Great French Revolution. It is the typical course of every first general reckoning of the revolutionary forces begotten within the womb of bourgeois society.

Its development moves naturally in an ascending line: from moderate beginnings to ever-greater radicalization of aims and, parallel with that, from a coalition of classes and parties to the sole rule of the radical party.

At the outset in March 1917, the "Cadets," that is the liberal bourgeoisie, stood at the head of the revolution. The first general rising of the revolutionary tide swept every one and everything along with it. The Fourth Duma, ultrareactionary product of the ultrareactionary four-class right of suffrage and arising out of the coup d'etat, was suddenly converted into an organ of the revolution. All bourgeois parties, even those of the nationalistic right, suddenly formed a phalanx against absolutism. The latter fell at the first attack almost without a struggle, like an organ that had died and needed only to be touched to drop off. The brief effort, too, of the liberal bourgeoisie to save at least the throne and the dynasty collapsed within a few hours. The sweeping march of events leaped in days and hours over distances that formerly, in France, took decades to traverse. In this, it became clear that Russia was realizing the result of a century of European development, and above all, that the Revolution of 1917 was a direct continuation of that of 1905-07, and not a gift of the German "liberator." The movement of March 1917 linked itself directly onto the point where, ten years earlier, its work had broken off. The democratic republic was the complete, internally ripened product of the very first onset of the revolution.

Now, however, began the second and more difficult task. From the very first moment, the driving force of the revolution was the mass of the urban proletariat. However, its demands did not limit themselves to the realization of political democracy but were concerned with the burning question of international policy — immediate peace. At the same time, the revolution embraced the mass of the army, which raised the same demand for immediate peace, and the mass of the peasants, who pushed the agrarian question into the foreground, that agrarian question which since 1905 had been the very axis of the revolution. Immediate peace and land—from these two aims the internal split in the revolutionary phalanx followed inevitably. The demand for immediate peace was in most irreconcilable opposition to the imperialist tendencies of the liberal bourgeoisie for whom Miliukov was the spokesman. On the other hand, the land question was a terrifying specter for the other wing of the bourgeoisie, the rural landowners. And, in addition, it represented an attack on the sacred principle of private property in general, a touchy point for the entire propertied class.

Thus, on the very day after the first victories of the revolution, there began an inner struggle within it over the two burning questions—peace and land. The liberal bourgeoisie entered upon the tactics of dragging out things and evading them. The laboring masses, the army, the peasantry, pressed forward ever more impetuously. There can be no doubt that with the questions of peace and land, the fate of the political democracy of the republic was linked up. The bourgeois classes, carried away by the first stormy wave of the revolution, had permitted themselves to be dragged along to the point of republican government. Now they began to seek a base of support in the rear and silently to organize a counterrevolution. The Kaledin Cossack campaign against Petersburg was a clear expression of this tendency. Had the attack been successful, then not only the fate of the peace and land questions would have been sealed, but the fate of the republic as well. Military dictatorship, a reign of terror against the proletariat, and then return to monarchy, would have been the inevitable results.

From this we can judge the utopian and fundamentally reactionary character of the tactics by which the Russian "Kautskyans" or Mensheviks permitted themselves to be guided. Hardened in their addiction to the myth of the bourgeois character of the Russian Revolution—for the time being, you see, Russia is not supposed to be ripe for the social revolution!—they clung desperately to a coalition with the bourgeois liberals. But this means a union of elements which had been split by the natural internal development of the revolution and had come into the sharpest conflict with each other. The Axelrods and Dans wanted to collaborate at all costs with those classes and parties from which came the greatest threat of danger to the revolution and to its first conquest, democracy.

It is especially astonishing to observe how this industrious man (Kautsky), by his tireless labor of peaceful and methodical writing during the four years of the World War, has torn one hole after another in the fabric of socialism. It is a labor from which socialism emerges riddled like a sieve, without a whole spot left in it. The uncritical indifference with which his followers regard this industrious labor of their official theoretician and swallow each of his new discoveries without so much as batting an eyelash, finds its only counterpart in the indifference with which the followers of Scheidemann and Co. look on while the latter punch socialism full of holes in practice. Indeed, the two labors completely supplement each other. Since the outbreak of the war, Kautsky, the official guardian of the temple of Marxism, has really only been doing in theory the same things which the Scheidemanns have been doing in practice, namely: (1) the International an instrument of peace; (2) disarmament, the league of nations and nationalism; and finally (3) democracy *not* socialism.

In this situation, the Bolshevik tendency performs the historic service of having proclaimed from the very beginning, and having followed with iron consistency, those tactics which alone could save democracy and drive the revolution ahead. All power exclusively in the hands of the worker and peasant masses, in the hands of the soviets — this was indeed the only way out of the difficulty into which the revolution had gotten; this was the sword stroke with which they cut the Gordian knot, freed the revolution from a narrow blind alley and opened up for it an untrammeled path into the free and open fields.

The party of Lenin was thus the only one in Russia which grasped the true interest of the revolution in that first period. It was the element that drove the revolution forward, and, thus it was the only party which really carried on a socialist policy.

It is this which makes clear, too, why it was that the Bolsheviks, though they were at the beginning of the revolution a persecuted, slandered and hunted minority attacked on all sides, arrived within the shortest time to the head of the revolution and were able to bring under their banner all the genuine masses of the people: the urban proletariat, the army, the peasants, as well as the revolutionary elements of democracy, the left wing of the Socialist Revolutionaries.

The real situation in which the Russian Revolution found itself, narrowed down in a few months to the alternative: victory of the counterrevolution or dictatorship of the proletariat — Kaledin or Lenin. Such was the objective situation, just as it quickly presents itself in every revolution after the first intoxication is over, and as it presented itself in Russia as a result of the concrete, burning questions of peace and land, for which there was no solution within the framework of bourgeois revolution.

In this, the Russian Revolution has but confirmed the basic lesson of every great revolution, the law of its being, which decrees: either the revolution must advance at a rapid, stormy and resolute tempo, break down all barriers with an iron hand and place its goals ever farther ahead, or it is quite soon thrown backward behind its feeble point of departure and suppressed by counterrevolution. To stand still, to mark time on one spot, to be contented with the first goal it happens to reach, is never possible in revolution. And he who tries to apply the homemade wisdom derived from parliamentary battles between frogs and mice to the field of revolutionary tactics only shows thereby that the very psychology and laws of existence of revolution are alien to him and that all historical experience is to him a book sealed with seven seals.

Take the course of the English Revolution from its onset in 1642. There the logic of things made it necessary that the first feeble vacillations of the Presbyterians, whose leaders deliberately evaded a decisive battle with Charles I and victory over him, should inevitably be replaced by the Independents, who drove them out of Parliament and seized the power for themselves. And that in the same way, within the army of the Independents, the lower petty bourgeois mass of the soldiers, the Lilburnian "Levellers" constituted the driving force of the entire Independent movement; just as, finally, the proletarian elements within the mass of the soldiers, the elements that went farthest in their aspirations for social revolution and who found their expression in the Digger movement, constituted in their turn the leaven of the democratic party of the "Levellers."

Without the moral influence of the revolutionary proletarian elements on the general mass of the soldiers, without the pressure of the democratic mass of the soldiers upon the bourgeois upper layers of the party of the Independents, there would have been no "purge" of the Long Parliament of its Presbyterians, nor any victorious ending to the war with the army of the Cavaliers and Scots, nor any trial and execution of Charles I, nor any abolition of the House of Lords and proclamation of a republic.

And what happened in the Great French Revolution? Here, after four years of struggle, the seizure of power by the Jacobins proved to be the only means of saving the conquests of the revolution, of achieving a republic, of smashing feudalism, of organizing a revolutionary defense against inner as well as outer foes, of suppressing the conspiracies of counterrevolution and spreading the revolutionary wave from France to all Europe.

Kautsky and his Russian coreligionists, who wanted to see the Russian Revolution keep the "bourgeois character" of its first phase, are an exact counterpart of those German and English liberals of the preceding century who distinguished between the two well-known periods of the Great French Revolution: the "good"

373

revolution of the first Girondin phase and the "bad" one after the Jacobin uprising. The liberal shallowness of this conception of history, to be sure, doesn't care to understand that, without the uprising of the "immoderate" Jacobins, even the first, timid and halfhearted achievements of the Girondin phase would soon have been buried under the ruins of the revolution, and that the real alternative to Jacobin dictatorship — as the iron course of historical development posed the question in 1793 — was not "moderate" democracy, but . . . restoration of the Bourbons! The "golden mean" cannot be maintained in any revolution. The law of its nature demands a quick decision: either the locomotive drives forward full steam ahead to the most extreme point of the historical ascent, or it rolls back of its own weight again to the starting point at the bottom; and those who would keep it with their weak powers halfway up the hill, it but drags down with it irredeemably into the abyss.

Thus it is clear that in every revolution only that party is capable of seizing the leadership and power which has the courage to issue the appropriate watchwords for driving the revolution ahead, and the courage to draw all the necessary conclusions from the situation. This makes clear, too, the miserable role of the Russian Mensheviks, the Dans, Tseretellis, etc., who had enormous influence on the masses at the beginning, but, after their prolonged wavering and after they had fought with both hands and feet against taking over power and responsibility, were driven ignobly off the stage.

The party of Lenin was the only one which grasped the mandate and duty of a truly revolutionary party and which, by the slogan — "All power in the hands of the proletariat and peasantry" — insured the continued development of the revolution.

Thereby the Bolsheviks solved the famous problem of "winning a majority of the people," which problem has ever weighed on the German social democracy like a nightmare. As bred-in-the-bone disciples of parliamentary cretinism, these German social democrats have sought to apply to revolutions the homemade wisdom of the parliamentary nursery: in order to carry anything, you must first have a majority. The same, they say, applies to revolution: first let's become a "majority." The true dialectic of revolutions, however, stands this wisdom of parliamentary moles on its head: not through a majority to revolutionary tactics, but through revolutionary tactics to a majority — that is the way the road runs.

Only a party which knows how to lead, that is, to advance things, wins support in stormy times. The determination with which, at the decisive moment, Lenin and his comrades offered the only solution which could advance things ("all power in the

374

hands of the proletariat and peasantry"), transformed them almost overnight from a persecuted, slandered, outlawed minority whose leader had to hide like Marat in cellars, into the absolute master of the situation.

Moreover, the Bolsheviks immediately set as the aim of this seizure of power a complete, far-reaching revolutionary program: not the safeguarding of bourgeois democracy, but a dictatorship of the proletariat for the purpose of realizing socialism. Thereby they won for themselves the imperishable historic distinction of having for the first time proclaimed the final aim of socialism as the direct program of practical politics.

Whatever a party could offer of courage, revolutionary farsightedness and consistency in a historic hour, Lenin, Trotsky and the other comrades have given in good measure. All the revolutionary honor and capacity which western social democracy lacked were represented by the Bolsheviks. Their October uprising was not only the actual salvation of the Russian Revolution; it was also the salvation of the honor of international socialism.

II. The Bolshevik Land Policy

The Bolsheviks are the historic heirs of the English Levellers and the French Jacobins. But the concrete task which faced them after the seizure of power was incomparably more difficult than that of their historical predecessors. (Importance of the agrarian question. Even in 1905. Then, in the Third Duma, the right-wing peasants! The peasant question and defense, the army.)

Surely the solution of the problem by the direct, immediate seizure and distribution of the land by the peasants was the shortest, simplest, most clean-cut formula to achieve two diverse things: to break down large landownership, and immediately to bind the peasants to the revolutionary government. As a political measure to fortify the proletarian socialist government, it was an excellent tactical move. Unfortunately, however, it had two sides to it; and the reverse side consisted in the fact that the direct seizure of the land by the peasants has in general nothing at all in common with socialist economy.

A socialist transformation of economic relationships presupposes two things so far as agrarian relationships are concerned:

In the first place, only the nationalization of the large landed estates, as the technically most advanced and most concentrated means and method of agrarian production, can serve as the point of departure for the socialist mode of production on the land. Of course, it is not necessary to take away from the small peasant his parcel of land, and we can with confidence leave him to be won over voluntarily by the superior advantages of social production and to be persuaded of the advantages first of union in

375

cooperatives and then finally of inclusion in the general socialized economy as a whole. Still, every socialist economic reform on the land must obviously begin with large and medium landownership. Here the property right must first of all be turned over to the nation, or to the state, which, with a socialist government, amounts to the same thing; for it is this alone which affords the possibility of organizing agricultural production in accord with the requirements of interrelated, large-scale socialist production.

Moreover, in the second place, it is one of the prerequisites of this transformation that the separation between rural economy and industry, which is so characteristic of bourgeois society, should be ended in such a way as to bring about a mutual interpenetration and fusion of both, to clear the way for the planning of both agrarian and industrial production according to a unified point of view. Whatever individual form the practical economic arrangements may take—whether through urban communes, as some propose, or directed from a governmental center—in any event, it must be preceded by a reform introduced from the center, and that in turn must be preceded by the nationalization of the land. The nationalization of the large and middle-sized estates and the union of industry and agriculture—these are two fundamental requirements of any socialist economic reform, without which there is no socialism.

That the soviet government in Russia has not carried through these mighty reforms—who can reproach them for that! It would be a sorry jest indeed to demand or expect of Lenin and his comrades that, in the brief period of their rule, in the center of the gripping whirlpool of domestic and foreign struggles, ringed about by countless foes and opponents—to expect that under such circumstances they should already have solved, or even tackled, one of the most difficult tasks, indeed, we can safely say, *the* most difficult task of the socialist transformation of society! Even in the West, under the most favorable conditions, once we have come to power, we too will break many a tooth on this hard nut before we are out of the worst of the thousands of complicated difficulties of this gigantic task!

A socialist government which has come to power must in any event do one thing: it must take measures which lead in the direction of that fundamental prerequisite for a later socialist reform of agriculture; it must at least avoid everything which may bar the way to those measures.

Now the slogan launched by the Bolsheviks, immediate seizure and distribution of the land by the peasants, necessarily tended in the opposite direction. Not only is it not a socialist measure; it even cuts off the way to such measures; it piles up insurmountable obstacles to the socialist transformation of agrarian relations.

The seizure of the landed estates by the peasants according to the short and precise slogan of Lenin and his friends — *"Go and take the land for yourselves"*— simply led to the sudden, chaotic conversion of large landownership into peasant landownership. What was created is not social property but a new form of private property, namely, the breaking up of large estates into medium and small estates, or relatively advanced large units of production into primitive small units which operate with technical means from the time of the Pharaohs.

Nor is that all! Through these measures and the chaotic and purely arbitrary manner of their execution, differentiation in landed property, far from being eliminated, was even further sharpened. Although the Bolsheviks called upon the peasantry to form peasant committees so that the seizure of the nobles' estates might, in some fashion, be made into a collective act, yet it is clear that this general advice could not change anything in the real practice and real relations of power on the land. With or without committees, it was the rich peasants and usurers who made up the village bourgeoisie possessing the actual power in their hands in every Russian village, that surely became the chief beneficiaries of the agrarian revolution. Without being there to see, any one can figure out for himself that in the course of the distribution of the land, social and economic inequality among the peasants was not eliminated but rather increased, and that class antagonisms were further sharpened. This shift of power, however, took place to the *disadvantage* of the interests of the proletariat and of socialism. Formerly, there was only a small caste of noble and capitalist landed proprietors and a small minority of rich village bourgeoisie to oppose a socialist reform on the land. And their expropriation by a revolutionary mass movement of the people is mere child's play. But now, after the "seizure," as an opponent of any attempt at socialization of agrarian production, there is an enormous, newly developed and powerful mass of owning peasants who will defend their newly won property with tooth and nail against every socialist attack. The question of the future socialization of agrarian economy — that is, any socialization of production in general in Russia — has now become a question of opposition and of struggle between the urban proletariat and the mass of the peasantry. How sharp this antagonism has already become is shown by the peasant boycott of the cities, in which they withhold the means of existence to carry on speculation in them, in quite the same way as the Prussian Junker does.

The French small peasant became the boldest defender of the Great French Revolution which had given him land confiscated from the *emigres*. As Napoleonic soldier, he carried the banner of France to victory, crossed all Europe and smashed feudalism

377

to pieces in one land after another. Lenin and his friends might have expected a similar result from their agrarian slogan. However, now that the Russian peasant has seized the land with his own fist, he does not even dream of defending Russia and the revolution to which he owes the land. He has dug obstinately into his new possessions and abandoned the revolution to its enemies, the state to decay, the urban population to famine.

(Lenin's speech on the necessity of centralization in industry, nationalization of banks, of trade and of industry. Why not of the land? Here, on the contrary, decentralization and private property.

(Lenin's own agrarian program before the revolution was different. The slogan taken over from the much condemned socialist-revolutionaries, or rather, from the spontaneous peasant movement.

(In order to introduce socialist principles into agrarian relations, the Soviet government now seeks to create agrarian communes out of proletarians, mostly city unemployed. But it is easy to see in advance that the results of these efforts must remain so insignificant as to disappear when measured against the whole scope of agrarian relations. After the most appropriate starting points for socialist economy, the large estates have been broken up into small units, now they are trying to build up communist model production units out of petty beginnings. Under the circumstances these communes can claim to be considered only as experiments and not as a general social reform. Grain monopoly with bounties. Now, *post-festum*, they want to introduce the class war into the village!)

The Leninist agrarian reform has created a new and powerful layer of popular enemies of socialism on the countryside, enemies whose resistance will be much more dangerous and stubborn than that of the noble large landowners.

III. The Nationalities Question

The Bolsheviks are in part responsible for the fact that the military defeat was transformed into the collapse and a breakdown of Russia. Moreover, the Bolsheviks themselves have, to a great extent, sharpened the objective difficulties of this situation by a slogan which they placed in the foreground of their policies: the so-called right of self-determination of peoples, or — something which was really implicit in this slogan — the disintegration of Russia.

The formula of the right of the various nationalities of the Russian Empire to determine their fate independently "even to the point of the right of governmental separation from Russia," was proclaimed again with doctrinaire obstinacy as a special battle cry of Lenin and his comrades during their opposition against Miliukovist, and then Kerenskyan imperialism. It constituted the axis of their inner policy after the October Revolution also. And it constituted the entire platform of the Bolsheviks at Brest-Litovsk, all they had to oppose to the display of force by German imperialism.

One is immediately struck with the obstinacy and rigid consistency with which Lenin and his comrades stuck to this slogan, a slogan which is in sharp contradiction to their otherwise outspoken centralism in politics as well as to the attitude they have assumed towards other democratic principles. While they showed a quite cool contempt for the Constituent Assembly, universal suffrage, freedom of press and assembly, in short, for the whole apparatus of the basic democratic liberties of the people which, taken all together, constituted the "right of self-determination" inside Russia, they treated the right of self-determination of peoples as a jewel of democratic policy for the sake of which all practical considerations of real criticism had to be stilled. While they did not permit themselves to be imposed upon in the slightest by the plebiscite for the Constituent Assembly in Russia, a plebiscite on the basis of the most democratic suffrage in the world, carried out in the full freedom of a popular republic, and while they simply declared this plebiscite null and void on the basis of a very sober evaluation of its results, still they championed the "popular vote" of the foreign nationalities of Russia on the question of which land they wanted to belong to, as the true palladium of all freedom and democracy, the unadulterated quintessence of the will of the peoples and as the court of last resort in questions of the political fate of nations.

The contradiction that is so obvious here is all the harder to understand since the democratic forms of political life in each land, as we shall see, actually involve the most valuable and even indispensable foundations of socialist policy, whereas the famous "right of self-determination of nations" is nothing but hollow, petty bourgeois phraseology and humbug.

Indeed, what is this right supposed to signify? It belongs to the ABC of socialist policy that socialism opposes every form of oppression, including also that of one nation by another.

If, despite all this, such generally sober and critical politicians as Lenin and Trotsky and their friends, who have nothing but an ironical shrug for every sort of utopian phrase such as disarmament, league of nations, etc., have in this case made a hollow phrase of exactly the same kind into their special hobby, this arose, it seems to us, as a result of some kind of policy made to order for the occasion. Lenin and his comrades clearly calculated that there was no surer method of binding the many foreign peoples within the Russian Empire to the cause of the revolution, to the cause of the socialist proletariat, than that of offering them, in the name of the revolution and of socialism, the most extreme and most unlimited freedom to determine their own fate. This was analogous to the policy of the Bolsheviks towards the Russian peasants, whose land-hunger was satisfied by the slogan of direct seizure of the noble estates and who were supposed to be bound thereby to the banner of the revolution and the proletarian government. In both cases, unfortunately, the calculation was entirely wrong.

While Lenin and his comrades clearly expected that, as champions of national freedom even to the extent of "separation," they would turn Finland, the Ukraine, Poland, Lithuania, the Baltic countries, the Caucasus, etc., into so many faithful allies of the Russian Revolution, we have witnessed the opposite spectacle. One after another, these "nations" used the freshly granted freedom to ally themselves with German imperialism against the Russian Revolution as its mortal enemy, and, under German protection, to carry the banner of counterrevolution into Russia itself. The little game with the Ukraine at Brest, which caused a decisive turn of affairs in those negotiations and brought about the entire inner and outer political situation at present prevailing for the Bolsheviks, is a perfect case in point. The conduct of Finland, Poland, Lithuania, the Baltic lands, the peoples of the Caucasus, shows most convincingly that we are not dealing here with an exceptional case, but with a typical phenomenon.

To be sure, in all these cases, it was really not the "people" who engaged in these reactionary policies, but only the bourgeois and petty bourgeois classes, who — in sharpest opposition to their own proletarian masses — perverted the "national right of self-determination" into an instrument of their counterrevolutionary class policies. But — and here we come to the very heart of the question — it is in this that the utopian, petty bourgeois character of this nationalistic slogan resides: that in the midst of the crude realities of class society and when class antagonisms are sharpened to the uttermost, it is simply converted into a means of bourgeois class rule. The Bolsheviks were to be taught to their own great hurt and that of the revolution, that under the rule of capitalism there is no self-determination of peoples, that in a class society each class of the nation strives to "determine itself" in a different fashion, and that, for the bourgeois classes, the standpoint of national freedom is fully subordinated to that of class rule. The Finnish bourgeoisie, like the Ukrainian bourgeoisie, were unanimous in preferring the violent rule of Germany to national freedom, if the latter should be bound up with bolshevism.

The hope of transforming these actual class relationships some-how into their opposite and of getting a majority vote for union with the Russian Revolution by depending on the revolutionary masses — if it was seriously meant by Lenin and Trotsky — repre-sented an incomprehensible degree of optimism. And if it was only meant as a tactical flourish in the duel with the German politics of force, then it represented dangerous playing with fire. Even without German military occupation, the famous "popular plebiscite," sup-posing that it had come to that in the border states, would have yielded a result, in all probability, which would have given the Bolsheviks little cause for rejoicing; for we must take into consid-eration the psychology of the peasant masses and of great sec-tions of the petty bourgeoisie, and the thousand ways in which the bourgeoisie could have influenced the vote. Indeed, it can be taken as an unbreakable rule in these matters of plebiscites on the national question that the ruling class will either know how to prevent them where it doesn't suit their purpose, or where they somehow occur, will know how to influence their results by all sorts of means, big and little, the same means which make it impossible to introduce socialism by a popular vote.

The mere fact that the question of national aspirations and tendencies towards separation were injected at all into the midst of the revolutionary struggle, and were even pushed into the foreground and made into the shibboleth of socialist and revo-lutionary policy as a result of the Brest peace, has served to bring the greatest confusion into socialist ranks and has actually destroyed the position of the proletariat in the border countries.

In Finland, so long as the socialist proletariat fought as a part of the closed Russian revolutionary phalanx, it possessed a posi-tion of dominant power: it had the majority in the Finnish parlia-ment, in the army; it had reduced its own bourgeoisie to complete impotence, and was master of the situation within its borders.

Or take the Ukraine. At the beginning of the century, before the tomfoolery of "Ukrainian nationalism" with its silver rubles and its "Universals" and Lenin's hobby of an "independent Ukraine" had been invented, the Ukraine was the stronghold of the Russian revolutionary movement. From there, from Rostov, from Odessa, from the Donetz region, flowed out the first lava-streams of the revolution (as early as 1902-04) which kindled all South Russia into a sea of flame, thereby preparing the uprising of 1905. The same thing was repeated in the present revolution, in which the South Russian proletariat supplied the picked troops of the pro-letarian phalanx. Poland and the Baltic lands have been since 1905 the mightiest and most dependable hearths of revolution, and in them the socialist proletariat has played an outstanding role.

How does it happen then that in all these lands the counterrevolution suddenly triumphs? The nationalist movement, just because it tore the proletariat loose from Russia, crippled it thereby, and delivered it into the hands of the bourgeoisie of the border countries.

Instead of acting in the same spirit of genuine international class policy which they represented in other matters, instead of working for the most compact union of the revolutionary forces throughout the area of the empire, instead of defending tooth and nail the integrity of the Russian Empire as an area of revolution and opposing to all forms of separatism the solidarity and inseparability of the proletarians in all lands within the sphere of the Russian Revolution as the highest command of politics, the Bolsheviks, by their hollow nationalistic phraseology concerning the "right of self-determination to the point of separation," have accomplished quite the contrary and supplied the bourgeoisie in all border states with the finest, the most desirable pretext, the very banner of the counterrevolutionary efforts. Instead of warning the proletariat in the border countries against all forms of separatism as mere bourgeois traps, they did nothing but confuse the masses in all the border countries by their slogan and delivered them up to the demagogy of the bourgeois classes. By this nationalistic demand they brought on the disintegration of Russia itself, pressed into the enemy's hand the knife which it was to thrust into the heart of the Russian Revolution.

To be sure, without the help of German imperialism, without "the German rifle butts in German fists," as Kautsky's *Neue Zeit* put it, the Lubinskys and other little scoundrels of the Ukraine, the Erichs and Mannerheims of Finland, and the Baltic barons, would never have gotten the better of the socialist masses of the workers in their respective lands. But national separatism was the Trojan horse inside which the German "comrades," bayonet in hand, made their entrance into all those lands. The real class antagonisms and relations of military force brought about German intervention. But the Bolsheviks provided the ideology which masked this campaign of counterrevolution; they strengthened the position of the bourgeoisie and weakened that of the proletariat.

The best proof is the Ukraine, which was to play so frightful a role in the fate of the Russian Revolution. Ukrainian nationalism in Russia was something quite different from, let us say, Czech, Polish or Finnish nationalism in that the former was a mere whim, a folly of a few dozen petty bourgeois intellectuals without the slightest roots in the economic, political or psychological relationships of the country; it was without any historical tradition, since the Ukraine never formed a nation or government, was without any national culture, except for the reactionary-romantic poems of Shevchenko. It is exactly as if, one fine day, the people living in the *Wasserkante* should want to found a new Low German (*Plattdeutsche*) nation and government! And this ridiculous pose of a few university professors and students was inflated into a political force by Lenin and his comrades through their doctrinaire agitation concerning the "right of self-determination including etc." To what was at first a mere farce they lent such importance that the farce became a matter of the most deadly seriousness—not as a serious national movement for which, afterward as before, there are no roots at all, but as a shingle and rallying flag of counterrevolution! At Brest, out of this addled egg crept the German bayonets.

There are times when such phrases have a very real meaning in the history of class struggles. It is the unhappy lot of socialism that in this World War it was given to it to supply the ideological screens for counterrevolutionary policy. At the outbreak of the war, German social democracy hastened to deck the predatory expedition of German imperialism with an ideological shield from the lumber room of Marxism by declaring it to be a liberating expedition against Russian czarism, such as our old teachers (Marx and Engels) had longed for. And to the lot of the Bolsheviks, who were the very antipodes of our government socialists, did it fall to supply grist for the mill of counterrevolution with their phrases about self-determination of peoples; and thereby to supply not alone the ideology for the strangling of the Russian Revolution itself, but even for the plans for settling the entire crisis arising out of the World War.

We have good reason to examine very carefully the policies of the Bolsheviks in this regard. The "right of self-determination of peoples," coupled with the league of nations and disarmament by the grace of President Wilson, constitute the battle cry under which the coming reckoning of international socialism with the bourgeoisie is to be settled. It is obvious that the phrases concerning self-determination and the entire nationalist movement, which at present constitute the greatest danger for international socialism, have experienced an extraordinary strengthening from the Russian Revolution and the Brest negotiations. We shall yet have to go into this platform thoroughly. The tragic fate of these phrases in the Russian Revolution, on the thorns of which the Bolsheviks were themselves destined to be caught and bloodily scratched, must serve the international proletariat as a warning and lesson.

And from all this there followed the dictatorship of Germany from the time of the Brest treaty to the time of the "supplementary treaty." The two hundred expiatory sacrifices in Moscow. From this situation arose the terror and the suppression of democracy.

IV. The Constituent Assembly

Let us test this matter further by taking a few examples.

The well-known dissolution of the Constituent Assembly in November 1917 played an outstanding role in the policy of the Bolsheviks. This measure was decisive for their further position; to a certain extent, it represented a turning point in their tactics.

It is a fact that Lenin and his comrades were stormily demanding the calling of a Constituent Assembly up to the time of their October victory, and that the policy of dragging out this matter on the part of the Kerensky government constituted an article in the indictment of that government by the Bolsheviks and was the basis of some of their most violent attacks upon it. Indeed, Trotsky says in his interesting pamphlet, *From October to Brest-Litovsk*, that the October Revolution represented "the salvation of the Constituent Assembly" as well as of the revolution as a whole. "And when we said," he continues, "that the entrance to the Constituent Assembly could not be reached through the Preliminary Parliament of Tseretelli, but only through the seizure of power by the Soviets, we were entirely right."

And then, after these declarations, Lenin's first step after the October Revolution was . . . the dissolution of this same Constituent Assembly, to which it was supposed to be an entrance. What reasons could be decisive for so astonishing a turn? Trotsky, in the above-mentioned pamphlet, discusses the matter thoroughly, and we will set down his argument here:

"While the months preceding the October Revolution were a time of leftward movement on the part of the masses and of an elemental flow of workers, soldiers and peasants towards the Bolsheviks, inside the Socialist Revolutionary Party this process expressed itself as a strengthening of the left wing at the cost of the right. But within the list of party candidates of the socialist revolutionaries, the old names of the right wing still occupied three-fourths of the places. . . .

"Then there was the further circumstance that the elections themselves took place in the course of the first weeks after the October Revolution. The news of the change that had taken place spread rather slowly in concentric circles from the capital to the provinces and from the towns to the villages. The peasant masses in many places had little notion of what went on in Petrograd and Moscow. They voted for 'Land and Freedom,' and elected as their representatives in the land committees those who stood under the banner of the *Narodniki*. Thereby, however, they voted for Kerensky and Avksentiev, who had been dissolving these land committees and having their members arrested. . . . This state of affairs gives a clear idea of the extent to which the Constituent

Assembly had lagged behind the development of the political struggle and the development of party groupings."

All of this is very fine and quite convincing. But one cannot help wondering how such clever people as Lenin and Trotsky failed to arrive at the conclusion which follows immediately from the above facts. Since the Constituent Assembly was elected long before the decisive turning point, the October Revolution, and its composition reflected the picture of the vanished past and not of the new state of affairs, then it follows automatically that the outgrown and therefore stillborn Constituent Assembly should have been annulled, and without delay, new elections to a new Constituent Assembly should have been arranged. They did not want to entrust, nor should they have entrusted, the fate of the revolution to an assemblage which reflected the Kerenskyan Russia of yesterday, of the period of vacillations and coalition with the bourgeoisie. Hence there was nothing left to do except to convoke an assembly that would issue forth out of the renewed Russia that had advanced further.

Instead of this, from the special inadequacy of the Constituent Assembly which came together in October, Trotsky draws a general conclusion concerning the inadequacy of any popular representation whatsoever which might come from universal popular elections during the revolution.

"Thanks to the open and direct struggle for governmental power," he writes, "the laboring masses acquire in the shortest time an accumulation of political experience, and they climb rapidly from step to step in their political development. The bigger the country and the more rudimentary its technical apparatus, the less is the cumbersome mechanism of democratic institutions able to keep pace with this development."

Here we find the "mechanism of democratic institutions" as such called in question. To this we must at once object that in such an estimate of representative institutions there lies a somewhat rigid and schematic conception which is expressly contradicted by the historical experience of every revolutionary epoch. According to Trotsky's theory, every elected assembly reflects once and for all only the mental composition, political maturity and mood of its electorate just at the moment when the latter goes to the polling place. According to that, a democratic body is the reflection of the masses at the end of the electoral period, much as the heavens of Herschel always show us the heavenly bodies not as they are when we are looking at them but as they were at the moment they sent out their light-messages to the earth from the measureless distances of space. Any living mental connection between the representatives, once they have been elected, and the electorate, any permanent interaction between one and the other, is hereby denied.

Yet how all historical experience contradicts this! Experience demonstrates quite the contrary: namely, that the living fluid of the popular mood continuously flows around the representative bodies, penetrates them, guides them. How else would it be possible to witness, as we do at times in every bourgeois parliament, the amusing capers of the "people's representatives," who are suddenly inspired by a new "spirit" and give forth quite unexpected sounds; or to find the most dried-out mummies at times comporting themselves like youngsters and the most diverse little *Scheidemaennchen* suddenly finding revolutionary tones in their breasts—whenever there is rumbling in factories and workshops and on the streets?

And is this ever-living influence of the mood and degree of political ripeness of the masses upon the elected bodies to be renounced in favor of a rigid scheme of party emblems and tickets in the very midst of revolution? Quite the contrary! It is precisely the revolution which creates by its glowing heat that delicate, vibrant, sensitive political atmosphere in which the waves of popular feeling, the pulse of popular life, work for the moment on the representative bodies in most wonderful fashion. It is on this very fact, to be sure, that the well-known moving scenes depend which invariably present themselves in the first stages of every revolution, scenes in which old reactionaries or extreme moderates, who have issued out of a parliamentary election by limited suffrage under the old regime, suddenly become the heroic and stormy spokesmen of the uprising. The classic example is provided by the famous "Long Parliament" in England, which was elected and assembled in 1642 and remained at its post for seven whole years and reflected in its internal life all alterations and displacements of popular feeling, of political ripeness, of class differentiation, of the progress of the revolution to its highest point, from the initial devout skirmishes with the crown under a speaker who remained on his knees, to the abolition of the House of Lords, the execution of Charles and the proclamation of the republic.

And was not the same wonderful transformation repeated in the French Estates General, in the censorship-subjected parliament of Louis Philippe, and even — and this last, most striking example was very close to Trotsky—even in the Fourth Russian Duma which, elected in the Year of Grace 1909 under the most rigid rule of the counterrevolution, suddenly felt the glowing heat of the impending overturn and became the point of departure for the revolution?

All this shows that "the cumbersome mechanism of democratic institutions" possesses a powerful corrective—namely, the living movement of the masses, their unending pressure. And the more democratic the institutions, the livelier and stronger the pulsebeat of the political life of the masses, the more direct and complete is their influence—despite rigid party banners, outgrown tickets (electoral lists), etc. To be sure, every democratic institution has its limits and shortcomings, things which it doubtless shares with all other human institutions. But the remedy which Trotsky and Lenin have found, the elimination of democracy as such, is worse than the disease it is supposed to cure; for it stops up the very living source from which alone can come the correction of all the innate shortcomings of social institutions. That source is the active, untrammeled, energetic political life of the broadest masses of the people.

V. The Question of Suffrage

Let's take another striking example: the right of suffrage as worked out by the Soviet government. It is not altogether clear what practical significance is attributed to this right of suffrage. From the critique of democratic institutions by Lenin and Trotsky, it appears that popular representation on the basis of universal suffrage is rejected by them on principle, and that they want to base themselves only on the soviets. Why, then, any general suffrage system was worked out at all is really not clear. It is also not known to us whether this right of suffrage was put in practice anywhere; nothing has been heard of any elections to any kind of popular representative body on the basis of it. More likely, it is only a theoretical product, so to speak, of diplomacy; but, as it is, it constitutes a remarkable product of the Bolshevist theory of dictatorship.

Every right of suffrage, like any political right in general, is not to be measured by some sort of abstract scheme of "justice," or in terms of any other bourgeois democratic phrases, but by the social and economic relationships for which it is designed. The right of suffrage worked out by the Soviet government is calculated for the transition period from the bourgeois capitalist to the socialist form of society, that is, it is calculated for the period of the proletarian dictatorship. But, according to the interpretation of this dictatorship which Lenin and Trotsky represent, the right to vote is granted only to those who live by their own labor and is denied to everybody else.

Now it is clear that such a right to vote has meaning only in a society which is in a position to make possible for all who want to work an adequate civilized life on the basis of one's own labor. Is that the case in Russia at present? Under the terrific difficulties which Russia has to contend with, cut off as she is from the world market and from her most important sources of raw materials, and under circumstances involving a terrific general uprooting of economic life and a rude overturn of productive relationships as a result of the transformation of property relationships in land and industry and trade—under such circumstances, it is clear that countless existences are quite suddenly uprooted, derailed without any objective possibility of finding any employment for their labor power within the economic mechanism. This applies not only to the capitalist and landowning classes, but to the broad layer of the middle class also, and even to the working class itself. It is a known fact that the contraction of industry has resulted in a mass-scale return of the urban proletariat to the open country in search of a place in rural economy. Under such circumstances, a political right of suffrage on the basis of a general obligation to labor, is a quite incomprehensible measure. According to the main trend, only the exploiters are supposed to be deprived of their political rights. And, on the other hand, at the same time that productive labor powers are being uprooted on a mass scale, the Soviet government is often compelled to hand over national industry to its former owners, on lease, so to speak. In the same way, the Soviet government was forced to conclude a compromise with the bourgeois consumers cooperatives also. Further, the use of bourgeois specialists proved unavoidable. Another consequence of the same situation is that growing sections of the proletariat are maintained by the state out of public resources as Red Guardists, etc. In reality, broad and growing sections of the petty bourgeoisie and proletariat, for whom the economic mechanism provides no means of exercising the obligation to work, are rendered politically without any rights.

It makes no sense to regard the right of suffrage as a utopian product of fantasy, cut loose from social reality. And it is for this reason that it is not a serious instrument of the proletarian dictatorship. It is an anachronism, an anticipation of the juridical situation which is proper on the basis of an already completed socialist economy, but not in the transition period of the proletarian dictatorship.

As the entire middle class, the bourgeois and petty bourgeois intelligentsia boycotted the Soviet government for months after the October Revolution and crippled the railroad, post and telegraph, and educational and administrative apparatus, and, in this fashion, opposed the workers government, naturally enough all measures of pressure were exerted against it. These included the deprivation of political rights, of economic means of existence, etc., in order to break their resistance with an iron fist. It was precisely in this way that the socialist dictatorship expressed itself, for it cannot shrink from any use of force to secure or prevent certain measures involving the interests of the whole. But when it comes to a suffrage law which provides for the general disfranchisement of broad sections of society, whom it places politically outside the framework of society and, at the same time, is not in a position to make any place for them even economically within that framework, when it involves a deprivation of rights not as a concrete measure for a concrete purpose but as a general rule of long-standing effect, then it is not a necessity of dictatorship but a makeshift, incapable of being carried out in life. This applies alike to the soviets as the foundation, and to the Constituent Assembly and the general suffrage law.

But the Constituent Assembly and the suffrage law do not exhaust the matter. We did not consider above the destruction of the most important democratic guarantees of a healthy public life and of the political activity of the laboring masses: freedom of the press, the rights of association and assembly, which have been outlawed for all opponents of the Soviet regime. For these attacks (on democratic rights), the arguments of Trotsky cited above, on the cumbersome nature of democratic electoral bodies, are far from satisfactory. On the other hand, it is a well-known and indisputable fact that without a free and untrammeled press, without the unlimited right of association and assemblage, the rule of the broad mass of the people is entirely unthinkable.

VI. The Problem of Dictatorship

Lenin says: the bourgeois state is an instrument of oppression of the working class; the socialist state, of the bourgeoisie. To a certain extent, he says, it is only the capitalist state stood on its head. This simplified view misses the most essential thing: bourgeois class rule has no need of the political training and education of the entire mass of the people, at least not beyond certain narrow limits. But for the proletarian dictatorship that is the life element, the very air without which it is not able to exist.

"Thanks to the open and direct struggle for governmental power," writes Trotsky, "the laboring masses accumulate in the shortest time a considerable amount of political experience and advance quickly from one stage to another of their development."

Here Trotsky refutes himself and his own friends. Just because this is so, they have blocked up the fountain of political experience and the source of this rising development by their suppression of public life! Or else we would have to assume that experience and development were necessary up to the seizure of power by the Bolsheviks, and then, having reached their highest peak, became superfluous thereafter. (Lenin's speech: Russia is won for socialism!!!)

In reality, the opposite is true! It is the very giant tasks which the Bolsheviks have undertaken with courage and determination that demand the most intensive political training of the masses and the accumulation of experience.

Freedom only for the supporters of the government, only for the members of one party—however numerous they may be—is no freedom at all. Freedom is always and exclusively freedom for the one who thinks differently. Not because of any fanatical concept of "justice" but because all that is instructive, wholesome

389

and purifying in political freedom depends on this essential characteristic, and its effectiveness vanishes when "freedom" becomes a special privilege.

The Bolsheviks themselves will not want, with hand on heart, to deny that, step by step, they have to feel out the ground, try out, experiment, test now one way, now another, and that a good many of their measures do not represent priceless pearls of wisdom. Thus it must and will be with all of us when we get to the same point — even if the same difficult circumstances may not prevail everywhere.

The tacit assumption underlying the Lenin-Trotsky theory of the dictatorship is this: that the socialist transformation is something for which a ready-made formula lies completed in the pocket of the revolutionary party, which needs only to be carried out energetically in practice. This is, unfortunately — or perhaps fortunately — not the case. Far from being a sum of ready-made prescriptions which have only to be applied, the practical realization of socialism as an economic, social and juridical system is something which lies completely hidden in the mists of the future. What we possess in our program is nothing but a few main signposts which indicate the general direction in which to look for the necessary measures, and the indications are mainly negative in character at that. Thus we know more or less what we must eliminate at the outset in order to free the road for a socialist economy. But when it comes to the nature of the thousand concrete, practical measures, large and small, necessary to introduce socialist principles into economy, law and all social relationship, there is no key in any socialist party program or textbook. That is not a shortcoming but rather the very thing that makes scientific socialism superior to the utopian varieties.

The socialist system of society should only be, and can only be, a historical product, born out of the school of its own experiences, born in the course of its realization, as a result of the developments of living history, which — just like organic nature of which, in the last analysis, it forms a part — has the fine habit of always producing along with any real social need the means to its satisfaction, along with the task simultaneously the solution. However, if such is the case, then it is clear that socialism by its very nature cannot be decreed or introduced by *ukase* [proclamation]. It has as its prerequisite a number of measures of force — against property, etc. The negative, the tearing down, can be decreed; the building up, the positive, cannot. New territory. A thousand problems. Only experience is capable of correcting and opening new ways. Only unobstructed, effervescing life falls into a thousand new forms and improvisations, brings to light creative force, itself corrects all mistaken attempts. The public life of countries with limited freedom is so poverty-stricken, so miserable, so rigid, so unfruitful, precisely because, through the exclusion of democracy, it cuts off the living sources of all spiritual riches and progress. (Proof: the year 1905 and the months from February to October 1917.) There it was political in character; the same thing applies to economic and social life also. The whole mass of the people must take part in it. Otherwise, socialism will be decreed from behind a few official desks by a dozen intellectuals.

Public control is indispensably necessary. Otherwise the exchange of experiences remains only with the closed circle of the officials of the new regime. Corruption becomes inevitable (Lenin's words, Bulletin No. 29). Socialism in life demands a complete spiritual transformation in the masses degraded by centuries of bourgeois class rule. Social instincts in place of egotistical ones, mass initiative in place of inertia, idealism which conquers all suffering, etc. No one knows this better, describes it more penetratingly; repeats it more stubbornly than Lenin. But he is completely mistaken in the means he employs. Decree, dictatorial force of the factory overseer, Draconic penalties, rule by terror — all these things are but palliatives. The only way to a rebirth is the school of public life itself, the most unlimited, the broadest democracy and public opinion. It is rule by terror which demoralizes.

When all this is eliminated, what really remains? In place of the representative bodies created by general popular elections, Lenin and Trotsky have laid down the soviets as the only true representation of the laboring masses. But with the repression of political life in the land as a whole, life in the soviets must also become more and more crippled. Without general elections, without unrestricted freedom of press and assembly, without a free struggle of opinion, life dies out in every public institution, becomes a mere semblance of life, in which only the bureaucracy remains as the active element. Public life gradually falls asleep, a few dozen party leaders of inexhaustible energy and boundless experience direct and rule. Among them, in reality only a dozen outstanding heads do the leading and an elite of the working class is invited from time to time to meetings where they are to applaud the speeches of the leaders, and to approve proposed resolutions unanimously — at bottom, then, a clique affair — a dictatorship, to be sure, not the dictatorship of the proletariat, however, but only the dictatorship of a handful of politicians, that is a dictatorship in the bourgeois sense, in the sense of the rule of the Jacobins (the postponement of the Soviet Congress from three-month periods to six-month period!). Yes, we can go even further; such conditions must inevitably cause a brutalization of public life: attempted assassinations, shooting of hostages, etc. (Lenin's speech on discipline and corruption.)

VII. The Struggle Against Corruption

A problem which is of great importance in every revolution is that of the struggle with the lumpenproletariat. We in Germany too, as everywhere else, will have this problem to reckon with.

The lumpenproletarian element is deeply embedded in bourgeois society. It is not merely a special section, a sort of social wastage which grows enormously when the walls of the social order are falling down, but rather an integral part of the social whole. Events in Germany — and more or less in other countries — have shown how easily all sections of bourgeois society are subject to such degeneration. The gradations between commercial profiteering, fictitious deals, adulteration of foodstuffs, cheating, official embezzlement, theft, burglary and robbery, flow into one another in such fashion that the boundary line between honorable citizenry and the penitentiary has disappeared. In this the same phenomenon is repeated as in the regular and rapid degeneration of bourgeois dignitaries when they are transplanted to an alien social soil in an overseas colonial setting. With the stripping off of conventional barriers and props for morality and law, bourgeois society itself falls victim to direct and limitless degeneration (*Verlumpung*), for its innermost law of life is the profoundest of immoralities, namely, the exploitation of man by man. The proletarian revolution will have to struggle with this enemy and instrument of counterrevolution on every hand.

And yet, in this connection too, terror is a dull, nay, a two-edged sword. The harshest measures of martial law are impotent against outbreaks of the lumpenproletarian sickness. Indeed, every persistent regime of martial law leads inevitably to arbitrariness, and every form of arbitrariness tends to deprave society. In this regard also, the only effective means in the hands of the proletarian revolution are: radical measures of a political and social character, the speediest possible transformation of the social guarantees of the life of the masses — the kindling of revolutionary idealism, which can be maintained over any length of time only through the intensively active life of the masses themselves under conditions of unlimited political freedom.

As the free action of sun's rays is the most effective purifying and healing remedy against infections and disease germs, so the only healing and purifying sun is the revolution itself and its renovating principle, the spiritual life, activity and initiative of the masses which is called into being by it and which takes the form of the broadest political freedom.

In our case as everywhere else, anarchy will be unavoidable. The lumpenproletarian element is deeply embedded in bourgeois society and inseparable from it.

Proofs:
1. East Prussia, the "Cossack" robberies.
2. The general outbreak of robbery and theft in Germany. (Profiteering, postal and railway personnel, police, complete dissolution of the boundaries between well-ordered society and the penitentiary.)
3. The rapid degeneration (*Verlumpung*) of the union leaders.

Against this, Draconian measures of terror are powerless. On the contrary, they cause still further corruption. The only antitoxin: the idealism and social activity of the masses, unlimited political freedom.

That is an overpowering objective law from which no party can be exempt.

VIII. Democracy and Dictatorship

The basic error of the Lenin-Trotsky theory is that they too, just like Kautsky, oppose dictatorship to democracy. "Dictatorship or democracy" is the way the question is put by Bolsheviks and Kautsky alike. The latter naturally decides in favor of "democracy," that is, of bourgeois democracy, precisely because he opposes it to the alternative of the socialist revolution. Lenin and Trotsky, on the other hand, decide in favor of dictatorship in contradistinction to democracy, and thereby, in favor of the dictatorship of a handful of persons, that is, in favor of dictatorship on the bourgeois model. They are two opposite poles, both alike being far removed from a genuine socialist policy. The proletariat, when it seizes power, can never follow the good advice of Kautsky, given on the pretext of the "unripeness of the country," the advice being to renounce the socialist revolution and devote itself to democracy. It cannot follow this advice without betraying thereby itself, the International, and the revolution. It should and must at once undertake socialist measures in the most energetic, unyielding and unhesitant fashion, in other words, exercise a dictatorship, but a dictatorship of the *class*, not of a party or of a clique — dictatorship of the class, that means in the broadest public form on the basis of the most active, unlimited participation of the mass of the people, of unlimited democracy.

"As Marxists," writes Trotsky, "we have never been idol worshippers of formal democracy." Surely, we have never been idol worshippers of formal democracy. Nor have we ever been idol worshippers of socialism or Marxism either. Does it follow from this that we may also throw socialism on the scrap-heap, a la Cunow, Lensch and Parvus, if it becomes uncomfortable for us? Trotsky and Lenin are the living refutation of this answer.

"We have never been idol worshippers of formal democracy." All that that really means is: We have always distinguished the social kernel from the political form of *bourgeois* democracy; we have always revealed the hard kernel of social inequality and lack of freedom hidden under the sweet shell of formal equality and freedom — not in order to reject the latter but to spur the working class into not being satisfied with the shell, but rather, by conquering political power, to create a socialist democracy to replace bourgeois democracy — not to eliminate democracy altogether.

But socialist democracy is not something which begins only

in the promised land after the foundations of socialist economy are created; it does not come as some sort of Christmas present for the worthy people who, in the interim, have loyally supported a handful of socialist dictators. Socialist democracy begins simultaneously with the beginnings of the destruction of class rule and of the construction of socialism. It begins at the very moment of the seizure of power by the socialist party. It is the same thing as the dictatorship of the proletariat.

Yes, dictatorship! But this dictatorship consists in the *manner of applying democracy*, not in its *elimination*, in energetic, resolute attacks upon the well-entrenched rights and economic relationships of bourgeois society, without which a socialist transformation cannot be accomplished. But this dictatorship must be the work of the *class* and not of a little leading minority in the name of the class — that is, it must proceed step by step out of the active participation of the masses; it must be under their direct influence, subjected to the control of complete public activity; it must arise out of the growing political training of the mass of the people.

Doubtless the Bolsheviks would have proceeded in this very way were it not that they suffered under the frightful compulsion of the World War, the German occupation and all the abnormal difficulties connected therewith, things which were inevitably bound to distort any socialist policy, however imbued it might be with the best intentions and the finest principles.

A crude proof of this is provided by the use of terror to so wide an extent by the Soviet government, especially in the most recent period just before the collapse of German imperialism, and just after the attempt on the life of the German ambassador. The commonplace to the effect that revolutions are not pink teas is in itself pretty inadequate.

Everything that happens in Russia is comprehensible and represents an inevitable chain of causes and effects, the starting point and end term of which are: the failure of the German proletariat and the occupation of Russia by German imperialism. It would be demanding something superhuman from Lenin and his comrades if we should expect of them that under such circumstances they should conjure forth the finest democracy, the most exemplary dictatorship of the proletariat and a flourishing socialist economy. By their determined revolutionary stand, their exemplary strength in action, and their unbreakable loyalty to international socialism, they have contributed whatever could possibly be contributed under such devilishly hard conditions. The danger begins only when they make a virtue of necessity and want to freeze into a complete theoretical system all the tactics forced upon them by these fatal circumstances, and want to recommend them to the international proletariat as a model of socialist tactics. When they get in their own light in this way, and

394

hide their genuine, unquestionable historical service under the bushel of false steps forced upon them by necessity, they render a poor service to international socialism for the sake of which they have fought and suffered; for they want to place in its storehouse as new discoveries all the distortions prescribed in Russia by necessity and compulsion—in the last analysis only by-products of the bankruptcy of international socialism in the present world war.

Let the German government socialists cry that the rule of the Bolsheviks in Russia is a distorted expression of the dictatorship of the proletariat. If it was or is such, that is only because it is a product of the behavior of the German proletariat, in itself a distorted expression of the socialist class struggle. All of us are subject to the laws of history, and it is only internationally that the socialist order of society can be realized. The Bolsheviks have shown that they are capable of everything that a genuine revolutionary party can contribute within the limits of the historical possibilities. They are not supposed to perform miracles. For a model and faultless proletarian revolution in an isolated land, exhausted by world war, strangled by imperialism, betrayed by the international proletariat, would be a miracle.

What is in order is to distinguish the essential from the non-essential, the kernel from the accidental excrescences in the policies of the Bolsheviks. In the present period, when we face decisive final struggles in all the world, the most important problem of socialism was and is the burning question of our time. It is not a matter of this or that secondary question of tactics, but of the capacity for action of the proletariat, the strength to act, the will to power of socialism as such. In this, Lenin and Trotsky and their friends were the *first*, those who went ahead as an example to the proletariat of the world; they are still the *only ones* up to now who can cry with Hutten: "I have dared!"

This is the essential and *enduring* in Bolshevik policy. In *this* sense theirs is the immortal historical service of having marched at the head of the international proletariat with the conquest of political power and the practical placing of the problem of the realization of socialism, and of having advanced mightily the settlement of the score between capital and labor in the entire world. In Russia the problem could only be posed. It could not be solved in Russia. And in *this* sense, the future everywhere belongs to "bolshevism."

AGAINST

CAPITAL PUNISHMENT

In September 1918 Germany's western front collapsed and a new strike wave ensued. The end of the war was clearly in sight. The government, anxious to broaden its base, in an attempt to save itself declared an amnesty for political prisoners. Karl Liebknecht was released on October 23 and carried triumphantly through the streets of Berlin to the Soviet embassy, but Rosa Luxemburg was apparently not covered by the amnesty, as she was being detained·by administrative order, not serving a definite sentence.

In late October the sailors at the Kiel naval base revolted, and councils of workers and soldiers, modeled on the Russian soviets, began to spring up throughout Germany, demanding that their authority be recognized. On November 9 a general strike broke out, forcing the government to abdicate. The chancellor, Prince Max of Baden, handed over power to Friedrich Ebert, the leader of the SPD. Under pressure from Liebknecht's call for the construction of a socialist republic, the social democrats abolished the monarchy and proclaimed Germany a democratic republic.

Rosa Luxemburg, still waiting in jail, was freed on November 9, as the masses in Breslau opened the prison gates. Grey-haired and considerably aged by her years in prison, she returned to Berlin to help lead Spartacus for the remaining two months of her life.

One of the first pieces she wrote after her release from prison was "Against Capital Punishment," published in *Rote Fahne* (Red Flag), the new journal of the Spartacus League. In it she condemns the inhumanity of capitalist "justice" and outlines the humanitarian goals of the socialist revolution and the treatment of prisoners.

"Against Capital Punishment" is reprinted from *Germany After the Armistice: A Report Based on the Personal Testimony of Representative Germans, Concerning the Conditions Existing in 1919* by Maurice Berger, translated from the French by William L. McPherson.

396

We did not wish for amnesty, not for pardon, in the case of the political prisoners, who had been the prey of the old order. We demanded the right to liberty, to agitation, to revolution for the hundreds of brave and loyal men who groaned in the jails and in the fortresses because, under the former dictatorship of imperialist criminals, they had fought for the people, for peace, and for socialism.

They are all free now.

We find ourselves again in the ranks, ready for the battle.

It was not the clique of Scheidemann and his bourgeois allies, with Prince Max of Baden at their head, that liberated us. It was the proletarian revolution that made the doors of our cells spring open.

But another class of unfortunate dwellers in those gloomy mansions has been completely forgotten. No one, at present, thinks of the pale and morbid figures which sigh behind prison walls because of offenses against ordinary law.

Nevertheless these are also the unfortunate victims of the infamous social order against which the revolution is directed — victims of the imperialistic war which pushed distress and misery to the very limit of intolerable torture, victims of that frightful butchery of men which let loose all the vilest instincts.

The justice of the bourgeois classes had again been like a net, which allowed the voracious sharks to escape, while the little sardines were caught. The profiteers who have realized millions during the war have been acquitted or let off with ridiculous penalties. The little thieves, men and women, have been punished with sentences of Draconian severity.

Worn out by hunger and cold, in cells which are hardly heated, these derelicts of society await mercy and pity.

They have waited in vain, for in his preoccupation with making the nations cut one another's throats and of distributing crowns, the last of the Hohenzollerns forgot these miserable people, and since the Conquest of Liege there has been no amnesty, not even on the official holiday of German slaves, the kaiser's birthday.

The proletarian revolution ought now, by a little ray of kindness, to illuminate the gloomy life of the prisons, shorten Draconian sentences, abolish barbarous punishments — the use of manacles and whippings — improve, as far as possible, the medical attention, the food allowance, and the conditions of labor. That is a duty of honor!

The existing disciplinary system, which is impregnated with brutal class spirit and with capitalist barbarism, should be radically altered.

But a complete reform, in harmony with the spirit of socialism, can be based only on a new economic and social order; for both crime and punishment have, in the last analysis, their roots deep in the organization of society. One radical measure, however,

397

can be taken without any elaborate legal process. Capital punishment, the greatest shame of the ultrareactionary German code, ought to be done away with at once. Why are there any hesitations on the part of this government of workers and soldiers? The noble Beccaria, two hundred years ago, denounced the ignominy of the death penalty. Doesn't its ignominy exist for you, Ledebour, Barth, Daeumig?

You have no time, you have a thousand cares, a thousand difficulties, a thousand tasks before you? That is true. But mark, watch in hand, how much time would be needed to say: "Capital punishment is abolished!" Would you argue that, on this question also, long discussions followed by votes are necessary? Would you thus lose yourselves in the complications of formalism, in considerations of jurisdiction, in questions of departmental red tape?

Ah! How German this German Revolution is! How argumentative and pedantic it is! How rigid, inflexible, lacking in grandeur!

The forgotten death penalty is only one little isolated detail. But how precisely the inner spirit, which governs the revolution, betrays itself in these little details!

Let one take up any ordinary history of the Great French Revolution. Let one take up the dry Mignet, for instance.

Can one read this book except with a beating heart and a burning brow? Can one, after having opened it, at no matter what page, put it aside before one has heard, with bated breath, the last chord of that formidable tragedy? It is like a symphony of Beethoven carried to the gigantic and the grotesque, a tempest thundering on the organ of time, great and superb in its errors as well as in its achievement, in victory as well as in defeat, in the first cry of naive joyfulness as well as in the final breath.

And now how is it with us in Germany?

Everywhere, in the small as in the great, one feels that these are still and always the old and sober citizens of the defunct social democracy, those for whom the badge of membership is everything and the man and the spirit are nothing.

Let us not forget this, however. The history of the world is not made without grandeur of spirit, without lofty morale, without noble gestures.

Liebknecht and I, on leaving the hospitable halls which we recently inhabited—he, among his pale companions in the penitentiary, I with my dear, poor thieves and women of the streets, with whom I have passed, under the same roof, three years and a half of my life—we took this oath as they followed us with their sad eyes: "We shall not forget you!"

We demand of the executive committee of the Council of Workers and Soldiers an immediate amelioration of the lot of all the prisoners in the German jails!

We demand the excision of capital punishment from the German penal code!

During the four years of this slaughter of the peoples, blood has flowed in torrents. Today, each drop of that precious fluid ought to be preserved devotedly in crystal urns.

Revolutionary activity and profound humanitarianism — they alone are the true breath of socialism.

A world must be turned upside down. But each tear that flows, when it could have been spared, is an accusation, and he commits a crime who with brutal inadvertency crushes a poor earthworm.

SPEECH TO THE FOUNDING

CONVENTION OF THE

GERMAN COMMUNIST PARTY

The last two months of Rosa Luxemburg's life were days and nights of almost uninterrupted mental and physical exertion. As one of the central leaders of the revolutionary wave sweeping Germany, she found little time to rest or recuperate from the harsh years in prison.

The period of November 9 to mid-January 1919 was one of continuing revolutionary ferment, with many ups and downs. In demonstration after demonstration, hundreds of thousands of workers poured into the streets, protesting every government move against their organizations or supporters. Mass meetings of thousands were held day after day as the war weariness of the masses and returning soldiers turned against the government and demanded satisfaction. It was much like the early months of 1917 in Russia, following the February Revolution.

On November 9, the day the monarchy fell, the immediate question became, "Who will govern Germany?" The SPD and USPD immediately began negotiations on the formation of a government. The USPD, in return for a generous offer of equal representation, withdrew its most radical conditions, and a Council of People's Commissars was established with three members of the SPD and three from the USPD. They immediately called for the election of a national assembly to take place as soon as possible.

Spartacus, which operated as an organized fraction within the USPD, denounced the Council of People's Commissars, and refused to participate in it. They called instead for all power to the Workers' and Soldiers' Councils. The Berlin Workers' and Soldiers' Council itself, however, met on November 10 and confirmed the six People's Commissars as the provisional national executive, leaving its own role and authority vague.

By and large, the majority of the Workers' and Soldiers' Councils formed in November were dominated by the SPD or politically unaffiliated soldiers and civilians of a somewhat conservative bent. The USPD controlled a number of the councils, and had a substantial minority in most of them. Spartacus controlled only a few, for a period of time, in Brunswick and Stuttgart. The extent of Spartacus's organizational weakness is evident in the fact that at the Reich Conference of Workers' and Soldiers' Councils held in mid-December in Berlin, there was apparently not even an organized Spartacus caucus, although Spartacus claimed ten delegates. The SPD had 288 and USPD eighty.

Throughout November and December Spartacus called repeatedly for new elections to the Workers' and Soldiers' Councils in an attempt to break the hold of the conservative forces over them, to make them more reflective of the growing radicalization of the masses. But such demands were vigorously rejected in most cases, especially in the crucial city of Berlin, and the Workers' and Soldiers' Councils increasingly handed over their power and moral authority to the SPD leaders, eventually joining hands with them in an attempt to crush the revolution.

Until early January the Spartacus leaders thought the revolutionary wave would continue to mount, although they did not expect an early or easy victory. But fundamentally, the relationship of forces grew worse and worse for the revolutionaries. Ebert, Scheidemann, Noske, and the rest of the SPD leaders were determined to bring "law and order" to Germany, and were fully conscious that it meant decapitating and destroying Spartacus. They were quite willing to use the most reactionary military and paramilitary forces to suppress the street demonstrations, hunt down the leaders on whose heads they had unofficially placed a price, capture the strongholds of the left wing, and destroy any support they might have with sections of the troops or police.

After a number of attacks on left-wing forces in December — confrontations which settled nothing — the USPD members of the Council of People's Commissars resigned, leaving the SPD in full command. At the beginning of January, the provisional government decided to try to provoke a military showdown and destroy the revolutionary forces. As their first move they fired the Berlin police chief, Emil Eichhorn, who was a member of the USPD, and replaced him with someone on whom they could rely. Eichhorn, however, refused to leave his office, claiming that he was responsible only to the Berlin Workers' and Soldiers' Council (which confirmed his dismissal a few days later).

A demonstration called on January 5 to protest the dismissal of Eichhorn turned out to be much larger than anyone had anticipated, and new demonstrations were called for January 6. It appeared to some of the left-wing forces that the question of taking power was on the agenda. A loose coalition of Spartacus (newly constituted as the Communist Party — KPD), the USPD, and the Revolutionary Shop Stewards formed a Revolutionary Executive, calling for continued struggle by the masses, the removal of Ebert and Scheidemann, the seizure of power by the council, and other measures.

It remains unclear whether the KPD representatives to the Revolutionary Executive — Liebknecht and Pieck — acted with KPD approval or not. According to Rosa Luxemburg's biographer, Paul Froelich, they did not have the support of the KPD leadership, and Rosa Luxemburg in particular upbraided Liebknecht for his dangerous and adventurist commitment of the party to a doomed insurrection. At any rate, it rapidly became evident to all that there was no hope of taking power with such an insecure base, and no attempt to take power was made. On January 10, with troops rapidly pouring into the city and counterrevolutionary paramilitary bands more and more taking the offensive, the KPD formally withdrew from the Revolutionary Executive — which had for all practical purposes already disintegrated. (Members of the USPD and the Revolutionary Shop Stewards were attempting to negotiate a truce with the SPD.)

At the same time, however, thousands of armed workers were in the streets, and the Spartacus leaders felt they had to stay with the masses and try to lead them in action so as not to loose contact with them.

On January 13, on SPD orders, troops attacked the *Vorwaerts* building which the revolutionary forces had occupied, and murdered the delegation sent to negotiate a surrender. Spies, agents, and armed vigilante bands were scouring the city in search of the Spartacus leaders, against whom a hysterical lynch campaign had been mounting for weeks. But Rosa Luxemburg and Karl Liebknecht adamantly refused to leave the city.

On January 15 a unit of troops raided the ill-concealed hiding place of Rosa Luxemburg and Karl Liebknecht. They were taken to the temporary headquarters of one of the paramilitary units that were operating freely with the SPD's full knowledge, if not open support.

Liebknecht was taken out and murdered "while trying to escape." Rosa Luxemburg was killed by a shot in the head, and her body thrown into a canal from which it was recovered only in May.

When the revolution began in early November, the Spartacus leaders decided to remain within the USPD as long as possible, to attempt to win over as many of the rank and file as they could reach. Rosa Luxemburg had a strong fear of loosing contact with the masses, which she was sure would result from any early attempt to found a new party totally separate from the USPD.

During November and December the Spartacus leaders expended their main energies on providing a political leadership for the mass movement that was swirling around them, and placed the construction of a tightly-knit, disciplined organization on a lower level of priority. The Spartacus League in reality was a few thousand members in a loose federation of groups scattered around Germany. While Spartacus leaders in Berlin made it clear that they had absolutely no use for the vacillating, centrist leadership of the USPD, the demarcation lines between the USPD and Spartacus tended to become more and more blurred the further one moved away from the top leadership circles into the provincial cities, or even among the ranks in Berlin itself.

It was only after the USPD leadership definitively refused to call a national congress—fearing the consequences of providing the Spartacus leaders with an opportunity to win larger numbers of supporters and clarify the deep differences that existed—only then that Spartacus decided to split from the USPD and found the Communist Party of Germany.

The founding congress of the KPD took place on December 30-31, 1918, and January 1, 1919, and it was at that congress that Rosa Luxemburg gave what was to be her last speech. On behalf of the executive committee she presented the draft program which the congress adopted. Paul Froelich, who was himself a part of the leadership of Spartacus, described her speech:

"The tension which developed at the congress between the sober wisdom of the leaders and the revolutionary impatience of the younger elements was lessened immediately [as] Rosa Luxemburg addressed the congress on the party program. The delegates had anxiously observed what a great effort of will was necessary before her exhausted body could triumph over the effects of long imprisonment, ceaseless excitement, nervous tension and serious illness, but no sooner had she begun to speak than inspiration worked wonders and she was suddenly her old self again. All her physical weakness fell away from her, all her energy returned, and, for the last time, her passionate temperament and brilliant oratory held her audience spellbound: convincing, gripping, stirring and inspiring. It was an unforgettable experience for all who were present."

The tension of the congress to which Froelich refers, and which Rosa Luxemburg mentions several times in her speech, developed over the question of what tactic should be adopted by the KPD toward the now inevitable elections for a national assembly. When it met in mid-December, the Reich Conference of Workers' and Soldiers' Councils had approved the Ebert government's call for elections. The executive committee of Spartacus proposed that the newly-formed KPD take advantage of the possibilities of reaching millions of people with revolutionary propaganda by participating in the elections. But the majority of the delegates taking a classically ultraleftist position, wanted nothing to do with the elections, and the congress voted sixty-two to twenty-three against the executive committee's resolution. In a letter to Clara Zetkin, Rosa Luxemburg characterized the vote as the result of a "somewhat childish, half-baked, narrow-minded radicalism" on the part of the young and impatient delegates, an attitude which she hoped and optimistically believed would rapidly disappear.

She also discusses at length Engels's preface to the 1895 German edition of *Class Struggles in France* by Marx. Her knowledge of Engels's uncompromising revolutionary positions led her to be somewhat suspicious of, or at least to reject, the interpretation of that preface that prevailed in the German SPD.

The preface had been written by Engels at the special pleading of the SPD leaders, who feared the passage of new antisocialist laws. But, unknown to Rosa Luxemburg, and virtually everyone else, even that specially designed preface had not pleased the SPD leaders and it had been grossly distorted by them. They edited out the sections of the preface in which Engels clarified his attitude toward nonlegal, nonparliamentary forms of struggle. On April 1, 1895, Engels had protested against this distortion of his views to Kautsky, saying, "I was astonished to see in today's *Vorwaerts* an extract from my introduction, reprinted without my approval and tailor-made in such a manner as to present me as a peaceful worshipper of legality at any price. I shall be all the more pleased to see the whole thing now reprinted in *Neue Zeit* to remove this unworthy impression." But the unedited preface was not printed in German until 1924.

It is a striking example of Rosa Luxemburg's deep understanding of revolutionary Marxism that she zeroed in on this passage as being somehow suspicious and out of step with everything Marx and Engels stood for, and it was not long before history vindicated her.

She also rejected the old division between a "minimum" and a "maximum" program, between demands to be struggled for here and now, and goals which were simultaneously held up as an inspiration for the future, yet considered irrelevant in terms of day-to-day practice. She found in that division one of the bulwarks of opportunism in the old SPD. The formulation of a single program, pointing the way from the present to the socialist future, was a decisive step in giving the KPD a truly revolutionary perspective and a means of struggling both for demands attainable under capitalism and for those that would inevitably lead the masses step by step toward the socialist revolution and its victorious completion.

Also in evidence is the old theme that ran through the mass

strike pamphlet and everything Rosa Luxemburg wrote about the 1905-06 Revolution. She predicts an imminent strike wave which will pass over from political to economic goals and ultimately bringing about a total economic and political transformation. Here again, as in 1905, she tends to overemphasize the effectiveness of the strike as the ultimate weapon.

The murder of Luxemburg and Liebknecht marked the end of the first phase of the German revolution, although even they, had they lived, could not have altered the immediate course of events. Their death was a tremendous blow to the new young party, one that deprived it of its most experienced leadership. Many more were to fall in the months to come as the counter-revolution swept Germany.

The murder of Luxemburg and Liebknecht was also a tremendous blow to the Russian Revolution, beseiged by civil war and invading forces and struggling to hold out long enough for victorious revolution in Germany to come to its aid. Speaking in the Petrograd Soviet on January 18, 1919, as word arrived confirming the murders of Luxemburg and Liebknecht and the defeat the revolution had suffered, Trotsky paid the highest revolutionary tribute to them:

"For us Liebknecht was not just a German leader. For us Luxemburg was not just a Polish socialist who stood at the head of the German workers. No, they are both kindred of the world proletariat and we are all tied to them with an indissoluble spiritual link. Till their last breath they belonged not to a nation but to the International!"

Rosa Luxemburg's final speech is translated by Eden and Cedar Paul. It follows a 1943 version published in *The New International.*

———

Comrades! Our task today is to discuss and adopt a program. In undertaking this task we are not actuated solely by the consideration that yesterday we founded a new party and that a new party must formulate a program. Great historical movements have been the determining causes of today's deliberations. The time has arrived when the entire socialist program of the proletariat has to be established upon a new foundation. We are faced with a position similar to that which was faced by Marx and Engels when they wrote the *Communist Manifesto* seventy years ago. As you all know, the *Communist Manifesto* dealt with socialism, with the realization of the aims of socialism, as the immediate task of the proletarian revolution. This was the idea represented by Marx and Engels in the Revolution of 1848; it was thus, likewise, that they conceived the basis for proletarian action in the international field. In common with all the leading spirits in the working-class movement, both Marx and Engels then believed that the immediate introduction of socialism was at hand. All that was necessary was to bring about a political revolution, to seize the political power of the state, and socialism would then immediately pass from the realm of thought to the realm of flesh and blood.

Subsequently, as you are aware, Marx and Engels undertook a thoroughgoing revision of this outlook. In the joint preface to the reissue of the *Communist Manifesto* in the year 1872, we find the following passage: "No special stress is laid on the revolutionary measures proposed at the end of section two. That passage would, in many respects, be differently worded today. In view of the gigantic strides of modern industry during the last twenty-five years and of the accompanying improved and extended organization of the working class, in view of the practical experience gained, first in the February Revolution, and then, still more, in the Paris Commune, where the proletariat for the first time held political power for two whole months, this program has in some details become antiquated. One thing especially was proved by the Commune, viz., that the 'working class cannot simply lay hold of the ready-made state machinery and wield it for its own purposes.'"

What is the actual wording of the passage thus declared to be out of date? It runs as follows:

"The proletariat will use its political supremacy: to wrest, by degrees, all capital from the bourgeoisie; to centralize all instruments of production in the hands of the state, i.e., of the proletariat organized as the ruling class; and to increase the total of productive forces as rapidly as possible.

"Of course, in the beginning, this cannot be effected except by means of despotic inroads on the rights of property, and on the conditions of bourgeois production; by measures, therefore, which appear economically insufficient and untenable, but which, in the course of the movement, outstrip themselves, necessitate further inroads upon the old social order, and are unavoidable as a means of entirely revolutionizing the mode of production.

"The measures will, of course, be different in different countries.

"Nevertheless, in the most advanced countries, the following will be pretty generally applicable:

"1. Abolition of property in land and application of all land rents to public purposes.

"2. A heavy progressive or graduated income tax.

"3. Abolition of the right of inheritance.

"4. Confiscation of the property of all emigrants and rebels.

"5. Centralization of credit in the hands of the state, by means of a national bank with state capital and an exclusive monopoly.

"6. Centralization of the means of communication and transport in the hands of the state.

"7. Extension of factories and instruments of production owned by the state: the bringing into cultivation of waste lands, and the improvement of the soil generally, in accordance with a concerted plan.

"8. Equal obligation upon all to labor. Establishment of industrial armies, especially for agriculture.

"9. Coordination of agriculture with manufacturing industries: gradual abolition of the distinction between town and country, by a more equable distribution of the population throughout the rural areas.

"10. Free education for all children in public schools. Abolition of children's factory labor in its present form. Combination of education with industrial production, etc., etc."

With a few trifling variations, these, as you know, are the tasks that confront us today. It is by such measures that we shall have to realize socialism. Between the day when the above program was formulated, and the present hour, there have intervened seventy years of capitalist development, and the historical evolutionary process has brought us back to the standpoint which Marx and Engels had in 1872 abandoned as erroneous. At that time there were excellent reasons for believing that their earlier views had been wrong. The further evolution of capital has, however, resulted in this, that what was error in 1872 has become truth today, so that it is our immediate objective to fulfill what Marx and Engels thought they would have to fulfill in the year 1848. But between that point of development, that beginning in the year 1848, and our own views and our immediate task, there lies the whole evolution, not only of capitalism, but in addition of the socialist labor movement. Above all, there have intervened the previously mentioned developments in Germany as the leading land of the modern proletariat.

This working-class evolution has taken a peculiar form. When, after the disillusionments of 1848, Marx and Engels had given up the idea that the proletariat could immediately realize socialism, there came into existence in all countries socialist parties inspired with very different aims. The immediate objective of these parties was declared to be detail work, the petty daily struggle in the political and industrial fields. Thus, by degrees, would proletarian armies be formed, and these armies would be ready to realize socialism when capitalist development had matured. The socialist program was thereby established upon an utterly different foundation, and in Germany the change took a peculiarly typical form. Down to the collapse of August 4, 1914, the German social democracy took its stand upon the Erfurt program, and by this program the so-called immediate minimal aims were placed in the foreground, while socialism was no more than a distant guiding star.

Far more important, however, than what is written in a program, is the way in which that program is interpreted in action. From this point of view, great importance must be attached to one of the historical documents of the German labor movement, to the preface written by Friedrich Engels for the 1895 reissue of Marx's *Class Struggles in France*. It is not merely upon historical grounds that I now reopen this question. The matter is one of extreme actuality. It has become our urgent duty today to replace our program upon the foundations laid by Marx and Engels in 1848. In view of the changes effected since then by the historical process of development, it is incumbent upon us to undertake a deliberate revision of the views that guided the German social democracy down to the collapse of August 4. Upon such a revision we are officially engaged today.

How did Engels envisage the question in that celebrated preface to the *Class Struggles in France*, composed by him in 1895, twelve years after the death of Marx? First of all, looking back upon the year 1848, he showed that the belief that the socialist revolution was imminent had become obsolete. He continued as follows:

"History has shown that we were all mistaken in holding such a belief. It has shown that the state of economic evolution upon the continent was then far from being ripe for the abolition of capitalist production. This has been proved by the economic revolution which since 1848 has taken place all over the continent. Large-scale industry has been established in France, Austria-Hungary, Poland, and of late Russia. Germany has become a manufacturing country of the first rank. All these changes have taken place upon a capitalist foundation, a foundation which in the year 1848 still had to undergo an enormous extension."

After summing up the changes which had occurred in the intervening period, Engels turned to consider the immediate tasks of the German Social Democratic Party. "As Marx had predicted," he wrote, "the war of 1870-71 and the fall of the Commune shifted the center of gravity of the European labor movement from France to Germany. Many years had naturally to elapse before France could recover from the bloodletting of May, 1871. In Germany, on the other hand, manufacturing industry was developing by leaps and bounds, in the forcing-house atmosphere produced by the influx of the French billions. Even more rapid and more enduring was the growth of social democracy. Thanks to the agreement in virtue of which the German workers have been able to avail themselves of the universal [male] suffrage introduced in 1866, the astounding growth of the party has been demonstrated to all the world by the testimony of figures whose significance no one can deny."

Thereupon followed the famous enumeration, showing the growth of the party vote in election after election until the figures swelled to millions. From this progress Engels drew the following conclusion: "The successful employment of the parliamentary vote entailed the acceptance of an entirely new tactic by the proletariat, and this new method has undergone rapid development. It has been realized that the political institutions in which the dominion of the bourgeoisie is incorporated offer a fulcrum whereby the proletariat can work for the overthrow of these very political institutions. The social democrats have participated in the elections to the various diets, to municipal councils, and to industrial courts. Wherever the proletariat could secure an effective voice, the occupation of these electoral strongholds by the bourgeoisie has been contested. Consequently, the bourgeoisie and the government have become much more alarmed at the constitutional than at the unconstitutional activities of the workers, dreading the results of elections far more than they dread the results of rebellion."

Engels appends a detailed criticism of the illusion that under modern capitalist conditions the proletariat can possibly expect to effect anything for the revolution by street fighting. It seems to me, however, seeing that today we are in the midst of a revolution, a revolution characterized by street fighting and all that this entails, that it is time to shake ourselves free of the views which have guided the official policy of the German social democracy down to our own day, of the views which share responsibility for what happened on August 4, 1914. [*Hear! Hear!*]

I do not mean to imply that, on account of these utterances, Engels must share personal responsibility for the whole course of socialist evolution in Germany. I merely draw your attention to one of the classical pieces of evidence of the opinions prevailing in the German social democracy — opinions which proved fatal to the movement. In this preface Engels demonstrated, as an expert in military science, that it was a pure illusion to believe that the workers could, in the existing state of military technique and of industry, and in view of the characteristics of the great towns of today, successfully bring about a revolution by street fighting. Two important conclusions were drawn from this reasoning. In the first place, the parliamentary struggle was counterposed to direct revolutionary action by the proletariat, and the former was indicated as the only practical way of carrying on the class struggle. Parliamentarism, and nothing but parliamentarism, was the logical sequel of this criticism.

Secondly, the whole military machine, the most powerful organization in the class state, the entire body of proletarians in military uniform, was declared on apriori grounds to be absolutely inaccessible to socialist influences. When Engels's preface declares that, owing to the modern development of gigantic armies, it is positively insane to suppose that proletarians can ever stand up against soldiers armed with machine guns and equipped with all the other latest technical devices, the assertion is obviously based upon the assumption that anyone who becomes a soldier, becomes thereby once and for all one of the props of the ruling class.

It would be absolutely incomprehensible, in the light of contemporary experience, that so noted a leader as Engels could have committed such a blunder, did we not know the circumstances in which this historical document was composed. For the credit of our two great masters, and especially for the credit of Engels, who died twelve years later than Marx, and was always a faithful champion of his great collaborator's theories and reputation, I must remind you of the well-known fact that the preface in question was written by Engels under strong pressure on the part of the parliamentary group. At that date in Germany, during the early nineties after the antisocialist law had been annulled, there was a strong movement towards the left, the movement of those who wished to save the party from becoming completely absorbed in the parliamentary struggle. Bebel and his associates wished for convincing arguments, backed up by Engels's great authority; they wished for an utterance which would help them to keep a tight hand upon the revolutionary elements.

It was characteristic of party conditions at the time that the socialist parliamentarians should have the decisive word alike in theory and in practice. They assured Engels, who lived abroad and naturally accepted the assurance at its face value, that it was absolutely essential to safeguard the German labor movement from a lapse into anarchism, and in this way they constrained him to write in the tone they wished. Thenceforward the tactics expounded by Engels in 1895 guided the German social democrats in everything they did and in everything they left undone, down to the appropriate finish of August 4, 1914. The preface was the formal proclamation of the nothing-but-parliamentarism tactic. Engels died the same year, and had therefore no opportunity for studying the practical consequences of his theory. Those who know the works of Marx and Engels, those who are familiarly acquainted with the genuinely revolutionary spirit that inspired all their teachings and all their writings, will feel positively certain that Engels would have been one of the first to protest against the debauch of parliamentarism, against the frittering away of the energies of the labor movement, which was characteristic of Germany during the decades before the war.

The fourth of August did not come like thunder out of a clear sky; what happened on the fourth of August was not a chance turn of affairs, but was the logical outcome of all that the German socialists had been doing day after day for many years. [*Hear! hear!*] Engels and Marx, had it been possible for them to live on into our own time, would, I am convinced, have protested with the utmost energy, and would have used all the forces at their disposal to keep the party from hurling itself into the abyss. But after Engels's death in 1895, in the theoretical field the leadership of the party passed into the hands of Kautsky. The upshot of this change was that at every annual congress the energetic protests of the left wing against a purely parliamentarist policy, its urgent warnings against the sterility and the danger of such a policy, were stigmatized as anarchism, anarchizing socialism, or at least anti-Marxism. What passed officially for Marxism became a cloak for all possible kinds of opportunism, for persistent shirking of the revolutionary class struggle, for every conceivable half measure. Thus the German social democracy, and the labor movement, the trade-union movement as well, were condemned to pine away within the framework of capitalist society. No longer did German socialists and trade unionists make any serious attempt to overthrow capitalist institutions or to put the capitalist machine out of gear.

But we have now reached the point, comrades, when we are able to say that we have rejoined Marx, that we are once more advancing under his flag. If today we declare that the immediate task of the proletariat is to make socialism a living reality and to destroy capitalism root and branch, in saying this we take our stand upon the ground occupied by Marx and Engels in 1848; we adopt a position from which in principle they never moved. It has at length become plain what true Marxism is, and what substitute Marxism has been. [*Applause.*] I mean the substitute Marxism which has so long been the official Marxism of the social democracy. You see what Marxism of this sort leads to, the Marxism of those who are the henchmen of Ebert, David, and the rest of them. These are the official representatives of the doctrine which has been trumpeted for decades as Marxism undefiled. But in reality Marxism could not lead in this direction, could not lead Marxists to engage in counterrevolutionary activities side by side with such as Scheidemann. Genuine Marxism turns its weapons against those also who seek to falsify it. Burrowing like a mole beneath the foundations of capitalist society, it has worked so well that the larger half of the German proletariat is marching today under our banner, the storm-riding

411

standard of revolution. Even in the opposite camp, even where the counterrevolution still seems to rule, we have adherents and future comrades-in-arms.

Let me repeat, then, that the course of historical evolution has led us back to the point at which Marx and Engels stood in 1848 when they first hoisted the flag of international socialism. We stand where they stood, but with the advantage that seventy additional years of capitalist development lie behind us. Seventy years ago, to those who reviewed the errors and illusions of 1848, it seemed as if the proletariat had still an interminable distance to traverse before it could hope to realize socialism. I need hardly say that no serious thinker has ever been inclined to fix upon a definite date for the collapse of capitalism; but after the failures of 1848, the day for that collapse seemed to lie in the distant future. Such a belief, too, can be read in every line of the preface which Engels wrote in 1895. We are now in a position to cast up the account, and we are able to see that the time has really been short in comparison with that occupied by the sequence of class struggles throughout history. The progress of large-scale capitalist development during seventy years has brought us so far that today we can seriously set about destroying capitalism once for all. Nay more, not merely are we today in a position to perform this task, not merely is its performance a duty towards the proletariat, but our solution offers the only means of saving human society from destruction. [*Loud applause.*]

What has the war left of bourgeois society beyond a gigantic rubbish-heap? Formally, of course, all the means of production and most of the instruments of power, practically all the decisive instruments of power, are still in the hands of the dominant classes. We are under no illusions here. But what our rulers will be able to achieve with the powers they possess, over and above frantic attempts to reestablish their system of spoliation through blood and slaughter, will be nothing more than chaos. Matters have reached such a pitch that today mankind is faced with two alternatives: It may perish amid chaos; or it may find salvation in socialism. As the outcome of the great war it is impossible for the capitalist classes to find any issue from their difficulties while they maintain class rule. We now realize the absolute truth of the statement formulated for the first time by Marx and Engels as the scientific basis of socialism in the great charter of our movement, in the *Communist Manifesto*. Socialism, they said, will become a historical necessity. Socialism is inevitable, not merely because proletarians are no longer willing to live under the conditions imposed by the capitalist class, but further because, if the proletariat fails to fulfill its duties as a class, if it fails to realize socialism, we shall crash down together to a common doom. [*Prolonged applause.*]

Here you have the general foundation of the program we are officially adopting today, a draft of which you have all read in the pamphlet *Was will der Spartakusbund?* [What Does Spartacus Want?]. Our program is deliberately opposed to the leading principle of the Erfurt program; it is deliberately opposed to the separation of the immediate and so-called minimal demands formulated for the political and economic struggle, from the socialist goal regarded as a maximal program. It is in deliberate opposition to the Erfurt program that we liquidate the results of seventy years' evolution, that we liquidate, above all, the primary results of the war, saying we know nothing of minimum and maximal programs; we know only one thing, socialism; this is the minimum we are going to secure. [*Hear! hear!*]

I do not propose to discuss the details of our program. This would take too long, and you will form your own opinions upon matters of detail. The task that devolves upon me is merely to sketch the broad lines in which our program is distinguished from what has hitherto been the official program of the German social democracy. I regard it, however, as of the utmost importance that we should come to an understanding in our estimate of the concrete circumstances of the hour, of the tactics we have to adopt, of the practical measures which must be undertaken, in view of the course of the revolution down to the present time, and in view of the probable lines of further development. We have to judge the political situation from the outlook I have just characterized, from the outlook of those who aim at the immediate realization of socialism, of those who are determined to subordinate everything else to that end.

Our congress, the congress of what I may proudly call the only revolutionary socialist party of the German proletariat, happens to coincide in point of time with a crisis in the development of the German revolution. "Happens to coincide," I say; but in truth the coincidence is no chance matter. We may assert that after the occurrences of the last few days the curtain has gone down upon the first act of the German revolution. We are now in the opening of the second act, and it is our common duty to undertake self-examination and self-criticism. We shall be guided more wisely in the future, and we shall gain additional impetus for further advances, if we study all that we have done and all that we have left undone. Let us, then, carefully scrutinize the events of the first act in the revolution.

The movement began on November 9. The revolution of November 9 was characterized by inadequacy and weakness. This need not surprise us. The revolution followed four years of war, four years during which, schooled by the social democracy and the trade unions, the German proletariat had behaved with intolerable ignominy and had repudiated its socialist obligations

413

to an extent unparalleled in any other land. We Marxists, whose guiding principle is a recognition of historical evolution, could hardly expect that in the Germany which had known the terrible spectacle of August 4, and which during more than four years had reaped the harvest sown on that day, there should suddenly occur on November 9, 1918, a glorious revolution, inspired with definite class-consciousness, and directed towards a clearly conceived aim. What happened on November 9 was to a very small extent the victory of a new principle; it was little more than a collapse of the extant system of imperialism. [*Hear! hear!*]

The moment had come for the collapse of imperialism, a colossus with feet of clay, crumbling from within. The sequel of this collapse was a more or less chaotic movement, one practically devoid of reasoned plan. The only source of union, the only persistent and saving principle, was the watchword, "Form workers' and soldiers' councils." Such was the slogan of the revolution, whereby, in spite of the inadequacy and weakness of the opening phases, it immediately established its claim to be numbered among proletarian socialist revolutions. To those who participated in the revolution of November 9, and who nonetheless shower calumnies upon the Russian Bolshevists, we should never cease to reply with the question: "Where did you learn the alphabet of your revolution? Was it not from the Russians that you learned to ask for workers' and soldiers' councils?" [*Applause.*]

Those pygmies who today make it one of their chief tasks, as heads of what they falsely term a socialist government, to join with the imperialists of Britain in a murderous attack upon the Bolsheviks, were then taking their seats as deputies upon the workers' and soldiers' councils, thereby formally admitting that the Russian Revolution created the first watchwords for the world revolution. A study of the existing situation enables us to predict with certainty that in whatever country, after Germany, the proletarian revolution may next break out, the first step will be the formation of workers' and soldiers' councils. [*Murmurs of assent.*]

Herein is to be found the tie that unites our movement internationally. This is the motto which distinguishes our revolution utterly from all earlier revolutions, bourgeois revolutions. On November 9, the first cry of the revolution, as instinctive as the cry of a newborn child, was for workers' and soldiers' councils. This was our common rallying-cry, and it is through the councils that we can alone hope to realize socialism. But it is characteristic of the contradictory aspects of our revolution, characteristic of the contradictions which attend every revolution, that at the very time when this great, stirring, and instinctive cry was being uttered, the revolution was so inadequate, so feeble, so devoid of initiative, so lacking in clearness as to its own aims, that on November 10 our revolutionists allowed to slip from their grasp nearly half the instruments of power they had seized on November 9. We learn from this, on the one hand, that our revolution is subject to the prepotent law of historical determinism, a law which guarantees that, despite all difficulties and complications, notwithstanding all our own errors, we shall nevertheless advance step by step towards our goal. On the other hand, we have to recognize, comparing this splendid battle cry with the paucity of the results practically achieved, we have to recognize that these were no more than the first childish and faltering footsteps of the revolution, which has many arduous tasks to perform and a long road to travel before the promise of the first watchwords can be fully realized.

The weeks that have elapsed between November 9 and the present day have been weeks filled with multiform illusions. The primary illusion of the workers and soldiers who made the revolution was their belief in the possibility of unity under the banner of what passes by the name of socialism. What could be more characteristic of the internal weakness of the revolution of November 9 than the fact that at the very outset the leadership passed in no small part into the hands of persons who a few hours before the revolution broke out had regarded it as their chief duty to issue warnings against revolution—[*hear! hear!*]—to attempt to make revolution impossible—into the hands of such as Ebert, Scheidemann, and Haase. One of the leading ideas of the revolution of November 9 was that of uniting the various socialist trends. The union was to be effected by acclamation. This was an illusion which had to be bloodily avenged, and the events of the last few days have brought a bitter awakening from our dreams; but the self-deception was universal, affecting the Ebert and Scheidemann groups and affecting the bourgeoisie no less than ourselves.

Another illusion was that affecting the bourgeoisie during this opening act of the revolution. They believed that by means of the Ebert-Haase combination, by means of the so-called socialist government, they would really be able to bridle the proletarian masses and to strangle the socialist revolution. Yet another illusion was that from which the members of the Ebert-Scheidemann government suffered when they believed that with the aid of the soldiers returned from the front they would be able to hold down the workers and to curb all manifestations of the socialist class struggle. Such were the multifarious illusions which explain recent occurrences. One and all, they have now been dissipated. It has been plainly proved that the union between Haase and Ebert-Scheidemann under the banner of "socialism" serves merely as a fig leaf for the decent veiling of a counterrevolutionary policy. We ourselves, as always happens in revolutions, have been cured of our self-deceptions.

There is a definite revolutionary procedure whereby the popular mind can be freed from illusion, but, unfortunately, the cure involves that the people must be blooded. In revolutionary Germany, events have followed the course characteristic of all revolutions. The bloodshed in Chaussee Street on December 6, the massacre of December 24, brought the truth home to the broad masses of the people. Through these occurrences they came to realize that what passes by the name of a socialist government is a government representing the counterrevolution. They came to realize that anyone who continues to tolerate such a state of affairs is working against the proletariat and against socialism. [*Applause.*]

Vanished, likewise, is the illusion cherished by Messrs. Ebert, Scheidemann & Co., that with the aid of soldiers from the front they will be able forever to keep the workers in subjection. What has been the effect of the experiences of December 6 and 24? There has been obvious of late a profound disillusionment among the soldiery. The men begin to look with a critical eye upon those who have used them as cannon fodder against the socialist proletariat. Herein we see once more the working of the law that the socialist revolution undergoes a determined objective development, a law in accordance with which the battalions of the labor movement gradually learn through bitter experience to recognize the true path of revolution. Fresh bodies of soldiers have been brought to Berlin, new detachments of cannon fodder, additional forces for the subjection of socialist proletarians — with the result that, from barrack after barrack, there comes a demand for the pamphlets and leaflets of the Spartacus Group.

This marks the close of the first act. The hopes of Ebert and Scheidemann that they would be able to rule the proletariat with the aid of reactionary elements among the soldiery, have already to a large extent been frustrated. What they have to expect within the very near future is an increasing development of definite revolutionary trends within the barracks. Thereby the army of the fighting proletariat will be augmented, and correspondingly the forces of the counterrevolutionists will dwindle. In consequence of these changes, yet another illusion will have to go, the illusion that animates the bourgeoisie, the dominant class. If you read the newspapers of the last few days, the newspapers issued since the incidents of December 24, you cannot fail to perceive plain manifestations of disillusionment conjoined with indignation, both due to the fact that the henchmen of the bourgeoisie, those who sit in the seats of the mighty, have proved inefficient. [*Hear! hear!*]

It had been expected of Ebert and Scheidemann that they would

416

prove themselves strong men, successful lion tamers. But what have they achieved? They have suppressed a couple of trifling disturbances, and as a sequel the hydra of revolution has raised its head more resolutely than ever. Thus disillusionment is mutual, nay universal. The workers have completely lost the illusion which had led them to believe that a union between Haase and Ebert-Scheidemann would amount to a socialist government. Ebert and Scheidemann have lost the illusion which had led them to imagine that with the aid of proletarians in military uniform they could permanently keep down proletarians in civilian dress. The members of the middle class have lost the illusion that, through the instrumentality of Ebert, Scheidemann and Haase, they can humbug the entire socialist revolution of Germany as to the ends it desires. All these things have a merely negative force, and there remains from them nothing but the rags and tatters of destroyed illusions. But it is in truth a great gain for the proletariat that naught beyond these rags and tatters remains from the first phase of the revolution, for there is nothing so destructive as illusion, whereas nothing can be of greater use to the revolution than naked truth.

I may appropriately recall the words of one of our classical writers, a man who was no proletarian revolutionary, but a revolutionary spirit nurtured in the middle class. I refer to Lessing, and quote a passage which has always aroused my sympathetic interest: "I do not know whether it be a duty to sacrifice happiness and life to truth. . . . But this much I know, that it is our duty, if we desire to teach truth, to teach it wholly or not at all, to teach it clearly and bluntly, unenigmatically, unreservedly, inspired with full confidence in its powers. . . . The cruder an error, the shorter and more direct is the path leading to truth. But a highly refined error is likely to keep us permanently estranged from truth, and will do so all the more readily in proportion as we find it difficult to realize that it is an error. . . . One who thinks of conveying to mankind truth masked and rouged, may be truth's pimp, but has never been truth's lover." Comrades, Messrs. Haase, Dittmann, etc., have wished to bring us the revolution, to introduce socialism, covered with a mask, smeared with rouge; they have thus shown themselves to be the pimps of the counterrevolution. Today these concealments have been discarded, and what was offered is disclosed in the brutal and sturdy lineaments of Messrs. Ebert and Scheidemann. Today the dullest among us can make no mistake. What is offered is the counterrevolution in all its repulsive nudity.

The first act is over. What are the subsequent possibilities? There is, of course, no question of prophecy. We can only hope to deduce the logical consequences of what has already happened, and thus to draw conclusions as to the probabilities of the future, in order that we may adapt our tactics to these probabilities. Whither does the road seem to lead? Some indications are given by the latest utterances of the Ebert-Scheidemann government, utterances free from ambiguity. What is likely to be done by this so-called socialist government now that, as I have shown, all illusions have been dispelled? Day by day the government loses increasingly the support of the broad masses of the proletariat. In addition to the petty bourgeoisie there stand behind it no more than poor remnants from among the workers, and as regards these last it is extremely dubious whether they will long continue to lend any aid to Ebert and Scheidemann.

More and more, too, the government is losing the support of the army, for the soldiers have entered upon the path of self-examination and self-criticism. The effects of this process may seem slow at first, but it will lead irresistibly to their acquiring a thoroughgoing socialist mentality. As for the bourgeoisie, Ebert and Scheidemann have lost credit in this quarter too, for they have not shown themselves strong enough. What can they do? They will soon make an end of the comedy of socialist policy. When you read these gentlemen's new program you will see that they are steaming under forced draught into the second phase, that of the declared counterrevolution, or, as I may even say, the restoration of preexistent, prerevolutionary conditions.

What is the program of the new government? It proposes the election of a president, who is to have a position intermediate between that of the king of England and that of the president of the United States. [*Hear! hear!*] He is to be, as it were, King Ebert. In the second place they propose to reestablish the federal council. You may read today the independently formulated demands of the South German governments, demands which emphasize the federal character of the German realm. The reestablishment of the good old federal council, in conjunction, naturally, with that of its appendage, the German Reichstag, is now a question of a few weeks only. Comrades, Ebert and Scheidemann are moving in this way towards the simple restoration of the conditions that obtained prior to November 9. But therewith they have entered upon a steep declivity, and are likely before long to find themselves lying with broken limbs at the bottom of the abyss. For by the ninth of November the reestablishment of the conditions that had existed prior to the ninth of November had already become out of date, and today Germany is miles from such a possibility.

In order to secure support from the only class whose class interests the government really represents, in order to secure support from the bourgeoisie — a support which has in fact been withdrawn owing to recent occurrences — Ebert and Scheidemann will be compelled to pursue an increasingly counterrevolutionary policy. The demands of the South German states, as published today in the Berlin newspapers, gave frank expressions to the wish to secure "enhanced safety" for the German realm. In plain language, this means that they desire the declaration of a state of siege against "anarchist, disorderly, and Bolshevist" elements; that is to say, against socialists. By the pressure of circumstances, Ebert and Scheidemann will be constrained to the expedient of dictatorship, with or without the declaration of a state of siege. Thus, as an outcome of the previous course of development, by the mere logic of events and through the operation of the forces which control Ebert and Scheidemann, there will ensue during the second act of the revolution a much more pronounced opposition of tendencies and a greatly accentuated class struggle. [*Hear! hear!*] This intensification of conflict will arise, not merely because the political influences I have already enumerated, dispelling all illusions, will lead to a declared hand-to-hand fight between the revolution and the counterrevolution; but in addition because the flames of a new fire are spreading upward from the depths, the flames of the economic struggle.

It was typical of the first period of the revolution down to December 24 that the revolution remained exclusively political. Hence the infantile character, the inadequacy, the halfheartedness, the aimlessness, of this revolution. Such was the first stage of a revolutionary transformation whose main objective lies in the economic field, whose main purpose it is to secure a fundamental change in economic conditions. Its steps were as uncertain as those of a child groping its way without knowing where it is going; for at this stage, I repeat, the revolution had a purely political stamp. But within the last two or three weeks a number of strikes have broken out quite spontaneously. Now, I regard it as the very essence of this revolution that strikes will become more and more extensive, until they constitute at last the focus of the revolution. [*Applause*]. Thus we shall have an economic revolution, and therewith a socialist revolution. The struggle for socialism has to be fought out by the masses, by the masses alone, breast to breast against capitalism; it has to be fought out by those in every occupation, by every proletarian against his employer. Thus only can it be a socialist revolution.

The thoughtless had a very different picture of the course of affairs. They imagined it would merely be necessary to overthrow the old government, to set up a socialist government at the head of affairs, and then to inaugurate socialism by decree. Another illusion? Socialism will not be and cannot be inaugurated by decrees; it cannot be established by any government, however admirably socialistic. Socialism must be created by the masses, must be made by every proletarian. Where the chains of capitalism are forged, there must the chains be broken. That only is

419

socialism, and thus only can socialism be brought into being.

What is the external form of struggle for socialism? The strike, and that is why the economic phase of development has come to the front in the second act of the revolution. This is something on which we may pride ourselves, for no one will dispute with us the honor. We of the Spartacus Group, we of the Communist Party of Germany, are the only ones in all Germany who are on the side of the striking and fighting workers. [*Hear! Hear!*] You have read and witnessed again and again the attitude of the Independent Socialists towards strikes. There was no difference between the outlook of *Vorwaerts* and the outlook of *Freiheit*. Both journals sang the same tune: Be diligent, socialism means hard work. Such was their utterance while capitalism was still in control! Socialism cannot be established in that way, but only by carrying on an unremitting struggle against capitalism. Yet we see the claims of the capitalists defended, not only by the most outrageous profit-snatchers, but also by the Independent Socialists and by their organ, *Freiheit*; we find that our Communist Party stands alone in supporting the workers against the exactions of capital. This suffices to show that all are today persistent and unsparing enemies of the strike, except only those who have taken their stand with us upon the platform of revolutionary communism.

The conclusion to be drawn is, not only that during the second act of the revolution, strikes will become increasingly prevalent; but, further, that strikes will become the central feature and the decisive factors of the revolution, thrusting purely political questions into the background. The inevitable consequence of this will be that the struggle in the economic field will be enormously intensified. The revolution will therewith assume aspects that will be no joke to the bourgeoisie. The members of the capitalist class are quite agreeable to mystifications in the political domain, where masquerades are still possible, where such creatures as Ebert and Scheidemann can pose as socialists; but they are horror-stricken directly profits are touched.

To the Ebert-Scheidemann government, therefore, the capitalists will present these alternatives. Either, they will say, you must put an end to the strikes, you must stop this strike movement which threatens to destroy us; or else, we have no more use for you. I believe, indeed, that the government has already damned itself pretty thoroughly by its political measures. Ebert and Scheidemann are distressed to find that the bourgeoisie no longer reposes confidence in them. The capitalists will think twice before they decide to cloak in ermine the rough upstart, Ebert. If matters go so far that a monarch is needed, they will say: "It does not suffice a king to have blood upon his hand; he must also have blue blood in his veins." [*Hear! hear!*] Should matters reach this pass, they will say: "If we needs must have a king, we will not have a parvenu who does not know how to comport himself in kingly fashion." [*Laughter.*]

It is impossible to speak positively as to details. But we are not concerned with matters of detail, with the question precisely what will happen, or precisely when it will happen. Enough that we know the broad lines of coming developments. Enough that we know that, to the first act of the revolution, to the phase in which the political struggle has been the leading feature, there will succeed a phase predominantly characterized by an intensification of the economic struggle, and that sooner or later the government of Ebert and Scheidemann will take its place among the shades.

It is far from easy to say what will happen to the National Assembly during the second act of the revolution. Perhaps, should the assembly come into existence, it may prove a new school of education for the working class. But it seems just as likely that the National Assembly will never come into existence. Let me say parenthetically, to help you to understand the grounds upon which we were defending our position yesterday, that our only objection was to limiting our tactics to a single alternative. I will not reopen the whole discussion, but will merely say a word or two lest any of you should falsely imagine that I am blowing hot and cold with the same breath. Our position today is precisely that of yesterday. We do not propose to base our tactics in relation to the National Assembly upon what is a possibility but not a certainty. We refuse to stake everything upon the belief that the National Assembly will never come into existence. *We wish to be prepared for all possibilities, including the possibility of utilizing the National Assembly for revolutionary purposes should the assembly ever come into being.* Whether it comes into being or not is a matter of indifference, for whatever happens the success of the revolution is assured.

What fragments will then remain of the Ebert-Scheidemann government or of any other alleged social democratic government which may happen to be in charge when the revolution takes place? I have said that the masses of the workers are already alienated from them, and that the soldiers are no longer to be counted upon as counterrevolutionary cannon fodder. What on earth will the poor pygmies be able to do? How can they hope to save the situation? They will still have one last chance. Those of you who have read today's newspapers will have seen where the ultimate reserves are, will have learned whom it is that the German counterrevolution proposes to lead against us should the worst come to the worst. You will all have read how the German troops in Riga are already marching shoulder to shoulder with the English against the Russian Bolsheviks.

421

Comrades, I have documents in my hands which throw an interesting light upon what is now going on in Riga. The whole thing comes from the headquarters' staff of the eighth army, which is collaborating with Herr August Winnig, the German social democrat and trade-union leader. We have always been told that the unfortunate Ebert and Scheidemann are victims of the Allies. But for weeks past, since the very beginning of our revolution, it has been the policy of *Vorwaerts* to suggest that the suppression of the Russian Revolution is the earnest desire of the Allies. We have here documentary evidence how all this was arranged to the detriment of the Russian proletariat and of the German revolution. In a telegram dated December 26, Lieutenant Colonel Buerkner, chief of general staff of the eighth army, conveys information concerning the negotiations which led to this agreement at Riga. The telegram runs as follows:

"On December 23 there was a conversation between the German plenipotentiary Winnig, and the British plenipotentiary Monsanquet, formerly consul-general at Riga. The interview took place on board H. M. S. *Princess Margaret,* and the commanding officer of the German troops was invited to be present. I was appointed to represent the army command. The purpose of the conversation was to assist in the carrying out of the armistice conditions. The conversation took the following course:

"'From the English side: The British ships at Riga will supervise the carrying out of the armistice conditions. Upon these conditions are based the following demands:

"' 1. The Germans are to maintain a sufficient force in this region to hold the Bolsheviks in check and to prevent them from extending the area now occupied. . . .

"' 3. A statement of the present disposition of the troops fighting the Bolsheviks, including both the German and the Lettish soldiers, shall be sent to the British staff officer, so that the information may be available for the senior naval officer. All future dispositions of the troops carrying on the fight against the Bolsheviks must in like manner be communicated through the same officer.

"' 4. A sufficient fighting force must be kept under arms at the following points in order to prevent their being seized by the Bolsheviks, and in order to prevent the Bolsheviks from passing beyond a line connecting the places named: Walk, Wolmar, Wenden, Friedrichstadt, Pensk, Mitau.

"' 5. The railway from Riga to Libau must be safeguarded against Bolshevik attack, and all British supplies and communications passing along this line shall receive preferential treatment.'"

A number of additional demands follow.

Let us now turn to the answer of Herr Winnig, German pleni-potentiary and trade-union leader:

"Though it is unusual that a desire should be expressed to compel a government to retain occupation of a foreign state, in this case it would be our own wish to do so, since the question is one of protecting German blood." [The Baltic Barons!] "Moreover, we regard it as a moral duty to assist the country which we have liberated from its former state of dependence. Our endeavors would, however, be likely to be frustrated, in the first place, by the condition of the troops, for our soldiers in this region are mostly men of considerable age and compara-tively unfit for service, and owing to the armistice keen on re-turning home and possessed of little will to fight; in the second place, owing to the attitude of the Baltic governments, by which the Germans are regarded as oppressors. But we will endeavor to provide volunteer troops, consisting of men with a fighting spirit, and indeed this has already in part been done."

Here we see the counterrevolution at work. You will have read not long ago of the formation of the Iron Division expressly in-tended to fight the Bolsheviks in the Baltic provinces. At that time there was some doubt as to the attitude of the Ebert-Scheide-mann government. You will now realize that the initiative in the creation of such a force actually came from the government.

One word more concerning Winnig. It is no chance matter that a trade-union leader should perform such political services. We can say, without hesitation, that the German trade-union leaders and the German social democrats are the most infamous scoun-drels the world has ever known. [*Vociferous applause.*] Do you know where these fellows, Winnig, Ebert, and Scheidemann ought by right to be? By the German penal code, which they tell us is still in force, and which continues to be the basis of their own legal system, they ought to be in jail! [*Vociferous applause.*] For by the German penal code it is an offense punishable by imprisonment to enlist German soldiers for foreign service. Today there stand at the head of the "socialist" government of Germany, men who are not merely the Judases of the socialist movement and traitors to the proletarian revolution, but who are jailbirds, unfit to mix with decent society. [*Loud applause.*]

To resume the thread of my discourse, it is clear that all these machinations, the formation of Iron Divisions and, above all, the before-mentioned agreement with British imperialists, must be regarded as the ultimate reserves, to be called up in case of need in order to throttle the German socialist movement. Moreover, the cardinal question, the question of the prospects of peace, is intimately associated with the affair. What can such negotiations lead to but a fresh lighting-up of the war? While these rascals are playing a comedy in Germany, trying to make us believe that they are working overtime in order to arrange conditions of peace, and declaring that we Spartacists are the disturbers of the peace whose doings are making the Allies uneasy and retarding the peace settlement, they are themselves kindling the war afresh, a war in the East to which a war on German soil will soon succeed.

Once more we meet with a situation the sequel of which cannot fail to be a period of fierce contention. It devolves upon us to defend, not socialism alone, not revolution alone, but likewise the interests of world peace. Herein we find a justification for the tactics which we of the Spartacus Group have consistently and at every opportunity pursued throughout the four years of the war. Peace means the worldwide revolution of the proletariat. In one way only can peace be established and peace be safeguarded—by the victory of the socialist proletariat! [*Prolonged applause.*]

What general tactical considerations must we deduce from this? How can we best deal with the situation with which we are likely to be confronted in the immediate future? Your first conclusion will doubtless be a hope that the fall of the Ebert-Scheidemann government is at hand, and that its place will be taken by a declared socialist proletarian revolutionary government. For my part, I would ask you to direct your attention, not on the apex, but to the base. We must not again fall into the illusion of the first phase of the revolution, that of November 9; we must not think that when we wish to bring about a socialist revolution it will suffice to overthrow the capitalist government and to set up another in its place. There is only one way of achieving the victory of the proletarian revolution.

We must begin by undermining the Ebert-Scheidemann government by destroying its foundations through a revolutionary mass struggle on the part of the proletariat. Moreover, let me remind you of some of the inadequacies of the German revolution, inadequacies which have not been overcome with the close of the first act of the revolution. We are far from having reached a point when the overthrow of the government can ensure the victory of socialism. I have endeavored to show you that the revolution of November 9 was, before all, a political revolution; whereas the revolution which is to fulfill our aims, must, in addition, and mainly, be an economic revolution. But further, the revolutionary movement was confined to the towns, and even up to the present date the rural districts remain practically untouched. Socialism would prove illusory if it were to leave our present agricultural system unchanged. From the broad outlook of socialist economics, manufacturing industry cannot be remodelled unless it be quickened through a socialist transformation of agriculture. The leading idea of the economic transformation that will realize socialism is an abolition of the contrast and the division between town and country. This separation, this conflict, this contradiction, is a purely capitalist phenomenon, and it must disappear as soon as we place ourselves upon the socialist standpoint.

If socialist reconstruction is to be undertaken in real earnest, we must direct attention just as much to the open country as to the industrial centers, and yet as regards the former we have not even taken the first steps. This is essential, not merely because we cannot bring about socialism without socializing agriculture; but also because, while we may think we have reckoned up the last reserves of the counterrevolution against us and our endeavors, there remains another important reserve which has not yet been taken into account. I refer to the peasantry. Precisely because the peasants are still untouched by socialism, they constitute an additional reserve for the counterrevolutionary bourgeoisie. The first thing our enemies will do when the flames of the socialist strikes begin to scorch their heels, will be to mobilize the peasants, who are fanatical devotees of private property. There is only one way of making headway against this threatening counterrevolutionary power. We must carry the class struggle into the country districts; we must mobilize the landless proletariat and the poorer peasants against the richer peasants. [Loud applause.]

From this consideration we may deduce what we have to do to ensure the success of the revolution. First and foremost, we have to extend in all directions the system of workers' councils. What we have taken over from November 9 are mere weak beginnings, and we have not wholly taken over even these. During the first phase of the revolution we actually lost extensive forces that were acquired at the very outset. You are aware that the counterrevolution has been engaged in the systematic destruction of the system of workers' and soldiers' councils. In Hesse, these councils have been definitely abolished by the counterrevolutionary government; elsewhere, power has been wrenched from their hands. Not merely, then, have we to develop the system of workers' and soldiers' councils, but we have to induce the agricultural laborers and the poorer peasants to adopt this system. We have to seize power, and the problem of the seizure of power assumes this aspect; what, throughout Germany, can each workers' and soldiers' council achieve? [Bravo!] There lies the source of power. We must mine the bourgeois state, and we must do so by putting an end everywhere to the cleavage in public powers, to the cleavage between legislative and executive powers. These powers must be united in the hands of the workers' and soldiers' councils.

425

Comrades, we have here an extensive field to till. We must build from below upwards, until the workers' and soldiers' councils gather so much strength that the overthrow of the Ebert-Scheidemann or any similar government will be merely the final act in the drama. For us the conquest of power will not be effected at one blow. It will be a progressive act, for we shall progressively occupy all the positions of the capitalist state, defending tooth and nail each one that we seize. Moreover, in my view and in that of my most intimate associates in the party, the economic struggle, likewise, will be carried on by the workers' councils. The settlement of economic affairs, and the continued expansion of the area of this settlement, must be in the hands of the workers' councils. The councils must have all power in the state. To these ends must we direct our activities in the immediate future, and it is obvious that, if we pursue this line, there cannot fail to be an enormous and immediate intensification of the struggle. For step by step, by hand-to-hand fighting, in every province, in every town, in every village, in every commune, all the powers of the state have to be transferred bit by bit from the bourgeoisie to the workers' and soldiers' councils.

But before these steps can be taken, the members of our own party and the proletarians in general must be schooled and disciplined. Even where workers' and soldiers' councils already exist, these councils are as yet far from understanding the purposes for which they exist. [*Hear! hear!*] We must make the masses realize that the workers' and soldiers' council has to be the central feature of the machinery of state, that it must concentrate all power within itself, and must utilize all powers for the one great purpose of bringing about the socialist revolution. Those workers who are already organized to form workers' and soldiers' councils are still very far from having adopted such an outlook, and only isolated proletarian minorities are as yet clear as to the tasks that devolve upon them. But there is no reason to complain of this, for it is a normal state of affairs. The masses must learn how to use power, by using power. There is no other way. We have, happily, advanced since the days when it was proposed to "educate" the proletariat socialistically. Marxists of Kautsky's school are, it would seem, still living in those vanished days. To educate the proletarian masses socialistically meant to deliver lectures to them, to circulate leaflets and pamphlets among them. But it is not by such means that the proletarians will be schooled. The workers, today, will learn in the school of action. [*Hear! hear!*]

Our scripture reads: In the beginning was the deed. Action for us means that the workers' and soldiers' councils must realize their mission and must learn how to become the sole public authorities throughout the realm. Thus only can we mine the ground so effectively as to make everything ready for the revolution which will crown our work. Quite deliberately, and with a clear sense of the significance of our words, did some of us say to you yesterday, did I in particular say to you, "Do not imagine that you are going to have an easy time in the future!" Some of the comrades have falsely imagined me to assume that we can boycott the National Assembly and then simply fold our arms. It is impossible, in the time that remains, to discuss this matter fully, but let me say that I never dreamed of anything of the kind. My meaning was that history is not going to make our revolution an easy matter like the bourgeois revolutions. In those revolutions it sufficed to overthrow the official power at the center, and to replace a dozen or so persons in authority. But we have to work from beneath. Therein is displayed the mass character of our revolution, one which aims at transforming the whole structure of society. It is thus characteristic of the modern proletarian revolution, that we must effect the conquest of political power, not from above, but from beneath.

The ninth of November was an attempt, a weakly, halfhearted, halfconscious, and chaotic attempt, to overthrow the existing public authority and to put an end to ownership rule. What is now incumbent upon us is that we should deliberately concentrate all the forces of the proletariat for an attack upon the very foundations of capitalist society. There, at the root, where the individual employer confronts his wage slaves; at the root, where all the executive organs of ownership rule confront the objects of this rule, confront the masses; there, step by step, we must seize the means of power from the rulers, must take them into our own hands. Working by such methods, it may seem that the process will be a rather more tedious one than we had imagined in our first enthusiasm. It is well, I think, that we should be perfectly clear as to all the difficulties and complications in the way of revolution. For I hope that, as in my own case, so in yours also, the description of the great difficulties we have to encounter, of the augmenting tasks we have to undertake, will neither abate zeal nor paralyze energy. Far from it, the greater the task, the more fervently will you gather up your forces. Nor must we forget that the revolution is able to do its work with extraordinary speed. I shall make no attempt to foretell how much time will be required. Who among us cares about the time, so long only as our lives suffice to bring it to pass? Enough for us to know clearly the work we have to do; and to the best of my ability I have endeavored to sketch, in broad outline, the work that lies before us. [*Tumultuous applause.*]

Appendix A

ON THE JUNIUS PAMPHLET

By V. I. Lenin

Lenin wrote this critique of the *Junius Pamphlet* in July 1916. It was subsequently published in *Sbornik Sotsial Demokrata,* number 1, in October 1916. This translation by Yuri Sdobnikov is reprinted from volume 22 of *Lenin, Collected Works.*

At last there has appeared in Germany, illegally, without any adaptation to the despicable Junker censorship, a social democratic pamphlet dealing with questions of the war! The author, who evidently belongs to the "left radical" wing of the party, takes the name of Junius (which in Latin means junior) and gives his pamphlet the title: *The Crisis of Social Democracy.* Appended are the "Theses on the Tasks of International Social Democracy," which have already been submitted to the Berne I. S. C. (International Socialist Committee) and published in number 3 of its *Bulletin*; the theses were drafted by the *Internationale* group, which in the spring of 1915 published one issue of a magazine under that title (with articles by Zetkin, Mehring, R. Luxemburg, Thalheimer, Duncker, Stroebel and others), and which in the winter of 1915-16 convened a conference of social democrats from all parts of Germany where these theses were adopted.

The pamphlet, the author says in the introduction dated January 2, 1916, was written in April 1915, and published "without any alteration." "Outside circumstances" had prevented its earlier publication. The pamphlet is devoted not so much to the "crisis of social democracy" as to an analysis of the war, to refuting the legend of it being a war for national liberation, to proving that it is an imperialist war on the part of Germany as well as on the part of the other Great Powers, and to a revolutionary criticism of the behavior of the official party. Written in a very lively style, Junius's pamphlet has undoubtedly played and will continue to play an important role in the struggle against the ex-Social Democratic Party of Germany, which has deserted to the bourgeoisie and the Junkers, and we extend our hearty greetings to the author.

To the Russian reader who is familiar with the social democratic literature in Russian published abroad in 1914-16, the *Junius Pamphlet* does not offer anything new in principle. In reading this pamphlet and comparing the arguments of this German revolutionary Marxist with what has been stated, for example, in the Manifesto of the Central Committee of our party (September-November 1914), ["The War and Russian Social Democracy" — Ed.], in the Berne resolutions (March 1915) ["The Conference of the R. S. D. L. P. Groups Abroad" — Ed.] and in the numerous commentaries on them, it only becomes clear that Junius's arguments are very incomplete and that he makes two mistakes. Before proceeding with a criticism of Junius's faults and errors we must strongly emphasize that this is done for the sake of self-criticism, which is so necessary to Marxists, and of submitting to an all-round test the views which must serve as the ideological basis of the Third International. On the whole, the *Junius Pamphlet* is a splendid Marxist work, and its defects are, in all probability, to a certain extent accidental.

The chief defect in Junius's pamphlet, and what marks a definite step backward compared with the legal (although immediately suppressed) magazine, *Internationale*, is its silence regarding the connection between social-chauvinism (the author uses neither this nor the less precise term social-patriotism) and opportunism. The author rightly speaks of the "capitulation" and collapse of the German Social Democratic Party and of the "treachery" of its "official leaders," but he goes no further. The *Internationale*, however, did criticize the "Center," i.e., Kautskyism, and quite properly poured ridicule on it for its spinelessness, its prostitution of Marxism and its servility to the opportunists. This same magazine *began* to expose the true role of the opportunists by revealing, for example, the very important fact that on August 4, 1914, the opportunists came out with an ultimatum, a ready-made decision to vote *for* war credits in *any* case. Neither the *Junius Pamphlet* nor the theses say *anything* about opportunism or about Kautskyism! This is wrong from the standpoint of theory, for it is impossible to *account for* the "betrayal" without linking it up with opportunism as a *trend* with a long history behind it, the history of the whole Second International. It is a mistake from the practical political standpoint, for it is impossible either to understand the "crisis of social democracy," or overcome it, without clarifying the meaning and the role of *two trends* — the openly opportunist trend (Legien, David, etc.) and the tacitly opportunist trend (Kautsky and Co.). This is a step backward compared with the historic article by Otto Ruehle in *Vorwaerts* of January 12, 1916, in which he directly and openly pointed out that a split in the Social Democratic Party of Germany was *inevitable* (the editors of *Vorwaerts* replied by repeating honeyed and hypocritical Kautskyite phrases, for they were unable to advance a single material argument to disprove the assertion that there were *already* two parties in existence, and that these two parties could not be reconciled). It is astonishingly inconsistent, because the *Internationale's* thesis number 12 *directly* states that it is necessary to create a "new" International, owing to the "treachery" of the "official representatives of the socialist parties of the leading countries" and their "adoption of the principles of bourgeois imperialist policies." It is clearly quite absurd to suggest that the old Social Democratic Party of Germany, or the party which tolerates Legien, David and Co., would participate in a "new" International.

We do not know why the *Internationale* group took this step backward. A very great defect in revolutionary Marxism in Germany as a whole is its lack of a compact illegal organization that would systematically pursue its own line and educate the masses in the spirit of the new tasks; such an organization would also have to take a definite stand on opportunism and Kautskyism. This is all the more necessary now, since the German revolutionary social democrats have been deprived of their last two daily papers; the one in Bremen (*Bremen Buerger-Zeitung*), and the one in Brunswick (*Volksfreund*), both of which have gone over to the Kautskyites. The International Socialists of Germany (I. S. D.) *alone* clearly and definitely remains at its post.

Some members of the *Internationale* group have evidently once again slid down into the morass of unprincipled Kautskyism. Stroebel, for instance, went so far as to drop a curtsey in *Neue Zeit* to Bernstein and Kautsky! And only the other day, on July 15, 1916, he had an article in the papers entitled "Pacifism and Social Democracy," in which he defends the most vulgar type of Kautskyite pacifism. As for Junius, he strongly opposes Kautsky's fantastic schemes like "disarmament," "abolition of secret diplomacy," etc. There may be two trends within the *Internationale* group: a revolutionary trend and a trend inclining to Kautskyism.

The first of Junius's erroneous propositions is embodied in the fifth thesis of the *Internationale* group. "National wars are no longer possible in the epoch (era) of this unbridled imperialism. National interests serve only as an instrument of deception, in order to place the working masses at the service of their mortal enemy, imperialism." The beginning of the fifth thesis, which concludes with the above statement, discusses the nature of the *present* war as an imperialist war. It may be that this negation of national wars generally is either an oversight, or an accidental overstatement in emphasizing the perfectly correct idea that the *present* war is an imperialist war, not a national war. This is a mistake that must be examined, for various social democrats, in view of the false assertions that the *present* war is a national war, have likewise mistakenly denied the possibility of *any* national war.

Junius is perfectly right in emphasizing the decisive influence of the "imperialist atmosphere" of the *present* war, in maintaining that behind Serbia stands Russia, "behind Serbian nationalism stands Russian imperialism," and that the participation of, say, Holland in the war would *likewise* be imperialist, for, first, Holland would be defending her colonies and, second, would be allied with one of the *imperialist* coalitions. That is irrefutable in respect to the *present* war. And when Junius stresses what for him is most important, namely, the struggle against the "phantom of national war," "which at present holds sway over social democratic policies" then it must be admitted that his views are both correct and fully to the point.

The only mistake, however, would be to exaggerate this truth, to depart from the Marxist requirement of concreteness, to apply the appraisal of this war to all wars possible under imperialism, to ignore the national movements *against* imperialism. The sole argument in defense of the thesis, "national wars are no longer possible," is that the world has been divided among a small group of "great" imperialist powers and for that reason any war, even if it starts as a national war, is *transformed* into an imperialist war involving the interest of one of the imperialist powers or coalitions.

The fallacy of this argument is obvious. That all dividing lines, both in nature and society, are conventional and dynamic, and that *every* phenomenon might, under certain conditions, be transformed into its opposite, is, of course a basic proposition of Marxist dialectics. A national war *might* be transformed into an imperialist war *and vice versa*. Here is an example: the wars of the Great French Revolution began as national wars and indeed were such. They were revolutionary wars — the defense of the great revolution against a coalition of counterrevolutionary monarchies. But when Napoleon founded the French Empire and subjugated a number of big, viable and long-established national European states, these national wars of the French became imperialist wars and *in turn* led to wars of national liberation *against* Napoleonic imperialism.

Only a sophist can disregard the difference between an imperialist and a national war on the grounds that one *might* develop into the other. Not infrequently have dialectics served — and the history of Greek philosophy is an example — as a bridge to sophistry. But we remain dialecticians and we combat sophistry not by denying the possibility of all transformations in general, but by analyzing the *given* phenomenon in its concrete setting and development.

Transformation of the present imperialist war of 1914-16 into a national war is highly improbable, for the class that represents *progressive* development is the proletariat which is objectively striving to transform it into a civil war against the bourgeoisie. Also this: there is no very considerable difference between the

431

forces of the two coalitions, and international finance capital has created a reactionary bourgeoisie everywhere. But such a transformation should *not* be proclaimed *impossible: if* the *European* proletariat remains impotent, say, for twenty years; *if* the present war *ends* in victories like Napoleon's and in the subjugation of a number of viable national states; *if* the transition to socialism of non-European imperialism (primarily Japanese and American) is also held up for twenty years by a war between these two countries, for example, then a great national war in Europe would be possible. It would hurl Europe *back* several decades. That is improbable, but *not* impossible, for it is undialectical, unscientific and theoretically wrong to regard the course of world history as smooth and always in a forward direction, without occasional gigantic leaps back.

Further, national wars waged by colonies and semicolonies in the imperialist era are not only probable but *inevitable.* About one thousand million people, or *over half* of the world's population, live in the colonies and semicolonies (China, Turkey, Persia). The national liberation movements there are either already very strong, or are growing and maturing. Every war is the continuation of politics by other means. The continuation of national liberation politics in the colonies will *inevitably* take the form of national wars *against* imperialism. Such wars *might* lead to an imperialist war of the present "great" imperialist powers, but on the other hand they might not. It will depend on many factors.

Example: Britain and France fought the Seven Years' War for the possession of colonies. In other words, they waged an imperialist war (which is possible on the basis of slavery and primitive capitalism as well as on the basis of modern highly developed capitalism). France suffered defeat and lost some of her colonies. Several years later there began the national liberation war of the North American States against Britain alone. France and Spain, then in possession of some parts of the present United States, concluded a friendship treaty with the states in rebellion against Britain. This they did out of hostility to Britain, i.e., in their own imperialist interests. French troops fought the British on the side of the American forces. What we have here is a national liberation war in which imperialist rivalry is an auxiliary element, one that has no serious importance. This is the very opposite to what we see in the war of 1914-16 (the national element in the Austro-Serbian War is of no serious importance compared with the all-determining element of imperialist rivalry). It would be absurd, therefore, to apply the concept imperialism indiscriminately and conclude that national wars are "impossible." A national liberation war, waged, for example, by an alliance of Persia, India and China against one or more of the imperialist powers, is both possible and probable, for it would follow from the national liberation movements in these countries. The transformation of such a war into an imperialist war between the present-day imperialist powers would depend upon very many concrete factors, the emergence of which it would be ridiculous to guarantee.

Third, even in Europe national wars in the imperialist epoch cannot be regarded as impossible. The "epoch of imperialism" made the present war an imperialist one and it inevitably engenders new imperialist wars (until the triumph of socialism). This "epoch" has made the policies of the present great powers thoroughly imperialist, but it by no means precludes national wars on the part of, say, small (annexed or nationally-oppressed) countries *against* the imperialist powers, just as it does not preclude large-scale national movements in Eastern Europe. Junius takes a very sober view of Austria, for example, giving due consideration not only to "economic" factors, but to the peculiar political factors. He notes "Austria's intrinsic lack of cohesion" and recognizes that the "Habsburg monarchy is not the political organization of a bourgeois state, but only a loose syndicate of several cliques of social parasites," and that "the liquidation of Austria-Hungary is, from the historical standpoint, only the continuation of the disintegration of Turkey and, at the same time, a requirement of the historical process of development." Much the same applies to some of the Balkan countries and Russia. And if the "great" powers are altogether exhausted in the present war, or if the revolution in Russia triumphs, national wars, and even victorious national wars, are quite possible. Practical intervention by the imperialist powers is *not* always feasible. That is one point. Another is that the superficial view that the war of a small state against a giant is hopeless should be countered by the observation that even a hopeless war is a war just the same. Besides, certain factors operating within the "giant" countries — the outbreak of revolution, for example — can turn a "hopeless" war into a very "hopeful" one.

We have dwelt in detail on the erroneous proposition that "national wars are no longer possible" not only because it is patently erroneous from the theoretical point of view — it would certainly be very lamentable if the "left" were to reveal a lighthearted attitude to Marxist theory at a time when the establishment of the Third International is possible only on the basis of unvulgarized Marxism. But the mistake is very harmful also from the standpoint of practical politics, for it gives rise to the absurd propaganda of "disarmament," since it is alleged that there can be no wars except reactionary wars. It also gives rise to the even more ludicrous and downright reactionary attitude of indifference to national movements. And such an attitude becomes chauvinism when members of the "great" European nations, that is, the nations which oppress the mass of small and colonial peoples, declare with a pseudoscientific air: "national wars are no longer possible"! National wars *against* the imperialist powers are not only possible and probable; they are inevitable, *progressive* and *revolutionary though* of course, to be *successful*, they require either the concerted effort of huge numbers of people in the oppressed countries (hundreds of millions in our example of India and China), or a *particularly* favorable conjuncture of international conditions (e.g., the fact that the imperialist powers cannot interfere, being paralyzed by exhaustion, by war, by their antagonism, etc.), or the *simultaneous* uprising of the proletariat against the bourgeoisie in one of the big powers (this latter eventuality holds first place as the most desirable and favorable for the victory of the proletariat).

It would be unfair, however, to accuse Junius of indifference to national movements. At any rate, he remarks that among the sins of the social democratic parliamentary group was its silence on the death sentence passed on a native leader in the Cameroons on charges of "treason" (evidently he attempted to organize an uprising against the war). Elsewhere Junius especially emphasizes (for the benefit of the Legiens, Lensches and the other scoundrels who are still listed as "social democrats") that colonial peoples must be regarded as nations along with all the others. Junius clearly and explicitly states: "Socialism recognized the right of every nation to independence and freedom, to independent mastery of its destinies"; "international socialism recognizes the right of free, independent and equal nations, but it is only socialism that can create such nations, and only it can realize the right of nations to self-determination. And this socialist slogan," Junius justly remarks, "serves, like all other socialist slogans, not to justify the existing order of things, but to indicate the way forward, and to stimulate the proletariat in its active revolutionary policy of transformation." It would be a grave mistake indeed to believe that all the German left social democrats have succumbed to the narrow-mindedness and caricature of Marxism now espoused by certain Dutch and Polish social democrats who deny the right of nations to self-determination even under socialism. But the *specific*, Dutch-Polish roots of *this* mistake we shall discuss elsewhere.

Another fallacious argument is advanced by Junius on the question of defense of the fatherland. This is a cardinal political question during an imperialist war. Junius has strengthened us in our conviction that our party has indicated the only correct approach to this question; the proletariat is opposed to defense of the fatherland in this imperialist war *because* of its predatory, slave-owning, reactionary character, *because* it is possible and necessary to oppose to it (and to strive to convert it into) civil war for socialism. Junius, however, while brilliantly exposing the imperialist character of the present war as distinct from a national war, makes the very strange mistake of trying to drag a national program into the *present, nonnational,* war. It sounds almost incredible, but there it is.

The official social democrats, both of the Legien and of the Kautsky stripe, in their servility to the bourgeoisie (who have been making the most noise about foreign "invasion" in order to deceive the mass of the people as to the imperialist character of the war), have been particularly assiduous in repeating this "invasion" argument. Kautsky, who now assures naive and credulous people (incidentally, through Spectator, a member of the Russian Organizing Committee) that he joined the opposition at the end of 1914, continues to use this "argument"! To refute it, Junius quotes extremely instructive examples from history, which prove that "invasion and class struggle are not contradictory in bourgeois history, as official legend has it, but that one is the means and the expression of the other." For example, the Bourbons in France invoked foreign invaders against the Jacobins; the bourgeoisie in 1871 invoked foreign invaders against the Commune.

In his *Civil War in France*, Marx wrote: "The highest heroic effort of which old society is still capable is national war; and this is now proved to be a mere governmental humbug, intended to defer the struggle of classes, and to be thrown aside as soon as that class struggle bursts out into civil war."

"The classical example for all times," says Junius, referring to 1793, "is the Great French Revolution." From all this, he draws the following conclusion: "The century of experience thus proves that it is not a state of siege, but relentless class struggle, which rouses the self-respect, the heroism and the moral strength of the mass of the people, and serves as the country's best protection and defense against the external enemy."

Junius's practical conclusion is this: "Yes, it is the duty of the social democrats to defend their country during a great historical crisis. But the grave guilt that rests upon the social democratic Reichstag group consists in their having given the lie to their own solemn declaration, made on August 4, 1914, 'In the hour of danger we will not leave our fatherland unprotected.' They *did* leave the fatherland unprotected in the hour of its greatest peril. For their first duty to the fatherland in that hour was to show the fatherland what was really behind the present imperialist war; to sweep away the web of patriotic and diplomatic lies covering up this encroachment on the fatherland; to proclaim loudly and clearly that both victory and defeat in the present war are equally fatal for the German people; to resist to the last the throttling of the fatherland due to the state of siege; to proclaim the necessity of immediately arming the people and of allowing the people to decide the question of war and peace; resolutely to demand a permanent session of the people's representatives for the whole duration of the war in order to guarantee vigilant control over the government by the people's representatives, and control over the people's representatives by the people; to demand the immediate abolition of all restrictions on political rights, for only a free people can successfully defend its country; and finally, to oppose the imperialist war program, which is to preserve Austria and Turkey, i.e., perpetuate reaction in Europe apd in Germany, with the old, truly national program of the patriots and democrats of 1848, the program of Marx, Engels and Lassalle — the slogan of a united Great German Republic. This is the banner that should have been unfurled before the country, which would have been a truly national banner of liberation, which would have been in accord with the best traditions of Germany and with the international class policy of the proletariat. .˙. . Hence, the grave dilemma — the interests of the fatherland or the international solidarity of the proletariat — the tragic conflict which prompted our parliamentarians to side, 'with a heavy heart,' with the imperialist war, is purely imaginary, it is a bourgeois nationalist fiction. On the contrary, there is complete harmony between the interests of the country and the class interests of the proletarian International, both in time of war and in time of peace; both war and peace demand the most energetic development of the class struggle, the most determined fight for the social democratic program."

This is how Junius argues. The fallacy of his argument is strikingly evident, and since the tacit and avowed lackeys of czarism, Plekhanov and Chkhenkeli, and perhaps even Martov and Chkheidze, may gloatingly seize upon Junius's words, not for the purpose of establishing theoretical truth, but for the purpose of wriggling, covering up their tracks and throwing dust into the eyes of the workers, we must in greater detail elucidate the *theoretical* source of Junius's error.

He suggests that the imperialist war should be "opposed" with a national program. He urges the advanced class to turn its face to the past and not to the future! In France, in Germany, and in the whole of Europe it was a *bourgeois*-democratic revolution that, *objectively*, was on the order of the day in 1793 and 1848. Corresponding to this *objective* historical situation was the "truly national," i.e., the national *bourgeois* program of the then existing democracy; in 1793 this program was carried out by the most revolutionary elements of the bourgeoisie and the plebeians, and in 1848 it was proclaimed by Marx in the name of the whole of progressive democracy. *Objectively*, the feudal and dynastic wars were then opposed by revolutionary democratic wars, by wars for national liberation. This was the content of the historical tasks of that epoch.

At the present time, the *objective* situation in the biggest advanced states of Europe is different. Progress, if we leave out for the moment the possibility of temporary steps backward, can be made only in the direction of *socialist* society, only in the direction of the *socialist revolution*. From the standpoint of progress, from the standpoint of the progressive class, the imperialist bourgeois war, the war of highly developed capitalism, can, *objectively*, be opposed only with a war *against* the bourgeoisie, i.e., primarily civil war for power between the proletariat and the bourgeoisie; for *unless* such a war is waged, serious progress is *impossible*; this may be followed — only under certain special conditions — by a war to defend the socialist state against bourgeois states. That is why the Bolsheviks (fortunately, very few, and quickly handed over by us to the *Prizyv* group) who were ready to adopt the point of view of conditional defense, i.e., defense of the fatherland on condition that there was a victorious revolution and the victory of a republic in Russia, were true to the *letter* of bolshevism, but betrayed its *spirit*; for being drawn into the imperialist war of the leading European powers, Russia would *also* be waging an imperialist war, even under a republican form of government!

In saying that the class struggle is the best means of defense against invasion, Junius applies Marxist dialectics only halfway, taking one step on the right road and immediately deviating from it. Marxist dialectics call for a concrete analysis of each specific historical situation. It is true that class struggle is the best means of defense against invasion *both* when the bourgeoisie is overthrowing feudalism, and when the proletariat is overthrowing the bourgeoisie. Precisely because it is true with regard to *every* form of class oppression, it is *too general*, and therefore, *inadequate* in the present *specific* case. Civil war against the bourgeoisie is *also* a form of class struggle, and only this form of class struggle would have saved Europe (the whole of Europe, not only one country) from the peril of invasion. The "Great German Republic," had it existed in 1914-16, would *also* have waged an *imperialist* war.

Junius came very close to the correct solution of the problem and to the correct slogan: civil war against the bourgeoisie for socialism; but, as if afraid to speak the whole truth, he turned *back*, to the fantasy of a "national war" in 1914, 1915 and 1916. If we examine the question not from the theoretical angle but from the purely practical one, Junius's error remains just as evident. The whole of bourgeois society, all classes in Germany, including the peasantry, were *in favor* of war (in all probability

437

the same was the case in Russia—at least a majority of the well-to-do and middle peasantry and a very considerable portion of the poor peasants were evidently under the spell of bourgeois imperialism). The bourgeoisie was armed to the teeth. Under such circumstances to "proclaim" the program of a republic, a permanent parliament, election of officers by the people (the "armed nation"), etc., would have meant, *in practice, "proclaiming" a revolution* (with the *wrong* revolutionary program!).

In the same breath Junius quite rightly says that a revolution cannot be "made." Revolution was on the order of the day in the 1914-16 period, it was hidden in the depths of the war, was *emerging* out of the war. This should have been *"proclaimed"* in the name of the revolutionary class, and *its* program should have been fearlessly and fully announced; socialism is impossible in time of war without civil war against the arch-reactionary, criminal bourgeoisie, which condemns the people to untold disaster. Systematic, consistent, practical measures should have been planned, which *could be carried out no matter at what* pace the revolutionary crisis might develop, and which would be in line with the maturing revolution. These measures are indicated in our party's resolution: (1) voting against war credits; (2) violation of the "class truce"; (3) creation of an illegal organization; (4) fraternization among the soldiers; (5) support for all the revolutionary actions of the masses. The success of *all* these steps *inevitably* leads to civil war.

The promulgation of a great historical program was undoubtedly of tremendous significance; not the old national German program, which became obsolete in 1914, 1915 and 1916, but the proletarian internationalist and socialist program. "You, the bourgeoisie, are fighting for plunder; we, the workers of *all* the belligerent countries, declare war upon you for socialism"—that's the sort of speech that should have been delivered in the parliaments on August 4, 1914, by socialists who had not betrayed the proletariat, as the Legiens, Davids, Kautskys, Plekhanovs, Guesdes, Sembats, etc., had done.

Evidently Junius's error is due to two kinds of mistakes in reasoning. There is no doubt that Junius is decidedly opposed to the imperialist war and is decidedly *in favor* of revolutionary tactics; and all the gloating of the Plekhanovs over Junius's "defensism" cannot wipe out this *fact.* Possible and probable calumnies of this kind must be answered promptly and bluntly.

But, first, Junius has not completely rid himself of the "environment" of the German social democrats, even the leftists, who are afraid of a split, who are afraid to follow revolutionary slogans to their logical conclusions.* This is a false fear, and the

---

* We find the same error in Junius's arguments about which is better,

left social democrats of Germany must and *will* rid themselves of it. They *are sure to do so* in the course of their struggle against the social-chauvinists. The fact is that they are fighting against *their own* social-chauvinists resolutely, firmly and *sincerely*, and this is the tremendous, the fundamental difference in principle between them and the Martovs and Chkheidzes, who, with one hand (*a la* Skobelev) unfurl a banner bearing the greeting, "To the Liebknechts of all countries," and with the other hand tenderly embrace Chkhenkeli and Potresov!

Secondly, Junius apparently wanted to achieve something in the nature of the menshevik "theory of stages," of sad memory; he wanted to *begin* to carry out the revolutionary program from the end that is "more suitable," "more popular" and more acceptable to the *petty bourgeoisie*. It is something like a plan "to outwit history," to outwit the philistines. He seems to say, surely, nobody would oppose a *better* way of defending the real fatherland; and the real fatherland is the Great German Republic, and the best defense *is* a militia, a permanent parliament, etc. Once it was accepted, that program would automatically lead to the next stage— to the socialist revolution.

Probably, it was reasoning of this kind that consciously or semiconsciously determined Junius's tactics. Needless to say, such reasoning is fallacious. Junius's pamphlet conjures up in our mind the picture of a *lone* man who has no comrades in an illegal organization accustomed to thinking out revolutionary slogans to their conclusion and systematically educating the masses in their spirit. But this shortcoming— it would be a grave error to forget this—is not Junius's personal failing, but the result of the weakness of all the German leftists, who have become entangled in the vile net of Kautskyite hypocrisy, pedantry and "friendliness" for the opportunists. Junius's adherents have managed, *in spite* of their isolation, to *begin* the publication of illegal leaflets and to start the war against Kautskyism. They will succeed in going further along the right road.

---

victory or defeat? His conclusion is that both are equally bad (ruin, growth of armaments, etc.). This is the point of view not of the revolutionary proletariat, but of the pacifist petty bourgeoisie. If one speaks about the "revolutionary intervention" of the proletariat— of this both Junius and the thesis of the *Internationale* group speak, although unfortunately in terms that are too general— one *must* raise the question from *another* point of view, namely: (1) Is "revolutionary intervention" possible without the risk of defeat? (2) Is it possible to scourge the bourgeoisie and the government of one's *own* country without taking that risk? (3) Have we not always asserted, and does not the historical experience of reactionary wars prove, that defeats help the cause of the revolutionary class? [V. I. L.]

439

Appendix B

FROM "NOTES OF A PUBLICIST"

By V. I. Lenin

The following selection is an excerpt from "Notes of a Publicist," which Lenin wrote at the end of February 1922. The essay was first published in issue number 87 of *Pravda* dated April 16, 1924. This translation is reprinted from *Lenin, Collected Works*, volume 33.

———

Paul Levi now wants to get into the good graces of the bourgeoisie — and, *consequently*, of its agents, the Second and the Two-and-a-Half Internationals — by republishing precisely those writings of Rosa Luxemburg in which she was wrong. We shall reply to this by quoting two lines from a good old Russian fable: "Eagles may at times fly lower than hens, but hens can never rise to the height of eagles." Rosa Luxemburg was mistaken on the question of the independence of Poland; she was mistaken in 1903 in her appraisal of menshevism; she was mistaken on the theory of the accumulation of capital; she was mistaken in July 1914, when, together with Plekhanov, Vandervelde, Kautsky and others, she advocated unity between the Bolsheviks and Mensheviks; she was mistaken in what she wrote in prison in 1918 (she corrected most of these mistakes at the end of 1918 and the beginning of 1919 after she was released). But in spite of her mistakes she was — and remains for us — an eagle. And not only will Communists all over the world cherish her memory, but her biography and her *complete* works (the publication of which the German Communists are inordinately delaying, which can only be partly excused by the tremendous losses they are suffering in their severe struggle) will serve as useful manuals for training many generations of Communists all over the world. "Since August 4, 1914, German social democracy has been a stinking corpse" — this statement will make Rosa Luxemburg's name famous in the history of the international working-class movement. And, of course, in the backyard of the working-class movement, among the dung heaps, hens like Paul Levi, Scheidemann, Kautsky and all that fraternity will cackle over the mistakes committed by the great communist. To every man his own.

Appendix C

HANDS OFF ROSA LUXEMBURG

By Leon Trotsky

Trotsky wrote this article in defense of Rosa Luxemburg from Prinkipo, Turkey on June 28, 1932. It was published in *The Militant* in two installments in the issues of August 6 and 13, 1932.

Stalin's article, "On Some Questions in the History of Bolshevism" reached me after much delay. After receiving it, for a long time I could not force myself to read it, for such literature sticks in one's throat like sawdust or mashed bristles. But still having finally read it, I came to the conclusion that one cannot ignore this performance, if only because there is included in it a vile and barefaced calumny about Rosa Luxemburg. This great revolutionist is enrolled by Stalin into the camp of centrism! He proves — not proves, of course, but asserts — that bolshevism from the day of its inception held to the line of a split with the Kautsky center, while Rosa Luxemburg during the time sustained Kautsky from the left. I quote his own words, "Long before the war, from about 1903-04, when the Bolshevik group had formed in Russia and when lefts first made themselves heard in the German social democracy, Lenin took the course toward a break, a split with the opportunists both at home, in the Russian Social Democratic Party, and abroad in the Second International, and the German social democracy in particular." That this, however, could not be achieved was due entirely to the fact that "the left social democrats in the Second International, and first of all, in the German social democracy composed a weak and impotent group . . . that was fearful even of uttering aloud the word, 'break, split.'" Such is the basic formulation of the article. Beginning with 1903, the Bolsheviks stood for a break not only with the right but also with the Kautsky center; while Rosa was afraid even to mention openly the word "split."

To put forward such an assertion, one must be absolutely ignorant of the history of one's own party, and first of all, of Lenin's ideological course. There is not a single word of truth

441

in Stalin's point of departure. In 1903-04, Lenin was, indeed, an irreconcilable foe of opportunism in the German social democracy. But he considered as opportunism only the *revisionist* trend, which was led theoretically by Bernstein.

Kautsky at the time was to be found fighting against Bernstein. *Lenin considered Kautsky as his teacher* and stressed this everywhere he could. In Lenin's work of that period as well as for a number of years following, one does not find even a trace of criticism in principle directed against the trend of Bebel-Kautsky. Instead one finds a series of declarations to the effect that bolshevism is not some sort of an independent trend, but is only a translation into the language of Russian conditions of the trend of Bebel-Kautsky. Here is what Lenin wrote in his famous pamphlet, *Two Tactics*, in the middle of 1905, "When and where did I call the revolutionism of Bebel and Kautsky 'opportunism'? When and where did any divergences come out into the open between me on the one hand and Bebel and Kautsky? . . . The complete solidarity of the international revolutionary social democracy in all major questions of program and tactic is an incontrovertible fact." Lenin's words are so clear, precise, and categorical as to entirely exhaust the question.

A year and a half later, on December 7, 1906, Lenin wrote, in the article "The Crisis of Menshevism," ". . . From the very first (see *One Step Forward, Two Steps Backwards*) we affirmed that we are not creating any special sort of bolshevist tendency; we only take our stand everywhere and at all times in defense of the point of view of the revolutionary social democracy. And within the social democracy, right up to the social revolution, there will inevitably be an opportunistic and a revolutionary wing."

Speaking of menshevism, as the opportunistic wing of the social democracy, Lenin compared the mensheviks not with Kautskyism but with revisionism. Moreover he looked upon bolshevism as the Russian form of Kautskyism, which in his eyes was in that period identical with Marxism. The passage we have just quoted shows, incidentally, that Lenin did not at all stand absolutely for a split with the opportunists; he not only admitted but also considered "inevitable" the existence of the revisionists in the social democracy right up to the social revolution.

Two weeks later, on December 20, 1906, Lenin greeted enthusiastically Kautsky's answer to Plekhanov's questionnaire on the character of the Russian Revolution, "What we have claimed — that our fight for the position of revolutionary social democracy against opportunism is in no manner whatsoever the creation of some 'original' bolshevist tendency — has been completely confirmed by Kautsky. . . ."

Within these limits, I trust, the question is absolutely clear. According to Stalin, Lenin, even from 1903, had demanded a break in Germany with the opportunists, not only of the right wing (Bernstein) but also of the left (Kautsky). Whereas in December, 1906, Lenin as we see was proudly pointing out to Plekhanov and the Mensheviks that the trend of Kautsky in Germany and the trend of bolshevism in Russia were—identical. Such is part one of Stalin's excursion into the ideological history of bolshevism. Our investigator's scrupulousness and his knowledge rest on the same plane!

Directly after his assertion regarding 1903-04, Stalin makes a leap to 1916 and refers to Lenin's sharp criticism of the war pamphlet by Junius, i.e., Rosa Luxemburg. To be sure, in that period Lenin had already declared war to the finish against Kautskyism, having drawn from his criticism all the necessary organizational conclusions. It is not to be gainsaid that Rosa Luxemburg did not pose the question of the struggle against centrism with the requisite completeness—in this advantages were entirely on Lenin's side. But between October 1916, when Lenin wrote about Junius's pamphlet, and 1903, when bolshevism had its inception, there is a lapse of thirteen years; in the course of the major part of this period Rosa Luxemburg was to be found in the opposition to the Kautsky and Bebel Central Committee, and her fight against the formal, pedantic, and rotten-at-the-core "radicalism" of Kautsky took on an ever increasingly sharp character.

Lenin did not participate in this fight and did not support Rosa Luxemburg up to 1914. Passionately absorbed in Russian affairs, he preserved extreme caution in international matters. In Lenin's eyes Bebel and Kautsky stood immeasurably higher as revolutionists than in the eyes of Rosa Luxemburg, who observed them at closer range, in action, and who was much more directly subjected to the atmosphere of German politics.

The capitulation of the German social democracy on August 4 was entirely unexpected by Lenin. It is well known that the issue of the *Vorwaerts* with the patriotic declaration of the social democratic faction was taken by Lenin to be a forgery by the German staff. Only after he was absolutely convinced of the awful truth did he subject to revision his evaluation of the basic tendencies of the German social democracy, and while so doing, he performed that task in the Leninist manner, i.e., he finished it off once for all.

On October 27, 1914, Lenin wrote to A. Schliapnikov, ". . . I hate and despise Kautsky *now* more than all the rest, the filthy, vile and self-satisfied brood of hypocrisy. . . . R. Luxemburg was right, she *long ago* understood that Kautsky had the highly developed 'servility of a theoretician' — to put it more plainly, he was ever a flunkey, a flunkey to the majority of the party, a flunkey to opportunism" (*Leninist Anthology*, Vol. II, page 200, my emphasis).

Were there no other documents (and there are hundreds), these few lines alone could unmistakably clarify the history of the question. Lenin deemed it necessary at the end of 1914 to inform one of the colleagues closest to him at the time, that "now," at the present moment, today, in contradistinction to the past, he "hates and despises" Kautsky. The sharpness of the phrase is an unmistakable indication of the extent to which Kautsky betrayed Lenin's hopes and expectations. No less vivid is the second phrase "R. Luxemburg was right, she *long ago* understood that Kautsky had the highly developed 'servility of a theoretician' . . . ." Lenin hastens here to recognize that "verity" which he did not see formerly, or which, at least, he did not recognize fully on Rosa Luxemburg's side.

Such are the chief chronological guideposts of the questions, which are at the same time important guideposts of Lenin's political biography. The fact is indubitable that his ideological orbit is represented by a continually rising curve. But this only means that Lenin was not born Lenin full-fledged, as he is pictured by the slavering daubers of the "divine," but that he made himself Lenin. Lenin ever extended his horizons, he learned from others and daily drew himself to a higher plane than was his own yesterday. In this perseverance, in this stubborn resolution of a continual spiritual growth over his own self did his heroic spirit find its expression. If Lenin in 1903 had understood and formulated everything that was required for the coming times, then the remainder of his life would have consisted only of reiterations. In reality this was not at all the case. Stalin simply stamps the Stalinist imprint on Lenin and coins him into the petty small-change of numbered adages.

In Rosa Luxemburg's struggle against Kautsky, especially in 1910-14, an important place was occupied by the questions of war, militarism and pacifism. Kautsky defended the reformist program, limitations of armaments, international court, etc. Rosa Luxemburg fought decisively against this program as illusory. On this question, Lenin was in some doubt, but at a certain period he stood closer to Kautsky than to Rosa Luxemburg. From conversations at the time with Lenin I recall that the following argument of Kautsky made a great impression upon him: just as in domestic questions, reforms are products of the revolutionary class struggle, so in international relationships it is possible to fight for and to gain certain guarantees ("reforms") by means of the international class struggle. Lenin considered it entirely possible to support this position of Kautsky, provided that he, after the polemic with Rosa Luxemburg, turned upon the rights (Noske and Co.). I do not undertake now to say from memory to what extent this circle of ideas found its expression in Lenin's articles: the question would require a particularly careful analysis. Neither can I take upon myself to assert from memory how soon Lenin's doubts on this question were settled. In any case they found their expression not only in conversations but also in correspondence. One of these letters is in the possession of Karl Radek.

I deem it necessary to supply on this question evidence as a witness in order to attempt in this manner to save an exceptionally valuable document for the theoretical biography of Lenin. In the autumn of 1926, at the time of our collective work over the platform of the Left Opposition, Radek showed Kamenev, Zinoviev and myself — probably also other comrades as well — a letter of Lenin to him (1911?) which consisted of the defense of Kautsky's position against the criticism of the German lefts. In accordance with the regulation passed by the Central Committee, Radek, like all others, should have delivered this letter to the Lenin Institute. But fearful lest it be hidden, if not destroyed, in the Stalinist factory of fabrications, Radek decided on preserving the letter till some more opportune time. One cannot deny that there was some foundation to Radek's attitude. At present, however, Radek himself has — though not very responsible — still quite an active part in the work of producing political forgeries. Suffice it to recall that Radek, who in distinction to Stalin is acquainted with the history of Marxism, and who, at any rate, knows this letter of Lenin, found it possible to make a public statement of his solidarity with the insolent evaluation placed by Stalin on Rosa Luxemburg. The circumstance that Radek acted thereupon under Yaroslavsky's rod does not mitigate his guilt, for only despicable slaves can renounce the principles of Marxism in the name of the principles of the rod.

However the matter we are concerned with relates not to the personal characterization of Radek but to the fate of Lenin's letter. What happened to it? Is Radek hiding it even now from the Lenin Institute? Hardly. Most probably, he entrusted it, where it should be entrusted, as a tangible proof of an intangible devotion. And what lay in store for the letter thereafter? Is it preserved in Stalin's personal archives alongside with the documents that compromise his closest colleagues? Or is it destroyed as many other most precious documents of the party's past have been destroyed?

In any case there cannot be even the shadow of a political reason for the concealment of a letter written two decades ago

445

on a question that holds now only a historical interest. But it is precisely the historical value of the letter that is exceptionally great. It shows Lenin as he really was, and not as he is being recreated in their own semblance and image by the bureaucratic dunderheads, who pretend to infallibility. We ask, where is Lenin's letter to Radek? Lenin's letter must be where it belongs! Put it on the table of the party and of the Comintern!

If one were to take the disagreements between Lenin and Rosa Luxemburg in their entirety, then the historical correctness is unconditionally on Lenin's side. But this does not exclude the fact that in certain questions, and during definite periods Rosa Luxemburg was correct as against Lenin. In any case, the disagreements despite their importance, and at times, their extreme sharpness, developed on the bases of revolutionary proletarian policies common to them both.

When Lenin, going back into the past, wrote in October 1919 ("Greetings to the Italian, French and German communists"), ". . . in the moment of the seizure of power and the creation of the Soviet Republic, bolshevism remained alone in the field, it had drawn to itself the best of *the tendencies closest to it in socialist thought*," I repeat, when Lenin wrote this, he unquestionably had in mind also the tendencies of Rosa Luxemburg, whose closest adherents, e.g., Markhlevsky, Djerjinsky and others, were working in the ranks of the Bolsheviks.

Lenin understood Rosa Luxemburg's mistakes more profoundly than Stalin; but it was not accidentally that Lenin once quoted the old couplet in relation to Luxemburg,

> Betimes the eagles down swoop and
> 'neath the barnyard fowl fly,
> But barnyard fowl with outspread wings will
> never soar amid the clouds in the sky.

Precisely the case! Precisely the point! For this very reason Stalin should proceed with caution before expending his vicious mediocrity when the matter touches figures of such stature as Rosa Luxemburg.

In the article "In Relation to the History of the Question of the Dictatorship," Lenin (October 1920) touching upon questions of the soviet state and the dictatorship of the proletariat, already posed by the 1905 Revolution, wrote, "Such outstanding representatives of the revolutionary proletariat and of the unfalsified Marxism as Rosa Luxemburg evaluated immediately the significance of the practical experience and came forward at meetings and in the press with critical analyses of it." On the contrary, "people, of the type of future Kautskyites . . . evinced an utter incapacity to understand the significance of this experience." In a few lines, Lenin fully pays the tribute of recognition to the historical significance of Rosa Luxemburg's struggle against Kautsky — the struggle, which Lenin himself had been far from immediately evaluating at its true worth. If to Stalin, the ally of Chiang Kai-shek, and the comrade in arms of Purcell, the theoretician of "the worker peasant party," of "the democratic dictatorship" of "nonantagonizing the bourgeoisie," etc. — if to him Rosa Luxemburg is the representative of centrism, to Lenin she is the representative of "unfalsified Marxism." What this designation meant coming as it does from Lenin's pen is clear to anyone who is even slightly acquainted with Lenin.

I take the occasion to point out here that in the notes to Lenin's works there is among others the following said about Rosa Luxemburg, "During the florescence of the Bernsteinian revisionism and later of ministerialism (Millerand), Luxemburg carried on against this tendency a decisive fight, taking her position in the left wing of the German party. . . . In 1907 she participated as a delegate of the S. D. of Poland and Lithuania in the London Congress of R. S. D. L. P., supporting the Bolshevik faction on all basic questions of the Russian Revolution. From 1907, Luxemburg gave herself over entirely to work in Germany, taking a left-radical position and carrying on a fight against the center and the right wing . . . . Her participation in the January 1919 insurrection has made her name *the banner of the proletarian revolution.*"

Of course, the author of these notes will in all probability on the morrow confess his sins and announce that in Lenin's epoch he wrote in a benighted condition, and that he reached complete enlightenment only in the epoch of Stalin. At the present moment announcements of this sort — combinations of sycophancy, idiocy and buffoonery — are made daily in the Moscow press. But they do not change the nature of things, "What's once set down in black and white, no ax will hack nor all your might." Yes, Rosa Luxemburg has become the banner of the proletarian revolution!

How and wherefore, however, did Stalin suddenly busy himself — at so belated a time — with the revision of the old Bolshevik valuation of Rosa Luxemburg? As was the case with all his preceding theoretical abortions so with this latest one, and the most scandalous, the origin lies in the logic of his struggle against the theory of permanent revolution. In his "historical" article, Stalin once again allots the chief place to this theory. There is not a single new word in what he says. I have long ago answered all his arguments in my book *The Permanent Revolution.* From the historical viewpoint the question will be sufficiently clarified, I trust, in the second volume of *The History of the Russian Revolution* (The October Revolution), now on the press. In the present case the question of the permanent revolution concerns us only insofar as Stalin links it up with Rosa Luxemburg's name. We shall presently see how the hapless theoretician has contrived to set up for himself a murderous trap.

After recapitulating the controversy between the Mensheviks and the Bolsheviks on the question of the moving forces in the Russian revolution and after masterfully compressing a series of mistakes into a few lines, which I am compelled to leave without an examination, Stalin indites, "What was the attitude of the left German social democrats, Parvus and Rosa Luxemburg, to these controversies? They concocted a utopian and a semi-menshevist schema of the permanent revolution. . . . Subsequently this semi-menshevist schema was caught up by Trotsky (partly by Martov) and turned into a weapon of struggle against Leninism. . . ." Such is the unexpected history of the origin of the theory of the permanent revolution, in accordance with the latest historical researches of Stalin. But, alas, the investigator forgot to consult his own previous learned works. In 1925 this same Stalin had already expressed himself on this question in his polemic against Radek. Here is what he wrote then, "It is *not true that the theory of the permanent revolution . . . was put forward in 1905 by Rosa Luxemburg and Trotsky.* As a matter of fact this theory was put forward by Parvus and Trotsky." This assertion may be consulted on page 185, *Questions of Leninism,* Russian edition, 1926. Let us hope that it obtains in all foreign editions.

So, in 1925, Stalin pronounced Rosa Luxemburg not guilty in the commission of such a cardinal sin as participating in the creation of the theory of the permanent revolution. "As a matter of fact, this theory was put forward by Parvus and Trotsky." In 1931, we are informed by the identical Stalin that it was precisely, "Parvus and Rosa Luxemburg . . . who concocted the utopian and semi-menshevist schema of the permanent revolution." As for Trotsky he was innocent of creating the theory, it was only "caught up" by him, and at the same time by . . . Martov! Once again Stalin is caught with the goods. Perhaps he writes on questions of which he can make neither head nor tail. Or is he consciously shuffling marked cards in playing with the basic questions of Marxism? It is incorrect to pose this question as an alternative. As a matter of fact, both the one and the other obtain here. The Stalinist falsifications are conscious in so far as they are dictated at each given moment by entirely concrete personal interests. At the same time they are semiconscious, in so far as his congenital ignorance places no impediments whatsoever to his theoretical propensities.

But facts remain facts. In his war against "the Trotskyist contraband," Stalin has fallen foul of a new personal enemy, Rosa

Luxemburg! He did not pause for a moment before lying about her and villifying her; and moreover before proceeding to put into circulation his stallion's doses of vulgarity and disloyalty, he did not even take the bother of verifying what he himself had said on the same subject five years before.

The new variant of the history of the ideas of the permanent revolution was indicated first of all by an urge to provide a dish more spicy than all those preceding. It is needless to explain that Martov was dragged in by the hair for the sake of the greater piquancy of theoretical and historical cookery. Martov's attitude to the theory and practice of the permanent revolution was one of unalterable antagonism, and in the old days he stressed more than once that Trotsky's views on revolution were rejected equally by the Bolsheviks as well as the Mensheviks. But it is not worthwhile to pause over this.

- What is truly fatal is that there is not a single major question of international proletarian revolution, on which Stalin has failed to express two directly contradictory opinions. We all know that in April 1924, he conclusively demonstrated in *The Questions of Leninism* the impossibility of building socialism in one country. In autumn, in a new edition of the book, he substituted in its place a proof (i.e., a bald proclamation) that the proletariat "can and must" build socialism in one country. The entire remainder of the text was left unchanged. On the question of the worker peasant party, of the Brest-Litovsk negotiations, the leadership of the October Revolution, on the national question, etc., etc., Stalin contrived to put forward, for a period of a few years, sometimes of a few months, opinions that were mutually exclusive. It would be incorrect to place the blame in everything on a poor memory. The matter reaches deeper here. Stalin completely lacks any method of scientific thinking, he has no criteria of principles. He approaches every question as if that question were born only today and stood apart from all other questions. Stalin contributes his judgments entirely depending upon whatever personal interest of his is uppermost and most urgent today. The contradictions that convict him are the direct vengeance for his vulgar empiricism. Rosa Luxemburg does not appear to him in the perspective of the German, Polish and international workers movement of the last half-century. No, she is to him each time a new, and, besides, an isolated figure, regarding whom he is compelled in every new situation to ask himself anew, "Who goes there, friend or foe?" Unerring instinct has this time whispered to the theoretician of socialism in one country that the shade of Rosa Luxemburg is irreconcilably inimical to him. But this does not hinder the great shade from remaining the banner of the international proletarian revolution.

Rosa Luxemburg criticized very severely and fundamentally

incorrectly the policies of the Bolsheviks in 1918 from her prison cell. But even in this, her most erroneous work, her eagle's wings are to be seen. Here is her general evaluation of the October overturn, "Everything that the party had the power to perform in the sphere of valor, of forceful action, of revolutionary farsightedness and consequentialness — all that was fully carried out by Lenin, Trotsky and the party comrades. All the revolutionary honor and the capacity for action, which the social democracy of the West so lacked, were demonstrated by the Bolsheviks. Their October insurrection was not only the true salvation of the Russian Revolution but it also saved the honor of international socialism." Can this perchance be the voice of centrism?

In the succeeding pages, Luxemburg subjects to severe criticism the policies of the Bolsheviks in the agrarian sphere, their slogan of national self-determination, and their rejection of formal democracy. In this criticism we might add, directed equally against Lenin and Trotsky, she makes no distinction whatever between their views; and Rosa Luxemburg knew how to read, understand, and seize upon shadings. It did not even fall into her head, for instance, to accuse me of the fact that by being in solidarity with Lenin on the agrarian question, I had changed my views on the peasantry. And moreover she knew these views very well since I had developed them in detail in 1909 in her Polish journal. Rosa Luxemburg ends her criticism with the demand, "in the policy of the Bolsheviks the essential must be distinguished from the unessential, the fundamental from the accidental." The fundamental she considers to be the force of the action of the masses, the will to socialism. "In this relation," she writes, "Lenin and Trotsky with their friends were the *first* who have set an example to the world proletariat. Even now they remain the *only ones* who can exclaim with Hutten, 'This, I have dared!'"

Yes, Stalin has sufficient cause to hate Rosa Luxemburg. But all the more imperious therefore becomes our duty to shield Rosa's memory from Stalin's calumny that has been caught by the hired functionaries of both hemispheres, and to pass on this truly beautiful, heroic and tragic image to the young generations of the proletariat in all its grandeur and inspirational force.

Appendix D

LUXEMBURG AND THE
FOURTH INTERNATIONAL

By Leon Trotsky

On June 24, 1935, Trotsky completed this article, which was subsequently published in the August 1935 issue of *New International.*

———

Efforts are now being made in France and elsewhere to construct a so-called Luxemburgism as an entrenchment for the left centrists against the Bolshevik-Leninists. This question may acquire a considerable significance. It may perhaps be necessary to devote a more extensive article in the near future to real and alleged Luxemburgism. I wish to touch here only upon the essential features of the question.

We have more than once taken up the cudgels for Rosa Luxemburg against the impudent and stupid misrepresentations of Stalin and his bureaucracy. And we shall continue to do so. In doing so we are not prompted by any sentimental considerations, but by the demands of historical-materialist criticism. Our defense of Rosa Luxemburg is not, however, unconditional. The weak sides of Rosa Luxemburg's teachings have been laid bare both theoretically and practically. The S. A. P. * people and kindred elements (see, for example, the dilletante intellectual "proletarian cultural": French *Spartacus,* the periodical of the socialist students appearing in Belgium, and oftentimes also the Belgian *Action Socialiste,* etc.) make use only of the weak sides and the inadequacies which were by no means decisive in Rosa; they generalize and exaggerate these weaknesses to the utmost and

———

* S. A. P. [Sozialistiche Arbeiterspartei — Socialist Workers Party]: a centrist German group formed in 1931 through a merger of left social democrats and former Right Communists, some of whose leaders briefly supported Trotsky's advocacy of a new international in 1933; most of its members eventually returned to the social democracy. [Ed.]

build up a thoroughly absurd system on that basis. The paradox consists in this, that in their latest turn the Stalinists, too —without acknowledging or even understanding it—come close in theory to the caricatured negative sides of Luxemburgism, to say nothing of the traditional centrists and left centrists in the social democratic camp.

There is no gainsaying that Rosa Luxemburg impassionately counterposed the spontaneity of mass actions to the "victory-crowned" conservative policy of the German social democracy especially after the Revolution of 1905. This counterposition had a thoroughly revolutionary and progressive character. At a much earlier date than Lenin, Rosa Luxemburg grasped the retarding character of the ossified party and trade-union apparatus and began a struggle against it. Inasmuch as she counted upon the inevitable accentuation of class conflicts, she always predicted the certainty of the independent elemental appearance of the masses against the .will and against the line of march of the officialdom. In these broad historical outlines, Rosa was proved right. For the revolution of 1918 was "spontaneous," that is, it was accomplished by the masses against all the provisions and all the precautions of the party officialdom. On the other hand, the whole of Germany's subsequent history amply showed that spontaneity alone is far from enough for success; Hitler's regime is a weighty argument against the panacea of spontaneity.

Rosa herself never confined herself to the mere theory of spontaneity, like Parvus, for example, who later bartered his social revolutionary fatalism for the most revolting fatalism. In contrast to Parvus, Rosa Luxemburg exerted herself to educate the revolutionary wing of the proletariat in advance and to bring it together organizationally as far as possible. In Poland, she built up a very rigid independent organization. The most that can be said is that in her historical-philosophical evaluation of the labor movement, the preparatory selection of the vanguard, in comparison with the mass actions that were to be expected, fell too short with Rosa; whereas Lenin—without consoling himself with the miracles of future actions—took the advanced workers and constantly and tirelessly welded them together into firm nuclei, illegally or legally, in the mass organizations or underground, by means of a sharply defined program.

Rosa's theory of spontaneity was a wholesome weapon against the ossified apparatus of reformism. By the fact that it was often directed against Lenin's work of building up a revolutionary apparatus, it revealed—to be sure, only in embryo—its reactionary features. With Rosa herself this occurred only episodically. She was much too realistic in the revolutionary sense to develop the elements of the theory of spontaneity into a consummate metaphysics. In practice, she herself, as has already been said, undermined this theory at every step. After the revolution of November 1918, she began the ardent labor of assembling the proletarian vanguard. Despite her theoretically very weak manuscript on the Soviet Revolution, written in prison but never published by her, Rosa's subsequent work allows the sure conclusion that, day by day, she was moving closer to Lenin's theoretically clearly-delineated conception concerning conscious leadership and spontaneity. (It must surely have been this circumstance that prevented her from making public her manuscript against Bolshevik policy which was later so shamefully abused.)

Let us again attempt to apply the conflict between spontaneous mass actions and purposeful organizational work to the present epoch. What a mighty expenditure of strength and selflessness the toiling masses of all the civilized and half-civilized countries have exerted since the world war! Nothing in the previous history of mankind could compare with it. To this extent Rosa Luxemburg was entirely right as against the philistines, the corporals and the blockheads of straight-marching "victory-crowned" bureaucratic conservatism. But it is just the squandering of these immeasurable energies that forms the basis of the great depression in the proletariat and the successful fascist advance. Without the slightest exaggeration it may be said: the whole world situation is determined by *the crisis of the proletarian leadership.* The field of the labor movement is today still encumbered with huge remnants of the old bankrupt organizations. After the countless sacrifices and disappointments, the bulk of the European proletariat, at least, has withdrawn into its shell. The decisive lesson which it has drawn, consciously or half-consciously, from the bitter experiences, reads: great actions require a great leadership. For current affairs, the workers still give their votes to the old organizations. Their votes — but by no means their boundless confidence. On the other hand, after the miserable collapse of the Third International, it is much harder to move them to bestow their confidence upon a new revolutionary organization. That's just where the crisis of the proletarian leadership lies. To sing a monotonous song about indefinite future mass actions in this situation, in contrast to the purposeful selection of the cadres of a new International, means to carry on a thoroughly reactionary work. That's just where the role of the S. A. P. lies in the "historical process." A left-wing S. A. P. man of the Old Guard can, of course, summon up his Marxian recollections in order to stem the tide of theoretical spontaneity-barbarism. These purely literary protective measures change nothing in the fact that the pupils of a Miles, the precious author of the peace resolution and the no less precious author of the article in the French edition of the *Youth Bulletin,* carry on the most disgrace-

453

ful spontaneity nonsense even in the ranks of the S. A. P. The practical politics of Schwab (the artful "not speaking out what is" and the eternal consolation of the future mass actions and the spontaneous "historical process") also signifies nothing but a tactical exploitation of a thoroughly distorted and bowdlerized Luxemburgism. And to the extent that the "left wingers," the "Marxists" fail to make an open attack upon this theory and practice of their own party, their anti-Miles articles acquire the character of the search for a theoretical alibi. Such an alibi first really becomes necessary when one takes part in a deliberate crime.

The crisis of the proletarian leadership cannot, of course, be overcome by means of an abstract formula. It is a question of an extremely humdrum process. But not of a purely "historical" process, that is, of the objective premises of conscious activity, but of an uninterrupted chain of ideological, political and organizational measures for the purpose of fusing together the best, most conscious elements of the world proletariat beneath a spotless banner, elements whose number and self-confidence must be constantly strengthened, whose connections with wider sections of the proletariat must be developed and deepened — in a word: to restore to the proletariat, under new and highly difficult and onerous conditions, its historical leadership. The latest spontaneity confusionists have just as little right to refer to Rosa as the miserable Comintern bureaucrats have to refer to Lenin. Put aside the incidentals which developments have overcome, and we can, with full justification, place our work for the Fourth International under the sign of the "three L's," that is, not only under the sign of Lenin, but also of Luxemburg and Liebknecht.

GLOSSARY OF NAMES
AND TERMS

Adler, Victor (1852-1918): Founder and leader of Austrian social democracy; member, International Socialist Bureau; a defensist during World War I.

Anarchism: Libertarian doctrine opposing all government and state coercion, popularized by Mikhail Bakunin and Pyotr Kropotkin, advocating social organization based upon free, autonomous, loosely associated communes of equal producers. Differs from Marxism in its opposition to parliamentary activity, political parties, centralized or "authoritarian" political and governmental bodies, even during the revolution itself, when insurrectionists are faced with the need of coordinated resistance to counterrevolution.

Andreyev, Leonid (1871-1919): Russian novelist, playwright, short-story writer, famous for his extreme pessimism; works include *The Red Laugh, He Who Gets Slapped,* and *The Seven Who Were Hanged.* An ardent patriot during World War I, he became an ardent anti-Bolshevik and went into exile where he called for foreign intervention to overthrow the Soviet regime.

Antisocialist laws: Also called socialist exception laws; laws, initiated by Bismarck, in effect in Germany from 1878 to 1890, forbidding organizations and publications from engaging in socialist propaganda. Social democrats were permitted only parliamentary activity.

Auer, Ignaz (1846-1907): Bavarian social democrat; secretary ôf German social democracy from 1875; reformist.

August 4, 1914: Date of collapse of the Second International. On that day the German Social Democratic Party members in the Reichstag voted for the war budget of the imperialist government, despite the party's antimilitarist stand up to that time. On the same day French and Belgian socialist parties issued manifestos declaring support of their governments in war.

Axelrod, Pavel (1850-1928): Early leader of Russian Social Democratic Party; supported Mensheviks.

Babeuf, Francois Noel (Gracchus) (1760-1797): A forerunner of French socialism; leader of so-called Conspiracy of the Equals in period of

Thermidorean reaction during French Revolution; sent to the guillotine, 1797.

Bakunin, Mikhail (1814-1876): A contemporary and antagonist of Marx in the First International; founder of anarchist movement.

Ballplatz: German foreign office, completely dominated by titled militarists.

Barth, Emil: USPD member; joined Ebert government in November 1918, resigned in December; headed Communist Party underground movement in 1921.

Baudelaire, Pierre (1821-1867): French poet; leader of the decadents, nineteenth-century French literary group; wrote *Les Fleurs du Mal.*

Beaumarchais, Pierre (1732-1799): French playwright known chiefly for *Le Barbier de Seville* and *Le Mariage de Figaro.*

Bebel, August (1840-1913): One of the founders and leaders of the German Social Democratic Party and the Second International; sentenced with Wilhelm Liebknecht to two years' imprisonment for treason in 1872; author of *Women and Socialism*; opponent of revisionist tendencies.

Belinsky, Vissarion (1811-1848): Russian literary critic and philosopher; a revolutionary democrat; his writings were the foundation of Russian literary criticism; regarded by Marxists as an intellectual forerunner of socialist thought in Russia.

Berchtold, Leopold, Count (1863-1942): Landowner, industrialist, richest man in Austria; diplomat; ambassador to Russia, 1906-11; foreign minister, 1912-15.

Bernhardi, Friedrich von (1849-1930): Prussian cavalry general and author of book preaching Pan-Germanism and glory of war.

Bernstein, Eduard (1850-1932): German social democrat; friend and literary executor of Engels; developed revisionist theory of evolutionary socialism; became leader of extreme opportunist wing of social democracy.

Bestuzhev, Aleksandr (1797-1837): Russian poet and author of many novels based on his life in the Caucasus; a leader of the Decembrist movement.

Bethmann-Hollweg, Theobold von (1865-1921): Chancellor of the German Empire, 1909-17.

Bismarck, Otto, Prince von (1815-1898): Reactionary Prussian and

German statesman; headed Prussian government, 1862-71; chancellor, German Empire, 1871-90; organized unification of Germany through Seven-Weeks' War against Austria and Franco-Prussian War; author of the antisocialist laws.

Blanc, Louis (1811-1882): French socialist; participated in government set up by February 1848 Revolution; later opposed the Paris Commune.

Blanqui, Jerome-Adolphe (1798-1854): French bourgeois economist; brother of the revolutionist, Louis Auguste Blanqui.

Blanqui, Louis Auguste (1805-1881): French revolutionary socialist whose name has become associated with the theory of armed insurrection by small groups of selected and trained men, as opposed to the Marxist concept of mass insurrection; participated in French Revolution of 1830; organized unsuccessful insurrection in 1839; freed by by Revolution of 1848; he was jailed again during its defeat; jailed on eve of Paris Commune. Broken in health by thirty-five years of prison life, he was pardoned in 1879 and elected the same year by the workers of Bordeaux to the Chamber of Deputies, but was declared ineligible by the government.

Boisguillebert, Pierre le Pesant, Sieur de (1646-1714): French classical bourgeois political economist.

Bolsheviks: Derived from the Russian word meaning *majority*. At the London Congress of Russian Social Democratic Labor Party in 1903, there was a split on the question of what kind of revolutionary organization should be built. The Bolsheviks, led by Lenin, were in the majority; the Mensheviks were in the minority. The Bolsheviks led the successful October Revolution of 1917.

Bonaparte Dynasty: Began with Napoleon I (1769-1821), France's postrevolutionary general and emperor, 1804-15; ended with Napoleon III (1808-1873), nephew of Napoleon I, who was emperor from 1852 to 1870.

Bourgeoisie: Word used in feudal times to denote town people, as opposed to country folk; came to mean the representatives of capital as opposed to landowning nobility, peasants, and wage laborers.

Brentano, Lujo (1844-1931): German economist, one of the "professorial socialists" who advocated "class truce"; thought that contradictions of capitalism could be overcome without class struggle through reformist trade unions which would permit capitalists and workers to reconcile their differences.

Brest-Litovsk: Town in Russia near Polish border where Russo-German peace treaty was signed March 3, 1918.

Briand, Aristide (1862-1932): Eleven times premier of France; originally a socialist; expelled from Socialist Party in 1906 for accepting office in capitalist cabinet; head of wartime coalition cabinet, 1915-17; representative to League of Nations.

Bucher, Karl (1847-1930): German bourgeois economist; adherent of "historical" school of political philosophy.

Buelow, Bernhard, Prince von (1849-1929): German foreign secretary, 1897; chancellor, 1900-09; ambassador to Italy, 1914.

Burgfriede: "Civil peace," based on old medieval custom which decreed the cessation of private quarrels when the castle was besieged. In Germany in 1914 it meant a halt to political opposition and class struggle on the part of the social democracy.

Byron, George Gordon, Lord (1788-1824): English romantic poet; partisan of revolutionary causes.

Cartel: Voluntary agreement among manufacturers producing the same kind of product to limit the competition among them by dividing up the markets, fixing prices, etc.

Cecil, Robert, Lord (1864-1958): Conservative British Member of Parliament from 1903; minister in charge of blockade, 1916-18; undersecretary of foreign affairs, 1918.

Center: Roman Catholic party of Germany which sat in center of Reichstag Chamber; maneuvered between government and left wing.

Charlemagne (742-814): King of the Franks; crowned Holy Roman emperor in 800.

Chartism: Great movement of British masses, which began in 1838 and extended through the early 1850s; a struggle for political democracy and social equality which reached near-revolutionary proportions; centered around a program (the Charter) for universal suffrage and other democratic political reforms, drawn up by the London Workingmen's Association.

Chauvinism: Term for exaggerated bellicose patriotism, similar to English "jingoism."

Chekhov, Anton (1860-1904): Great Russian dramatist and short-story writer.

Chernyshevsky, Nikolai (1828-1889): Russian author and literary critic; his novel *What Is To Be Done?* influenced Russian Populist movement.

Chkheidze, Nikolai Semenovich (1864-1926): Menshevik member of Third and Fourth Dumas; was centrist in war; chairman of Petrograd Soviet, 1917.

Clemenceau, Georges, E. C. (1841-1929): French physician, editor, politician; in his youth a socialist; later became leader of big bourgeoisie; premier in 1906-09 and in 1917-19.

Communard: One who participated in the Paris Commune of 1871.

Cunow, Heinrich (1862-1936): German social democrat and university professor who was theoretician of the group led by Scheidemann; before war considered himself an orthodox Marxist and consistently fought against revisionism; during war became a social patriot.

Daeumig, Ernst (1866-1922): German social democrat; member of USPD; led Revolutionary Shop Stewards' movement in 1918; headed Communist underground; left Communist Party in 1921.

Dan, Feodor (1871-1947): Menshevik leader; physician; pacifist during war; member of Petrograd Soviet, 1917; opponent of October Revolution.

D'Annunzio, Gabriele (1863-1938): Italian poet, dramatist; aviator during World War I; when angered at Versaille Treaty's failure to give Fiume to Italy, he led an armed seizure of the city and proclaimed it an independent state.

Dante, Alighieri (1265-1321): Italian poet; author of *The Divine Comedy*, allegorical trip through Hell, Purgatory, and Paradise.

Darwin, Charles Robert (1809-1882): Great English naturalist; formulated theory of evolutionary biology; author of *Origin of Species*.

David, Eduard (1863-1930): Right-wing member of German social democracy; revisionist; supported imperialist war; minister without portfolio, 1919-20; first president of National Assembly, 1919.

Defensist: Social democrat who believed in prosecuting the war as a war in defense of the fatherland.

Dittman, Wilhelm (1874-1954): German social democrat closely associated with Hugo Haase; secretary of Haase's Social Democratic Labor Fellowship, 1916; later leader of Independent Social Democratic Party (USPD); supported USPD affiliation with Comintern, but refused to accept the twenty-one points for affiliation stipulated by the Communist International.

Dobrolyubov, Nikolai (1836-1861): Russian journalist and critic; considered an originator of revolutionary activity in Russia.

459

Dostoyevsky, Feodor (1821-1881): Russian novelist; wrote *Crime and Punishment, The Idiot, The Possessed, The Brothers Karamazov.*

Dreyfus, Alfred (1859-1935): Central figure in greatest political case of nineteenth century; Jewish officer on French Army General Staff framed-up in 1894 on charge of selling military secrets to Germany; the attempts to expose frame-up divided France politically into two camps — monarchist, anti-Semitic and clerical versus republican, leftist and anticlerical. Dreyfus was freed from prison in 1899 and fully vindicated in 1906.

Duehring, Eugen Karl (1833-1921): German petty bourgeois economist and philosopher; now remembered mainly because of Engels's criticism of his view in *Anti-Duehring.*

Duncker, Hermann: German social democrat who became member of Spartacus League and Communist Party.

Ebert, Friedrich (1870-1925): German Social Democratic Party leader in Reichstag; during war was a social-chauvinist; entered government in 1918 to prevent revolution and save the monarchy; when this failed he became premier of provisional government; first president of Weimar Republic, 1919-25.

Eisner, Kurt (1867-1919): German socialist and editor; member of USPD; prime minister of Bavaria, 1918; assassinated by army officer.

Erfurt Program: Drafted by Karl Kautsky and adopted at German Social Democratic Congress, Erfurt, 1891, replacing Gotha Program; introduced concept of the "minimum program," supposedly capable of achievement within the framework of capitalism, and the "maximum program," a more distant socialist goal. Program stopped short of dictatorship of proletariat and the full significance of this omission only became clear during November 1918.

Fabian: Member of Fabian Society in England, or one sharing its views; moderate evolutionary socialists.

Favre, Jules (1809-1880): French politician; a member of provisional government after 1848 Revolution; a leader of Republican Opposition under Louis Napoleon; helped crush Paris Commune.

February Revolution: French revolution of February 23-25, 1848, in which Louis Philippe was overthrown. The liberal bourgeoisie and the workers won the struggle against the monarchy, big financiers and industrialists, and the Second Republic was proclaimed.

First International: see International Workingmen's Association.

Fischart, Johann (Mentzer) (1546-1590): German satirist and poet.

Fourier, Francois Marie Charles (1772-1837): French utopian socialist and critic of capitalism.

France, Anatole (pseudonym of Jacques Thibault) (1844-1924): French satirist, humorist; a Dreyfusard, anticleric and sympathizer of the left.

Francis, Sir Philip (1740-1818): English government official and writer; one of those reputed to be author of the Junius letters (1768-72) attacking the British ministry.

Franz, Ferdinand (1863-1914): Archduke of Austria and heir to Habsburg throne; assassinated with his wife Sophie at Sarajevo, Austria, by a Serbian patriot; the assassination provided the excuse for Austria's ultimatum to Serbia, and the declaration of war, July 27, 1914.

Galilei, Galileo (1564-1642): Italian astronomer and physicist; advocated Copernican solar system, for which was tried by Inquisition and forced to deny that the sun is the central body around which earth and planets move; he allegedly replied to the inquisition following his recantation *Eppur si muove* (Nevertheless it [the earth] does move).

Galsworthy, John (1867-1933): English playwright and novelist; author of *The Forsyte Saga*.

Gapon, Father Georgiy (1870-1906): Russian orthodox priest who led peaceful workers' demonstration to czar's Winter Palace requesting constitutional rights and improved labor conditions; police fired on demonstrators, sparking Revolution of 1905.

Girondins: Moderate bourgeois republicans during French Revolution; overthrown and expelled from Convention by the Jacobins in 1793.

Goethe, Johann Wolfgang von (1749-1832): Poet and dramatist; Germany's greatest man of letters; wrote *Faust*.

Goetterdaemmerung: Literally, the twilight of the gods; the title of the fourth and final opera of Richard Wagner's *Ring of the Nibelungen* cycle; signifies a stage of collapse and dissolution accompanied by catastrophic violence and disorder.

Gogol, Nikolai (1809-1852): Russian author, called the father of realism in Russian literature; wrote *Dead Souls* and *The Inspector General*.

Gorky, Maxim (1868-1939): Russian author of realistic stories; became a social democrat and Bolshevik sympathizer; in 1917 opposed October Revolution, but later gave it critical support; ended all public criticism of Stalin in 1930s.

Griboyedov, Aleksandr (1795-1829): Russian statesman and poet, wrote *Gore ot Uma* (Woe from Wit).

Gruen, Karl (1817-1887): Spokesman for "true" socialism — a reactionary trend in Germany in the 1840s among petty bourgeois intelligentsia who substituted sentimental preaching of brotherhood and love for socialism, and denied need for bourgeois democratic revolution.

Guesde, Jules (1845-1922): Communard; founder of Marxist Socialist Party in France and leader of Marxist wing of United Social Democratic Party (SFIO), but became a social patriot upon outbreak of World War I and entered coalition government.

Haase, Hugo (1863-1919): Succeeded Bebel in 1913 as leader of Social Democratic Party; held pacifist views during war but submitted to majority discipline and voted for war credits till he resigned as party head in 1915; leader of Independent Social Democratic Party (USPD), 1916; one of USPD ministers in coalition government set up in November 1918 following Kaiser's abdication; resigned at end of December in protest to government's counterrevolutionary course; murdered in 1919.

Habsburg Dynasty: Ancient ruling family of Austro-Hungarian Empire; last ruler, Emperor Karl, abdicated in face of revolution of November 1918.

Hardenburg, Karl A., Furst von (1750-1822): Prussian minister who abolished serfdom and reformed army and education, completing work of Stein and Scharnhorst.

Hauptmann, Gerhart (1862-1946): German author famous for social protest plays, especially *The Weavers*.

Heine, Heinrich (1797-1856): German revolutionary lyric poet; spent most of life in exile in France; friend of Marx and Engels.

Heine, Wolfgang (1861- ?): German social democrat; one of Bernstein's most ardent supporters in revisionist struggle; social patriot during war.

Herzen, Aleksandr (1812-1870): Russian author and political writer; after several terms in Siberia went into exile in France and England, where he edited revolutionary journal, *The Bell*, which was smuggled into Russia and had great influence on the intelligentsia in the 1860s. He was the father of Narodnik (Populist) theory.

Hindenburg, Paul von (1847-1934): Prussian militarist who fought in war against France, 1870-71; German commander-in-chief in World War I and later became president of Weimar Republic. In 1932 social democrats supported him for reelection as "lesser evil" to Nazis; he appointed Hitler chancellor, January 1933.

Hofmannsthal, Hugo von (1874-1929): Austrian playwright and poet.

Hohenstaufen Dynasty: A medieval German dynasty which provided Holy Roman emperors in eleventh to thirteenth centuries.

Hohenzollern Dynasty: Ruling family of Prussia and, from 1871, of Germany; overthrown in 1919.

Hutten, Ulrich von (1488-1523): German humanist and poet, theoretician of nobility who were for reform of empire by eliminating princes and secularizing church property.

Hyndman, Henry Mayers (1842-1921): English socialist; one of the founders of the Social Democratic Federation, 1884; expelled from British Socialist Party for support of the war, 1916.

International Socialist Bureau: The Executive Committee of the Second International, established by decision of the Paris Congress of 1900; headquartered in Brussels.

International Workingmen's Association (First International): Founded by Marx and Engels in 1864, the First International survived the defeat of the Paris Commune in 1871, when the center was moved from England to the United States. The last conference was held in Philadelphia in 1876.

Jacobi, Johann (1805-1877): German publicist and politician; led Prussian left in struggle against Bismarck; became a social democrat in 1872.

Jacobins: Members of the Jacobin Club, the most radical political faction in the French Revolution, which ruled from the overthrow of the Gironde until Thermidor and the execution of Robespierre et al. in July 1793.

Jaures, Jean (1859-1914): Most prominent leader of French socialists; founded the newspaper L'Humanite in 1890; after Dreyfus affair, Jaures formed the bloc between the Socialists and the Radicals to support Millerand in the bourgeois government; a strong opponent of militarism and war; assassinated July 31, 1914; his patriotic murderer was acquitted.

Jena Resolution: The resolution concerning the tactic of the general strike passed by the Congress of the Social Democratic Party of Germany in Jena in 1905; the party's position declared support for the tactic, but was strategically vague.

Jevons, William Stanley (1835-1882): English economist and logician; developed theory of utility.

Jogiches, Leo (Tyszko) (1867-1919): Leader of Polish social democracy; founding member of International Group and Spartacus League;

arrested and assassinated in 1919 a month after similar murders of Liebknecht and Luxemburg.

Junkers: Members of the Prussian landed aristocracy; holders of extreme militarist and antidemocratic views.

Kaclerovic, Trisa (1879- ?): Founder of Serbian social democracy, Serbian Communist Party, and Independent Labor Party; antimilitarist; with Laptchevic voted against war credits in parliament.

Kaledin, Alexei Maximovich (1861-1918): Czarist general, chief of Don Cossacks in 1917; after October he started civil war against Soviets; was defeated both by Red Guards and defections among Cossacks and committed suicide.

Kant, Immanuel (1724-1804): German idealist philosopher.

Kasprzak, Martin (1860-1905): Polish revolutionary; friend and mentor of Rosa Luxemburg; worked with German SPD; spent most of his life in prison, and ended on gallows.

Katzenjammer: Discordant clamor, cacophony.

Kautsky, Karl (1854-1938): German social democrat; leading theoretician of Second International; during war was pacifist centrist; violent opponent of bolshevism and Soviet government.

Kennan, George (1845-1924): American engineer who became expert on Siberia. His writings on political prisoners and deportees there, especially his *Siberia and the Exile System* (New York, 1891), were much appreciated and cited by all Russian opponents of czarism; they were translated into many languages and were world famous.

Kerensky, Alexander F. (1881-   ): Russian social revolutionary; patriot during war; vice-chairman of Petrograd Soviet; held several ministerial posts during 1917; premier of provisional government, overthrown by October Revolution.

Kladderadatsch: A great noise.

Korolenko, Vladimir (1853-1921): Russian novelist whose best-known works are *Makar's Dream, The Blind Musician, The Rustling of the Woods, Bad Company,* and *Murderer.*

Krupp, Alfred (1812-1887): Big German industrialist, munitions manufacturer, and steel tycoon; at founding of German Empire, 1871, was leading industrialist.

Krylov, Viktor (1838-1906): Russian playwright.

Landsberg, O.: German social democrat; in Ebert cabinet, 1918.

Lange, Friedrich Albert (1828-1875): German neo-Kantian philosopher and social reformist.

Laptchevic (1864- ?): Serbian social democrat; antimilitarist who with T. Kaclerovic opposed war credits in parliament, 1914.

Lassalle, Ferdinand (1825-1864): German socialist; founder of General Union of German Workers in 1863, which later fused with Marx's followers to form the Social Democratic Party.

Ledebour, Georg (1850- ?): German social democrat; collaborator of Bebel and Haase; opposed war and signed Zimmerwald Manifesto; joined USPD.

Legien, Carl (1861-1920): Social democratic head of German trade unions from 1890; opposed idea of general strike; supported war; after Bebel's death in 1913 he and Ebert were actual leaders of SPD.

Lensch, Paul (1873- ?): German social democrat; prior to war, member of left wing; his newspaper printed articles of Luxemburg, Mehring, etc.; upon outbreak of war he became a fierce chauvinist; rightward evolution continued after war and he became editor for Hugo Stinnes, industrialist and press magnate; expelled from SPD in 1922.

Lermontov, Mikhail (1814-1841): Russian poet and novelist of revolutionary views who wrote *A Hero of Our Time* and *The Demon*.

Lessing, Gotthold (1729-1781): German dramatist, editor and philosopher of eighteenth-century Enlightenment, who fought for freedom of thought.

Levi, Paul (1883-1930): German social democrat; well-known defense lawyer; friend of Rosa Luxemburg; member of Spartacus League and later Central Committee of German Communist Party; split from Communist Party in 1922 and reentered SPD.

Liebknecht, Karl (1871-1919): Son of Wilhelm Liebknecht; from his youth a left-wing militant in SPD; sentenced for high treason in 1907 for his book *Militarism and Anti-Militarism*; first to vote against war credits in Reichstag in 1914; drafted during war; imprisoned for anti-war activity, 1916-18; leader of International Group and Spartacus League; arrested and assassinated with Rosa Luxemburg in 1919.

Liebknecht, Wilhelm (1826-1900): Participated in German Revolution of 1848; went into exile in England where he became a disciple of Marx and Engels; returned to Germany after 1860 amnesty and built Marxist party which united with Lassallean party to form SPD; jailed for high treason in 1872; upheld Marxist orthodoxy against revisionist attempts in SPD.

Louis Philippe (1773-1850): King of France, brought to throne by July Revolution (1830); overthrown by February Revolution (1848).

Lumpenproletariat: That layer of proletariat which has been declassed or ejected from the productive process — unemployables, cripples, elderly paupers, beggars, petty criminals, etc.

Malthus, Thomas Robert, Rev. (1766-1834): English clergyman and economist who theorized that human population will outstrip the food supply.

Mandeville, Bernard (1670-1733): English philosopher and satirist whose major work *The Fable of the Bees* is a satire in verse which maintains that social welfare rests on the self-seeking efforts of individuals.

Mann, Thomas (1875-1955): German author; works include *Buddenbrooks, Death in Venice, The Magic Mountain.* He supported German government in World War I, went into exile under Hitler and supported Allied governments during World War II.

Manteuffel, Edwin von (1809-1885): Prussian field marshal; in October 1849, Prussian home secretary; commanded armies in Seven-Weeks' War against Austria and Franco-Prussian War of 1871; headed army of occupation in France, 1871-73; military governor of Alsace-Lorraine, 1879-85.

March Revolution: The German Revolution of 1848.

Martov, L. (Yulii Ossipovich Tsederbaum) (1873-1923): One of the founders of Russian social democracy; in early years a close associate of Lenin; later a left-wing Menshevik leader; opposed October Revolution; emigrated to Germany in 1920.

Mehring, Franz (1846-1919): German scholar and historian; biographer of Marx; left-wing social democrat; leading member of International Group and Spartacus League.

Menger, Carl (1840-1921): Austrian political economist.

Menshevik: Derived from the Russian word meaning *minority*; party led by Plekhanov, Martov, Dan, Tseretelli, etc. (See "Bolshevik.")

Mignet, Francois August Marie (1796-1884): French liberal historian of the Restoration.

Miliukov, Pavel Nikolaievich (1859-1943): Leader of liberal bourgeois Constitutional Democratic (or Cadet) Party; minister of foreign affairs in Russian provisional government, March-May 1917; opponent of Bolshevik Revolution; inspired many counterrevolutionary attempts.

Millerand, Alexandre (1859-1943): French socialist who entered bourgeois government of Waldeck-Rousseau. This was a first in social democratic history. Subsequently expelled from Socialist Party; formed Independent Socialist Party; president of French Republic, 1920-1924.

Ministerialism: Tendency in socialist movement advocating socialist participation in capitalist coalition ministries.

Moliere (pseudonym of Jean Baptiste Poquelin) (1622-1673): Great French playwright of the seventeenth century.

Monti, Vincenzo (1754-1828): Italian poet.

Narodniks: Also called Populists; organization of Russian intellectuals of late nineteenth century who concentrated on liberating peasants, went to the countryside; used conspiratorial and terrorist tactics.

National Liberals: German political party of industrialists and shipowners.

Nekrasov, Nikolai (1821-1877): Russian poet and editor; works include *To Whom Is Life in Russia Worth Living?* and *Fatherland.*

Neupauer, Dr. Joseph Ritter von: German bourgeois economist whose views were recommended by Bernstein.

Nicholas I (1796-1855): Russian czar, 1825-55.

Nietzsche, Friedrich (1844-1900): German idealist philosopher.

Noske, Gustav (1868-1946): Right-wing social democrat; as minister for military affairs was responsible for murder of Luxemburg and Liebknecht.

Novikov, Nikolai (1744-1818): Russian journalist who satirized serfdom, foreign influence in Russian life, and other social conditions.

Old Believers: Also known as *Raskolniki* (Splitters); a religious sect which regarded the revision of Biblical texts and liturgical reforms of 1654 by the Russian Orthodox Church as contrary to the true faith; persecuted under czarism.

Oppenheimer, Franz (1864-1943): German sociologist and socialist.

Owen, Robert (1771-1858): English industrialist, reformer and utopian socialist.

Paris Commune: First dictatorship of the proletariat. At the end of the Franco-Prussian war, the people of Paris, led by workers' organizations, created their own government and resisted efforts of the bourgeois government of Versailles to disarm it. The Commune withstood the attacks of the Versailles army from March 18 to May 21, 1871, when it was crushed after a bitter struggle in which 30,000 Communards were killed.

Parliamentary cretinism: Term applied by Marx to those who think that all history is decided by motions, votes, and points of order in parliamentary debate.

Parvus (Alexander Helphand) (1869-1924): Prominent in prewar years as Marxist theoretician in Eastern Europe; reached conclusions similar to Trotsky's theory of permanent revolution; Trotsky broke with him in 1914 when Parvus became one of the leaders in the prowar wing of the German social democracy. In 1917 he tried in vain to reconcile the German party with the Bolsheviks and later the Independent Socialists with the Ebert-Noske leadership.

Pereira, Isaac (1806-1880): French economist; bourgeois apologist.

Petty bourgeoisie: Small proprietors such as peasants, artisans, and tradesmen.

Pieck, Wilhelm: Member of Spartacus League, official of German Communist Party from its founding; spent World War II years in Moscow; returned to East Germany and headed Socialist Unity Party, the government party.

Plekhanov, George Valentinovich (1856-1918): Founder of Russian Marxism; editor of *Iskra* and *Zarya*, journals of Russian social democrats; became social-patriot during war; opposed the Bolsheviks.

Potter-Webb, Beatrice (1858-1943): Fabian socialist; wife of Sydney Webb; co-author with him of numerous books.

Prince Max of Baden (1867-1927): Had been appointed chancellor of Germany ten days before overthrown by workers' demonstrations, November 9, 1918.

Progressives or Radicals: German middle-class party opposed to the Junkers and Bismarck; free-traders; led by Eugene Richter (1838-1906).

Proudhon, Pierre Joseph (1809-1865): French utopian socialist who envisioned a society based on fair exchange between independent producers and considered the state less important than the workshops which he believed would replace it; author of *Philosophy of Poverty*, which was replied to by Marx in his *Poverty of Philosophy*.

Pushkin, Aleksandr (1799-1837): Russian poet who participated in the

Decembrist uprising; author of *Boris Godunov, Eugene Onegin,* and *The Captain's Daughter.*

Quesnay, Francois (1694-1744): French physiocrat; first to attempt systematic presentation of capitalist economic structure in his *Tableau Economique,* 1758.

Rabelais, Francois (1494-1553): French satirist; author of the two novels *Gargantua* and *Pantagruel.*

Rabener, Gottlieb (1714-1771): German satirist, who principally mocked middle-class life.

Ricardo, David (1772-1823): English representative of the classical school of bourgeois economy.

Rodbertus, Karl Johann (1805-1875): German economist who held socialist but not revolutionary views; Engels deals with his views in detail in the introduction to Marx's *The Poverty of Philosophy.*

Rohrbach, Paul (1869- ?): German journalist and semiofficial commentator on military affairs.

Roscher, Wilhelm Georg Friedrich (1817-1894): German economist; founder of historical school of political economy.

Rubicon: River dividing ancient Gaul from Italy, crossed by Julius Caesar when he marched his troops on Rome in defiance of the Senate, hence, to cross the Rubicon is to take an irrevocable step or decision.

Ryleyev, Kondrati (1795-1826): Russian lyric poet; Decembrist.

Sainte-Beuve, Charles (1804-1869): French literary historian and critic; first French critic to break away from classical dogmas and promote Romantic movement.

Saint-Simon, Claude Henri (1760-1825): French utopian socialist.

Saltykov-Shchedrin (real name Mikhail Saltykov; pseudonym N. Shchedrin) (1826-1889): Russian writer; works include *Contradictions, Provincial Sketches,* and *Satires in Prose.*

Sansculottes: French, literally without kneepants, i.e., those who did not wear the costume of gentlemen, but the long pantaloons of the lower classes; the revolutionary street masses who accomplished the French Revolution.

Say, Jean-Baptiste (1767-1832): French bourgeois economist; popularizer of Adam Smith; Say's law was the thesis that every act of production created the necessary purchasing power to buy the product.

Scharnhorst, Gerhard Johann David von (1755-1813): General who reorganized Prussian army after Peace of Tilsit in 1807.

Scheidemann, Philip (1865-1937): Right-wing social democratic leader in Germany; actively supported the war; appointed state secretary by Kaiser Wilhelm in 1918, but was unable to save monarchy; was minister in Ebert coalition cabinet and worked to crush Spartacus uprising.

Schippel, Max (1859-1928): Right-wing revisionist in German social democracy; defended imperialist, expansionist, and aggressive policies of Germany.

Schmidt, Konrad (1863-1932): German economist and social democrat who corresponded with Engels; became a revisionist.

Schmoller, Gustav (1838-1917): Economist and historian; founded schools of social and economic history in Germany.

Second International: In contrast to unmistakably revolutionary trend of First International and its centralized character, the Second International, founded in 1889, was a loose association of national socialist parties of all varieties. The International Socialist Bureau, created in 1900, was its center. At the Amsterdam Congress of 1904 the revisionism of Bernstein and ministerialism of Millerand and Jaures were condemned. However, the theory and practice of reformism gradually gained dominance, climaxing in 1914 when the International collapsed morally and politically as most national sections voted for war credits. It was revived after World War I, and still exists in name.

Shaw, George Bernard (1856-1950): Irish playwright; Fabian socialist; plays include *Man and Superman, Major Barbara, Pygmalion,* and *St. Joan.*

Shevchenko, Taras (1814-1861): Ukrainian poet.

Sisyphus: Mythological king of Corinth who in the nether world was condemned to roll to the top of a hill a huge stone, which constantly rolled back again, making his task incessant.

Smith, Adam (1723-1790): English economist; foremost representative of the "classical" school; author of *The Wealth of Nations.*

Social Revolutionary Party: Heterogenous petty bourgeois formation in Russia formed in 1901, generally considered to represent the interests of the poor peasants and agrarian reformers. In October 1917, the party split, with the left wing forming a coalition government with the Bolsheviks. This broke up when the Left SRs turned against the Soviet government for signing the peace of Brest-Litovsk with Germany.

Soloviev, Vladimir (1853-1900): Russian religious philosopher, critic and poet.

Stein, Heinrich Friedrich Karl, Baron von (1757-1831): Prussian statesman and reformer; was in employ of czar until the anti-Napoleonic coalition gained victory; began emancipation of serfs and many other reforms in administration and local government in Prussia.

Sterne, Laurence (1713-1768): English novelist known for his *Life and Opinions of Tristram Shandy* and *A Sentimental Journey*.

Stewart, Dugald (1753-1828): Scottish philosopher.

Stroebel, Heinrich: German social democrat; took internationalist position at beginning of war; member of German USPD; contributed to magazine published by Luxemburg and Mehring; later joined social-chauvinists.

Swift, Jonathan (1667-1745): English satirist particularly known for *Gulliver's Travels* and *A Modest Proposal*.

Syndicalism: A manifestation of anarchism in trade-union field; opposes parliamentary action and all political parties; stresses the complete independence of trade unions and the concept that they are sufficient to accomplish the emancipation of the working class from capitalism.

Thalheimer, August (1884-1952): German social democrat, close collaborator of Luxemburg in Spartacus League; became a leader of German Communist Party and editor of central party organ, *Rote Fahne* (Red Flag); when expelled from CP along with Heinrich Brandler in 1929, they set up the KPO or German Right Opposition.

Thiers, Louis-Adolphe (1797-1877): French politician and historian; premier in 1836, 1840; president of French Republic, 1871-73, crushed Paris Commune.

Tolstoy, Lev (1828-1910): Russian novelist; author of *War and Peace* and *Anna Karenina*.

Troelestra, Pieter Jelles (1860-1932): Leader of Dutch social democracy; member of International Socialist Bureau; defensist during war.

Tseretelli, Iraklii G. (1882-1959): Russian Menshevik; supported the war; held ministerial positions March-August, 1917; strong opponent of Bolsheviks; emigrated 1919.

Turgenev, Ivan (1818-1883): Russian novelist; author of *Fathers and Sons, A Sportsman's Sketches,* and *Virgin Soil*.

Uspensky, Gleb Ivanovich (1840-1902): Russian novelist of peasant life.

Va banque: French idiom meaning a sheer gamble, staking everything.

Vaillant, Edouard (1840-1915): French socialist; prominent in Paris Commune; friend and disciple of Blanqui; one of the organizers of the unified French Socialist Party in 1905; member of International Socialist Bureau of Second International; an active antimilitarist before war, he became a social patriot upon outbreak of war.

Via Dolorosa: Literally, path of sorrow; Christ's road to Calvary.

Viviani, Rene (1863-1925): French politician; originally a socialist; joined Clemenceau cabinet, 1906, ousted from Socialist Party; made appeal for sacred union and became premier of national defense ministry upon outbreak of war; his cabinet fell in 1915 and he became minister of justice.

Vollmar, Georg Heinrich von (1850-1922): Leader of Bavarian social democracy; in 1891, years before Bernstein, urged reformist views, thus becoming pioneer of German reformism.

Waldeck-Rousseau, Pierre (1846-1904): French republican statesman; as premier he chose ministers from the left, including the first socialist cabinet member (Millerand), and the right; resigned, 1902.

Webb, Sydney (1859-1947): Chief English theoretician of gradualist socialism; a founder of Fabian Society; co-author with wife Beatrice of numerous books on cooperation and trade unionism; became colonial minister in Labour Party government; made Lord Passfield; he and wife became apologists for Stalinism in 1930s.

Wedekind, Frank (1864-1918): German playwright and poet whose works include *The Earth Spirit, Pandora's Box,* and *Love Potion.*

Weitling, Wilhelm (1808-1871): First German proletarian writer; collaborator with Blanqui; an egalitarian utopian socialist.

Wiener Hofburg: Imperial palace in Vienna where emperor held court.

Wilde, Oscar (1854-1900): Irish dramatist and poet who wrote *The Picture of Dorian Gray, The Importance of Being Earnest* and *The Ballad of Reading Gaol.* Though his interests were mostly aesthetic, he declared himself a socialist and wrote several essays to that effect. In 1895 he was jailed for homsexuality in one of the great scandals of the epoch.

Will of the People (Narodnay Volya): Terrorist wing of split in Land and Freedom movement; attacked czarism from 1879 to 1883 by means of terrorist acts; succeeded in assassinating Alexander II in 1881.

Winnig, August (1878- ?): Influential German trade unionist; social democrat of extreme "imperialist" wing; believed in furthering interests of German working class through conquest of world market by Ger-

472

man industry; advisor to German imperialists in intervention against Soviet Republic.

Wolf, Hugo (1860-1903): Austrian composer; disciple of Wagner.

Wolff, Julius (1862- ?): German bourgeois economist.

Wrangel, Ernest von, Count (1784-1877): Prussian general; real power behind throne in 1848.

Zemstvo: Rural assemblies in czarist Russia, late nineteenth and early twentieth centuries, with very limited powers, having only economic and cultural functions.

Zetkin, Clara: (1857-1937): Associated with Rosa Luxemburg in German social democracy before war; editor of party's paper for women; a founder, theoretician, and activist in women's movement; founding member of Spartacus League; leading figure in German Communist Party and Communist International.

Zola, Emile (1840-1902): French novelist; founder of naturalistic school; played prominent role in exposing frame-ups of Dreyfus.

Zubatov, Sergei Vasilievich (1864-1917): Revolutionist who turned police agent in 1880s and became head of the Okhrana (secret political police); brought Russian police methods up-to-date with fingerprinting, photography, etc.; inspirer of "police socialism" whereby workers were organized under police auspices as a preventive measure; when some of these "company" unions got out of hand and became nucleus of general strike movement, he was fired; rehired in 1905; committed suicide after February 1917 Revolution.